DATTOPANT THENGADI

The Activist Parliamentarian

DATTOPANT THENGADI

The Activist Parliamentarian

Introduction

S Gurumurthy

Editors

Anirban Ganguly | Navin Kalingan

Published by
PRABHAT PRAKASHAN PVT. LTD.
4/19 Asaf Ali Road,
New Delhi-110 002 (INDIA)
e-mail: prabhatbooks@gmail.com

ISBN 978-93-90366-34-7
DATTOPANT THENGADI : The Activist Parliamentarian
Ed. Anirban Ganguly • Navin Kalingan

Edition
2025

Price
₹ 1000.00 (Rupees One Thousand only)

Printed at
Narula Printers, Delhi

Editor's Note

This volume was conceived and initiated by late Shri Anil Madhav Dave, environmental thinker and activist who served as Union Minister for Environment, Forest and Climate Change (2016-2017). Shri Dave, then member of the Rajya Sabha from Madhya Pradesh was, besides being a deft political organiser, an active parliamentarian with interest in varied fields ranging from governance to environment, river rejuvenation to national security and strategic issues. With assistance from Shri Navin Kalingan, he had started working on the volume and the collation of Dattopant Thengadi's speeches and interventions in the Upper House had taken off.

In my interactions with Dave, over the last few years, I came to know that he had started this work. My own interest in independent India's political history and evolution made me enquire, from time to time, about the progress of the volume. However, his sudden demise in 2017 had left this endeavour hanging. At the renewed initiative of Shri Suresh Soni and Shri Dattatreya Hosabale, Sah Sarkaryavahs of Rashtriya Swayamsevak Sangh (RSS), Shri Prabhat Kumar of Prabhat Prakashan and Dave's private secretary and associate, Shri Kartik Shirish Sapre, the work of compiling Dattopant Thengadi's parliamentary speeches was resumed. The aim was to try and complete the project in his centenary year. With his vast experience in Parliament's reference and library sections, Navin Kalingan undertook the herculean task of gathering and listing the speeches. This volume stands as a tribute to the *karyakarta*-leader that Anil Madhav Dave was. Thengadi himself never lost connect with the *karyakarta* within him. His speeches, the issues he raised in Parliament, the manner with which he championed democratic rights of the marginalised made him stand apart from many others.

This compilation is a selection and covers almost all of Thengadi's major interventions in Parliament. His very brief interventions, in form of a single sentence, and questions which elicited brief answers have been omitted. We have left these out in order to avoid making the work too voluminous. This volume is not exhaustive, nor are the annotations extensive, it provides an insight into the parliamentary dimension of Thengadi's personality. It lays a foundation for the future scholar to undertake a more detailed study of this aspect of his public action.

Thengadi entered Rajya Sabha in the biennial elections of 1964 from Uttar Pradesh, representing Bharatiya Jana Sangh (BJS). At that time, as General Secretary of Bharatiya Mazdoor Sangh (BMS), he was in the thick of organising the labour movement and expanding the organisation's footprints. Giriraj Kishore Kapoor, president of the Madhya Pradesh unit of BJS, and 'a popular and witty speaker at the Jana Sangh meetings' also entered the Upper House with Thengadi. Kapoor died in August 1965. When he entered Rajya Sabha in April 1964, Thengadi had as company then BJS and later Bharatiya Janata Party (BJP) stalwart, Atal Bihari Vajpayee, who was serving his first term in the Upper House (1962-1967). When Thengadi was into his second and last term in the Upper House, he had as company the other BJS and BJP stalwart L.K. Advani, who had made his debut in parliamentary politics (1970-1976). Advani was elected BJS President in 1973. The other BJS stalwart who was in the Rajya Sabha with Thengadi was Sunder Singh Bhandari, who entered the Upper House for the first time in 1966. Bhupesh Gupta of the Communist Party of India who was in the Rajya Sabha since 1952, Chandra Shekhar, who made his parliamentary entrée as a 'consensus nominee of PSP' in 1962 and Chitta Basu, veteran Forward Bloc leader who entered the House in 1966 were some of the other well-known political leaders of the period. In 1964, Pandit Deendayal Upadhyaya, the indefatigable General Secretary of BJS continued to lead its organisational expansion and electoral consolidation.

It is interesting to note that Thengadi's tenure in the Rajya Sabha started at the end of Nehru's tenure as Prime Minister. Nehru died in May 1964 and by the time it ended, Nehru's daughter, Indira Gandhi had clamped Emergency in the country. Thengadi would switch roles and from the portals of Parliament, he would soon emerge as one of the leading lights of the resistance against this clampdown on democracy and democratic rights. Discussing the Emergency, Thengadi once wrote, "An Emergency is an extraordinary situation...putting an end to it requires extraordinary struggle. An extraordinary struggle of courage and valour." Thengadi displayed that extraordinary courage and valour in the struggle against Emergency.

Thengadi's parliamentary tenure was witness to some of the most momentous developments in India's national and political life. It was witness to the India-Pakistan war 1965; the Tashkent Declaration, 1966; Lal Bahadur Shashtri's death, 1966; the firing on anti-cow slaughter protestors in front of Parliament and the killing of *Sadhus*, 1966; culmination of the Punjabi Suba movement, 1966; the end of the Congress' electoral hegemony with losses in state elections, 1967 and the emergence of BJS and Swatantra Party as major opposition formations within Parliament and the formation of several non-Congress ministries in the states; Pandit Deendayal Upadhyaya's election as BJS president, 1967; his assassination, 1968; nationalisation of Banks, 1969; split in the Congress, 1969; abolition of Privy Purses, 1971; Bangladesh Liberation War, 1971; Simla Agreement, 1972; all India Railway Strike, 1974; Pokharan–I, 1974; Emergency 1975. Internationally, some of the dominant developments were Vietnam War; China's hydrogen bomb explosion 1966; Apartheid; an accentuated Cold War; decolonisation in Africa, the Six-Day War, 1967; Henry Kissinger's secret trip to China with Pakistan's assistance, 1971; China's (PRC) admission to the UN, 1971; US President Richard Nixon's visit to China, 1972; the first United Nations Conference on Environment at Stockholm, 1972. Not all of these have been discussed, but while reading Thengadi's speeches these are the broad political developments and milestones – national and international – that one would do well to place as a backdrop. It gives a view into the political world that saw Thengadi the organiser, the thought-leader emerge as the activist parliamentarian.

In a foreword he wrote to a book sometime in 1994, two decades after his parliamentary innings had come to an end, Thengadi had observed, "the essence of sovereignty lies in the full right to take all decisions concerning national life. Dr Syama Prasad Mookerjee and Pandit Deendayal Upadhyaya expressed the view that preservation and promotion of national self-interest within the framework of world welfare and human happiness should be the objective of the foreign policy of every nation." In his exhortations in Parliament, Thengadi always seemed to keep this formulation at the forefront while arguing for preserving and perpetuating India's 'national self-interest'.

Known and revered as a one of the greatest trade union leader of post independent India, Thengadi was also a profound social and political thinker. While championing workers' rights in Parliament, undertaking his cyclonic action in organising labour across India, Thengadi also formulated fundamental positions on these issues. In an interview to Organiser in April 1965, a year after he had entered Parliament, he spoke on the '*Bharatiya* tradition' of industrial establishments, according to which, he argued, "every industrial establishment is an industrial family with all those working within it as its industrial coparceners. Workers, including technicians and managers, are coparceners of their respective industries."

In his twelve years in Parliament, Thengadi, representing BJS, ceaselessly championed the working people's interests and helped in further expanding the party among that important section. It was an expansion that he systematically effectuated throughout his parliamentary tenure. He also brought in a lot of intellectual heft and parliamentary excellence to BJS, which saw a phenomenal electoral and political rise.

But he was not a rigid doctrinaire and well saw the need to re-structure, re-state, re-evaluate and re-direct a position and movement whenever it was required. For instance, participating in a number of debates on the Railway Budget in the House, Thengadi felt that there was a need to abolish the Railway Board, which should be replaced, he argued, by an autonomous corporation. Thengadi's excellence and mastery in the field of labour and employment issues has been well recognised, but one also saw streaks of the radiance of his thought, his forthrightness, his intellectual prowess, his capacity for analysing challenges in a number of other fields as well. Some of these appear throughout the volume and it will be relevant to refer to some of them in this prefatory note. I cite some extracts in Thengadi's own words since he had an inimitable style of parliamentary speech which cannot be paraphrased or replicated.

Participating in a discussion regarding the appointment of a committee to check the influx of rural population in urban areas, (1974) Thengadi anticipated the problems that would arise from unplanned urbanisation and neglect of villages and indicated a way ahead, when he told the House:

> Our Planning Commission has not taken cognisance of this problem and therefore we find that our rural areas are almost totally ignored. Is it not a fact that thousands of villages are not having access even to drinking water in the summer season? The very first economic problem before the country was what should be the character of our industrialisation?
>
> Urbanisation, over-urbanisation, has its own problems. Because of over-urbanisation, those who come from the rural areas are cut off from their moorings and they do not have the family life and it affects their total personality and also the problems of sanitation and transport and other such problems we have not been able to solve in the cities. Moreover, we also find that because of over-urbanisation our cultural standards are also going down. Instead of concentrating our industries in the urban areas, if we decentralise our industries in the rural areas, it will be possible for us to have equitable distribution of wealth and, at the same, to have a healthier atmosphere.
>
> If we channelise all the small sums available in the rural areas into industrial investment through small-scale savings and again investing them in small-scale industries, the very industrial map of India would have been altered. Therefore, I suggest that an expert committee should be appointed to study the technological and locational aspects of our industries. I say this because in the rural areas there is not sufficient electrification and we have not tried to imitate the Japanese way. In Japan, electricity is there in all the huts in the villages and the hamlets and the processes of production are decentralised and in every hut some part of a commodity, some part of an article, is being produced according to specifications and standards and all such parts produced separately are assembled at one place and in this way, sir, the agricultural population, which is underemployed and unemployed for at least five or six months in a year, gets additional employment without losing its contact with its land. If we adopt some such techniques, it is possible for us also to decentralise the processes of production and in this fashion, industrialisation suited to our conditions can take place in our rural areas.

> If the technology is changed – I am sure, our technologists, if properly engaged, are competent enough to take care of this problem – if technology is changed to suit the Indian conditions, it should be possible for us to have widely scattered small and medium-size industries throughout the rural areas so that our problems of economics and equality will be solved, and, sir, simultaneously the problems arising out of over-urbanisation which are mainly cultural in character, will be solved.

Discussing the Maternity Benefit Bill in 1965, Thengadi made a strong case for enhanced security of service for women and called for realising the dream of a comprehensive social security:

> It is a matter of great regret that even today, that is to say, 19 years after our attaining Independence, we are not free from the inadequacies, the defects and the drawbacks of the maternity benefit legislation, and have not been able to ensure fully the two essential features of a maternity benefit scheme, namely, compensation and medical care. Whatever legislation is there, suffers from the absence of proper enforcement. Insecurity of service is still a menace that women workers are required to face constantly.
>
> In the past we had evolved a characteristically *Bharatiya* socio-economic order which ensured fullest social security to all, but that order is now disintegrating. And a new order is not yet evolved. Thus, ours is a case of unborn tomorrow and dead yesterday. Against this background, I urge upon the government to make an early and determined effort to realise our long-cherished dream of full comprehensive social security.

Discussing the report of the University Grants Commission (UGC) in 1964, Thengadi displayed a deep empathy and reverence for all Indian languages and emphasised the need for strengthening them, for launching a comprehensive translation project and for preserving manuscripts. He called for teaching as many foreign languages as possible and not leave the dominance to English alone and looked forward to the day when Indian languages would also become international languages. Each Indian language for Thengadi was a national language, he wanted Indian languages to become the medium of instruction. His own phenomenal linguistic skill and mastery and his work across the country made him symbolise linguistic integration and synthesis:

> It becomes imperative that the translation work should be expedited – translation of scientific and technical terminology from foreign to our Indian languages. There should be one central agency for the preservation and utilisation of manuscripts. A translation service should be efficiently organised for translating select passages of literature from one Indian language into all other Indian languages. That would bring about National Integration. For example, why should not the entire Thirukkural by Thiruvalluvar be translated into all other Indian languages? Similarly, the southern languages should be made compulsory in the northern universities.
>
> We have no particular hatred for the English language. They say it is an international language; there are other international languages also. We aspire that our own Indian languages should become international languages as early as possible but, at the same time, while we may give the status of international languages not only to English but to German, French and other languages also, as medium of instruction.
>
> To my mind, all the languages spoken by Indians are national languages and Hindi is the state as well as the national language. Therefore, all the national languages should be recognised as mediums of instruction. I should like our hon'ble Minister of Education to enlighten us on one point – whether the advanced non-Anglo-Saxon countries have accepted English as medium of instruction and if not, whether they have suffered for want of English as medium of instruction?

Thengadi's interventions in the discussion on the Jawaharlal Nehru University (JNU) Bill, in 1965, for instance, was prescient and prophetic. He opposed the objective of setting up of the university, which he feared would carve out an '*ism*' out of Nehru's philosophy and argued that the University to be named instead, 'Rashtriya Vishwavidyalaya.' The discussion also saw him weave his argument with supporting thoughts and citations from Buddha and Ambedkar:

> Now all of us have a very high regard for the late revered Pandit Jawaharlal Nehru. He was one of the greatest leaders of humanity and scientific outlook was his special characteristic. Now through this wording, I think we are trying to create almost a church out of the theories or ideals that he stood for. This task, howsoever noble, comes hardly within the legitimate jurisdiction of a university. This is the work of a church, not of a university. The university should be expected to

> encourage and to conduct research in the philosophy of Pandit Nehru, but not to 'fulfil the ideals' he stood and worked for. Madam, through this fulfillment of the ideals through the medium of a university, I fear we will be carving an 'ism' out of his philosophy.
>
> To put the thing in a nutshell, what I want to say is, whether it is intended by the hon'ble Education Minister today or not, in course of time, this is going to convert this university into a sort of school of thought, if the First Schedule is adopted. Therefore, we want to repeat that this formulation of an *ism* is going to do some injustice and damage to the memory of Pandit Nehru, and that for two reasons. I shall try to put it as briefly as I can. First of all, *isms* are static, while situations are dynamic. Again, all *isms* are close systems of thought while the frontiers of human knowledge are ever expanding. And so, I think to convert any institution into a school of thought and associate that institution with the name of any great dignitary would be doing injustice to that great dignitary...

Participating in the Banaras Hindu University (BHU) Amendment Bill, 1965, Thengadi was emphatic that the word 'Hindu' could not be dropped from the name of the university and if denominational titles were to be banned, he argued, why not bring a separate Bill 'banning all denominational titles of educational institutions':

> I feel that there is no case for changing the original name of the Benaras Hindu University. The term 'Hindu' is not denominational; it is national...Now during the last five decades nobody could prove that the insertion of the word 'Hindu' had created any communalism in the Benaras Hindu University. Actually, even those who have raised an objection against the word 'Hindu' have conceded that originally the word 'Hindu' was inserted in the title of the Act in the national sense and not in the denominational sense. Secondly, even if it is taken for granted that all denominational names should be dropped, then it would be more appropriate to bring forward a separate Bill banning all denominational titles of educational institutions, so that in one Bill we can achieve the purpose, which is sought to be achieved. Thirdly, it would be more appropriate to allow the educational institutions themselves to decide what names they should adopt or should not adopt, instead of our legislating on the point. In view of the fact that the word 'Hindu' denotes national and not denominational sense, I oppose the dropping of the word 'Hindu'.

Many who closely saw Thengadi in his avatar as a parliamentarian and now scan his speeches and debates, will notice the wide acceptance and respect that he commanded cutting across party lines. He remained staunch and unflappable in his defence of democracy and democratic rights, in his faith in Constitutional norms and propriety and in his fundamental conviction that India's democracy needed to be preserved, protected and nurtured. It was this spirit of his which, in later years, saw him plunge headlong into the anti-Emergency struggle. His advocacy for the marginalised was equally matched by his unflinching advocacy of democracy and India's democratic spirit. He did not display such an approach keeping political considerations in mind, he demonstrated it whenever he felt democracy was in danger. In Parliament too, he repeatedly opposed the Congress' degenerative political habit of imposing President's Rule in states which had non-Congress governments. It did not matter to him, if the ones he was defending were communists who were at the receiving end of the Congress' Article 356 largesse! This was amply displayed in the discussion on the continuation of President's Rule in Kerala in 1966. Thengadi told the House:

> The Congress Government is opposed to the Communist Party. We are also opposed to it. But at the same time the votaries of democracy would not like the Communist Party to be defeated by undemocratic methods. Even if it is to be defeated in the battle of the ballot box, it should be through democratic measures. And therefore, as a votary of democracy, though I am opposed to Communism, I am very much against the spirit of this Resolution and I feel that we would be strengthening the forces that are against democracy by adopting such measures.

There are no recorded instances to show whether communists and their parties demonstrated a reciprocal gesture in defence of democracy! Thengadi once succinctly described the kind of democracy that was needed, "democracy without allowing it to degenerate into licentiousness, and discipline without allowing it to degenerate into regimentation."

Thengadi's public persona, his intellectual and spiritual dimension were greatly influenced and shaped by two giants of our modern India – Sri Guruji M.S. Golwalkar and Dr B.R. Ambedkar. This core dimension of his personality has been amply brought out in Shri S Gurumurthy's introduction to the volume; we are grateful to him for having penned it. Having closely worked with Thengadi, Gurumurthy's introduction brings great authenticity to the assessment. Shri Saji Narayanan, former president of BMS, has written an inspiring life-sketch of Thengadi, under whose guidance he actively worked in the organisation.

We gratefully acknowledge the support of Dr B.C. Joshi, Shri Pradosh Panda and Shri Suresh Chand, officials of the Lok Sabha Secretariat who assisted at different stages of the finalisation of the draft. We are grateful to Shri Adarsh Tiwari, Shri Abhay Chandel, Shri Amit Kumar, Shri Rangaswamy, Shri Ayush Anand and Shri Shailendra Shukla – all part of the team at Dr Syama Prasad Mookerjee Research Foundation (SPMRF).

A lot of what Thengadi had aspired for and envisaged is coming to gradual fruition today. India's capacity, to take in full sovereign rights, her decisions for preserving and pursuing her national self-interest is more evident today than at anytime before in her history as an independent nation. The renewed discussion on globalisation in the post-pandemic era, the increasing search for new normals of living and of global engagement, Prime Minister Narendra Modi's call for the need of a 'new type of human centric globalisation', his call for being 'vocal about local' and the need to make this a people's movement and a part of our daily existence, his emphasis on self-reliance which essentially means developing our national capacity to take decisions based on our national strength which will bring about a comprehensive economic reconstruction is placing the spotlight on many of Thengadi's thoughts. It is clearly an echo of what Thengadi once wrote:

> For *Bharat*, the term *swadeshi* has special significance. Here it is not a mere economic movement but is a means of bringing about economic reconstruction of the country. It is not a mere political slogan but is the essence of declaration of political independence. As a matter of fact, it is a spiritual movement which comprises not only the objectives of economic development and political independence but also all other aspects of national consciousness.

A greater global turning towards India and her civilisational ways, the increasing dissemination of the knowledge of Indian – *Bharatiya* – approaches towards a healthy and harmonious global living is imparting greater relevance and contemporaneity to Thengadi's thoughts, his vision and articulation. He continues to emerge as a '*seer*', a visionary of ages and of paradigms.

In one of his opuses, 'The Third Way', discussing renaissance and reform in the Indian rubric, Thengadi quoted a moving observation made by G Subramania Iyer, legendary social reformer, freedom fighter, doyen of Indian journalism:

> Statesmen, poets, men of science, inventors of mechanical contrivances, all these no doubt contribute to progress, but cannot impart the initial moving force, which come from those great men who by the power of their lofty character and sublime deeds and burning enthusiasm impart idealism to masses of men, sweep away abuse and falsehood, sort out superstitions, open new paths and establish fresh ideals for the elevation and advancement of the human race.

One could easily fit Dattopant Thengadi himself, within the contours of this fascinating description.

—Dr Anirban Ganguly

Vijaya Dashami

Vikram Samvat 2077

(25th October, 2020)

Introduction

—S Gurumurthy*

I am delighted, even feel fortunate, to write an introduction to this book 'Dattopant Thengadi : The Activist Parliamentarian' which is a collection of his speeches in the Rajya Sabha over his two terms in the august house.

My association with Dattopant Thengadi dates back to the 1980s. And from 1992 it became more intense with my active participation with him in the Swadeshi Jagaran Manch he had founded in the face of the onslaught of undefined globalisation which hit India like a tsunami. My close association with him over the next two decades yielded the most instructive experience of my life. Thanks to my interactions with him, I undertook extensive travel across the country which made me experience the real and entrepreneurial India at work in the hundreds of communitarian competitive industrial clusters from Ludhiana in Punjab to Thoothukudi in Tamil Nadu. My understanding of the Indian economy underwent a paradigm shift. I owe a lot of my unlearning and learning experiences to my association with him.

The gigantic personality of Thengadi built on his massive work in his illustrious life spent entirely in the cause of the nation cannot be comprehended from his role and speeches in the Rajya Sabha in the political and constitutional domain. It is actually the other way round. The content and essence of his speeches in the Rajya Sabha are a product of his comprehensive world view shaped by his unbelievably multidimensional and exceptionally versatile life and experience. Some add value to the institution they adorn and for some the institution they are in adds lustre. Thengadi added value to the institution of Rajya Sabha.

---

* Eminent Thinker, Chairman, Vivekananda International Foundation & Editor, Tughlaq.

Unless that larger Thengadi, of which his tenure in Rajya Sabha is a smaller part, is presented, even the picture of him as a Parliamentarian will be incomplete.

Unbelievable Bandwidth

Thengadi, whose bandwidth of connects and activities in Indian public life ranged from being a lifelong missionary of RSS to being the understudy of Babasaheb Ambedkar for 4 long years; from the toddy tapping community of Kerala to the global conferences of labour; from the discipline of RSS *shakhas* to the turbulence of trade unionism; and from the corridors of Rajya Sabha to secret underground cells during the Emergency; and from sleeping in the unlettered unorganised labourers' homes to the company of the commanding heights of high power intellectualism, was a human dynamo that operated non-stop till it broke down under the weight of its overwork throughout his life till it ground to a halt when he was 84.

A Nationalist takes over the Communist Terrain

For a communist, the trade union movement is a logical extension of his ideology and natural part of his public activity. But Thengadi was an RSS man and more a self-declared one, whose philosophy would be dismissed as disagreeable if not repugnant to the trade union ecosystem. Yet he, from the nationalist school of thought, took to trade unionism ideologically shaped by the conflict between communism and capitalism as compatible with only the former, like a fish takes to water and built the largest trade union network in India, the Bharatiya Mazdoor Sangh (BMS) in just three decades. Formed in 1955, it overtook the largest Indian trade union INTUC, where, ironically, Thengadi had apprenticed on the ABC of trade unionism for a year in 1951, by the mid-1980s. By 1989, BMS had reached a strength of 31 lakhs plus. That was more than the combined strength of CITU and AITUC who were, till then, the monopolists of the Indian trade union movement. In the next 12 years, its membership exceeded the collective strength of most other trade unions.

War against Class War

Thengadi, a stranger to the class war terrain of communism and communists, opposed their class enemy ideology and stormed their citadel and captured it from them. Never a Socialist, he vanquished them in their own territory. He waged an open war, an inclusive war, against their exclusive ideology, and defeated them in a straight battle, not in any guerrilla fight. He proved that honest trade unionism is the essence of worker protection, while class war makes the worker an instrument of a larger political agenda of a global ideological mission. He was not needed to use his strength to support or prop up an ideology. He never called a *bandh*, the normal weapon of large trade unions, never brought any city to stand still to show his might. His unions never indulged in violence. His unions were never part of any political party. He broke the rules of the game of ideologically directed and politically controlled unions and changed the paradigm of the trade union movement in India.

A trade union leader, yes, he was, but he was no urbanite like most trade unionists. Rooted in ancient Indian rural culture like Gandhiji, he handled the urban and cosmopolitan India without being affected or polluted by it. He built the largest union of agriculturists in India, the Bharatiya Kisan Sangh. Still he was not a village versus town man, or agriculture versus industry man. For him, nationalism was the melting pot of all sectional views and interests. Being not a believer in war between classes, he never promoted enmity between the rich and the poor, but stood for collective national interests. He carried nationalism and integral humanism to the territories monopolised by class hatred and class war and rendered the class idea almost irrelevant by promoting and institutionalising honest practice and fair bargain in the trade union movement.

Nationalism as the Alternative for Globalisation: The founding of SJM

When globalisation challenged India in early nineties and every one helplessly just opposed it or blindly welcomed it, he recalled the spirit of the freedom movement, the *Swadeshi* idea, to show the way to handle it with an indigenous paradigm. He formed the Swadeshi Jagaran Manch (SJM) which articulated an alternative endogenous economic model, not just opposition to globalisation. It emerged as the bulwark against mindless globalisation and succeeded in creating a vision for India as a global power. The forces of globalisation shaped the psychology of the Indian establishment to accept the world as the core and nation as the additive instead of the nation as the core and world as additive. The SJM became a trans-political and trans-party movement and took on the national discourse dominated by the powerful forces of globalisation which threatened to question the very concept of nation. The SJM emerged as the principal opinion maker on economic ideas centred on nationalism and national interests. The SJM saw globalisation as a passing phase when the entire world and Indian thinkers held it out as the final global order ever. In just under 25 years, as Thengadi had predicted, globalisation is over. He waged a war against the WTO. Now the US/West is waging a war against it. It is unfortunate that Thengadi, who had the conviction that the idea of the nation would prevail over the ideology of globalism is not alive today to hear the President of United States which was the principal driver of globalisation in 1990s, speak 'patriotism, not globalism as the future'. It is again unfortunate that he is not alive to read the Economist magazine which led the intellectual warhorse of globalisation to write the obituary of globalisation titled 'Globalisation is dead'.

A Ceaseless Activist and Astounding Intellectual

He was more. He was an astounding intellectual with a remarkable grasp of history and economics, sociology and politics. Yet he rarely appeared in public or even rarely allowed himself to be photographed or interviewed by mass media. In his view, nation builders do better things than stand before cameras. He was in politics, in the Rajya Sabha for two terms. But that did not make any difference to his definition of himself. He was an activist, who did in one life what was doable in ten lives. Yet massive activity did not interfere with his contemplative genius. He found time amid chaotic activity to think, read and write. He authored innumerable books of originality and high intellectual content — some 50 books in all, 27 in Hindi, 12 in English and 10 in Marathi. He has presented innumerable papers on profound subjects in national and international conferences. He learnt five languages apart from Marathi and English. He founded, inspired, managed and advised over a hundred organisations! And found time for all activities, yet time to talk and chit chat with thousands of ordinary workers! He could discover the 25th hour in the day and the 13th month in the year.

He predicted the Fall of Communism, Foresaw the End of Capitalism as Well

He was a seer. Decades before, he saw and theorised the collapse of communism as, he perceived, it went against human nature. It has happened. He has also theorised that capitalism too will collapse as that too is against human spirit and nature. This is waiting to happen. Even in philosophising the resistance to globalisation, he foresaw the national spirit as the greatest defence against global forces. He unveiled the hidden element of globalisation as the competition between nations. Result, not just in India but, all over the world today the real resistance to globalisation comes from perceived national interest, that is, *Swadeshi* at individual national level.

As Ambedkar's Understudy

Thengadi was the understudy of Babasaheb Ambedkar. 'Gurumurthy, I do not agree with Arun Shourie's conclusions on Babasaheb Ambedkar', he once told me. I pointed out to him that Arun's book was fully completely documented. He asked me: 'Do you mean to say that the lives of people who had had to face the greatest of challenges can be captured in records and documents?' He added that the complex times and the challenges that *Baba*—this is how he called Babasaheb Ambedkar—faced could not be read from records. 'In fact, most of the recordings cosmetise the real facts, more bluntly, they conceal, not bring out, the truth. So, records cannot capture the challenging life of Babasaheb Ambedkar'. Thengadi could talk with authority about Babasaheb Ambedkar because he was a full-time understudy with Ambedkar in the last four years of Babasaheb's life.

What Thengadi told me further was stunning. He said: 'I was an eyewitness to Babasaheb's tensions and problems'. He recalled 'Babasaheb wanted the Hindu *sants* and religious heads to declare openly that untouchability did not have the sanction of Hindu religious scripts'. RSS efforts in this direction were not bearing fruit. But Babasaheb told Thengadi that time was running out. His health was deteriorating fast in 1954. Babasaheb told Thengadi that 'I have faith in the process of the RSS in removing untouchability. But that is too slow. I cannot wait because I will not live to see the end of the problem'. Thengadi also recalled what made Babasaheb embrace Buddhism, in Babasaheb's own words thus: 'If I did not show the way for this helpless community, they would be hunted down by the Christian church and the communists.' What Babasaheb wanted the Hindu religious leaders to do in 1954, RSS could persuade them to do only a decade later, in 1965, in a conference of Hindu religious leaders in Udupi organised by the Vishwa Hindu Parishad. Thengadi's unique knowledge of Babasaheb made many, including me, insist that Thengadi write on his experiences with Babasaheb. A couple of months before he died Thengadi did that too, and his book on Babasaheb Ambedkar was also released.

A Meticulous Parliamentarian

The dimension of Thengadi that has been brought out in this volume is his role as a parliamentarian in the debates in the Rajya Sabha for two terms from 1964 to 1976. What stands out from the extracts of his speeches and interventions in the august house are his meticulous presentation of facts, highly referenced propositions and dignified response to counter viewpoints. His intense intellectualism and his diverse fields of knowledge are manifest in the range of subjects he has handled, each an area of specialisation for an expert. He has spoken on Economy and Finance, Agriculture, Food and Civil Supplies, Industry and Company Affairs, Railways, Petroleum, Mining and Power, Labour and Employment, External Affairs, Defence, Media, Home Affairs, Education, Judiciary and other matters of general public Importance. This volume is a lesson for the young and the elder parliamentarians of today to learn from the extracts of Thengadi's speeches in the Rajya Sabha how to be an efficient, competent and elegant parliamentarian. Today's parliamentary proceedings are least conducive to development of high-quality parliamentarians and debates. This book is an invaluable guide for contemporary parliamentarians

His Sole Inspiration and Drive: The RSS

What inspired him to such unbelievable mental, physical and intellectual activity beyond all known reserves of human energy? What drove him to attempt and accomplish the un-attempted impossible? The RSS. The much misunderstood and much maligned open-air university that trains patriots of high commitment in this country even today. He became a full time *pracharak* of RSS at the age of 22 and continued to work full time till he breathed his last. His creations, the BMS, the Kisan Sangh, and the SJM, are well known and powerful in thought and action. Thengadi, unknown to most, was the creator of institutions known, popular and powerful but was himself not known. No office attracted him. He could have occupied any position in public life. But for people like him positions added nothing.

He Owned the Country—and Nothing Else

He owned nothing, not a house or a car, no cell phone or else. He lived in a small room in Delhi provided by the BMS and in other's houses elsewhere. His needs, a few *kurtas* and *dhotis*, were accommodated in a suitcase. He travelled in overnight buses and mostly second-class trains.

Never thought of marriage as his time was exhausted by the cause he had taken up in life. A *rishi*, a *tapasvi*, he was. Like most *tapasvis*, he was also little known. National newspapers which waste thousands of tons of newsprint on what retired or prancing cine stars do in the morning and evening never even reported on this great man's work, much less on his greatness. Having seen him closely and known him intimately and learnt from him immensely, the only thing I could do is to let a few others know by my homage to him through an article in The New Indian Express titled 'Dattopant Thengadi—A *Tapasvi* Dies Unnoticed' when the great soul passed away on October 14, 2004 unnoticed by the media.

(15th September, 2020)

Rishibhisthulyam
Dattopant Thengadi : A Life Sketch

In Valmiki *Ramayana* (2.19.20), Kaikeyi asks Rama to leave for the forest at the earliest. Rama happily accepts it saying he is not after worldly wealth; he always wanted to live like a *rishi* (ऋषिभिस्तुल्यं) entirely devoted to *Dharma* alone (केवलं धर्ममास्थितम्). India's history is the creation of a long chain of such sacrificing *rishi* like figures who reigned in different walks of our social life. Shri Dattopant Thengadi is the latest shining link in the chain. Hence he is honoured by the term '*Rashtra Rishi*'.

Shri Dattatreya Bapurao Thengadi alias Dattopant Thengadi was born in 1920 in Arvi in Wardha District of Maharashtra. Like many other great personalities of the past, he was also very much influenced and oriented by his spiritually inclined mother, Janakibai. Even during school days, Thengadiji displayed his intellectual and multifaceted brilliance.

Sri M.S. Golwalkarji (Sri Guruji) became the second Sarsanghchalak of RSS in 1940. He adopted an aggressive and proactive organisational strategy to reach all walks of national life. During his tour from 1940 to 1942, Sri Guruji called upon youth at every place to come out as *pracharaks* in order to spread the work and the message of the Sangh. He said: "Today for Bharatmata *pooja*, we require flowers which are untouched, unsmelt, not dried up, and not worn in the head; retaining fragrance, honey and charm." On his call, hundreds of youth from various *shakhas* came out leaving their home, parents, wealth, jobs, friends, villages, towns etc. They readily went to places which they had not seen or even heard of, with full self-confidence of emerging victorious. The first batch of *pracharaks* was ready in 1942 to fan out to the nook and corner of the country in order to spread RSS' work. Young Thengadiji was one among them who became a *pracharak* after completing his studies in law in flying colours. His father, being a well-known lawyer, wanted his son to join his profession, but Thengadiji had already made up his mind to dedicate his life for the nation through RSS work, with which he was associated from his school days.

One fine morning in 1942, Sri Guruji sent Thengadiji to Kozhikode, Kerala to start RSS work there with an introduction letter to a well-known lawyer of the town. Kerala was unknown to him, and the only advantage Thengadiji had was that he could speak fluent English. Thengadiji met the lawyer, and after hearing about the assignment, the lawyer affectionately advised him to return at the earliest, since such work, he observed, was not suited for a region like Kerala. However, the young *pracharak* did not get disappointed, he stayed back and in a short time built a strong foundation of RSS work in Kerala. From 1944 to 1948 he worked as *state pracharak* in Bengal including the area of Assam.

In 1949, Congress leader and the then home minister of Madhya Pradesh, Dwaraka Prasad Mishra, while supporting the lifting of the ban on RSS, invited Thengadiji to work in the INTUC, to strengthen it organisationally. Sri Guruji asked Thengadiji to accept it as he saw it as an opportunity to gain first-hand experience which would be useful to create later a labour organisation based on Bharatiya values and tradition. At that time, the trade union movement was in the control of communists. In October 1950, Thengadiji became a member of the national executive committee of INTUC. Interestingly between 1952 and 1955, he worked as the State Organising Secretary of AIBEA (All India Bank Employees Association), a communist organisation for bank employees. He worked with unions in sectors like postal, banking, LIC, railway, textiles and coal and was an office-bearer of several unions. Thus in Sri Guruji's own words, Thengadiji 'single-handedly' completed the task assigned to him when he started Bharatiya Mazdoor Sangh (BMS) in 1955.

For several years after the formation of BMS, Thengadiji continued as Member of the National Executive Committee of Bharatiya Jana Sangh (BJS). He is also remembered by some as the energetic and deft Organising Secretary of Bharatiya Jana Sangh (BJS) for Madhya Pradesh during 1952-1953 and for south India during 1956-57. He was associated with the formation of many Sangh inspired organisations like Akhil Bharatiya Vidyarthi Parishad (ABVP), Bharatiya Jana Sangh, Bharatiya Kisan Sangh, Swadeshi Jagaran Manch, Akhil Bharatiya Grahak Panchayat, Samskar Bharati, Akhil Bharatiya Adhivakta Parishad, Samajik Samrasata Manch,

Bharatiya Vichar Kendram. Some of them were founded by Thengadiji. His organisational vision directly benefitted BMS the most. In 1984, at the Hyderabad Conference of BMS, he declared war against the hegemony of multinational companies and their agents in India. Thus he conceived the idea of Swadeshi Jagaran Manch that was formed later in 1991. He launched a struggle against government's new economic policies initiated in 1991 as a result of international structural changes in the aftermath of the Dunkel proposal. Within the BMS, he created the Sarva Panth Samadar Manch for harmonious relations among labourers belonging to different religions and Paryavaran Manch for environmental protection and promotion.

As Rajya Sabha Member

Thengadiji was elected to the Rajya Sabha for two terms, 1964-1976. During this period, he developed close relationships with leaders of all parties and various labour organisations. He had many friends in the Congress. Regular exchange of ideas took place between Thengadiji and Communist leaders like S.A. Dange, Hiren Da (Hiren Mukherjee), Chaturanan Mishra, P. Ramamurti, Bhupesh Gupta, Jyotirmoy Basu, Beni and Roza Deshpande and CITU leader Dr M.K. Pandhe. K. Damodaran, one of the early theoretical builders of the Communist Party in Kerala, visited Thengadiji regularly. K.R. Malkani, the famous journalist, former editor of the Organiser weekly and BJP leader, in his reminiscence during the 61st birth anniversary of Thengadiji, writes in his usual investigative style: "I feel that I am not cheating by disclosing a secret; in the year 1969, when the entire opposition including the left-wing parties unanimously proposed the name of Dattopant Thengadiji for the post of deputy speaker in Rajya Sabha... the proposal was rejected by the then ruling party."

When CITU General Secretary P. Ramamurthy completed and celebrated 75 years of his life, along with other Communist Party leaders, he invited Thengadiji. After the Emergency when communist youths in Kerala started joining RSS, there was a fiery reaction from the CPI(M) to prevent the outflow by indulging in murderous attack on RSS workers. Pained by this Thengadiji and P. Ramamurthy jointly tried to bring about an amicable solution. However, Ramamurthy later admitted that he did not have control over his cadre.

Whenever there was some rally or programme in Delhi, workers from other parts of the country used to troop in to Thengadiji's MP quarters in

57 South Avenue, they would sleep inside and on the lawn outside even in his absence. There were occasions when Thengadiji returned at 2 a.m. at night and could not find space for himself, he found some corner and went to sleep without a murmur.

Emergency was imposed on 25th June, 1975, and RSS was banned on 4th July. During the dark phase of Emergency, after the arrest of Nanaji Deshmukh and later Ravindra Verma who were Secretaries of the Lok Sangharsh Samiti, Thengadiji fearlessly took over charge as its Secretary from February 1976. His responsibility as General Secretary in BMS was handed over to Ram Naresh Singhji who had by then been released from detention under NSA. For about 13 months, Thengadiji toured the country in disguise carefully evading the tentacles of the secret agencies of the government and led the underground movement organising people against the tyranny. He frequently met opposition Chief Ministers like Sheikh Abdullah, Karunanidhi, Babu Bhai Patel and leaders of Sarvodaya, Akali Dal, Lok Dal, Congress (O), socialist and labour organisations in order to associate them in strategic planning. His efforts led to a unified fight against Emergency while many other political leaders were afraid and gradually withdrew from activities. On 18th January 1977, Indira Gandhi suddenly declared elections for March. By that time, Thengadiji had well prepared the ground for a political fight. He played a significant role in the formation of the Janata Party on 23rd January, and along with Ravindra Verma, he drafted the constitution of the new party and its organisational setup. He remained one of the few underground leaders who could not be arrested during the entire period of Emergency. Many have rightly said, Thengadiji is the real hero of the anti-Emergency struggle.

The Life of a *Rishi*

Though many positions of power and awards came to him, he rejected all of them with utmost humility. After Emergency in 1977, many seniors requested him to become a minister or MP in the Janata Party regime. However, he rejected all such requests as he had decided to leave political and parliamentary life forever. From that time onwards, Thengadiji freed himself from all posts even in BMS and worked for the organisation till the end only as a guide without any formal position. He continued to inspire thousands of activists in various fields of nation building. When his name was proposed for Padma Bhushan in 2003, he respectfully refused to accept it.

Thengadiji regularly toured the country to address RSS swayamsevaks in meetings and training camps. He meticulously maintained contacts all over India through the 'person to person, heart to heart and door to door' approach. Senior activists always sought his guidance on organisational and other matters. After the passing of both Deendayal Upadhyayaji and Sri Guruji, Thengadiji continued to be the most senior thought-leader of Sangh and *Parivar* organisations.

At the Kanpur conference of BMS in 1970, Thengadiji declared that communism would soon disappear from the world. Within 20 years, the world witnessed the fall of communism in all Communist countries. Similarly in his book *The Third Way* (1995 edition p.114) he wrote: "The days of capitalism are numbered; it will not last even up to 2010 A.D. The search is already going on for *The Third Way.*" In mid-September, 2008, when a global financial crisis started from Wall Street and spread to all streets, many proponents of capitalism termed it as the 'demise' of capitalism. While the famous prophecies of Karl Marx were proved false by the passage of history, Thengadiji's true vision transcended time and place. He was a *drashta* (visionary seer) in the real sense.

As an ardent RSS swayamsevak, wherever he worked, his life was his message. To cite an example, once, Thengadiji came to Tatanagar to attend a BMS meeting. He stayed in the quarter of a labourer. On the same day, the well-known Communist leader S.A. Dange also came to attend another meeting in the same town and stayed in a luxury hotel. Dange's followers questioned their leader on this issue. Thengadiji usually felt no difference in travelling in the second and third class compartments of trains. Such living examples have contributed to the growth of our organisation immensely.

Thengadiji authored a large number of books with originality and high intellectual content which emanated not only from his ideological conviction but also from his first-hand experience of the relevant issues. His declared position, 'no compromise on fundamentals' might have displeased some. His forewords written for many books were also evidences of his intellectual mastery. Three books authored by him during the last phase of his life, namely *The Third way, Karyakarta* and *Dr Ambedkar aur Samajik Kranti ki Yatra* are his masterpieces. He profusely quoted the ideas of personalities ranging from A.K. Gopalan of the Communist Party, Charu Mazumdar of CPI(ML) to Khalil Gibran and also from world literature. He was fluent in Marathi, Hindi, English, as well as Malayalam and Bangla.

Thengadiji had extensively travelled to almost all parts of the world except the pacific region. On 28th April, 1985, during his visit to China as a part of a BMS delegation, Beijing Radio broadcasted his speech for twenty minutes in Hindi with Chinese translation. A World Trade Union Conference was held in Moscow in November 1990 in which he participated. It highlighted the failure of the market economy as well as communism and raised the big question as to what the third alternative was. Thengadiji had already turned to consolidate the ideas of a third alternative, which later came out as the famous book '*The Third Way*'. In his Washington speech in 1993, he argued that human beings everywhere prefer to be status-quo-ist and self-complacent. However, the international economic order will be provoked by circumstances to turn to Indian ideas. Sarcastically he quoted John Milton's God, who said:

> "If not goodness, let calamity
> Toss him unto my Bosom."

Thengadiji's Association with Dr Ambedkar

During 1952 elections, Dr Bhimrao Ramji Ambedkar felt extremely let down when Jawaharlal Nehru put up a candidate against him but not against the Communist Party's A.K. Gopalan so that Gopalan could win uncontested. Such was the Congress's antagonism towards Dr Ambedkar. The CPI's founding member S.A. Dange went to the extent of telling people openly: "Spoil your votes but don't vote Dr Ambedkar." Thus, when both the Indian National Congress and the Communist Party of India treacherously tried to defeat him in elections, Dr Ambedkar turned to RSS at the fag end of his life. In the 1952 elections, in Madhya Pradesh, Bharatiya Jana Sangh, Dr Ambedkar's Shetkari Federation and Samajwadi Dal formed an alliance. In the Bhandara Lok Sabha constituency by-election held in April 1954, Dr Ambedkar chose RSS *pracharak* Thengadiji as his election convenor after getting Sri Guruji's approval. But his association with RSS was short-lived for two years till Dr Ambedkar's death in 1956. Thengadiji's book on *Dr Ambedkar aur Saamajik Kranti ki Yatra* (Hindi) describes Dr Ambedkar's close relationship with RSS. In order to realise Ambedkar's dream, Thengadiji founded Samajik Samarasta Manch in 1983. When Arun Shourie wrote a book accusing Dr Ambedkar of colluding with the British, it deeply pained Thengadiji.

End of a Lifelong *Tapasya*

During the final years of his life in the midst of his increasing illness, Thengadiji took two years to complete the book on Dr Ambedkar. After finishing the work in July 2004, he was seen relaxed and expressed his immense happiness. Thengadiji's last message to BMS activists at the organisation's Surat meet was: "In future, ardent *tapasya* is required." He was reminding us that at a time when recognition and honours pour upon the organisations, our *tapasya* should not be lost.

Dattopant Thengadiji's parents were devotees of Bhagavan Dattatreya whose temple stands at Ganagapur, in Gulbarga district of Karnataka and his parents had deep faith that Thengadiji was born due to the blessings of Bhagavan Dattatreya. Thus the child was named Dattatreya. Thengadiji did not speak till the age of 4. The worried parents worshipped at the temple, tonsured the head of the child as part of the religious offering. Relatives recall that during the return journey, the boy uttered his first words at the station. On 14th October, 2004, *Sharad Navratri*, Thengadiji's soul left his body at the age of 84 in Pune, while taking a bath. Prominent personalities from all walks of life paid tributes to this great *rishi*. Recalling him as a great labour leader, organiser and ideal patriot, the Rajya Sabha paid rich tribute to him.

A question naturally arises: Will a void be created by the demise of people like him? Thengadiji himself had answered it at the time of the death of Badebhai Ram Naresh Singhji, a stalwart of BMS. Thengadiji had then said: "When Ganga is flowing continuously, we take a bucket full of water. We may think that there will be a vacuum in Ganga. However, the moment the bucket is raised, in no time, water from the surroundings will fill the gap and Ganga will continue to flow uninterruptedly. Even if you and I are gone, the great divine organisation will go on uninterruptedly." The ideal life that he lived would continue to shed light through the activities of lakhs of dedicated workers inspired by him, who will fill the void created by his departure.

The entire world now wants to get an insider view of RSS which has built the edifice of a strong nation today and which is deeply rooted in all walks of public life including politics, labour, culture, religion and so on. These achievements of RSS is due to the inspirational lives of personalities like Thengadiji.

Thengadiji's thoughts will be remembered through works such as the present volume. This volume provides the signature he left on parliamentary work. Deriving experience from his activities in labour and other fronts, Thengadiji raised such issues and problems and insisted upon the government for follow-up actions through policies and attendant legislation. His primary concern was the nation and its common people, and on matters of national interest on several occasions, he went beyond the ideological division between the 'Right' and the 'Left' which is amply documented in this work. We can pay off our *rishi-rina* (debt) to him by disseminating the fundamentals of his thoughts, his vision and his selfless-work and by trying to mould ourselves in those values and ideals that shaped him and which he pursued throughout his inspiring and fascinating life.

—Saji Narayanan
Former President
Bharatiya Mazdoor Sangh (BMS)

Rajya Sabha (1966-1968)

P.T.O.

Shri Dattopant Thengadi (encircled) with other Rajya Sabha Members

Contents

1

Economy and Finance

While participating in the general discussion on Union Budgets in the Rajya Sabha, Thengadi felt that the Budget should always be consumer-oriented. The government should take the common masses in confidence while preparing the Budget as well as the plans. The Budget should lay adequate focus on employment generation, national wage policy and national price policy. In his speeches, Thengadi welcomed moves towards simplification of taxation and searches and raids to unearth black money.

Thengadi spoke for an integrated social security scheme and also highlighted the plight of pensioners. He urged the government to appoint a Pension Commission to address the relevant issues. He favoured progressive liberalisation of the industries and felt concerned about the pattern of industrial ownership.

Agriculture, according to Thengadi, had not received the attention it deserved. He felt the need to develop agro-industries. He was of the opinion that Minimum Wages Act should be extended to agro workers and extensively spoke about income disparities, problem of capital formation, employment, price rise, etc. He also spoke about promoting professionals for public administration and emphasised the need for changes in the composition of RBI and felt that the autonomy of RBI would lead to better economic policy formulation.

Regarding planning, Thengadi was of the opinion that there should be wide consultations while finalising the plans. He observed that instead of being formulated in the air-conditioned rooms, the plans must evolve from the level of the people. He held responsible the traders and black marketeers for frequent price rise and advocated parity between the prices of agricultural and manufactured goods.

Motion Regarding Draft Fourth-Five Year Plan (1969-71)[1]

Sir, now that we are discussing the draft Fourth Plan, I think it is necessary for us to have some introspection and see why the three previous plans have admittedly failed to generate enthusiasm amongst the people. The reason was that they were not people's plans. The plans are being formulated in air-conditioned rooms and not being evolved from the bottom, that is, from the level of the people themselves. I think we are putting the cart before the horse while formulating these plans because the right procedure would be that the various economic interests of the country should be properly organised. There should be mutual consultations. There should be a round table conference of all the organised as well as unorganised economic interests in which every economic interest should be allowed to state its difficulties, its aspirations, its pledge for contribution during the plan period and, thus, by mutual consultation, through consensus, the targets and other items in the plan should be decided upon. We know, sir, that in a small country like Israel, they have successfully implemented this method. It is true that ours is a very vast country but still if we try to evolve this procedure, I think there is no reason why we should not succeed. Now, in this respect, we see that there are certain organised sections, for example, labour, employees, administration, some sections of *kisans*, self-employed persons, and so on. If instead of imposing any plan from above, the Planning Commission inspires each economic interest to have its own plan and then tries to coordinate the various plans of the different economic interests and, thus, evolves a national plan on the fashion of Israel,[2] then, I think the people would accept that plan as the people's plan and then naturally enthusiasm would be generated amongst the people to implement the plan and even to make sacrifices for its implementation. Now in this plan, we do not find anything that would inspire the poorer sections of the population. As a matter of fact, it was expected that against the background of our experience of the three Plans, at least now in this Fourth Plan, there would be an endeavour to evolve a national income policy, a national price policy,

1. *Rajya Sabha Debate* dated 14th May, 1969.
2. Typically, Israel prepares a national plan on the basis of zones. Each national plan is further enhanced and detailed by more local plans that discuss its implementation in greater detail. National outline plans are drafted by the National Planning and Construction Committee of Israel or the National Infrastructure Committee, and approved by the Government of Israel. Thengadi was perhaps referring to the need for more detailed grassroots plans rather than a top-heavy one.

a national productivity policy and a national employment policy. No such systematic efforts seem to have been made while drafting the plan and, therefore, I again reiterate our original demand for a round table conference of different economic interests to evolve through consensus all these four national policies during the Fourth Plan period.

Only one more point. Much has been said about public sector undertakings. Certainly, they are suffering from bureaucratism and the bureaucrats are not known for either business acumen on the one hand or for sufficient knowledge of industrial psychology, on the other. In the present conditions, it is a problem for us how to handle the public sector undertakings. I would like to suggest that taking some courage in both hands, we should have some experiment at least in two or three of the public sector undertakings of auto management, that is, experiment of workers managing their own undertakings with the help of the government. Let us take the workers into confidence and give them a fair trial and see whether, if the same technical and financial aid which the government would have given to any undertaking if it had been run by the bureaucrats, is made available to the workers, the workers through their co-operative council could manage their own undertakings, and whether they could manage them in a better way, more efficiently and more profitably. That trial should be given to them.

Calling Attention Motion Regarding Inordinate Delay in the Finalisation of the Draft Fourth Five-Year Plan[3]

D. Thengadi: Sir, the Planning Minister said that after devaluation, comprehensive re-examination of all aspects has become necessary. It is true there is inflation and from various points of view, the impact is quite considerable. May I point out what the report submitted by six experts, appointed by the Organisation for European Economic Co-operation[4] after studying the experience of 20 countries over a period of eight years, has observed:

"For the stabilisation authorities, to have a wage policy, therefore, seems to us the only appropriate and reasonable means of facing the problem of wage push inflation."

---

3. *Rajya Sabha Debate* dated 10th August, 1966.
4. Committee of European Economic Co-operation (CEEC) met in Paris between 12th July, 1947 to 22nd September, 1947, to discuss Europe's post World War-II economic recovery and to work out the implementation of the Marshall Plan.

Against the background of this experience, may I seek an assurance from the Planning Minister that the government will formulate a national wage policy[5] for the Fourth Plan period and for that purpose, will convene a round table conference of all the parties to industrial relations.

Resolution Regarding Appointment of a Parliamentary Committee to Enquire into the Soaring Prices of Essential Commodities and to Suggest Remedial Measures*[6]

D. Thengadi: Madam, before I go to the subject proper, let me clarify one point which was raised earlier that the theory of wage price spiral is unscientific. There is no necessary correlation between the two. That is, there can be price rise not preceded by a wage increase and a wage increase not followed by a price rise.

Now, it has been said that diagnosis is half the cure. I am sorry to say that there is an attempt either deliberate or inadvertent to minimise or undermine the magnitude of the problem. Take the example of our index numbers. We are told that there was a rise of 11.3 between March 20 and August 21. Now this pertains to wholesale prices. No consumer can obtain anything in the market at the prices published by the government because the average consumer purchases everything at retail shops. As a matter of fact, it was necessary that our index numbers should have taken cognisance of retail prices rather than of wholesale prices. In the same way, it is necessary to assess correctly the difference between the existing price level and also the minimum requirements of the common man. This has again become impossible because of the faulty and unscientific cost of living index numbers. I would suggest that in this respect, the report of the committee[7] on the Middle Class Cost of Living Index should be accepted as the basis for compiling the index numbers for the common man. Now we are facing this problem of inflation for a number of years. I wonder why we did not make any attempt at formulating a national price policy as well as a national wage policy. Had we evolved such a policy for price as well as for wage, it would have been possible for us to cope with events and contingencies. We could have taken assistance of the different agencies that are available. We have got a banking

5. A policy was incorporated in the First Five Year Plan to fix labour wages in different sectors.
6. *Rajya Sabha Debate* dated 10th September, 1965.
7. A Committee constituted by the Ministry of Labour and Employment, Govt. of India, in 1959.

system here. I remember that in Australia in 1949, when the nationalised banking system was denationalised, one of the two tasks entrusted to the denationalised banking system was to maintain the price line. It was also one of the tasks entrusted to the eight *sardars* of the banking industry of Canada and if any of the banks in Canada failed to make its own contribution in maintaining the price line, the practice was that it would forfeit its lease after a period of 10 years. Now in our country, we are facing a number of problems so far as prices are concerned, but I must say that, as a matter of fact, this inflation is not a disease in itself; it is a symptom even as eczema or asthma is not said to be a disease but only a symptom of some other disease. Similarly, inflation is a symptom of a number of other diseases and they are broadly psychological and material. Psychologically, we know that the traders and the middlemen about whom much is said are not patriots. They are responsible for the price rise. Unless an atmosphere and environment of patriotism is created, it would not be possible for us to control prices only through legal measures. Now on the material level, there are certain difficulties. There should be a proper parity between the prices of agricultural produce and those of the manufactured goods. Our *kisans* would have no spurt to production unless the prices are production-oriented but the consumer would be finished if our indices are not consumption-oriented. Now because we are not having consumption-oriented indices, it would be suicidal to have production-oriented prices. And that is the paradox of the situation. So far as the psychological aspect is concerned, as I have already referred to the case of traders and middlemen, I must also say that the consumers in general and the workers in particular can be trained to bear the burden of increased prices if there is an atmosphere of patriotism. Only a couple of days back... (*Interruptions*)

It is possible to create an atmosphere in which people can bear this strain. For example, just before a couple of days, the British Trade Union Congress endorsed and accepted the present or proposed price policy of the British Labour Party. So far as material factors are concerned, I may say that they can be divided under three heads. One is deficit financing, the second is profiteering and the third is natural scarcity. So far as deficit financing is concerned, everybody is well aware of its evils and yet we are pursuing that because we are enamoured of our bookish approach to the plan. What I should like to suggest is that unless we bring about drastic changes in regard to the basis of our Five-Year Plans, it would not be possible for us to regulate the price level of the country. Secondly, there is profiteering. Much need not be said about this. Surely, national discipline must be followed even by commerce and industry. Thirdly, there is the problem of scarcity. I would like to suggest that it is possible there are scientific methods to have a cause-wise break-up of all these three factors. So far as scarcity is concerned, it can be assessed fairly correctly on the strength of the balance of payments deficit. If we evolve this method of cause-wise break-up of inflation, it would be possible for us to have the allocation of responsibility on all the three, i.e. the producer, the profiteer and the government. In that case, it would be possible for us to regulate prices. At this juncture, because of the national Emergency,[8] I would not like to say anything very harsh against the present policies of the government. I support the resolution of our hon'ble friend, Jagat Narainji,[9] in the hope that the findings of the committee appointed because of this resolution would be properly considered and implemented by the government.

Resolution Suggesting Steps to be taken by the Government for Providing Greater Employment Opportunities and Bringing about Uniformity in the Working of Industrial Undertakings[10]

Sir, I welcome the resolution. I am of the opinion that the introduction of 40 hours per week will be helpful in increasing productivity and production. It has been experienced that if the same quantum of work is spread over a longer period, it gets itself spread and the entire time is taken by the same work. If a shorter period is allotted for the work, then the same work is finished within a shorter period also. According to Parkinson's Law, whatever extra time is allotted for the same quantum of work is exhausted by that work. Therefore, the introduction of 40 hours per week will be helpful in increasing productivity and production. And again, we will be able to work our plants, our machines with greater efficiency for longer hours if seven days per week we managed to run all the plants, all the factories with this provision that every worker will have 40 hours per week.

---

8. A reference to the emergency situation in the country that had arisen because of the India-Pakistan war in1965.
9. Lala Jagat Narain (1899-1981) – freedom fighter, for three decades member of the AICC, detained under MISA during the Emergency imposed by Indira Gandhi in 1975, editor, member of the Punjab Legislative Assembly, Member of Parliament, founder of *Punjab Kesari*, founder of the *Hind Samachar* media group, Narain was shot dead by Khalistani terrorists for opposing their demand for Khalistan.
10. *Rajya Sabha Debate*, dated 11th June, 1971.

Then, I cannot reconcile myself with the idea that the age of retirement should be 60 years. That is too much. The present limit of 58 years is quite enough. We should also give opportunity to younger elements.

So far as the ceiling of Rs. 4,000 is concerned, I am of the opinion that this should not be considered in isolation. It is a part of the bigger problem. It would be better if we begin from the other end, that is, of determining the ratio between the minimum and the maximum expendable incomes in the country should be 1:20 and an effort should be made to bring it down to 1:10. With that end in view, we should decide the ratio between the minimum and the maximum, and not merely the ceiling of the supervisor or the managerial staff. With the difference of opinion, I support the Resolution.

The Union Budget (General) 1965-66[11]

Responsibility towards Consumers Remains Unfulfilled

D. Thengadi: Mr. Deputy Chairman, sir, I support the plea for the simplification of the taxation structure and of the law governing it. Regarding the foreign investors' role, I would like to warn the government that their collaboration should not be allowed to usher an era of dollar imperialism or rouble imperialism.

Regarding the searches and raids for unaccounted money, we welcome the gesture. It has helped a lot. For example, I know that if the results of the raids on the residence of the proprietors of the Edward Mills at Bombay[12] are publicised, the workers of the mills would be able to secure all their legitimate dues. Consequently, we welcome this gesture. So far as the working class is concerned, I must say that the present Budget is not a workers' Budget. As a matter of fact, workers constitute a major bulk of consumers and since every Budget is expected to be consumer-oriented, and since the working class does not stand to gain much through this Budget, I have to say that the Budget has not fulfilled its responsibilities towards the consumer.

The much-trumpeted reduction in certain excise duties has been preceded by an earlier rise in those duties and, therefore, this measure is only deceptive, if not fraudulent. Moreover, the government itself is not confident that the benefit arising out of such reduction will pass on to the consumers. In this Budget, we expected that more funds would be allotted for the benefit of workers, industrial, agricultural, forest, etc. Nothing

11. *Rajya Sabha Debate* dated 10th March, 1965.
12. A cotton mill in Girangaon area of Mumbai started in the colonial era.

has been said about the working class. As a matter of fact, the Central Government has in its employ nearly 21 million people. Their plight has been completely ignored. As we all know, the recommendations of the Das Commission[13] have not been implemented fully and the plea of the workers for merging of dearness allowance with the basic salary has not been accepted.

The agricultural labour has been ignored. Actually, they are receiving less than 60 paisa every day. Agriculture has not been given the priority it deserves. Even tractors are not manufactured in our country.

So far as the workers are concerned, there has been a demand for a Wage Board for the Railways and a Third Pay Commission for the rest of the Central Government employees. And since this demand has not been conceded, the workers would not be enthused.

Now, sir, I come to a certain major problem of our Indian economy. Much has been said about the price-wage-price spiral. I am convinced that consumers cannot stand to gain unless three objects are achieved: (i) full employment, (ii) evolution of a National Wage Policy, and (iii) evolution of a National Price Policy. If the trend of money wages is compared with the rate of growth of national income, I must say that the wages have not outstripped the rate of production. Our basic problem is to provide a steady and equitable rise in real income without affecting adversely the price stability. For this purpose, we must have a clear analysis of the various causes that contribute to the changes in prices in a given period and the computation of differential weightage that these factors exercise. It is wrong to think that such an analysis will be unnecessary if we resort to the way of controls because the utility of controls is only limited. They do not eliminate the basic pressures leading to higher prices. Broadly three factors are at work behind the screen, viz. scarcity, inflation and profiteering. In view of these factors, we must work out the break-up of a consumer price-index number for working, middle or agricultural classes on a cause-wise basis. The present pattern of expenditure of these sections of population is distributed over such essentials of life that all scarcity in these commodities is fairly represented in consequential imports.

It is essential for the stability of economy that we evolve a National Wage Policy. We are on the threshold of the Fourth Five-Year Plan[14] and

13. Das Commission – The Second Pay Commission set up by the Government of India in 1957. It submitted its report two years later and was headed by Jaganatha Das.
14. Launched by the Indira Gandhi government in the period 1969-1974.

the wage policy during the plan period must be determined. Sir, here I would like to point out to an observation in a recent report produced by the Organisation for European Economic Cooperation titled, *The Problem of Rising Prices.*[15] It says:

"The enunciation of a wage policy would itself constitute an enormous step forward to combat inflation and it would be a step that would attract others in its train... It would lead to a greater understanding of the working of the economy and of the considerations that must underlie public policy."

Now, while determining our national wage policy, we must consider two aspects: (i) a cause-wise response of money wages to the results of index breakdown as proposed earlier, and (ii) a determined rate of growth in real wages on the basis of planned productivity. The effect of scarcity on the price situation should be absorbed equally by all as a national concern. Some qualifications can be proposed, such as protecting the lower grades at minimum level at the expense of the higher ones and giving a proportionate right to workers in the ownership of capital to the extent that the investment policy is responsible for the creation of scarcity. As regards neutralisation of the effects of inflationary policies pursued by the government, the decisions will have to be taken from time to time with a special reference to the defence requirement. On the other hand, there needs to be no compromise on profiteering, though a reasonable return on capital up to a determined maximum of total allowable gain should not be in dispute.

As regards the problem of sharing the gains of productivity, the following formula suggested by Dr P.S. Lokanathan,[16] the founder chairman of the National Productivity Council, deserves serious consideration. He states:

"Where the wage is below the minimum wage, the management should get zero per cent, and labour 100 per cent. Where the wage is between the minimum and the fair wage, the management should get 20 per cent, and labour 80 per cent. Where the wage is at or above the fair wage level, the management should get 50 per cent, and labour 50 per cent."

15. May 1961.
16. Dr Palamadai S. Lokanathan (1894-1972) – economist, taught economics at Madras University, editor of Eastern Economist, first Executive Secretary of the United Nations Economic Commission for Asia and the Far East (ECAFE), later UNESCAP. The National Productivity Council was launched in 1958.

By working in this fashion, we can work out a National Wage Policy and a National Price Policy and ensure fullest employment. We can be assured of the real satisfaction of the average consumer.

The Union Budget (General), 1966-67[17]

Need for an Employment-oriented Budget

D. Thengadi: Sir, we have always insisted that the Five-Year Plan or the one-year plan, that is, our Annual Budget should be employment-oriented. But I am sorry to note that even in this year's Budget, there is no employment orientation. I should like to assert that after the completion of this Budget period, the ratio of the unemployed and the underemployed to the total population of the country would be bigger than what it is today. Distribution of all cultivable waste land to landless labourers, particularly to those belonging to the Scheduled Castes and Scheduled Tribes, introduction of subsidiary industries in the rural areas of the country, development of peculiarly Bhartiya technology with a view to decentralising the processes of production with the help of electrification in the rural areas, special protection to the cottage- and small-scale industries, demarcation between the spheres of the small-scale industries and the large-scale industries, fixation of the national minimum and of the ratio between the minimum and the maximum, expendable monthly incomes in the land, proper correspondence between the prices of the agricultural produce and those of the manufactured goods, enunciation of the national price policy and substantial reduction in the indirect taxes – these among others are some of the measures which are calculated to ease economic tension of unemployment and underemployment. I am sorry to say that none of these measures has found a place in the Budget under discussion.

On the contrary, there is a definite attempt to increase unemployment by various devices, such as introduction of automation in the Life Insurance Corporation, and admission in the agricultural industry of Punjab to big capitalists. These are some of the examples of this official policy, leading to large-scale unemployment. The government should give up all such anti-employment policies and accept the golden rule that there should be no retrenchment without alternate employment. An unemployment insurance scheme should also be introduced.

This Budget is bound to give a rude shock to consumers in general and workers in particular. While the plight of the general consumers has been

---

17. *Rajya Sabha Debate* dated 21st March, 1966.

already discussed elaborately, I should like to draw the attention of the House to the plight of workers who are the worst sufferers. It has become imperative now to chalk out the National Wage Policy.[18] Nothing has been done in this direction in the Budget under discussion. Workers can be inspired to perform supreme sacrifices for national prosperity. They have proved their patriotism during the Sino-Indian conflict as well as the Indo-Pak conflict. But they must feel that they are being taken into confidence. They must feel that their viewpoint also has been taken into consideration by the Finance Minister that the Budget and the plan are theirs, that it is the people's plan and the people's Budget and that their sacrifices are not going to be in vain. For this purpose, I request the government to take the workers, along with other sections of the population, into confidence while preparing the Budget and the plan.

For evolving the National Wage Policy, it is necessary, in the first place, to have a working-class family budget enquiry conducted in all industrial centres and on the basis of such an enquiry to compile the working class cost of living index. I want to mention the report of a committee appointed in 1959 for compiling the middle class cost of living and I would suggest that there should be a regular compilation of the middle class cost of living which should be treated henceforth as the working class cost of living index because, as a matter of fact, looked at scientifically, the recommendations of the Middle Class Cost of Living Index Enquiry Committee[19] are applicable to the working class cost of living also. I would further suggest that the scheme of D.A. wherever it prevails should be abolished because dearness allowance is not a temporary phase now since there is no possibility of the prices coming down to the pre-1939 level and, therefore, dearness or the spiral of prices being a permanent phase, the D.A. should be merged fully, that is 100 per cent, in the basic wage and the entire pay package should be linked with the cost of living index number.

Great discontent prevails among the workers on account of the provisions of the Payment of Bonus Act.[20] As a matter of fact, national prosperity certainly depends upon production and production has been impaired during the last few weeks because of the various strikes. I may just

18. National Wage Policy – A policy of consistent and continuous improvement of real wages and standard of living of workers as well as productivity, adopted by Govt. of India.
19. A Committee constituted by the Ministry of Labour and Employment, Govt. of India, in 1959.
20. The Payment of Bonus Act, 1965.

refer to the lockout in the DCM,[21] the general strike in the Bombay Textiles, etc. and all these are on account of the defective provisions of the Act. Without going into the details, I would suggest that the government should accept realistically the principle that bonus is a deferred or supplementary wage until there is a gap between the living wage and the actual wage and on the basis of the acceptance of this principle, the government should be prepared to recast or re-mould the Payment of Wages Act. If that is done, many of the industrial strikes will be automatically eliminated. We will head towards industrial peace, greater production and greater prosperity. It has become necessary to ensure that our workers are given the right to rest, in the absence of which productivity is hampered. The regulation of workload, regulation of working hours and appropriate leave facilities must be properly taken care of and this is the responsibility of the government so far as the different industries are concerned. We have different pieces of legislation regarding social security, such as different workmen's compensation, Provident Fund, gratuity, ESI[22] and other things but the workers have been demanding and demanding rightly that there should be an integrated social security scheme evolved and what acts in the way of such an evolution, it is difficult for me to comprehend.

In this Budget, there has been no progress made in the direction of thinking about social security schemes and, therefore, I urge that this aspect of industrial sphere should not be lost sight of. We have been told that along with foodgrains and cloth, housing is also one of the most important problems of the masses but we know that though the Centre has allotted various amounts for industrial housing to the different states, the same have not been utilised either by the employers or by the state governments. I would like to suggest that now we should begin from the other end, so that the Centre should take the initiative in industrial housing and realise the due amounts from the state governments and the employers subsequently. That is the only way to accomplish our programme of industrial housing.

When I am speaking of a National Wage Policy, I cannot ignore the plight of our pensioners who have no trade union right and the monetary value of whose pensions has already gone down and therefore, I request

21. DCM Textile Mills earlier known as the Delhi Cloth & General Mills Ltd. founded in 1889.
22. Employees' State Insurance (abbreviated as ESI) – The Employees' State Insurance Corporation (ESIC) which manages the ESI is a statutory body under the Ministry of Labour and Employment, Govt. of India.

that though this class is ignored and ineffective, the government should itself take care of this particular class and see that justice is done by restoring the monetary value of their original pension. There must be some basic rethinking on the problem of the pattern of industrial ownership. I am happy to note that the government seems to have relieved itself of its doctrinaire and academic thinking on this problem. As a matter of fact, various industries have various characteristics and each industry should have the appropriate pattern of ownership suited to its peculiar characteristics and, therefore, there can be regulated private enterprise, municipalisation, co-operativisation and along with that, I would suggest labourisation, and democratisation. By labourisation, I mean (1) co-partnership in which the worker, labour is evaluated in terms of share and he is made a shareholder of his concern, (2) by labour co-operativisation, I mean whenever there is an occasion to snatch an industry from the hands of the capitalists, the same should be handed over to the workers and their cooperatives should be allowed to run the industries, and (3) there should be autonomous corporations with Board of Directors of Management consisting of the various interests including those of employees and, in the same way, by democratisation, I mean that the industry's shares should be thrown open. Every share should be small and it should be a rule that only the low-income group people should be allowed to purchase the shares. The employees should have priority in the purchase of shares and none should be allowed to purchase more than 5 or 6 shares and in the way the industries can be labourised and democratised. All these various patterns, without any regimentation of thought, should be tried, so as to suit the peculiar characteristics of the different states and if this is done, we will be able to make good progress in the industrial sphere.

For greater production, industrial peace is necessary. Contented labour, enlightened employers, alert public opinion and just and fair government, these are the four pre-requisites for industrial peace. This would necessitate change of outlook on the part of the employers and also of the government and because the government is the biggest employer, it is necessary that it should function as a model employer so that it would have a moral right to bring appropriate pressure to bear on the employers in the private sector.

While I have dealt with the working class, I would like to refer within a minute to the present situation and its demands. Today it seems we are on the brink of national disintegration. Various demands are raised. There is a demand for Punjabi Suba, for Vidarbha, for Bhojpuri state and for a

Konkan state, and probably like the Athens' Sparta, we are going to have so many states. The time is so ripe when we should seriously consider the propriety of moving in the direction of a unitary form of government.

The Union Budget (General), 1967-68[23]

Employment-oriented Industry Needs Attention

D. Thengadi: Sir, obviously this Budget is not consumer-oriented. Instead of the government providing relief to the people, the people are required to provide relief to the government and the people are being required to pay for the government's sin of devaluation. In the present Budget, there is no indication that there would be elimination of evasion of taxes nor have any effective measures been suggested for unearthing and uncovering black money. All the indirect taxes raised in this Budget are unjustified and the government has no moral right to do this because the present situation is one of the government's own making. The government has not come forward with any suggestion for drastic reduction of civil expenditure by introducing economy at the top instead of at the bottom. Our licensing system, it has become obvious, should be revised on the basis of the conclusions and recommendations contained in the Hazari Report.[24] The foreign petroleum companies should be taken over. We have land ceiling provisions in some of the States. But even on urban expendable incomes, some ceiling must be prescribed. The co-operative sector has not been paid the attention which it deserves, particularly the agricultural credit structure should be given more serious thought. I would urge that the government should study whether it would be advisable to set up a separate monetary authority at par with the Legislature, the Judiciary and the Executive, which would look after the monetary policy of the country, which would be respected by the government and which would coordinate and co-operate with the fiscal policy of the government. Whether the setting up of such a separate monetary authority would be helpful in formulating and implementing our agricultural and industrial credit policy should be studied. This, I submit, is an important suggestion which deserves serious consideration.

---

23. *Rajya Sabha Debate* dated 20th June, 1967.
24. The Committee on Industrial Licensing set up by Govt. of India in 1966, under the chairmanship of Professor R.K. Hazari, (1932-1986), industrial economist, professor at Bombay University, later Deputy Governor, RBI, then a Planning Commission consultant, to review the Industrial Licensing System under Industries Development and Regulation Act, 1951.

In the agricultural sector, it was assured long ago that about two million acres of land, which has been rendered surplus on account of the land-ceiling provision, would be distributed among the landless labourers in our country. That has not been done so far. Crop insurance scheme has not been implemented in the different states. Now there are certain problems outside agriculture which I should like just to mention. We are facing the problem in Bihar of making available to us agricultural implements. Now on good authority, I learn that on the surplus capacity of Railway workshops, we can manufacture our agricultural implements. I urge that this should be tried.

Now, in our country, next to the food problem, we are confronted with the problem of industrial housing. Top priority should be given to the solution of that problem. Regarding public sector undertakings, it has been our experience that they are not run either efficiently or economically and that in the name of nationalisation, we are doing nothing but bureaucratisation and these bureaucrats do not know either industrial psychology or business tactics. Therefore, they are running in loss and they are also oppressive so far as their employees are concerned. I should like to suggest that the pattern of ownership and management in public sector should undergo some drastic change. Every public sector undertaking should have a Board of Management with representatives of interested parties on it and technical and experts' aid should be made available to it. In view of the fact that because of the wrong policies of the government we apprehend in the immediate future unprecedented spiralling of prices and also in view of the fact that the recommendations of the Dearness Allowance Commission have been quite disappointing, it is high time that the government came forward with a proposal for the appointment of a Third Pay Commission for all the Central Government employees excluding Railwaymen, and a separate Wage Board for Railwaymen because of the large number of employees and categories in the Railways.

Pensioners all over the country deserve our sympathetic consideration because we know that their pensions are static while the prices are spiralling. Therefore, I should like to suggest that with a view to having a proper adjustment of the pensions, a Pension Commission should be appointed.

Now the government is not correct in saying that every wage rise or rise in emolument is necessarily responsible for price rise. We are of the considered opinion that wage rise can be held responsible for price rise only to the extent that the wage rise exceeds the productivity rise; not in all cases.

The government is responsible for offering employment to all. The right to work should be included in the list of fundamental rights under our Constitution. And accordingly, government should not allow schemes leading to mass retrenchment schemes, such as automation, simplification, mechanisation, etc. because the stage of our industrial growth does not justify such automation.

The government has violated the letter and spirit of the joint consultation machinery by declaring unilaterally the retirement age as 50. On 29th and 30th May, a deadlock has been created in the joint consultation machinery because of the adamant attitude of the government and if the deadlock persists, the administration, if not collapse, at least will be adversely affected and, therefore, I urge that the government should revise its attitude towards its own employees.

Now, there are some industries to which I think it is necessary to make some reference. A very small industry, the stone quarry industry, which is employing 25,000 workers is facing a serious crisis. They are demanding that welfare measures should be introduced in the stone quarry industry.

In textiles, it is good that a corporation is to be set up, but at the same time, there are problems, we realise, of outmoded and outdated machinery still. The government should ensure that not a single textile worker is thrown out of employment. While we welcome the setting up of the corporation, we should also like to insist that an experiment should be made of labourisation of the mills. I mean that some of the mills should be handed over to the workers and they should be allowed to run them and the financial and technical aid which would have been made available to the mills had they been taken over by the corporation should be made available to the workers of the mills.

Our sugar industry is also facing a serious crisis. If in the absence of adequate prices the cane-growers change the pattern of their production, the sugar mill employees would be the worst sufferers. In view of this, the government must come forward in a big way to give subsidy to the sugar industry. The controlled sector of sugar production should be protected from the competition of the uncontrolled sector of khandsari [unrefined sugar] and jaggery production.

The government should not reduce the quantum of Central assistance to states. It should agree to a moratorium on the loans given to states so that the latter can divert these funds to irrigation and other productive purposes.

The Budget does not take us further in the direction of the evolution of a national income policy. Now that we are on the eve of the Fourth Five Year Plan, it would be advisable on the part of the government to convene a round table conference of all the economic interests in the country to evolve details of the Fourth Plan. We will be able to describe only such a plan evolved on the basis of the consensus of such a round table conference as the people's plan, which will be capable of inspiring people to greater sacrifices. I think if such a round table conference of all economic interests is convened, all of us are patriotic and through mutual exchange of views, we will be able to evolve a plan for which we can all sacrifice.

The Finance Bill, 1964[25]

Reduction in Prices and Increase in Real Income

D. Thengadi: Now, coming to the Finance Bill, I must say that the Finance Bill will not be received with much enthusiasm by the consumers in general and the workers in particular inasmuch as it does not ensure either reduction in prices or increase in the quantum of real wages to workers or provide employment to the unemployed ones. True, an attempt has been made to bring the tax-evaders to book. It is good and noble so far as it goes but that is not enough. The workers must be assured that whatever has been realised from the tax evaders would proceed to the workers and, therefore, this is my humble suggestion that in the case of industrial employers, whatever is realised from them by way of penalty for wrong assessment should be utilised specifically for making up the gap between the real wage and the actual wage of the employees working under them.

Now, the Finance Bill has given wide powers to the income-tax officials. We want to punish the tax-evaders no doubt, but in our enthusiasm to curb one evil, we should not raise another Frankenstein and I want this assurance from the Finance Minister that the income-tax officials will have sufficient character and integrity not to misuse the powers given to them under this Act. Our experience as workers in this respect has not been very encouraging. While, on the one hand, it can be apprehended that the

25. *Rajya Sabha Debate* dated 24th April, 1964.

Income-tax officials can abuse their powers against the income-tax payers, we, the workers, have often experienced that whenever income-tax officials choose to conspire with or to have unholy alliances with the industrial employers, both of them put together can deprive the workers of their legitimate dues. I want to cite one concrete example, that of the Edward Mills in Bombay. In the case of this Edward Mills, for the last four months, the employees have publicly alleged that the accounts are fraudulent and yet the income-tax officials have conveniently connived at the whole thing and there is every reason to allege that there is a conspiracy between the income-tax authorities and the management of the Edward Mills. I would request the Government of India to hold an impartial enquiry into our allegations against the management of the Edward Mills. Of course, this is incidental, yet I would request the Government of India to hold an enquiry into our allegations against the management of the Edward Mills.

Now, various aspects of our general economy are also under discussion. There is discussion about the advisability of expansion of the public sector. Now, the prosperity of any country must depend upon production and production, in its turn, upon the enthusiasm of the producers. How would the producers be inspired to work more if the workers are told that they have only two choices? Their choice is only between two evils, private capitalism and State capitalism in the name of nationalisation; they are required to choose between the devil and the deep sea, between the frying pan and the fire. In such circumstances, they would have hardly any enthusiasm to work sincerely. The workers in general require a third solution which would steer clear of both the evils: the evils of private capitalism and State capitalism in the name of nationalisation. It would be wrong to presume that any one particular pattern of ownership is a panacea for all industrial evils. There are patterns and patterns and different industries have different characteristics, which necessitate different patterns. At the same time, wherever the question of ending private ownership arises, the workers must be assured that precedence would be given not to the 'statisation' of industry but to labourisation of that industry so far as possible through schemes of co-partnership or labour co-operativisation. Therefore, I request the Government of India to give serious consideration to schemes of labourisation also. As a balanced thinker, I believe no one particular pattern would suit all industries and the pattern would have to be different from industry to industry – restrained and regulated private enterprise, co-operative economy, municipalisation, even nationalisation in case of basic industries and defence industries and also labourisation. The tendency today to prescribe nationalisation as a panacea and not even to think of labourisation through co-partnership and labour co-operativisation is not likely to arouse enthusiasm among the workers for producing more and more. I think, so far as the Finance Bill is concerned, on behalf of the poorer sections of the population, these comments should suffice.

Finance (No. 2) Bill, 1971[26]

Agriculture and Industrial Sectors need more Attention

D. Thengadi: Sir, I am sorry to say that the government has not yet taken cognisance of some of the basic and long-standing demands of workers, though the government expects them to work hard for the prosperity of the country. For example, the workers' demands are that the right to work should be included in the Schedule of Fundamental Right in our Constitution. They should have a security of service, the need-based minimum wage, initial pay of a Class IV or unskilled worker, the wage differential based upon the scientific process of job evaluation, linking pay packet with the cost of living index, conversion of Wage Boards into tripartite forums, treating the bonus as deferred or supplementary wage so long as there is a gap between the living wage and the actual wage; since the government is unable to check the price line, fair-price shops for wage-earners, introduction of 40 hours' work, passing legislation on gratuity and unemployment insurance and evolution of a comprehensive integrated social security scheme, promotion of industrial housing to be tackled on a war footing, etc. As a matter of fact, workers' co-operation should be encouraged and the employers, who are not willing to offer housing facilities to their employees, should be charged with specific housing tax and the amounts recovered from such housing tax should be handed over to the workers' co-operatives for this purpose. There are various industries that are undergoing a crisis – textile, engineering, sugar, etc. We had long back urged upon the government that as in Great Britain, so in our country also a system of efficient audit should be introduced in all these three industries. In the case of engineering industries, the heavy excise duty on steel does not enable the engineering industry to maintain the price level of its products. Therefore, such excise duty should be withdrawn or reduced. We had further demanded that in every

26. *Rajya Sabha Debate* dated 4th August, 1971.

sector, whether private, public, co-operative or otherwise, there should be progressive liberalisation of industries; by which I mean that the labour of every worker should be evaluated in terms of share and the worker made a shareholder, contributing his labour and, thus, having his voice in the decision-making process – decision-making even on important matters, like deployment of capital. And, in this way, he should be made to feel that he also has a vested interest in the industry as much as the employer or the government. We had further demanded that a separate provision of public administrators should be created with statutory recognition: that arbitration boards, with workers' representatives included in them, should be there to settle all industrial disputes instead of allowing them to linger on under adjudication. So far as textile mills are concerned, the process of sick mills being taken over by the government and then handing them over to the original employees was severely condemned by the workers' representatives. And, today, we find that a number of textile mills that are sick are still waiting to be restarted by some agency or the other.

At this stage, I want to make a particular reference to the Usmanshahi Mill[27] at Nanded in Maharashtra. There, in the tussle between Haridas Mundhra[28] and his creditors, the mill was closed down, and the day before yesterday all the workers and all the citizens of Nanded observed 'Nanded Bandh' simply to express their sympathy with the demands of the workers. The mill should be taken over by the government and started without any further delay. Regarding development rebate, workers are of the view that small-scale industries, industrial corporations and our

27. Osmanshahi Mills Private Limited was a non-govt company, incorporated on 31st July 1963. The company was primarily into the business of agriculture and allied activities.

28. Haridas Mundhra was a Calcutta-based stock speculator who was found guilty and imprisoned in the first mega scam of independent India. The scam, known as the Mundhra scandal, exposed the links between Nehru's government at various levels, stock market speculators and business groups. It was a perfect case of crony capitalism promoted by the Nehruvian establishment. "In June 1957 the public-sector Life Insurance Corporation (LIC) had bought 1.24 crore, or 12.4 million rupees, worth of fraudulent stock in six companies owned by Haridas Mundhra, a Calcutta-based businessman. The investment was the largest that LIC had made in its short history, but contrary to regulations, its investment committee had not been consulted on the decision." (Samanth Subramanian, *Long View: India's Very First Corruption Scandal* in India Ink, Blogs at *New York Times*, May 9, 2012) Nehru's son-in-law Feroze Gandhi, then a Congress Member of Parliament from Rae Bareli, had first exposed the scam in Parliament and made it a countrywide issue. The M.C. Chagla Committee of Enquiry appointed to look into the allegations exposed in greater detail the politician-bureaucracy-business nexus, leading to the resignation of the then Union Finance Minister, T.T. Krishnamachari (TTK).

young electronic industry should be given the benefit of development rebate but not the rest.

Industrial housing, as I was referring, is also necessary to restrain the would-be employers from initiating setting up of any further industry without previously making adequate arrangements for the housing of their workers.

The problem of housing also leads to the problem of slums. We are sorry to say that in the name of slum clearance, workers are thrown out of their houses. They should be improved and handed over to workers' co-operatives.

In the industrial sector, we are confronted with some of the major problems on which decisions must be immediately taken. The number one problem is the problem of technology. It is obvious that Western technology cannot be suitable to our Indian conditions and traditions and, therefore, in tune with our requirements of indigenous technology, a Bharatiya technology must be developed and, for this purpose, I urge upon the government to consider very seriously whether what is described as 'intermediate technology' or 'appropriate technology' could be utilised for the purposes of various industries. I do not say that the intermediate technology or the appropriate technology is the only technology useful for the country. There is no such technology which is universally useful but, still, the utility, the efficacy and the advisability of intermediate technology or appropriate technology in the case of different industries should be scrutinised.

In the same way, we are also confronted with the problem of the pattern of industrial ownership. I urge that there should be no dogmatism on this point. Our considerations and our decisions should be based upon realism. There can be various patterns of industrial ownership. There can be regulated private capitalism; there can be State capitalism and a co-operative sector; there can be municipalisation; even a joint sector and, in some cases, even democratisation of some of the industries as was done by Germany some six years ago.

In Germany, a large share capital of 800 crore Marks in the industrial estates was thrown open to the people on four conditions: (1) every share was to be small, (2) no one was allowed to purchase more than five shares, (3) only those who could produce low-income group certificates were entitled to purchase shares, (4) the employees of the industrial estates got priority in the matter of purchase of shares. So, this process of democratisation can also be utilised in some cases, but a high-power committee to go through the problem of the patterns of industrial ownership should be appointed and the problem should be decided not on the basis of any prejudice or dogma, but on the considerations of pragmatism and national prosperity.

The problem of location of industries also has acquired considerable importance in recent times, particularly because we are facing a very paradoxical situation of over-urbanisation on the one hand and rural unemployment, on the other. For this purpose, diversification of industries is necessary; decentralisation of procedures of production is necessary. Also it is necessary to raise colonies in the vicinity of big cities and allow people to occupy them on appropriate charges, and also to develop medium-sized cities with appropriate facilities, such as water, electricity, etc.

If in this way, we take particular care about the location of the industry, it would be possible for us to have a balanced picture of industrial development. Even the ecological problems, such as problems of air pollution, water pollution, etc. would be minimised, if not eradicated.

Then, while we are talking of industrial sector, sir, I cannot forget the fact that the infrastructure for industrial prosperity, leads to industrial growth which leads to the growth of agriculture. Even in the countries which are industrially advanced today, agriculture was properly taken care of. It is a sad plight that in our country, agriculture has not received the attention that it deserves. A number of problems are there that must be tackled immediately. This morning, hon'ble Mr. Shinde[29] had given us the recommendations or broad guidelines of the Land Reforms Committee,[30] but there must be a comprehensive picture of the whole thing. I am sorry that he has missed one important section of our rural

29. Annasaheb Shinde (b. 1922-), then Minister of State for Ministry of Food, Agriculture, Community Development, Co-operation and Irrigation, Govt of India in 1966-1967. Shinde, a Congress Member of Parliament from Ahmednagar, in Maharashtra, held various responsibilities as Minister of State in the food, agriculture and development ministries in 1960s and 1970s.

30. The National Development Council of the Indian Planning Commission constituted a committee in 1963 with the then Union Minister of Home Affairs, S. Gulzari Lal Nanda, as chairman and the then Minister of Food and Agriculture Sardar Swaran Singh, the member in-charge of land reforms in the Planning Commission and five Chief Ministers who were vice-chairman of the zonal councils, as members, to review the progress of land reform in different states and to propose measures for ensuring its implementation.

population, that is, the share-croppers. They should be immediately protected by immediate registration. Most of the actual cultivators have no right as tenants today under various tenancy laws. Also he has missed the point of reconsolidation of land. We very much want to know as to what Land Records Committee has to say on this question because after the redistribution of land, there are uneconomic holdings scattered all over the village areas and uneconomic holdings that are not contiguous, that are not compact, create problems of development. Even service co-operatives cannot render much service to such scattered uneconomic holdings. In Egypt, we know that after the construction of Aswan Dam, lands with uneconomic holdings were distributed to landless labourers. The lands were contiguous and, therefore, through the utilisation of service co-operatives, uneconomic holdings could be rendered economic. For the purpose of rendering these uneconomic holdings into economic ones, reconsolidation of land would be necessary and the government and the Land Reforms Committee must take cognisance of this particular problem.

Then, sir, it is generally admitted that our farmer or our village artisan or a small young person trying to come up in the world in rural areas does not get adequate loan facilities even from the nationalised banks. Similarly, rural indebtedness is a very big problem and debt relief measures are not being properly implemented in different states. There should be a planned development in a widespread manner. Irrigation projects and those who are to benefit from these irrigation projects should be encouraged, should be enthused, should be asked to participate in the process by giving loans to state governments on interest.

It is not as if only the government has to impose rural reconstruction upon the people who are to benefit by power projects and irrigation projects, but they are not implementing the projects for want of proper funds. In this case, those who are to benefit by such of these projects should be asked to give loans to the government and to participate in the rural prosperity. This voluntary enthusiasm should be created amongst the public.

The network of approach roads should be extended to the maximum possible extent and necessary transport facilities should be offered to farmers.

The adulteration in commodities supplied to farmers, such as petrol, diesel, kerosene, lubricant diesel, fertilisers, insecticides, seeds, etc.

must be stopped. Supply of these commodities must be pure. With this end in view, the work of various agencies, such as FACT,[31] the National Seeds Corporation, oil companies, etc. must be properly geared up. For proper maintenance and utilisation of tractors, there should be adequate provision of standard spares, standard fuel and lubricants, skilled mechanics, efficient drivers, etc.

Only such of the farm implements as are certified by the ISI should be supplied to the farmers. Steady supply of electric power should be ensured for the benefit of pumping sets run by electric motors and the number of tube-wells maximised. New farm machinery, such as bulldozers, levellers, etc. should be rented to the farmers by the state governments during the appropriate seasons. Farmers should be saved from the exploitation of middlemen so far as prices of their commodities are concerned. Wherever FCI [Food Corporation of India] has not spread its network, it is necessary to ensure that the farmers are not deprived of the average prices of foodgrains and other articles as recommended by the Agricultural Prices Commission. It is further necessary to ensure in such areas that the middlemen do not cause delays in cash payments and irregularities in payment. The schemes of cattle and crop insurance should be taken up without delay. The research institutes, such as the ICAR [Indian Council of Agricultural Research], the IARI [Indian Agricultural Research Institute] should be required to bring down the level of their research from the class level to the mass level for day-to-day purposes. A central body or cell should be set up to bring about proper coordination between the various official and unofficial agencies dealing with the peasants' needs and problems. Agro-industries or subsidiary industries must be developed and there should be set up an organisation to serve as a proper liaison between the *kisans* or their organisations and the government. At the same time, for the agricultural workers, the provisions of the Minimum Wages Act should be extended to the agricultural workers in the country and for village artisans, the marketing cooperatives must be given utmost facility so that the spirit of co-operativism is inculcated among our village artisans. I have just stated a few points that need immediate attention of the government but one thing is certain that by merely imposing plans or projects from above, no nation can be reconstructed. If I remember aright,

31. The Fertilisers and Chemicals Travancore Limited or FACT, a fertiliser and chemical manufacturing company founded in 1943 and headquartered at Kochi, Kerala.

Mr. M.N. Roy[32] had said at one place that wherever there is a revolution, the revolutionary cadres after the revolution culminate into success and convert themselves into bands of active nation-builders. In our case, such bands of active nation-builders are lacking and so long as there is no such nucleus of active workers who are endowed with the spirit of patriotism, it would not be possible for us to undertake programmes or plans of national reconstruction. This is a problem and I do not know whether it is properly within the jurisdiction of the Finance Ministry but this is a problem which must be taken up by all the patriots, irrespective of party politics.

The Finance (No. 2) Bill, 1974[33]

Protecting Consumers

D. Thengadi: Sir, I do not see which of the professed objects of our government are going to be fulfilled by the introduction of this Finance Bill. It was earlier said that this was a step in the direction of curbing inflation. But now the government has to admit that this is not going to help curb inflation. It was said that it was not going to hit the common man or the common consumer. But you know, sir, that the whole burden will be indirectly passed on to the consumers. For example, cigarettes are, of course, used by the common people. Now, it is true that tyres will be purchased by bus owners. But ultimately, fares will be increased and the common passengers will have to suffer. Oils, asbestos, cement, iron rods – these are also commodities which are useful for the common people. Then rubber goods and diesel oil are intermediates for finished goods. That means, the cost of the finished goods will increase. But indirect taxation will be there. In the last Budget, there was an indirect taxation of Rs. 200 crores. Now, this will be added to Rs. 232 crores of this indirect taxation, and the whole will be borne by the common people of the land. Sir, in this respect, it is worthwhile to note that while the luxury goods give a tax return of Rs. 749 crores, consumer goods give a tax return of Rs. 1,049 crores.

32. M.N. Roy – Manabendra Nath Roy (1887-1954) (Narendra Nath Bhattacharya) was an Indian revolutionary who was actively associated with the early revolutionary nationalists led by Jatindranath Mukherjee (Bagha Jatin) (1879-1915). Attracted to Marxism later, Roy founded the Marxist Communist Party and the Communist Party of India and was also member of the Comintern's Presidium. In later years, Roy, a prolific political theorist, moved away from Marxism and formulated his philosophy of radical humanism.

33. *Rajya Sabha Debate* dated 26th August, 1974.

Now, the taxation rates in the case of sugar rose from Rs. 4419 lakhs in 1960-61 to Rs. 15,300 lakhs in 1974-75. In the case of tea, it rose from Rs. 747 lakhs to Rs. 4,140 lakhs. In the case of cigars and cigarettes, it rose from Rs. 1,12,797 lakhs to Rs. 17,800 lakhs. In the case of motor spirit, it rose from Rs. 4,046 lakhs to Rs. 40,180 lakhs. In the case of kerosene, it rose from Rs. 892 lakhs to Rs. 13,000 lakhs. The same is the case with other commodities also. What I mean is that while the consumer goods industries are being discouraged, luxury goods are being encouraged, and, thus, the pattern of production is gradually being altered in favour of luxury goods.

Sir, our professed projects are not being fulfilled to any extent through this Finance Bill. For example, this is not going to check the price rise. *Mr. Chavan*[34] had earlier talked of a package deal. What he means by package deal, I fail to understand, because though he has come with a heavy hand on the working class and introduced through the Compulsory Deposit Scheme not only wage freeze but wage cut, actually, still that is not going to help curbing the price rise. Secondly, this is not going to help generation of employment also. The government also does not claim that this is going to improve the employment position. Thirdly, it has not been established that the growth rate will increase because of the provisions in this Finance Bill. What he stated is that the deficit will be minimised. That means, while the government itself is responsible for the extravagant expenditure, the ordinary people will be asked to pay for the sins of the government in such irresponsible expenditure. Now, if the government had suggested that this Finance Bill will have the effect of reducing disparities of income, that was understandable. But this is not going to reduce disparities in income. The government could have introduced consumption tax. They could have said that any expenditure over Rs. 2,000 will bear consumption tax. But they have not done so. All this goes to suggest that this is just a hoax and there is no package deal.

And this dose of taxation is going to increase the prices, is going to cause hardships to common people, is going to hit the pockets of common consumers and it is not just a burden on the rich and the affluent. No effective measures have been adopted to deal with the problem of black money which is the most important problem of our economy. The government has refused to accept the recommendations of the Wanchoo

34. Y.B. Chavan (1913-1984), then Finance Minister in Indira Gandhi's government.

Committee[35] regarding demonetisation; their measures against hoarders and blackmarketeers are also only farcical. Regarding smugglers, Mr. K.R. Ganesh[36] has come with some bravado before the people. It is ridiculous for a minister to say that he will offer *satyagraha*. Nevertheless he has chosen to say so. Even against smugglers, no effective measures have been adopted. Under these circumstances, we have every reason to believe that the government is not very serious about either providing appropriate relief to the unemployed and underemployed or to enhance growth rate or to bring down the prices. They just want to have some sort of patch work. Therefore, I should like to ask whether they can assure us that during this year itself, the Finance Minister will not come before this House with another proposal for taxation, direct or indirect. That clarification I seek from him. On all these grounds, we are not very enthusiastic in supporting this; rather, we are positively against the provisions of this Finance Bill and we think it is anti-consumer, anti-people and it is against all the professed objectives of our national economy.

The Finance (No. 2) Bill, 1967[37]

Protecting the Interest of Wage and Salary Earners

D. Thengadi: Madam, coming from U.P., I am seriously aware of the crisis in our sugar industry. We have insisted throughout that three conditions must be fulfilled regarding this industry: (i) the yield of cane must be 30 tonnes per acre; (ii) sugar recovery must be 11 per cent; and (iii) duration of the crushing season must be seven months. If this is done, we feel the sugar production capacity will come to 50 lakh tonnes, while the actual average production today is 25 lakh tonnes. Thus, 50 per cent of the capacity is going waste on account of shortage of raw material and its poor quality. The remedy lies in increasing the yield of cane per acre

35. The Justice Wanchoo Committee on Demonetisation submitted an interim report in 1971 and suggested demonetisation of high value currency notes. The recommendation was turned down by then Prime Minister Indira Gandhi and Finance Minister Y.B. Chavan.

36. K.R. Ganesh (1922-2004) – freedom fighter, was the first elected Member of Parliament (Lok Sabha) from Andaman and Nicobar Islands, member of fourth Lok Sabha 1967-1970 & fifth Lok Sabha, 1971-1977, was Deputy Minister and Minister of State in Finance, Petroleum ministries between 1970 and 1975. Ganesh – also called Ganesh babu by his acolytes and constituents, became a household name when he undertook a drive, as MoS Finance, against smuggling. Fell out with Indira Gandhi over imposition of Emergency, formed Congress for Democracy with Jagjivan Ram, Nandini Sathpathy, Hemvati Nandan Bahuguna *et al.*

37. *Rajya Sabha Debate* dated 1st August, 1967.

and its sucrose content in the field, and larger duration of crushing season and sugar recovery in the factories. This will increase the productivity of land, labour and the factories. This will ensure cheap sugar for internal consumption as well as for exports. Our actual consumption of sugar today is only 25 to 30 lakh tonnes. It will be detrimental to convert rice-production area to sugar-production area by giving loans and licences for establishing new factories or for expanding the capacity of the existing ones. If the above conditions are fulfilled, there will be no need or justification for such loans and licences.

We can increase the yield of cane and sugar recovery by installation of 5,000 tubewells in U.P. alone, which will cost only Rs. 50 crores, spread over a period of five years and by giving Rs. 16 crores worth of fertilisers on loan to the cane-growers. This will enable us to produce 24 lakh tonnes from the factories in U.P. alone against their production of 7 lakh tonnes in 1966-67 and expected production of 4 to 5 lakh tonnes in 1967-68.

The expenditure of Rs. 200 crores for the installation of new machinery, whether for establishing new factories or for expansion of the existing ones, must be stopped forthwith. All that money should be placed at the disposal of the state government for intensive development of cane, irrigation and fertilisers. This will give an additional income of Rs. 200 crores per year from the existing factories of U.P. at the present rate of sugar price of Rs. 1,400 to 1,500 per tonne. This will also enable us to reduce the area under cane in the reserved areas of sugar factories from the average acreage of 22 lakh to 11 lakh acres. They will also be able to manufacture 10 lakh tonnes of *gur*, valued at Rs. 100 crores, in addition to the supply of full requirements of cane to the factories. There is also a dispute about the supplies of cane between the vacuum-pan factories and power crushers. I would suggest that the areas of the two should be clearly demarcated and the owners of power-crushers should be made responsible for the development of cane along the lines suggested earlier. The government should help both with money and material to obtain quick results. Remission of 50 per cent of purchase-tax and excise duty on excess cane crushed and sugar produced, over and above the average of the last 5 years, is also a measure I should like to suggest. This would give an additional income to the Central Government as well as the state governments, without putting any financial burden or responsibility on them. I would like to urge that an expert in sugar industry from Lucknow, one Mr. Thakurdas Sahni, has conducted research in this respect. He has submitted his suggestions to the Government of India and I would urge that the government should take him into confidence and discuss with him the pros and cons of the scheme suggested by him.

Regarding agriculture, I am sorry to find that there is no strict implementation of the various provisions of the Land Reforms Act, particularly those regarding ceilings and the cultivable waste land; the land rendered surplus on account of the ceiling has not yet been distributed among the landless labour. If I remember aright, a couple of years back, the government had assured that such land would be distributed among the landless labourers, particularly those belonging to the Scheduled Castes and the Scheduled Tribes, but it has not yet been done. It is also necessary that the flow of agricultural credit should be freed from or cleared of political influence. In the field of industry, it is necessary that industrial peace should be maintained because unless there is extra production, there cannot be any distribution but it is the responsibility of the government to function as model employer. Then alone it will have any right or authority to guide properly the industrialists or the employers in the private sector, but I am sorry to state that the government has failed so far to carry out its responsibilities as model employers. Particularly, the practice of government of going back on its words is responsible for much of the discontent and heart-burning. The case of the employees of the Ministry of Food and Agriculture whose services have been transferred to the Food Corporation of India is one of such instances. They are government servants and when they entered the service, they were given certain undertakings about their service conditions, the continuity and security of their service and the pensionary and other retirement benefits. When certain functions of the Food Ministry were transferred to the Food Corporation, these functionaries also were simultaneously transferred. Now the government cannot deny them any of the benefits to which they would have been entitled, had they continued formally as government servants, because their services are transferred to the Corporation. Again the government cannot absolve itself of its responsibilities towards these employees even if the Food Corporation is wound up or there is shrinkage of work of the Food Corporation. Under any of these contingencies, it is the government's responsibility to see that their continuity of service conditions and the retirement benefits as government servants are ensured. The government should come forward with a clear assurance that it will carry out its responsibilities under any circumstance.

Recently, there has been a case of breach of trust in the LIC. An agreement was arrived at between the National Federation of Insurance Field Workers and the LIC authorities on 24th December, 1966 to the effect that there would be negotiations between the two about the question of D.A. in case there is any rise in the cost of living index. Now the LIC have come forward with a plea that they will not consider any rise in D.A. which is in excess of Rs. 155 and which is the existing ceiling for government employees. Regarding the clause in the agreement, regarding house rent allowance also, the authorities are going back upon their word. Regarding other items, the authorities have refused to conduct negotiations, though such negotiations are a 'must' under the agreement. This is a case of breach of trust and I hope the Finance Minister will look personally into the matter.

There is yet another instance of the breach of trust. When the 'work-to-rule' agitation of the Telegraph Traffic III employees was withdrawn, the hon'ble minister for Communications had given certain assurances on the floor of this House. Those assurances have not yet been fulfilled. There is a feeling that the fulfillment of those assurances could have been possible had the Finance Ministry extended a helping hand in the matter and I think it is high time that the minister should come forward with the helping hand so far as the problems of the Telegraph Traffic III employees are concerned.

The employees of the Rehabilitation Department are facing the danger of large-scale retrenchment on account of the anti-labour decisions of the Staff Inspection Unit of the Ministry of Finance. In this department, there appears to be an unholy alliance between the higher officials on deputation and the Ministry of Finance to effect a drastic cut in the staff strength. I must warn the government that if they implement the suggestions of the Staff Inspection Unit and retrench workers without offering them earlier alternative jobs with similar grade and seniority, they will have to thank themselves if they are required to confront a mass agitation.

Yes, then there is our moral responsibility towards the employees who have come to India from Pakistan. Counting of service for pension, in respect of displaced temporary government servants coming from NWFP (North-West Frontier Province) and Sind has been defective. They have been discriminated against in the matter of counting their pre-migration of temporary service towards pension. In the case of those whose service records have not been received from the Government of Pakistan, it has been provided that the temporary service declared by them on the basis of collateral evidence will count only to the extent of five years. This is unjust. In their case, the basis of collateral evidence should be accepted as sufficient. For, they are in no way responsible for the non-receipt of their service records from the Government of Pakistan.

The employees of the Survey of India all over the country have recently launched an agitation. The recommendations of the Survey Reviewing Committee were accepted in principle by the government. Hon'ble Ministers of Education, Kabir and Chagla[38] assured on the floor of the Parliament that the pay scales of these employees would be revised but the Ministry of Finance is refusing to fulfill these assurances. Apart from the large army of the unemployed and the underemployed, the largest single section of the working classes is that of casual labour. Curiously enough, lakhs of workers under the various employing ministries are continued for years as casual for a number of years, even for 12 or 13 years.

The recommendations of the Second Pay Commission in regard to the policy relating to the employment of casual labour and regulations of the terms and conditions of their employment have not been followed by the employing ministries in the case of their casual labour. It is for the minister to ensure that these recommendations are properly followed.

Then there is the general question of the Central Government employees. Today the Finance Minister is very well aware that 22 lakhs of Central Government employees are extremely agitated because of the reluctance of the government to give its own decision on the recommendations of the Gajendragadkar Commission[39] and also because of some news item in the papers that the hon'ble minister is thinking of a wage freeze. So far as the recommendations of the Gajendragadkar Commission are concerned, the employees have expressed clearly that those are not satisfactory. I do not know whether there were limitations on the Commission because of the terms of reference but one thing is certain that they have not received what they expected to and, therefore, there is much discontent even about the recommendations as such. The low-paid employees who are on subsistence level have not been given any

38. Kabir and Chagla – Humayun Kabir, Union Education Minister (01.09.1963 to 21.11.1963) and M.C. Chagla, Union Education Minister (21.11.1963 to 13.11.1966).

39. Gajendragadkar Commission was constituted by Govt of India, in 1971, headed by P.B. Gajendragadkar (1901-1980), the 7 Chief Justice of India. It was mandated to submit a report on the adequacy of the Dearness Allowance permissible to Central Government employees.

neutralisation. The Commission has failed to enunciate any principle about the protection of real wage and, therefore, full neutralisation has not been granted even to those who are paid less than Rs. 300 because, according to us, the economic limit of subsistence level should be considered at Rs. 300 even as that of vulnerability at Rs. 750 while the Commission has treated it at the level of Rs. 575. At the same time, they have recommended that if there is a 10-point rise in the course of a year, there should be negotiation started. As a matter of fact, we had suggested that after every six months and after a rise of 5 points, there should be a fresh consideration. The Commission has itself suggested that there is likely to be a price rise. We think that because of the wrong economic policy of the government, there would be an unprecedented price rise in the near future and because the recommendations made are quite unsatisfactory and a price rise is inevitable, it is but proper that the government should immediately declare the appointment of a Third Pay Commission for all Central Government employees, excluding the Railwaymen, for whom a separate Wage Board should be appointed. The subject of wage freeze has been referred to. It has also been asked whether the government is prepared for a profit freeze, a price freeze and an expenditure freeze. But we are told that there would only be a freeze in the case of wages. As a matter of fact, it is not possible for the government.

So far as the prices are concerned, it seems that it is not within the competence of the government to control prices. Every time we are confronted with the price spiral and this talk of wage freeze becomes irrelevant. What is needed is a basic approach. That basic approach should be about our planning itself. The size of the plan is not material, but the character of the plan is. It is necessary that the projects in our plan should be of the production-type, labour-intensive and depending least upon foreign aid. I welcome the appointment of our revered Gadgil Sahib[40] to the Planning Commission. I wish that the entire Planning Commission should be a body of economic experts, freed from politicians. I also wish that our central banking authority, the Reserve Bank of India should also be guided by the advice of economic experts and not by bureaucrats. If the plan changes its character and if more and more employment

40. D.R. Gadgil (1901 1971) – economist, vice-chairman of the Planning Commission of India, founder Director of the Gokhale Institute of Politics & Economics. Gadgil was the originator of the Gadgil formula, which determined the quantum of Central assistance for states under the five-year plans.

opportunities are offered, only then will it be possible for us to increase the purchasing power, the purchasing capacity of every individual citizen. Therefore, without effecting any basic changes in the character of our Plan, it would be wrong to think of a wage freeze. It would only invite or provoke the Central Government employees to further agitation. I learn – I am not sure whether I am correct – that the leaders of the Central Government employees wanted to wait upon the hon'ble Finance Minister. But he is reported to have said that such discussions would be of no avail. I do not think this is a correct approach. He should be free to be converted to the other's point of view if there are genuine arguments on the other side. In this way, if he keeps his mind open, there is every possibility that matters will not be precipitated and the Central Government employees would not be required to launch an agitation. I urge upon the Finance Minister to consider this aspect seriously and to ensure that he gives a lead to the Central Government as a model employer and to the other industrialists, in maintaining industrial peace. I say this because very often in our country, it is found that because of the wrong and adamant attitude of the employers, the workers are forced to adopt measures which they otherwise would not have adopted. Therefore, this is a golden opportunity for the hon'ble Finance Minister to give correct lead not only to the other employing ministries but also to the industrialists in the private sector. I hope he will not miss this particular opportunity.

The Kerala Budget, 1966-67[41]

Industrial Potential Underutilised

D. Thengadi: Sir, the feeling obtaining in Kerala that the state is discriminated against is not without justification. Under the rule of the Centre, Kerala is certainly becoming poorer and poorer, day by day. Industries, proposed or licensed for the state, are shifting elsewhere because of official delay and apathy. Administrative inefficiency has caused substantial amounts of grants, voted for essential services, to be surrendered unutilised. Unemployment has been on the increase and by the end of the Fourth Plan, the number of educated unemployed is estimated to be as high as one million. Steps have not been taken, as explained by my friend, Koya,[42] to bring about overall uniformity between

41. *Rajya Sabha Debate* dated 12th May, 1966.
42. K. Nalla Koya Thangal (b. 1924) was appointed by the President of India to serve as Member of Parliament from Lakshadweep constituency between 1957 and 1967.

the Malabar region and the rest of the state, so that people in that region say that even if Vasco da Gama were to reappear, he would not miss any lane or bylane in Calicut.

Ours is a socialist government. Sir, I do not know the precise meaning of the technical term 'socialism' but if it has anything to do with equality, I must accept that this government is really socialistic in that it robs all sections of the population, equally alike without discrimination. Therefore, there is a rising tide of discontent among all sections of our population.

The entire population of Kerala is extremely disturbed because of the major crisis of power-cut. Formerly, it used to affect only the industrial consumption. Since January this year, even domestic consumption is being affected by the power-cut. I can hardly overstress the need for a major thermal station in Kerala. In the absence of such a major thermal station, we are incurring huge losses. The fertiliser factory there has suffered a loss, during the last four years, of nearly Rs. 10 crores. The expenditure on the thermal station, I am sure, would be more than compensated. I request the government to shake off its indifference and procrastination in this matter. Apart from power-cut, the paucity of raw materials, particularly that of iron, is a great handicap in the way of small-scale industrialists. The government must come forward to do the needful and remove this obstruction in the way of the progress of the small-scale industries there.

The millions of fishermen of Kerala have not received from the government the protection that they deserve. The Fisheries Corporation cannot be treated as a substitute for fishermen's co-operatives. The latter should be encouraged and subsidised. A law should be passed, enabling the fishermen to become owners of their own boats and appropriate relief should be granted to them during the off-season period. Development of the Cochin Port also deserves top priority.

The general wage-level in Kerala is low. The wages have no relation whatsoever either with the productivity of labour or with the cost of living obtaining today. The wage structure in Kerala presents a picture of anarchy.

The Kerala Labour Department is not being helpful to labour. It is paying scant regard to tripartite meetings and national labour conferences in the name of economy.

The provisions of the Kerala Land Reforms Act regarding land ceiling have not been implemented. Consequently, the surplus land has not been made available for distribution among the landless labourers who are the worst sufferers. They are not being given the minimum wages or alternative rural employment during the offseason period.

In the north Malabar region, particularly Tellicherry and Cannanore [Kannur], there have been unlawful encroachments on the private forest areas, due to the connivance of the Devaswom managers. The government should take over those private forests and help the forest workers to organise their own co-operatives.

The *kisans* are grumbling over the complicated procedures of agricultural income-tax assessment, procurement levy, restriction on the inter-district movement of foodgrains, inadequate supply of loans, seeds and other materials and the anti-peasant lacunae in the Land Reforms Act. Sir, it is regrettable that while the state of Kerala is full of industrial potentialities, they have not been utilised and developed fully by the government. It has not given proper direction to the private sector. It has also failed to conduct efficiently the affairs of the public sector undertakings. The record of this failure is too long to be narrated here. I may, however, by way of illustration, state a few facts here. This is not an exhaustive enumeration of the government's mistakes of commission and omission which, if narrated, would be too long. Sir, to take the first example, the Kerala Ceramics Ltd.,[43] Kundara is an illustration of the government's policy of procrastination. Out of the total amount representing the share-capital of Rs. 1 crore, only Rs. 8,58,100 worth of shares have been issued. Even after two years of the formation of the company, the government's sanction for the issue of the remaining shares has not been received.

There has further been the mistake of basing the entire expansion programme with export as the mainstay without carrying out any market studies. In view of the inevitable competition with traditional exporters of high-class crockery, the mass-scale production by foreign manufacturers and the practice of the foreign manufacturers to spend large sums on product design and development, the present policy of the company seems to be unrealistic and is leading to yet another financial disaster. The company is depending too much on foreign collaboration. It is not making any effort to develop something Indian. The Indian tradition in porcelain manufacture is an ancient one and it deserves revival with

43. Launched in 1963, the Kerala Ceramics Limited, a fully owned Government of Kerala ceramics products manufacturing company, at Kundara, Kollam. Started in 1963.

adaptation to modern needs. The neglect of this aspect of the matter is capable of being interpreted as a symptom of the lack of patriotism. This policy should be reversed.

The Travancore Titanium Products Limited,[44] Trivandrum provides us with an example of government's lack of confidence in Indian technicians and its tendency to lean heavily upon foreign collaboration, even when the same is uncalled for. The TTP had already suffered because of British Titanium Products' financial interest in the company. Further negotiations for foreign collaboration were entirely uncalled for.

Further, it is necessary that import substitution should be coupled with Indian technical know-how, wherever it is available. Indian technical personnel should be afforded the fullest opportunity.

It is surprising that this company has not so far utilised modern concepts of programme and performance budgeting. This should be done at the earliest.

There has been a shortfall in the production of the Trivandrum Rubber Works Limited,[45] Trivandrum. The reasons ascribed by the management for the shortfall are not convincing. True, power-cut is a problem common to all the Kerala government companies, but the plea that non-availability of materials affected the production of Travancore Rubber Works[46] is not convincing.

Actually, the company had not planned the procurement of raw materials in time, in the context of its scale of operation anticipated in the ensuing years, nor had it introduced modern methods of materials management. The development of materials, required by the company indigenously, should have also been encouraged. It would have avoided shortages of the required materials.

The Travancore-Cochin Chemicals Ltd.,[47] Udyogamandal, incurred a loss of Rs. 11.09 lakhs during the year 1963-64 by selling hydrogen

44. Travancore Titanium Products Ltd., a leading manufacturer of anatase-grade titanium dioxide in India, the company was incorporated in 1946 in Thiruvananthapuram, by the erstwhile ruler of Travancore.
45. Trivandrum Rubber Works Limited – a public sector manufacturing industry based in Thiruvananthapuram, Kerala. It was promoted by the Kerala State Industrial Development Corporation (KSIDC) in 1963.
46. Another name for Trivandrum Rubber Works Limited.
47. Travancore Cochin Chemicals, a public sector undertaking owned by the government of Kerala and situated in Udyogamandal industrial district of Kochi was launched in 1950.

chloride gas and hydrochloric acid at rates lower than their costs. The company had entered into a 6-year contract with Messers Hindustan Insecticides Ltd.,[48] Udyogamandal, for the supply of chlorine at Rs. 250 M.T. as against the actual cost of production of Rs. 430 during 1963-64.

As a matter of fact, an ancillary industry to manufacture chlorine-based products could have been located at Alwaye[49] or nearabout, and it could be possible to build up an export-oriented industry as, for instance, the manufacture of benzene hexachloride. There should be other such chloride-based products which have good export possibilities. The recommendations of the Tariff Commission are valuable, and the D.G., T.D. and the Ministry of Commerce should make a detailed study in this respect in consultation with other manufacturers.

Regarding the Plantation Corporation of Kerala Ltd.,[50] Kottayam, it is worth noting that the target for planting rubber during the Third Plan period was originally fixed at 20,000 acres. Subsequently, it was reduced to 15,000 acres. The reason given was paucity of land, but paucity of land is not a new or an unforeseen development. Having once approved the programme for planting 20,000 acres, the government should have ensured that the required land was released to the Corporation in time. On the contrary, there have been a number of instances of delays in the release of land.

Again, proper care was not taken in selecting the pieces of land. For example, in regard to Vettilappara Estate,[51] the Management Consultant has observed:

"It is unfortunate that a large plantation corporation, such as Plantation Corporation of Kerala (PCK) should have undertaken to develop at all, in the first instance, an estate like Vettilappara. It is not only poorly located across the river in relation to the main estate in the Kaladi group, but is also unfavourably spread over a large geographical area in bits and pieces, too small to be effectively maintained and managed as an integral part of a group of large estates."

48. Hindustan Insecticides Limited, a Government of India enterprise under the Ministry of Chemicals and Fertilisers, was incorporated in 1954 and headquartered in Kochi.
49. A municipality and a northern suburb of the city of Kochi in Kerala.
50. The Plantation Corporation of Kerala Ltd., was formed in 1962, by the government of Kerala.
51. Rubber plantations, which are located in Vettilappara village of Malappuram district in Kerala.

This is only one of the many examples of lapses and misjudgements. Sir, in case of the Traco Cable Co. Ltd.,[52] Ernakulam, the Committee on Public Undertakings,[53] in its report, stated that "the financial position of the promoters should have been verified by the state government and the Central Government before recommending their case and at the time of issuing the industrial licence in 1958. In its absence, a valuable period of 4 years (upto 1962) was lost in raising the necessary capital, by which time the factory was originally expected to be commissioned. It will also be seen that the state government which had originally agreed to participate in the share capital of the new company to the extent of only 25 per cent, and had no intention of running it as a government concern, was compelled to take over a larger liability than anticipated."

Regarding the Kerala PREMO Pipe Factory Ltd.,[54] Trivandrum, the committee has said:

"Even five years after the setting up of the factory, it is not being run to its full-rated capacity. The factory was, no doubt, given by the Indo-Norwegian Foundation[55] as a gift, but the productive resources should have been fully utilised. It was expected of the management to study the pattern of demand for pre-stressed concrete pipes at the very beginning and to arrange production accordingly. It is surprising that despite the many advantages, which the use of pre-stressed concrete pipes offers over cast iron pipes, the company has not been able to promote their sales. It is also surprising that the state government did not insist on its full productive capacity being utilised. What is worse, the policy of restricting production of pre-stressed pipes to the orders received has been followed all these years and, in order to utilise the available capacity, the production of RCC pipes had to be taken up."

---

52. Traco Cable Co. Ltd., PSU in Kerala established in 1964 and was a supplier of cables and conductors to State Electricity Boards, Indian Railways, BSNL, etc.
53. Parliamentary Committee for examining reports and accounts of the public sector undertakings of Govt. of India.
54. Kerala PREMO Pipe Factory Ltd., a Kerala state Govt. company, incorporated in 1961. Its major products are polymer, synthetic, PVC water storage tanks and other plastic products.
55. Formed in 1953 by the Govt. of India and the Norwegian government for assistance in areas such as fisheries in Kerala, health, sanitation, water supply, etc. through Norwegian technical and financial assistance. Between 1952 and 1972, Norway provided technical and financial assistance to India for technological upgradation in these fields.

Though there is a large variety and number of undertakings in the public sector, the Industries Department has not yet organised a well-equipped and suitably-staffed technical planning cell to concentrate on the broader technical and economic aspects of the projects. The committee has said that such a cell should be entrusted with the task of examining the projects from the point of view of their technical feasibility, economic soundness, etc., studying the various stages of their execution and co-ordination at the policy and administrative levels. Setting up of such a cell would have contributed to the speedy implementation of the industrial projects and to their efficient working. Nothing has been done in this direction so far by the government.

The Committee on Public Undertakings was not generally impressed with the manner and circumstances under which most of the public sector undertakings were established in the state.

A proper study has not been conducted to find out what the shortcomings of the companies, that were to be taken over, had been, and how best they could be set right.

Insofar as new industries were concerned, a proper techno-economic feasibility study was not usually conducted before the venture was undertaken, or before expansion took place, with the result that some of the undertakings are not economically viable.

Kerala, sir, abounds in important industrial raw materials. It has good transport facilities by road, rail and waterways. It has a major port. And it can boast of a literate and intelligent labour. In view of these industrial potentialities of Kerala, one cannot but conclude that the present industrial backwardness of the state is mainly due to the wrong policies of the government. I should like to quote specifically yet another case of the governmental procrastination. As per the recommendations of an expert committee, the 10 factories directly managed and run by the Department of Industries and Commerce, Kerala were converted into five joint stock companies, all the shares being owned by the government of Kerala on 24th February, 1964. This had a far-reaching repercussion on the service conditions of the staff members working in the erstwhile Malabar area under the three establishments of (i) Kerala Soap Institute, (ii) Government Oil Factory, and (iii) Government Hydrogenation Factory, all situated at Kozhikode (now formed into a company under the name and style of 'Kerala Soaps and Oils Ltd.') which were all previously run by the Department of Industries and Commerce of the Madras government and then by the Kerala government. Most of the staff members were recruited as government servants by the Public Service Commission – this is important – and ruled by the Madras Service Rules or Kerala Service Rules and are all allotted personnel.

The original G.O., according to which the joint stock companies were formed, allowed option to the staff members to work under government or the newly formed company. But a later G.O., which clarified the above G.O., indirectly refused the option to the staff members.

Some staff members filed a writ petition to quash the latter G.O. upon this, the High Court observed:

"It will be open to the petitioners to file representations before the government, stating their grievance and the government will pass appropriate orders after taking into consideration all relevant circumstances."

The matter is now pending with the Kerala government. The service conditions of the staff members have not so far been defined, even though two full years have elapsed after the formation of the joint stock company.

Then, sir, the grievances of the NGOs are there. These 2 lakhs of NGOs in Kerala are, for the first time, forced to resort to direct action. These demands, it is needless to stress, are thoroughly justified and would receive moral and substantial support from all the Central labour organisations. It would be in the fitness of things if in the state, which is directly under the Centre, the disparity between the emoluments and the dearness allowance of the Central Government employees and the state government employees is done away with.

The Kerala Appropriation (No. 3) Bill, 1966; The Kerala Appropriation (No. 4) Bill, 1966; and The Kerala Appropriation (No. 5) Bill, 1966[56]

Discrimination against the People of Kerala

D. Thengadi: Madam, the people of Kerala are convinced that the much-trumpeted Consultative Committee is no substitute for the self-government. There are a number of things on account of which they feel that their state is being discriminated against. One small, but important, point which does not fit in the financial involvement is about the declaration of Malayalam as the state language. There is no reason why this should have been postponed so far. As a matter of fact, language is so dear to the people

56. *Rajya Sabha Debate* dated 1st December, 1966.

that even in our own country, people are threatening even bloodshed for inducting a village or two or a *tehsil* or two in their own state; they may not be so enthusiastic about China or Pakistan. Nevertheless, after the President's Rule, there has been inordinate delay or postponement about the declaration of Malayalam as the state language.

Then, madam, the people have demanded that the provisions of the Kerala Land Reforms Act,[57] particularly those belonging to the land ceiling should be implemented immediately. As a matter of fact, they were not satisfied with the Land Reforms Act and the provisions about the land ceilings because, as compared to the other neighbouring states, the ceiling fixed in Kerala was already too high, but even those provisions have not been implemented so far.

Co-operative societies of fishermen have not been receiving adequate financial assistance from the Centre. The demand of the fishermen and the assistance actually given to them have no proportion between the two. The industries in Kerala have not been given technical aid for their development. No steps have been taken to develop fisheries on scientific lines.

No systematic efforts have been made to develop centres of tourism in Kerala. As a matter of fact, we feel that Kerala can be another Kashmir from the tourist point of view. Development of hydel projects has not been properly attended to. The rivers have not been harnessed for this purpose. As a matter of fact, on account of geographical and other situations, I feel that it is quite possible for us to circulate power in villages from hamlet to hamlet, to have de-centralisation of productive processes on the strength of machinery run by power, and, thus, we can develop a number of small-scale industries, giving employment to a large number of persons. In Kerala, the problem of unemployment is very severe. At the end of the Third Plan, we were told that 5,50,000 was the number of unemployed persons, out of whom 1,50,000 was the number of educated unemployed and we are alarmed to learn that at the end of the Fourth Plan, there would be an increase of unemployed persons to the tune of seven lakhs. As a matter of fact, planning should have taken proper cognisance of this most important economic problem of this state and should have adjusted itself accordingly. For this purpose, the planners should have given priority to labour-intensive schemes and also to the programmes of diversification of

57. Passed in 1957 by the EMS Namboodiripad government. K.R. Gowri Amma, one of the most well-known communist leaders of Kerala, who was expelled in 1994 from the party, was then Revenue Minister and piloted the Bill in the Assembly.

industries in the rural areas but both these aspects have not been properly taken care of. The difference in the per capita incomes of the country as a whole and of Kerala in particular is really significant. The difference would be 40 by the end of the Fourth Plan, which means that there is clearly a discrimination against the state of Kerala. The problem of students and teachers in Kerala had assumed alarming proportions a few months back. It is a matter of some satisfaction that now the teachers' dispute has been settled but I learn from reliable sources that the government was forced to come to some terms with the teachers, whose number is 1,35,000 and who are assisted by the students running to more than 4 million because of the fact that the police in Kerala refused to support the government measures, particularly if they were repressive and they conveyed to the government very frankly that in order to suppress the agitation of the teachers, the government would have to bring in the military and could not depend upon the police. I reliably learn that because of this stand taken by the Police Department, the government was forced to come to terms with the teachers. Anyway, even today, we would like to insist that the recommendation pertaining to the pay scales and other emoluments of teachers should be implemented in Kerala, which is directly under the Centre. The state government employees are also discontented and they, along with the state government employees of other state governments, have taken a decision to go on a token strike on 5th January. It is also significant that the venue of the conference in which this decision was taken was Trivandrum. This problem is unnecessarily being allowed to continue as a lingering one and it is for the Centre to ensure that the state government employees of Kerala are not forced to join hands with other agitators because unlike other states, Kerala is being managed by the Centre itself. On 5th December, the employees of the State Electricity Board of Kerala are to start their agitation. This is really alarming. We used to hear that God said: 'let there be light' and there was light but if the Centre does not intervene in proper time, then we would have to say that the government said: 'let there be darkness' and there was darkness in Kerala. All these should be attended to immediately and urgently. On all these points, the people of Kerala are feeling aggrieved, are feeling that they are discriminated against and, therefore, it would be a very sad commentary on the role of the Centre if there is no enthusiasm among the people of Kerala to support this particular demand for additional grants. On this account, I oppose this demand for further grants.

Appropriation (No. 2) Bill, 1970[58]

Need to Implement Recommendations of the National Labour Commission

Sir, we do not find any justification for the government to come forward with any additional demands because the government has failed to fulfil even the primary expectations of the people. For example, it has been rightly stated that unemployment and underemployment are the most vital problems of our Indian economy but planning, not being conducive to the eradication of unemployment, has failed so far to solve the problem. In this context, I should like to know from the government one thing. Our President,[59] though in his personal capacity, has given a sort of thesis or a comprehensive plan for eradication of unemployment, I would like to know whether the government has studied this comprehensive plan by V.V. Giri, though it is in his personal capacity, and what are the reactions of the government to this plan? Particularly, in the rural areas, the problem of unemployment and underemployment is assuming dangerous proportions. The government is aware – though not much has been done in this respect – that land reforms have not been properly implemented in the different states, that surplus lands consequent to land legislations have not been distributed to the landless labourers, particularly those people belonging to the Scheduled Castes and the Scheduled Tribes and the provisions of the Minimum Wages Act have not been extended to agriculture in the entire country, though there has been a persistent demand for this on behalf of the agricultural labourers. We also know that we have not cared to develop agro industries which would be helpful as subsidiary industries to provide employment during the off-season period to peasants and also to agricultural workers.

Regarding industrial workers, the entire labour in the country is agitated because the government has not taken any decision on the recommendations of the National Labour Commission. The Commission submitted its recommendations on 31st August last and nothing has been done so far, not even deliberations, with a view to giving a proper shape to the labour policy of the Government of India. We should like to

58. *Rajya Sabha Debate* dated 4th May, 1970.
59. V.V. Giri (1894-1980) was the fourth President of India, from 24th August, 1969 to 24th August, 1974 and a well-known labour leader. Founder of the All India Railwaymen's Federation, Giri also served as president of the All India Trade Union Congress, India's first High Commissioner to Sri Lanka, as Union Labour Minister, Vice President of India, etc.

know when that will be done and how it will be expedited. The industrial workers throughout the country are discontented because they are not getting their legitimate demands met. The Wage Boards have failed to give them their legitimate due and now the time has come when the very character and composition of the Wage Boards should be changed. They should be converted into tripartite forums for collective bargaining with the representative of the government only to help the process of mutual consultation, mediation and final agreement. Even it is necessary to change or to introduce appropriate changes in industrial laws, particularly with a view to bringing all those who are in employer-employee relationship within the framework of industrial laws. Therefore, it is necessary to define industry as any activity in which the employer-employee relationship persists. It is also necessary that in order to preserve and promote industrial peace, a sense of responsibility must be inculcated in the workers. That cannot be done by mere speeches. For that, it is necessary that there should be progressive labourisation of industries by which I mean that labour should be evaluated in terms of shares. Thus, every worker should be a shareholder of his respective industry, whether it is in the private or in the public sector. But we are sorry to note that the Government of India, which is the biggest employer in the country, is not conducting itself as a model employer. For example, we are aware how its own employees were compelled to resort to a token strike on 19th September, 1968 and how the government came down with a heavy hand on the strikers and even now some of the cases are pending.

Now the government has announced the appointment of the Third Pay Commission but the government employees are not satisfied with this announcement for various reasons. In the first place, no labour representative or representative of the Central Government employees is included in the body of the Pay Commission. Secondly, the government employees expected that interim relief would be declared even before the Commission commenced its work in the light of the increased cost of living but the matter has been postponed. It has been entrusted to the Commission which may take its own time. Thirdly, no time limit has been prescribed for the completion of the Commission's work. And again there has been no firm commitment on the part of the government regarding the need-based minimum wage and the protection of the real wage. In the absence of such assurance, the entire work of the Pay Commission would become useless, would come to nothing. In view of all these factors, government servants are not quite satisfied with the composition and terms of reference of the Pay Commission.

Simultaneously, Railway employees, who number 16 lakhs, are demanding that a separate Wage Board should be constituted for them in view of the large number of categories of employees in the Railways and if a stand was taken that such a separate Wage Board is not possible, at least a separate cell within the Pay Commission should be constituted to go through their pay scales.

And with a view to normalising the employer-employee relationship in the Central Services, I urge that the government should withdraw whatever cases are going on as a consequence of the strike of 19th September. The Government of India, as I said, has failed to fulfill its duty as employer and the recent strike of the Himachal Pradesh employees is another example of it. In Himachal Pradesh, the employees have been demanding Punjab scales and the government of Himachal Pradesh, which is strictly under the Central Government, has come forward with a statement that they would have fresh recruitment on the basis of permanency. This is highly undemocratic. This is snatching away the right to strike and the government must be aware that the right to strike is the legitimate weapon in the armoury of the workers and if that is snatched away, the workers will have no other alternative but to resort to revolution. It is not desirable and, therefore, the government must protect, safeguard and respect the right to strike of the Himachal Pradesh employees and come out with an assurance that there won't be any vicitimisation, that there won't be any fresh recruitment and that Punjab pay scales would be granted to them. Though we have now crossed the threshold of the Fourth Five-Year Plan, I am sorry to say that we have not yet finalised national policies on employment, productivity, prices and incomes during the Fourth Plan period. Finalisation of these policies is necessary; otherwise at the end of the Fourth Plan period, we will find ourselves in conditions worse than what exist today.

There has been much talk about socialism. I do not go by words. Prophet has said that the letter killeth.[60] I do not know whether socialism is one such word. Even now we find that not much has been done effectively to minimise the disparity in income. For example, even now a major portion of all unearned incomes has not been properly diverted into public utilities. Appropriate measures, such as consumption tax, have not

60. Referred in the book of Isaiah in terms of solving the problems of people.

yet been taken to minimise the disparity. As a matter of fact, there should be a fixation of ratio between the minimum and the maximum expendable incomes in the country at 1 to 20 immediately. I personally suggest that a constant and conscious endeavour should be made to reduce the same to 1 to 10. It is not merely an economic problem as some of our socialist friends presume; the problem is more psychological because the problem is how to reconcile incentive with equality. If equality is established with the materialistic values of life, where only material advantages are prime considerations, then it would be impossible to have incentives for personal development without having disparity in incomes.

Therefore, it is necessary that we introduce in our public life, in the entire atmosphere, not only materialistic values of life, but also a coordinated system of the materialistic and non-materialistic values of life, under which social status will be an incentive over mere material gains and in which the higher the social status, the smaller would be the sphere of enjoyment and the wider the sphere of enjoyment, the lower will be the social status. In this way, there should be a coordinated system of enjoyment and social status introduced. Then alone it is possible to bring about equality. This is one thing which I want to suggest at this stage.

Even for capital formation, the government has not taken suitable measures. The problem of capital formation has not been properly dealt with. It is not necessary to presume that the process of capital formation is an integral part of capitalism. These are two different things, but nothing has been done, for example, regarding the revival of the spirit of *swadeshi* or regarding introducing changes in our consumption pattern or for the fullest utilisation of the installed capacity in our industry, for a vigorous drive for import substitution, for the rationalisation of imports, for the imposition of still higher excise duties on luxury goods or for a reduction in all unnecessary, unproductive and superfluous expenditures. As you are aware, the Public Accounts Committee[61] has recently observed that losses were avoidable and infructuous expenditure in the various government departments examined by them during 1969-70 totalled Rs. 42 crores. A drastic curtailment in the administrative expenditure and an intense drive for household and other domestic savings is necessary. In the name of socialism, we have taken certain measures. Banks have been nationalised and the chapter is almost closed. Have we taken the follow-up

61. The Parliament's Public Accounts Committee (PAC). In 1970 the PAC was headed by Atal Bihari Vajpayee.

measures properly? Have we pursued the matter properly? For example, it was expected that once the banks are taken over, a proper structure would be given to the banking industry. The government may differ from us, but we had suggested that an autonomous monetary authority should be constituted with the object of price regulation through currency control and fullest employment through credit control. For this purpose, a financial consultation service should be constituted for micro-planning in the rural areas for the benefit of the peasant and his family in the villages, but nothing of the sort has been done so far.

Regarding nationalisation, I feel that we have not started the process of nationalisation from the right quarter. In fact, the first to be nationalised should have been foreign banks, insurance of foreign trade and also the export and import of trade with the communist countries for rupee payment, but this we have failed to do. Also, we had suggested that the foreign industry should be indianised. What has happened to Indianisation in industry? For example, in regard to tea, the foreign industry can be taken over and its share capital thrown open to the Indian general public with a pre-condition that only the low-income group would be entitled to purchase the shares. It has been found practical in some other countries for the low-income group to purchase shares in the industry and to run the industry. The process of democratisation of industry should be followed. Then, I come to a very vital problem and that is the pattern of ownership. I think that even the ruling party with its experience of the last one year or so must have come to the conclusion that relying on empty slogans does not pay much either politically or in the economic sphere. There must be some rational basis for our thinking. A mere label of isms will not help. Some constructive, practical thinking is necessary. I suggest that a national commission on the pattern of industrial ownership should be appointed and it should be asked to go thoroughly into the problem of the ownership of the different industries. Different industries have their different characteristics. There are various kinds of ownership, for example, private enterprise. What should be its place in the total scheme of things? The right to property may be fundamental, but it cannot be an absolute right. In the present scheme of things, what should be the place of industry? To the extent it can be entrusted to private enterprise, what other industries should be nationalised, what other industries should be entrusted to workers themselves, to what extent there should be co-operativisation, municipalisation, labourisation and even democratisation; also, in the case of foreign industries, whether Indianisation can be suitably introduced. All these things should be reconsidered and for this purpose, it is necessary that a national commission should be appointed to consider the patterns of industrial ownership. They should go to the very basis of the problem. Again, even as we are thinking of taking over industries from private capitalists, there may or may not be justification for it, we will have to consider how to make our public sector undertakings more efficient. Even though there is a clamour for nationalisation, nationalisation under the present state is only governmentalisation and bureaucratisation. It has been extremely difficult to make the public sector undertakings perfectly accountable to the general public, that is, to Parliament. I understand there is a problem – how to strike a balance between autonomy and accountability of public undertakings. This has to be entrusted to the national commission, as I suggested.

Similarly, I am of confirmed view that we have to rethink on the problem of de-departmentalisation of certain services. It is not only a question of taking over same industries from the private capitalists. We have also to consider what departments should be taken over from the government and entrusted to public bodies. So, de-departmentalisation should also be considered. There should be established a national profession of public administration with its defined professional standards, both substantive and ethical, with its own professional discipline, training and progressive activities. This profession should be granted statutory recognition. Retaining the departmental structure only the strictly governmental functions, for which direct ministerial responsibility to Parliament is essential, it is advisable to convert all other functions, whether routine payment, technical or specialist services, trading and economic services, judicial and equity administration or regionalised or localised services – into non-governmental public agencies under commissions, tribunals or boards, to be managed by the public administrators, and subject only to supervision at the highest level by Parliament through a specially constituted Ministry of Public Agencies, thus achieving the ideal of fewer ministries and a slimmer civil service, by relieving the Cabinet and bureaucracy of certain departmental functions. For example, it can be considered whether the Cabinet can be relieved of some of its functions, such as health, education and youth services, information, broadcasting and tourism and Railways, posts and telegraphs and shipping. This classification can be made and, in this way, we can consider in what ways we can relieve the public sector of certain industries, if necessary, and relieve the government of certain functions, if necessary. For all this, it is absolutely necessary that a national commission on the pattern of industrial ownership should be appointed. If it is appointed, I think, without going into a war of words and without fighting for mere slogans, it will be possible for all thinking people in the country to come together and chalk out and finalise a concrete plan for our economic reconstruction.

Taxation Laws (Amendment and Miscellaneous Provisions) Bill, 1965[62]

Measures to Discourage Dishonesty and Corruption

D. Thengadi: Madam Deputy Chairman,[63] as a layman, I have been unable to understand the logic underlying the different economic measures of the government. A few weeks back, the government introduced the Gold Control Bill[64] knowing fully well how adversely it was going to affect not less than 2 million members of goldsmith families, and though the Akhil Bharatiya Swarnakar Sangh,[65] which was about to launch an agitation, refrained from doing so as a gesture of goodwill and patriotism because of our armed conflict with Pakistan, our hon'ble Finance Minister had not a word of appreciation for these poor starving goldsmiths, and now he has come forward with a measure patronising officially the black marketeers and anti-social elements.

The obvious implication of this Bill is that honest payment of taxes is a folly and not a virtue. This Bill confirms my previous impression that the government is specialising itself in the art of pleasureless sin.

One after the other, the government is presenting to the people measures that enlarge the premium on dishonesty and corruption. But while the premium is being increased, the returns from these three

62. *Rajya Sabha Debate* dated 29th November, 1965.
63. Violet H. Alva (1908-1969) – first woman to preside over Rajya Sabha, lawyer, journalist and politician belonging to the INC from Karnataka. Elected to Rajya Sabha in 1952, Alva became Deputy Minister for Home in 1957 and was Deputy Chairperson of the Rajya Sabha from 1962-1969.
64. Gold Control Bill – The Gold (Control) Act, 1968 is a repealed Act of the Parliament of India which was enacted to control sale and holding of gold in personal possession.
65. Akhil Bharatiya Swarnkara Sangh, all India organisation of artisans, traders, workers of the gem-jewelry industry, founded in 1963.

consecutive measures are progressively disappointing. It is interesting to measure the achievement of each consecutive scheme in the light of the fact that the total amount of evaded income tax is of the order of Rs. 3,400 crores; and gold in India is estimated at Rs. 4,000 crores, 80 per cent in the form of ornaments and 20 per cent in the form of bullion. This Bill exempts the subscriber from a number of taxes – Wealth Tax, Gift Tax, Capital Gains Tax, Estate Duty. It has been laid down, persons who have acquired the gold, subscribed by them towards the Bonds, out of their income which they have not disclosed for the purposes of income-tax, excess profits tax, business profits tax, super-profit tax or surtax, will not be liable to any of these taxes on such income, in assessments for any assessment year made after 19th October, 1965, if the income had not been detected by the income-tax officer before the date on which the gold was subscribed towards the Bonds and the gold offered for subscription had not been seized under any law before the date of the subscription. The assets represented by such undisclosed income will not be liable to inclusion in the net wealth of such persons, and courts will be barred from requiring any public servant to give any evidence pertaining thereto. The criminals are assured of full negotiability, pledge, sale, and what not. No question can be asked of the subscriber about the source of the gold subscribed. No searches, no harrying, no penalties, no payments.

Obviously, this is legalising the illegal, the immoral, the criminal and the sinful acts of the wealthier sections of the population. As I said earlier, through this Bill, the government is committing a sin; but, what is more, it is a sin without any compensating pleasure.

According to the latest information, the stock market is worried about the discouraging response to the new Gold Bonds.

During the first 21 days after launching the scheme, the collection of gold amounted to 1,538 kilograms, which works out to more than Rs. 2 crores at the Indian price. It is equivalent to Rs. 82 lakhs only in terms of international price. There is a progressively downward trend in the prices of the new bonds. When the scheme was inaugurated, the bonds were unofficially transacted at the rate of Rs. 100 per 10 grams. Trading in the bonds was officially started in the stock market in the middle of the current month; the price then dropped to about Rs. 89 or so per 10 grams. But the rate has since declined to the low figure of Rs. 83 per 10 grams.

The new bonds carry an interest of Rs. 2 per 10 grams for I5 years. So, the total interest of Rs. 30 will accrue at the time of redeeming the bonds by gold. Taking into account the international price of gold at Rs. 53.58 per 10 grams, the value of the bond on maturity should not amount to more than Rs. 83.58 per 10 grams.

Although the collection this time was in the initial stage better than that in the earlier two bonds, i.e. of 1962 and of March 1965, it is far short of expectations. The over-optimism in the official circles about the materialisation of the declared estimate of Rs. 500 crores is based upon unrealistic calculations. Even the Prime Minister's modest target of Rs. 200 crores seems to be quite unattainable.

The main object was to compensate for the acute shortage of foreign exchange. True, unless enough gold is collected, we cannot maintain the working of our industries that will suffer consequently from the shortage of raw materials, spare parts and components. That is all right. But the way devised by the government is not effective. It is highly improper. Is there no other remedy available, except offering sinful allurements to the anti-social capitalists? On account of this tendency of the government, those anti-social elements are bound to bring pressure upon the government to give further concessions to their sins.

In view of the steady progress, the government has been registering in the art of pleasureless sin, I am led to believe that sooner, rather than later, the government will announce that the Gold Bonds shall be Bearer Bonds. Direct conversion of unaccounted money into gold and subsequently into Gold Bonds may also be facilitated. That is my apprehension based upon the present policy of the government. I feel that this is not the proper way to meet squarely the economic crisis. The only appropriate method would be to appeal to the patriotic feelings of countrymen. All of us have reasons to believe that, if appealed to properly, our citizens would be prepared to offer everything they possess at the altar of the motherland. Our nation has a glorious tradition of complete, unreserved self-sacrifice at the altar of the Motherland – from Sage Dadhichi[66] of Vedic times to the hon'ble recipients of gallantry awards[67] at the hands of the President during the last week. There is absolutely no cause or justification for nervousness on

66. Sage Dadhichi, sacrificed himself so that *devatas* (gods) could make a weapon out of his bones to defeat the *asuras*. He symbolises the spirit of supreme sacrifice of *Tyaga* and *Dāna*, for a larger and benevolent cause. The weapon, vajra, made out of Sage Dadhichi's bones, figures as the emblem of India's highest gallantry award, the 'Param Vir Chakra.'

67. Gallantry Awards instituted by the Government of India to honour the acts of bravery and sacrifice of the officers/personnel of the Armed Forces and other forces.

this score. Even at this stage, I request the government to withdraw this unlawful and immoral measure.

Madam, revered Mahatmaji [Mahatma Gandhi] always insisted upon purity of the means. He never subscribed to the communist theory of 'ends justifying the means.' He would not even welcome *Swaraj* if it entered India through the gates of immorality. Economics divorced from ethics was disastrous, according to Mahatmaji. I am confident that if he were really able to be in the House at the time of introduction of this Bill, he would certainly exclaim in Shakespearean style: 'What a fall, my Finance Minister!"

The Banking Laws (Amendment) Bill, 1968[68]

Accord better Status to Bank Employees

D. Thengadi: Madam Deputy Chairman, in the first place, I think the hon'ble Deputy Prime Minister[69] will agree with me that it is not customary to include provisions regarding allowances in this type of Bill that is presented before us today. Secondly, there is no reason why deputation allowance should be denied. Because the employees are working under different managements for the time being and working under different working conditions, their promotional avenues and seniority claims are not adversely affected. Therefore, why should deputation allowance be denied to them?

Thirdly, it is a well-known fact that transfer is an instrument in the hands of the management to victimise whomsoever they do not like and, therefore, this clause, giving them this handle, is likely to be misused to the detriment of the employees' interest. On all these grounds, I urge that this clause should be withdrawn. Therefore, we oppose it.

Madam, I am not very particular about the third reading, because in the first place, this may be a cry in the wilderness. Secondly, madam, I do not think that our Deputy Prime Minister is not wise enough to understand the disastrous implications and consequences of the Bill. It is easy to awaken one who is asleep, but difficult to awaken one who pretends to be asleep. That is the difficulty. The government should not cultivate the knack of rousing antagonism where it does not exist. Therefore, I again

68. *Rajya Sabha Debate* dated 4th and 5th December, 1968.
69. Morarji Desai (1896-1995) –fourth Prime Minister of India (1977 to 1979). Desai was Deputy Prime Minister and Finance Minister in the Indira Gandhi cabinet between 1967-1969. One of the most well-known Gandhian Congressman and freedom fighter, Desai's was a dominant presence in post-independent India's public life.

urge that the entire Bill should be withdrawn. Otherwise, unnecessary hostility, antagonism and bitterness will be created and probably our hon'ble Deputy Prime Minister will have the distinction of being the architect of trade union units in the banking industry which was difficult so far.

D. Thengadi: Madam, one clarification, not interruption. Will the hon'ble minister agree with me when I say that in the composition and structure, there is a vast difference between the Reserve Bank of India and the Federal Reserve Board of the US?

Morarji R. Desai: There is bound to be. They are quite different things. They work in a different manner. We need not copy one federal structure or the other.

D. Thengadi: I understand it. That is why, we want that the very composition and objectives should be changed.

D. Thengadi: Again, madam, on a clarification, I am not interrupting him.

D. Thengadi: The hon'ble minister said that these two objectives cannot be the objectives of the Reserve Bank. For clarification, may I ask whether in Australia, the banking industry is not entrusted with these two functions, viz. full employment and regulation of the price structure, whether it is not carrying out these functions?

D. Thengadi: Madam, to put the records straight I should mention one thing. Mr. Shejwalkar[70] who was a member of the Select Committee[71] had sent a telegraphic dissent which unfortunately on technical grounds could not be included in the eport of the Select Committee. It read: "Not received draft report as yet. I want to put dissent note regarding Section 36AD and even regarding taking over of banks, kindly record my dissent." It is just to put the records straight that I am mentioning this.

Now, the hon'ble minister has not explained how Section 7 of the Criminal Law (Amendment) Act[72] does not cover the present provision. Secondly, even when that Criminal Law (Amendment) Act was passed, we

70. N.K. Shejwalkar (1923-2000) – Jana Sangh leader, Mayor of Gwalior, was elected to the Lok Sabha from Gwalior to the 6th and 7th Lok Sabha, was also member of Rajya Sabha (1968-1974).
71. Parliamentary Select Committee for looking into Indian banking laws and status for Bank employees in 1969.
72. The Criminal Law (Amendment) Act, passed by the Lok Sabha and by the Rajya Sabha, which provided for amendment of Indian Penal Code, Indian Evidence Act and Code of Criminal Procedure in 1952.

had referred that the British government had assured on the floor of the then Assembly that the provisions of Section 7 would not be applicable to trade union activity. Then, madam, the government proposes to constitute a Banking Commission. In that case, we do not understand why there should be this indecent haste in bringing about such a provision which prejudices the work of the Banking Commission. Thirdly, the National Labour Commission is already trying to evolve a common labour code and we were given an impression by the Home Ministry that the government wants to pay respect to and maintain the dignity of the National Labour Commission and that was precisely why the government refused to refer to arbitration the demand of the Central government employees for a need-based minimum wage. The argument was that a reference to arbitration of this particular demand which is already pending before the National Labour Commission, would prejudice the work of the National Labour Commission. My point is why the same argument could not be made applicable in this case because it is clear that Section 36AD prejudices the work of the National Labour Commission. On all these grounds, we oppose this particular clause and we again appeal to the Deputy Prime Minister to consider deleting this clause.

The Banking Laws (Amendment) Bill, 1968[73]

Vision about the Banking Industry

In the first place, I think I should confine myself to a few remarks which should be taken into consideration by the Select Committee to be constituted.

First of all, there is great agitation in the whole country about section 36AD. I must say that through this section, the Finance Ministry has encroached upon the legitimate jurisdiction of the Home Ministry and the Labour Ministry, because law and order is within the jurisdiction of the Home Ministry and industrial relations fall within the jurisdiction of the Labour Ministry and both these functions are being taken by the Finance Ministry through this section.

Regarding demonstrations within the premises, it should be possible in an ideal condition for the government to regulate industrial relations through mutual consent, negotiations and consultation, and legislation should not be resorted to because psychological handling is much more important in the field of industrial relations. Even then we cannot ignore

73. *Rajya Sabha Debate* dated 20th August, 1968.

the fact that disciplinary action, punishments – major and minor, misconduct – major and minor, all these aspects were taken into consideration and a verdict was given on all these matters in different awards, i.e. the Sen, Sastri, Desai and Iyer Awards.[74] There is no reason to have any further legislation because in all these four cases, competent persons, judicially-minded persons have prescribed certain major and minor punishments for major and minor misconduct and, therefore, this is not at all necessary.

Again, in our criminal law, there are adequate provisions. Now, every citizen is governed by the Indian Penal Code and it should have been sufficient if the bank employees also were governed by the IPC in the normal course, but it seems that bank employees were born in sin and, therefore, they are doubly governed, i.e. by the IPC and proposed Section 36AD. They are being deprived of the privileges of a normal citizen through this section.

Again sub-clause (1) (c) says:

"Act in any manner calculated to undermine the confidence of the depositors in the banking company."

This is a very vague provision. It can be used for suppression of truth or to cover the misdeeds of authorities-that be to the detriment of the depositors themselves. Now, this would afford protection to mischief-mongers and, thus, defeat the very purpose. From all these points of view, bank employees are extremely agitated over this provision and not only token strikes, but even indefinite strikes are in the offing and this time our Select Committee should take into consideration the reason why the minds of bank employees are so agitated.

---

74. In 1949, the Govt. of India constituted a Tribunal headed by Justice. K.C. Sen, retired judge of Bombay High Court to look into certain industrial disputes. "The award of the Tribunal evolved a formula for fixing the bonus payable to employees of banks. But that award was set aside by the Supreme Court on account of the defect in the constitution of the Tribunal which rendered its proceedings invalid." [accessed at: *https://indiankanoon.org/doc/1269580/?type=print* (30.8.2020)]
    - Government of India constituted a tribunal under Justice S. Panchapagesa Shastri, former Judge of the Madras High Court to look into, among other things, on the issue of the bonus payable to the bank employees.
    - National tribunal constituted by the Government of India under Justice K.T. Desai, then Chief Justice of High Court of Gujarat. The Desai Tribunal's mandate was same as that of the earlier two with some variations.
    - S. Ramachandra Iyer was the Chief Justice of Madras High Court from 1961-1964; he had delivered the judgement regarding the dispute between The Indian Bank Ltd. vs The Indian Industrial Tribunal and Ors. on 18th January, 1963.

Again, under the proposed Section 55-A, sub-clauses (2) and (3), the Reserve Bank employees are denied deputation allowance and they are put in a very awkward position. They do different types of work at different places under different circumstances, very often under dual control and still, though they may lose promotion and seniority, they will not be given by way of compensation any deputation allowance. There is no propriety in this particular section.

Regarding the constitution of the Board of Directors, first of all, it is not expected or it will not include the representatives of employees and customers. This is highly undemocratic. Employees and customers must have a right to elect their own representatives to the Board of Directors. The employees should be treated as subjects of the institution and not merely as its objects. In other developed countries and developing countries, a better status is accorded to bank employees in the scheme of things.

Now, power to reconstitute, admittedly by the Board which is biased, is given to the same Board. That means that through the backdoor, they can bring in their own men under a different disguise and have their own majority. So, the appointing authority should not be vested in the Board of Directors.

Now, there is the question of control. Our experience about governmental control has not been very happy. The Reserve Bank of India was constituted to hold the value of the money, since metallic backing to the money was not given. But the Government of India went on printing one-rupee notes, which made the position of the Reserve Bank of India ineffective. This is the history of our monetary control. The same thing about credit. Now, though in theory, on paper, the Reserve Bank of India as our central bank has many rights and many powers; in practice, we find that it is completely dominated by the government. It is not an autonomous body. I should like to suggest – and the Select Committee should give serious thought to the matter – that the very composition of the Reserve Bank of India should be changed. Instead of being manned by a majority of ICS [Indian Civil Service] officers and bureaucrats, it should be managed, manned, controlled and directed by independent economists with experience in the field of economics and that too preferably an economist drawn on a contract basis, for a few years, so that no one will have a sense of being a government employee. If, in that way, the Reserve Bank is managed, manned, directed and controlled by independent economists, there is every hope that the functions of the Reserve Bank, i.e. the central bank, will be properly carried out.

In this connection, I should like to state that in this Bill, there is no clarity of vision about the objectives of the banking industry. The objectives of the banking industry must be: (1) to regulate prices; and (2) to offer the fullest employment. Banking is meant for currency and credit policies. Through currency, the price-line should be held and through their credit policies, the fullest employment should be given. That should be the responsibility of the banking industry in general and of the Reserve Bank in particular. We find that in the constitution of the Central Bank of Japan, these objectives are specifically laid down and it has been stated that the banking authority would be an autonomous monetary authority. Government will have all fiscal powers. Though the monetary authority should co-operate with the fiscal authority, that is, the government, the fiscal authority should pay respect to the decisions and recommendations of the monetary authority. It should be mutually respected. At the same time, the independence of the monetary authority must be established and even as we are now having three wings, i.e. the Legislature, the Executive and the Judiciary, there should be a fourth wing or fourth arm, i.e. the monetary authority. Unless this is done, everything will be dominated by the government, which we know is famous or notorious for its knack of mismanaging affairs.

Now, regarding agricultural finance, today we know that agricultural financing through the co-operative sector is not being properly used. Even in this Bill, the Reserve Bank of India has not been given the power to control the utilisation of these funds, which the state governments are using for political ends. So, there are innumerable bad debts in agricultural finance and there is a vast unorganised money market flourishing in the country. The control that is sought to be established through this Bill will be governmental and political, but not social. Even this control is not entirely to the dissatisfaction of our present bank lords. The word used is 'social' control, but it is significant to note that our bank lords are very happy at the introduction of this Bill. In their memorandum to the Finance Minister, they have said:

"We have the honour to observe that most of the provisions of the Banking Laws (Amendment) Bill, 1967 introduced in the Lok Sabha on 23rd December are in conformity with the conclusions arrived at in the informal meetings of the representatives of our association with you."

That means that they are quite happy at the introduction of this Bill and, in fact, this Bill is likely to introduce an element of capitalism even in the field of agriculture. We know that small peasants will not be receiving credit since they are not creditworthy and only the creditworthy people, i.e. the bigger ones will be receiving credit. In this way, a sort of capitalism would be introduced even in the agricultural sector.

Yes, when I say that our objectives must be laid down, I also want to state that the functional specialisation of the banking industry must be stressed upon. That is to say, every bank is expected to deal with every industry. That will not do. In a number of countries, every bank is entrusted with this functional specialisation, to deal with special functions or industries or operations. That is being introduced in certain countries, like Russia and Finland statutorily, and in other countries by customs. This functional specialisation has helped a lot in the development of those respective countries. Now, today we find that our banking industry being dominated by capitalists has failed so far to organise its credit policy so as to give proper relief to medium-sized small-scale industries and agriculture. But there is no guarantee, madam, that through this social control Bill or Act,[75] proper help will be rendered. And, therefore, we think that from all the points of view, it is necessary to scrap the Bill, to throw it out lock, stock and barrel and to have a rethinking, a fresh thinking about the structure of our banking industry and to see that our banking industry performs its functions properly and fulfils the objectives of maintaining the price-line on the one hand and the fullest employment, on the other.

The Banking Laws (Amendment) Bill, 1968[76]

Autonomy of the RBI

D. Thengadi: In the first place, I want to question the propriety of the Section, namely AD36. This Bill is supposed to be a Money Bill or Financial Bill and this was not the proper Bill in which to introduce something in connection with the curtailment of the trade union rights. This belongs to some other department, namely the Labour Department and this was not the occasion for introducing a provision curtailing the trade union rights because this is a Money Bill. Secondly, precisely on this point, that is, about disciplinary action, then punishments – major and minor – misconduct –

75. Social control was imposed through Act No.58 of 1968 which was an amending Act to the banking regulation Act, and which came into force in 1969. The expression 'social control' in connection to banks and banking came into usage around December 1967.
76. *Rajya Sabha Debate* dated 2nd December, 1968.

major and minor, all these matters have been gone through by four competent persons, namely Sen, Sastri, Desai and Iyer and now to come forward with another provision would amount to a sort of no-confidence in these competent persons.

Again government has not said even during the last discussion that there was any need for introduction of such a provision in that there was any occasion where the employees became uncontrolled, that they committed some violence; that is, there was no justification put forward by the government during the last discussion.

Again, madam, as has been rightly said by our friends, there are various Sections of the Indian Penal Code; certain Sections have been referred to, such as 339, 340, 426, 441, 504 and 511. Because of these Sections of the Indian Penal Code, this Section 36AD becomes redundant. More than that, I want to say that when the Criminal Law Amendment Act was passed in 1931, when Section 7 was passed at that time, even the British government had assured that the provisions of Section 7, which pertained to restrictions on peaceful picketing, would not be made applicable to trade union activities. That is to say, when even the foreign government was so considerate to the trade union activities, it is tragic. Madam, that our own government should come with a heavy hand on our employees.

Again, madam, the wording of Section 36AD is very vague; it is capable of being misused. It says in clause (c):

"act in any manner calculated to undermine the confidence of the depositors in the banking company."

Now what does it mean? 'Calculated' means who will calculate? The employees or the employers or the general public or the customers or the government? That means much is left to the discretion of the employers only. And if the employees try to uncover, try to expose the misdeeds or defalcations or some such matters on the part of the employers, then it would be calculated to undermine the confidence of the depositors. Again, madam, if the government says that this is only to maintain law and order, then the proper procedure would have been, instead of saying, 'No person shall' etc. Government ought to have said in this clause, 'No person other than a worker or an employee,' etc. In that case, probably the bona fides of the government would not have become challengeable. Again, madam, so far as the demonstrations by the employees are concerned, the standing orders and the provisions in the Industrial Disputes Act have been quite adequate in public sector undertakings and in private industries to deal with such eventualities. And, therefore, in a way, the Finance Ministry has encroached upon the legitimate jurisdiction of the Home Ministry on the one hand, and the Labour Ministry, on the other by introducing this Section 36AD. As a matter of fact, we were thinking that both the Home and the Labour Ministries would come out with a protest against the Finance Ministry, not merely to protect or safeguard the interests of employees, but to safeguard their own legitimate jurisdiction. But I am sorry to see that even the Labour Ministry is silent on this point.

Madam, there is another Section, Section 54 AA sought to be inserted in the Reserve Bank of India Act, 1934, which denies deputation allowance to the Reserve Bank of India employees. This is also detrimental to their interests and is unjust to them. In the first place, whoever is sent on deputation, has to work under different managements under different working conditions. Even his promotion and seniority may be jeopardised, and under such circumstances, it would be cruel to deny him any deputation allowance. And, secondly, deputation allowance is an item which properly belongs to the sphere of collective bargaining, and should not have fallen part and parcel of this Bill.

Now so far as the general contents of the Bill are concerned, the Finance Minister has referred to Clause 2 which deals with banking policy. I am of the opinion that, instead of laying down the banking policy, the time is ripe when the objectives of banking industry should be prescribed. And according to us, banking industry must be given two objectives. Number one, regulation of price structure through currency control, and number two, maintaining full employment through control of credit policy. Now, in this respect, I should like to suggest that the very composition of the Reserve Bank should be changed. The Reserve Bank should be entrusted with both these functions, that is, regulating price and maintaining full employment. This would become possible because through currency, prices can be maintained. Only thing, government should not interfere with the work of the Reserve Bank. But today, government is issuing one-rupee notes and that is interference. And if in this fashion, the Reserve Bank is entrusted with these two functions, and if its composition is changed, I am sure the whole economic picture of the country would undergo some drastic change. For these purposes, we want to suggest that the composition should be changed in the sense that bureaucrats or ICS officers should not be in the majority. The Board of Directors should consist of independent economists, preferably drawn on a contract basis, so that they should not have a feeling that they are government employees depending upon the mercy of the government. Only the Secretary may be a bureaucrat or an ICS officer. And, in this fashion, if the Reserve Bank is really made an independent or autonomous monetary authority, it would be possible for us to have a better economic policy because, in that case, being autonomous, the Reserve Bank would have the right, not only to differ with the government on economic matters, but also to express its difference of opinion publicly, and to initiate a public debate on any matter of difference so that, whenever on any economic policy there is a difference between the Government of India and this monetary authority that would be autonomous, naturally the matter would come to the Parliament before being finalised, and Parliament's verdict would be the final verdict. In this way, we propose that even as we have three wings, the Legislative, the Judiciary and the Executive, we should also introduce this fourth wing or arm, that is, this monetary authority. And that can be done if the composition of the Reserve Bank is altered.

Secondly, madam, it has been said that those who deserve to be given credit but are denied the same today, would benefit through this Bill. The hint is obviously to the small-scale industries, the medium-sized industries and the agricultural sector. But this Bill does not empower the Reserve Bank to control the utilisation of funds advanced to agriculture through the co-operative banking sector, and various state governments are exploiting this for the political ends of their party. Thus, there are innumerable bad debts in agricultural finance, and there is a vast unorganised money market flourishing in the country. Creditworthiness should not be a precondition for advancing credit. Otherwise, only big *kisans* or big people would be receiving credit. This will introduce capitalism even in agriculture. Efforts should be made to advance money to small *kisans* who are not creditworthy today. It is the point that credit should be advanced to those who are not creditworthy today and they should be helped by the banks giving credit through a financial counselling system of their own to become creditworthy. That is true financial counselling. Those *kisans* should be advised how best to utilise the credit given to them and the responsibility for financial counselling should lie with the banks giving credit.

So far as the Board of Directors is concerned, I think the provisions in the Bill are disappointing. In the first place, the representatives of customers or employees are not to be found in the Board of Directors and so long as the employees and the customers are not having their own representatives on the Board of Directors, they would not be inspired with the zeal to work and they would have no confidence in the conduct of affairs. With these few remarks which are incidental but mainly condemning Section 36AD and section 54AA I, oppose the provisions of the Bill which I feel must be thrown out lock, stock and barrel and, in particular, Clause 15 which is anti-labour.

State Bank Laws (Amendment) Bill, 1973[77]

Banking and Management Practices

D. Thengadi: I welcome this Bill because it is good so far as it goes. But it ought to have been more comprehensive. At least, it should have covered such of the aspects as required to be amended. But, unfortunately, it is a piece-meal legislation as usual.

Now that it has become obvious that the nationalised banking industry has failed, not only regarding profit-making, but regarding rendering services, we should have a complete review of the whole canvas and take into account some of the valuable suggestions that were made at the time of nationalisation, but were not taken cognisance of. For example, there was a valuable suggestion that the Reserve Bank of India should be raised to the status of an autonomous monetary authority entrusted with the responsibility for price regulation through currency control and full employment through credit control. Autonomy we demand because the fiscal authority should not be competent to override the decisions of monetary authority unilaterally and if there be any difference of opinion between the monetary authority and the fiscal authority, the matter should be brought before the Parliament and the verdict of the Parliament should be final. I think it is high time that this valuable suggestion is considered seriously by the government and implemented.

Another aspect is about the financial consultation services. This service has not been organised in the nationalised banking industry. This is the most important reason for our failure in evolving appropriate credit policies. The discussion has been whether the criterion of creditworthiness should be suitably altered. But I should like to say that the basic problem is how to convert the uncreditworthy poor person into a creditworthy one. If the banking industry is to support only creditworthy people, then, probably the bulk of our population would not be entitled to receive any

77. *Rajya Sabha Debate* dated 30th July, 1973.

help from the banking industry. We had suggested that the nationalised banking industry should organise financial consultation service so that the poor peasants with economic or uneconomic holdings, the average artisans and even agricultural workers are free to have their own micro-plans regarding their own small industries. These micro-plans should be submitted to the financial consultation service and scrutinised by them and loans advanced according to the merit of the plan. There should be supervision by the consultation service regarding the spending of the loan amounts. This consultation service should ensure that through these micro-plans properly implemented, the un-creditworthy poor peasants are turned into creditworthy persons. That was the need of the hour, but that has been overlooked and that is why, we feel that this discussion on the criterion of creditworthiness is futile so far as the requirements of the country are concerned. Then what are the tightening measures envisaged by the government so that there should be no repetition or recurrence of incidents like the Nagarwala affair?[78] Some tightening measures were necessary. But that aspect was also neglected.

So far as introduction of the scheme of worker-directorship is concerned, I welcome it whole-heartedly. At the same time, I should like to know what would be the mode of appointment or nomination of worker-director. I suggest that it is better to have elections to the directorship and it should not be left to the sweet will of a few individuals. Another important matter is there, sir. This scheme of worker-directorship is a step in the right direction, but it does not go far enough. It is inadequate. The experience in Great Britain has been that while between 1930 and 1945, the British Trade Union Congress was clamouring for the introduction of the scheme of worker-directorship, after 1945, when the Labour Government came to power, the enthusiasm of the British Trade

78. Nagarwala case was one the most widely discussed scandal of its era, exposing the politican-banking nexus under the Indira Gandhi regime. On 24th May, 1971, Rustom Sohrab Nagarwala mimicking the voice of then Prime Minister Indira Gandhi, called up chief cashier Ved Prakash Malhotra, of the State of Bank of India, Parliament Street branch, in New Delhi and instructed him to withdraw Rs 60 lakh and deliver it to a 'Bangladeshi'. Malhotra, without verifying the caller's veracity, followed the instructions. Nagarwala was nabbed the same day and the cash recovered. The incident shocked the entire country with the political opposition questioning the whole method of withdrawal and disbursement. It generated a strong perception that there existed a deep nexus between Indira Gandhis' Congress Party and the nationalised banks. Nagarwala died in prison while the investigating officer, D.K. Kashyap, died in a mysterious car accident.

Union Congress for this scheme died down, because it was found that the worker-director was not strong enough, was not stationed well enough, to influence the decisions of the Board of Directors, but, on the contrary, his commitment to the policy of the Board of Directors became a sort of commitment or estoppel for the militant trade union organisation and, therefore, though not as a rule or as an article of their constitution, but as a convention, the British Trade Unions have seen to it that those who are appointed or nominated as Directors are no longer members of the executive or other office-bearers. Therefore, sir, this experience of Great Britain should be taken into consideration. Though I concede that whatever holds good for other industries cannot be made equally applicable to the banking industry because it has its own special characteristics, still I feel that if the Government is earnest about ensuring workers' participation in management, it should try to study the experiment in Yugoslavia where, within the framework of national planning and national targets, the entire decision-making is left to the workers in the plant right from the purchase of raw materials to the marketing organisation and, in this way, the workers are made to feel this responsibility for the running of their industries properly.

Sir, some kind words have been said by my friend, Kulkarni,[79] about the responsibility of the employees. I fully agree with him. But, sir, he has also said and said rightly that the sense of responsibility should proceed from the top. It cannot proceed from below and move upwards. Can we say confidently that at the top, there is a sense of responsibility so far as financial affairs are concerned? I should like to suggest that if the State Bank employees are getting more pay than they should be getting, in that case, this criterion should be made applicable at all levels and let us have a rule in our country that the ratio between the minimum and the maximum of incomes in our country should be 1:10 and even the highest personality in this country should not be allowed to violate this rule. If some such self-discipline is observed by those in authority, then it is possible for us to convince the workers that financial discipline is necessary. But, when we find that financial discipline is not being observed by the authorities themselves, to come with a piece of advice only for the low-paid employees is inequitous and is a cruel joke.

79. A.G. Kulkarni (1917-1992) – Congress leader from Maharashtra, was, a four-term Member Rajya Sabha, and served in the Upper House between 1967 and 1992. Kulkarni was also Vice Chairman of Rajya Sabha between 1978-1982.

Sir, the employees of the banking industry are sufficiently educated. It is possible for us to persuade them to take proper line of action. But the leaders should come forward with examples also rather than with precepts.

Another aspect of the problem of industrial peace is that today, sir, we are confronted with the fact of multiplicity of unions. I stand for the principle: 'one industry, one union'. But what is the proper method for translating this principle into action? I think it is no good to patronise or boost up any trade union as against the others. The proper way would be to pass a legislation that in every industry, there should be only one union so that the position of a single union would be analogous to the single Parliament in the country, while today the position of such unions in the same industry is analogous to the position of different political parties in the country. That would be a 'parliament' of workers in that particular industry. At the same time, it would be necessary, not only to abolish different unions within the industry, but also to abolish all the central labour organisations. And when such single unions are established in different industries, their representatives should be sent to the single National Federation of Labour, and that would constitute the real unity among the working classes. But so long as there is no such legislation passed or any such step taken, it is necessary to be realistic and to live with the fact of multiplicity of trade unions. And when there is a multiplicity, it is necessary that the management should be judicious in its behaviour, in its attitude, towards its employees. This judiciousness of the management is necessary to inspire confidence. I am sorry to say that in certain cases, this judiciousness is absent. For example, on the Parliament Street, in the head office of the State Bank of India, there was an incident on 22nd June last, when there was a conflict between two groups of employees. One of the employees was injured and sent to hospital. But I am sorry to say that the management has not taken any step to bring the culprits to book. If such judiciousness is absent, then the workers would be sceptic and they would be reluctant at least to co-operate with the management.

Sir, at this juncture, while I was welcoming this workers' directorship, I also want to suggest that government should evolve a wider and a more broad-based scheme for workers' participation in management. And so far as discipline and other things are concerned, government should ensure that the thing should start with the government itself. The doctor must heal himself first and then give advice to others.

The Mineral Oils (Additional Duties of Excise and Customs) Amendment Bill, 1964[80]

Consumer Protection

D. Thengadi: Sir, in the first place, whatever amounts accrue as a result of this measure must be passed on to the consumer. It has been argued that the amount is too small. If the benefits are too small, that is an additional argument why the government should not hesitate to pass it on to the consumer. As a matter of fact, there is a widespread impression in the country that the government is not consumer-conscious and this impression must be removed. It has been said that the burden arising out of this measure will not be passed on to the consumers but, at the same time, we all know that these companies have a knack of passing on the burden over their shoulders to the consumers and the government invariably finds itself helpless in such matters. Therefore, we will not be prepared to accept any assurance from the ministry that the road transport will not be dearer on account of this measure. Even if it is decided that the benefits accruing from this shall not be passed on to the consumers, it is necessary that the amount recovered should be appropriated to the Roads Fund because we have not yet fulfilled the targets set out in the Nagpur plan.[81] According to my information, probably with the only exception of West Bengal, no other state has fulfilled the Nagpur Plan targets. If the amount is appropriated to the Consolidated Fund, we are not confident that it would be properly utilised or that it would be utilised specifically for the development of road transport. And I need not emphasise the need to develop road transport at the present stage of our economic development. Sir, the hon'ble minister may or may not express it in so many words but it is certain that as a consequence of this measure, the burden of taxation is bound to increase. I am more interested in reduction of prices of some essential commodities, such as kerosene, diesel or petrol. All these commodities are of common use and the government must assure us that their prices would be reduced. It will not do for the hon'ble minister to shirk the responsibility and say that reduction in their prices or taxation on these commodities or such matters pertain properly to the Budget and

80. *Rajya Sabha Debate* dated 15th December, 1964.

81. The 1934 conference convened in Nagpur, of chief engineers from the provinces and the Govt of India –then British India – to prepare a road development plan. The conference spoke of a 20 years' road development plan between 1943 and 1960 which came to be known as the Nagpur Plan.

that this Bill is something different and, therefore, this matter of reduction of prices should not be brought in at this stage. I should like to say that we must have an integrated financial policy and such an integrated policy cannot suffer separation of the Budget from other Acts or Bills concerned with finance.

One more point I should like to add. The government has given a certain guarantee about profits to these various companies. I should like to point that foreign companies like the Burmah Shell,[82] and ESSO[83] are giving indecent treatment to their employees. It is not merely a question of employer-employee relationship. The Finance Ministry cannot absolve itself of its responsibility by saying that employer-employee relationship is a matter entrusted to the Labour Ministry. Unless you close the nose, the mouth will not be opened. It is a question of our national honour. Our employees in Burmah Shell and ESSO are not likely to get decent treatment unless and until the Finance Ministry emphatically and boldly asserts that no guarantee of profits can be given unless these foreign companies assure the government that they would give a fair and decent treatment to their employees.

With these words I close.

Discussion under Rule 176 on the Report of the Third Central Pay Commission, 1973[84]

Due Consultation with the Central Government

D. Thengadi: Sir, the decision of the government on the recommendations of the Third Pay Commission is going to be a very important event in the history of our trade union movement. It would be important not only for the Central Government employees, but it would also be a pace-setter. All the subsequent Wage Boards and collective bargaining would have this decision as the guideline. Even the committee appointed for the fixation of pay scales of the employees of our Rajya Sabha and the Lok Sabha is sure to finalise its recommendations in consultation with the representatives of the employees on the basis of the guidelines furnished by this decision on the recommendations of the Third Pay Commission.[85]

82. A British oil business company launched in 1886. In 1966, Castrol was acquired by Burmah Shell, was renamed as Burmah Castrol. BP Amoco (now BP) purchased the company in 2000.
83. ExxonMobil, a major US based petroleum company.
84. *Rajya Sabha Debate* dated 20th August, 1973.
85. Constituted in April 1970 and submitted its report in March 1973.

Therefore, the importance of this decision is to be noted in the interest of not only the Central Government employees, but the entire trade union movement. The plea made by my hon'ble friend, Mr. Gadgil – I cannot use any harsh language – is certainly anti-labour. It would appear from his arguments as if the Class IV employees under the Central Government are demanding that whatever is due to the agricultural labourers and artisans in our rural areas should be snatched away and given to them so that they would be responsible or they are responsible for the sub-subsistence level of our toiling millions. Till recently, the government used to say that every wage rise leads to price rise while the economists contradicted it with the plea that every wage rise is not responsible for price rise. The wage rise is responsible for price rise only to the extent to which the wage rise is in excess of productivity rise, but even the National Labour Commission has categorically stated that in our country, after Independence, the productivity rise has been greater than the wage rise; the wage rise has not caught up with the productivity rise and the price rise is still higher, so that wage rise is chasing the productivity rise and both of them are chasing the price rise. Under this condition, it is wrong to say that wage rise is responsible for price rise. Similarly, the plea made by Mr. Gadgil is not in consonance with the observations of the Third Pay Commission. I will quote on page 21 in para 25, the Pay Commission says:

"A large section of the government employees had not received their due share of the increase in the national product. When per capita national income at current prices increased by 95.2 per cent, the Class IV employees alone received an equivalent increase of 95 per cent. The emoluments of all the other categories had lagged far behind. The increase in their monetary emoluments ranged from 51 to 74 per cent for clerical categories, 25.4 per cent for Class II and 11 to 16.7 per cent only for Class I employees."

In para 23, the Commission says:

"The normal tendency in countries which have to assume new functions and responsibilities for development is for the wages and salaries bill to increase more than in proportion to the increase in revenue and expenditure. It would, therefore, appear that there is some leeway for raising the wage and salary levels without placing an undue strain on the exchequer."

In para 22, it has given the ratio for the various categories between wage and salary bill and revenue and expenditure. The Commission says:

"...there was a declining trend in the wages and salaries bill of the Government of India as a percentage of total revenue expenditure from 1960-61 to 1970-71 when it fell from 33.5 per cent to 28.3 percent. The wage bill as a proportion of revenue receipts also showed a steadily declining trend from 32.2 per cent in 1960-61 to 25 per cent in 1965-66; but since then, it has been rising and reached 27.2 per cent in 1970-71, which is 5 per cent less than the position in 1960-61. Over the years, therefore, both revenue expenditure and revenue receipts have increased faster than the wages and salaries bill."

These are not the observations of any trade union or service association but these are the observations of the Pay Commission. It goes on to say:

"From 1960-61 to 1970-71, the wages and salaries Bill increased by 184.7 per cent when revenue receipts went up by 235.7 per cent and revenue expenditure by 236.4 per cent."

If these observations of the Pay Commission are taken into consideration, I think that would give a lie to whatever arguments have been advanced by my hon'ble friend, Mr. Gadgil, against the demands of the Central Government employees. Sir, the Third Pay Commission has raised very high hopes in the minds of our brethren, the employees, but the way in which it has functioned is really somewhat wonderful. It has taken years to complete its work and after the completion of the work, it has said that it did not precisely know the definition of either Central Government employees or service conditions as specified in the terms of reference. All these years what prevented the Pay Commission from seeking clarification from the government on the definition of these terms, I cannot understand, but this has created some ridiculous position. For example, they have omitted a large number of categories from the purview of their work. They themselves have enumerated them and I need not go into all that. Even the pensioners have been excluded from the purview of its work. It has already been stated how essential it is that pensioners should be meted out justice. With the rise in price level, they also should be given increased emoluments and I need not stress on that. While some categories have been excluded, some others have been placed in the wrong way. For example, it has placed the employees of the Audit and Accounts Department in the wrong category. Instead of treating the Audit and Accounts Department as an independent entity, the Commission has taken it to be a subordinate office and has made the salary structure of subordinate offices applicable to audit employees in utter disregard of the specific suggestions given by the CAG in a memorandum submitted to it. This is at variance with the requirements of Article 148 (5) of the Constitution. Now, it is the duty of the government to set aside the Pay Commission's recommendations so far as they relate to the Audit and Accounts Department and cause a *de novo* determination of a revised wage structure for the officers and staff of this department. Apart from this, the very fact that the Pay Commission could not seek clarification about the definition of 'Central government employee' and also 'service conditions' from the Government of India in the course of all these years is a sad commentary on the efficiency of work of the Commission. Now, we all know that the Commission was set up directly, though the government would like to deny it, as a result of the 1968 strike.[86] That strike was mainly on the demand for a need-based minimum wage. Even then the government employees had said that the norms and standards laid down by the 15 Indian Labour Conference[87] were outdated and new norms and standards should be prescribed. This was said by the Central Government employees even in 1968. That apart, based on those norms and standards, the Commission has worked out the figure of Rs. 343.69 as the need-based minimum wage for manual labourers. Having stated it, the Commission has also said that, in view of the incapacity of the government to pay it, they are prescribing Rs. 185 as the present minimum. In prescribing it, the Commission has taken for granted, if you go through their calculations – I will not take much time – that an employee gets one meal for 50 to 75 paise and a quarter for the rent of Rs. 14.71. I should like our Finance Minister to make these facilities available to all the Central Government employees. Instead of granting cent per cent neutralisation under this condition of an unprecedented price rise, the recommendations of the Commission have, in fact, sanctified the erosion of real wages. It is interesting to note the extent of erosion sanctified by the Third Pay Commission with reference to wages the Central Government employees had been given on the basis of the recommendations of the First Pay Commission. In the case of Class IV employees, "the extent of erosion is from Rs. 1 to Rs. 33. In the case of Class

86. 19th September, 1968 countrywide strike by Central Government employees demanding a need-based minimum wage.

87. 15th Indian Labour Conference held in 1957 and focused on defining categories of needs essential for workers on which wages ought to be fixed. It focused primarily on safeguarding the interests of workers in the unorganised sector.

III employees, the extent of erosion is from Rs. 44 to Rs. 190. In the case of assistants, it is to the tune of Rs. 267. And those who received Rs. 245, as per the recommendations of the First Pay Commission, suffer an erosion of Rs. 327, if we consider the value of the rupee at the price-level obtained today. The Commission has not conducted its work on any scientific basis. Only a few examples I will cite within the limited time I am allowed. The first example relates to LDCs. The pay scale of LDCs [Lower Division Clerk] comes to the stage of stagnation after 19 years of service. Now, a boy enters service at the age of 19 or 20. That means for nearly 20 years, the LDC will have to go without any further increment. He will have to stagnate.

Though the Commission has expressed its view that 'wherever duties and responsibilities are similar or qualification standards comparable, each such common category should have uniform scale of pay', it has not cared to cater justice to a number of such categories. To cite one example, the telegraphists of the P&T Department[88] are at par with the junior telegraphists of the Overseas Communication Service, but their pay scales are not made equal.

It is a general convention that the existing facilities and amenities should not be curtailed. But the Commission is guilty of violation of this convention. To cite a few examples, according to the recommendations of the Commission, administrative offices are required to increase half-an-hour, the receipts of the house rent allowance are required of even the low-paid employees which was not the case earlier and the percentage of the City Compensatory Allowance has been reduced. At the same time, the Commission has not taken the trouble of re-classifying the cities on a scientific basis of price levels. The Commission does not stand for minimising disparities of incomes in the services. It stands for the ratio of 1 : 25.8 between the minimum and the maximum remuneration within the services.

While this ratio between the minimum and the maximum remunerations within the services is 1 : 8.7 in the United States, 1 : 9.6 in Australia and 1 : 10.2 in Canada, on the contrary, the Commission has blessed the surreptitious designs of the IAS officers, of conferring additional benefits upon themselves. I will just refer to this problem. You know, sir, when there was the Indo-Pak war on 1st September, 1965, the IAS officers had granted themselves some further benefits. Now, the Second Pay Commission, with a view to decreasing the disparity of ratio

88. P&T – Post & Telegraph Department

did not increase the salary given to them by the First Pay Commission. Now, the salary recommended by the First Pay Commission and also approved by the Second Pay Commission, if it is compared with the salary increase ordered in 1st September, 1965 and the salary now approved by the Third Pay Commission, we arrive at a position that a Secretary who used to receive Rs. 3000 has increased his own pay to Rs. 3,500 which has been approved by the Third Pay Commission, that is, Rs. 500, then in the case of the Additional Secretary, it is Rs. 250, in the case of a Joint Secretary, the increase is Rs. 250–Rs. 500. There is a surreptitious increase given by the IAS officers to themselves, which has been legalised, offering them an increase of Rs. 500 to Rs. 250, which, in terms of minimum wage, would be equivalent of salary of 4 to 2 Class IV servants.

It is a matter of opinion. It can be established. It is already proved.

Now, there is a discrimination in the incremental rates granted. Incremental rates provided for in the revised scale also tell a story of discrimination. Class IV category rates of increments are Rs. 2, 3, 4, 5, 6 and 8 which range from 1.1 per cent to 3.6 per cent of their respective minimum wages. Class III categories have been given the incremental rates of Rs. 6, 8, 10, 12, 15 and 20, the percentage to their respective minimum wages varying from 2.3 per cent to 5.2 per cent. Class II, non-gazetted categories have been given incremental rates of Rs. 15, 20, 25 and 30, the percentage to their minimum ranging from 3.5 to 5.4 per cent. Class II gazetted categories have increments of Rs. 30, 35 and 40, and percentage to their minimum varies from 4.5 to 6.1 per cent.

Class I officers' increments are Rs. 40, 50, 60 and 100 and the percentage to their minimum ranges from 3.3 per cent to 8.0 per cent.

The discrimination in increments is quite obvious. The workers' demand has been for one day wage or 5 per cent of minimum of scale and also that the ratio between the initial and the last pay packet within a span of 20 years should be 1 : 2 so that after retirement, the pension ratio should be equal to the initial pay packet.

Regarding house rent allowance and also pensionary benefits, there has been discrimination in favour of the Class I and other officials which I will not go into details.

Then, sir, there has been the fixation formula which is, if not fraudulent, at least defective. One or two cases I will cite. The Commission has devised a very defective formula for fixation of pay in the time scale recommended by them. Denial of accrued benefits has been achieved thereby. A Class IV employee who enters the service on 1-3-73 would get Rs. 185, and one who had entered the service on 1-3-68 would also get Rs. 185. The Pay Commission recommended Rs. 185 as minimum wage on the plea that it would be only after 5 years that an employee would be supporting a family of 3 consumption units when he would be getting Rs. 196. But, as a matter of fact, he would be fixed only at Rs. 185 even after completing the five years' service. A Class IV employee with 14 years of service will only be fixed at Rs. 195. Thus, what has been proposed to be given at the commencement of sixth year by way of minimum wage by the Pay Commission is actually permitted by them in the fifteenth year only. All these factors are to be taken into consideration and we will, naturally, arrive at the conclusion that the recommendations of the Third Pay Commission cannot be accepted as they are and they cannot satisfy the legitimate demands or aspirations of the Central Government employees. Against this background, I should like to request the government that without falling a prey to the false notion of prestige, they should have consultations with the representatives of the Central Government employees. Whether inside the JCM[89] or outside the JCM, that is immaterial. With the consent of the Central Government employees, they should finalise their decision on the recommendations of the Third Pay Commission. This is the only way to ensure industrial peace in this vital sector.

Calling Attention to a Matter of Urgent Public Importance Regarding Threatened Strike by Employees of the Life Insurance Corporation of India[90]

D. Thengadi: May I refresh the memory of the hon'ble Finance Minister because his statement suffers from certain serious inaccuracies? Regarding annual increments, the Memorandum of Settlement between the Life Insurance Corporation and the National Federation of Insurance Field Workers[91] clearly states:

"NFIFWI has been demanding that the present system of appraisals should be ended and Development Officers be granted regular annual increments in the time scale of pay. The Development Officers have under certain appraisal formulae developed the organisation of business for

89. JCM – Joint Consultative Machinery, a platform for resolution of disputes between the government as employer and the employees.
90. *Rajya Sabha Debate* dated 8th March, 1965.
91. National Federation of Insurance Field Workers of India (NFIFWI), formed in 1957 is a union of Development Officers of Life Insurance Corporation of India (LIC).

the past eight years. The time has now come when the introduction of a regular annual increment in the time scale of pay may be considered. The LIC, therefore, agrees with NFIFWI that introduction of a regular annual increment in the time scale of pay would be feasible as it gives a sense of security to Development Officers. Both sides agree that a regular annual increment in the time scale of pay should ultimately but progressively result in greater efficiency in developing business of LIC, on sound and healthy lines," etc.

Then in the monthly magazine of the Life Insurance Corporation of India, *Yogakshema* published from its Central office in the month of August 1964, there is a speech by the Chairman of the LIC reported therein, and he has said on 18th July, 1964:

Mr. Chairman: Mr. Thengadi, if it is a speech, it is bound to be long. So, will you please give the purport of what you want to say?

D. Thengadi: Yes, sir; in his speech also, he has admitted that the principle of annual increments has already been accepted by the LIC. In a recent letter from the LIC to the Federation of Insurance Field Workers dated 30th January, 1965, it is stated:

"As you are aware, the principle of regular annual increment in the time scale of pay has been accepted by the Corporation."

In view of this, the statement by the hon'ble Finance Minister is certainly incorrect and there is no justification whatsoever for denying regular annual increments to them. Regarding the method of implementation, it has already been suggested that provision No. 2 of sub-clause (2) of Section 56 of the Staff Regulations should be deleted, and Section 39 of the Staff Regulations should be used, as it is used for purposes of penalty, as a disciplinary action against all employees. Secondly, the question of house rent also was accepted, but it is not being given. So are we to understand...

Mr. Chairman: Everything has been conceded, it seems. What is the trouble about?

D. Thengadi: No, what we want to say is...

A.B. Vajpayee:[92] Not implemented.

D. Thengadi: What we want to ask is: Is it a sort of loss of memory that whatever had already been accepted is not now being remembered by the government? It is all in black and white, particularly the principle of annual increments. It has been accepted and yet now it is being said by the

92. Atal Bihari Vajpayee was a Member of the Rajya Sabha in 1962 and 1986.

hon'ble Finance Minister that they are not in a position to do so; so many arguments are being advanced...

Mr. Chairman: He said that it was not automatic; he gave the reasons.

Calling Attention Motion Regarding Abnormal Delay in Grant of Interim Relief[93]

Is it not a fact that the name of Mr. E.X. Joseph[94] was suggested by a majority of the unions and associations of the Central Government employees, and, if so, why has not the government accepted the name? Secondly, is the government aware that the compilation of the cost of living index is faulty? For example, the wholesale price is taken into consideration while compiling the index number, while the poor workers have to purchase goods at retail prices. Has the government advised the Pay Commission that there should be a recompilation of the index number on the basis of realism? Only on that basis, the quantum of interim relief should be decided. Thirdly, may I know whether the Pay Commission has been asked to grant interim relief on the basis of the index number which should be recompiled or whether the capacity to pay has also been brought in even for determining the interim relief?

May I know whether the question of capacity to pay has been brought in for determining the interim relief?

---

93. *Rajya Sabha Debate* dated 19th August, 1970.
94. E.X. Joseph (respondent) was a Central Govt. servant and the Secretary of the Civil Accounts Association of non-gazetted staff. This Association was recognised by the Govt. which was subsequently withdrawn because it was preparing for a general strike. Mr. Joseph was asked by the government to disassociate himself but he refused to do so. As a result, the government initiated departmental proceedings against him as per Rules 4(A) and 4(B) of Central Civil Services (Conduct) Rules, 1955. Mr. O.K. Ghosh (Petitioner) was the Accountant-General of Maharashtra who held the enquiry and found Mr. Joseph to be guilty on: 4(A) provided that that no govt. servant shall participate in any demonstration or resort to any form of strike in connection with any matter pertaining to his condition of service, and 4(B) restricted the employees from joining any association which has either not been recognised or recognition has been withdrawn. Mr. Joseph challenged the constitutional validity of the said rules. The constitutional validity of Rule 4(A) was upheld but the proceedings under it were quashed as mere preparation could not be equated with actual strike and Rule 4(B) was held to be invalid.

Pay and Allowances to the Central Government Employees – Payment of Dearness Allowance in Installments to the Central Government Employees[95]

D. Thengadi: In the first place, I should like to point out that the last increase in the dearness allowance was given with effect from 1st April, 1974. Four instalments of increase are now due to the employees. Secondly, you have rightly pointed out that the Third Pay Commission had recommended that should the price level rise above the 12th monthly average of 272 points, the government should review the position and decide whether dearness allowance scheme should be extended further or the pay-scales themselves should be revised. In this respect, we should like to have a categorical statement from the minister whether the government is going to revise the wage structure in view of this rise in index. The argument of the government that payment of D.A. may cause further price rise does not seem to be valid in view of the fact that it is a recognised principle of economics that every wage rise is not responsible for price rise. Wage rise is responsible for price rise only to the extent where the wage rise is in excess of the productivity rise. In our country always, we have the wage rise lagging behind the productivity rise. In view of this fact, I should like the hon'ble minister to make a categorical statement giving the specific date by which all the instalments that are now due would be paid. I would also like to enquire why the recommendations of the Committee of Parliament appointed to report on the structure of pay, allowances, leave and pensionary benefits for the officers and staff of the Rajya Sabha and Lok Sabha Secretariats have been made applicable only to officers and not the employees of the Lok Sabha and Rajya Sabha? Why this discrimination against the employees of Parliament?

Can you give an approximate date?

Sir, I want a clarification from the Minister. The hon'ble minister is repeating 'the instalments'. I should like to know whether it is not four instalments? In our view, it should be four instalments because the last payment was on the 1st of April.

You should kindly clarify the position.

□

95. *Rajya Sabha Debate* dated 8th December, 1974 .

2
Agriculture, Food and Civil Supplies

Thengadi considered agriculture as the food-giving industry in our country. He stood for land reforms while opposing collectivisation of agriculture. Underlining the important role played by bovine species in rural life, he sought for legislation on cow slaughtering. Regarding compulsory procurement of essential commodities, he pointed out that a lot of discontent prevailed among farmers on this count. Highlighting deficiencies in the procurment system, he suggested that only marketable surplus should be procured through levy.

Resolution Regarding Appointment of a Parliamentary Committee to Enquire into Agricultural Co-operatives and to Suggest Measures for Strengthening them[96]

D. Thengadi: In the first place, I think I must clarify the position of Jana Sangh because there was reference to it in the speech of our friend, Mr. Chandra Shekhar.[97] Mr. Chandra Shekhar was vehement without being logical and I can tell him that his vehemence was based upon ignorance of Jana Sangh's manifesto. I do not know whether he would like to go through the manifesto of Jana Sangh because once he understands what is *Jana Sangh,* he would be deprived of his 'holier than thou' attitude which is thoroughly unjustified. That might embarrass him. I must tell him that though he may be quite happy with his own paradise, the position of Jana Sangh is different from what he thinks it to be. Now, unlike the

96. *Rajya Sabha Debate* dated 11th September, 1964.
97. Chandra Shekhar-(1927-2007) – one of the most well-known socialist leaders, who started his political career with the Praja Socialist Party, Chandra Shekhar closely worked with stalwarts, such as Acharya Narendra Deva, and had a political career that spanned more than five decades. Elected to the Rajya Sabha in 1962, Chandra Shekhar joined the Congress in 1965, was elected General Secretary of the Congress Parliamentary Party in 1967. Eventually becoming a centre of dissent within the Congress party against Indira Gandhi, Chandra Shekhar was arrested

Swatantra Party,[98] the *Jana Sangh* stands for land ceiling, but unlike the communists, the *Jana Sangh* is opposed to collectivisation. *Jana Sangh* is all for the cooperative movement. It is also not in favour of co-operative farming simply because, as our communist friend here has just pointed out, collective farming is calculated to be a step ahead in the direction of collectivisation. I think our friend, Mr. Chandra Shekhar, has mistaken co-operation for coercion and the cooperative movement for collectivisation. That is unjustified, we are all in favour of co-operation. At the same time, we will not tolerate collectivisation and particularly this subject has a practical aspect also. It should not be merely a doctrinaire discussion. It has a practical aspect and that is that agriculture is the food-giving industry. It is the biggest industry of the land and no adventurism in the name of any doctrine can be permitted, can be tolerated in this vital industry of our country. Therefore, while opposing collectivisation, we stand for land ceiling. Thus, we have differentiated and distinguished our stand from both Swatantra on the one hand and communists, on the other.

Now, coming to the resolution, the subject matter of the resolution is very important because, as I said just now, it deals with the biggest and the food-giving industry of the country. It has been our feeling that in all the consecutive plans, agriculture has been discriminated against,

---

during Emergency despite being a member of the Congress Working Committee. Post Emergency, he became the president of the Janata Party, after the collapse of the Janata Party government and electoral setbacks, the Janata Dal was formed by merging various factions of the Janata Party and other parties. V.P. Singh led the National Front coalition government comprising of the Janata Dal and other parties between 1989-1990, after the Congress's defeat under Rajiv Gandhi. The BJP extended external support to the coalition. Chandra Shekhar fell out with V.P. Singh, formed his Samajwadi Janata Party and became the eighth Prime Minister of India, between 10th November, 1990 and 21st June, 1991, heading a minority government with outside support from the Congress. Rajiv Gandhi soon withdrew support to Chandra Shekhar's government leading to its collapse. Chandra Shekhar continued to retain his Lok Sabha seat till his death in 2007. Another high point in Chandra Shekhar's career was when he undertook a *Padayatra* from Kanyakumari to Rajghat in 1983 to renew mass contact.

98. Party founded by C. Rajagopalachari, in 1959, in response to Nehruvian hegemony. A party in the classical liberal mode, supporting market-based economy, representing the economic right so to say, opposing the stifling 'License Raj' structures of the Nehruvian economy among other things, the Swatantra Party had stalwart leaders, such as N.G. Ranga, Minoo Masani, K.M. Munshi, Piloo Moody, V.P. Menon and others. In the 1967 General Elections to the 4th Lok Sabha, the Swatantra Party emerged as the single largest Opposition party winning 44 seats and more than 8 per cent of the votes. After 1971, the party rapidly declined and eventually merged with the Bhartiya Lok Dal in 1974.

so that we have not spent as much on agriculture as we ought to have done. Therefore, we are of the opinion that henceforth more attention should be paid to agriculture, particularly by the Planning Commission, so that our *kisans* should be able to avail themselves of credit facilities not merely for production but also for consumption, not on the strength of their borrowing capacity but on the strength of their genuine needs. Unless that is done, our *kisan* will not be enthused, will not be inspired to conduct his operations and give us greater production.

So far as the Resolution is concerned, while I agree entirely with the sentiments of the mover, I think rural life cannot be compartmentalised. There are various aspects of rural life which are inter-related. They cannot be isolated and, therefore, it is necessary to take an integrated view of the entire rural life. For example, I agree with the mover when he says that there are three aspects, i.e. land, labour and capital, and that agricultural co-operatives deal mainly or only with the capital aspect of it. Now, how can we isolate the capital aspect from the other aspect, that is, labour? There are millions upon millions of landless labourers and we know that their difficulties, their maladies have had no remedy so far. I have experienced myself. In order to give relief to agricultural workers, we tried to implement the Minimum Wages Act and some other Acts, but these Acts could not provide proper relief to landless labourers. Are they to form their own labour co-operatives or trade unions or should some subsidiary industries be started in the rural areas for their benefit? All these are interlinked, inter-related problems and, therefore, to consider any one aspect of rural life in isolation would be doing injustice to the integrated view of rural life.

There is another aspect of it which is also equally important. The mover has referred to the role of the bovine species in our rural life, particularly in the agrarian economy. The bovine species have a very important role to play. It is unfortunate that this aspect has escaped the attention of the government. Otherwise, the government would have already banned, as was demanded, cow slaughter and the slaughter of the bovine species. I remember that on this particular point, the biggest ever petition submitted to the Head of a State was submitted to our President a few years ago, but the entire thing was put in cold storage. It was very kind of the mover that he has referred to the bovine species. Also, he tells us that we have got the lowest yield per annum from a cow, which is very unfortunate. Therefore, I take this opportunity of requesting the government to be more serious about this matter, to legislate on the banning of cow slaughter and the slaughter of the bovine species and allow the bovine species to play the important role that it is designed to play.

Much has been said about the absence of co-operation. It has been aptly said by one authority that in India, there is no co-operation in the co-operative movement. That is true. As a matter of fact, for the success of the co-operative movement, it is necessary that a particular psychological environment should be created. I must say that the co-operative mind should precede the co-operative movement. That is what happened in the Scandinavian countries where the co-operative movement has been a great success. Now, we have put the cart before the horse. Probably, there was no other alternative. Now, appropriate steps should be taken to create that environment and that would be a subject-matter not of any particular Party. There again, some co-operative effort, wherein all should put their shoulders together, would be required.

As I said, the subject matter of this Resolution is very important. It is very urgent. It cannot allow, it cannot admit of any dilatory tactics. While agreeing with the sentiments of the mover, I must say that because I am in entire agreement with the objective of the Resolution, I oppose the Resolution because, as has already been experienced by many of us, by all of us, the appointment of a committee is just only another way of postponing the matter. If you do not want to expedite a matter, appoint a committee. Delay would naturally be there. Because I want that the matter should be expedited and also because I think that we are already having sufficient data on the matter, I feel that there should be no appointment of a committee. Therefore, I oppose the Resolution. At the same time, I think that even without the appointment of a committee, the matter can be expedited.

Reference to Incidents Relating to the Anti-cow Slaughter Agitation[99]

D. Thengadi: I have also been an eyewitness to what I have seen myself, and with all sense of responsibility, with at least as much sense

99. *Rajya Sabha Debate* dated 7th November, 1966. Anti-Cow Slaughter Agitation - In 1966 several organisations under the Go-Raksha Maha Abhiyan Samiti headed by Prabhudatt Brahmachari, gathered before Parliament to press the Indira Gandhi government for banning cow-slaughter. A large number of Hindu religious and social leaders were active in the anti-cow slaughter movement which saw wide mass response. Personalities like Hanuman Prasad Poddar of the Gita Press, Gorakhpur,

of responsibility as Mr. Shah[100] possesses, I can say that the provocation by the police has been responsible for this ugly scene. Had there not been a teargas shell thrown on the dais, making it impossible for the leaders to direct the mob, they would have certainly directed it properly. But the provocation came from the police, and to find that out, I request the government to assure us that an impartial inquiry into the police firing will be held, and the Home Minister should make a statement clarifying the whole thing.

Calling Attention to a Matter of Urgent Public Importance Regarding Serious Food Situation in Kerala[101]

D. Thengadi: Specifically, taking a lesson from all these disturbances and crises, will the Central Government take a firm decision about the abolition of the zonal system?

---

was the treasurer of the Samiti with the then Sadguru of the Namdhari Sikhs being its vice chairman. The demonstration culminated in police firing which saw 17 demonstrators, *sadhus* among them, killed. It was an unprecedented situation which saw *sadhus* being fired upon and killed. Even CPIM member in the House, Niren Ghose, came down hard on the government's order of firing on protestors, Ghose demanded, a judicial enquiry, "I demand that a judicial inquiry should be held into the entire affair, into all aspects of the matter including the shootings, so that truth could be established and these things might not be repeated. Killings and shootings are not the way in which you are going to rule the country." Minister of State in Home Ministry Jaisukhlal Hathi made a statement in the Upper House on 7th November 1966, his statement was countered in detail by Atal Bihari Vajpayee on how the events actually unfolded. On 16th November 1966, when the House debated the issue, Atal Bihari Vajpayee also demanded a judicial enquiry in the issue when he called for the following to be added at the end of the motion, "having considered the same, this House is of opinion that immediate steps must be taken to institute a judicial enquiry into the incidents of November 7, 1966..." Following the episode Gulzari Lal Nanda, then Union Home Minister, resigned from the Indira cabinet. For a detailed understanding of the event see e.g. Atal Bihari Vajpayee's intervention in Rajya Sabha on 16th November, 1966 on the issue, in N.M. Ghatate edited, *Atal Bihari Vajpayee: Four decades in Parliament*, Vol.1, Delhi: Shipra Publications, 1996, pp.658-662.

100. K.K. Shah (1908-1986) – Congress leader, member of the Rajya Sabha from 1960 to 1971, held a number of portfolios as Union Minister, such as Information and Broadcasting, Health & Family Welfare, Housing & Urban Development, leader of the Rajya Sabha, 1969-1971, Governor of Tamil Nadu, 1971-1976.

101. *Rajya Sabha Debate* dated 17th November, 1964.

D.R. Chavan:[102] I have already stated that this matter will be considered today at the Chief Ministers' Conference, and also tomorrow.

D. Thengadi: The attitudes or inclinations of the concerned state governments notwithstanding, once having come to know their attitude, what administrative measures were adopted by the Central Government to ensure such coordination between the Central Government and the concerned state government to meet the crisis?

Essential Commodities (Amendment) Bill, 1966[103*]

Supply of Essential Commodities

The Bill provides for, in an indirect way, compulsory procurement of essential commodities. That means levy, and it is well known that a lot of discontent prevails among *kisans*. Can the government claim that because of the levy system, they could bring down prices last year?

The *kisans* should be paid the market price and not the post-harvest price. These post-harvest prices can in no way be described as remunerative or supporting prices. Government should enter the market and purchase foodgrains, etc. according to the market price and not at the prices arbitrarily fixed by the government.

This enactment will discourage producers from producing food crops. They will be more interested in the production of cash crops, like tobacco, cotton, sugarcane, etc. Further, production of food crops will be affected adversely.

Besides, the system of procurement is also defective. The cultivator has to go to the *tehsil* office to secure the price of the produce sold.

Again, the extent of levy is fixed on the acreage and not on the quantity of produce. This creates anomalies.

This Bill also provides for the forfeiture and confiscation of packages, vehicles and animals. This is wrong. This is out of all proportion. The prices of articles thus confiscated may, in many cases, be many times more than the amount of fine intended to be imposed.

This Bill confers extensive powers – this is most objectionable – on the Collector and the Executive. This is misused everywhere. This has

102. D.R. Chavan (1916-1973) – Member, All-India Peasants' and Workers' Party (1948-55), All India Mazdoor Kisan Party (1955-60) and later member of the Congress party, member of the 2nd Lok Sabha, 1957-62, 3rd Lok Sabha, 1962-67, 4th Lok Sabha, 1967-70 and 5th Lok Sabha, 1971-1977, served as Deputy Minister, Minister of State, Minister in several ministries such as Defence, Food & Agriculture, Labour & Employment, Law Petroleum & Chemicals, Supply.

103. **Rajya Sabha Debate* dated 3rd September, 1966.

given rise to the Bastar incident. Even the DIRs have been utilised for such oppression. To show how *kisans* are suffering because of these powers already given or conferred upon the Collector and the Executive, I will read out the relevant portion of our petition from Madhya Pradesh, which has been signed by more than 5,000 *kisans*. The petition says, I will read out the relevant portion:

This is just a sample of the result of the powers that the Collector and the Executive are already enjoying.

Deputy Minister in the Ministry of Food, Agriculture, Community Development and Cooperation (*Annasahib Shinde*):[104]

All that the orders of the state government provide for is that enough quantities should be provided for the families and only the surplus should be procured through levy.

D. Thengadi: I quite agree with the intention of the Bill, I do not disagree with it, but the difficulty is that for various reasons with which the hon'ble minister is quite well acquainted, the Executive authorities do misuse their powers, and I am just bringing to your notice how these powers are being misused. Fortunately, while in the original Bill, there was no right to appeal to the judicial court and only the state government was to be approached for appeal after the Collector's order, now there is an amendment but I should like to insist that the judicial authority must be announced immediately; otherwise if there is delay, the cases would remain pending subject to the arbitrary authority of the Collector.

The government has already become the biggest monopolist. For example, in Madhya Pradesh, the government procured *jowar* at Rs. 33 per quintal and sold it to the consumer at Rs. 43 or Rs. 44 per quintal. That is, the government has taken Rs. 11 per quintal as profit.

In the case of wheat, the Madhya Pradesh government has purchased wheat at Rs. 65 per quintal and sold it at Rs. 75 or Rs. 80 per quintal.

Thus, government is itself profiteering. Similar reports are received from other states also. On account of this, prices shall not come down and the very purpose of this Bill would be defeated. The object of price-control is that the producer should get better prices and the consumer should get at cheaper rates. But today both are dissatisfied. Producers are not getting remunerative prices. The consumers also suffer. The reason is that

104. Annasahib Shinde, Congress leader from Maharashtra, participated in Quit India Movement, led peasant movements, member of the 3rd, 4th, 5th & 6th Lok Sabha, was Deputy Minister and Minister of State for Food, Agriculture and Irrigation.

the zonal system has not been abolished and there is no free movement on the plea that black-marketing would increase on account of the abolition of the zonal system. That plea does not hold good because even today when the zonal system is prevailing, the black marketeers are having their heyday.

There are some suggestions about some clauses in the Bill. Whatever is confiscated by the Collector must be put up with the challan for the witnesses. The very article that is confiscated must be produced before the court, otherwise identification of the article would be difficult. Another thing is, where an order under Section 6A is modified or annulled or where in a prosecution instituted for the contravention of the order in respect of which an order of confiscation has been made under Section 6A, the person concerned is acquitted and if in either case, it is not possible for any reason to return the foodgrains or edible oilseeds or edible oils seized, such persons should be paid, therefore, the market price obtaining then, and not as provided for in Section 6(c)(2), the price as if these commodities had been sold to the government with reasonable interest calculated from the day of the seizures of these commodities. For, more often than not, by the time we reach the stage of repayment, the actual price would have risen far above the price envisaged by Section 6(c)(2).

□

3
Industry and Company Affairs

Thengadi differentiated between the businessmen and industrialists. According to him, an industrialist identifies himself with the industry while the businessman's focus is on profit. In the backdrop of industrial sickness and mismanagement of public sector units, he felt that a system of efficiency audit and early warning should be introduced. He advocated for renouncing 'unfair labour practices'. In the case of closure, he opined that the mills or factories or the industrial establishments should be invariably handed over to the workers. Thengadi desired that so far as labour productivity was concerned, proper productivity indices need to be drawn up in the country. In his speeches on industrial relations, he demanded that the workers should have an effective voice in the decision-making processes with adequate say in the management. He suggested that whenever there were any agreements on awards for the workers of textile industry, the same should be made applicable to the workers of the sick mills too. Speaking on the Companies (Amendment) Bill, 1964, he categorically stated that the Bill was an inadequate step though in the right direction.

Industries (Development and Regulation) Amendment Bill, 1966 (to amend Section 15) Motion for Consideration[105]

Sir, Mr. Arjun Arora[106] has rendered a signal service to the cause of labour by bringing in this Bill. We are all aware that unfortunately in our country, though there may be 75 industrial houses, only a few of them, by way of exception, are industrialists; most of them are businessmen. I think that an industrialist is one who identifies himself with the industry. He rises and falls with the rise and fall of the industry. But businessmen are those who are interested only in fattening their bank balance and in

105. *Rajya Sabha Debate* dated 21st August, 1970.

106. Arjun Arora (1912-1981) – Congress Member of Rajya Sabha from Uttar Pradesh between 1960-1972.

their profit motive, and, therefore, they sabotage the industry started earlier in order to earn huge profits and cause new industries to be started elsewhere from the profits accrued from the original industries. Therefore, this mismanagement is a deliberate affair. It is not inadvertent. And, therefore, it is necessary that the provisions of the Industries (Development and Regulation) Act, 1951[107] should have been strictly implemented. But I am sorry to say that while there is much scope for improved management under the Act, even the original provisions have not been properly implemented. For example, according to the Act, if there is a price rise in the product of an industry, an investigation into the price rise should be conducted. But during the last 19 years, there has not been a single instance where in case of a price rise, there was any investigation instituted. Price rise of products is a very usual and common phenomenon during the last 19 years. But in not one single case has there been an investigation.

Then again we know the results of the investigation. It is necessary that they should be made public because as in the public sector, we come to know who are the officials that are working to the detriment of the industry. They cannot be entrusted with the management of the industry. We also should be in a position to know what particular employers and personnel from the managerial cadre are equally irresponsible and see that they do not deserve to be entrusted with the management of the industries. Unless these documents are the results of the investigations are made public, it would not be possible for us to man the affairs in the private sector.

Simultaneously, I should like to say that the laws regarding the mismanaged units of the different industries are also helpful to such offending employers, to such employers who are deliberately mismanaging their industries. For example, we know that in some of the industries, like textiles, a law has been passed in some of the states that if the units are sick, their management would be taken over by the government. Then the workers would be paid less than their usual wages. And when, with the sacrifices of the workers and the efforts of the government, the sick units again become healthy by any standard, they are again handed over to those employers who are really responsible for the sickness of their units. And, thus, this has become a new passport, a new concession, to the

107. The Act aimed at bringing under the central government the regulation and development of certain deemed to be important industries.

employers that they should mismanage their industries for their profit motive, then they would place their industry on the lap of the government and the government should nourish it at the cost of labour welfare and then again the industry should be taken over by the employers. Such an action is going on regarding the sick units in the various industries. Thus, instead of punishing severely the employers and the managers who are responsible for the sickness and mismanagement, actually they are encouraged by the different laws in the different states according to which the sick units are taken over for management by the government.

Now, we know that it is necessary to have some sort of restraint. It cannot be a laissez faire, as they say. Unless there are proper restraints imposed on the managements of the private sector, we will be confronted with a very unhappy situation, that is with two alternatives – either we should allow the private sector with such deliberately mismanaging employers and managers to run them or the units should be nationalised or should be placed under the public sector, which means that they should be bureaucratised. So, between the devil and the deep sea, between the private employers and the bureaucrats, that will be the only choice left to us. Therefore, it is necessary that proper restraints must be imposed. For this purpose, I should like to suggest that by way of experiment, at least in some of our industries, like textiles, engineering, etc., we should introduce the system of efficiency audit and early warning, as has been introduced in some of the industries in Great Britain.

There, even in the private sector, the efficiency is audited by government officials, and if it is found that there is mismanagement, inadvertently or deliberately, early warning is issued and these employers cannot say that because of some unforeseen circumstances, their units have become sick. I think it is necessary that the system of efficiency audit and early warning should be introduced even in our industry.

Secondly, it is necessary that in the process of decision-making regarding deployment of capital in the industry, workers should have a right to participate because workers are also vitally interested in the prosperity of the industry. Now if they are partners in the industry and if they are not allowed to participate in decision-making regarding deployment of capital, it would be grave injustice not only to the workers and the industry but also to the nation, because we know that for prosperity, the only way is maximum production and equitable distribution. So, workers must be given the right to participate regarding deployment.

Similarly, I should like to reiterate that even for the private sector, as I have suggested regarding the public sector, a separate profession of public administrators must be created. Even the General Managers should be a regular cadre, properly trained and properly equipped. Only from this cadre, managers and administrators should be drawn in the public sector as well as private sector. If this arrangement is made, some extra restraint also would be imposed upon the private sector units.

With all these suggestions, sir, I support this Bill. I am very thankful to Mr. Arjun Arora for having brought the Bill which would help us a lot in mending the affairs before we are required to end them by a change in the pattern of industrial ownership.

Industrial Disputes Bill, 1971[108]

D. Thengadi: Sir, I must say that this Bill that has been brought forward is a step in the right direction though, as probably the hon'ble minister is also aware, it does not go long enough. In the first place, this measure is not really fool-proof. The Labour Court, Tribunal or National Tribunal has to rely on the materials on record and shall not take any fresh evidence in relation to the matter. Now, this places the aggrieved worker in a very disadvantageous position. In domestic inquiry, the worker is extremely helpless. Leave alone lawyers, even an office-bearer of a registered trade union is not allowed to assist a worker in domestic inquiry. Managements are all-powerful. They bring all sorts of pressure and the poor worker cannot withstand or resist the pressure. In hundred cases out of hundred, I can say without exaggeration that the evidence recorded in domestic inquiry is tilted heavily in favour of management and against the worker. Justice is denied to the worker in domestic inquiry. Now, if the Court of the Tribunal is not to record fresh evidence in a free atmosphere, the very purpose of setting up the Court or the Tribunal will be defeated. Either the domesticity of domestic inquiry should be finished, or there should be a statutory provision in the procedure to be followed in domestic inquiry according to which the worker will not be discriminated against, or, the Tribunal itself – and this is the safest course – the Tribunal or the Court to be set up under this measure, itself, should be empowered to record fresh evidence, so that whatever injustice has been done in the course of domestic inquiry can be undone by the Tribunal. Again, we are apprehensive whether, even if Tribunal does justice to the worker, dilatory tactics will not be followed

108. *Rajya Sabha Debate* dated 16th November, 1971.

by the employers by resorting to or by approaching the High Court or the Supreme Court on points of law, thus defeating partly the purpose of this measure. Secondly, the amendment to Section 25FFF[109] is subject to the condition that no retrenchment compensation would be payable to the workmen concerned if the employer provides them with alternative employment with effect from the date of closure at the same remuneration as he was entitled to receive, and on the same terms and conditions of service as were applicable to them, immediately before the closure. In this respect, on the strength of the experience so far, I should like to say that it is necessary to take the precaution that the employers concerned do not take to dilatory tactics or devices to circumvent this provision and to drag the worker into unnecessary and endless litigation on this score, just by way of caution. Now, if it is proved before the Tribunal that the dismissal of an employee was malafide – not in good faith – by way of victimisation, the employer concerned should be brought to book and subjected to deterrent punishment. Presently, only workers are proceeded against for misconduct. At the most, workers may secure justice; that is all. But, under the present law, an employer cannot be proceeded against for mala fide dismissal of his employee, though he may resort to such malpractices times without number. This omission must not be allowed to persist. For employers also, varieties of misconduct must be prescribed, particularly in their dealings with their employees.

Now, this Bill provides for payment of full compensation to workmen in the event of the closing down of a mining undertaking due to exhaustion of its reserves subject to certain conditions.

This is a welcome precedent, a welcome principle. Precisely because of that, I should like to urge that the same principle should be extended, by analogy, to similar situations in some other industries. Particularly basing on this principle, I urge that in all seasonal factories, retaining allowance should be granted to workers during the offseason period as has been the practice followed in the sugar industry. Ginning and pressing and other factories are instances in point.

Now, in this Bill, the government proposes to declare service in, or in connection with, the working of major ports and docks as a permanent public utility service. This is justifiable only when there is simultaneous declaration of a national emergency. Under normalcy, such a measure is highly undemocratic and, therefore, objectionable. On this ground, I

109. Section 25FFF Compensation to workmen in case of closing down of undertakings.

oppose this.

I also seek clarification on one point from the hon'ble Labour Minister. Once having declared major ports and docks as a permanent public utility service, will the hon'ble minister assure that, among other things, the Government will take responsibility for the pay scales and service conditions of workers under private contractors connected with ports and docks?

Now, as usual, though this is a welcome measure, it is not comprehensive. It is a piecemeal legislation. If at all the government sought to amend the Industrial Disputes Act, they should have brought forward a comprehensive measure. For example, it was agreed on all sides that the definition of 'workman' should be uniform in all Acts, and comprehensive. This has not been done through this measure.

It is further necessary, by way of legislation – I am giving one or two points – to define precisely 'unfair labour practice'. It would be advisable to prescribe on all-India level the prohibition of, and penalties for unfair labour practices as specified in the Report of the Maharashtra government Committee on Unfair Labour Practices [1968] based upon which some legislation also has been passed, though not to the complete satisfaction of the workers.

Industry-wise additional lists of unfair labour practices should also be prepared, such as, for example:

(i) short payments, unwarranted deductions, extra deduction for absenteeism – in tanning;

(ii) circumvention of law by distributing material to workers and requiring them to return finished products – in *bidi* and tanning;

(iii) evasion of legal provisions by splitting a concern into a number of smaller units – in *bidi*, powerloom, etc.

So, such industry-wise lists also should be prepared.

Then, it is also necessary–and I hope the hon'ble minister would agree with me – that some sort of protection, either of the Industrial Disputes Act or of special laws enacted for the purpose, should be extended to workers say, for example, all educational institutions, social welfare organisations, hospitals, domestic employees, co-operatives other than workers' co-operatives, construction work, small-scale industries, seasonal industries, *mallah* work, etc. Here also I should like to suggest that on the model of the Maharashtra *Mathadi* [head-loaders], *Hamal* [porters] and other

Manual Workers (Regulation of Employment and Welfare) Act[110] a special law should be enacted for unprotected labour in general.

Now, if some of the suggestions would have been taken into consideration and a comprehensive measure been brought forward, it would have been most welcome. As it is, with reservation, we support this measure and the reasons for our reservation I have already stated.

Industrial Disputes (Second Amendment) Bill, 1972[111]

D. Thengadi: While welcoming the Bill, I would remind our Minister that he himself had admitted earlier the necessity of introducing a comprehensive Bill regarding industrial relations because the present ID Act is admittedly just one of the relics of the British regime not adequate to deal with the present situation. So, a simple Conciliation-cum-Arbitration Bill would serve the purpose better than all such complicated provisions. Secondly, I would reiterate my earlier suggestion that in every undertaking in the private sector, efficiency audit system should be introduced. Because, in that case, mismanagement and other things will naturally be curbed. Thirdly, in the Statement of Objects and Reasons, it has been rightly stated that there are four reasons for closure – mismanagement, labour unrest, financial difficulties and non-availability of raw materials but obviously various parties are responsible for the factors responsible for closure. So far as labour unrest is concerned, it is all the more necessary now, particularly when there has been an appeal from the President and the Prime Minister for a three-year moratorium on strikes and lock-outs, that justice should be cheap and expeditious, that there should be Joint Management Councils in every industry or industrial establishment either in the public or private sector and every decision should be taken only unanimously by the Council, whether that decision pertains to disciplinary action or deployment of capital and without the approval of the workers' representative, no decision should be taken. So, it is high time that such Councils are set up in every industry. That is the way to overcome the difficulty of labour unrest.

---

110. "An Act for regulating the employment of unprotected manual workers employed in certain employments in the state of Maharashtra to make provision for their adequate supply and proper and full utilisation in such employments" (1969) (https://www.ilo.org/dyn/natlex/docs/ELECTRONIC/17861/110575/F-1301927122/IND17861.pdf.)

111. *Rajya Sabha Debate* dated 6th April, 1972.

Coming to the present Bill, I have a few suggestions. I will not put up any formal amendment because it is of no use. In Section 3, the punishment prescribed for employers should be progressively more deterrent and by that, I mean the larger the establishment, the more deterrent should be the punishment. Then in Section 2, it is stated:

"The appropriate government may, if it is satisfied that owing to such exceptional circumstances as accident in the undertaking or death of the employer or the like, it is necessary so to do, by order, direct that provisions of sub-section (1) shall not apply, etc."

Here there should be such a provision that before issuing such a directive for exemption, the appropriate government must consult the representatives of the workers therein and secure their prior approval for exemption from the operation of Section 1. That is imperative. Then in sub-section (1) of Section 2, some exceptions are being provided and there is a list of industries. Here I would stress that no industry should be exempted from the provision of notice of 60 days. The only exception, if it is to be made, can be in the case of cottage industries employing less than 20 workers; otherwise, the provisions of the Bill should be applicable to all other industries and no exception should be made. Then whenever there is a notice for closure, there should invariably be constituted a Committee of Enquiry consisting of a representative of the workers also and that committee should be required to determine the real causes and the validity of the notice for closure.

In case of closure, retaining allowance must be given to all workers. So far as the payment is concerned, if the Committee of Inquiry comes to find that the responsibility for closure is on the employers, then the retaining allowance should be paid by the employers themselves and if it is found it is non-availability of raw materials that is responsible for the closure, in that case, the retaining allowance should be paid jointly by the employer and the government.

Then, sir, in case of closure, the mills or factories or the industrial establishments should be invariably handed over to the workers therein unless they shirk the responsibility of managing their own affairs and the government must come forward with the requisite technical and financial aid. There are certain cases where we may have reasons to believe that the closure is mala fide. In that case, the workers should have the right to stage a strike in the reverse. By strike in the reverse, I mean that the workers will not quit the premises; they will continue to occupy the premises and they will run the mills and the government should come forward with appropriate help to the workers in case of such a strike in the reverse.

Industrial Disputes (Amendment) Bill, 1970 (to amend Section 2)

Motion for Consideration[112]

D. Thengadi: Sir, the amendment introduced by our friend, Mr. D.L. Sen Gupta,[113] is quite in keeping with the spirit of Section 2 of the Industrial Disputes Act. Rather, when Section 2 was framed, I am quite confident that such a case was meant to be covered, but afterwards it was an omission which was inadvertent, and not deliberate. There is an analogy; there is a similar provision in Civil Procedure also as mentioned by our friend, Sen Guptaji.

Under the circumstances, I think it should not be very difficult for the hon'ble minister to accept the amendment, particularly in view of the fact that the much trumpeted Industrial Relations Bill is yet to be introduced. We were told that the Industrial Relations Bill was going to be introduced before several sessions. That propaganda has been going on continuously and still the Bill has not been placed before the House. Now, before the introduction of the Industrial Relations Bill, our friend has suggested this amendment. I think it should not be difficult for the hon'ble minister to insert this amendment also in the Industrial Relations Bill. Simultaneously, I should like to suggest that the very definition of 'workman' needs to be revised. It was demanded by the working class and conceded by the authorities that such of the workers as are wage earners and not yet covered by the Industrial Disputes Act should be brought within the purview of that Act. For example, the employees of educational institutions, hospitals and also, if I may add, social and social welfare organisations should be covered. So far as the social welfare organisations are concerned, we know that they are meant for social work. But, at the same time, those who serve there serve for remuneration and not as missionaries. It has been difficult to maintain any discipline in the educational institutions so far as the wages and working conditions are concerned because the managements are not susceptible and amenable to any provisions of the Industrial Disputes Act. Regarding hospitals, I

112. *Rajya Sabha Debate* dated 13th December, 1970.

113. Dwijendra Lal Sen Gupta (b 1916-) – two term independent Member of Rajya Sabha from West Bengal, Member, West Bengal Legislative Council, 1960-64 and Member, Rajya Sabha, 1964 to 1970 and 1970 to 1976.

do agree that the case is slightly different. But some provisions can be introduced with a view to regulating relations there. Sir, I further feel that the very definition of industry should be changed and any activity involving employer and employee relationship should be considered as an industry. Again, sir, so far as the dismissed worker is concerned, when we say "during the pendency of the proceedings", that means that proceedings are there and these proceedings arose out of the arbitrary authority given to the management or the employers for dismissal, discharge, termination, retrenchment, etc. Now, if we want to maintain industrial peace or industrial relationship, it is necessary that some basic thinking should be done regarding this right to dismiss or discharge or terminate or retrench. To my mind, it would be more appropriate and helpful if it is indicated that the management shall not have the right to victimise workers or to proceed against the workers without prior consultation or with the consent of Workers' Committees wherever they are constituted or the workers' representatives where the Workers' Committees are not constituted, so that any action against an employee or worker should be with the consent of the workers' representatives either within or outside the Workers' Committees. I think, now that the Industrial Relations Bill is about to be introduced–not in this session, but most probably in the next session–I hope that all these basic considerations should be in the mind of the hon'ble minister so that when the new Bill comes, it would be possible for us to welcome it whole-heartedly.

Sir, the hon'ble minister should categorically make a statement about two things. Firstly, he should say whether it is only consideration or acceptance of the whole thing, the whole amendment, in principle.

One more clarification I want to know from the hon'ble minister whether this comprehensive Industrial Relations Bill is really going to be introduced at any time and if so, can he give some date?

Can you give a firm date?

During the next session at least will it be introduced?

The Industries (Development and Regulation) Amendment Bill, 1965[114]

D. Thengadi: Madam, this Bill is quite non-controversial. It is true that it is difficult to envisage the entire period for which extension would be required and also it is correct that longer than necessary period should

114. *Rajya Sabha Debate* dated 23rd March, 1965.

not be availed of. In view of both these considerations, this amending Bill deserves our support.

On this occasion, I should like to put forth a few suggestions. In the first place, there should be some Standing Committee[115] to decide which particular industrial establishment deserves to be taken over by the government because there have been cases when decisions are taken arbitrarily and the demand of the workers that the establishment should be taken over is ignored. I should like to suggest that a Standing Committee consisting of representatives of the Central Labour Organisations[116] should be constituted and that committee should be empowered to take decisions regarding the taking over of industrial establishments. Further, whenever there is a demand by the workers, it should be taken proper note of. For example, both the textile mills at Sholapur [Maharashtra] are not functioning for the last so many months, and the workers of those mills have been demanding such a step from the government but their demand has been completely ignored. There are a number of examples and there have been a number of examples of this type where the workers have been demanding but their voice was quite ignored.

One more suggestion which I would like to put forth is that before the government takes over any particular industrial establishment, an opportunity should be given to the workers of that particular establishment to run that establishment themselves because I am confident that, even as the government has to avail of the services of technicians when the mills or establishments are taken over and also have to divert some of its funds for running them, if the same aid, that is, in the form of services of technicians and in the form of funds, is given to the workers, it is very likely – rather I am sure – that the workers would be able to conduct their own industrial establishments. Aided by the government, if the workers are given this opportunity, we will have started a new experiment of labourising the industry which would be more beneficial as compared to the governmentalisation of the industry.

There are some other complaints regarding the functioning of the industries or establishments taken over by the government. I would only like to suggest that there should be no discrimination in the treatment given to the workers in other private establishments and in those taken over by the government.

115. Standing Committee – Parliamentary Standing Committee.

116. Central Labour Organisations – Union of India's labour organisations.

Motion Regarding Crisis in the Textile Industry[117]

D. Thengadi: Mr. Deputy Chairman, I want to urge in the first place that there must be a national textile policy evolved with a view to coordinating the various interests, i.e. those of cotton growers, textile employers, textile workers and consumers on the one hand and those of textile mills, powerlooms, handlooms and khadi, on the other. For this purpose, some special committee may be appointed or I will not grudge if the hon'ble minister can give us an assurance that the proposed Textile Corporation shall undertake this task of evolving a national textile policy. In any case, the formulation of such a policy is a must and I urge that the government should without delay undertake this work.

Now we have been insisting since long that there should be, as in England, a continuous efficiency audit of all our textile mills. In England, they have practised this in the case of a number of industrial units and they have been successful. Along with this continuous efficiency audit, there should also be a financial counsel service, so that a timely warning can be issued to any mill or industrial unit facing the danger of being closed. In case that industrial unit refuses to abide by the financial counsel given by such service, it will have to be taken over by the Textile Corporation. Much has been said about the productivity of our workers even in this context but I must say that proper productivity indices are not being drawn up in our country and whenever employers use the word 'productivity', probably they only imply labour productivity, while in India, productivity per unit of capital is most important, and since all our resources are not being fully utilised, it would be wrong or impossible to arrive at any productivity indices with regard to labour productivity only. Therefore, we insist that productivity per unit of capital should be given its due importance, so that mismanagement of mills and diversification of profits from textile units are immediately stopped. Then serious efforts should be made to find new markets for our textile machinery and textile goods. I know it is difficult but, at the same time, I want to know from the hon'ble minister whether such efforts have been made, particularly in some of the Asian and African countries which, I think, can provide us some market, at least so far as our textile goods and machineries are concerned.

It is really sad to note that the government is taking a long time – there is inordinate delay – in the organisation of this Textile Corporation. This should be expedited.

117. *Rajya Sabha Debate* dated 1st August, 1968.

Regarding excise duty, I would agree with Mr. [A.G.] Kulkarni that excise duty on fine and superfine cloth may be increased and proportionately there should be a reduction in the duty on other varieties which are meant for the poorer sections of the population. Regarding control and decontrol, I think we should not adopt any doctrinaire approach.

Now for the proper functioning of the textile industry, I think the banking system of the country has to play a very important role, because efficiency audit and financial counselling can be done only through the banking system or by the banking authority which, in this case, would be the Reserve Bank. It should be the responsibility of the Reserve Bank to see that all the mills are issued a warning before they are closed and at the same time, the workers thrown out of employment are provided with alternate employment, because the credit policy of the entire country is controlled by the Reserve Bank and the authority which controls the credit policy should be responsible for the fullest employment in the country.

Calling Attention to a Matter of Urgent Public Importance Regarding Reported Direction by Indian Cotton Mills Federation[118] to Textile Mills to Close Down for a Fortnight[119]

D. Thengadi: As has been stated here, the other day we are conducting negotiations for a further import of cotton to the tune of 2 to 4 lakh bales. May I know whether the government has information about the number of mills having surplus cotton stocks and the extent of surplus? Further, in view of the stiff attitude taken by the Indian Cotton Mills Federation and in view of the fact that all the other concerned interests are out to support the government in its present difficulty, does the government propose to convey to the office-bearers of the Indian Cotton Mills Federation tomorrow that if they persist in their determination to close down the mills for a fortnight, the office-bearers of the Federation will be proceeded against under the Defence of India Rules?

118. Confederation of Indian Textile Industry (CITI) industry chamber for the textile and clothing industry, was founded in 1958 and was initially known as the Indian Cotton Mills Federation (ICMF).

119. *Rajya Sabha Debate* dated 30th November, 1966.

Calling Attention to a Matter of Urgent Public Importance Regarding Accident in the Birla Technical Institute of Textiles[120] at Bhiwani[121*]

D. Thengadi: Is the government aware that even when the building was complete, the workers through their union had repeatedly lodged protests saying that it was not in a proper condition? Secondly, why was there such inordinate delay in clearing the debris because, according to our information, there was wilful obstruction on the part of the management? May I know whether this has been ascertained by the government?

D. Thengadi: Obviously, the judicial enquiry cannot be entrusted with the work of proceeding against the culprits. What is the provision for it?

Deputy Chairman: He has no information on it.

Calling Attention Regarding Closure of the Delhi Cloth Mills and Reported Indiscriminate *Lathi*-charge by the Police on the Workers of the Mills[122]

Is it not a fact that the token strike on the 1st of February was quite peaceful but the management subsequently tried to provoke the workers by serving false charges? Niranjan Singh of the dyeing department of the Mills, who was that day attending the funeral of his nephew at Nigambodh Ghat, was charged with having taken part in some violent activities in the Mills' premises. And, secondly, is it not a fact that with a view to discrediting the peaceful agitators, the management has appointed its favourites to conduct undesirable and provocative activities? And in view of all these facts, will the government conduct an impartial enquiry into the incidents just now referred to so that the real culprits could be brought to book? Again, is the government aware of the fact that if at this stage, these anti-labour activities of this particular management are not restrained, then they will give rise to a chain of such anti-labour activities among textile labour throughout the country, leaving no other way for the workers except resorting to general agitation?

---

120. Founded in 1943 by G.D. Birla.

121. **Rajya Sabha Debate* dated 24th August, 1966.

122. **Rajya Sabha Debate* dated 25th February, 1966.

Calling Attention to a Matter of Urgent Public Importance Regarding Shortage of Scooter Tyres and Tubes[123*]

श्री दत्तोपंत ठेंगड़ी : मैडम, जहाँ यह बात सही है कि कॉन्सिलिएशन प्रोसीडिंग्स फायरस्टोन के बारे में चल रही हैं, वहाँ इतने दिनों से क्या सरकार ने यह एसर्टेन करने का प्रयास किया है या नहीं कि यह जो देरी हो रही है, उसके लिए किसकी हठधर्मिता कारण है—फायरस्टोन की या मजदूरों की? कौन इसके लिए जिम्मेदार है? क्या इसे एसर्टेन करने का प्रयास सरकार ने किया?

दूसरा प्रश्न है कि स्कूटर-टायर का मैन्युफैक्चर करनेवालों में विदेशी कंपनियाँ कितनी हैं और स्वदेशी मैन्युफैक्चरर्स कितने हैं? क्या यह बात सही है कि हमारे जो स्वदेशी निर्माता हैं, वे स्पर्धा में कुछ कठिनाई अनुभव करते हैं? इस दृष्टि में स्वदेशी मैन्युफैक्चरर्स को कौन सी सहायता देने का प्रयास किया है?

तीसरी बात यह है, जो अभी पूछी गई थी कि इसे एसेंशियल कमोडिटी घोषित करने में कौन सी आपत्ति है?

श्री फखरुद्दीन अली अहमद : तीसरी बात का जवाब मैंने अभी दिया कि जो ऑनरेबिल मेंबर का सजेशन है, उसपर मैं गौर करूँगा।

जहाँ तक स्ट्राइक की बात पूछी है तो उनसे स्टेट गवर्नमेंट का ताल्लुक है। वह मैटर स्टेट गवर्नमेंट के पास है, कॉन्सिलिएशन बोर्ड के पास है, इसलिए मेरा इस वक्त कोई राय देना मुनासिब नहीं होगा कि किसकी गलती है और किसकी गलती की वजह से यह स्ट्राइक चल रही है।

जहाँ तक देशी और विदेशी कंपनियों की बात है तो मैं ऑनरेबिल मेंबर को यह यकीन दिलाना चाहता हूँ कि देश की कंपनियों में प्रोडक्शन बढ़ रहा है और उनको हर तरह से सहूलियतें दी जा रही हैं, ताकि वे किसी तरह से प्रोडक्शन बढ़ा सकें।

Regarding Statement on Sugar Policy for 1967-68[124]

D. Thengadi: Some 10 days back, a comprehensive scheme which claims to ensure extension of crushing season to 7 months, 11 per cent recovery of sucrose content, elimination of the additional expenditure of 200 crores on installation of new machinery, demarcation of the spheres of controlled sugar and uncontrolled *gur* and *khandsari* [unrefined '*desi*' sugar–muscovado], consequent reduction in the price of sugar here and abroad, etc. has been submitted to the Government of India by Mr. Thakurdas Sawhney of Lucknow? He is an expert in the matter. He had also seen the minister, Shinde, and explained the scheme on the last 10th. Has the government gone through the scheme and arrived at any conclusions?

123.**Rajya Sabha Debate* dated 11th December, 1967.

124. *Rajya Sabha Debate* dated 18th August, 1967.

Calling Attention to a Matter of Urgent Public Importance Situation Arising out of Delayed Start in Sugarcane Crushing Factories and the Imminent Threat to Sugarcane Growers and Consequent Unemployment[125]*

D. Thengadi: Revision of the policy may take some time but in the meanwhile, the situation stands today in U.P. and Bihar, the sugar mills will be running for a lesser period this year, and the problem of the sugar mill workers is going to become very acute because, as the hon'ble minister is aware, they get only a retaining allowance which is only a nominal wage. So, their total pay packet this year is going to be less. They have no other alternative employment. So, what measures government proposes to adopt in order to give relief to these sugar mill workers who will get lesser pay packets during this year?

Calling Attention to a Matter of Urgent Public Importance Regarding Imminent Grant of Industrial Licence to M/s Remington Rand of India Limited to Manufacture Portable Typewriters with Foreign Collaboration[126]*

D. Thengadi: Will the minister assure at least now that before considering the proposal for foreign collaboration, he will have discussions with our indigenous manufacturers and assure them that the government will give adequate aid so that they can produce them in this country?

Calling Attention Motion Regarding Reported Threat of Closure of Cotton Textile Mills in the Country[127]

D. Thengadi: Sir, to wait and watch helplessly till the mills close and then to place the sick mills on the lap of the National Textile Corporation,[128] I think, is viewing socialism from the wrong end. Instead, why does the government hesitate to introduce the system of efficiency audit in all the textile mills, so that we will have before us the cost-wise break-up of the reasons that lead to the closures, because the cotton crisis may be one of the main causes of the closures.

---

125. *Rajya Sabha Debate* dated 26th November, 1968.
126. *Rajya Sabha Debate* dated 26th November, 1968.
127. *Rajya Sabha Debate* dated 4th June, 1971.
128. Is a Government of India public sector enterprise under the Ministry of Textiles incorporated in 1968. Its mandate was to manage sick textile undertakings in the private sector, that had been taken over by the Government of India.

The government is well aware that this cotton crisis can be utilised as just a pretext for closures which might have been actually brought about due to various other reasons. So, why is not the government introducing efficiency audit even at this late stage?

Then, particularly wherever there are groups of mills, why every group should not be treated as one industrial family for this particular purpose so that even when one sick mill is taken over by the National Textile Corporation, its deficit can be made up at least partially from the profits of the other mills within the same group? Why is not such a system introduced?

The first question is, though the cotton crisis may be due to valid reasons, still it can be utilised as a pretext for closures which have been brought about for various other reasons, such as mismanagement or speculative activities of the employers and other things. So, why does not the government introduce a system of efficiency audit in all the textile mills so that we will have before us the cost-wise break-up of the factors responsible for the closures?

Secondly, wherever there are groups of textile mills, why should not each group be treated for this purpose as one industrial family so that when one sick mill is taken over by the National Textile Corporation, its deficit can be made up at least partly from the profits of the other mills from the same group?

Half-an-Hour Discussion on Points Arising out of Answers to Starred Question No. 735 on 31st August, 1966 Regarding Withdrawal of Complaint against Laxmi Ratan Cotton Mills Limited[129*]

D. Thengadi: Is it not a fact that no attempt was made to investigate into the charge of conspiracy against the Directors of the Laxmi Ratan Cotton Mills for causing deliberate loss of foreign exchange and there was no justification for the withdrawal of the criminal case? Again why was no action taken on the application of the Life Insurance Corporation for the arrest of Mr. Ram Ratan Gupta[130] for non-payment of arrears; and thirdly, has the government ensured that the companies floated by Mr. Ram Ratan Gupta outside India are not operating in furtherance of the foreign

129. *Rajya Sabha Debate* dated 2nd December, 1966. Laxmi Ratan Cotton Mills Limited, a Kanpur-based Cotton Mill.

130. Director in M/s Laxmi Ratan Cotton Mills Ltd.

exchange racket, such companies being, apart from the India-China Enterprises Ltd., Hong Kong, (1) Industrial Developments Ltd., Singapore, (2) Singapore Thermit Corporation, Singapore, and (3) the Hindustan Import and Export Co. Ltd., Australia?

Half-an-Hour Discussion Regarding Manufacture of Small Car[131]

D. Thengadi: The explanation by the hon'ble minister that the government has not been yielding to the pressures of the monopolists is not very much convincing. Nevertheless, one thing is certain that the government is following a policy of vacillation and procrastination. We want to know categorically whether the government is inclined to give preferential treatment to any foreign concern, for considerations other than economic, instead of to any Indian concern?

Secondly, much is talked of about foreign exchange. That is true. But why is the government unwilling to divert a part of foreign exchange that is made available to big car manufacturers for import of different materials for small car projects?

Thirdly, may I know whether, in order to enable a small car project, when it comes into being, the government is prepared to give some sort of relief in excise duty, taxes, etc. or whether the government is hesitating and is reluctant because of this point also?

Statutory Resolution Seeking Disapproval of the Industries (Development and Regulation) Amendment Ordinance, 1971[132*]

D. Thengadi: The question of re-starting closed industrial units is of vital importance to the workers as well as to the nation. But I am sorry

131. **Rajya Sabha Debate* dated 2nd June, 1967. Fakhruddin Ali Ahmed then Minister for Industrial Development gave the following reply: "some questions have been raised which are outside my purview. So far as the question of taxes, excise duties are concerned, these are matters which should be referred to the Finance Minister because what I am concerned with is the cost of production of the car ex-factory without the excise duty and other taxes. It is only a matter of opinion. I have already said that s0 far as we are concerned. We have not yielded to any pressure. If that notion I cannot remove by my statement, I &o not know what is the other way of removing that impression from the mind of the hon. Member. As I have already pointed out, it is my desire that as far as possible this project should be taken up in the public sec- tor. But if any private entrepreneur has to be considered, then certainly preference will have to be given to one within our own country." By 1967, the discussion on small car manufacturing was gaining ground in political circles in Delhi, with Prime Minister Indira Gandhi pushing it.

132. **Rajya Sabha Debate* dated 22nd December, 1971.

to say that our repeated requests to take care of provision rather than cure in this respect have been ignored. We had suggested that an efficient audit system or appraisal audit system or early warning system should be introduced in the engineering and textile industry. Had this been done, probably the present calamity could have been minimised.

While we welcome the move to restart the closed units by taking them over, we are sorry that many of the provisions of the Bill are against the interests of the working class. In the first place, I should like to point out that while this Ordinance was promulgated on the 1st of November, it was in direct contravention of the unanimous decision taken by the Indian Labour Conference hardly a week earlier. The decision read thus:

"Consequent upon the take-over, there should not be any reduction in employment or emoluments, nor there any adverse effect of service conditions or benefits."

This was the unanimous decision of the Labour Conference and to pay scant regard to the unanimous decisions of the Indian Labour Conference[133] will create a very bad precedent and will affect adversely the future industrial relations in private and public sector units.

Then, this Bill provides for the contingency of liquidation. But we know that mismanagement is one of the many reasons responsible for the closure. In the *Economic Times*, it had been stated authoritatively that there are at least three reasons for closure of the mills. I am quoting:

"At least a third of the closed factories suffer from depletion of finances and shortage of working capital; about 20 per cent suffer from technological obsolescence and about 10 per cent suffer from shortage of raw materials and managerial inefficiency." Thus, mismanagement, lack of raw materials and bad industrial relations leading to strikes, lock-outs, etc. are the three main factors for closure. Out of these three, the latter two factors have not been taken care of by this Bill. Along with mismanagement, the supply of raw-materials is an important factor. And, sir, it is the government's responsibility to ensure that there is an adequate and steady flow of raw materials necessary for the various industries. I should like to suggest that there should be a sort of pool of

133 . The Indian Labour Conference (ILC), the apex consultative committee in the Ministry of Labour and Employment with central trade unions, employers organisations and the concerned Central and state government ministries and departments as part of it. Modelled on the International Labour Conference, the tripartite conference has been convened under this nomenclature since 7th August, 1942. In 1942, the Conference had Dr B.R. Ambedkar as its Chairman.

raw materials and there should be proper distribution of raw materials in keeping with or in proportion to the production or employment in the different industrial establishments.

Sir, regarding strikes and lock-outs, which are, to a minor extent, responsible for closures, I should like to suggest that our industrial relations machinery should be streamlined, because under the present system, there are delays and delay defeats the very purpose of the industrial relations machinery. Now, sir, in this Bill, it has been provided that after the take-over, the new management can retrench any worker, can terminate the services of anybody and, again, it has not specified which particular type of persons would be appointed as the authorised persons. Our experience so far has been very disappointing in this respect. Very often, the same original employer or his representative is appointed as the authorised person and if he is allowed to administer, allowed to conduct, his unit in his own fashion, according to his own sweet will, and if he is authorised to terminate the services of anybody, then, in that case, his original vindictiveness will follow and many trade union workers in that unit will be victimised and no law would be there to protect their legitimate interests. Therefore, it is necessary that this right of the management that is specified in this Bill to terminate the services of anybody should be withdrawn. Similarly, the workers are not to be treated as re-employed, because re-employment has its own implications. They would be deprived not only of the emoluments, but also of the various other benefits and, therefore, their continuity of services, their seniority, etc. should be guaranteed.

Now, sir, there is a provision that normal labour laws would be suspended. The Minimum Wages Act is one of the three Acts that will be suspended under this Bill. Now, we know that the Minimum Wages Act does not provide for the need-based minimum wage. It is a statutory minimum and that statutory minimum is admittedly on the starvation level. If even this sub-subsistence wage is to be denied to the workers, I think the very purpose of the unemployment relief measure would be defeated. So, there is no point in withdrawing the protection of the Minimum Wages Act to the workers after the takeover. Similarly, there are the Standing Orders. I cannot imagine how any industrial establishment can be run without the Standing Orders. If they are withdrawn, if the protection under the Industrial Disputes Act is withdrawn, in that case, it will be a day of dictatorship and authoritarianism and the workers will be completely defenceless. So, this provision, withdrawing the protection of certain industrial Acts should be withdrawn.

Now, sir, when you are refusing the protection of the Minimum Wages Act to the workers, are you taking into consideration the fact that the present wage level, that is, the wage level that will be introduced after the take-over, will be continued till the units are handed over, if at all they are handed over, the original employers and in that case, the original employers, after taking over the administration or the management, will not fail to continue the same subsistence level of wage and it will be a permanent loss to the workers? In any case, the protection of industrial Acts should not be withdrawn.

Then, sir, there is the question of payment of the legitimate dues to the workers. The legitimate dues are not to be withheld under any condition. Now, the question arises whether it would be possible for the new management to pay all the dues which may be to the tune of some lakhs and, if it is an unemployment relief measure, how the concern can be run after making such a huge payment; this question may arise. I may suggest that in the first place, payment must be made. And, secondly, if payment in cash cannot be made, in that case, whatever amount is due to the workers should be treated as their share in the industry. They should be made shareholders of the respective industries, and as shareholders, they should have voice in the management of their undertaking.

Similarly, sir, after the take-over, as I have suggested, it will be a very disappointing feature of the Bill if the management is entrusted to the same culprits who have been responsible for mismanagement or to their representatives. I suggest that the management should be entrusted to the workers themselves. All the financial aid and technical aid, which would have been made available to the concern, had it been managed by the so-called authorised persons, should be made available to the concern managed by workers. I am quite confident that the workers, having their own vested interests in the running of the industries, smooth running of the industries, would be competent enough to run their own units. So, instead of entrusting the management to any authorised persons of doubtful competence and doubtful bona fides, I suggest, emphatically suggest, that the management should be entrusted to the workers themselves.

So far as the formulation of the scheme is concerned, it is said that various interests will be consulted before the scheme is finalised. Now, the words are like this:

"The Central Government may make such modifications, if any, in the draft scheme as it may consider necessary in the light of the suggestions and objections received from the company, from the registered trade unions, of which the employees of the company are members and from any members or creditors of the company."

This does not satisfy us because the workers or creditors or members of whatever interests represented, will have no effective voice in the decision-making process of the scheme. So, I demand that the workers should have an effective voice in the decision-making process of the scheme and that the management should be entrusted to them.

Statutory Resolution Seeking Disapproval of the Sick Textile Undertakings (Nationalisation) Ordinance, 1974 (No. 12 of 1974); and the Sick Textile Undertakings (Nationalisation) Bill, 1974[134]

D. Thengadi: Sir, I move –

'That this House disapproves the Sick Textile Undertakings (Nationalisation) Ordinance, 1974 (No. 12 of 1974) promulgated by the President on 21st September, 1974.

Sir, when the textile workers learnt of the proposal to take over the sick textile mills, they had certain apprehensions because their earlier experience of take-over was not a very happy one. In the first place, there was a large-scale retrenchment in such mills as were taken over, and even the security officers were threatened. They, however, hoped that the earlier mistakes would be rectified and a foolproof Bill would be introduced in the Parliament. But, sir, I am sorry to say that in this Bill, there is no assurance that all the past dues or arrears of workers would be paid. There is no justification for differentiating between one set of dues or arrears and the other, and the government should come with an unequivocal assurance that every single pie that is due would be paid by the government. Secondly, sir, it has not been provided here that whenever there are any agreements or awards for the workers of textile industry, the same would be made applicable to the workers of the sick mills also. Because there is a loose talk about the nationalisation of the remaining textile mills also, it is necessary that the management of the mills that are taken over is conducted in an ideal manner. For this purpose, there should be an assurance that even indirectly there would be no retrenchment, that

134. *Rajya Sabha Debate* dated 16th December, 1974.

every single pie would be paid without any differentiation, and that all the awards and agreements would be made applicable to the sick textile mills also.

Sir, it has also been said that the Bill has been introduced with a view to reorganising and rehabilitating such sick textile undertakings so as to subserve the interests of the general public. Now, if the mills are to be re-organised, it becomes essential that the workers are allowed to participate in all the decision-making processes of the management, right from the purchase of raw materials to the marketing organisation and also about the manner in which the capital has to be deployed. If the workers are not allowed to participate in all the decision-making processes, they would hardly have any enthusiasm to work to the optimum. Similarly, sir, when we are thinking of the sick mills, it is also necessary to ensure that other mills do not become sick. With that purpose in view, we had suggested earlier that in all the textile mills, the system of early warning and efficiency appraisal should be introduced. This system has worked very well in Great Britain in engineering and other units. Though the mills are owned by private parties, the government has a right to have an appraisal of the efficiency of every unit, and whenever any omission or lacuna is found, earlier warning is issued. If such a system is introduced in our country, probably the other mills will not become sick as they are now.

In view of all these facts, sir, we disapprove of this Ordinance, and we request the government to come forward with an assurance regarding the payment of the arrears and the application of awards and agreements to sick mills also.

I may add that presently in our country, nationalisation is nothing but bureaucratic capitalism. What Mr. Misra[135] wants is socialisation which is distinct from bureaucratic capitalism.

Sir, the word 'nationalisation' has special connotation; it need not be confused with other ideas.

Sir, I was sorry to note yesterday that the hon'ble minister was not kind enough to concede the one demand which had been endorsed by all the members from both sides who spoke on the Bill. Any liability arising

135. Lokanath Misra (1921-2009) – Three term Rajya Sabha member from Odisha between 1960-1978, Mishra, son of Godabarish Mishra, one of Odisha's most well-known poet-politician, was a versatile personality. Mishra joined the Ganatantra Parishad, was editor of the newspaper Ganatantra and entered the Rajya Sabha in 1960. Between 1991-1997 Mishra was Governor of Assam and held additional charge of Nagaland and Arunachal Pradesh.

out of wages, salaries and other dues of the employees of the sick mill undertakings in respect of any period not only after, but, even prior to the period when the management of such undertakings had been taken over by the Central Government should be the liability of the Central Government. That has been the unanimous verdict of this House. The natural corollary would be that any liability arising out of such amounts as may have been paid from the Provident Fund of the workers as loans to the sick undertakings at any period prior to or after the management of such undertakings had been taken over by the government and such amounts as may have been paid by small depositors as fixed deposits to the sick undertakings in any period prior to the taking over by the Central Government should also be the liability of the Central Government. I hope that even at this late stage, the hon'ble minister would reconsider the whole situation and give appropriate assurance in this respect.

Sir, the House has discussed the various aspects of this problem of the prosperity of the textile industry as well as of the sick mills. As has been rightly pointed out, cotton production in our country has fallen because proper price was not paid to the cotton growers. In 1971-72, production was 65 lakh bales and in 1973-74, the production was 60 lakh bales. Before April 30 last, the Cotton Corporation[136] used to sell cotton to any buyer, either mill or private trader. On April 30, the decision was taken that the Corporation could sell its stocks directly to the mills. That means till April 30, there was full scope for speculation by traders. Why such loophole was left, it is difficult to understand. The Cotton Corporation had given till that period to the private traders, 5 lakh-odd bales and to the mills, 3,01,024 bales. Sir, it is necessary for balanced development that we must ensure remunerative prices to cotton growers, catalogue prices for cotton, that is, cost price plus 1 per cent commission as service charges to mills, reasonable price for cloth to consumers and rational wages to workers. There should be some relationship between the purchase price of cotton and the sale price of finished cloth. Such a relationship does not exist today.

Sir, the textile mills have been concentrating their attention and vying with one another for producing sophisticated high-priced varieties and that too non-cotton and mixed fibre fabrics. The nationalised mills should

136. The Cotton Corporation of India Limited, a Government of India agency engaged in procurement, export and trading of cotton, was incorporated in 1970 under the Companies Act 1956.

concentrate on the requirements of the masses and produce standardised variety, say Janata *dhotis*, sarees, shirting, etc. According to a report of the Textile Committee[137] of the Ministry of Commerce, that is, consumer purchases of textile, 1973, the per capita consumption of cotton textile declined by 10 per cent after a fall of 6.4 per cent in per capita availability and the rise of 17 per cent in prices. It is true that the prices of cotton have gone up specially from January 1974 by 40 per cent and during the last one year, by 30 per cent. The nationalised mills should manage to purchase cotton at the right time on a centralised basis. It is their moral duty to build a wide network of fair-price shops for the distribution of their cloth and bring down the prices, particularly of the coarse and medium varieties of cloth. It is also their duty to spin more yarn for the handloom sector.

Sir, yesterday there was some discussion on the desirability of nationalisation. Personally, I consider nationalisation today is nothing but bureaucratic capitalism. I would prefer, instead of bureaucratic capitalism, labourisation, by which I mean that the labour or effort of the worker should be evaluated in terms of shares and workers raised to the status of shareholders. This can be done. Moreover, there can be democratisation of mills also under which the shares of the company should be thrown open to the low-income group only, so that they can also participate as shareholders. Co-operatisation has also been tried, to an extent successfully, in this country. Nevertheless, it seems that while the very concept of industrial ownership deserves to be reconsidered, today, at least when we are discussing this Bill, the question whether these mills should be nationalised is only of academic interest. Even when the management of the mills was taken over under the Industries (Development and Regulation) Act and the Sick Textile Undertakings Act, 1972 it was made clear that the mills would not be handed over to the original owners. An expenditure of Rs. 108 crores has been earmarked during the Fifth Plan for expansion and modernisation of these mills. Already about Rs. 10 crores worth of new machinery is reported to have been received up to June end. True, some of these mills are mere scrap or crippled or limping with no machinery worth the name. They have only heavy liabilities. Still the number of working mills today is 96 out of 103. Reorganisation and rehabilitation of these mills is a 'must'.

137. The Textiles Committee is a statutory body under the Ministry of Textiles; earlier it was under the Ministry of Commerce.

It is true that the production of cloth and capacity utilisation of government-managed mills has been progressively increasing during the last three years. It is also a fact that, while the prosperity of the mills is increasing, the share of the workers in that prosperity, that means their relative wages, has not increased correspondingly or proportionately. It should be ensured that with modernisation, retrenchment is not effected. Presently, the total number of workers in these sick mills is 1,63,000. It constitutes almost 18 per cent of the total number of textile workers.

Just one clarification. Can the Hon'ble minister categorically state that he would treat the workers' dues at par with banker's dues? In the name of technicalities, he is going to rob the workers of their dues. It is a highway robbery.

If the hon'ble minister's contention is accepted, then the NTC[138] should be prepared to abandon the claim to all the loans and other governmental moneys from the 1st of April to this day when the Bill is being passed. If he is not prepared to abandon that claim, then it only means that between the claims of the government and the claims of workers, there is discrimination. That is the point.

Sir, apart from the workers' dues, I just want to seek clarification from the hon'ble minister on a few points. Can the minister assure us that there would not be any retrenchment in the process of modernisation? We want a categorical assurance regarding retrenchment. Secondly, will he assure us that the workers of the sick mills will be paid relative wages, that is, their share in the prosperity will not dwindle and there would be a corresponding proportionate rise in their wages with the rise in the prosperity of the plant? Thirdly, he has not mentioned anything about the applicability of the agreements and awards in the textile industry to the sick mills. Lastly, sir, I would like to know whether the government will accept responsibility for the distribution of coarse and medium cloth at cheap rates.

Motion Regarding of Monopolies Inquiry Commission 1966[139]

D. Thengadi: The Monopolies Inquiry Commission has rendered a signal service to the cause of national reconstruction. We all know that monopoly and democracy cannot go together. Political democracy, under the conditions of concentration of economic power, is an impossibility. We

138. NTC – National Textile Corporation.

139. *Rajya Sabha Debate* dated 8th December, 1966.

are opposed to all monopolies, whether it be private monopolies or State monopolies, because while through private monopoly...

D. Thengadi: While through private monopoly, a few individuals can control the State apparatus, through State monopolies also a few individuals in the ruling party manage the freedom and democracy of the entire nation. Therefore, we are opposed to both types of monopolies. So far as the various aspects of the report are concerned, much has been said and I need not cover the whole ground again. How we have been ineffective to deal with the managing agencies or interlacking directorships of people in resisting the concentration of the economic power, all these have been explained already. What I feel is that it is not exactly the failure of the ruling party. Probably, the ruling party never meant to do it. I remember definitely the definition of politics as quoted by Sir Stafford Cripps.[140] The definition is that politics is a gentle art of getting votes from the poor and collecting funds from the rich by promising to protect each from the other. If this definition is accepted, probably the ruling party consists of successful politicians. So, they never meant it. But if socialism, as professed by the ruling party, is to be taken with any seriousness, then it is very clear from this report that there is a wide divergence between the profession and practice of the ruling party. So far as the Indian monopolies are concerned, they are hand-in-glove with the ruling party – it goes without saying – and a number of instances have been given. There is another alarming feature of their collusion with the foreign capitalists also. We are apprehensive that in the name of foreign collaboration, probably our Indian industrialists are being utilised as sappers and miners for the advent of the economic imperialism of the USA in India and from this point of view, it is absolutely necessary to scrutinise the terms and conditions of all the foreign collaborations. So far as the basic problem of abolition of monopolies themselves is concerned, mere legislation and an anti-Monopolies Commission are not going to be of much help. The basic approach to the problem must be changed. Fresh thinking should be brought to bear upon this subject. I think it is necessary to have re-thinking about the suitable patterns of industrial structure in

140. Stafford Cripps, (24th April, 1889-21st April, 1952) was one of the most well-known British Labour Party political leader of his era, became member of the British War Cabinet under Winston Churchill, led the Cripps Mission to India in March 1942, for trying to elicit support of Indian parties for the War efforts. The Cripps Mission failed, leading to the Quit India Movement in August 1942. After the War, Cripps was also member of the Attlee ministry as Chancellor of the Exchequer.

India and suitable patterns of industrial ownership in India. When I speak of industrial structure, I mean that once it was fashionable to have a craze for large-scale industries indiscriminately and during the latter half of the last century, steel was the only basis for mechanisation but now the circumstances have changed. Since steam could not be decentralised, the processes of production could not be de-centralised and there could not be decentralisation of production and of economic power. But now we have power and we have got atomic energy which can be decentralised and which can be circulated to every village and every hearth and hamlet. Following the example of Japan, we can turn every hearth and home into a centre of production and mechanised production can be had with the help of power. There can be decentralisation of the processes of production which would help in the abolition of monopolies, though by instalments.

Another thing is that we have neglected all these 20 years to give adequate protection to the small-scale and medium-size industries. As a matter of fact, they have suffered adversely in the competition. It is necessary to see that managerial skill which can be useful for the small-scale and medium-size industries should not be allowed to go waste and that the capital which can be used only in such industries should not be allowed to lie idle. Unless adequate protection is given to extend small-scale and medium-size industries, this would not be possible.

India has been famous for the sector of the self-employed persons. They are neither masters nor servants of anybody else. Mechanisation needs to be introduced in their crafts also. Their crafts need to be encouraged properly and if that is done, we will have built up the people's sector where the employer-employee relationship would be completely absent.

Even as I am speaking about the pattern of industrial structure, I must say that an even more important point is the pattern of industrial ownership. There is the misconception in some quarters that there are only two alternatives, i.e. private enterprise or State-isation or governmentalisation or bureaucratisation. I beg to differ from this. I think that there are a number of other alternatives, if we do not allow ourselves to be enslaved by any slogans and if our approach is pragmatic, it would be possible for us to devise a number of patterns of ownership of industries. Take a few examples which would convince us that these are not the only two alternatives. There can be others. I shall cite the example of the banking industry in Greece. In Greece, private capital is not admitted into the banking industry. In the State enterprise, the State takes only 10 per cent of the share capital. The rest 90 per cent of the capital is owned by the historically grown social welfare organisations of Greece. What term or what particular brand it can be described? It is neither private enterprise, nor can it be described as State-isation or nationalisation. In Denmark, though there is a central bank, most of the banking industry is under cooperativisation. It is neither private capitalism nor State capitalism. To cite another example, the Preussag industry[141] in West Germany was developed by Hitler. There was a decision of the West German government to denationalise the industry which had a total share capital of 800 crore marks. It was actually denationalised. According to certain fanatics, there should be nationalisation of all private enterprises. But when this denationalisation was undertaken, they had four conditions. One was that every share was to be small. The second was that no one was allowed to

---

141. Preussag Industry – founded in Berlin in 1923 as (Prussian Mine and Foundry Company) "out of a collection of iron, lead, zinc, coal, oil, amber, and potash mining, foundry, and processing works formerly owned by the German State of Prussia." Exempted by the "Prussian government from the restrictions imposed by the State Budget, the new company's management was charged with building Preussag through the profit opportunities of the free market." In 1932, after he took over as Chancellor of Germany, Hitler initiated a military and infrastructural expansion that offered Germany's steel industry some protection from the stagnant world steel market, and by 1933, Preussag's gross profits had bounced back to RM [Reichsmark currency of the Third Reich] 60.1 million." Hitler's implementation of the four-year economic plan in 1936, "effectively placed the German economy on a war footing – the German iron and steel industry" submitted to the needs and objectives of the State's industrial policy. "Benefitting from the armaments-led expansion of the economy, between 1935 and 1938, Preussag's gross profits rose from RM 78 million to almost RM 100 million, and its work force climbed to 34,000." Soon after the War, "the Allied powers pursued a policy of Entflechtung, or decartelisation, in which many German firms were dismantled and large industry groups were broken up into separate companies with a maximum permitted share capital of RM100,000 each. In 1951 the dismantling of German plants was halted and bans, controls, and restrictions on German industry were lifted" Preussag diversified into coal, and as "European reconstruction spurred a boom in the demand for steel, Preussag's work force grew to 22,800. In 1952, the lifting of limits on German steel production finally enabled German steel companies to once again become competitive in the world market." In 1958 the German government, "in an attempt to spread the interest in German companies to a wider portion of the public (specifically, Preussag employees and low-income individuals), decided to initiate a partial privatisation of Preussag ... As world demand for steel began to decline around 1960 and the overproduction of steel of the 1950s created a global glut that lasted until the end of the 1960s, a newly privatised Preussag turned to diversification and acquisition."

(Read more: https://www.referenceforbusiness.com/history2/15/Preussag-AG.html#ixzz6XiNBSQzR accessed on: 9.9.2020)

purchase more than five shares. The third was that only those producing a low-income group certificate would be entitled to purchase shares. The fourth condition was that if simultaneously more than one person came for purchase of shares, then the employee of that particular concern would get priority. With these four conditions when there was denationalisation of the Pressaug industry in West Germany, I would ask the government whether this denationalisation means private capital being encouraged. There can be a number of patterns of ownership and we in India will have to find out our own pattern. It would be wrong to have regimentation or to be dogmatic in the sphere of economics. Our approach should not be dogmatic. We want fresh thinking and according to the conditions, we must be able to adopt and evolve our own model. In case we adopt or we evolve such a fresh thinking on the pattern of industrial ownership, it would be possible for us to abolish monopolies and to establish in the country economic democracy. For example, in the large-scale industries and even in the public sector undertakings, why should there not be introduced the concept of co-partnership of labour? Even as money is capital, labour is also capital. Therefore, labour should be affiliated in terms of shares and every worker should be made a shareholder or a partner in his industry. In the same way, we shall, whenever any concern is to be snatched away from private hands, why should it go directly to the government? That means bureaucratisation. Why should not the workers concerned be allowed to manage their own industry? In the autonomous corporations that we may set up or that we have already set up, why should the workers not be their own representatives? Why should there not be labourisation of industry? Even the British Labour Party has come to the conclusion that regimentation on the pattern of ownership is already obsolete and out of date and that there can be as many patterns as there are characteristics of industries. For every characteristic, there would be a different pattern. I wish the government would bring fresh thinking to bear upon this subject without being the slave of any particular dogma and adopt a pragmatic attitude. That way we could have different patterns of ownership suited to the conditions and institutions of the country. If this is done, I think that would be more effective than just having some pieces of legislations or appointing anti-monopoly commissions.

Half-an-Hour Discussion Regarding Loans to Sen Raleigh Company[142]

I want some clarification on one point. Firstly, is the government aware as to who are the officials that are responsible for granting loans on different occasions? Sir, I do not want the government to disclose their names at this stage. But I want to know whether the minister is aware of those names.

Secondly, sir, what has prevented the government from taking over the Company for such a long period? What obstructions were there and what considerations were there? Why was the process delayed?

Thirdly, sir, I want to know whether any investigation was conducted into the causes, for the present deterioration in the company's affairs and whether it is not a fact that it was not the labour productivity, but the capital productivity, that went down and, if that be so, whether any investigation was there and what are the findings of such an investigation?

Fourthly, may I know whether there are any rules about interlocutory directorships and whether those rules were not violated?

Reference to Closure of Ayodhya Textile Mills[143*]

D. Thengadi: Sir, for the last three days, the workers of the Ayodhya Textile Mills have been staging a *Dharna* before the residence of the Prime Minister, in connection with their demand that the Mill which has been closed since March 1971, should be reopened, and for that purpose, the Government of India should take over the mill so that they can resume their work. Sir, I request the government to realise the urgency of the matter because more than 250 workers are affected. The government should come out with a firm decision and announcement that the mill will be immediately taken over and the workers will be allowed to resume work.

---

142. *Rajya Sabha Debate* dated 4th August, 1971. Sen-Raleigh Ltd. private company, incorporated in 1949, based out of Kolkata, used to be a major cycle manufacturing company. One of its main production unit, started functioning in 1952 near Asansol in West Bengal. Then Minister for Company Affairs, K.V. Raghunatha Reddy responded thus to the points raised by Thengadi, "Sir, the question raised by Mr. Thengadi is, who are the officials responsible for granting these loans? The State Bank of India has given the loans on hypothecation and this is the normal practice. Unless something abnormal is seen, it is presumed to be the normal practice." The discussion was an intense one, CPI's trade union leader Kalyan Roy, who had initiated the discussion, also demanded a CBI enquiry into the loan defaulting proprietors of the company.

143. **Rajya Sabha Debate* dated 1st April, 1971.

The Companies (Amendment) Bill, 1964[144*]

D. Thengadi: Mr. Vice Chairman, at the very outset, I would like to congratulate the Ministry on having brought forward this Bill which is the need of the hour, particularly when we are out to weed out large-scale corruption. It is true that enquiries under the provisions of Sections 235, 237, 239, 247, 248 and 249 of the Companies Act, cannot be properly conducted unless the employees are extended adequate protection. The government is further justified in anticipating difficulties in connection with the collection of facts for referring to the Tribunal under Section 388-B of the Companies Act, cases of fraud, etc. against the managerial personnel. The employers are not justified in drawing a line of demarcation between informants and informers. No informer can render any damage to any company if the affairs of the company are, as they say, like Caesar's wife, above suspicion. Again, the information conveyed to the investigating officer would be secret and it would not be publicised. So, no danger would accrue to the company, whether these people are described as informants or as informers. The employers have again taken exception to sub-section (4) of this proposed section and they think that this would tantamount to ousting the rule of law. As a matter of fact, it is casting aspersions on the integrity of our tribunals and, therefore, there is no basis or foundation whatsoever for this apprehension.

While I congratulate the government for introducing this Bill, I do feel that this is an inadequate step, though in the right direction. The Bill is for a limited purpose but unfortunately the protection extended by the Bill to the employees is also limited because only during the pendency of the enquiry would the workers enjoy protection. Now, the employers are of the view that the period of protection must be specified. This demand of the employers suggests that they want to victimise, to dismiss or discharge the employees furnishing information to the investigating inspectors once this specified period is over.

Therefore, no worker or no officer would come forward and co-operate freely with the inspectors if he is also not assured that he would not be victimised even after the culmination of the enquiry. Now, there are ways of victimising workers. It is not necessary for the employers to say in so many words that after the culmination of the enquiry, they would proceed against the employees for furnishing information. We all know

144. **Rajya Sabha Debate* dated 28th September, 1964.

in the field of labour that under various disguises, by giving different charge-sheets, the employers victimise their employees. As a matter of fact, it would work like vengeance and, therefore, it is necessary that even after the culmination of the enquiry, protection should be extended to the employees. The case of officers drawing more than five hundred rupees per month would be still more precarious for it is this particular class that is in a position to give effective co-operation to the investigating officers because they are in possession of important statistical facts of the company and again it is this particular class of officers drawing more than five hundred rupees per month that is all the more defenceless even as compared to the workmen because the workmen enjoy protection under the Industrial Disputes Act,[145] whereas even this protection is not available to the officers.

Therefore, those very officers whose co-operation would matter would be most unwilling to co-operate with the inspectors for the simple reason that they would have no protection after the enquiry is over. I would, therefore, request the hon'ble minister to suitably amend this amending Bill so that even after the enquiry is over, the employees, whether they are workmen or officers, get adequate protection. Then alone would the workman or the officer have the courage to extend co-operation to the investigating officers. I hope that this suggestion of mine would be taken seriously into consideration. With these words and suggestions, I support the Bill.

□

145. The Industrial Disputes Act, 1947 extends to the whole of India and is "an Act to make provision for the investigation and settlement of industrial disputes".

4
Railways

Speaking in various debates on Railway Budget in the House, Thengadi felt that there was a need to abolish the Railway Board, which should be replaced by an autonomous corporation. He raised the problems of Railway employees in greater details and wanted to have a separate Wage Board for them. He was against continuing of the casual workers for a longer period and not only spoke about the plight of the gangmen, but also highlighted the general conditions of Class-IV employees of the Railways. He was of the opinion that officers dealing with personnel and welfare matters of the staff should have proper training in industrial psychology. Thengadi wanted Railways to be made fully autonomous with reduced number of zones and with one General Manager. He raised voice against 'contract' system.

On the operational side, Thengadi was of the view that government should further streamline the methods by which surveys are undertaken. He was of the opinion that safety organisation, machinery and equipment of the Railways should be subjected to periodical reviews by a Parliamentary Committee.

About the historic strike by the Railway employees in 1974, he said that it was imposed on them by the government. The employees wanted a negotiated settlement with the Railway Ministry. He categorically said that the employees were deprived of their legitimate trade union rights. Thengadi also spoke in detail on victimisation of employees by the government.

Budget (Railways), 1965–66[146]

Need to Make Railways Autonomous

D. Thengadi: I share the general feeling that the additional burden imposed by this Budget upon the poorer sections of the Railway users should be withdrawn forthwith. As is well known, the cost of living in India today is five times more as compared to the 1939 level, and there is

146. *Rajya Sabha Debate* dated 23rd February, 1965.

no corresponding increase in incomes. Actually, the real wages have been going down and according to this Budget, the freight rates would be five times more and the passenger fares roughly three times more. This is all unfair and unjust, and, therefore, at least the burden imposed through this particular Budget should be withdrawn.

The plight of casual labour has already been referred to. It is a mockery of the word 'casual' because persons are continued as 'casual' workers for years together. They should be confirmed after six months and their rates should be enhanced in the light of the latest working-class cost of living index figure. Before the recommendations of the J.A. Bell Committee in 1931, 12 gangmen used to look after a bit of 3 miles length. Subsequently, in keeping with that recommendation, 9 gangmen looked after a bit of 4 miles. During this period, the traffic has increased at least 20 times more. So, at least the pre-1931 arrangement should be restored and the number of gangmen should be correspondingly increased.

Every Railway employee should be provided with appropriate housing accommodation, and the quarters for the Class IV workers must be at least consisting of two rooms of 12 ft. by 8 ft. with an open space of 5 sq. ft. There should be the immediate appointment of a Wage Board for Railway employees, and while the Wage Board would be considering the problem of the pay scales and other emoluments of all those in service, I would request the government to entrust to the Wage Board the work of considering the demands of the retired Railwaymen also. I say this because the plight of the retired Railwaymen is particularly unfortunate. They are not having their regular trade unions to conduct collective bargaining and they are neglected folk who are most uncared for.

Railway employees should not be deprived of their right to bonus. Bonus should be given also to those in the public sector. Also, the Railway Administration should invariably extend the protection of the provisions of the Industrial Disputes Act to these employees. There is no justification for denying this protection to them.

Railway employees in India should be allowed the same rights and privileges and all civic and political rights as are being enjoyed by their counterparts in Great Britain and other civilised countries. It is very unfortunate that once a man enters the Railway service, it is presumed that he has become a slave. His civil and political rights should remain unhampered.

So far as dearness allowance is concerned, it has already been mentioned that this discriminates between employee and employee and, as such, this discrimination should be done away with and even those drawing higher salaries should be brought within its purview; they should be extended the benefit of the recommendations of the Das Commission. We are particularly of the opinion that now the time is ripe when the scheme of this dearness allowance should be dropped because this scheme of dearness allowance was introduced as a temporary measure during war-time so as to deprive the workers of their legitimate dues by way of bonus, gratuity, Provident Fund and pensions. In Western countries, there was a corresponding increase in wages or salaries, but in India, we introduced this temporary measure. Now, in view of the fact that dearness has come to acquire a permanent character, this dearness allowance should be merged cent per cent, with the basic wages and the total wage or the entire salary should be linked to the cost of living index. The government should take particular note of the middle-class cost of living index number and at every important centre, such middle-class cost of living index should be compiled and this should be utilised while determining the wages and salaries and other emoluments of Railway employees.

In keeping with the recommendation of the Stores Committee,[147] stores should not exceed the sum of Rs. 50 crores. When most of the goods required were being imported from abroad, we followed strictly this limit of Rs. 50 crores. Now we are told that at least 75 per cent of the goods are being manufactured in our own country. So, there is no propriety in maintaining such large quantities of goods in the stores, because it leads to unnecessary losses and wastage.

There are certain lines, though small, owned by foreign concerns and managed by the Railway Administration. This is not satisfactory. The Railway Administration should immediately take over these lines. The Railways have failed to evolve a machinery for speedy settlement of any type of claims – for loss of goods, parcels, surrendered or unused tickets. The longer the time taken for settlement, the bigger would be the claim and consequent loss to the tax-payer. I suspect that the money spent for resisting claims would be more than double the amount of claims resisted. In order to reduce the amount of claims, may I suggest that Traffic

147. Committee constituted by the Railway Ministry to look into the purchases of the Railway Board.

Inspectors, etc. should be authorised to settle the claims on the spot and the Claims Act of 1890[148] should be amended suitably to meet the needs of the changed circumstances?

The compilation and publication of statistics of ticketless travellers is absurd. It encourages wrong tendencies. Usually ticketless travellers are short-distance passengers. It is almost impracticable to obtain correct statistics and the practice of publishing these statistics should be put an end to. Specific criteria should be prescribed for declaring any Railway area as suburban area and the criteria so prescribed should be strictly adhered to. The Railways must keep statistics of trains running late, individually. Today the practice followed is to furnish total hours of late running per month. This does not lead us to any correct conclusion. While detaining or delaying trains that are already late, the convenience of passengers should be taken into consideration. The present speed of Railway traffic and the workload of the employees demand changes in the General and Subsidiary Rules which were prepared in 1929.[149]

These rules are practically unworkable today. The time schedule for different operations should be suitably revised. These rules cannot ensure the previous objective of maximum safety.

It is absolutely necessary that there should be uniformity in service conditions, responsibilities and facilities extended to different categories of workers on all the zones without, in any way, curtailing the existing facilities. After retirement, Class IV employees should be given the same facility regarding passes and PTOs[150] as are granted to Class III people. The pension rules should be revised in the light of the recommendations of the Central Pay Commission. Standardisations of nomenclature of the staff and the adoption of the scientific process of job analysis should be completed on all the zones.

The nomenclature should normally indicate the nature of the job and responsibilities.

---

148. The Revenue Recovery Act, 1890: Recovery of public demands by enforcement of processes in other districts than those in which they become payable.

149. In 1962, the Railway Accidents Committee had advocated the need to revise these rules, subsequently in 1968, another Railway Accidents Inquiry Committee reiterated the demand. A committee comprising of officers from the traffic and signal department of the Railways was then constituted and it submitted its report in 1970; the rules were eventually reframed and reworked in 1976.

150. PTO – Privilege Ticket Order; are paid passes issued to serving Railway employees and officers for travel on a concessional rate of one-third of the ordinary single.

I would like to know whether proper precautions have been taken to coordinate and integrate plans for the development of road transport, water transport and the Railways. Such an integrated policy is necessary. Regarding the starting of new lines, I should like to suggest that our previous plans have not been properly executed. The example of the Delhi-Bombay line is there where doubling has not yet been completed. Plans should not be influenced by any political considerations.

Much has been said about the zones. It has already been brought to the notice of the Administration that there is much discontent, particularly in the Solapur Division[151] regarding the carving out of the South Middle Zone. The merits or demerits of that case apart, I should like to suggest that the zonal system, as it exists today, has failed to achieve its important objective, viz. economy. The increase in the number of General Managers has not meant a corresponding increase in efficiency. I suggest that there should be only one General Manager in the country with a number of Deputy General Managers to assist him in the different zones. It will ensure economy as well as efficiency. The number of zones should be reduced to six and a high-powered committee of experts should be appointed to demarcate and adjust the zones. Again, political considerations should not be allowed to influence the demarcation of zones.

After much thought, I have to suggest that the Railways should be made really autonomous under an autonomous corporation, with experts and representatives of users, i.e. the consumers and employees on its Board of Management. The autonomy should be real and not fictitious. The present Railway Board should be abolished.

The Budget (Railways), 1966-67[152]

Need for a Wage Board for Railway Employees

D. Thengadi: Regarding inauguration of new lines, the government has taken certain definite decisions. Nevertheless, I should like to ask questions. We are told that surveys on Singareni-Katni and Siliguri-Jogighopa lines have been completed. How far have we undertaken the construction work on these lines?

Surveys were conducted on Kota-Chittorgarh (Rajasthan) and Tirunelveli-Kanyakumari (Tamil Nadu), but there is no decision on either of those lines in the current year's proposals.

---

151. Solapur Railway Division is largest division of the Indian Central Railway Zone and spans 10 districts of the state of Maharashtra, Karnataka and Telengana.

152. *Rajya Sabha Debate* dated 9th March, 1966.

There is a very heavy traffic on the Ghaziabad-Saharanpur (Uttar Pradesh) section. There must be made some additional arrangements to ease the pressure.

The Kotkapura-Fazilka (Punjab) section, which is only 83 Kms, is metre-gauge today. From the strategic point of view, it is necessary to make it broad-gauge.

From the same point of view, a new line from Pokharan to Jaisalmer (Rajasthan) should be given top priority.

Regarding Railway lines, I have a few suggestions. There are certain lines, though small, owned by foreign concerns, and managed by the Railway Administration. This is unwise. The Railway Administration should immediately take over these lines.

Existing trains should not be discontinued. It is learnt that Dharwad-Hubli (Karnataka) local train will be discontinued. This is going to cause great inconvenience to industrial and loco-workshop employees.

There should be no general ban on inaugurating new lines if they are considered essential for, and helpful to, the general prosperity of the country, essential movement of foodgrains and increase in the Railway revenue.

The new train, I propose, should be run from Ahmedabad to Calcutta via Bhopal, Itarsi, Nagpur. For the movement of foodgrains and the general industrial development of Kerala, which has become a trouble spot now, and Marathwada, which is the industrially backward region of Maharashtra, I make certain suggestions. From north Kerala to Cochin, it is broad gauge. From Cochin to further south, it is metre gauge. This creates difficulties for transport of goods as well as of passengers. The entire line should be made broad gauge. Also, these new lines should be laid down, i.e. Trivandrum to Kanyakumari, Trichur to Guruvayur, Mangalore-Calicut-Bangalore direct line and Kollengode to Trichur (Kerala). The introduction of these lines is essential for easing the recurring food crisis in Kerala as well as for its general prosperity.

In Marathwada, I suggest that the line from Pardi (Gujarat) to Baijnath (Himachal Pradesh) and Latur-Kurduwadi-Miraj (Maharashtra) and from Kolhapur to Ratnagiri (Maharashtra) should be converted into broad gauge line. Broad gauge would be essential for the development of that region.

Next I come to certain administrative problems. Now that at least 75 per cent of the goods are being manufactured in India, we should faithfully follow the recommendation of the Stores Committee, so that the Standing Stores should never exceed the sum of Rs. 50 crores. There is no propriety in maintaining large quantities of goods in the stores. It leads to avoidable losses and wastage.

The administration has failed so far to evolve a machinery for speedy settlement of any type of claims for loss of goods, parcels, surrendered or unused tickets. The longer the time taken for settlement, the bigger would be the claim and consequent loss to the tax-payer. The money spent for resisting claims would be more than double the amount of the claims resisted. In order to reduce the amount of claims, Traffic Inspectors and others should be authorised to settle the claims on the spot and the Claims Act of 1890 should be amended suitably to meet the needs of the modern conditions.

The practice of publishing statistics of ticketless travellers should be put an end to. These are usually short-distance passengers and it is impracticable to obtain their correct statistics. Such publication only encourages wrong tendencies.

Specific criteria should be prescribed for declaring any Railway area as suburban area, and the criteria so prescribed should be strictly adhered to.

The Railways must keep statistics of trains running late, individually. Today, the practice followed is to furnish total hours of late running per month. This does not lead us to a correct conclusion. While detaining or delaying trains that are already late, the convenience of the passengers should be taken into consideration.

The General and Subsidiary Rules, prepared in 1929, are unworkable today because of the present speed of the Railway traffic and the increased workload of the employees. Appropriate changes should be introduced therein. The time-schedule for different operations should be suitably revised. These rules cannot ensure their original objective of 'maximum safety'.

Sir, though I do not intend to discuss the language policy of the country here, I insist that Railway Newsletters and other notifications should be published in all regional languages. I request the hon'ble minister to inform us whether this is already being done. I draw his attention, for example, to one complaint. The Dakshina Railway Karmik Sangh [Southern Railway Workers Union attached to the BMS] has written to the Chairman, Railway Board, that the Southern Railway Administration has not taken any action on their request that the newsletters should be published in Kannada language also. This injustice should be done away with.

Sir, it must be admitted by the government that the recent increase in dearness allowance is quite inadequate. We are doubtful about the so-called 'new methods' of compensating the workers. The rising cost of living must be fully neutralised. For this purpose, it is necessary to hold the price line. As S.K. Das stated in his report, "If the price line was not held in future, even a 90 per cent neutralisation may prove illusory." In view of this fact, I suggest evolution of our National Price Policy and the National Wage Policy during the Fourth Plan period (1969-1974). In the meanwhile, the opening of cheap grain-shops in all centres should not be delayed.

Sir, with all the emphasis that I can command, I want to submit that it is absolutely imperative to appoint a Wage Board for Railway employees. In view of their vast number, it is obviously imprudent to club them with the general Central Government employees for the purpose of wage determination. They must have a separate Wage Board.

The Dearness Allowance of the employees should be merged fully, that is to say 100 per cent, with their basic wage, and the consolidated wage or their pay packet should be linked with a scientifically recompiled middle-class cost of living index number, which should henceforth be treated as the genuine working class cost of living index number.

There is no justification whatsoever for depriving the Railway employees of their right to bonus. In the first place, bonus under the present conditions is only deferred wage, inasmuch as there exists a wide gap between the living wage and the actual wage. Secondly, Railways have been earning huge profits. When the Railway employees demand bonus, they are told that they are departmental employees and, hence, they are not entitled to bonus. When they demand other facilities as departmental employees, they are brushed aside on the plea that they are 'industrial' workers. Thus, the Railway employees are receiving not the best but the worst of both the words. This should be put an end to and their right to bonus should be accepted ungrudgingly. Similarly, they should not be deprived of the protection of the Industrial Disputes Act.

There has already been an inordinate delay in the introduction of the Whitley Council Machinery.[153] The Railway employees had been

153. Primarily Joint Industrial Councils, in England comprising of representatives of labour and management for settlement of industrial unrest. Named after J.H. Whitely, British politician, later Speaker of the House of Commons, who was appointed to head such a committee to look into the 'Relations of Employers and Employees.'

sceptical so far about its utility and efficacy, because of the pre-conditions prescribed by the government. They had not yet crossed this stage of scepticism, though they welcome the recent change in the government's policy regarding the worker's right to strike. Railway employees will enthusiastically welcome the Whitley Council Machinery, only if it is modelled after the original British pattern.

Again, the mere form of joint consultative machinery will bring us no good if the bureaucrats persist in their present attitude. The appropriate spirit must precede the form. I request the hon'ble minister to take suitable steps for this purpose.

Sir, the magnitude of the problem of casual labour can hardly be overemphasised. Lakhs of workers are continued for years together as 'casual' which is a mockery of that word. They should be confirmed after six months, and their rates should be enhanced in the light of the latest working class cost of living index number.

Sir, the plight of the gangmen deserves special attention. Before the recommendation of the J.A. Bell Committee in 1931, 12 gangmen used to look after a length of 3 miles. Subsequent and consequent to the Bell Committee recommendations, 9 gangmen are required to look after 4 miles. During the last three decades, there has been a tremendous increase in the traffic. Therefore, I would request the government to at least restore the pre-1931 arrangement and to increase the number of gangmen correspondingly.

Sir, the housing problem of the Railway employees is a very important one. So far, we have been able to make provision for only one-third of the regular employees. This is quite inadequate. Every Railway employee must be provided with appropriate housing accommodation. The quarters for the Class IV employees must be at least consisting of two rooms of 12 ft. by 8 ft. with an open space of 5 sq. ft. The problem of additional space can be solved by a few measures. First of all, we can curtail the accommodation facility of the Railway officials and bringing them on par with the other Central Government officials in this respect. And, secondly, we can make the buildings already available to the Railway Administration multi-storeyed. For the staff that is liable to periodical transfers, the quarters should be allotted on priority basis. The Railway lands on both sides of the Railway line and also beyond the outer signal should be made available to the Railway employees.

Sir, I understand that the Second Pay Commission did not revise the pay scales of guards. I submit that their case for promotion and better scales of pay deserve consideration.

On certain Railways, the rules for promotion of firemen and shunters have been changed unfavourably for the working employees. In the past, there was a ratio of 6:1 for promotion from second fireman to fireman, that is to say, while 6 second working employees working as second firemen were promoted as firemen, only one was taken from outside. Also 25 per cent of the posts were reserved for departmental candidates. The changed rules are very unfavourable to working employees.

While I am happy to learn that some of the demands of the stenographers and typists are being conceded, the basic demand of the stenographers for parity of pay scales with the stenographers working in the Railway Board Office still remain unfulfilled. The typists cannot rise beyond the post of a head typist. Typists cannot become chief clerks or Superintendents. I submit that their long-standing grievances should be looked into and removed.

In the Engineering Department, sir, there exists an anomaly. The staff who are recruited as *khalasis* [helpers] even when they are promoted to higher posts as AIOWs [Assistant Inspector of Works], IOW [Inspector of Works] during the course of their service, are not confirmed for many years.

The majority of workers in the workshops are in the recruitment grade and they have hardly any chance of advancement with the result that there is a regular flow of skilled workers leaving the service and joining private industries where attractive salaries are offered. The conditions must be comfortable for this category of people. I understand that instead of bettering their lot with a view to attracting more people, the existing facilities given to trade apprentices in workshops are being curtailed. Their stipend is proposed to be revised from Rs. 75 per month to Rs. 25 per month. This is not in the larger interests of the Railways. The ex-grain shop staff, the justness of whose demands is known to the ministry, should be given justice. The incentive scheme in workshops has not been made applicable to all the workers contributing to increased production directly or indirectly. Even those entitled to the benefits of this scheme directly are not getting a chance to earn incentive bonus because of short supply of raw material. Their time is lost and they are booked idle. Evidently there is something wrong in the planning. This should be looked into.

The general conditions of Class IV staff are miserable. The recommendations of the Class IV Staff Promotion Committee have not been implemented. Though there are definite orders to set aside 10 per cent of the vacancies for the promotion of Class IV staff to Class III categories, the necessary examinations are not being held and educated qualified Class IV staff are being deprived of their chances of promotion. Worse is the condition of gangmen in the Engineering Department who have hardly any chance of advancement with the Railway Administration installed I.B. machines costing crores of rupees. They are, however, giving only a meagre special pay of 15 rupees to the operators while elsewhere it is over 50 rupees. Again, this amount is not allowed to be merged with basic pay at the time of promotion of the machine operators. This should be done. Night allowance should be granted to all those who work during nights. There should be no discrimination in this respect. The conductors on night trains should be provided with one berth during nights. The duration of night duty should be regulated. The maximum number of nights that an employee from the running staff would be required to spend out of the headquarters should also be prescribed. The effects of dieselisation are slowly being felt by the Railway employees. Initially, when the representatives of staff expressed their apprehensions that this would lead to retrenchment, the Administration was quick in announcing that nobody would lose his job but would be given alternate employment. The experience of the staff, however, shows that they have not been properly treated by the government. On the pretext of giving alternate employment, they are being thrown in the different departments. It is generally known that while in 1948 there were only 15 Under-Secretaries in one government department, now there are one 150. This seems to apply equally to the Railways and this excessive number of posts of officers should be minimised. The officers dealing with personnel and welfare matters of staff should have proper training in industrial psychology because sometimes they become so indifferent to staff difficulties that their genuine requests are not acceded to and every issue is made a prestige issue for the Administration. This results in great resentment among the staff. While it is needless to say that corruption is rampant, and while I agree with the statement that spread of corruption-consciousness is at least as harmful as the spread of corruption itself, I should like to draw the attention of the ministry to some main spots of corruption against which the employees have to fight. Motivated transfer, against which introduction of transfer allowances is a protection – Non-confirmation of staff and denial of increment and timely promotions. This can be checked if the staff responsible for errors is taken to task by the Administration, booking and posting of the staff. Prescription of proper basis for determination of seniority can do away with this type of injustice, selections and suitability tests. Constitutional setting up of Trade Testing Panel and Selection Boards consisting of reputed officers is the only way to eliminate this evil. During the last decade, selection rules have been changed at least 10 times – sometimes giving due credit to senior persons for length of service and sometimes doing away with this. This smacks of vested interest every time the selection rules are changed. I feel that a well-thought-out policy should be laid down once for all and senior men should be given credit for their long, faithful and efficient service. Standardisation of nomenclature of the staff and the adoption of the scientific process of job analysis should be completed on all the zones. The nomenclature should normally indicate the nature of the job and responsibilities. There should be uniformity brought about in service conditions and responsibilities and facilities extended to different categories of workers in all the zones, without in any way curtailing the existing facilities.

The South Central Zone is to be carved out. At this juncture, I reiterate the demand of the employees to retain Sholapur Division in the Central Zone and to add Guntakal Division to the South Central Zone. Further, much precaution needs to be taken regarding seniority claims of the staff that would be absorbed in this new zone. The seniority of the MSM *[Mechanical Signal Maintainer]*. Staff that was absorbed in the Southern Zone was adversely affected and even to this date, those aggrieved have not been able to secure justice. The same mistake should not be repeated this time. I request the ministry to consider seriously the demand of the workers to confine the scope of options to the concerned division. Again, sir, on the eve of the carving out of the South Central Zone, the problem of reversion of Class III promotees in the Southern Zone has become a burning problem. I request the Administration to allow them to continue, without reversion. The staff that had opted for Pakistan in the year 1947 but subsequently returned to India have not been given the due seniority and the CPC arrears till today. This should be remedied immediately.

Sir, among other things, I demand treatment as running staff, as public servants and as essential staff for the ticket-checking category, abolition of overlapping grades from commercial category and ticket-checking staff as well as the Station Masters and Assistant Station Masters and change in the pattern of uniforms for the TTEs, firemen, drivers and crane drivers of loco workshops and loco sheds.

Among the broader issues, Railway employees in India should be allowed the same rights and privileges, all civic and political rights as are being enjoyed by their counterparts in Great Britain. It should not be presumed that once a person enters the Railway service, he becomes a wage-slave. The reply given by the hon'ble minister for Railways in the Rajya Sabha on 24th March, 1965, in the case of Mukund Parekh of Western Railway is completely incorrect, and the government knows it to be so.

The question of pensionary benefits to Railway staff who have retired prior to 1st April, 1957 is still hanging fire. On 27th February, 1965, the hon'ble S.K. Patil[154] had assured V.R. Ghule, president of the All-India Retired Railwaymen's Federation that he would give sympathetic attention to this question, but I am sorry to state that nothing in this respect has been done so far. In this context, I should like to challenge the figures given by the Railway Board earlier. In February 1964, Ramaswamy,[155] the then Deputy Minister for Railways, stated in Parliament that there were approximately three lakhs of such people and that the cost of pension thereon would work out to 150 crores of rupees spread over six years. I assert there are not more than 25 thousand such people living and that the cost of pensions thereon can never exceed one crore of rupees per year.

I would request the government to do justice expeditiously to these retired Railwaymen who had rendered splendid service to the country.

Apart from the case of this particular section of the retired Railwaymen, I should like to request the government to consider sympathetically the problem of pensions to all retired Railwaymen. The price-level has been rising constantly. The quantum of pension is the same. Consequently, they are, in fact, receiving less real monetary relief. They have no trade union rights to protect themselves. Sir, among retired Railway staff, there should

154. S.K. Patil (1898-1981) – freedom fighter, veteran Congress leader, once the principal leader of the Congress in Maharashtra, thrice Mayor of Bombay, one of the chief fund-raisers for the party, three-time Member of Parliament from Mumbai and Mumbai South, Minister of Railways and Information & Broadcasting in Nehru cabinet. Patil was among the six Union Ministers who resigned under the Kamaraj Plan in 1963. In 1969, Patil sided with Nijalingappa, Kamaraj, Morarji Desai, Atulya Ghose to form the Congress (Organisation).

155. S.V. Ramaswamy (b.1906-), Member of Parliament from Salem, Tamil Nadu, Member of 1st Lok Sabha, 2nd & 3rd Lok Sabha, became Deputy Minister of Railways in 1958.

be made no distinction or discrimination between class and class. For example, after retirement, a Class IV employee should be given the same facility of passes and PTOs as are granted to a Class III employee.

Sir, on 16th September, 1965, the hon'ble minister of State for Railways stated in the Rajya Sabha:

"Representation has been given to the Passengers' Associations on the Zonal Railway Consultative Committee at the rate of one on each committee." Specific representation has not been given to the Passengers' Associations on the National Railway Users' Consultative Council, as the representatives of Parliament, Chambers of Commerce, elected members of the Zonal Railway Users' Consultative Committees' special interests, etc. on the council, in their capacity as general rail users adequately represent the interests of passengers."

I am sorry to state that this statement fails to do justice to the passengers' interests.

I was dealing with the problem of representation of passengers' associations and their Federation, on the different Railway users' committees. In the first place, if we take into consideration the total number of members of the different zonal Railway users' consultative committees, it would be discerned that the passengers' associations are given only 2 per cent representation. The commercial interests get representation under three different heads, namely chambers of commerce, merchants and industries and, thus, they are represented by 19 members on an average out of an average of 48, whereas the passengers' interests are represented by only one member. The proportion of earnings from these two interests is 37 per cent from passengers and 63 per cent from commercial interests. It is, therefore, in the fitness of things to give additional representation to passengers' interests.

Secondly, the argument forwarded by the Minister of State for not granting specific representation to the passengers' interests on the National Railway Users' Consultative Council is not satisfactory. It has been argued that Members of Parliament elected from different categories to represent different interests from different parts of the country in their capacity as general Railway users adequately represent the interests of passengers and, therefore, specific representation need not be given for passengers' interests. But he was not fully dependent on the Members of Parliament to represent other interests from whom Railway income is derived. He thought it necessary to give specific representation to them, viz. the commercial interests. If other interests, who are responsible for 63 per cent of the revenue, are fit to be given specific representation, why should passengers who are responsible for 37 per cent of the revenue be deprived of a similar privilege? Therefore, I request the hon'ble minister to consider this problem in the broader aspects. National interest requires that consumer consciousness should be roused and developed properly in the country because consumer consciousness is the nearest economic equivalent to national consciousness. From this point of view, every effort should be made to encourage passengers' consciousness also.

Sir, with a view to achieving the twin objects of economy and efficiency, I suggest certain drastic changes in the administrative set-up:

1. The Railways should be made really autonomous under an autonomous corporation with experts and representatives of Railway users and Railway employees on its Board of Management. The autonomy should be real and not nominal. The present Railway Board should be abolished.
2. The number of zones should be reduced to six and a high-powered committee of experts, and not of politicians, should be appointed to demarcate and adjust the zones. Political considerations should not be allowed to influence the demarcation of zones.
3. There should be only one General Manager in the country with a number of Deputy General Managers to assist him in the different zones. This is necessary for both economy as well as efficiency.
4. A proper coordination and integration of plans for the development of road transport, water transport and the Railways should be ensured.

I am confident that the hon'ble Railway Minister will take cognisance of all these suggestions.

The Budget (Railways), 1967-68[156]

Protection of the Employees' Interests

D. Thengadi: I think the Railways have been following a policy of false economy all these years. While, on the one hand, for Class I officials, the Railways have become a training ground, there is a tendency to accommodate a greater number of Class I officers through the different

156. *Rajya Sabha Debate* dated 29th March, 1967.

zones which are being carved out. There is also an attempt to retrench, directly or indirectly, the Class III and Class IV employees. For example, there has been a ban on the creation of clerical posts and, therefore, an increase in the workload of clerks. One can understand this but, at the same time because new zones have been carved out, the number of Class I officials is increased and, therefore, the burden on our economy is also increased. Retrenchment is being effected through various ways, as I said directly or indirectly. For example, when we introduced mechanisation in the Accounts Department, it led to indirect retrenchment; it blocked the promotional avenues. There is no substantial reduction in the cost, and actually it has increased our dependence on the USA for mechanics, spare parts and other materials. After electrification and dieselisation, there is bound to be large-scale retrenchment and the government has not assured that the principle of no-retrenchment without alternative employment would be followed and there has been no attempt or effort to train the workers who would be declared surplus, in the various jobs, including that of electrification and dieselisation.

Regarding the various facilities that should be naturally and justifiably given to the employees, there is much room for discontent. A few important problems I would like to refer to. Firstly, there is the housing problem. Less than one-third of the total Railway employees are provided with quarters. Some of them are in service for 15 or 20 years and still they are without quarters, staying in big cities. We know that there is no free suburban services also and much hardship is caused to the Railway employees on account of this lack of housing facilities. More quarters should be constructed. Some vigorous programmes for industrial housing must be undertaken by the Railways. The officers are given big bungalows. As a matter of fact, their bungalows also can be utilised for some construction purposes.

Then there is complaint about inadequate and inefficient medical services. The workers are not satisfied with the present facilities and if they approach doctors outside, their bill will not be reimbursed. At least, the CHS[157] should be extended to the Railway employees.

Regarding selection tests also there is much discontent. In the name of merit, favouritism is rampant and it is necessary to see that there is no room for any grievance so far as selection is concerned and also to see that

157. Central Health Scheme under the Govt. of India for providing comprehensive health-care facilities for the Central Govt. employees and pensioners and their dependents.

seniority is given its due place. Now the Emergency has been practically over though not legally probably, but the extra half-an-hour has not been curtailed and alternate Sundays have not been declared as holidays. This should be done immediately.

We now come to some big problems. There has been no uniformity in the different zones about the service conditions and even in the same zone, there is no uniformity in the payment of different allowances, such as overtime or night allowances.

Night allowance should be granted to all those who work during nights but, unfortunately, many of the categories that have to work during nights are not given night allowance. This should be rectified.

We come to the most important problem, that is of wage. The Railway employees have been demanding a separate Wage Board, and there is justification for the demand. In the first place somehow, a number of categories were not properly represented before the Second Pay Commission. Therefore, the Second Pay Commission could not do justice to these categories. Now even the Second Pay Commission's period is over and there is no talk in the air about the appointment of a Third Pay Commission. Even if there is one, I find that it is not going to solve the problem because our experience with the first two Pay Commissions has been that the Railways being a very huge concern comprising more than one-and-a-half million workers consisting of a number of categories, it is not possible to have a very comprehensive study of the Railway employees' plight by a Pay Commission which is also to look after all the various Central Government departments and, therefore, the demand for a separate Wage Board is perfectly justified. I would request the minister not to make it a prestige point and to concede this just demand of the Railway workers.

Then we took pride last year in saying that 45 lakhs of workers have been brought within the purview of the right to bonus. As a matter of fact, bonus is not actually profit-sharing so far as our present conditions are concerned because it has been accepted by economists all over the world that bonus is nothing but a deferred wage so long as there is a gap between living and actual wage and it assumes the character of profit-sharing only after the actual wage attains the level of a living wage, but even assuming for the sake of argument that it is profit-sharing. There is no reason why the right to bonus should be denied because the Railways have earned huge profits, last year more than Rs. 13 crores, and it was because of the sweat and blood of the Railway employees. So, they should be given the right to bonus.

Now there are some other facts that are causing discontent among the Railway employees. For example, rules are not strictly followed regarding many vital matters, such as decasualisation. It is really shameful to see that lakhs and lakhs of workers are kept as casual for years together and as temporary for years together and, therefore, there should be strict implementation of the rules of permanency and of decasualisation.

The contract system, the government has declared, would be abolished but it is really unfortunate to see that on their own Railways, the contract system still prevails and the principal employer is not held responsible for all the rights and remuneration of the employees. Now it is necessary to revise, in view of the increased traffic load during the last three decades, the various time schedules for the different operations, the number of personnel in every department, the working rules, etc. because all these have become obsolete. For example, the compensation after an accident is being governed by an Act of 1890. It is really obsolete. So, all these should be rectified and should be brought up-to-date. If all these suggestions are taken into consideration and if we try to curtail the number of Class I officials, if we resolve not to retrench the Class III or Class IV employees and if all these rights and amenities are granted to the workers, a contented labour would be an asset to the Railway Administration.

Nothing about the employees' plight?

C.M. Poonacha:[158] As for the employees' plight, I might take this opportunity to explain that in the Railways, the welfare of the staff is of paramount importance. We give great importance to this matter and personnel management is one of the most important functions of the Railway Administration today. As my hon'ble friend himself is aware, we have ever so many commissions and tribunals appointed from time to time to examine specific problems and the government has accepted

158. C.M. Poonacha (1910-1990) – freedom fighter, member of AICC 1938, elected to Coorg Legislative Council in 1945, member of the Constituent Assembly and Provisional Parliament, Chief Minister of Coorg from 1952-1956, Minister of Home & Industries in the newly formed Mysore state, elected to the Rajya Sabha in 1964. From 1964 to 1966 Poonacha held various portfolios as Minister of State, in Ministry of Finance and Ministry of Transport, Aviation, Shipping and Tourism, Union Minister for Railways from 1967 to 1969 and Minister for Steel and Heavy Engineering in 1969, appointed Governor of Madhya Pradesh in 1978 and of Odisha in 1980.

each and every recommendation of such commissions and tribunals that were appointed from time to time. Not only that. We have implemented them fully. So, it could not be said that the Railway Administration or the Government of India are indifferent to the welfare of labour and staff who are employed by them. At the same time, hon'ble members would be knowing that this is an undertaking which employs the largest number of labour. We have about 1.5 million bodies working. We run about 11,000 trains per day and as was mentioned by my hon'ble friend on the other side, we carry 5.7 million passengers every day. It is a huge operation and, in this, there are ever so many problems coming up daily, say, hourly. Each hour we have a problem. They are being tackled continuously. It is not as if during these exercises, the welfare of labour is given a low order of priorities. No. The welfare of labour is given the highest priority.

General Discussion on Railway Budget, 1968-69

D. Thengadi: Construction as such is permanent work, though construction at a particular place may be temporary.

तो इस दृष्टि से कैजुअल को परमानेंट और टेंपोरेरी इस प्रक्रिया में डालने में कौन सी आपत्ति है ? डिकेजुअलाइजेशन के बारे में मैं आग्रह करना चाहूँगा। वही बात टेंपोरेरी के लिए है। सालो-साल लोगों को कॉन्फर्म नहीं किया जाता। आपको आश्चर्य होगा कि जहाँ तक क्लास फोर कर्मचारियों का संबंध है, मैं ऐसे उदाहरण दे सकता हूँ कि वे 18-20 साल तक टेंपोरेरी के नाते काम करते हैं और 80 रुपए तक उनकी तनख्वाह है। ऐसे उदाहरण हमें यहाँ प्राप्त होते हैं।

आज रेलवे कर्मचारियों के सामने एक बड़ी भारी कठिन समस्या उनके वेतन और एलाउंसेज की है। आश्चर्य की बात है कि एमेलगेमेशन के बाद इतने साल हो गए, सर्विस कंडीशंस में जिस प्रकार की एकरूपता आनी चाहिए, वह अभी तक नहीं आ पाई। मुझे स्मरण है कि मैं एक जोन से पास कर रहा था कि मुझे एक अच्छे पढ़े-लिखे इंप्लाई ने यह बताया कि एक डिवीजन में यूनिफॉर्म दिया जाता है, दूसरे डिवीजन में बिल्कुल नहीं दिया जाता और उसने अंग्रेजी में बताया—there is no uniformity in the Railways even about uniforms. तो सर्विस कंडीशंस में एकरूपता नहीं है; यह बड़े आश्चर्य की बात है। दूसरी बात, जबकि उसका एकत्रीकरण हो चुका है और उनकी वेतन-श्रेणियों के बारे में कोई अच्छी व्यवस्था आज भी नहीं हुई कि किसको कितनी तनख्वाह, इसका आधार क्या, ऑरबीट्रेरी आधार पर सब तनख्वाहें रखी जाएँ तो उसको न्याय नहीं कहा जा सकता। वैसे भी, रेलवे में इतनी ज्यादा केटेगरीज हैं कि सभी केंद्रीय कर्मचारियों के लिए एक ही पे-कमीशन नियुक्त किया जाए और उसके अधीन रेलवे कर्मचारियों का सवाल रखा जाए तो मैं समझता हूँ कि संपूर्ण सदिच्छाओं के बावजूद वह पे-कमीशन रेलवे कर्मचारियों से न्याय नहीं कर सकता। फिर सेकेंड पे-कमीशन के सामने विभिन्न कैटेगरीज की ओर से जिस तरह का रिप्रजेंटेशन होना चाहिए था, वह नहीं हुआ। इसके कारण एक असंतोष फैल गया। फिर सेकेंड पे-कमीशन की मियाद खत्म हो गई और बीच में जो कमीशन आए, वे महँगाई भत्ते के बारे में थे। और आज जो उनकी तनख्वाह है, उसके लिए कोई भी शास्त्रीय आधार नहीं। शास्त्रीय आधार से

मेरा यह मतलब है कि रेलवे में जितनी केटेगरीज हैं, सब केटेगरीज का जो इवेल्युएशन होना चाहिए और इसके आधार पर उनके वेज-डिफरेंशियल्स तय होने चाहिए और इस तरह से हम सारे ग्रेड्स तय करें, तभी शास्त्रीय आधार पर वेजेज तय होंगे। यह करने के लिए वेज बोर्ड की आवश्यकता है। आज जो वेतन श्रेणियाँ हैं, उनमें इतनी एनोमेलीज हैं कि काम करने वाले एक सीनियर और एक जूनियर··· (interruptions)

The Minister of State (Defence Production) in the Ministry of Defence (*L.N. Mishra*):[159] If there is job evaluation, it might result in retrenchment also.

D. Thengadi: It will not, we will see to it.

L.N. Mishra: There is that obligation also.

D. Thengadi: It has various aspects.

L.N. Mishra: All right, go ahead.

दत्तोपंत ठेंगड़ी : तो वेतन श्रेणियों में इतनी एनोमेलीज के रहते हुए वेज बोर्ड की नियुक्ति करने में क्यों देर की जा रही है, यह आश्चर्य की बात है। अभी-अभी इन एनोमेलीज के बारे में दो हाईकोर्टों ने अपना अभिप्राय प्रकट किया है। मद्रास हाईकोर्ट ने Assistant Surgeons in the Railway Medical Services with LMP qualification के बारे में जो रेलवे बोर्ड का ऑर्डर था, उसको क्वेश कर दिया। जस्टिस वेंकट चारी ने कहा है—

"It was discriminatory and violative of Articles 14 and 16 (1) of the Constitution."[160]

6 फरवरी को आंध्र हाईकोर्ट ने रेलवे एडमिनिस्ट्रेशन, जिसको न्यू डील कहना है, यानी 1956 से जो पे-स्ट्रकचर आया है, उसके बारे में कहा है कि यह डिस्क्रिमिनेटरी है—

Andhra High Court:

"Discriminatory and violative of Articles 14 and 16 of the Constitution."

---

159. Lalit Narayan Mishra (1923-1975) – understudy of Sri Krishna Sinha (Sri Babu) first Chief Minister of Bihar, member, AICC 1950, Member of 1st, 2nd and 5th Lok Sabha, member of Rajya Sabha, Mishra started his political career in Delhi as Parliamentary Secretary under Jawaharlal Nehru, was Deputy Minister and Minister of State between 1964-1970 in Ministry of Home, Ministry of Finance, Minister of State for Defence Production (1967-1970), 1970-1973, Minister for Foreign Trade, 1973-1975, Union Minister of Railways. One of the chief fundraisers of the Congress, Mishra was assassinated in a bomb explosion in Samastipur, Bihar on 2nd January, 1975. The trial into his assassination continued for 39 years, and concluded in 2014when four men, accused of Mishra's murder, were found guilty. However, his death and its reasons continued to be shrouded in mystery.

160. Article 14: "The State shall not deny to any person equality before the law or the equal protection of the laws within the territory of India". Article 16: " Equality of opportunity in matters of public employment."

और फिर कहा—

"It is indeed curious that such things should be happening like the employees of the superior cadre being paid less than those in the inferior cadre."

"It is true," Mr. Justice Narasimhan remarked in his judgement "that the petitioners – a dozen Station Masters and of the South Central Railway are getting less pay than those in the inferior cadre of commercial clerks to which they had been originally recruited.

और फिर इस एनोमेली के लिए जस्टिस नरसिम्हन कहते हैं—

"worse form of discrimination."

आगे वे कहते हैं—

"He was unconvinced that this matter could be explained away by the Railway authorities as an anomaly in pay structures, remediable only by a Pay Commission appointed by Parliament, and that they (the authorities) were helpless, which meant that the discrimination had to be suffered (by the affected employees)."

फिर वे कहते हैं—

"The authorities may not nonchalantly term it an anomaly and get away with discrimination."

और फिर कहते हैं—

"It is strange that they, being in a superior cadre, should seek reversion to the inferior cadre of commercial clerks, which only explains their deep frustration at their service conditions."

और फिर सुझाव देती हैं जस्टिस नरसिम्हन—

"The High Court was of the view that the authorities could find appropriate ways of remedying the adverse effects caused to the petitioners by the implementation of the 'new deal'."

इस तरह से दोनों जजों के जजमेंट से यह बात स्पष्ट हो जाती है कि इतनी एनोमेलीज रेलवे में हैं कि the Ministry of Railways can be described as the Ministry of Anomalies. इस दृष्टि से मैं यह समझता हूँ कि नए वेज बोर्ड की नियुक्ति आवश्यक हो जाती है।

जहाँ वेजेज के बारें में हमारा सवाल है, वहाँ दूसरी बात हम यह नहीं समझ पाए कि दो-ढाई साल पहले उस समय के मंत्री महोदय ने जब बोनस का बिल पेश किया था, तब बड़े अभिमान से यह कहा था कि 45 लाख ज्यादा लोगों को हम यह बेनिफिट एक्सटेंड कर रहे हैं। फिर हमारे रेलवे कर्मचारियों को बोनस के अधिकार से क्यों वंचित किया जाए? बोनस प्रॉफिट-शेयरिंग नहीं कहा जा सकता; देर से दिया हुआ वेतन डेफर्ड वेज, यह उसका स्वरूप है। आज जो हमारा प्रत्यक्ष वेतन है, वह लिविंग वेज से बहुत कम है। जब तक जीवन वेतन और प्रत्यक्ष वेतन में खाई है, तब तक डेफर्ड वेज विलंबित वेतन के नाते बोनस का अधिकार मिलना ही चाहिए।

अभी हमारे मंत्री महोदय ने कहा था कि बड़ी तेजी से आगे कर्मचारियों की छँटनी हो रही है। डिकेजुअलाइजेशन के फलस्वरूप ड्राइवर्स, कंडक्टर्स का प्रमोशन रुक गया है। फोरमैन, फिटर्स और यार्ड खलासीज को बड़ी संख्या में सरप्लस घोषित किया गया है और उनका रिवर्शन भी किया गया है। पाँच साल से ऊपर की श्रेणी में काम करने वाले लोग भी इसमें रिवर्ट किए गए हैं। ऑटोमेटिक सिगनलिंग का ठीक यही परिणाम पॉइंट्समैन के ऊपर हुआ है। मित्शा मशीन, जो आप ला रहे हैं, उसके कारण क्लास फोर के गैंगमैनों की बड़ी संख्या में छँटनी हो रही है। यह जो बस इंजन ओनली सिस्टम, जो छोटे सेक्शनों पर चल रहा है, उसके कारण ए.एस.एम. कॉमर्शियल क्लर्क्स वगैरह सरप्लस हो रहे हैं और होंगे। फिर जो नया पेमेंट का प्रोसीजर है, उसके कारण आप क्लर्क्स की संख्या भी घटा रहे हैं।

इंसेंटिव स्कीम लाने के कारण वर्कशॉप में हजारों पोस्ट पहले ही सरप्लस घोषित हो चुके हैं और यह जो सरप्लस स्टाफ है, इसको दूसरी तरफ एबजॉर्ब भी किया जाता है तो उनकी जो सीनियरिटी है, ग्रेड है, उनका प्रोटेक्शन ऑफ पे है, यह सारा देखा नहीं जाता और इसके कारण घोर असंतोष फैल रहा है इसी के कारण कई आर्टिजन और सुपरवाइजर्स की तरक्की रुक गई है। एकाउंट्स डिपार्टमेंट में आप जो सिंपलीफिकेशन और मेकैनाइजेशन लाए हैं, उसके कारण भी सरप्लस स्टाफ की संख्या बढ़ रही है। फिर ऑटोमेशन है, अत: मैं समझता हूँ कि उसके विरोध में बहुत विस्तृत वर्णन करना चाहिए, किंतु संक्षेप में कहना हो तो कहूँगा कि ऑटोमेशन के कारण एक तरफ तो बहुत बड़ी संख्या में छँटनी होगी और दूसरी ओर हमारे औद्योगिक प्रगति की आज की जो अवस्था है, उस अवस्था में हम ऑटोमेशन के फलस्वरूप आने वाले कंप्यूटर्स का फुल्लेस्ट यूटिलाइजेशन भी नहीं कर सकते और इसके कारण दूसरे देश के आर्थिक साम्राज्य के चंगुल में भी फँस जाएँगे। खैर, वह तीसरा कंसीडरेशन अलग है, लेकिन यह निश्चित है कि इसके कारण बहुत बड़ी संख्या में और छँटनी होने वाली है। जो अच्छी, एडवांस्ड कंट्रीज हैं, उन्हें भी ऑटोमेशन का डोज बरदाश्त नहीं हो रहा है। अत: हमें कहाँ तक इसे स्वीकार करना चाहिए, इस पर गंभीरता से पुनर्विचार करने की आवश्यकता है।

अब इकोनॉमी के नाम पर ये सारी बातें की जाती हैं। क्लास थ्री और क्लास फोर के कर्मचारियों की छँटनी इकोनॉमी के लिए होती है, लेकिन इधर क्लास वन के ऑफिसर की संख्या बढ़ाई जाती है और इस दृष्टि से जहाँ-जहाँ इकोनॉमी के लिए गुंजाइश है, वहाँ इकोनॉमी नहीं की जाती, जैसे कि कंस्ट्रक्शन के बारे में है, इंडिज ऐंड वेगन यूसेज के बारे में, लाइन कैपेसिटी के बारे में है, स्टोर्स की यूटिलाइजेशन के बारे में है कि वहाँ काफी वेस्टेज होता है और उधर ध्यान नहीं दिया जाता। तो, मैं तो यह कहूँगा कि जहाँ क्लास थ्री और क्लास फोर स्टाफ की छँटनी करते हैं, वहाँ जबरदस्ती क्लास वन और क्लास टू ऑफिसर्स की संख्या बढ़ाने की क्या आवश्यकता है ? यदि वास्तव में रेशनलाइजेशन करना है तो हम सुझाव दे सकते हैं कि बड़ी तनख्वाह पाने वाले अफसरों की भी बराबर छँटनी होनी चाहिए और उनको भी कहीं दूसरी जगह एब्जॉर्ब करना चाहिए। वैसे हम तो बहुत से उदाहरण दे सकते हैं, लेकिन एक उदाहरण देता हूँ—जैसे ए.डी.जी.एम. की पोस्ट है, उसका काम एकोमोडेशन का है, वह जनरल मैनेजर के असिस्टेंट सेक्रेटरी के जिम्मे दें तो वे बराबर काम कर सकते हैं। इसी तरह से हेडक्वार्टर्स में ऑफिस सुपरिंटेंडेंट और असिस्टेंट सेक्रेटरी का

काम इकट्ठा किया जा सकता है। इसी तरह विजिलेंस में कई उच्च-अधिकारियों को कम करने से एफिशियंसी कम नहीं होगी। तो इस तरह से जहाँ क्लास थ्री और क्लास फोर की छँटनी का विचार कर रहे हैं, वहाँ क्लास वन के आफिसर्स के लिए भी विचार करें। जो वेस्टेज हो रहा है, उसको रोकें और यह भी सोच लें कि किसी भी देश की अर्थनीति में जहाँ हम कैपिटल फॉर्मेशन की बात कहते हैं, वहाँ कैपिटल की परिभाषा में न केवल मनी ऐंड मैटीरियल, मशीन ऐंड मैटीरियल ही आती है बल्कि जो हमारी मैन-पावर है, वह भी कैपिटल है और उसकी फुल्लेस्ट यूटिलिटी होनी चाहिए। यह विचार करें तो हम लोगों को कुछ अलग नीति अपनानी पड़ेगी, यह स्पष्ट है।

फिर यह निवेदन है कि जिनको आप सरप्लस घोषित करते हैं, उनको दूसरी जगह एब्जॉर्ब तो करते हैं, उनको दूसरी ओर ले जाते हैं, लेकिन होता यह है कि एक तो उसको रिवर्ट किया जाता है और उसका प्रमोशन ब्लॉक्ड हो जाता है, जहाँ उसका जो पुराना कौशल-स्किल थी, उसका उपयोग नहीं हो पाता और नए काम के लिए जो आवश्यक स्किल है, उसके लिए उसको ट्रेनिंग नहीं दी जाती। तो इस तरह की बातें भी खयाल में रखने की आवश्यकता है।

फिर हम यह बताएँगे कि जहाँ एक ओर इकोनॉमी के नाम पर छँटनी हो रही है, वहाँ आश्चर्य की बात है कि दूसरी ओर लोगों के काम का बोनस भी बढ़ रहा है। 1951 ई. के फेडरल फाइनेंशियल इंटीग्रेशन के पश्चात् आज तक रूट किलोमीट्रेज, नंबर ऑफ गुड्स ऐंड पैसेंजर ट्रेंस, वॉल्यूम ऑफ गुड्स ऐंड पैसेंजर ट्रैफिक ऐंड रोलिंग स्टॉक, इन सबमें कई गुना वृद्धि हुई है, किंतु उस मात्रा में कर्मचारियों पर काम का बोझ बढ़ गया है। जो ड्यूटी रोस्टर है, उनमें ऑवर्स ऑफ इंप्लायमेंट रेगुलेशन के अनुसार कुछ नहीं चलता है और विभिन्न ऑपरेशंस के लिए जो टाइम शेड्यूल निश्चित किया गया है, वह भी बहुत पुराना है। 30 साल का पुराना है और अब बीस गुना ज्यादा ट्रैफिक बढ़ गया है। इसके कारण अगर पुराने ट्रैफिक शेड्यूल के मुताबिक बराबर काम हो तो 24 घंटे भी रेल का काम नहीं चल पाए। अगर वर्क टू रूल्स प्रोग्राम आ जाए तो किसी भी कैटेगरी में काम नहीं हो पाए और रेलवे को बहुत अधिक धक्का पहुँचे। वास्तव में आनंद होता है कि कर्मचारी बेचारे ऐसा नहीं करते। यों एकॉर्डिंग टू रूल्स वे करें "This should be a matter of satisfaction. But they are working." तो ये जो टाइम शेड्यूल रूल्स हैं, ये बड़े डिफेक्टिव हैं। तो इस दृष्टि से भी इन सब बातों को देखते हुए और बढ़ते हुए ट्रैफिक को खयाल में रखते हुए इसमें कुछ परिवर्तन करने की आवश्यकता है। खासकर यह देखने की आवश्यकता है कि काम का बोझ ज्यादा न पड़े। रेलवे को आर्थिक दृष्टि से भी नुकसान होता है।

The Deputy Chairman: You have taken twenty minutes.

D. Thengadi: Three, four minutes more.

A.D. Mani:[161] He is making very good points.

दत्तोपंत ठेंगड़ी : रेलवे को भी नुकसान होता है, जैसे कि मैं कहूँगा कि क्लेम्स के बारे में है। पहली बात तो मैं यह स्पष्ट करना चाहता हूँ कि गुड्स ट्रैफिक के बारे में रेलवे और रोड के कंपिटिशन को यह समझकर विचार किया जाता है कि यह ठीक नहीं, तो वह हमारे लिए घातक होगा। रेल, रोड और इनलैंड वॉटर ट्रांसपोर्ट—इन तीनों का कोऑर्डिनेशन किस तरह हो सकता है,

161. A.D. Mani (1910-1978) – Independent Member of Rajya Sabha from Madhya Pradesh for two terms, 1960 to 1966 and 1966 to 1972, was also managing editor of *Hitavadi*.

इसकी कुछ प्रक्रिया होनी चाहिए, क्योंकि जब तक यह कंपिटिशन है, तब तक और अच्छा है। मैं यह सोचता हूँ। हमारे सम्मानित मंत्री महोदय ने कहा कि रोड से बहुत ट्रैफिक इधर डाइवर्ट किया है, बड़े आनंद की बात है, लेकिन यह इससे भी इफेक्टिव हो सकता है कि हम दूसरी तरफ भी ध्यान दें। जैसे हम देखें कि क्लेम्स आफिस में, जो आज नहीं के बराबर होता है, जो वहाँ विलंब होता है, उस वजह से भी रेलवे का रोड की ओर बहुत ट्रैफिक जाता है। ऐसे कई ऑफिसेज हैं, कंपेनसेशन क्लेम्स ऑफिसेज हैं, जहाँ के सुपरिंटेंडेंट्स ने, चीफ कॉमर्शियल सुपरिटेंडेंट्स ने कई बार माँग की है कि यहाँ नई पोस्टों की भरती होनी चाहिए। उदाहरण के लिए, मैं यहाँ की एक बात कहूँगा कि कश्मीरी गेट कंपेनसेशन क्लेम्स ऑफिस में 72 पोस्ट सेंक्शन हो गई। इनको कई साल हो गए, पर अभी तक इनकी भरती नहीं हुई। इसके कारण यहाँ इनएफिशिएंसी आ जाती है और डिले हो जाती है। फिर एक जो नई पद्धति इंट्रोड्यूस की है, ऑफ्टर सेल्स सर्विस टू सेलेक्टेड कस्टमर्स। इसके अंतर्गत यह कहा गया है कि जो पार्टीज मार्केटिंग और सेल्स ऑर्गेनाइजेशन जो आपका है, इसके द्वारा मिनिमम गुड्स ट्रैफिक की गारंटी देंगी। उनके क्लेम्स तुरंत किए जाएँगे। अब अवश्य ही इसमें रेलवे का ज्यादा खर्चा आएगा। लेकिन इतना ही किया जाए कि जो पोस्ट खाली हैं, यदि मात्र उनको भरा जाए तो कम खर्चा आएगा और इससे ज्यादा लोगों को काम मिलेगा, साथ-ही-साथ आपका काम भी अविलंब हो जाएगा। तो इस तरह से जो काम का बोझ पड़ता है, उसके बारे में कोई रेशनल एटीट्यूड लेने की, रेशनल व्यू लेने की आवश्यकता है और यह भी देखना है कि रेलवे को नुकसान भी न हो। अत: यह हम चाहते हैं।

अब सबसे इंपोर्टेंट प्रॉब्लम जो है, वह क्वार्टर्स की है। हम जानते हैं कि एक तो क्वार्टर की रिपेयरिंग क्लास थी, पर फोर स्टाफ की होती नहीं और दूसरी ओर क्लास वन के क्वार्टर की रिपेयर पर काफी खर्च किया जाता है। खैर, हम यहाँ उसकी शिकायत नहीं करेंगे, लेकिन क्वार्टर्स के बारे में कोई एक अच्छी व्यवस्था होनी चाहिए। हम चाहेंगे कि जिस तरह से सी.पी.डब्ल्यू.डी.[162] में (That is Central Estate Office) में यह पद्धति है कि डेट ऑफ एपॉइंटमेंट से ही कर्मचारियों का क्लेम क्वार्टर के लिए रजिस्टर होता है, लेकिन रेलवे में डेट ऑफ दि एप्लीकेशन से क्लेम रजिस्टर होता है, इस कारण से जिनका ट्रांसफर हो जाता है, उन्हें काफी नुकसान होता है। तो ऐसे ट्रांसफर होने वाले कर्मचारियों की डेट ऑफ एपॉइंटमेंट से रजिस्ट्री क्वार्टर के लिए होने चाहिए और सभी केंद्रीय कर्मचारियों के लिए यह बात होनी चाहिए। यह सिर्फ रेलवे की ही बात नहीं है। क्वार्टर्स की दृष्टि से सबका एक ही कॉमन पूल हो सके, एक ही कॉमन एजेंसी हो सके और एक ही कॉमन प्रोसीजर हो सके तो मैं समझ सकता हूँ कि उसके कारण सबके साथ एक न्याय हो है।

मैं एक छोटी-सी बात बताकर समाप्त कर दूँगा। मैं आपको यह बताना चाहता हूँ कि दक्षिण-मध्य रेलवे के नाम से जो एक नए जोन का निर्माण हुआ है, उसकी कई प्रॉब्लम्स हैं और उसकी ओर विशेष रूप से ध्यान देना होगा। इसमें ऑप्टीज का झमेला खड़ा हुआ है, जिसे मंत्री महोदय अच्छी तरह से जानते हैं। जोनल और डिवीजनल ऑफिस में स्थान की कमी है, पोस्टिंग ऐंड प्रमोशन के बारे में इरैगुलरिटीज की शिकायतें हैं। रेलवे बोर्ड का जो पत्रक है (नं. 621 डी.एस. डी.ए. डेटेड 6-12-1966), उसको मैं पढ़ना नहीं चाहता हूँ, क्योंकि समय नहीं है; लेकिन इतना

162. Central Public Works Department.

बताना चाहता हूँ कि वहाँ उसको इम्प्लीमेंट नहीं किया गया है। तो मैं आपको यह जानकारी कराना चाहता हूँ। फिर वहाँ क्वार्टर्स के सब जगह निर्माण करने की आवश्यकता है। फिर एम.एस. रेलवे की सेवा की शर्त के बारे में जिन कर्मचारियों को लिया या उनके प्रमोशंस के बारे में और रिवाइज्ड पे स्केल्स वगैरह के बारे में कठिनाई है तो इन सब पर ध्यान देने की आवश्यकता है।

अब आम हड़ताल के फलस्वरूप डिसमिस होनेवाले कर्मचारियों को दूसरी जगह काम पर लगाया गया और कई कर्मचारियों को नहीं लिया गया तथा सस्पेंड किए हुए कर्मचारियों का सस्पेंशन पीरियड रेगुलराइज नहीं किया गया, तो यह भी तुरंत करने की आवश्यकता है।

तीसरी बात, रेलवे के हित की दृष्टि से भी कहना चाहता हूँ कि लालगुड़ा वर्कशॉप का विस्तार होना चाहिए, सिकंदराबाद रेलवे प्रिंटिंग प्रेस का भी विस्तार होना चाहिए, बॉक्स वैगन इस्टैब्लिशमेंट का वहाँ पुनर्निर्माण होना चाहिए, क्योंकि इस प्रकार के वैगन्स की माँग हंगरी और साउथ कोरिया में ज्यादा बढ़ी है। यही नया जोन होने के कारण इसकी सुविधा के बारे में भी विशेष रूप से विचार होना चाहिए। विशेष मैं केवल एक ही प्रार्थना करता हुआ··· (interruptions)

ए.सी. गिल्बर्ट:[163] डेफिसिट दूर करने के बारे में आपने नहीं बताया?

विपुल कुमार मन्नालालजी चौराड़िया:[164] चेंबर में मिलिए।

दत्तोपंत ठेंगड़ी: आखिर में मैं मंत्रीजी से इतनी ही प्रार्थना करूँगा कि आनेवाले समय में हम यह देखना चाहते हैं कि रेलवे का कारोबार मंत्री महोदय की इच्छा के और डिस्कशन के अनुसार चलता है, न कि रेलवे बोर्ड के ब्यूरोक्रेट्स के अनुसार। इतना ही हमें एश्योरेंस मिलेगा तो भी··· कुछ कार्य हुआ है, ऐसा हम मानेंगे।

The Appropriation (Railways) No. 5 Bill, 1968 and The Appropriation (Railways) No. 6 Bill, 1968[165]

Need to Set up an Autonomous Corporation Replacing Railway Board

I could not appreciate the procedure as followed by the Railway Ministry in suggesting that only after the Planning Commission has indicated its quantum of money to be allotted for construction of new lines, the ministry will be in a position to determine which new lines are to be taken up. I think, madam, this is putting the cart before the horse. As a matter of fact, the Railway Ministry ought to make up its own mind about its plan and then place it before the Planning Commission and press for its implementation. Unless this method is adopted, the construction of new Railway lines is bound to suffer adversely. Secondly, madam, the

163. Albert C. Gilbert (1908-1990) – Congress member of Rajya Sabha from Uttar Pradesh, 1960 to 1964 and 1964 to 1970; Died.
164. Vimalkumar Mannalalji Chordia (1924-) – Jana Sangh member of Rajya Sabha from Madhya Pradesh, member, Madhya Bharat Legislative Assembly, 1952-57, Madhya Pradesh Legislative Assembly, 1957-62 and member, Rajya Sabha, 1962-1968; was also vice-president, Madhya Pradesh Jana Sangh.
165. *Rajya Sabha Debate* dated 19th December, 1968.

surveys that are taken so often are not really profitable. I do not mean that after every survey, there must be construction. That cannot be. That I can understand. But more often than not, these surveys are not followed up by any construction work. I think the government must reconsider the method in which this survey has to be undertaken.

Regarding the staff side, I think if this staff side is handled properly, probably the Railway Ministry will not have to come forward with demands for additional sums. For example, now more than 4,500 Railway employees are being proceeded against and victimised. This litigation is bound to cost a lot. If all these cases are withdrawn, I think a lot can be saved. There is no point in victimising those who have gone only on a token strike. That apart, it seems that the government is not earnest either about the efficiency or economy of the Railway administration, otherwise, it would not have taken so long, that is 21 years, either to revise the time schedule for different operations which have become obsolete, or to revise the pay scales through the appointment of a separate Wage Board for the Railway employees or reassess their workload and evaluate all the various jobs on Railway and abolish finally the Railway Board which is only a bureaucratic apparatus without efficiency and set up an autonomous corporation for Railways. Since all these things have not been done for the last 21 years, one is justified in suspecting that the government is not very earnest either about the efficiency or the economy of the administration. I take this opportunity of suggesting and appealing to the hon'ble minister that all these measures should be taken and adopted without delay, and if this is done and particularly if the labour force is kept contented for which now the government has an opportunity of showing a gesture of goodwill by withdrawing all the cases and also saving a lot, which it will have to spend on litigation, I think next time it will not have to come forward with a fresh demand for additional grants.

The Budget (Railways), 1969-70[166]

Railways Using Wrong Strategy in the Name of Economy

D. Thengadi: I will confine myself to a few remarks about the plight of Railway employees. Recently, the Railway Board ordered upgradation of certain Class I posts which carried certain grades of pay; such upgradation carrying with it better scale of pay. It would cost an additional expenditure of Rs. 12 lakhs. But nothing is being done for Class III and Class IV staff. The

166. *Rajya Sabha Debate* dated 12th March, 1969.

former Railway Minister, Mr. Poonacha, had instructed that 10 per cent upgradation in the Class III categories of Railway staff should be finalised by the end of January 1969. The Railway Board is delaying action in the matter. The Railway Board is anxious to remove stagnation of promotions of Class I officers, but it is unmindful of the stagnation of Class III staff.

The total number of gazetted posts of Railways in 1966-67 was about 6,000; it is 7,000 in 1967-68. The number of non-gazetted staff was about 13,63,000 in 1966-67; in 1967-68, it was 13,55,000. The Efficiency Bureau of the Railway Board examines the question of economy. But this bureau suggests economic measures in a very perverse manner.

The benefits accruing to Railway employees because of the merger of Dearness Allowance with basic pay, as given effect to from 1st December, 1968, would give the employees only nominal benefits. Fulfilment of their long-standing demand for a separate Wage Board for a scientific revision of pay scales, workloads and promotional prospects will only keep them satisfied, not this patch-work, because in this merger, employees in certain pay ranges will actually suffer a reduction in their total emoluments. Those in the pay ranges between Rs. 390 and Rs. 490 – who were getting, prior to the merger, 15 per cent of their basic pay as house rent allowance, have not only lost it; also, even if they produced rent receipts, they have to bear 10 per cent, of their basic pay plus Dearness Allowance, which amounts to Rs. 50 and Rs. 70 per month. The orders should be suitably revised.

The New Year gift promised to Class III employees by the former Railway Minister should be announced and similar benefits extended to Class IV employees. Then there is urgent need to expand cadres in different departments to give the much-needed fillip to the Railway working and to bring about greater spurt in its earnings. The tendency of the Railway Board to curtail Class III and Class IV posts while increasing Class I and Class II posts should be stopped forthwith. The Railway Board, which never cared for implementation of Class IV Employees' Promotion Committee's Recommendations, exhibited unseemly haste increasing the pay scales and promotional prospects of Class I officers. An unbridgeable hiatus is now being developed between Class I and Class II officers on one side, and Class III and Class IV staff, on the other, between the higher class and the lower class. The tendency on the part of higher officials to circumvent rules and procedures is on the increase. Ostentatious living on the part of high officials in the form of salons, air-conditioned chambers and expensive accommodation should be curbed.

Staff becoming surplus due to introduction of modernisation programmes should be suitably readjusted without affecting adversely their senior grades, etc. Unified grades for accountants, stock verifiers and TIAs[167] in Accounts Department, and running grades for ministerial staff should be introduced. The special allowance given to machine operators and comptists should be increased. Typists should be given special allowance. A stenographer should not be attached to more than one officer. Console operators to work on computers should be drawn from the Statistical Department; qualification restrictions should be done away with. The condition of the broad-gauge goods brake vans should be improved so that the health of the broad-gauge guards might not be impaired. Incentive bonus should be given to Chargemen 'A' in mechanical workshops. Foremen and assistant foremen in workshops should be given special pay on par with their counterparts in production units. A higher percentage of posts should be reserved for unskilled staff for promotion to semi-skilled and skilled grades in workshops, loco sheds, TXR[168] and other departments. Ticket-checking staff should be treated as Running Staff. All staff at wayside stations should invariably be provided with quarters. Mobile medical units should be introduced on Railways. Corrupt practices in payments to staff should be stopped. The rules governing reimbursement of school tuition fee should be suitably relaxed to ensure full reimbursement in respect of children studying in government-aided and unaided schools. The system of casual labour and contract labour should be abolished, and till such time as it is abolished, in all Class IV recruitments, casual labour should be given priority. Recognition of unions should not be on political considerations. The Joint Consultative Machinery should be constituted with representatives elected by staff through secret ballot. Recognition of unions must be through secret ballot by those who are members of one union or the other.

The work of the Wanchoo Commission,[169] going into Railway accidents, should not go the way of the Kunzru Committee[170] whose recommendations are not in the least heeded to or implemented by the government.

---

167. Travelling Inspector of Station Accounts.

168. Train Examining Department.

169. Railway Accidents Inquiry Committee 1968 headed by K.N. Wanchoo.

170. Railway Accidents Committee 1962 headed by Hridaya Nath Kunzru.

The safety organisation, machinery and equipment on Railways should be subjected to a periodical review by a Parliamentary Committee. Railwaymen's representatives should invariably be associated with all Committees and commissions regarding Railways. The Payment of Bonus Act, 1963[171] should be extended to Railwaymen, and interest on their Provident Fund holdings should be brought on par with the bank rate.

I want to specifically mention the fact that the recent relaxation or liberalisation regarding Section 4 of the Essential Services (Maintenance) Ordinance[172] has not been implemented in a number of places. In particular, I want to draw attention to the cases on the Olavakkot Division of the Southern Railway where those suspended under Section 4 are still continuing to be under suspension. This should be immediately rectified.

Pension rules should be liberalised and employees retired after 1st May, 1968 but before 31st December, 1968, should be allowed to opt for pension. Class IV employees should be treated at par with Class III for purposes of complimentary passes after retirement, and employees' privilege of free travel in two-tier and three-tier bogies should be restored.

Recognition to unions whose recognition was withdrawn in the wake of the strike must be restored and also the M.R.K. Sangh, which deserves recognition on the basis of the criteria laid down in that regard, must be recognised without delay.

The Personnel Departments on the Railways should be decentralised for promptly dealing with staff matters.

Quarters to Railway staff should be provided on a large scale in big cities. Option to avail CGHS services should be allowed to Railway employees wherever it is feasible. Non-matriculate steam-side senior drivers and firemen should be sent for training in dieselisation and given promotions according to their original seniority.

The strikers in Delhi should be treated at par with the strikers in other parts of the country. Cases against Railway employees under Section 188 should be dropped and employees convicted under Section 4 of ESO and Section 188 of IPC should be allowed to join duty.

I am sorry that the government is using wrong strategy in the name of economy. As a matter of fact, there is scope for reduction, substantial

171. Act of Parliament to provide for the annual payment of bonus to employees of certain establishments (including factories and establishments employing 20 or more persons).

172. The Essential Services Maintenance (ESMA) – Act of Parliament to ensure the delivery of services, which if obstructed would affect the normal life of the people.

reduction, in the posts of Class I officials. For example, there are many gazetted posts, such as vigilance officers, in different zones. First of all, their number can be reduced without affecting efficiency and, secondly, I should like to suggest that in every zone, only those who are not employees of that particular zone should be appointed as vigilance officers. Otherwise, if they are employees of the same zone, they would not be in a position to carry out their work efficiently.

Lastly, I am sorry that in spite of all our arguments, the government has not thought it wise to abolish the Railway Board. As a matter of fact, the Railway Board has proved itself thoroughly incompetent to handle the job and, therefore, I should like to suggest that the Railway Board should be thrown out lock, stock and barrel and an autonomous corporation should be set up and the Board of Management of that autonomous corporation should comprise of representatives of passengers, commercial interests, Railway employees and Parliament.

Appropriation (Railways) Vote on Account Bill, 1971: Motion for Consideration and Appropriation (Railways) Bill, 1971[173]

Creation of a Special Cell in the Pay Commission for the Railway Employees

D. Thengadi: This year our Rashtrapati in his address to the joint session has laid particular stress on maintenance of industrial peace which is very much relevant so far as the biggest public undertaking of our land, that is the Railways, is concerned. For this purpose, it is necessary that the administration should scrupulously observe certain norms and standards in their dealings with the employees. For example, our friend Lokanath Misra had rightly pointed out the miserable plight of the casual labour. The process of de-casualisation or regularisation of casual labour has not been followed in the Railways properly. Similarly, the rules regarding confirmation have not yet been strictly adhered to so that we find hundreds of thousands of employees are continuing as temporary workers for 10 years or 15 years. So, the rules of confirmation must be strictly adhered to. Even today, the contract labour system is not completely abolished in the Railways, though the Government of India itself has expressed, through a Bill, its opposition to the continuance of the contract labour system. Again, there is much hard bickering amongst the employers because no firm and scientific promotion policy has been evolved and followed, and so far as

173. *Rajya Sabha Debate* dated 27th March, 1971.

transfers are concerned, the measures are taken arbitrarily according to the sweet will of the officials.

Very often it is said that the Railway employees are not given the quantum of work they are expected to perform, but on the other hand, there is also a complaint by workers that the workload has increased. I suggest that the Railway Ministry should introduce productivity indices so that hard bickering on this score will be removed.

The most important thing of all is naturally about the remuneration of the workers. Gulzarilal Nanda, when approached, had assured the employees that at least a separate cell would be created within the body of the Pay Commission exclusively for catering justice to the Railway employees when their demand for a separate Wage Board was rejected. I request Mr. Hanumanthaiya[174] to fulfil the promise of his predecessor so that a separate cell should be created, and when such a cell is created, at least one representative of the Railway employees should be included in the personnel of such a cell, and the government should prescribe a time-limit for the completion of the work either of the cell so constituted, if it is constituted, or of the Pay Commission. If a time-limit is not prescribed, probably by the time the work of the Pay Commission is completed, the prices would have spiralled up and whatever concession is granted will not do justice to the workers. Similarly, the government should come forward with a firm commitment that (1) the demand for need-based minimum wage would be considered; (2) that the real wage would be protected; and (3) that the recommendations of the Pay Commission or the cell would be implemented in consultation with the representatives of the employees within the Joint Consultation Machinery. Again I think an enlightened minister like Mr. Hanumanthaiya would agree with me that the terms of reference for the Pay Commission should be modified in the interests of justice. It is true that the capacity to pay of the employer should be taken into consideration. Today, the Pay Commission is required to take into account the capacity not only of the Central Government but of the state

174. K. Hanumanthaiya (1908-1980) – freedom fighter, Congress leader, member of the Constituent Assembly, member of the 3rd, 4th and 5th Lok Sabha, accomplished parliamentarian, second Chief Minister of Mysore state, leader who unified Karnataka, built the uniquely designed Vidhan Soudha – Legislative Assembly building – in Bangalore, was deputy leader of the Congress Party in Parliament, Minister of Law and Social Welfare, Minister of Railways. In 1964 when Parliament debated for three months the abrogation of Article 370, Hanumanthaiya strongly spoke in favour of abrogating Article 370. Was also the Chairman of the Vivekananda Rock Memorial Committee for Mysore State.

governments, the public undertakings and the local self-governing bodies, and all that. I think this is irrelevant. The capacity of the employer only should be taken into consideration and appropriate modification should be insisted upon by our enlightened minister.

Again, so far as the colonies of the Railway employees are concerned, it is necessary to pay more attention to the cleanliness and other requirements of these colonies. For example, recently, I visited the Kishanganj Railway Colony and I was surprised to find that even the basic human requirements that they had insisted upon were not being fulfilled. I request that all these colonies should be paid particular attention, and basic human needs of the residents should be fulfilled.

Our friend, Gulab Rao Patil[175] has referred to the problem of reservation of posts for the Scheduled Castes and the Scheduled Tribes. I would like to suggest that mere reservation would not suffice. Apart from reservation or alongwith reservation, special training classes or refresher courses should be conducted for the candidates from the Scheduled Castes and the Scheduled Tribes so that they can be on par with the other candidates.

The system of publishing statistics of the ticketless travellers is really very ridiculous. It is not possible to have real statistics of the ticketless travellers because the statistics that you are publishing only indicate the number of travellers who are caught and from whom money has already been realised. So, I think this practice should be totally stopped.

The Claims Office should be re-organised so as to make it more efficient.

The hon'ble minister has spoken of coordination between the Railway system and road transport. If coordination among Railway, road, inland water transport and air service is taken into consideration, it would be increasing our efficiency and also economy.

So far as the administration is concerned, it is necessary to reduce the number of Class I and Class II officials and also to reduce their remuneration. Much of the staff in Class I and Class II is superficial and superfluous. Their number and remuneration should be reduced. And at least, let the Railways take the initiative in introducing the ratio between the minimum and maximum pay scales which should not exceed 1:10 so

175. Gulabrao R. Patil (1921-1989) – Congress leader from Maharashtra, was a leading figure in the state's cooperative movement, was president of the Maharashtra Congress and served two terms in the Rajya Sabha from 1966-1972, 1972-1978.

that the minimum and the maximum should be within the ratio of 1:10. Let the Railway Administration take the initiative in this respect.

One more suggestion. For the sake of the administration, it is necessary to decentralise power or to decentralise the decision-making authority, to delegate that authority at the lower level. And as we have said, so long as the present structure of the Railway Board continues, it is not possible either to have economy or efficiency or justice to the employees and the passengers. The Railway Board should be scrapped and it should be replaced by an autonomous corporation, the Board of Management, which should comprise the representatives of passengers, commercial interests, Parliament and Railway employees, if such an autonomous corporation is set up, it would be possible to do justice to all the concerned parties.

One more suggestion I would like to make and I will conclude my speech. It would be worthwhile to study whether the entire administrative set-up of the Railways cannot be altered profitably. For example, there are 13 different trades. It is worthwhile to examine whether all these or some of them can be converted into autonomous enterprises and whether such a conversion of the different trades into autonomous enterprises would not be conducive to economy and efficiency. In Yugoslavia, particularly, this experiment of carving out different enterprises out of the Railway system has been tried and it is reported – I do not know about the authenticity or veracity of it – that it has helped their economy and efficiency. I think it is worthwhile for some committee or commission to go through the problem of the administrative set-up and to find out the desirability or otherwise of splitting up the Railway administration into autonomous enterprises.

Railways (Employment of Members of the Armed Forces) Bill, 1965[176]

Smooth Functioning of the Railways

D. Thengadi: I am aware of the fact that this Bill does not mean, even by implication, that our Railway employees have failed, so far, in carrying out their duties during the national emergency. As a matter of fact, the entire nation has congratulated our Railway employees on their dutifulness, discipline and even risking their lives for the sake of the motherland. The present Bill is non-controversial. I welcome particularly Clause 2 of the Bill which says that it extends to the whole of India, which means that it includes Jammu & Kashmir also. If I am right, probably this is the first Bill

176. *Rajya Sabha Debate* dated 24th November, 1965.

of this type and I congratulate the hon'ble minister on this gesture. I urge that all subsequent measures that will be introduced in this House should follow this pattern.

Whenever Armed Forces are inducted for the assistance of the Railway Administration, it becomes necessary that they should be given protection under the Indian Railways Act of 1890. Otherwise, they will not be able to perform their duties in an efficient way, to handle Railway property or to give instructions. Actually, this is not doing the Armed Forces any favour. Their very efficiency requires that the protection under the Railways Act of 1890 should be extended to them. Clause 3 of the Bill thus removes the main handicap in the way of our Armed Forces fulfilling their responsibility. While protection under the Railways Act of 1890 is extended to the Armed Forces, there is a proviso that so far as Chapter VIA is concerned, it does not apply to them. Now, this chapter deals with hours of work and periods of rest. This is also proper. The Armed Forces would be required to assist the Railway Administration only during periods of emergency and during such periods, it would not be possible to abide by the hours of employment and periods of rest according to the Railways Act.

It is also in the fitness of things that so far as the discipline and control of the armed personnel are concerned, the Railways Act should not apply to them. Otherwise, there would arise administrative difficulties, both for the Railways and the Defence Ministry. It is also quite understandable that the Army would be required to take over certain sections of the Railway only under emergency conditions. The Railways Act, which is meant for normal times, would be unworkable during such emergency. Only the Army Act should be applicable to Army personnel so inducted. Emergency conditions would necessitate emergency measures.

We are already in conflict with Pakistan and the so-called 'cease-fire' is only a 'decrease-fire', and that, too, only from our side. The emergency persists and the possibility of an armed conflict with both Pakistan and China cannot be ruled out. As has been said, hope for the best, but prepare for the worst. The provisions of this Bill are essential for our national security. During the last emergency, some Territorial Army troops were inducted into the Railway Administration, but in the conflict to come, it may be necessary for us to send even the regular Army units to assist the Railways, to transport troops, patients, goods and equipment. In view of this fact, the Bill was already overdue. In fact, the Bill is clothing in legal terminology much of what is being already done in practice.

There are certain points which are not very clear to me. It has been said that they are exempted from the operation of Chapter VIA of the Railways Act. As a matter of fact, when I went thoroughly through the Act, I found that Chapter VIA was the only chapter which gave any protection whatsoever to the Railway employees. To say that they are exempted from this provision, though I have no quarrel with the exemption, would mean that no particular protection is available to them through the extension of the Railways Act. Now, in Chapter VIA itself, there are certain categories that are excluded from the limitation of hours of employment, that is, "armed guards or other personnel subject to discipline similar to that of the Armed Police Forces". In the Railways Act, another exemption is made under Section 71(4):

"Temporary exemptions may be made in any emergency which could not have been foreseen or prevented."

Therefore, it would have been possible for us to take shelter under this particular section and make appropriate amendments to the Railways Act itself instead of introducing a new piece of legislation. That is my impression and I should like the hon'ble minister to throw some light on the technical aspects of this problem.

Again, we are thinking of the Armed Forces running or taking charge of the Railways, but there is one more aspect. Today nearly 17,000 Railway men are in the Territorial Army. It is reported that during the recent war, [1965 India-Pakistan war] in a number of places in Punjab, nearly one thousand Railwaymen, who were in the Territorial Army, were sent on active service to man the Railway installations and assist in running the Railways. I feel that Railway employees, who have undergone military training, should be given priority whenever there arises any occasion for the Armed Forces to run the Railways.

Even as we are thinking of the Armed Forces that would be required to run the Railways, we will have to give some consideration to the Armed Forces, though not within the purview of this Act. The Armed Forces which used to guard or patrol Railway lines or installations are not covered by this Bill, which comes into play only when they are employed to do the work of Railway employees. Their role is also certainly very important. In view of the national emergency, even as we have thought of and clothed in legal terminology certain provisions for the running of the Railways by the Armed Forces, we cannot ignore the same contingency in the case of water transport and road transport. Water transport also constitutes an important part of our civil and military transport. Therefore, in the case of merchant navy also, similar provisions should be extended. According to the Navy Act, our Navy can utilise the services of the employees of the merchant navy and to that sphere also, it is necessary to extend similar provisions.

The role of road transport has been very important, particularly during the last conflict in Punjab. The employees of the road transport services and particularly the truck drivers, who in most cases were self-employed persons, have rendered splendid service to the country in the cause of national defence. It is necessary that some sort of protection should be offered to these people also, so that if water transport, road transport and Railways, all these three are given proper consideration and the employees thereunder are given adequate protection, it would be possible for us to inspire confidence and also to ensure the smooth functioning of all the three forms of transport and, thus, augment our defence effort.

Discussion Under Rule 176 Regarding Reported Harassment, Victimisation, etc. of Railway Employees for Participation in Recent Strike[177]

Employees Deprived of their Trade Union Rights

D. Thengadi: Sir, before I come to the subject proper, I must make one clarification. Approaching the International Transport Workers' Federation is not tantamount to seeking foreign intervention; otherwise, India's membership of the United Nations also would be treated as such. So, that misunderstanding should not be there.

Sir, you must have been amused at the bravado of some of the members on that side. All of us know that the strike was imposed upon the Railway employees, who wanted a negotiated settlement with the

177. *Rajya Sabha Debate* dated 6th August, 1974. The nationwide Railway strike called by the All India Railwaymen Federation, led by George Fernandes and others demanding an eight-hour working day and a hike in wages that had remained stagnant for years. It was the biggest and most crippling strike, which lasted for 20 days and saw participation by 17 lakh workers. The Indira Gandhi government's crackdown on the strike was brutal and Fernandes was arrested. The complete strike showed for the first time how the country's supplies could be crippled with its lifeline coming to a halt. *The New York Times* reporting on the historic strike had then observed, that "The restless mood in New Delhi was underscored in a message from prison by George Fernandes, a 44-year-old Socialist party leader and organiser of the strike. Mr. Fernandes, who is one of the more than 1,000 union leaders and Railway workers recently arrested, said: "The time for action has come. For Railwaymen it is now do or die."

Railway Ministry. We also know that there was no sabotage or violence anywhere in the country. So, the strike was nationwide and continued for 20 days – in some places it was for more than 20 days – for which the Railway employees should have been congratulated by the other side. We also know that while the Railway employees went in for industrial action, the government greeted them with semi-military operation and tried to crush them as if it was an array of China or Pakistan, and not their own brethren, flesh of their flesh and blood of their blood. And then, our friends on that side boasted here of suppressing the Railway strike as if they have suppressed a rebellion or a revolution. It is quixotic, sir, you must have heard the story of Don Quixote as you are well versed in all these things. Now, the government has said that the strike was illegal and technically they can say so...

This strike has been declared as illegal. Yesterday, I was surprised to hear from Mr. Qureshi[178] that it was illegal because the strike ballot was not taken on the demands for which the strike was launched. In the first place, this is a misrepresentation or a misunderstanding because whatever might have been said in the course of negotiations, one tiling is certain that the demands for which the strike was launched were precisely the demands for which the strike ballot was taken. That is one thing. Apart from that, I want to know whether according to the hon'ble minister, the strike would have been legal had the strike ballot been taken afresh on the same demands because, according to us, the strike became illegal as there was a notification from the President that the Railways are the essential services. And on the strength of that notification, it was declared illegal. Does the hon'ble minister mean to say that had the strike ballot been taken, notwithstanding the notification by the President, the strike would have been considered as legal? Against this background, I want to ask, can there be any occasion or any period or any circumstance under which the Railwaymen in our country would have an opportunity to stage a legal strike because, every time when there is a likelihood of a strike by the Railwaymen, some such notification by the President would be there. And, therefore, virtually the Railway employees have been deprived of their legitimate trade union rights because strike is a legitimate trade union

178. M. Shafi Qureshi (1928-2016) – Congress leader from Jammu & Kashmir, elected to the Rajya Sabha in 1965, elected to the Lok Sabha from Anantnag in 1971 and again 1977. Between 1966 and 1977 Qureshi held various portfolios as Deputy Minister Commerce, Steel and Railways, was appointed Governor of Bihar in 1991, Madhya Pradesh 1993 and Uttar Pradesh in 1996.

right. And I would like the hon'ble minister to specify the circumstances under which they will have an opportunity to stage a legal strike.

Now, I will not go into all the details of the government action during the strike. But I should like to inform the House that even after the strike was called off, victimisation is persisting. I said, and it was not contradicted by either of the Ministers, that on July 18th, the services of four lady employees of Tinsukia in Assam were terminated while there was no sabotage or violence in the vicinity. And in mid-July, the services of three members of the running staff in Kanpur were terminated. And there are reports from other places also. Sir, the hon'ble minister has given some information about victimisation. But, it is not a total picture of victimisation. He has gone on technicalities. Only the number of dismissed employees has been given by the hon'ble minister. It was 10 thousand and odd. But, sir, victimisation comprises not only dismissal but removal, termination, discharge, compulsory retirement, discontinuance without any sort of communication, etc. Now, sir, if the Members of Parliament inquire as to what is the total number of dismissed employees, they are not going into the technicality of difference between removal and termination and discharge and dismissal. They want to know the total picture of victimisation. But, standing on technicality, only the number of dismissed employees has been given, which is not only inaccurate and incomplete but misrepresents the total picture. To give one example only, in the Ajmer Division, in this month, i.e. two months after the strike is over, notices for compulsory retirement have been served on about 180 employees. Now, sir, according to rules, it is true that there can be compulsory retirement and notices can be given but I would like to know when that rule was made. Pandit Jawaharlal Nehru had assured that it would be used very sparingly and only in cases of corruption and gross inefficiency and in cases of danger to national security. But, in the case of these 180 employees, it has not been proved that either they suffered from corruption or gross inefficiency or that they constituted danger to national security. Nor even a committee for scrutinising their cases was constituted. Arbitrarily, they were served with notices for compulsory retirement, which is also as much victimisation as dismissal.

Now, the Railway Establishment code says that transfers should not be ordered by way of punishment and here, after the strike, a large number of employees have been transferred without rhyme or reason by way of punishment.

It is a convention that transfer in the same grade can be ordered normally before the academic year starts. But, after the strike, there have been large-scale transfers even before the commencement of the academic year. Even gangmen, who are normally not transferred, are being transferred. The implication of this should be properly understood. In the case of certain divisions, transfers within the same division also mean inter-state transfers. Take, for instance, Ratlam Division. It comprises areas from three States – Gujarat, Rajasthan and Madhya Pradesh So, the medium of instruction, text-books, curriculum, etc. changes. This certainly causes great hardship to the children of the employees.

Now, in the event of a transfer, the administration has to give Rs. 200 to each employee and they are giving it. This is unnecessary expenditure on the part of the administration and it is only to satisfy the personal vendetta of some of the officials. All these cases should have been gone into by the Railway Ministry.

The extent of vindictiveness can be understood by the fact that there are cases where people have been dismissed on the ground of having gone on strike while, in fact, they were arrested before the commencement of the strike. That will just give the idea as to how vindictiveness is playing its own part.

There are cases of employees who have been refused permission to occupy their quarters during the pendency of their appeals. While the appeals are pending, employees are employees and, as such, they should be allowed to occupy their residential quarters. But they are being evicted, thrown out bed and baggage, though their appeals are still pending. There are also cases where employees were thrown out. Again, they were asked, giving a latitude, to re-occupy their residences and once again they are served with notices that before I5th of August, they must quit; otherwise they will be thrown out forcibly.

We had in this House and also in the other House reported a number of cases of police atrocities. Even there was manhandling of females in Railway colonies but no enquiry has been instituted in all such atrocities which any civilised government should have done by now.

After the strike, though it has been said by the Railway Minister that the Railways, constitute one family, he is just ahead of the family of the Railway employees and now the free movement, of Railway employees which was a normal feature till the strike has been restricted. They are not allowed to move. You will be wonderstruck, sir, they are not allowed to move out of the office buildings or workshop buildings even during lunch hours. Virtually, they are prisoners during office hours. The employees were normally required to mark their attendance once in a day but they are required to mark their attendance thrice, i.e. at 10 a.m., at I3.35 hours and at 17 hours. Probably, as some psychologist said that whatever is in subconscious mind is revealed by unconscious gestures. A very significant gesture has been there in Delhi that the boundary walls of the office of the Divisional Superintendent at New Delhi have been raised, after the strike, further by six to 10 feet. Probably, they are strengthening the walls between themselves and the employees. Names of all the employees attending gate meetings are noted and reported by Railway intelligence. At Jagadhari, some employees are being chargesheeted for attending gate meetings, which is a normal trade union right.

There was no system of appealing in 1960 and 1968. Now this appeal system has been introduced. But, in appeals, it was decided, we were told, that no humiliation would be inflicted upon the employees. It was a gentleman's agreement that what is to be given in writing should be that I have been dutiful and I will continue to be dutiful; I have been loyal and I will continue to be loyal in future. But, in practice, in order to break the morale of the re-instated workers, they are compelled to write something humiliating. Those whose break-in service has been condoned after due consideration are also forced to give similar humiliating undertakings. I may say with confidence that the number of those suffering from break-in service was much higher than 2.5 lakhs when the minister declared that figure on the floor of the House. Subsequently, the officials had to hurry up the process of condoning, in order to bring down the number to 2.5 lakhs. In the process, they got this in writing from the poor employees merely as a face-saving device for themselves.

Personal venom of officials is playing havoc in appeals. The cases are rejected in spite of earlier clearance after scrutiny.

According to the policy, now 'hard core' is to be kept out, but what is 'hard core'? In a number of cases, we know, important office-bearers are being taken back while ordinary workers are kept out just to satisfy the sense of personal revenge. With whomsoever they have quarrels, officers are keeping them out and some of them are described as 'hard core', the others as blacklisted but it is just venom and nothing else.

Quite unusually the SPs and District Magistrates have been required to consult the D.S. of Railways for the purpose of finalising as to which cases should be withdrawn in spite of the fact that the group of workers is chargesheeted and, apart from FIR, earlier screening by the Departmental Security Officer and Police Department, nothing new can now be added. Even there are cases in which the entire group thus chargesheeted is categorised for being taken back and then, subsequently, a few of them have been omitted on the advice of Railway officials. For example, at Agra, two employees, Ranbir Singh and Man Singh, have been left out deliberately, while the entire group, whose members were chargesheeted together, has been taken back. Temporary staff, who can be taken back, have been deliberately kept out, describing them as casual or substitutes. In workshops or open lines, there can be no substitutes. Still they are so described and maliciously kept out. Preferential treatment to the so-called loyal workers is bound to create a permanent division among employees, which is not in the interests of the smooth running of the administration. Recently, there has been en masse upgradation of officers, while simultaneously reduction has been effected in certain categories, such as stenographers, etc. I should like to know whether the Labour Ministry has become defunct so far as Railway officials are concerned. It is not functioning in the normal way. RLCs [Regional Labour Commissioners] are not taking cognisance of the complaints of Railway employees. PNM[179] meetings are not being held and, thus, all the doors are closed. This is bound to aggravate discontent further.

It is very unfortunate and unusual that the Railway Ministry is trying to interfere in the democratic trade union movement. You will be surprised to hear that at every level, from top to bottom, the office-bearers of the recognised unions are told that they must throw out Mr. George Fernandes[180] from the presidentship of AIRF [All India Railwaymen's

179. Permanent Negotiating Machinery –aims to maintain contact with labour and to resolve disputes and differences which may arise between Railway labour and Administration.

180. George Fernandes (1930-2019) – one of the most well-known Socialist leader and trade union leaders, Fernandes entered Lok Sabha in 1967, and went on to win nine elections till 2004; firebrand trade unionist, Fernandes led the historic Railway strike in 1974; was among those leaders who challenged Indira's and Congress's hegemony; was arrested during Emergency; stood for elections from prison and won the Muzaffarpur seat from Bihar; became Industries Minister in the Janata Party government. Fernandes was Railway Minister in the short-lived V.P. Singh National Front Government; he formed the Samata Party in 1994 and allied with the BJP. Fernandes was the convenor of the National Democratic Alliance (NDA) and Defence Minister in the Vajpayee government between 1998-2004, his tenure as Defence Minister saw, among other things, India's nuclear testing in Pokhran in May 1998 and the Kargil War in 1999.

Federation]. Otherwise, victimisation will not be withdrawn. I must say that this is quite undemocratic and dictatorial. It is for the workers to decide who should be their president. Still I should like to announce here that if the legitimate demands of the workers are met, i.e. all the arrested persons are released; the victims' families are compensated; all victimisation is withdrawn; all the notices for the de-recognition of unions are withdrawn; negotiations with the NGCRS are resumed; if all these demands are conceded by the Railway Ministry, here and now Mr. George Fernandes is prepared to resign from the presidentship of AIRF. I want to know from the government whether they are prepared to concede these legitimate demands, instead of interfering like a totalitarian State in the democratic trade union rights of the Railway employees.

Decision by the Railway Unions to go on Indefinite Strike and Cancellation of a Large Number of Trains[181]

D. Thengadi: Well, I do not know whether I should congratulate our hon'ble Railway Minister for himself initiating the Railway strike more efficiently and promptly than the labour leaders. Probably, his name will go down as the first striking minister of India because by the cancellation of trains, he has himself initiated the strike but may I enquire from him whether his plea of conservation of coal is not a lame excuse because most of the trains that are cancelled are run on diesel or electricity, but not on coal. That is number one.

Secondly, he should inform us what is the composition of the negotiations table. He seems to be very earnest about a negotiated settlement. Now the very preliminary prerequisite for the success of any negotiation is the definition of the parties to the negotiation. They must be properly defined and mutually agreed upon. Here Mr. George Fernandes is asserting at the negotiations table that he is there not in his capacity as president of the AIRF but as convenor of the National Co-ordination Committee for Railwaymen's Struggle and that the representatives at the negotiations table are representing the Action Committee of the NCCRS which comprises of, apart from the All-India Railwaymen's Federation, the Bharatiya Railway Mazdoor Sangh, the All-India Railway Workers' Federation, the Confederation of Category-wise Associations, Locomen's Association and CITU [Centre of Indian Trade Unions]. Now, the workers' representatives are saying that they are the parties to the negotiation

181. *Rajya Sabha Debate* dated 26th April, 1974.

while the hon'ble minister is saying that he is not talking with the people who are representing the Action Committee. May I know – first this is the preliminary prerequisite for the success of any negotiation – whether he will accept or he is accepting the version given by the workers' representatives or under the pressure from the bureaucrats of the Railway Board who are prestige officers, whether he will allow the negotiations to break down on this unrealistic ground because you are talking with them and you are saying that you are not talking with them? This is not even gentlemanly. So, first of all, what is the composition at the negotiating table and will he allow the negotiations to break down on the unrealistic plea that you are not talking with the people for whom you are talking? That is No. 1. Secondly, regarding financial demands, we are not convinced with the figures worked out by the hon'ble minister about the additional burden. He has not informed the House and the general public that the workers' representatives have offered to enter into a public debate with the government on the adjustability of their financial demands within the framework of the existing national economy. They have suggested that there should be held a round table conference of all economic interests to formulate national policies on employment, productivity, prices and income and if such a national incomes policy is formulated, Railwaymen are quite prepared to adjust their demands within the framework of such a national incomes policy. Is the government prepared to accept this suggestion? He has not informed the House and the public about certain important figures. According to 109th report of the PAC [Public Accounts Committee of Parliament], the growth rate in the productivity of Railwaymen is 3.5 per cent annually. In 1965-66, it was 164 and in 1971-72 it is 193. It shows a 3.5 per cent steady annual growth rate in productivity by Railwaymen. The same report states that the percentage of staff cost to the total working expenses is the lowest in India. In India, it is 54.2 and in Britain it is 62. Also, the report states the staff expenses for 1,000 traffic units are 18.19 in 1971-72 in India and on the British Railways, it is 122.18. Thus, staff expenses per 1,000 traffic units are the lowest in India. He has kept the House in darkness about many such figures relating to financial demands.

Then, there are some non-financial demands by which I mean demands which are not predominantly financial, for example, extension of full-fledged trade union rights and rationalisation of working hours. What are the difficulties? Why are they standing on false prestige? Why are they adopting a stiff attitude in this regard? Again, now that we are members of the ILO, why is the government hesitating to implement the conventions of the ILO about treating Railwaymen as industrial workers?

Then, the most important problem before any disinterested, impartial and objective thinker is about the sincerity of the Railway Minister to arrive at a negotiated settlement. Some facts are against our accepting his sincerity. For example, the Railway Ministry initiated no move for negotiation till after the expiry of the strike notice period on April 10. The negotiations started after April 10. Even after that period, the Ministry has shown no sense of urgency in conducting negotiations expeditiously. In the meanwhile, the Railway Administration has been provoking the workers to launch agitations which is evident from the strike at the Mysore workshops and the agitation in the DS[182] office and accounts office in Ajmer. I may inform you that in the case of Mysore workshop, workers belonging to Mr. Anandan's union started the strike. Again, while the negotiations are inconclusive and they are in process, the Administration has got at least 500 trade union workers arrested. In fact, they were arrested under DIR [Defence of India Act] and MISA (Maintenance of Internal Security Act) for their legitimate trade union activities, though apparently some vague charges were levelled against them. May I ask the hon'ble minister whether, in order to create an atmosphere and environment congenial to a negotiated settlement, he will withdraw all such cases, he will get all these people released and he will settle amicably the disputes at the Mysore workshop and the DS office and the accounts office at Ajmer and also see that the representatives who are sitting at the negotiation table are named by their proper names? Why is the Railway Minister fighting shy of mentioning the party with whom he is talking? Is he like an orthodox Hindu wife fighting shy of taking the name of her husband? What is the matter? He should explain it to us?

Reference to Arrest of George Fernandes[183]

D. Thengadi: This is a matter of very great magnitude. Actually, today the representatives of the workers were invited for negotiations at 10 a.m. Mr. L.N. Mishra had informed them earlier that the Prime Minister would be arriving today and after her arrival, she would be apprised of the progress of the negotiations and then a final decision would be taken.

182. Divisional Superintendent.

183. *Rajya Sabha Debate* dated 2nd May, 1974.

In the meanwhile, we are hearing this news of his arrest. Sir, workers' representatives, representatives of all the sections of Railwaymen are eager for a negotiated settlement. If there is a Railway strike, the dimension, the magnitude of the strike is unpredictable. Workers are willing, workers are eager, are prepared to avert this strike, and the government is forcing the strike upon the workers by precipitating the matter through such arrests. This is a breach of trust as Goray[184] said. This is treachery. So, I request you – this is a problem of such a magnitude that we, here in this House, cannot sit as helpless spectators watching the national tragedy like Nero's fiddling while Rome is burning – to adjourn the House till the government comes out with a proper solution and if the government is incompetent to have that proper solution, the only hon'ble course for the government would be to resign and quit and not sit tight in office.

Reference to Situation Arising out of Railway Strike[185]

D. Thengadi: In spite of the false propaganda by All India Radio to the contrary the fact remains that the Railway strike has been a grand and unprecedented success.

Truth cannot be shouted down. The pitch of the voice is no indication of the truth.

Yesterday the Action Committee of the NCCRS[186] reiterated its readiness to resume negotiations in a statement issued after its meeting. The committee appealed to the public to bring pressure on the government to arrive at a negotiated settlement and bring about an end of the strike. The hardships being faced by the travelling public, the effects on our national economy, all this could be overcome according to the Committee if the government abandons its adamant attitude and takes steps to resume negotiations without further delay. That has been the reaction of the committee. Now in this connection, we all remember that one so-called 3-point formula initiated by the government, subsequently disowned by the government, came before the public. The implications

184. N.G. Goray (1907-1993) – freedom fighter, Congress Socialist party leader, general secretary, Praja Socialist Party (PSP), member of 2nd Lok Sabha, 1957-1962, member of Rajya Sabha 1970-1976, Goray was also part of the first batch of *satyagrahis* for the liberation of Goa in 1955 and was sentenced to 10 year imprisonment by the Portuguese government. Goray was also India's High Commissioner to the United Kingdom between 1977-1979 and was a prolific writer in Marathi.

185. *Rajya Sabha Debate* dated 13rd May, 1974.

186. National Coordination Committee for Railwaymen's struggle.

of the 3-point formula are to be understood by the House and by the general public.

It is customary in all civilised countries – and we are one of them – to conduct negotiations while a strike notice has been served. In the terminology of the government's spokesman, the threat of strike is hanging over the head of the government. Under such conditions, usually and invariably, negotiations are conducted. Even under the Industrial Disputes Act, the Labour Department initiates conciliation proceedings after the strike notice is served. So, there is nothing uncommon and unusual about this procedure. Again, sir, this House and the general public are probably not fully aware of the implications of the formula. We have to understand that strike notices were served by 110 trade unions and a resolution to that effect was passed in a full-fledged conference of all the 110 trade unions' representatives and for withdrawing the strike notice, again there has to be a conference of those representatives. It is reported and I believe that the report may be correct, the Prime Minister has said that if after all this exercise we again come to... (*interruptions*)

It would be a futile exercise to resume negotiations, because there is no primary clarification about the position of the government on the financial demands. We might again reach the same stage of deadlock. In view of all these facts, unless the government's position about the financial commitments is somewhat clarified to the Action Committee and unless the government does not insist on the withdrawal of the strike notice, it is not possible for the Action Committee, within its limitations, to proceed further. The Action Committee has done a signal service to the cause of industrial peace and the country by expressing in unequivocal terms their readiness for a negotiated settlement. Now, sir, this eagerness for a negotiated settlement is being responded to by the government, thus, I am very sorry to say that throughout the country, a reign of terror has been let loose on Railway employees. There are many centres from which we have received reports. There is a systematic effort to force the Railway workers to vacate their quarters. This procedure is not followed in any of the civilised countries of the world.

During the strike period, people are not forced to vacate their quarters. The day before yesterday, Mr. D.L. Sen Gupta, M.P. and myself and yesterday Mr. L.K. Advani,[187] M.P., Dr Ramkripal Sinha,[188] M.P., Mr. Hukam Chand Kachwai,[189] M.P., Lok Sabha, Mr. Sundar Singh Bhandari,[190] Jana Sangh general secretary and Mr. Jagdish Prasad Mathur,[191] Secretary, Jana Sangh, visited the Kishenganj Railway colony. In this colony, we were sad to find that there was the police ordering indiscriminate arrests of people. Even small children were beaten up and male policemen handled females. All these atrocities are going on.

Water supply and electricity supply which are directly under the management of the Railway Administration were stopped from 6.00 a.m. of 8th May. Also we have received various reports from the different centres about the repressive measures but I am not going into details. And I will confine myself to the time you have given to me... (*interruptions*)

This hardly indicates the willingness of the government for a negotiated settlement; this strengthens the suspicion of the Railway employees that the previous eagerness of the government for a negotiated settlement is only a pretext, is only a diplomatic device to mislead and antagonise the people against the Railway employees. In the interests of industrial peace as well as national economy, I wish to urge upon the government (1) that the government should immediately stop all such repressive measures, (2) that the government should immediately release all the arrested workers and their leaders unconditionally, (3) that the

---

187. L.K. Advani, then, a first term member of Rajya Sabha from 3-4-1970 to 2-4-1976.
188. Dr Ram Kripal Sinha (1934-) – BJP leader, was member of the Bihar Legislative Council in 1968, was a minister in Bihar Chief Minister Karpoori Thakur's ministry, member of Rajya Sabha from 1974-1980, Minister of State for Labour & Parliamentary Affairs, 1977-1979, Janata Party government. Sinha was also the office secretary of the BJP's parliamentary party's executive committee.
189. Hukam Chand Kachwai (1933-1996) – trade union leader associated with Jana Sangh and BMS from Madhya Pradesh, closely associated with several workers' movements, member of the 2nd, 3rd, 4th, 5th and 6th Lok Sabha (1957-1980).
190. Sunder Singh Bhandari (1921-2005) – among the first generation Pracharaks who joined the Jana Sangh at inception (1951) Bhandari was General Secretary of the party from 1951-1964 and again from 1967-1977. An indefatigable organiser and political worker, Bhandari was instrumental in spreading the party at the grassroots and served in the Rajya Sabha for three terms, 1966-1972 from Rajasthan, 1976-1982 from Uttar Pradesh, 1992-1998 from Rajasthan. Bhandari also served as vice president of BJP and as Governor of Bihar and Governor of Gujarat.
191. Jagadish Prasad Mathur (1921-2007) – leader of the Jana Sangh and later BJP. Joined Jana Sangh in 1952, was national secretary of Jana Sangh between 1956-1977, became secretary of the BJP in 1986, was a two-term member of Rajya Sabha from 1978-1984 and 1990-1996. A meticulous chronicler of his party's growth and history, Mathur's contribution was immense in terms of documenting the Jana Sangh's growth.

government should immediately withdraw all cases of victimisation against the Railway workers, and (4) that the government should without further delay resume negotiations with the Action Committee from the stage that negotiations had reached on the evening of April 30th.

Situation Created in the Course of the Negotiation Between the Government and the Railwaymen by the Arrest of George Fernandes and Others[192]

D. Thengadi: Before coming to the main problem, I take this opportunity to clarify certain points regarding which the hon'ble Railway Minister has made some wrong statements. Mr. George Fernandes did not say, as has been alleged by the Railway Minister, that the negotiations were a meaningless exercise. What he said was that job evaluation, without commitment on the part of the government regarding reclassification or regradation, was a meaningless exercise – job evaluation was meaningless and not the negotiations. His statement has been misrepresented by the minister. Whether it was done deliberately or inadvertently, I will leave it to you for judgement. The minister did not tell the truth to the House when he said, as he mentioned in his letter to Mr. Fernandes, that the representatives of AIRF had absented themselves from the meeting on 1st May to draw up the minutes of agreement. On behalf of the Action Committee of the NCCR,[193] Mr. George Fernandes had sent Mr. Gokhale and Smt. Parvathi Krishnan[194] for the purpose. Both of them attended the meeting on behalf of the entire NCCR and not as representatives of either Bharat Railway Mazdoor Sangh or Indian Railway Workers' Federation. The minister knew his position. Still he wrote giving a different version.

A friend of mine in the trade union field has, in his anxiety to prove that the strike move is politically motivated, said that the workers' representatives did not even know as to what was meant by trade union activities and that they took nearly four hours to arrive at the agreed definition. Is it a statement of fact? The fact is that the existing service

192. *Rajya Sabha Debate* dated 3rd May, 1974.

193. National Coordination Committee for Railwaymen's Struggle (NCCRS), the umbrella body of trade unions which spearheaded the 1974 Railway strike.

194. Parvathi Krishnan (1919-2014) – Communist Party of India leader, trade unionist, secretary AITUC, was active in the Railway strike of 1974, member of Rajya Sabha, 1954-1957, member of the 2nd Lok Sabha, 1957-1962, 5th Lok Sabha, 1974-1977. Krishnan's father P. Subbarayan was the Chief Minister of Madras Presidency, India's ambassador to Indonesia and Union Minister of Transport and Communication in Nehru's cabinet.

rules have become outdated, anachronistic and are in some respects in contravention of the legitimate trade union rights. The service rules need modification. Mr. Qureshi himself appreciated this fact and offered to examine the service rules in the light of this context and agreed to modify them whenever they contravened the legitimate trade union rights. This was the factor responsible for prolonged discussion on the point. I am sorry to find that my trade unionist friend is more loyal than the Deputy Railway Minister himself.

There has been another case of misrepresentation also. It has been alleged that the workers' representatives wanted to increase the burden on the common man by revising the freight and fare structure. It is wrong. What all they wanted was that concessions to big business and monopoly houses be withdrawn. Their suggestion was directed against monopoly houses and not against common man.

Now, regarding the stage of negotiations, at the time when Mr. Fernandes was arrested, negotiations were in progress. Workers' representatives as well as Mr. Qureshi must be credited for the spirit of mutual understanding and accommodation. On a number of questions, agreement was arrived at. And, in this process, both Mr. Qureshi and the NCCR representatives showed commendable spirit of accommodation and reconciliation – neither side taking a rigid stand. Victimisation, working hours, de-casualisation of casual labour and job evaluation – on these four points, working agreement had been arrived at. Both the parties to negotiations adopted reasonable and flexible attitude. On the remaining problems, i.e. on supply of subsidised foodgrains and predominantly financial demands, it was mutually agreed to conduct negotiations on May 2nd. Thus, the position was that when Mr. Fernandes was arrested, agreement was arrived on some points. Differences were narrowed down regarding remaining points. Negotiations were to be conducted on May 2nd. At such a juncture, the government launched this major offensive.

Then, there are certain other misrepresentations by the government and I also want to mention about them. Who was eager for a negotiated settlement? Hon'ble minister has times without number expressed his eagerness in his House about a negotiated settlement. But, at the same time, we know, sir, that before and even during the pendency of the negotiations, the administration caused penal transfers and arrests of trade union workers of Railways. In fact, this should have been a sufficient justification for the Railway labour leaders to discontinue talks and to come out of negotiations. But, with great self-restraint, they refrained from any such move and conducted negotiations in spite of the ungentlemanly behaviour of the Railway Ministry. It is noteworthy, sir, again, my friend, Mr. Brahmananda Panda,[195] has talked about financial potentialities and other things. But he does not know that in the last sitting, i.e. on 30th April, the workers' representatives did not take any rigid stand on the financial demands. They did not say that these are our demands, these must be fulfilled. How to raise financial resources for the same is your headache and not ours. This position they did not take. On the contrary, they suggested that the authorities and the representatives of labour workers should jointly explore further availability of funds and that this should be a joint exercise. They expressed their willingness to share the responsibility of finding out finances to meet their demands. Does this not clearly manifest their sense of responsibility and reasonableness? To be fair, I must say that Mr. Qureshi gave appropriate response to this gesture of the labour leaders. Now, sir, while all these facts I am placing before the House, these are by way of just clarification because the Railway Minister has misrepresented a number of things.

Now I must come to the main problem which is, who is responsible for the breakdown of the negotiations? Whether the demands were justified or not, that question has receded into the background; that is not relevant just now but the most relevant and pertinent question now is who is responsible for the breakdown of the negotiations and, for this purpose, it is necessary to state in brief how the negotiations proceeded. I will not go into details but the main salient features I want to highlight. On 27th February, as you all know, there was a national convention of the NCCRS in which a resolution was passed giving a time limit up to April 10th and up till 10th April, the Railway Minister made no move to contact the representatives of the workers or even to initiate a talk about negotiations. It is true that during this period, the Minister for Labour, Raghunatha Reddy,[196] contacted the different Railway unions separately

195. Brahmananda Panda (1922-1996) – Congress leader from Odisha, was two-term member of Rajya Sabha, 1967-1972 and 1972 -1978; Panda was also a short story writer and poet.

196. K.V. Raghunatha Reddy (1924-2002) – Congress leader from Andhra Pradesh, was a three term Rajya Sabha member, from 1962 to 1968, 1968 to 1974, 1974 to1980. Reddy also served as Union Minister holding portfolios of Industrial Development and Company Affairs, Labour and Rehabilitation, 1967- 77, served as Governor of Tripura, West Bengal and Odisha.

and on 11th April, it was after the 10th April, he convened a meeting of the representatives of the different unions in the Railways as well as the central labour organisations and, sir, I must say that he tried to understand the problem. He made an earnest effort to grasp the niceties and subtleties of the problem and made up his mind properly on the composition of the negotiations table, the issues for negotiation and the status of the negotiators which are the primary prerequisites for even the beginning of any negotiations. I must add here that on all these three important points, the Railway Minister had no clear idea of his own and had not made up his mind till almost the last phase of the negotiations. Sir, on April 11th, while the Labour Minister had concluded his talks with the workers' representatives – Mr. George Fernandes received a letter from Mr. Mishra saying that he along with his colleagues could come for talks as if it was a dinner party, as if with some friends from the club, he was to go for a dinner party at Mr. Mishra's place. He did not specify who were to be the parties to the negotiations.

It is the primary prerequisite about which you did not make up your mind or you did not understand your own mind almost till the 18th. That is my allegation. I am charging you that up to 18th April, you had not made up your mind about the primary prerequisite as to the composition of the negotiations table. Then on April 12th Mr. Mishra said that the labour leaders could sit along with Mr. Warrier, member of the Railway Board on April 15th. Now whoever comes as a negotiator must have powers to negotiate. And April 15th had a special significance – in view of the fact that the NCCRS was to meet again on the same date to take a decision about the strike. So, simultaneously, these two meetings were to be held but it was necessary that the negotiations should not fail. The Minister should have ensured that at least on his part, there will be no lacuna. He should have ensured that the negotiations are at least in the process of continuance but what actually happened was that Mr. Warrier was not armed with any powers for negotiations, so that when... (*Interruptions*)

I have no doubt of his ability or competence as a negotiator but he was not given any powers so that the poor fellow had to admit that he was just a postman and not a negotiator. This shot the confidence of the workers in the bona fides, sincerity, earnestness of the Railway Minister for a negotiated settlement and that is why on 15th, they took a decision to go on strike. Had Mr. Warrier been given adequate powers as a negotiator, there was no occasion for the convention of the NCCRS to take a decision about the strike. So, Mr. Mishra is responsible for the resolution passed on that day by the convention of NCCRS. Then, sir, subsequently Mr. Fernandes wrote to Mr. Mishra that he was meeting him on 18th. I am concluding. I am not talking anything irrelevant. On 18th, they met and on 20th, Mr. Mishra appointed Mr. Qureshi for the purpose of negotiations. Negotiations just commenced and unfortunately – we are very sorry – his father expired. He had to go. This is understandable. Was Mr. Mishra ignorant of the fact that, according to the resolution of the convention of NCCRS, 23rd was the appointed date for serving strike notices? If Mr. Mishra did not prove his bona fides and his sincerity about a negotiated settlement, workers would have no other alternative but to serve strike notices. 21st and 22nd, two important days, he lost. Actually, Mr. Fernandes requested Mr. Mishra that in place of Mr. Qureshi, he should resume negotiations. He refused to do so. Had he resumed negotiations, there would have been no occasion for the workers' unions to give strike notices. He is responsible for precipitating matters. Again, after the return of Mr. Qureshi, as I said earlier and I need not repeat it, he picked up the threads and conducted negotiations. He showed a reasonable attitude to the workers' representatives and they were also reasonable, co-operative and helpful. Differences were narrowed down, but here again, the same mistake as was committed on April 15th, was committed partially. When it came to financial commitments, it was obvious that Mr. Qureshi was not given any powers to negotiate. I am sure had Mr. Qureshi been given powers regarding financial commitments, he would have continued the talks in a satisfactory manner. But he was not given the powers and that is why, he had to say that he could not even clearly and categorically state whether this was a matter of principle or finance. At a later stage, when Mr. Mishra intervened, he invited the labour leaders or the Action committee of the NCCRS on May 2nd for negotiations. In the meanwhile, in the early hours of May 2nd, Mr. Fernandes was arrested. The whole history of the negotiations clearly proves that there was either lack of earnestness in the part of Mr. Mishra or lack of efficiency on the part of Mr. Mishra and if Mr. Mishra's acts of commission and omission are owned by the ruling party. I must tell our friends that side that history will have to record that great problems came to them for solutions, but they did not deal with them greatly.

Reported Staying Away from Duty of a Large Number of Firemen in Certain Sections of the Southern Railway[197]

D. Thengadi: The role of recognised federations has been referred to. I should like to know whether the grievances of these firemen were taken on the agenda of the Permanent Negotiating Machinery (PNM) by any of the affiliated federations and if so, on what particular date it was taken on the agenda, and how many months or years are required to consider these demands? If their demands were not considered by these Federations, what other form or method would the hon'ble minister advise them to take in order to focus the attention of the government on their problems?

C.M. Poonacha: As a result of the modernisation of the Indian Railways, that is to say, consequent on the introduction of diesel engines and the electrification of some lines and so on, certain work-programmes have got to be re-drawn and for that, a simplification procedure has been recommended and certain guidelines have been prescribed. These guidelines have been discussed by the two Federations at the Federation level. The two Federations have generally approved of these simplification procedures, subject to certain local anomalies being set right as and when they are noticed. This general approval of the federations at the federation level to the simplification procedures has been indicated. Now, subsequently, in certain sections, when it is put into practice, certain types of anomalies have been noticed. These matters would be gone into. I do not know if at the divisional level, the PNM has been used in this particular matter. But before that, certain sections of firemen in these divisions have gone on mass sick leave.

Calling Attention to a Matter of Urgent Public Importance[198]

Situation Arising out of Countrywide Railway Strike

Mr. Deputy Chairman: Mr. Thengadi. I am calling Mr. Thengadi because he is connected with the Railways.

D. Thengadi: This is not an occasion for passionate outbursts by either side. This is a very grave occasion and I should like to ask one specific question. The hon'ble Railway Minister has refrained from giving details of whatever happened in the meeting of PM with the Opposition leaders but I should like to know the reaction of the Railway Ministry or the Government to one specific suggestion from some political quarters;

197. *Rajya Sabha Debate* dated 3rd August, 1967.

198. *Rajya Sabha Debate* dated 10th May, 1974.

that is, without standing on prestige because this is a question affecting the entire national economy, by prior mutual agreement on both sides to fix up a zero hour when simultaneously three things should happen – release of all arrested workers and leaders to be followed by negotiations and declaration and suspension of the strike by the National Coordination Committee. I want to know whether the government is in a position or wants to accept this suggestion so that with prior agreement, we can fix up a zero hour when all the three things must happen simultaneously.

In Response to the Statement by Minister of Railways Regarding Strike Situation in Railways[199]*

D. Thengadi: Times out of number, hon'ble member raised the point about negotiated settlement. He has not reiterated his stand in today's statement. I do not know whether this is deliberate or inadvertent.

Then, some leaders of the Opposition sought permission for interview with Mr. George Fernandes in the jail. The permission was refused. I should like to know why the permission was refused, whether it is in keeping with the profession of the government that they are very eager for negotiated settlement.

Secondly, we are told that in her talk with the opposition leaders, the Prime Minister had indicated that even on financial demands, the government would not take a rigid stand, though there are obviously some limitations on how far they can go.

But yesterday evening, Mr. L.N. Mishra is reported to have told press reporters, "Nothing doing, no negotiations unless the strike notices are withdrawn." This is going back on whatever has been said by the Prime Minister that day. So, we should like to know where the government stands so far as a negotiated settlement is concerned. Our friend, Mr. Kali Mukherjee[200] has asked, "Negotiation with whom?" I may only suggest, negotiations with those with whom the government was conducting negotiations already on the evening of April 30th. It is not a very difficult thing. Then, the government says that they want a negotiated settlement. The Action Committee has said that they are also eager for a negotiated settlement, and they find the 3-point formula unworkable. There are

199. *Rajya Sabha Debate* dated 14th May, 1974.

200. Kali Mukherjee (1916-1989) – Congress trade union leader from West Bengal, was member of the West Bengal Legislative Assembly, 1952-57 and member, Rajya Sabha, from 1972 to 1978; Mukherjee was also secretary of the West Bengal PCC and president, INTUC, West Bengal.

obviously limitations. We have already mentioned them. In brief, I may say that withdrawal of strike notices cannot be made a precondition for the simple reason that in every civilised country, negotiations are being conducted while strike notices are there. Even during the pendency of a strike, even when a strike is going on, negotiations are conducted and even this government has conducted negotiations when strikes were going on. Secondly, even in our Industrial Disputes Act, conciliation proceedings are initiated after strike notices are served. So, this cannot be a pre-condition. Again the government is very well aware that strike notices were served by 110 unions in a full-fledged conference of the National Co-ordination Committee. If the notices are to be withdrawn, a full-fledged conference of the representatives of all the 110 unions should again meet because they alone are authorised to withdraw the strike notices. The Action Committee is not in a position to meet in a full-fledged manner because some of them are in prison. All these facts indicate, sir, that the 3-point formula is unworkable. The Action Committee has said that they are very eager for a negotiated settlement and the government is quite aware of the difficulties in the way. Therefore, the government itself should come forward with a proposal that is workable, and the Action Committee will very willingly think over it and give an appropriate response.

I would like to know from the hon'ble minister whether their stand about a negotiated settlement has changed because we are suspecting their stand on account of the various reports we have received and whatever we have seen. Even in Railway colonies like Kishanganj, Shakurbasti and Tughlaqabad, there are repressive measures by police. Womenfolk are being beaten up and manhandled. Even their wages are being withheld. A number of repressive measures are being adopted. There is victimisation, dismissal and suspension. Thousands are arrested. In view of all these facts, we doubt the bona fides – I am using the word 'bona fides' with all sense of responsibility – of the Railway Minister when he declared in the first place that he was very eager for a negotiated settlement. This is a grave problem. The entire national economy is involved. I would urge that at this stage, the government should not stand on any false notion of prestige because whatever be the consequences, whatever be the result of this strike, it is not that the government will lose or the Railway workers will lose. Primarily, it is the nation that stands to lose today. Therefore, I urge that the government should not stand on any false notion of prestige. They should give a workable proposal that can be acceptable to the Action

Committee.

Late Running of Trains Due to Work-to-Rule Agitation by the Railway Signal Staff[201]

D. Thengadi: In view of the fact that the current system of recognition is one of the main factors responsible for this industrial unrest, may I ask the hon'ble minister whether he is aware that in the seminar of representatives of workers in public undertakings held in December last and also in the seminar of the representatives of administration and workers of public undertakings held in February last, a consensus was arrived at that, howsoever laudable may be the principle of 'one industry, one union', it is not likely to be achieved in the near future, and that we have to live with the fact of multiplicity of unions and for that purpose, the present system of recognition of bargaining agency needs to be altered, changed and improved upon? And may I know whether he is aware of the fact that recently we have seen how in the case of locomen's strike in the Sholapur Division and other in other cases, the present system of recognition has proved thoroughly inadequate? May I ask whether the government would reconsider the question of recognition because, not only the question of category-wise association, but there is a general federation – Bharatiya Railway Mazdoor Sangh – which has now grown in strength and stature in most of the divisions and in some of the divisions, it is stronger than the affiliates of the recognised federation and the obstinate or ostrich – like attitude of the hon'ble minister in not recognising the facts as they are, is standing in the way of our helping the cause of industrial peace on the Railways, because the government is clinging to the original system of recognition though the power position amongst the employees has now changed? In view of these facts, may I ask whether until such time as the laudable objective of one industry, one union, as has been dreamt by the hon'ble minister, is achieved – it may take some decades – for the immediate solution of industrial problems, the government would reconsider its policy of recognition so that the largest number of employees are taken into confidence and a new type of bargaining agency is evolved?

201. *Rajya Sabha Debate* dated 29th November, 1973.

In Response to the Statement by Deputy Minister (Railways) Regarding Financial Position of the Railways[202]

D. Thengadi: With regard to this particular problem, even before the strike was called off, the Railway Minister had assured that there would be no victimisation. He also said so on the day the strike was called off. Just 24 hours before that, the Rashtrapati had made an appeal from Madras that the strike should be called off. And in deference to his advice, the Action Committee of the NCCRS had called off the strike. In view of the fact that it was in deference to his advice that the strike was called off, the victimisation ought to have been withdrawn even before this time. Now, the Railway Minister is making contradictory statements in the same breath. He does not contradict whatever report that has appeared about the advice rendered to him by President Giri and, at the same time, he is not prepared to abide by the advice. Under the situation without going into the constitutional niceties, I should like to say that it is not in keeping with the ordinary decency and decorum to pay slight or scant regard to the President and to continue victimisation. Since this is a collective responsibility, I should like the Prime Minister, who is fortunately present here, to clarify the position and ensure that no damage is done to our sense of decency and decorum, and that the victimisation is withdrawn, as assured by the Railway Minister earlier, and subsequently as advised by the President to the Railway Minister.

□

202. *Rajya Sabha Debate* dated 21st August, 1974.

5
Petroleum, Mining and Power

Participating in the discussion on motion regarding report of the Cochin Refineries Limited, Thengadi questioned the reasons for not providing cause-wise break up of increase in the expenditure. According to him, most of the reasons given for the increase in the expenses were not unforeseeable. Thengadi expressed deep concern over the underground explosion in colliery and wanted to know measures taken by the government after nationalisation to revise the safety rules and to tighten implementation machinery. In the power sector, he felt concerned about workers who had been affected due to closure of factories as a result of frequent power-cuts.

Motion Regarding Report of the Cochin Refineries Limited for the Year 1964-65[203]

D. Thengadi: Madam, certain information which ought to have been furnished has not been furnished in this report. For example, the reasons for the resignation of Mr. Shiralkar are not given. Are they strictly personal or on policy matters?

Secondly, while the main reasons for the increase in the estimated expenditure are enumerated, the cause-wise break-up of this increase has not been given, which was necessary. I request the government to furnish us at least at this stage with such cause-wise break-up.

We are assured through this report that the mistakes committed in the case of other refineries would not be repeated in the case of this Cochin Refinery. We want to be reassured that such mistakes will not be repeated because our experience in the past has been very sad. For example, madam, in the case of the Noonmati Refinery,[204] the trouble had been unduly aggravated by the serious mistakes

203. *Rajya Sabha Debate* dated 7th April, 1966.

204. Guwahati Refinery was set up at Noonmati in Guwahati on 1st January, 1962, the first public sector refinery in India belonging to Indian Oil Corporation Limited.

in carrying out hydraulic testing. The crude distillation unit of the refinery was commissioned in haste. In the case of Barauni,[205] if the decision about location had been taken only on technical grounds, the extra expenditure of approximately Rs. 96 lakhs would have been avoided. The original time schedule was not carried out in the case of Barauni Refinery which led to an increase in the estimated cost. The civil engineering talent has frequently been allowed to be wasted. In the case of the Cochin Refinery, we should now profit by the earlier mistakes. Will the government assure us that at least the same or similar mistakes will not be repeated in this case?

Madam, while I concede that in case of refineries, there can be certain unforeseen factors, I do assert that most of the reasons given for an increase in the estimated expenditure were not unforeseeable. What was the unforeseeable factor in the case of:

a) the cost of land in the Cochin area;
b) the cost of preparing it to accept heavy construction;
c) construction of a new 2-mile road; and
d) the scale of the length of the necessary pipe and rail lines?

Unforeseeability of the increase in the import duty during the year can, of course, be conceded.

The additional capital outlay, now required according to the report, is to the tune of approximately Rs. 4 crores. I think the calculation is incorrect. It would be approximately Rs. 5 crores or Rs. 4.92 crores. The figures should be checked up.

Madam, the report states that "the defaulting shareholders have been served with notice that failure to pay the amount due from them by 15th September, 1965 will entail forfeiture of their shares by the company." How many shares, the allotment money with interest on which have not been fully paid by 15th September, 1965 have been forfeited so far? How many shareholders have made the payment before the prescribed dates? The respective figures of the total value of the shares forfeited, of those paid up, and also of those not paid before the prescribed date and yet not forfeited should be given.

Further, madam, the government must do some basic thinking on the lack of enthusiasm among the prospective shareholders about the Cochin Refinery. The report states that as on 31st March, 1965, an amount of

205. Barauni Refinery situated in Bihar, built with Soviet collaboration, went into operation in 1964.

Rs. 3,75,750 remained as call in arrears. Is it because the people have lost faith in the efficiency of administration and commercial prospects of such undertakings? Research on this point is necessary. The construction of the refinery was to be completed by the end of May 1966. I should like to know whether this time schedule would be properly maintained.

Cochin is the only refinery having no captive thermal plant. Consequently, there are losses in millions. The expenditure on the thermal plant would not be a waste; it would be more than compensated and it would be a wise investment. Cochin is a natural port situated on the shores of the Arabian Sea. Thus, it is best suited for the location of the oil refinery. And here we are setting up a comparatively smaller refinery. Before taking up refineries at any other place, Cochin should have been given better financial assistance. The Cochin port deserves to be developed. The oil tanker that would be able to enter Madras Port should also be able to enter the port of Cochin.

Madam, one of the pleas against the development of Cochin Refinery is that the crude oil price would be higher in Kerala. On good authority, I learn that the price in Kerala could be and would be on the same level as that at Madras. It is quite practicable, as Mr. Arjun Arora has put it, to implement the recommendations of the Damle Committee.[206]

I would also like to know the latest position regarding the petrol complex industry that was promised to Kerala.

And, lastly, madam, the pattern of ownership and that of management should be modified suitably so as not to allow the foreign companies to become de facto proprietors. Particularly, the distribution should be entirely in Indian hands. The foreign companies should be allowed to enjoy their present status on two conditions, namely:

(i) maintenance of proper industrial relations; and
(ii) maintaining the price line.

---

206. Government of India appointed an Oil Price Enquiry Committee in 1960 under K.R. Damle, then Secretary, Ministry of Food and Agriculture. "Various pricing committees appointed by the government during the 1960s including the Damle Committee (1961) and Talukdar Committee (1965) under the chairmanship of K.R. Damle and T.N. Talukdar, respectively advocated fixing of prices of petroleum products on import parity basis as the bulk of the crude oil and the major petroleum products were being imported into the country from West Asia..." (Reference note on petroleum prices, issued by Member's Reference Service, Lok Sabha Secretariat, 2013).

Coal Mines Provident Fund and Bonus Schemes (Amendment) Bill, 1965: Continued[207]

D. Thengadi: Sir, the administration of the Coal Mines Provident Fund scheme must be made more efficient. A sum of more than Rs. 16 crores is held by the Coal Mines Provident Fund in what I may describe as 'suspense account'. A large number of workers have not received their annual statements showing how much money is lying to their credit in the account, what is the interest accrued, how much is the contribution of the employer and how much more is due. Under the Act, it is actually obligatory for the Fund to do so. The problem of non-receipt of contribution cards from employers deserves to be mentioned. The employer does not give in a number of cases the card showing his contribution.

One more interesting aspect of the working of this scheme is the number of non-effective or dead accounts. The number of workers is 5 lakhs while the number of accounts is more than 15 lakhs. The utilisation of the Provident Fund amounts should be given special attention. In the first place, the present top-heavy pattern of administration should be re-organised, bringing down the administrative charges to the minimum. secondly, if we accept the suggestion of scrapping the present scheme for coal mines and amalgamate it with the Employees Provident Fund Scheme, we will be saving a huge amount which is now being spent to maintain this organisation.

Then the Provident Fund which amounts to Rs. 50 crores should be utilised for launching certain schemes, such as unemployment insurance, non-contributory old-age pension, etc. It is well known that coal miners become disabled earlier than other average workers.

The contribution of the workers should be invested in securities giving a higher return than what we are securing to it now. The employers are required to contribute 3 per cent towards administrative charges of the Provident Fund and the bonus scheme. Now it is to be reduced to 2.4 per cent. The benefit of this reduction should be given to the workers. There should be proportionate reduction in the workers' contribution and the levy rate of 3 per cent, from the employers should continue as before. The funds obtained from the coal mines should be utilised for the development of ancillary industries.

Modernisation and mechanisation of coal mines, if undertaken, would render a considerable number of workers superfluous. They can

207. *Rajya Sabha Debate* dated 1st December, 1965.

be absorbed in such ancillary industries. The wealth obtained from the coal industry should be invested in the coal industry itself. This would ensure further development of the industry. What is most important, the coal-mine workers have demanded that there should be no separate scheme of Provident Fund for them. This scheme should be merged with the Employees' Provident Fund Scheme. This will ensure economy, justice and labour welfare.

Now, the workers have also demanded the abolition of a separate bonus scheme for coal-mine workers. They want that the provisions of the Payment of Bonus Act should be extended to them also. The bonus they have been receiving so far is merely attendance bonus. It is not a production bonus, not an incentive bonus, nor even a profit-sharing bonus. As a matter of fact, we have demanded that, under the present conditions, bonus should be treated as a deferred wage, so long as there is a gap between the living wage and the actual wage. The present system of bonus in coal mines is not even connected with the profits of the industry or of the individual units. The present bonus scheme is beneficial to employers only. The price of coal includes the cost of payment of bonus. The employers are experts in the various malpractices arising out of the peculiar nature of the mineworkers' bonus. Measures devised so far to counteract these malpractices have been a failure. The present bonus system has in no way contributed to the stability or development of the coal industry. Irregularities in the payment of bonus have also become a regular feature. While the quarterly average number of workers who received bonus went up from over 2,70,000 in 1962 to 3,05,000 in 1963, the quantum of bonus decreased over this period from Rs. 4.26 crores to Rs. 4.22 crores. The inspectorate detected as many as 3,747 irregularities in 1963. Under the bonus scheme, the bonus amount is forfeited when a strike is declared illegal. We know how workers are often forced to resort to illegal strike because there remains no other alternative for the redressal of their grievances. Because of the illegality of their strike, they are already deprived of a considerable quantum of their other emoluments. To reduce the quantum of their bonus also would be highly inhuman, particularly when they have actually earned the bonus amount. Today only 50 per cent of the underground workers, whose nature of work is very hazardous, receive bonus, while 97 per cent of the supervisory staff gets it. This anomaly must be removed.

A more comprehensive Bill providing for Provident Fund, welfare, unemployment insurance, old-age pension and bonus of different kinds should have been introduced. What we are demanding is an integrated scheme of social security. The Study Group recommended in 1947 the amalgamation of the three organisations, i.e. those dealing with the Employees' State Insurance Scheme, the Employees' Provident Fund Scheme and the Coal Mines' Provident Fund Scheme, all into one. It is possible to implement this recommendation without affecting adversely the economic aspect of it, though the ESI is implemented area-wise, the EPF industry-wise and establishment-wise and the CMPF [Coal Mines Provident Fund] coal-mine-wise. Only the pattern of the consolidated machinery would be different from the routine one.

Lastly, I urge upon the government to come forward with an integrated scheme of social security, instead of bringing forward such piece meal legislation.

D. Thengadi: I want some clarifications. Firstly, I want to know what technical difficulty stands in the way of extending the provisions of the Payment of Bonus Act to the coal-mine workers. That, in express terms, the hon'ble Deputy Minister has not said so far. Secondly, I want to know whether his ministry proposes to take over the administration of the Coal Mines Labour Welfare Fund also? At least, has the ministry worked out the implication in terms of efficiency and economy of the administration of any such proposal?

The Gold (Control) Bill, 1964[208]

D. Thengadi: Sir, according to Clause 3, sub-clause (3) self-employed goldsmiths have been permitted to accept any ornament having gold of any purity for the purpose of making, manufacturing or preparing new ornament or ornaments having gold of a purity not exceeding 14 carats. In this context, we demand that permission should be granted to self-employed goldsmiths to make or manufacture ornaments of 14 carat purity with the help of jewellers or *sarafs*.

Again according to Clause 13(7), 150 grams of primary gold can be obtained by the self-employed goldsmiths in the process of making, manufacturing or preparing new ornament or ornaments. First of, all, this clause is not clear. Our demand is for as much ornament as is received by the self-employed goldsmiths from the customers, they should be permitted

208. *Rajya Sabha Debate* dated 31st August, 1965.

to have primary gold to facilitate their work and, secondly, the quantity of 150 grams mentioned in sub-clause (7) should be the quantity over and above that received from customers. This is for practical convenience.

V.M. Chordia:[209] Sir, I beg to move:

18. "That at page 11, lines 39-40, after the words and figures 'the 10th day of January, 1963', the words 'or if he has undergone training for one year under a certified goldsmith, or in any government institution, or any institution maintained for the purpose of such training' be added."

(The amendment also stood in the name of D. Thengadi.)

19. "That at page 11, lines 41-42, the words 'or a certified goldsmith or other dealer' be deleted."

(The amendment also stood in the name of D. Thengadi.)

20. "That at page 12, lines 5-6 be deleted."

(The amendment also stood in the name of D. Thengadi.)

21. "That at page 13, after line 4, the following sub-clause be inserted, namely:

'(6A) Any person aggrieved by an order rejecting an application for grant of a certificate made under sub-section (2) or by an order cancelling a certificate under sub-section (5) may within 30 days from the date on which the said order is communicated to him, appeal to such appellate authority as may be prescribed and the authority shall dispose of such appeal in such manner as may be prescribed'."

(The amendment also stood in the name of D. Thengadi.)

Dahyabhai V. Patel:[210] I beg to move:

22. "That at page 13, line 13, for the words 'one hundred and fifty grams', the word 'gold' be substituted."

V.M. Chordia: I beg to move:

23. "That at page 13, line 22, after the word 'polishing', the words 'and the like' be inserted."

(The amendment also stood in the name of D. Thengadi.)

The questions were proposed.

---

209. Vimal M Chordia (1924-) was a member of Madhya Bharat Legislative Assembly (1952-57) and of Madhya Pradesh Legislative Assembly (1957-62). Chordia served as vice-president of state unit of Bharatiya Jan Sangh and was member of Rajya Sabha from 1962 to 1968. [may be removed]

210. Dahyabhai Patel (1906-1973) – Sardar Vallabhbhai Patel's son, left the Congress in 1957, joined the Maha Gujarat Janata Parishad, was member of Rajya Sabha, 1958-1964, 1964-1970, 1970-1973, Dahyabhai was also vice-president of the Swatantra Party.

In Response to the Statement Regarding the Accident in Dhori Colliery on 28th May, 1965[211]

D. Thengadi: From the statement, it is obvious that the employers are using dilatory tactics. What measures are the government going to take so that these tactics do not succeed? Again, if according to the interim report, safety rules have been violated, when will their interim report be published and, secondly, may I know if any action would be taken on that score?

Calling Attention to a Matter of Urgent Public Importance Regarding Reported Negotiations by the Government with an American Firm for Collaboration in a Copper Project (Agnigundala) in Andhra Pradesh[212]

D. Thengadi: May I know if it is not a fact that with this favoured technical management, they will be in a dictating position for obvious reasons and, therefore, they would be virtually controlling the whole thing? Therefore, has the Government of India under contemplation any programme to train our personnel to develop our own technical know-how within the shortest possible time? And how are they going to eliminate the possibility of virtual control by the American firm?

S.K. Dey:[213] Sir, that question does not arise because the management control of the firm still remains with us, only the technical control being vested in them. Simultaneously, we are working our own project at Khetri. This is completely under Indian management with assistance, technical as well as financial, from France. Also, we are trying to develop a new deposit at Rakha[214] and we are trying to begin it at a very slow pace with assistance from the National Metallurgical Laboratory and the National Mineral Development Corporation and others. So, it is not that there will be something of a monopoly of copper knowledge in Agnigundala. We thought that we could have these two or three different projects each under a different management, with assistance from different people, competing with each other. Of course, the intention is to train our own

211. *Rajya Sabha Debate* dated 16th August, 1965. On the night between the 27th and 28th of May, 1965, one of the biggest accidents in the coal-mining sector in India occurred at Dhori Colliery in Dhanbad, killing 268 persons.

212. **Rajya Sabha Debate* dated 1st August, 1966.

213. Surendra Kumar Dey, (1906-1989) was member, Rajya Sabha, 1957-1962; Union Minister, Community Development Co-operation and Panchayati Raj – the first minister after the ministry was created; recipient of Padma Bhushan, 1955.

214. A copper deposit owned by the Hindustan Copper Ltd. in Singhbhum district in Jharkhand.

people in the shortest possible period of time.

Calling Attention Motion Regarding Underground Explosion in Jitpur Colliery on 18th March, 1973[215*]

May I know what precisely was the time lag between the accident and the commencement of rescue operations and what factors were responsible for this time lag? I think this can be replied to even on the strength of the enquiry conducted by the hon'ble minister yesterday without waiting for months for the findings of the court of enquiry. Secondly, sir, there seems to be some confusion in government's mind about the adoption and implementation of the recommendations of previous courts of enquiry. Will the hon'ble minister lay on the table of the House the recommendations that have been adopted and implemented? Apart from that, I should like to know what measures were introduced by the government after nationalisation to revise the safety rules which were so much needed and to tighten the implementation machinery? An impression is gaining ground that after such accidents, either the culprits are not brought to book properly or the punishments prescribed are not so severe as to be deterrent. Will the government think of prescribing deterrent punishments for the culprits? So far as this particular accident is concerned, I would like to know whether, in general, many of the persons who are functioning as custodians now are those who were functioning as Managers in the old order?

Calling Attention Motion Regarding Cut in Power Supply in Kerala Resulting in Closing of Factories and Unemployment of Workers[216]

The Minister of Irrigation and Power (*Fakhruddin Ali Ahmed*):[217] Sir, because of the failure of the usual monsoons and unprecedented drought, the reservoirs in Kerala did not get completely filled. As a result, the

215. **Rajya Sabha Debate* dated 21st March, 1973.

216. *Rajya Sabha Debate* dated 21st March, 1966.

217. Fakhruddin Ali Ahmed (1905-1977) – veteran Congress leader from Assam, freedom fighter, member of Rajya Sabha 1954-1957, 1966-1967, minister in Assam, between 1966-1967, Union Minister of Irrigation and Power and Education, Member 4th Lok Sabha, 1967-1970, was also Union Minister for Industrial Development and Company Affairs, and Union Minister for Food, Agriculture, Community Development and Co-operation. Ahmed became the fifth President of India from 1974 to 1977 and gave assent to the imposition of Emergency by Indira Gandhi in 1975. Ahmed was the second President to die in office, the first being Zakir Hussain, the third President of India, who died in 1969.

generating capability of the system since the dry weather season of 1966 has dropped to about 14 lakh units per day.

A power cut of 25 per cent in the consumption of electrical energy by all industrial consumers, cinemas and commercial establishments was imposed with effect from 15th November, 1965. From 11th December, 1965, this power cut was enhanced to 50 per cent in the case of industrial consumers and cinemas, 25 per cent cut was imposed on domestic consumers also. Restrictions were imposed on display lightings, street lighting and on connecting up of new loads. Certain categories of consumers like defence service establishments, agricultural loads, other essential services, etc. were exempted from the restrictions.

At present, there is no proposal for a further cut in Kerala. However, the power position will remain critical till the middle of April 1966. All industries were allowed three months' quota, based on 50 per cent of their power consumption during October 1965, to be used as required by them till March 1966. Most of the industries have exhausted their quota within two months and these industries are being disconnected. Several big industries, such as M/s Travancore-Cochin Chemicals, Rare Earths Factory, Kerala government Ceramics, etc. as also various minor industries have been affected.

The exact number of workers affected by the closure of factories as a result of power cuts in Kerala has not been assessed as yet. However, it is estimated that roughly about 12,000 workers have been affected.

In order to mitigate the power shortage, arrangements were made to provide Kerala with a part of the surplus power of Mysore over the Madras grid. Kerala is, at present, drawing an average of 3 lakh units per day from Mysore through Madras transmission system. Construction of a direct 110 KV transmission line from Mangalore in Mysore to Kasergode in Kerala has been taken up on a priority basis. With the commissioning of the first unit of Sholayar Power Station and two units of Sabarigiri[218] by about the middle of April 1966, it is expected that the position will improve. With the onset of monsoons from June 1966 onwards, the power supply position in the state is expected to ease considerably.

As the power supply position in the state is entirely dependent on the timely onset and intensity of monsoons, the provision of thermal power station at Cochin to back the hydropower in the state is considered necessary. Steps are being taken to expedite the construction of Cochin Thermal Station.

218. Sabarigiri Hydroelectric Project is located in Kerala and is operated by Kerala State Electricity Board and was commissioned in 1966.

The Minister of State in the Ministry of Irrigation and Power (*Dr K.L. Rao*):[219]

It is a fact that the Kerala aluminium factory has been affected. A number of projects have been sanctioned in Pamba, Sholayar and Idukki.[220] But we should have reservoirs with much more capacity so that there may not be this kind of failure which at present obtains from the existing small stations. In addition to that, we envisage a thermal station because of the oil project which gives 40,000 tonnes per year. Therefore, we would establish a project which will be backed up with oil, and when more oil is forthcoming and when other sources of energy are forthcoming, then the thermal generation of power will be increased.

D. Thengadi: What is the total amount of compensation for these 12,000 unemployed workers? And secondly, will the government assure us that the decision regarding the Cochin Thermal Station will be taken on the advice of experts and not on the advice of politicians.

Fakhruddin Ali Ahmed: The question of compensation does not arise. Information was given to the industries concerned beforehand about the shortage of power. And as I have already pointed out earlier, early action is being taken to establish this thermal power station.

Calling Attention Motion Regarding Serious Crisis due to Power Shortage in the Country[221]

D. Thengadi: Sir, while big projects are being pursued, as an immediate measure I would like to ask whether government is contemplating any scheme to require bigger industrial units in affected areas to have their own generators, as an immediate measure. Secondly, since your ministry is responsible for loss of wages to workers, will you consider how to subsidise through government or joint efforts, particularly to those who are temporary, casual or *badli* workers? Thirdly, will you also consider, in consultation with other concerned ministries, shortening the working hours, i.e. from 8 to 6 hours, without any loss of wages?

You can advise them.

□

---

219. Dr K.L. Rao (1902 1986), often referred to as the father of India's water management, irrigation and agriculture, Rao was instrumental in designing some of the major dams of the Nehru era. Rao was Minister of State for Irrigation and Power from 1963-1973. He was awarded the Padma Bhushan in 1963.

220. Pamba reservoir is constructed across Pamba river in Kerala. The power project was commissioned in 1966.

221. *Rajya Sabha Debate* dated 20th February, 1973.

6
Labour and Employment

Thengadi took great interest in the Bills pertaining to labour and employment, which were close to his heart. He spoke profusely on Bills pertaining to payment of bonus, industrial disputes, Trade Union and Labour Provident Fund Laws, to mention a few. He spoke in great detail on the Contract Labour Bill,[222] *as well as on the Essential Services Maintenance Bill. He took part in the discussions on the government's policy on PSUs and delay in the implementation of the Gajendra Gadkar Commission Report.*[223] *He spoke in detail on the resolution seeking disapproval of the Essential Services Maintenance Ordinance, resolution seeking disapproval of the Payment of Bonus (Amendment) Ordinance and resolution seeking disapproval of the Additional Emoluments (Compulsory Deposit) Ordinance.*

Besides the above subjects, Thengadi participated in the discussion on matters of urgent public importance which included boycott of the one-man independent body for DA by the Central Government Employees Union, strike by the employees of PTI (Press Trust of India), agitation by the employees of the office of the C & AG (Comptroller and Auditor General of India), demonstration by the Development officers of LIC (Life Insurance Corporation), strike by the government employees, strike by the All India Port and Dock Workers' Federation, strike by the tea garden workers in West Bengal, demonstration by the state government employees in New Delhi, situation arising out of jute workers' strike in West Bengal and Central Government employees' strike in September, 1968.

All the above subjects reveal the fact that Thengadi's focus was on the welfare and protection of the interest of the working class. He was

---

222. The Contract Labour (Regulation and Abolition) Act, 1970 aims at regulating employment of contract labour so as to place it at par with labour employed directly.

223. The first National Commission on Labour was set up on 24th December, in 1966 under the chairmanship of Justice P.B. Gajendragadkar (1901-1981), 7th Chief Justice of India, 1964-1966. The commission submitted its report in August 1969.

relentlessly concerned about the well-being of the working community and made efforts to ensure that they were not exploited by their employers. His speeches on the floor of the House are a testimony to the fact that he had total command over and grasp of the subject matter. He always participated in the discussions with full facts and figures.

Speaking on the payment of Bonus Bill, he observed that the Bill had virtually excluded a large number of employees from the benefit rather than those included in it. He felt that the government was in half mind to concede that bonus as a deferred wage. He wanted 'bonus' to be defined properly. He was worried about the fate of the 'contract workers'. He did not find any justification for excluding the monopolistic undertakings in the public sector from the benefits of bonus. He wanted the government-run industries to be brought within the purview of the Bonus Act.

Thengadi was in favour of workers to be given right to go through the accounts and inspect the balance sheet to have a correct assessment of the company's performance and to participate in the decision-making processes. He was against bureaucratisation of the PSUs. He argued that there was a need to create a regular cadre of public administrators. He was of the view that the workers of PSUs were patriotic and responsible enough to manage the PSUs efficiently.

Regarding the Industrial Dispute Amendment Bill, Thengadi felt that the entire Bill was a piece-meal legislation which was not going to serve the purpose for which it was brought for approval of the Parliament. He wanted to make it more comprehensive and welfare-oriented to ensure that the legislation should cater justice to the workers without any favour or bias.

While welcoming the Indian Trade Unions (Amendment) Bill, he feared that the amendment disqualifying persons convicted of moral turpitude could be exploited to the disadvantage of the genuine trade union workers by the vested interests. He wanted to have a legislation on 'one industry and one union' so as to have one single union in every establishment. Thengadi wanted to have a legislation to deal with unfair labour practices based on the report of the committee constituted by the government of Maharashtra on this subject.

Speaking on the issue of Provident Fund, he desired to have a Provident Fund Committee in every factory. This he said in the backdrop of the problem of steadily growing arrears of the Provident Fund. So far as defaulting employers are concerned, he opined that workers should take over in such a situation and manage it. He was in favour of an integrated social security law under an integrated social security authority.

The Payment of Bonus Bill, 1965[224]

D. Thengadi: Mr. Chairman, it is for the first time that any piece of legislation has been brought in this context, and, therefore, this is something commendable. One of the objects of this legislation was to minimise the litigation on bonus which had become a regular feature of our industrial sphere, but I am sorry to say that for various reasons, this object is not going to be achieved.

It seems there was a certain amount of pressure on the government because I know that the hon'ble Labour Minister and the hon'ble Deputy Labour Minister are men of the masses and they are quite earnest about labour welfare, but still the Bill goes against the spirit of labour welfare, and that is why, I am led to believe that there was some pressure from certain quarters. We have been hearing so far about protection being granted to minorities, that is, on the basis of religion or language, but now it seems that the government is also determined to give protection to economic minorities, that is, the capitalists of the country. The government has set a bad precedent by introducing modifications in the recommendations of the Bonus Commission.[225] To say that these are modifications would be a gross understatement of facts. As a matter of fact, some of the unanimous and majority recommendations have been torpedoed, because among other things, the very basis for the computation of the distributable, whether it be described as available or allocable surplus for bonus, has been changed drastically. One thing I may say confidently, and the hon'ble Labour Minister may agree with me, that the distributable surplus under the present government formula would be generally less than that available under the Bonus Commission's formula, and that available under the Bonus Commission's formula would be generally or I may say invariably lesser than that available under the LAT [Labour Appellate Tribunal] formula. We are certainly grateful to the hon'ble Labour Minister for the provision of the minimum bonus of 4 per cent, or of Rs. 40, whichever is higher. But we fear that in case this provision is struck down by Court, the workers would be left defenceless because there are no other provisions in this Bill. It is not a sweeping generalisation but after careful scrutiny, I

---

224. *Rajya Sabha Debate* dated 20th September, 1965.

225. Commission set up by the Government of India with M.R. Mehar as its chairman, in 1961 to look into the question of payment of bonus. The Mehar Commission's watershed observation was that "Bonus is a right of the work as the worker has a share in the prosperity of the company."

am saying this. There are no other provisions in this Bill that are rather favourable to the workers. Again, this provision for minimum bonus, though actuated with the best of the intentions, is likely to be taken advantage of and exploited by the employers. I learn from Kanpur that some of the employers have already reduced the quantum of bonus taking advantage of this provision of minimum bonus. While the principle of minimum bonus is understandable, it is not clear what is the propriety in prescribing the ceiling of 20 per cent, because the hon'ble Labour Minister has been at pains to explain that there is a saving clause which would protect the interests of workers who used to get more than 20 per cent, earlier. Let me say that Clause 34(2) does not fulfil the assurance given by him on 18th September, 1964. The clause fails to protect the earlier formula or scheme of computation. I am not saying anything about quantum. It may vary. But even the formula under which they used to get bonus earlier and which was more favourable has not been protected. But what the hon'ble minister seeks to protect through this clause is only the ratio, which is neither here nor there. Practically, I fear, this will become a protective clause to the industrialist class who used to pay more than 20 per cent, bonus earlier.

A word about the retrospective effect. The commission had recommended that their recommendation should be given retrospective effect from the accounting year on any day in 1962, i.e. with regard to bonus issues relating to the financial year 1961-62. Clause 33 does not fulfil this condition. The government should not have been afraid of reopening the disputes which were decided on principles inconsistent with those underlying this Bill.

Madam, this Bill contains certain provisions which are in contravention of the provisions of the Industrial Disputes Act. For example, under the Industrial Disputes Act, the apprentices are included in the category of 'workmen'. But this Bonus Bill excludes them from that category.

Again, 'travelling concession' is included in the definition of 'wage' under the Industrial Disputes Act. But that is excluded from 'wages' under this Act. These are the contraventions of the Industrial Disputes Act.

The hon'ble Labour Minister has stated that 45 lakhs of workers would be getting bonus for the first time because they were not getting bonus earlier, by virtue of this piece of legislation. It is true and we are thankful to him for his help but I would request him to kindly work out the number of those who are excluded by virtue of the exclusion clauses, i.e. Clauses 20 and 32. Apart from the categories enumerated therein, regarding which I may make some reference subsequently, there are certain other sections of the working population that are excluded also. The contract labour in general and those employed in constructional and building work in particular, the seasonal workers, the ministerial staff, the departmental employees, etc., why should they be excluded? What is a department? Is road transport a department? Then the Railways are a full-fledged, regular, profit-earning industry. Why should the Railway employees be deprived of their right to bonus? Again, it is worth noting that the LIC employees who are excluded by the operation of Clause 32 had already secured through agreement with the management, their bonus previously. Also, the Chamber of Commerce at Calcutta was granting the *puja* bonus[226] customarily to its employees; in West Bengal, there is only the *puja* bonus. Also the government is aware that the Bombay Dock Labour Board[227] was thinking of making provision for payment of bonus to its employees and that also the Boards at Calcutta and Madras were contemplating to follow suit.

Madam, clauses 20 and 32 are the exclusion clauses and with the number of workers thus excluded, it may be more–I am not sure–than the 45 lakhs claimed by the hon'ble Labour Minister as having been included.

Faulty drafting has created some difficulty. To my mind, there is inconsistency between the provisions of clause 32 and those of clause 34(3).

Clause 20 of the Bill is discriminatory. It places the public sector undertakings on a different footing. The public sector should be a model employer. As a matter of fact, the leaders of the government are giving advice to the private sector employers and we agreed with them on that. But, at the same time, in order to bring the appropriate pressure to bear upon the employers in the private sector regarding the proper maintenance of industrial relations, it is necessary that wherever the government appears as an employer, the industrial relations should be proper and it should function as a model employer. It seems that because of the 20 per cent competitive character, it would be very difficult to ascertain which category of employees in the public sector will be entitled

226. Puja Bonus is given to employees before Durga Puja.

227. In colonial India, dock workers had no security of employment, lacked safety provisions with wages varying and dependent on contractors. The setting of the Bombay Dock Labour Board ensured some security to the dock workers.

to bonus. There would be a continuous stream of litigation to determine whether public sector undertakings are covered by this Act. This will further add to confusion and difficulties. In the Fourth Five-Year Plan, we are contemplating increasing expansion of the public sector. That means that the employees under the public sector would be increasing in number and all those employees would be excluded from the benefit of bonus. Thus, this Bill has virtually excluded a larger number of employees from the benefit rather than those included under it. government is well aware that it is extremely difficult to determine with any amount of accuracy whether the 20 per cent competitive character exists or not.

There are a number of other points, for example, the development rebate. Under the Income-tax Act, it is not obligatory to claim a development rebate. Because of the Bonus Act, this would become rather a regular feature. The employers will be inclined to claim it. It may be noted that the Adarkar Committee[228] does not give development rebate as a prior charge to the employer and no Court has accepted so far the development rebate as a prior charge. Even Mr. Dandekar[229]who represented the employers had not suggested it. The Bonus Commission had not conceded it. But the government is offering to the employers what they themselves did not demand. This is going out of the way. There are a number of other points which I should like to discuss when there is the clause-by-clause consideration. But one important point I wish to make and that is, it is essential at this stage to define the concept of bonus in the Bill. The provision is 4 per cent or Rs. 40, whichever is higher. The principle of minimum bonus goes to indicate that the government was in half mind to concede that bonus is a deferred wage. But it has not conceded it actually. Now, unless 'bonus' is properly defined, it would be very difficult to work out any principles and, therefore, I would like to suggest that this definition should have been incorporated in the Bill itself.

The Payment of Bonus Bill, 1965: Continued[230]

D. Thengadi: Madam, I move:

92. "That at page 3, lines 38 to 40 be deleted."

---

228. In 1943, the then Government of India appointed a commission under Professor B.P. Adarkar to submit a report on a possible health insurance scheme for industrial workers. The report formed the basis of the Employment State Insurance (ESI) Act 1948.

229. Member of the Bonus Commission, 1964.

230. *Rajya Sabha Debate* dated 21st September, 1965.

93. "That at page 3, lines 41 to 44 be deleted."

94. "That at page 4, line 1, the brackets and words (other than an apprentice) be deleted."

95. "That at page 4, at the end of line 6, after the words 'implied', the words 'and includes all persons employed by or through a contractor' be inserted."

96. "That at page 4, line 13, after the words 'so named' the words 'and in the case of contract labour, the principal employer' be inserted."

97. "That at page 4, line 18, after the word 'agent', the words 'and in the case of contract labour, the principal employer' be inserted."

98. "That at page 5, lines 11 and 12 be deleted."

The Deputy Chairman: Let Mr. Thengadi first speak on his amendments and you can speak afterwards.

D. Thengadi: With respect to my amendment No. 92, I only request the government to follow exactly what the Bonus Commission has prescribed. I now refer to my amendment No. 93. It is obvious that if other taxes are also included in 'direct tax', then, naturally, the slice of the workers would be curtailed, and there is no justification whatsoever for adding, just by notification in the Official Gazette, any other tax to the direct tax and, thus, cut down the slice of the workers.

Then comes my amendment No. 94. Here, as I pointed out yesterday, this provision is in contravention of the provision in the Industrial Disputes Act because, under that Act, apprentices are included in the definition of 'workman', and there is also the apprehension that, if this is allowed, naturally, the apprentices would be continued as apprentices and would not be regularised for years to come.

Then I come to my amendment No. 95. Here the fate of contract labour has been totally ignored by the hon'ble Labour Minister, and unless they are given specifically, in clear terms, this protection, and included in the definition of 'employee', naturally, they would be left defenceless.

Then comes my amendment No. 96. Here again the same consideration holds good. Contract labour is already defenceless and, therefore, it is necessary to provide specially that the principal employer should be responsible for payment of bonus to them.

I take up now amendment No. 97. Here also the same principle applies; contract labour should not be ignored in this fashion.

Now comes amendment No. 98. Here it refers to the deletion of the Bill provision 'any other allowance which the employee is for the time-being entitled to'. There are allowances which should be included in the wage. Also I had said yesterday about the inclusion of travel concessions and other allowances that they also should be included in the wage.

D. Thengadi: Madam, I move: 'That at page 6, lines 31 to 33' be deleted.

D. Thengadi: Madam, it would be improper to put it as either by way of development rebate or development allowance. As a matter of fact, both these items should have been considered separately. As I said yesterday, development rebate has not been conceded by any Court, not suggested by the Adarkar Committee, not even considered by the Bonus Commission and not even demanded by the employers themselves. That is the mysterious part of it and still the government is going out of its way to give something which they themselves did not demand. Formerly, the rebate was 20 per cent. Now, it is 35 per cent generally and 40 per cent in the case of shipping companies. It is a big proportion, and, therefore, to deprive the worker of such a big amount would be highly unjust. I request the hon'ble Labour minister to consider this and withdraw the development from this clause.

D. Thengadi: Madam, I move:

101. "That at page 7, lines 36-37, the brackets and words (other than development rebate or development allowance)' be deleted."

D. Thengadi: The Labour Minister seems to be over-optimistic about the attitude of the employers but I may suggest that this development rebate is going to be a regular feature now after the enactment of this measure and, therefore, this wording should have been dropped. I very much doubt whether he will accept this amendment because my earlier argument has not gone home. Nevertheless I press my amendment.

D. Thengadi:

102. "That at page 8, after line 14, the following proviso be inserted, namely: 'Provided that he is convicted by the appropriate court for any of the above offences'."

D. Thengadi: The point is whether he has earned an amount of bonus or not. If he has committed any offence, he is punished for it. Secondly, it is an everyday occurrence that straightway workers, particularly trade union workers, are proceeded against by the managements, and false charges are levied against them, and in view of this, it is necessary to amend the clause and I am suggesting that the proviso "provided that he is convicted by the appropriate Court for any of the above offences" be inserted at the end of Bill clause 9, because only departmental enquiry would not do; it should be the appropriate Court that would punish him, and only in that case, he should be deprived of his right to bonus. Another small point, under the Criminal Procedure Code, theft of Rs. 250 is a compoundable offence. So, there is no reason why theft should be included in this particular clause.

D. Thengadi: What is the practice in communist countries?

Bhupesh Gupta:[231] The practice in the communist countries is to refer the matter to the Swatantra Party. The point raised by such a ridiculous question can only be answered in so ridiculous a manner.

D. Thengadi: Madam, the government is not willing to allow the reopening of the cases that are already decided but the point is that in this Bill, the government has evolved certain principles for payment of bonus and there is no reason why if the decisions taken are in contravention of the principles involved or set out in this Bill, in that case, reopening should not be allowed. The argument put forward by the Labour Minister is that if such reopening is allowed, industrial peace would be disturbed. It may be the other way round; probably, if reopening is not allowed, industrial unrest may be created and, therefore, this amendment should be accepted.

D. Thengadi: What about the cases decided earlier?

D. Sanjivayya: I have already made it very clear that we do not want to reopen the cases which have been settled either by awards or by Tribunals or through mutual negotiations.

D. Thengadi: Madam, I move:

104. "That at page 8, lines 30-31, the words 'subject to a maximum of twenty per cent, of such salary or wage' be deleted."

D. Thengadi: Madam, my amendment No. 104 virtually means... (*interruptions*)

D. Thengadi: Madam, my amendment No. 104 virtually means that there should be no ceiling on the percentage of the salary to be paid as bonus. The reasons are obvious. Firstly, the Bill lays down certain basis for the computation of the quantum of bonus. No doubt the basis is not as favourable as the LAT formula or the Bonus Commission formula. Nevertheless, some basis has been prescribed. In view of that, there is no propriety in putting down a ceiling of 20 per cent.

---

231. Bhupesh Gupta (1914-1981) – veteran leader of the Communist Party of India (CPI), secretary of the national council of the CPI, was a five-term member of Rajya Sabha from 1952-1981. One of the most vocal communist leaders in the Upper House and among the party's most well-known parliamentary faces, Bhupesh Gupta led the CPI to support Indira Gandhi's imposition of Emergency in 1975.

The hon'ble Labour Minister has been very earnest, and he has expressed it very often, to protect the higher quantum of bonus the workers used to get earlier according to different formulae or agreements. But, I must say with regret that Clause 34 does not give adequate or assured protection to the workers. Secondly, it is not guaranteed or assured that the set on amounts would not go to the coffers of the employers but would come back to the workers. That assurance is lacking. In view of all this, I think there should be no ceiling on the percentage or the quantum of bonus.

The Payment of Bonus Bill, 1965: Continued[232]

D. Thengadi: Sir, I move:

106. "That at page 9, line 18, the words 'with salary or wage' be deleted."

107. "That at page 9, after line 23, the following be inserted, namely:

'(e) he has been locked out or has been on strike not declared illegal by any competent authority'."

(These amendments also stood in the name of V.M. Chordia.)

The questions were proposed.

D. Thengadi: This deals with the computation of working days for the purposes of bonus. The days on which a worker has been laid off either with or without compensation should also be computed as working days. All cases of lay off may not necessarily be covered by an agreement or by the standing orders, or by the Industrial Disputes Act. Even where they are, it would not be clear in all cases whether they are entitled to compensation or not for those days of lay off. Such instances may occur, as are not covered specifically by agreement. In some cases, a worker may be entitled to compensation for a period of lay off but not for the balance of it. Even if a worker has not been paid compensation, he has been laid off for no fault of his and that should not be counted against him when it comes to the computing of working days. Then regarding leave, leave is generally authorised.

It may be with salary or wage or without salary or wage. Particularly, persons coming from rural areas to industrial centres generally go to the respective places with authorised leave, without salary or wage. Because the leave is authorised, there is no justification for leaving out those days in computation of the working days. Then sick leave without pay should also be counted. Then I have suggested that wherever a worker

232. *Rajya Sabha Debate* dated 22nd September, 1965.

has been locked out or has been on strike not declared illegal by any competent authority, those days also should be included for the purpose of computation. The reasons are obvious. Our provision for legal strike under labour laws would be rendered superfluous if we do not accept this position that if he has been out of work because of a legal strike, those days should be computed. Otherwise that provision is meaningless. Also, whenever he is locked out for no fault of his, t hose days also should be included. There may be a few cases only where employers may be in a position to say that the workers are responsible for lock-out, but generally that does not happen. So lock-out days also should be included while computing working days.

D. Thengadi: Madam, we already opposed the imposition of ceiling on the quantum of bonus yesterday. Now at this stage, I should like to request the hon'ble Labour Minister that he should assure us and arrange accordingly that the 'set on' amount should profit the employees and not go to the coffers of the employer. At least that can be done by the hon'ble Labour Minister.

D. Thengadi: After four subsequent years, what will happen to the set-off amounts?

D. Thengadi: I move:

108. "That at page 10, line 17, for the word 'sixth', the word 'second' be substituted."

109. "That at page 10, line 35, the words 'and losses' be deleted."

(These amendments also stood in the name of V.M. Chordia.)

The questions were proposed.

D. Thengadi: I will first speak on amendment No. 109. I would like to say that losses stand on a different footing as compared to depreciation. Therefore, it cannot deserve the same priority as depreciation. Regarding the bonus holiday of six years, apart from fraudulent dealings that may be given rise to because of this provision, there is another feature which deserves our attention. Now that the development rebate is enhanced, naturally to make up the total cost of development if formerly five years were required, now within three years or less than three years, the whole thing would be made up. So, there is no reason why this period of six years should be prescribed. Therefore, I have said that the word 'sixth' should be replaced by 'second'. Then in the same clause, sub-clause (2) seeks to apply that provision so far as may be to new departments or undertakings or branches set up by existing establishments. This seems to be wrong.

It is absurd that 1,200 workers of the concern should secure bonus but 50 workers of a newly established foundry or other concern of the same parent concern should be deprived of the right to bonus. Now the proviso to this clause is helpful to establishments which have been paying bonus even before 1965 but if the establishment has not actually been able to pay bonus before 1965, the old department will not qualify itself for the payment in 1966 or 1967 simply because the employees there were not paid before 1965, while people of the new department would be qualifying themselves for bonus. This is something unjust and, therefore, I wish that the whole thing should be redrafted.

D. Thengadi: Madam, I move:

110. "That at page 11, lines 24 and 25 be deleted."

(The amendment also stood in the name of V.M. Chordia.')

In Bengal, *puja* bonus was a customary bonus, and actually, when the custom evolved, there were no particular principles that were followed in determining the percentage or quantum of bonus, and, therefore, it would be unfair to bring in Puja bonus here for purposes of diminishing the workers' share by way of bonus.

The question was proposed.

D. Thengadi: I move:

111. "That at page 11,

(i) in line 33, after the word 'guilty', the words 'by a court of law' be inserted;

(ii) in line 34, for the word 'misconduct', the words 'gross misconduct' be substituted."

(The amendment also stood in the name of V.M. Chordia.)

The questions were proposed.

D. Thengadi: Madam, when we speak of guilt, who is to decide whether a worker is guilty or not? Therefore, I have suggested that it should be a court of law; it should be a court of law and not an employer because, in the latter case, whomsoever the employer does not like in his establishment would be victimised. Secondly, the word 'misconduct' is likely to be misused. All standing orders contain a huge list of offences which are technically described as misconduct. There are as many as 39, madam, and it would be very difficult for the employers to resist the temptation of victimising straightway the workers, particularly trade union workers, and, therefore, they would avail of this particular clause and, thus, dispense with them. Now, if any trade union leader or worker is dismissed on account of a legal strike, say, four months after the year ending, should his right to bonus, which he has already earned, be denied to him? Now there is the question of negligence. Now, through which procedure can we work out the amount of loss incurred on account of negligence, or on account of late-coming? And, therefore, I am moving these amendments.

D. Thengadi: Madam, I beg to move:

112. "That at page 12, line 14, for the word 'two', the word 'one' be substituted."

(The amendment also stood in the name of V.M. Chordia.)

Now, the object of this clause is obviously to expedite payment of bonus which is quite a laudable one but because there is provision for extending the period up to two years under special circumstances, I feel that the very purpose of this Bill has been defeated. It has been stated that the extension would be granted for sufficient reasons. This is a very ambiguous term and this word 'sufficient' has not been precisely defined or in any way defined. I am suggesting that instead of two years, the period should be confined to one year only. In order to expedite the payment of bonus, extension should be confined to one year and not to two.

D. Thengadi: Madam, firstly, it would be extremely difficult and government is well aware that to determine precisely or accurately, the 20 per cent competitive character of any public sector undertaking is bound to give rise to a lot of litigation, while through this Bill, what we seek is minimising, if not completely eliminating, the litigation. Again, as usual, we are quite reluctant to accept any balance sheet, be it from the public sector or private sector, at its face value. So, the litigation is bound to increase. Moreover, there is no justification whatsoever for the exclusion of monopolistic undertakings in the public sector from this benefit of bonus. I request the hon'ble Labour Minister to go through the balance sheets and the profit and loss accounts of road transport concerns in the different states. It would be obvious, if he examines those profit and loss accounts and the balance sheets, that whenever there was partial nationalisation of road transport, the profits earned by the nationalised road transport were less as compared to the period when nationalisation was complete, because there was monopoly, there was no fear of competition and, therefore, profits increased. And this is an additional argument in favour of the employees of the monopolistic industrial undertakings in the public sector for securing the right to bonus.

The Railways and road transport – it is well known – are earning huge profits. So, why should their employees whose number is running into lakhs be excluded from this particular benefit? Again, during the Fourth Five-Year Plan, we are trying to expand the sphere of the public sector, which means an ever-increasing number of public-sector employees. If this class is exempted, then naturally the ever-increasing number of employees will be denied this right to bonus. In view of all this, this is a sad commentary on the shape of socialism to come. Therefore, this clause should be deleted.

D. Thengadi: Madam, there is obvious contradiction in the provisions of Clause 21 and those of Clause 10. There should be no objection on the part of the hon'ble Labour Minister to provide that the provision of Clause 21 should be subject to that in Clause 10.

D. Sanjivayya:[233] Madam, I am not in a position to accept the amendments for the following reasons. I am not in a position to think of a case where bonus would be payable at once in settlement or agreement at least, if not award. Even Clause 10 does not contemplate straightway payment of bonus. It is again subject to Clause 13. Clause 13 says:

"Where an employee has not worked for all the working days in any accounting year, the minimum bonus of 40 rupees or, as the case may be, of 25 rupees, if such bonus is higher than 4 per cent, of his salary or wage for the days he has worked in the accounting year, shall be proportionately reduced."

It is also covered by Clause 14 according to which you have to calculate the number of days he is supposed to be on duty. There are days on which he is on leave. The question is whether those days should be accounted. All these calculations will have to be made and minimum bonus will have to be proportionately given.

Secondly, even if it is 4 per cent, the minimum is conceded, but 4 per cent, of what? 4 per cent of the total annual earnings of the worker. How many days he has worked, how much basic pay he has got, what is the Dearness Allowance, all these factors will have to be calculated. All

233. D. Sanjivayya (1921-1972) – freedom fighter, Congress leader from Andhra Pradesh, president of the Indian National Congress, 1962-64, was member of the Provisional Parliament, 1950-52, Madras Legislative Assembly, 1952 and member, Andhra Pradesh Legislative Assembly, 1952-64; minister, Governments of Madras and Andhra Pradesh, 1952-60 and Chief Minister of Andhra Pradesh, 1960-62. Sanjivayya was member of the Rajya Sabha, 1964-1970 and 1970-1972; he was also Union Minister of Labour and Employment and Industry, 1964-67 and 1970-71.

this will involve a lot of work which can be settled by mutual agreement. Therefore, if the hon'ble members could suggest an illustration, which would go to show that straightway amount will become due under this Act, I am prepared to accept. This was raised in the Lok Sabha also.

D. Thengadi: In the case of companies other than banking companies, the workers should have the right to go behind the balance sheets and accounts and seek clarifications and other things adequately. They should have the right to challenge and the balance sheets should be open to them.

D. Sanjivayya: Clause 23(2) gives the right to get clarification which Mr. Thengadi wants and after such clarifications and after seeing the balance sheets produced before the Tribunal, the trade union leaders or workers will be in a position to point out the loopholes which will be taken note of by the Tribunal. I hope the purpose will be served.

D. Thengadi: Sir, I move:

114. "That at page 16, for lines 6 to 11, the following be substituted, namely:

'(5) Nothing contained in Section 34A of the Banking Companies Act, 1949 shall prevent an inspector from requiring a banking company to furnish or disclose any statement or information or to produce, or give inspection of any of its books of account or other documents'."

(The amendment also stood in the name of V.M. Chordia.)

Now the difficulty lies in this. We can understand in the case of banking companies the employees are not being given the right to go through the documents or balance sheets, etc. but there must be some authority – that is more important – that should have the right to inspect these documents; otherwise there is every reason to apprehend that fraudulent affairs would continue and so I have suggested that the inspector should be given that right. Whether it is the inspector or some other authority, that authority must be given to somebody. Otherwise there is no end to fraud in the case of banking companies.

The question was proposed.

D. Sanjivayya: Banking companies are specifically given this privilege that they will not be asked to produce documents under Section 34A of the Banking Companies Act, 1949.[234] Therefore the same privilege should be continued.

---

234. The Banking Regulation Act, 1949 is a legislation in India that regulates all banking firms in India.

D. Thengadi: I move:

115. "That at page 16:

(i) in line 19, for the words 'or with fine' the words 'and with fine' be substituted; and

(ii) in line 20, the words 'or with both' be deleted."

(The amendment also stood in the name of V.M. Chordia.)

The clause reads like this:

"If any person:

(a) contravenes any of the provisions of this Act or any rule made thereunder; or

(b) to whom a direction is given or a requisition is made under this Act fails to comply with the direction or requisition, he shall be punishable with imprisonment for a term which may extend to six months, or with fine which may extend to one thousand rupees, or with both."

Now in amendment No. 115, I have suggested that the words 'or with fine' should be substituted by the words 'and with fine', and then in the following line, in line 20, the words 'or with both' be deleted. Now the reasons are obvious. The employers are generally not deterred by mere fine, but if there is a provision for fine plus imprisonment, then naturally it would be a deterrent clause. In order to make the provision in this clause more effective, I have proposed my amendment. The question was proposed.

D. Thengadi: I move:

116. "That at page 17, lines 6 to 8 be deleted."

(The amendment also stood in the name of V.M. Chordia.)

The questions were proposed.

D. Thengadi: Sir, our experience about the authority of the government to refer cases to an appropriate authority is not very happy. Therefore, we suggest that any worker or a registered trade union on his behalf should have the right to approach the Court and the matter should not be left to the sweet will of the government.

D. Thengadi: Sir, clause 32 imposes a blanket ban on the right to bonus to a number of categories, whose numerical strength, I very much fear, may be more than 45 lakhs, of course, including both Clauses 32 and 20. Therefore, I am totally opposed to both these clauses and I seek the omission of clause 32.

Now, sir, so far as general insurance is concerned, it has been rightly said that it is in the private sector. It is competitive and there is no justification whatsoever for eliminating that from the benefit of bonus. So far as LIC is concerned, as I said earlier, the employees of LIC have already entered into an agreement and through that agreement, they have already got their bonus. Cement, I think, is a very peculiar case. The government is trying to help them through one measure and is encroaching upon their right to bonus through another measure. This is not proper. The Bonus Commission has said that stevedore labour should not be ineligible for bonus, but this has not been accepted in this Bill. Regarding contract labour also, the position taken by this Bill is different from that of the Bonus Commission. Construction labour, whose number may be anywhere between two to three million, I believe, should not be excluded, because most of the construction companies are conducting their work on a permanent basis. A particular construction work may be temporary, but the work of construction companies as such is on a permanent basis and there are very big organisations of contractors which are doing big business. So, there is no justification for excluding them from the purview of this Bill. Also, this particular clause contains certain categories which were not recommended for exclusion by the Bonus Commission, e.g. any Financial Corporation, etc. This is not justified.

So far as educational institutions are concerned, true, it has been observed by the Supreme Court that they are non-profit-making institutions. Yet I may say from practical experience of many of the institutions that that observation does not hold good. That apart, the government is aware that many of the labour laws in a number of states are not applicable to the employees of educational institutions.

[The Deputy Chairman in the Chair] This is all the more reason why they should have been given the protection of this particular Bill and its benefits.

D. Thengadi: Regarding Chambers of Commerce, I said that in Calcutta, they used to pay *puja* bonus. Also, I had mentioned yesterday about the Bombay Dock Labour Board and those in Madras and Calcutta. The Bombay Dock Labour Board was making a provision for the payment of bonus and Calcutta and Madras were to follow suit.

Regarding the Reserve Bank of India, it is well known that the Reserve Bank had explained its position before the Supreme Court, namely once the capacity of other commercial banks to pay is determined, the Reserve Bank would be prepared to pay something more than other commercial banks. That means the capacity to pay is not lacking. It is also true that the Reserve Bank employees are not getting a living wage. Since there is a gap between their actual wage and the living wage and since the Reserve Bank of India has the capacity to pay, there is no moral justification for denying the Reserve Bank employees their right to bonus. In view of these considerations, I am opposing the inclusion of this clause in the Bill. I hope the hon'ble Labour Minister will consider it favourably, because the clause is of such a character that if it stands as it is, I may say that the very name of the Bill will have to be changed. Instead of calling it the Payment of Bonus Bill, we will have to call it the 'Non-payment of Bonus Bill'.

D. Sanjivayya: He suggested payment of minimum bonus Bill.

D. Thengadi: Madam, I move:

120. "That at page 19, after line 14, the following be inserted, namely:

"Explanation XI – A dispute shall also be deemed to be pending if the payment of bonus was not made due to non-availability of surplus."

(The amendment also stood in the name of V.M. Chordia.)

The questions were proposed.

D. Thengadi: My amendment says:

"That at page 19, after line 14, the following be inserted, namely:

'Explanation II – A dispute shall also be deemed to be pending if the payment of bonus was not made due to the non-availability of surplus'."

Madam, the Bonus Commission has recommended that their recommendation should have retrospective effect from the accounting year on any day in 1962, that is, regarding the bonus issue relating to financial year 1961-62. Now our hon'ble minister has said that he does not want to reopen the cases that are already decided because in that case, the industrial peace would be disturbed. We can appreciate that to some extent. Nevertheless, since now in this Bill, we have laid down the principles according to which, the quantum of bonus is to be computed. If there are any decisions or cases where bonus was denied and that denial was not consistent with, or was in contravention of, the principles laid down in this particular Bill, then the hon'ble Labour Minister should not hesitate to reopen those cases and, therefore, I have suggested that wherever the bonus was not paid due to the non-availability of surplus, such cases should be taken into consideration again. He should not be afraid of reopening such cases.

D. Thengadi: Madam, I move:

121. "That at page 19, lines 30 to 37 be deleted."

(The amendment also stood in the name of V.M. Chordia.)

The questions were proposed.

D. Thengadi: Madam, on September 18th, I had specifically asked, "Where there is no agreement, will the LAT formula prevail?" And the hon'ble Labour Minister had replied, "Yes, if there is no agreement, the bonus will be calculated both on the basis of the LAT formula and the present formula, whichever is higher, the worker will get it." I beg to submit, madam, that sub-clause (2) of Clause 34 does not fulfil the assurance given by the hon'ble Labour Minister on 18th September, 1964. No employer would be foolish enough to offer something more if a protection is given to him otherwise. Then one more point – there seems to be some inconsistency between two clauses, that is, Clause 32 and sub-clause (3) of Clause 34. Anyway, in view of the fact that the hon'ble Labour Minister was himself convinced of the justice of his own assurance on 18th September, I request him to withdraw this clause.

D. Thengadi: Madam, I move:

88. "That at page 1, lines 8-9, the words 'in which 20 or more persons are employed on any day during an accounting year' be deleted."

91. "That at page 1, line 13, for the figure '1964', the figure '1962' be substituted."

(These two amendments also stood in the name of V.M. Chordia.)

The questions were proposed.

D. Thengadi: Madam, my second amendment – No. 91 – is in keeping with the letter and spirit of the Bonus Commission's recommendation and much light has already been thrown upon this matter. Regarding amendment No. 88, I must say that I am opposed to the numerical floor of '20 or more persons employed', for one reason that the government is aware that in a commercial establishment, various devices or tactics are employed by the employers for evading the operation of labour laws. Employers employing more than 20 persons generally float another establishment to show less than 20 persons at both the places. Thereby, though they actually employ more than 20 persons, they avoid the legal responsibility of payments in the case of both establishments which are only for the sake of evading the operation of labour laws. In view of this and in order to give adequate protection even to the employees covered by the Shops and Establishments Act [1953], I am opposed to this numerical floor of 20.

The Payment of Bonus Bill, 1965: Continued[235]

D. Thengadi: I am very sorry that our arguments have not gone home. We expected that even at this stage, the hon'ble Labour Minister would give some consideration to our amendments and speeches. But all of them have been of no avail. I, however, expect that in time to come, since I am confident or convinced of his sincerity and earnestness, I expect that in time to come, if it is proved by experience that the attitude he has exhibited is now that of over-optimism, he would come forward with amendments to his own Bill so that, ultimately, the Bill, as amended, would stand in favour of workers.

Payment of Bonus (Amendment) Bill, 1966 (To Amend Sections 10, 12, 13 and 32 and to Omit Sections 11, 15 and the Fourth Schedule and Substitution of New Section for Section 20) – Motion for Consideration[236*]

I stand to support the Bill introduced by my friend, Basu.[237] When the Bonus Bill was being discussed and passed, the Labour Minister today was in charge of the Labour Ministry and I hope he will remember that even at that stage, in the course of discussion we had said that the drafting was defective and that it would not stand the scrutiny of the judiciary. Now this has come true. The main point is, unless the definition of bonus is incorporated in the Bill itself, it is difficult to support some of its other provisions. Unfortunately, there is some misunderstanding about the concept of bonus. Bonus is not profit-sharing. It has two characters. In the first place, bonus is only a deferred or supplementary wage so long as there is a gap between the living wage and the actual wage and only after the actual wage attains the level of the living wage, bonus assumes the character of profit-sharing and in view of the fact that the large bulk of our workers do not receive a living wage, it is but proper that it should be treated by and large as deferred or supplementary wage. If this definition is incorporated in the Act itself, many of the complications arising now

235. *Rajya Sabha Debate* dated 22nd September, 1965.

236. **Rajya Sabha Debate* dated 8th May, 1970.

237. Chitta Basu (1925-1997) – veteran Forward Bloc leader from West Bengal, Basu joined the party in 1945 as a student leader and rose to become its general secretary in 1979, a post he held till death. Basu was elected member of the West Bengal Legislative Assembly, 1957-62, member of the Rajya Sabha, 1966-1972 and 1985-1989, he was elected to the Lok Sabha from Barasat in West Bengal in 1977, 1980, 1989,1991 and 1996.

may be avoided. Secondly, regarding the statutory minimum bonus, it has been demanded that this should be raised to 1/12th of the actual income of the employee in the establishment and that means, it is one month's pay and I think our wage scales are so low that this demand to raise the statutory minimum to 1/12th is perfectly justified. There are some other aspects of the Act that deserve our consideration. Many establishments have been excluded and exempted from the operation of the Act. I would urge that all the establishments, whether in the public or private sector, even government industries, should be brought within the purview of the Act and the number of employees in the establishment should not be the criterion for including or excluding any establishment from the operation of this Act. Even if in a certain establishment, there are only one or two or four employees, even then they should be given the right to bonus because the actual wages are very far short of the living wage. The upper limit of 20 per cent is also not justified. This upper limit and the consequent setting-off and setting-on will give an opportunity to the employers to manipulate their accounts in such a way as to deprive the workers of their legitimate bonus and, therefore, it is necessary that the upper limit should be removed.

Another important factor is that the workers must be given the right to go through the accounts and inspect the balance sheet because unless they are given such a right to inspect the profit and loss account specifically, it would be very difficult for them to have any correct assessment. As a matter of fact, we are of the opinion that the workers, being partners, of the industrial establishment should be consulted in matters of deployment of capital and as a first step in that direction, it is necessary that it would be advisable that they should be given the right to inspect the profit and loss account. In this context, I would mention that the Bombay Stock Exchange has initiated a very good measure, that is, of publishing a sort of a directory comprising the profit and loss accounts and balance sheets of the preceding 10 years of all the important establishments particularly. Of course, the field workers in the labour can utilise this particular service of the Stock Exchange but over and above that it is necessary that such a right should be given. I think if all these suggestions are taken into consideration and the Bonus Act is redrafted, then it will be and it will not be susceptible to any onslaught from any quarter.

Payment of Bonus (Amendment) Bill, 1966: Motion for Reference to a Select Committee[238]

To begin with, I take strong exception to the principle enunciated by my progressive friend, Mr. Dharia,[239] that the quantum of bonus should be linked with productivity because we all know that labour productivity is not the only responsible factor for total productivity. There are many other factors, including the attitude of the management. We have very often seen that managements are responsible for reducing production because of the law of demand and supply. If production goes on unhampered, there will be additional supply which will reduce the price and, therefore, the profit margin. I personally know of instances where employers have even bribed or tried to bribe some of the trade unionists to bring about strikes so that production could be hampered and consequently the prices can go up and the profit of margin also can go up. When all such examples are there, it would be wrong to link the quantum of bonus with productivity.

For want of time, I am not entering into a debate.

Therefore, to link the quantum of bonus with productivity is highly unfair. Secondly, the whole discussion has arisen, the whole controversy has arisen, because the definition of bonus has not been incorporated in the Act itself. Bonus is not, as many of our friends would have us believe, merely profit-sharing. In the first place, so long as there is a gap between the living wage and the actual wage, bonus is only a deferred wage or a supplementary wage, and, as such, it deserves to be given all priority. Only after the actual wage attains the level of the living wage, the profit-sharing character of bonus commences. And, therefore, to say that since there are no profits, no bonus should be given, is irrelevant. If the living wage is being given to the workers, then profit can be the basis for computation of the quantum of bonus. So long as we have not reached the level of

238. *Rajya Sabha Debate* dated 11th December, 1970.

239. Mohan M. Dharia (1925-2013) – Congress leader from Maharashtra, associated with the Praja Socialist Party (PSP), later with the Bharatiya Lok Dal leader, was a freedom fighter, thinker, farmers' rights activist, environmentalist, associated with trade union movements and former Union Minister. Dharia was elected to the Rajya Sabha in 1964 and 1970, was member of the 5th Lok Sabha, 1971-77 was Minister of State for Planning, 1971, Minister of State for Works & Housing, 1974-1975. Dharia resigned from the Indira Gandhi ministry months before Emergency in March 1975, arguing that a dialogue must be held with Jayaprakash Narayan and other leaders. As a Bharatiya Lok Dal member, Dharia, was Minister of Commerce, Civil Supplies and Co-operation in the Morarji Desai ministry. He was conferred the Padma Vibhushan in 2005.

living wage, it is only a wage, deferred or supplementary. And, as such, the workers should not be denied their right to wage.

Even about the public sector undertakings, there has been a public debate going on about how to balance properly its autonomy and its answerability to Parliament. We know that in the name of nationalisation, there is an excessively heavy dose of bureaucratisation in the public sector undertakings. Even in countries like Great Britain, a Thinkers' Group of the socialist MPs of the Labour Party has come to the conclusion that because of bureaucratisation, it has not been possible for them to make the public sector undertakings completely answerable to Parliament. Therefore, I should like to suggest that even in regard to the public sector undertakings, rethinking is necessary. Bureaucratisation must be removed. And, for this purpose, I would like to suggest that a regular cadre of public administrators should be created. These public administrators should be given statutory recognition. The public sector undertakings should be placed under their charge. And, by way of experiment, it would be worthwhile to entrust at least two or three of the public undertakings to the Workers' Councils, that is, councils of the workers within the industry. And all the financial and technical aid which is generally made available to public undertakings if they are under the bureaucrats' charge should be made available to the workers also. And I am very confident that our workers are patriotic and responsible enough to manage the public undertakings as efficient at least as the bureaucrats are.

Then so far as the private industry is concerned – and as a matter of fact, this can be generalised and extended to the public undertakings also – it is necessary that the quantum of bonus should be increased because of the rising cost of living. Four per cent was the prescribed minimum. But we know how in the private sector, employers have turned this minimum into maximum so that even those who used to give 16, 17 or 20 per cent, are now giving only 4 per cent, and saying that their statutory obligation is over. So, the minimum is converted into maximum. In order to eliminate all controversies regarding bonus, it is necessary that our workers should be given the right to go behind, inspect and scrutinise the balance sheets and profit and loss accounts of their own concerns and, secondly, they should have a right to participate in the process of decision-making on deployment of capital of their own industry and, thirdly, it should be recognised as a principle that as money is the capital of any industry, labour also is the capital, though of a different type. As such, the labour of every worker should be evaluated in terms of shares. Every worker should be elevated to the status of a shareholder and, as shareholders, our workers should have a right to send their representative even to the Board of Directors. If such an arrangement materialises, there will be no controversy regarding bonus in our country. So long as that is not done, it is necessary that the Bill by Mr. Chitta Basu should be passed. It should be sent to the Select Committee and the right to bonus of the workers, irrespective of the number of employees in any particular undertaking, or its public or private character, irrespective of all these considerations, every worker who is earning a living wage must have a right to the deferred or supplementary wage, that is, bonus. This should be incorporated in the Act itself.

With these suggestions, I support the move for sending the Bill to the Select Committee.

The Payment of Bonus (Amendment) Bill, 1972[240]

D. Thengadi: Sir, I beg to move the following Resolution:

"That this House disapproves the Payment of Bonus (Amendment) Ordinance, 1972 (No. 8 of 1972) promulgated by the President on 23rd September, 1972."

To begin with, I must say that the workers have welcomed one gesture, i.e. the raising of the minimum quantum of bonus from 4 per cent or Rs. 40, whichever is higher to 8.33 per cent or Rs. 80, whichever is higher, but there are other factors which are prompting us to bring forward this resolution of disapproval. Firstly, the gesture is discriminatory in character. Bonus is, in fact, deferred wage. The number of wage-earners in the country, whose wage is below the living wage, is at least 13.5 million while by a rough estimate, this gesture is going to extend the benefit of bonus only to 3.5 million people. Now, since the definition of the bonus is not incorporated in this Bill or in this ordinance, naturally there is a possibility that even some of the welcome provisions could be struck down by the appropriate judicial authorities. So, this care has not been taken. As a matter of fact, it should be clearly stated that bonus assumes the character of profit-sharing only after the actual wage attains the level of a living wage. But till then, it is nothing but a deferred wage and as such, the payment of bonus should receive the priority as the payment of wage does. It should also be defined that so long as in any establishment, the last worker does not receive a

240. *Rajya Sabha Debate* dated 11th December, 1972.

living wage, the so-called profits are nothing but unpaid wages. This discrimination against the vast majority of the workers is being resented and, therefore, the better organised sections among the employees are organising demonstrations and other things of which our hon'ble minister is very well aware. So far as the Central Government employees are concerned, we know that after the strike of 19th September, 1968,[241] the Third Pay Commission was appointed but its work is being prolonged and nobody is sure when it would submit its report and also whether the recommendations would be commensurate with the difficulties and the hardships that the Central Government employees are undergoing because of the price rise during the last few months, and actually, price rise is a continual phenomenon in our country. Even the state government employees are organising themselves to secure the right to bonus, and it would be useless to make any differentiation amongst employees and employees on the basis that some of them are industrial employees and others are non-industrial employees. The point is not whether the workers belong to the industrial class or the non-industrial class, the main point to be borne in mind is whether they are receiving a living wage or not and if even the non-industrial employees of the Central Government or the state government do not receive a living wage to which they are entitled, they should be given the right to bonus as deferred wage. As a matter of fact, every wage-earner in our country, be he the employee of the Central Government or the state government or of the local self-government or body – even a domestic servant because he also has to purchase grain or cloth – or be they the members of the staff of the Rajya Sabha or the Lok Sabha, whoever is the wage-earner who has not been receiving a living wage, he must be given the right to bonus as a deferred wage. The hon'ble minister is aware that even some of the classes which are supposed to be privileged but are not so privileged actually, the journalists are agitating. In Punjab, journalists and non-journalists are on a strike for an increase in their wages. Even the need-based minimum wage is not being granted to the vast majority of the workers. It is wrong to say that a living wage is not a common thing. Therefore, every worker should be brought within the purview of the benefit of bonus.

---

241. One-day strike by Central Government employees numbering nearly 40 lakhs, demanding, among other things, a grant of minimum wages that had been recommended by the 15th Labour Conference of 1957. The Indira Gandhi government cracked down on the strikers, arresting leaders and workers, dismissing them from service and victimising them.

Secondly, the present provision in the Act stipulating that if the number of employees in any establishment is less than 20, then they would be deprived of their right to bonus, must be done away with. Even if in any establishment, there is a single employee, he should have the right to bonus. Again, when the industries start functioning and a worker gets his employment, his right to bonus should also start. There should be no such provision that for a number of years, the establishment should have an exemption from the obligation to pay bonus.

Again, it has been stated:

"Where the percentage of the salary or wage of an employee payable by way of bonus under this Act (including Section 34) in the accounting year commencing on any day in the year 1971 is higher than that paid or payable by way of bonus under this Act (including Section 34) to such employee in respect of the accounting year immediately preceding the aforesaid accounting year, so much of the amount calculated with reference to the difference in such percentages shall be remitted by the employer to the authority maintaining the Provident Fund account of such employee for crediting the same in that account and the balance shall be paid in cash to the employee within the time-limit specified in sub-section (1)."

Sir, we are demanding bonus to meet the price situation as existing today. If some of the amounts are credited to the Provident Fund account, that means they will be useful in future. In view of the fact that our demand for bonus is to meet the price rise today, this is quite unjust, unfair and cruel. So, this provision should also be withdrawn.

There were certain demands of the workers which deserve serious attention of the government, considerateness on the part of the government. But, in this measure, these demands of the workers have not been taken cognisance of. For example, they were demanding that they should have a right to scrutinise the balance sheet and profit and loss account. This provision is not there. Actually, the manipulations of employers in this regard are so well known. For example, in the award given by S.N. Mukherjee in the case of Bihar Sugar Mills, bonus dispute, he has clearly stated that it had become the practice with the employers of sugar factories not to submit correct accounts since the rule linking bonus to profits was authoritatively laid down. Now this rule to go behind the balance sheet and profit and loss account has been challenged. The various expenditures must be made known to the workers if the workers are to be treated as partners, morally and legally.

Secondly, in the name of depreciation, workers are deprived of their legitimate dues. We suggest that depreciation should be statutorily allowed at the flat rate of 3 per cent. This method was adopted by the Tata Iron and Steel Co. in the five-year agreement with the Tata Iron and Steel Company. The hon'ble minister is very well aware of it.

Then, sir, some regulation should have been there about the rate of return on capital. We suggest that this should be linked with the level of workers' wages. So long as the workers' wages are below the need-based minimum, return on capital should be 4 per cent, that is, 2 per cent, below the bank rate. When the level is above the need-based minimum wage, but below the living wage, the return on capital should be 6 per cent, that is bank rate. And above the living wage, it should be 8 per cent, that is bank rate plus 2 per cent.

Now, regarding reserve, the reserve should be treated as the joint property of the labour and employer. There the management should also be joined, and whenever bonus shares are to be issued to the shareholders out of the accumulated reserves, workers should also be given bonus shares out of these reserves.

Regarding prior charges, one of the suggestions was that income tax should be allowed as a prior charge. Direct taxes, super profit tax and surtax should not be included in the computation of tax. These were some of the demands of the workers which have not been taken cognisance of while framing this new measure. Whenever workers demand more money on any score, the pet argument of the government is that if they pay more money, there would be price rise. Probably, the hon'ble minister is very well aware that this is a misleading argument. Every wage rise is not responsible for price rise.

Wage rise is responsible for price rise only to the extent to which wage rise is in excess of productivity rise. And even a third party such as the National Labour Commission has said that in India, wage rise has lagged behind productivity rise, while productivity rise and wage rise both have failed to keep pace with the price rise. So, this pet argument of the government will not do. Secondly, the very economic thinking of the Government of India needs to be reoriented. As a matter of fact, our main problem is how to put money into the pockets of the lowliest of the low. According to economics, if the lowest paid man is given more money, a new cycle of economics can be started. The hon'ble minister is aware that Prof. Dandekar and Rath[242] in their thesis have said that the minimum desirable consumption level in urban areas should be at the price level of 1968-69, at least Rs. 486, if the entire economy is to receive a boost. With the present price level, it would come to Rs. 536 for urban areas.

Now, with all these considerations, we have brought forward this reservation of disapproval. Though, as a matter of fact, we are highly obliged to the hon'ble minister, Mr. Khadilkar, for the efforts he has made in securing the raising of the minimum quantum of bonus from 4 to 8.33 per cent. I hope that he would further exert his influence on the government and see that the coverage of the Bonus Act is increased, and that every wage-earner is given the benefit of the right to bonus as deferred wage.

The Minister of Labour and Rehabilitation (*R.K. Khadilkar*):[243] Mr. Vice Chairman, sir, I beg to move:

"That the Bill further to amend the Payment of Bonus Act, 1965, as passed by the Lok Sabha, be taken into consideration."

The Bill seeks to replace the Payment of Bonus (Amendment) Ordinance, 1972. Hon'ble members are aware of the demands that were made in this House as well as outside for amendment in the Payment of Bonus Act, 1965, so as to increase the quantum of minimum and maximum bonus payable under the Act. A Bill on the subject was introduced in this House by Chitta Basu. In the course of the debate on that Bill, I had stated that the bonus scheme embodied in the Act would be reviewed. Accordingly, a committee known as the Bonus Review Committee was set up by a resolution of the government, dated 20th April, 1972; to review the operation of the Payment of Bonus Act, 1965. This committee is headed

242. In 1971, V.M. Dandekar and N. Rath, for the first time, made a comprehensive assessment "of poverty in India, based on National Sample Survey (NSS) data from 1960-61. They argued that the poverty line must be derived from the expenditure that was adequate to provide 2250 calories per day in both rural and urban areas. This generated debate on minimum calorie consumption norms while estimating poverty and variations in these norms based on age and sex." (accessed at: https://www.prsindia.org/tags/dandekar-and-rath) (13.9.2020)

243. R.K. Khadilkar (1905-1979), Congress leader from Maharashtra, freedom fighter, later joined the Peasants and Workers Party, rejoined Congress in 1962, was member, 2nd Lok Sabha, 3rd Lok Sabha, 4th and 5th Lok Sabha, Deputy Speaker, Lok Sabha, 1967-1969; between 1969 and 1971, Khadilkar held a number portfolios as Minister of Supply and Minister in the Ministry of Finance, 1969- 1970; Minister of Supply 1971; Minister of Labour and Rehabilitation from 1971 onwards. It was during his tenure as Labour Minister that the Punekar Committee was set up to review 'the operation of the Payment of Bonus Act, 1965.'

by Dr B.K. Madan[244] and it includes as members, economists and persons representing employer-and-workers' interests. The committee has been given detailed terms of reference and its work is in progress. It has, however, given its finding on one of the terms of reference relating to the raising of the minimum bonus payable under the Act. Unfortunately, the committee could not come to unanimous conclusions on the subject. Its findings were given in two separate reports, one signed by the Chairman, Dr S.D. Punekar,[245] N.S. Bhat and Harish Mahindra, and the other by R.P. Billimoria, Mahesh Desai, G. Ramanujam and Satish Loomba.[246] After a careful consideration of both the reports, government decided that the statutory minimum bonus payable to the workers covered by the Payment of Bonus Act for the accounting year commencing on any day in 1971 should be raised from 4 per cent of the wages or salary to 8-1/3 per cent.

At the same time, the government did consider it necessary to take some protective measures so that the benefit of the higher minimum bonus might not get eroded by any aggravation of the existing inflationary pressures on the economy. It was accordingly decided that only the minimum bonus be paid fully in cash but where payments above the rate of 8-1/3 per cent are to be made, the plus difference, if any, between the payments to be made during the accounting year 1971-72 and the payments made during the accounting year 1970-71 should be deposited in the Provident Fund account of the beneficiary. These two main decisions were given effect to by the Payment of Bonus Amendment Ordinance 1972 which was promulgated by the President under Clause (1) of Article 123 of the Constitution on 23rd September, 1972 and which the Bill before the House seeks to replace. Opportunity has been taken while drafting the Bill to clarify one or two points raised after the Ordinance was promulgated. It was pointed out that while the percentage of wages or salaries declared as bonus in the year 1970-71 and 1971-72 may be the same, the amount actually payable in the later year could be higher due to increase in the wages and salary of an employee and that it should not be necessary to deposit the excess amount in such cases in the Provident Fund accounts.

244. B.K. Madan, economist, secretary of the Indian delegation to the Bretton Woods Conference (United Nations Monetary Conference), 1944, served for many years with the Reserve Bank of India (RBI) from director research to Deputy Governor, he was India's first Executive Director at IMF and World Bank; served for two terms as Executive Director of IMF.

245. S.D. Punekar, Chairman, Bonus Review Committee 1972-1974.

246. Bonus Review Committee Members.

It was also pointed out that in the case of employees who were not in service for the whole year 1970-71, a comparison between the amount of bonus paid in 1970-71 and 1971-72 for the purpose of determining the excess to be deposited in the Provident Fund would lead to an anomalous situation. These anomalies have now been removed by making suitable provisions in the Bill. As I have said earlier, the present Bill only seeks to replace the ordinance already promulgated. I may also add that the provisions made in the Bill will relate only to the payment of bonus for one year, namely the accounting year commencing on any day in the year 1971. The provisions in the Bill are, therefore, transitional and temporary in nature. The government may have to come up with more comprehensive proposals for amendment when the final report of the Bonus Review Committee is received and examined. Meanwhile, the present Bill may be taken into consideration.

Payment of Bonus (Amendment) Bill, 1973[247]

D. Thengadi: Mr. Deputy Chairman, sir, the hon'ble minister has rightly said that the Bill is non-controversial. It has been our experience that wherever payment is involved, the employers are not generally amenable to a mere advice by the government. So, this Bill was a must. It is also true that the Bonus Review Committee has not yet completed its work and, certainly, the sad demise of our friend and colleague, Satish Loomba, has caused irreparable loss to the working class movement in general and to the working of the Bonus Review Committee in particular. But, sir, now that the amending Bill has been introduced, the government could have very well incorporated certain other non-controversial provisions in the same amending Bill so that it becomes more effective. For example, whatever be the formula presented by the Bonus Review Committee after it completes the work, the principle of bonus should have been incorporated in this amending Bill and probably it would have saved us of so much of industrial unrest. The Bill should have specifically stated that bonus is not merely profit-sharing, but that so long as there is a gap between the living wage and the actual wage, bonus is a deferred wage and only after the actual wage attains the level of the living, wage, bonus assumes the character of profit-sharing. If this definition is not incorporated in the law itself, industrial unrest is bound to persist.

247. *Rajya Sabha Debate* dated 16th August, 1973.

Secondly, sir, I endorse the views expressed by Anandan[248] that like charity, justice also should begin at home and, therefore, in view of the fact that bonus is nothing but a deferred wage for the Class III and Class IV employees also of the Central Government, the Government of India should have gracefully come forward with the proposal to offer the right to bonus to the Class III and Class IV employees, whether they are industrial workers or non-industrial workers.

We have to establish that the Government of India is a model employer. I am not entering into the discussion here but, very unfortunately, the Pay Commission has absolved the Government of India of its responsibilities of becoming a model employer. It has just said that the Government of India is a demanding employer and not an ideal employer. Had the Government of India given a lead, then the employers in the private sector would have been forced to follow the lead and give justice to their workers. Even at this late stage, I urge upon the government to offer this right of bonus to all its employees and prevail upon the state governments to cater this right to their own employees. This is really a non-controversial Bill. The only thing is that it ought to have been more comprehensive. With these comments, I support the Bill.

Statutory Resolution Seeking Disapproval of the Payment of Bonus (Amendment) Ordinance, 1972 (No. 8 of 1972) Promulgated by the President on 23rd September, 1972[249]

D. Thengadi: In the first place, I should like to repeat that every wage rise is not responsible for price rise. The wage rise is responsible for price rise only to the extent to which the wage rise is in excess of productivity rise and during the last 25 years, productivity rise is in excess of wage rise. And that is according to the National Labour Commission.

Sir, I quite appreciated the patriotic feeling expressed by my friend, Babubhai Chinai[250] but I should like to know from him whether out of his enthusiasm for national re-construction he and his colleagues are

248. T.V. Anandan (1904-1999) – two-term Independent member of Rajya Sabha from Tamil Nadu between 1964 1970 and 1970 to 1976.

249. *Rajya Sabha Debate* dated 11th December, 1972.

250. Babubhai M. Chinai (1913-1975) –Member of Parliament from Maharashtra. Chinai was Member, Bombay Legislative Council, 1952-58 and member, Rajya Sabha, 1958-1964, 1964-1970 and 1970-1975. Chinai was also president of the Swadeshi League and was conferred the Padma Bhushan in 1966.

prepared to concede to the workers the right to scrutinise the balance sheet and profit and loss accounts.

To challenge the propriety of different expenditures and to participate in the process of decision-making on the deployment of capital, I want specific answers for these.

Sir, I was really surprised to hear from our friend, Bipinpal Das[251] the term 'economism'. That term was used contemptuously by Lenin in a different context under different circumstances. Means must be suited to the ends and the ends visualised by Lenin were very clear. He was very unequivocal. I do not know whether my friend stands for the same type of dictatorship. If we are to follow the parliamentary democratic system, then this term 'economism' cannot be used so contemptuously. It is true that 22 crores of our people, that is 40 per cent of the total population, is below the subsistence level, but that is no fault of the employees of the Central Government or the state governments or the local self-government bodies. It is the outcome of the faulty and defective policies of the Government of India and the different state governments. The state government and the Central Government employees should not be made to pay for the sins of commission and omission on the part of the different governments. The Government of India has dealt with the problem of economic reconstruction very casually and lightly. Just to give one or two illustrations, all of us know that unemployment is the biggest economic problem of the country but we are surprised that today neither the Planning Commission nor the Government of India is in a position to give us a correct assessment of the magnitude of the problem of unemployment and the Fourth Plan document says that the very methodology for assessment of unemployment in a country like India is not available with us. That shows beyond all doubt how this matter has been treated casually and lightly by the authorities. Therefore, it would be wrong to punish the employees of the Central and state governments for the sins committed by government itself. I was really amazed to learn from our socialist friends that differentiation should be made between the employees of the private sector and the public sector and government

251. Bipinpal Das (b.1923-) – Praja Socialist Party leader and later Congress leader, was Secretary, Assam PSP, joint secretary, All India PSP, general secretary, All India Socialist Party, 1956 and 1957; Member, Rajya Sabha, 1970-1976 and 1976-1982. Das was also Union Deputy Minister of External Affairs, 1974-1977 and was elected to the Lok Sabha from Tezpur, Assam in 1984.

departments. That means the government wants to introduce socialism only at the cost of somebody else.

Charity does not begin at home. Socialism does not begin at home. The government is not prepared to concede the right to bonus to its own employees, but socialism has to be brought about at the cost of the last penny of the last private employer. We are not in favour of private capitalism, but we do not understand how a socialist government can afford to say that it will not do justice to its own employees, while passing a law for doing justice to employees in the private sector. During the last war, it used to be said that Great Britain would fight to the last drop of blood of the last Frenchman. Probably, that is the procedure through which the government wants to bring in socialism, not at its own cost but at the cost of somebody else. I again urge upon the Government of India to do justice to its own employees, not to provoke the employees of the Railways, the Posts and Telegraphs Department, Civil Aviation, Defence Production, who are described as industrial employees, and also the employees of the Secretariat and other departments who are not industrial employees, to go on the warpath. It is not graceful for the government to allow its own employees to fight the battle for bonus, the battle for deferred wage, a very reasonable thing in the ethics of socialism. So, without making it a prestige issue, I request the government to concede the right to bonus to all the employees of the Central and state governments and also to consider seriously how the same right can be extended to every wage-earner in the country.

By way of clarification, I should like to ask whether, while the employees of the non-competitive public sector undertakings are given the benefit of the minimum bonus formula, they should also be covered by the general bonus law.

Then, it was a surprise when I heard from one of our members that the concept of bonus is new. Probably, all of us know that a so-called reactionary Prime Minister of a reactionary state – I am referring to the late Sir C.P. Ramaswamy Aiyar[252] of Travancore state – had made it a rule that every employer must pay 4.25 per cent as compulsory, minimum

252. C.P. Ramaswami Iyer (1879-1966) – administrator, jurist, educationist, social reformer, thinker best known for his contributions as Diwan of the state of Travancore, before Independence, where his positive contributions were irrigation, industrialisation, temple-entry legislation and many other progressive socio-economic steps. During the last phase of the freedom struggle when Partition was being discussed, C.P. at one time contemplated an independent Travancore; this was one of his most negative

bonus, whether the concern was running in profit or loss.

Then, sir, so far as the ceiling or maximum limit on bonus is concerned, I should like to suggest that the bonus should form part of a sound unit and the appropriate accounts should be made on this basis for the purpose of computation of the gross profit. There should be no ceiling or maximum limit on the quantum of bonus. The present ceiling of 20 per cent should be done away with and, consequently, the system of set-on and set-off should be discontinued.

That ceiling should not exist. Our objection is for the ceiling. No maximum limit should be statutorily prescribed. That is what we want.

With these observations, I close my speech.

The Industrial Disputes (Amendment) Bill, 1963[253]

D. Thengadi: I want to know from the Minister whether in the light of his past experience, it is desirable to introduce a new system, that is, of secret ballot and whether the Parliament is not a competent body to set aside the decision of the Indian Labour Conference even if it is necessary to set aside.

D. Thengadi: This particular amendment is quite in keeping with the original intentions of the government in this regard. So, I request the hon'ble Deputy Minister not to refuse it, as if refusal is part of a ritual.

Ratanlal Kishorilal Malviya:[254] Madam, the rights of the workers, so far as their permanency is concerned, are protected by the Employees' Standing Orders Act.[255] Every concern worth the name has got Standing Orders in which the service conditions of a worker are defined. The complaint which has been made by Mr. Kumaran[256] is correct. We have

---

moments. He later came round in support of an Indian Union. Post-independence CP contributed in many ways, mainly in the field of education as Member of the UGC, Vice Chancellor of Benaras Hindu University and Annamalai University etc.

253. *Rajya Sabha Debate* dated 8th September, 1964.

254. R.K. Malviya (1907-1985) – Congress leader from Madhya Pradesh, freedom fighter, for sometime secretary of Harijan Sevak Sangh, labour leader, president of the Madhya Pradesh unit of the INTUC, member, Constituent Assembly, 1948-50 and Provisional Parliament, 1950-52. Malviya was member of the Rajya Sabha, 1954-1960 and 1960-1966; was parliamentary secretary to the Union Minister of Labour and Employment and later was Union Deputy Minister for Labour and Employment, 1962-66.

255. Act of an Indian Parliament regarding industrial establishments to formally define conditions of employment.

256. P.K. Kumaran (1921-1991) – CPI leader from Andhra Pradesh, was member of the Rajya Sabha (1968-1962).

also got complaints to the effect that if there is a provision in the Standing Orders to have a temporary worker only for a period of three months, six months or for a period of one year. But even in cases of work of permanent nature, unscrupulous employers terminate their services before the end of three months, six months or one year and after a few days, they will again be taken back in service on a fresh contract. So far as law is concerned, this practice is against the Standing Orders. It is for the trade unions to strengthen themselves and protect the rights which have already been conferred on the workers. This amendment, therefore, is not the remedy to protect such workers who are turned out of service before the period expires. The remedy lies elsewhere. I would request my hon'ble friend to seek remedy elsewhere and not by means of this amendment. I am sorry I cannot accept the amendment.

D. Thengadi: Madam, while I will not like to reiterate what has already been said by way of comments on different clauses in the Bill, I would just like to emphasise that the entire Bill is a piece-meal legislation which is not going to serve the purpose it is meant to serve and, therefore, it is quite necessary to introduce a more comprehensive Bill. Therefore, I request the government that instead of rushing this Bill through, the government should take more time and bring in a more comprehensive Bill. Then, that would be to the benefit of the workers and all concerned.

The Industrial Disputes (Amendment) Bill, 1963[257]

D. Thengadi: Sir, this measure is not as comprehensive as it could have been or should have been. In the first place, it has been suggested by workers that the jurisdiction of the Industrial Disputes Act should be co-extensive with the areas of industrial disputes or at least with the jurisdiction of the Indian Trade Unions Act. There is no reason why this Act should not be extended to such of the industries and services where industrial disputes exist. Even where certain negotiation machinery has been set up, as is the case in the Railways, there is no harm in extending this Act. It would be helpful; it would simplify matters and not complicate them. Educational institutions and even social service organisations for that matter should not be excluded so that the jurisdiction of this Act should be co-extensive with the areas of industrial disputes.

257. *Rajya Sabha Debate* dated 9th June, 1964.

When I am uttering the word 'comprehensive', I am reminded of the objection taken by our hon'ble friend, Mr. Abid Ali,[258] to this word, and he has said that he does not understand, though I know that he understands, as to what needs to be dealt with in a comprehensive Bill. Now, only in an illustrative way, I would put forth a few points.

In a comprehensive Bill, our workers would like that in clause (k) of Section 2 of the principal Act, the words 'Dismissal, removal, termination or retrenchment of a workman mean a dispute between employer(s) and such workman' should be added, that in Clause (g) of Section 2 of the principal Act, the following sub-clause (iii) should be added:

"(iii) In relation to the workman employed in connection with the main business of the industry or the jobs connected with the main business, through contractors, the principal employer."

They would like that Section 10 of the principal Act[259] dealing with reference to disputes to Boards, courts or tribunals should be recast that Section 17A of the principal Act should be deleted, that the proviso to Clause (1) of Section 25FFF of the principal Act be deleted, that notwithstanding the present amendment, Section 33C of the principal Act dealing with the recovery of money due from an employer be recast, that sub-section (3) of Section 36 of the principal Act dealing with the right to be represented by a legal practitioner be revised. I am giving these only by way of illustration. This is not an exhaustive list and am sure that all concerned would be convinced that it is necessary, rather inevitable, to have a comprehensive amending Bill and that the piece-meal measure as is brought forth now would not serve the purpose.

Now, so far as this measure is concerned, there are a few points which I would like to place before the House. In this amending Bill, Clause 6(a) is unjustified. There should be no provision for an even number of arbitrators. In case the parties can agree to have one common person as the umpire, why can't they agree beforehand to have the same person as the arbitrator? This would save considerable time.

Clause 6(b) of the Bill should be deleted. A period of 14 days is quite enough for the purpose. Why should it be made one month? It would save avoidable delay.

---

258. Abid Ali (1899-1973) – Congress leader from Maharashtra, trade union unionist and one of the founding members of the INTUC, served for four terms in the Rajya Sabha between 1952-1970. Was Union Deputy Minister for Labour between 1952 and 1962.

259. Main portion of the Industrial Disputes (Amendment) Bill, 1963.

Clause 3 of the amending Bill seeks to amend Section 7 of the principal Act and I think that amendment is necessary so as to enable the lawyers practising industrial law for not less than five years to fill up the posts. I must emphasise here the fact that while in other branches of justice, it is necessary to adhere to legal justice, in industrial law social justice is to be looked after and probably the minds that are trained in the art and psychology of legal justice are not quite capable of dealing with the problems of social justice. If they are efficient in one branch, that is of legal justice, they would be justified in not being so efficient in the other branch, that is of social justice. Therefore, instead of confining the sphere only to judges who are trained in the art and psychology of legal justice, the posts should be open to lawyers also who have practised industrial law for not less than five years.

The Deputy Chairman (*Akbar Ali Khan*):[260] But our judges have risen to the occasion and they take into consideration social developments also.

D. Thengadi: I do not want to exclude them, Sir. I just want to include the lawyers.

Now, the principle of voluntary arbitration is quite good so far as it goes but it has been our experience that the attitude of even the Government of India in its own departments has not been very helpful in this respect. We should like to request the Government of India to change its own attitude first so that it could have the moral authority to give appropriate advice to the employers in the private sector.

Now, there has been some discussion about the word 'majority' and the use of the device of secret ballot. Of course, I agree with the hon'ble minister that some sanctity should be attached to the decisions of the tripartite conferences. But if I am right – and I should like to be wrong – there are occasions when certain ministries have informed the Pay Commission that the government or at least that particular Ministry does not treat the decisions of the Tripartite Labour Conference as final and binding on it. If that be the attitude of the government in one case, why should so much sanctity be attached and it be said that the decisions are final and binding? After all, that is not the last word of wisdom. If we

260. Akbar Ali Khan (1899-1994) – Congress leader and educationist from Andhra Pradesh, a three term Rajya Sabha Member between 1954 and 1972, was Deputy Chairman of Rajya Sabha for twelve years, was awarded the Padma Bhushan in 1965. Khan was also Governor of Uttar Pradesh and Odisha.

grow in wisdom through experience, there is no reason why we should not change whatever has been decided when it is proved erroneous or mistaken subsequently. And, therefore, I should like to suggest that this device of secret ballot which is more accurate should be adopted in deciding the majority of the workers. Of course, I entirely agree with the suggestion that expiry of leave and other things should not affect adversely the continuity of service. This much about the amending Bill.

Now, sir, there are certain aspects which deserve serious consideration when we are dealing with this amending Bill. Now, as patriots, we are very much in favour of industrial peace and I suggest that patriotism is not the monopoly of any one particular organisation. I respect all patriots but I differ from some of them when they claim to be the sole claimants to patriotism. So, instead of identifying patriotism with pro-capitalism, let us call a spade a spade and without bringing into consideration patriotism here where it is irrelevant, let us say clearly that our legislation would cater justice to the workers and that while catering justice to the workers, the government would see that no union is discriminated against and that no favour or partiality is shown to any one particular central labour organisation. I am referring to the INTUC. Now, it has been established that the government very often goes out of its way in supporting the claims of the INTUC. I can very well understand it, and it would be more honest if we passed a legislation that in India, no central labour organisation excepting the INTUC should be allowed to survive. Such a legislation would be more honest.

Arjun Arora: That would be fascism.

D. Thengadi: I cannot say but at the same time...

Abid Ali: Workers will decide it.

D. Thengadi: And, therefore, we want secret ballot for which you should have no objection. (interruptions) Let us have secret ballot, and I can say and challenge that 95 per cent, of the INTUC unions having recognition today will lose their recognition by secret ballot.

Then there are a few other considerations which I should like to place before the House. The main difficulty which arises is regarding wages. I request the House to take into consideration the suggestion of setting up a Standing National Wage Council on the model of our conciliation machinery to go through the entire problem of region-cum-industry-wise wages and make appropriate recommendations from time to time. Also there is some difficulty experienced by labour and trade unionists on account of a certain chaos in the procedures. Therefore, it would be advisable to compile Labour Procedure Code on the model of the Civil Procedure Code and the Criminal Procedure Code. Also we will have to consider at some future date, in order to maintain industrial peace, whether it is not desirable to change the structure of industry and to introduce such a pattern as would eliminate the employer-employee relationship itself through a measure of labourisation of industry, that is, through co-partnership and labour co-operativisation. All these suggestions should be considered. Against this background, I suggest that this measure should not be rushed through. We should take some time to have a more comprehensive measure on the same subject so that it will be more effective and we will not be required to pass another piece-meal legislation on the same point.

The Industrial Disputes (Amendment) Bill, 1964[261]

D. Thengadi: Madam, these amendments have to be considered on two different levels. The amendments in themselves are quite welcome. They seek to give more relief to the workers and their families. At the same time, I agree with Mr. Arjun Arora that this time-limit of one year should be dispensed with or done away with. I also welcome sub-section (5) of the proposed Section 33C, because it simplifies the procedure in favour of workers. Also, the amendment to Clause 20 is welcome because it will avoid procedural delays. At the same time, madam, I should like to know from the hon'ble minister why, if at all he intended to bring certain amendments here, he did not try to introduce more comprehensive, if not Bill, at least amendments, because there were certain important points made out during the last discussion, and he could have availed of this opportunity to introduce those amendments also. In brief, I should like to mention some of them so that the hon'ble Labour Minister could clarify the position.

Particularly there was much discussion about the criterion for ascertaining the majority and, if my memory be correct, he had said that he would not hesitate to revise the method under certain conditions. I want to know why a secret ballot should not be adopted, and I think that though the decisions of the Indian Labour Conference are to be respected, much fetish should not be made about them, because we know that one of the most important decisions of the Indian Labour Conference, that is regarding the norms and standards of the need-based minimum wage,

261. *Rajya Sabha Debate* dated 26th November, 1964.

was not accepted by the Government of India as final and binding. At the same time, there was discussion last time about the express permission of the Tribunal or the Court which should be sought by the employer before proceeding by way of dismissal of any worker. But that also has not received the proper attention of the Labour Ministry.

Then regarding sub-section (5) of Section 33, the redrafting of it was suggested by hon'ble R.K. Malviya himself. Without going into the matter, I would only suggest that he should stick on to his point.

Deputy Chairman: How long will you take?

D. Thengadi: Two or three minutes.

Deputy Chairman: There is a motion to follow after this. Please finish in two or three minutes.

D. Thengadi: All right, madam. At the same time, it was emphasised last time that references should be automatic and also that workers thrown out of employment because of an occupational injury or major accident should be given retrenchment benefits. I am not giving an exhaustive list, but this is only illustrative. I should like the hon'ble minister to explain to us why he did not take the trouble of bringing a comprehensive Bill before us or introducing all these amendments because we are again considering the original amendment.

Industrial Disputes (Second Amendment) Bill, 1964[262]

D. Thengadi: Sir, this amending Bill is quite a healthy one and on behalf of workers, I think we would be justified in welcoming the various provisions of the Bill. It was but natural and justifiable that the Indian Airlines and the Air India Corporation should be brought within the jurisdiction of the central sphere. But, at the same time, I take this opportunity to bring one particular fact to the notice of the Labour Ministry that the provisions of the Industrial Disputes Act are not being properly extended to the concerns that have already been brought under the jurisdiction of the Centre. I am referring to the Railways. As a matter of fact, the Industrial Disputes Act is applicable to the Railways, but it is well-known that the administration has persistently refused to abide by the provision and, therefore, I should like to request the government that they should be very particular about the effective implementation of the provisions of the Industrial Disputes Act in the various concerns which are brought within its purview, that the dispute between an employee and employer, individual workman, should

262. *Rajya Sabha Debate* dated 18th February, 1965.

be per se an industrial dispute. This is a long-felt need. No doubt we stand for the growth of a strong trade union movement and as such, we should like to see that every workman is represented through the union, and that every industry should have only one union so that the principle of one-industry one-union should be brought into practice. Nevertheless, under the present circumstances, it would be unjustifiable to deny the workers their right to get their cases represented through a union or through their own lawyers, or themselves. As such, this particular provision under the present circumstances deserves to be welcomed, though we should like to see that in times to come, there should be growth of healthy trade union movement under which every workman would be represented through some union or the other.

The lay-off compensation would become payable for all the days of lay-off beyond the first 45 days, whether the period is continuous or not. This is also a welcome feature of this Bill because as we all know, our employers have been experts in depriving labour of its legitimate dues. Various devices have been adopted to this effect. I would like particularly to mention the device of continuing workmen for years together as temporary just through some technical lacuna and I would also like to request the Labour Ministry that even as they have been graceful enough, kind enough or just and fair enough to bring in this amendment, there should be some provision which would ensure confirmation of workers in their respective jobs and which would disallow the employers' practice of continuing the workers as temporary for years and years together. But so far as this particular provision is concerned, we welcome it wholeheartedly. At the same time, a provision for enhanced penalty in the event of continued breach of settlements or awards by employers was also demanded by the workmen and this is also a fulfillment of a long-felt need. On the whole, this entire Bill is worth being welcomed by the working class of our country.

The Indian Trade Unions (Amendment) Bill, 1964[263]

D. Thengadi: Madam Vice Chairman, I appreciate the omission of the word 'Indian' from subsection (1) of Section 1 of the principal Act since that word has by now become superfluous. I also welcome the replacing of the word 'officer' by the word 'office-bearer' because the latter is more in keeping with the spirit and environment of the trade-union field. I also welcome the amendment proposed to Section 28, which will now provide

263. *Rajya Sabha Debate* dated 25th November, 1964.

for the submission of the statistics by the end of the calendar year. Of course, we in the trade unions will take some time in the initial stages to get psychologically adjusted to this change, but nevertheless there will be this adjustment before long. At the same time, I should like to suggest that in the near future, if not immediately, an attempt should be made to have this calendar year the Bharat year. I think this should be possible.

I also welcome the amendment disqualifying any person, who has been convicted by a Court of moral turpitude, from becoming or continuing as member of the Executive or any other office-bearer of a registered trade union. But the provision of the period of 5 years, I dare suggest, should be dropped, though just now we have heard from the hon'ble Education Minister, Chagla[264] that a similar provision of 5 years is there in the various other Acts also, one of which relates to Members of Parliament. I think that the other Acts should be cast in a different mould and this provision of 5 years should be dropped.

There is one particular warning that I want to give at this stage. While the amendment disqualifying persons convicted of moral turpitude has been introduced with the best of intentions and with the noblest of intentions, probably this can be exploited to the disadvantage of genuine trade union workers by vested interests because there is a dangerous tendency amongst interested parties to malign their adversaries. I fear that the introduction of this amendment is likely to give rise to a campaign of character assassination against trade union workers. As an example of this particular tendency, I may cite here a recent episode at Bombay. I will not take much time. This episode will indicate the tendency that is there on the part of vested interests. As everybody knows, on August 12th last, there was a general token strike in Maharashtra and also in Bombay, in the course of which lakhs and lakhs of workers had resorted to strike. But the management of the Reserve Bank of India sought the help of the Police Department to put some of its employees in the wrong. The Police Department did not oblige them, it must be said in fairness to that department. The Police Department did not oblige the management, but 21 days after that strike, show-cause notices were issued and now after 3 months, on 17th November, 43 of the workers have been charge-sheeted. This is wrong. At the same time, I want to mention how they tried to seek the help of the Police Department and how that department did not oblige them. I am just giving it as an example of the tendency on the part of the

264. M.C. Chagla was Union Education Minister between 1963-1966.

management. Here is the letter of the Inspector of Police concerned to the management of the Reserve Bank of India.

Palton Road Police Station, Bombay.

26th August, 1964

The Manager,

Reserve Bank of India, Bombay-1.

Sir,

Apropos your telephonic conversation with Deputy Commissioner of Police, Zone I, Daphale regarding the demonstrations of the bank employees in the Reserve Bank of India on 12-8-1964.

The list of the Reserve Bank employees who demonstrated inside the bank on 12-8-64 is enclosed. Since no cognisable offence was disclosed, no action was feasible at this end. You may, if you deem fit, take any departmental action against the demonstrators.

Yours faithfully,

Inspector of Police, Palton Road Police Station.

This is just an example of the tendency. Because of the noble intentions that have prompted the introduction of this amendment, I support this amendment and also the entire Bill. At the same time, I would like the Labour Ministry of the Government of India to take proper precautions against any such campaign of character assassination and malignment by interested parties.

D. Thengadi: One clarification. I said in the near future, not immediately. We have no objection to have either the 'Vishu' in Kerala or the Tamil New Year day in Tamil Nadu or any other year.

P. Ramamurti:[265] You may have no objection, but other people will have objection in this county. It is not decided by one Mr. Thengadi. There are other people. For example, if I speak for Tamil Nadu I am absolutely certain if not Mr. Thengadi, there will be hundreds of other people from the north to oppose it. (interruption)

Arjun Arora: I will not understand the Tamil year.

D. Thengadi: The only suggestion is you know that we are heading towards National Integration.

---

265. P. Ramamurti (1908-1987) – CPI-M leader, Politburo member, one of the founding members of the CPI in Tamil Nadu, earlier with the Congress Socialist Party (CSP), ideologue, trade unionist, later was part of the breakaway faction which formed the CPI-M, became the first General Secretary of the CITU in 1970, Ramamurti was member, Madras Legislative Assembly, 1952-57; leader of the Opposition in the Madras Legislative Assembly, 1953-57 and member, Rajya Sabha, 1960-1966 and 1977-1983.

The Indian Trade Unions (Amendment) Bill, 1964[266]

D. Thengadi: Madam, I have already expressed serious apprehensions about the amendment disqualifying persons convicted of moral turpitude from becoming office-bearers and as an example of the tendency to indulge in character assassination by vested interests, I cited the example of the Manager of the Reserve Bank of India attempting it in Bombay. I also request the hon'ble Labour Minister to explain to us how legitimate trade union workers would be protected from such campaigns of character assassination. Nevertheless, I view this particular amendment not in an isolated manner but as part and parcel of our general programme to improve the standard of public life. Now that we are trying to evolve a code of conduct for ministers and politicians and what not, I think there should be no objection to any attempt to evolve a code of conduct for trade union leaders also. Therefore, though this particular amendment has its own defects – and I have already referred to them – I think there is some merit about it also. Every effort should be made to make it workable and to make it practicable.

I am very much grateful to my hon'ble friend Bhupesh Gupta for furnishing us with a new piece of information that morality can be classified under different heads, such as capitalist morality, patriotic morality and the morality of those who have extra-territorial allegiance, and so on.

M. Ruthnaswamy:[267] Proletarian morality.

D. Thengadi: With this request that proper safeguards against deliberate malignment and character assassination should be provided for, I support the provision.

D. Sanjivayya: The hon'ble member, Shri Thengadi supported the amendment but he wanted that safeguards should be provided and protection given to good workers against character assassination that may be carried on. I assure him that all possible precautions would be taken.

---

266. *Rajya Sabha Debate* dated 26th November, 1964.

267. M. Ruthnaswamy (1885-1977) – educationist, thinker from Tamil Nadu, Ruthnaswamy was with the Justice Party in his initial years and later on went on to become one of the founding members of the Swatantra Party and represented it for two terms in the Rajya Sabha. Ruthnaswamy was vice president of the Swatanatra Party and one of its most visible representatives in the Upper House. He was member, Madras Legislative Council, 1921-25, Central Legislative Assembly, 1927 and member, Rajya Sabha, 1962-1968 and 1968-1974 and was conferred the Padma Bhushan in 1968.

The Industrial Disputes (Amendment) Bill, 1967[268*]

D. Thengadi: Madam, so far as this Bill is concerned, we welcome it; it is good, but at the same time, I must say that it is not adequate. As a matter of fact, government has very often said that they are waiting to have a common labour code and the matters will be finalised after the recommendations of the National Labour Commission are out. In that case, I do not see why this should have been expedited in this fashion, but if the government is convinced that there are certain matters which are more urgent and cannot await the publication of the recommendations of the National Labour Commission and their examination by the government, then we are justified in saying that other matters equally urgent should have been taken up for legislation. Now regarding closure, the first thing I want to suggest is that prevention is better than cure and from that point of view, we urge that there should be a system of continuous efficiency audit of the different industrial establishments. In Great Britain, this system has been working quite efficiently.

A.D. Mani: For example?

D. Thengadi: In textiles, in engineering particularly.

Bankey Behary Das:[269] Not in newspapers?

D. Thengadi: In case of continuous efficiency audit, it becomes possible for the government to issue a warning beforehand that the capital is being managed in an improper manner. The government can suggest ways and means of proper deployment of capital and it becomes possible for the government to locate the responsibility for the closure or failure of the industrial establishment. So, in India also, it should be possible for us to evolve this system of efficiency audit.

Secondly, this Bill deals with closure, no doubt, but it does not prescribe any penalty for employees whose mismanagement has been responsible for the closure because in more than 50 per cent of the cases, it is not the natural causes or causes beyond the control of the employers, but the rivalries between the employers themselves or mismanagement on their part that is responsible for the closure of the establishments or factories. In such cases, some deterrent punishment or penalty should be prescribed for those who are found guilty of mismanagement.

---

268. **Rajya Sabha Debate* dated 26th November, 1968.

269. Bankey Behari Das (1923-2001) – Praja Socialist Party leader from Odisha, was member, Odisha Legislative Assembly, 1957-61 and member, Rajya Sabha, 1966-1971.

D. Thengadi: Thirdly, the workers should have the right to scrutinise the balance sheet, even to go behind it. This is very essential because without this right to go behind the balance sheet, the workers will not be able to contribute their mite to the proper management of the industrial establishment. This will serve as a sort of deterrent and the workers will also have a sense of participation. And I am quite confident that if workers are given the right to scrutinise the balance sheet, probably the eventuality of closure may not arise at all. So, the workers should be given this right. Fourthly, the term 'industrial dispute' should be redefined and industrial matter should include the deployment of capital also. That means the workers should have the right to suggest or to recommend in what particular way the capital should be deployed. Today the term 'industrial dispute' does not include or cover this particular aspect; it covers only employer-employee relationship. Therefore, we urge that the term 'industrial matter' should cover this aspect also, that is, deployment of capital and the workers should have the right to suggest in what particular way capital should be deployed. I think if these suggestions are accepted by the government, the effectiveness of the Bill will be all the more greater.

D. Thengadi: The hon'ble minister has not given his reaction about the system of efficiency audit; secondly, about the right of workers to go into the balance sheet, to scrutinise the balance sheet; also to raise an industrial dispute regarding the deployment of the capital.

Trade Unions (Amendment) Bill, 1970[270]

I am here to support the Bill. I fully endorse all the views expressed by my hon'ble friend, Sen Gupta. Over and above what has been already said, I want to put forth a few more facts for consideration.

Now, this question of recognition has been treated very shabbily for all these 26 years. Government has been enamoured of a slogan which is ideal but which is at variance with realities. The slogan is 'one industry, one union'. Government must consider why this ideal condition has not materialised in spite of the fact that everybody is shouting the slogan of 'one industry, one union'. What is the real way to achieve this ideal condition? It is not by bringing about some sort of a political agreement between the different unions. Either the workers themselves must be made trade-union conscious so that they bring appropriate pressure to

270. *Rajya Sabha Debate* dated 31st August, 1973.

bear upon their respective leaders or else, under the present conditions, when trade union conscience is lacking, at least to the extent necessary amongst the workers, the only possible way is to have a legislation on 'one industry, one union', and then to abolish all the various unions at plant level or industrial level, to set up one single union in every establishment and industry, and with their representatives at the central level, to form one single national federation of labour. That is the only possible way of bringing about unity in the trade union movement. But if this is to be followed, the implication would be that different unions operating at plant and industrial level will have to be disbanded; the different affiliating central labour unions will have to be dissolved, and then a fresh national labour federation will have to be set up. If the government has got that courage, it is good, it is welcome. But, if the government fails to gather that much courage, then it must accept a realistic view, and learn to live with the fact of the multiplicity of unions.

So far as the problem of recognition is concerned, we know how the problem has been dealt with so far in an unrealistic manner. My hon'ble friend Sen Gupta has pointed out the case of the locomen's strike. We are clinging to the fossils that have no life as such. The federations recognised – it is doubtful whether they continue to be as strong as they used to be once. The situation has changed, the power position has changed. New unions and central labour organisations are now in the field, and still we are clinging to the same old position.

Now, regarding the multiplicity of trade unions, we will have to give fresh thought, and, therefore, I welcome the important suggestion in this Bill that wherever the status of a union is to be decided, the decision should be based upon the process of secret ballot and not just verification of membership, which can be partial, full of frailties and other things. I welcome this particular provision. But more than that, I should like to suggest that today in the different industries, it has become necessary to seek the co-operation of all the workers in order to maintain industrial peace. It means that the number of employees should be involved in any agreement for which purpose it is necessary that a composite bargaining agency should be set up at the plant and industrial level. By composite bargaining agency, I mean that all the unions having a sizeable membership should be a party to any negotiation. Now, sir, in the banking industry, we are going to have negotiations after a few months. Now, if different unions of sizeable strength are omitted or ignored, you cannot be sure of industrial peace in that vital sector. By composite bargaining agency, I mean that there should be a secret ballot. The number of representatives should be fixed. And if in this fashion, there is a secret ballot for 10 or 12 seats, then naturally whichever union commands any strength will have, in proportion to its strength, representation on the composite bargaining agency.

So, it has become necessary now to change the traditional pattern of thinking on the industrial front, to have a fresh thinking regarding industrial relations and, thus, to take into consideration the factors that have newly arisen in the industrial field of the country. What holds good about recognition of a single union is also equally valid regarding the recognition as a Central Labour Organisation. I am very happy that the government has undertaken this particular work of reconsideration, of revising its decision regarding the central recognition, but it should be expedited. Since, because of various factors – I do not want to mention them – the decision is likely to take some time; in the meanwhile, before the matter of central recognition is decided, I should like to suggest emphatically that all of the tripartite committees that will be set up, the claims of the Bharatiya Mazdoor Sangh and the Central Trade Union, both these organisations should not be ignored; their representatives should be included in the various tripartite committees till a final decision is taken on the question of central recognition or the government should assure us that the final decision of central recognition will be expedited and a date should be fixed by which time the decision would be available.

Sir, so far as the various definitions in this Bill are concerned, I should like to give a few suggestions. The minister has already assured us that in the proposed legislation on industrial relation, the definition of 'workman' will be expanded so as to include employees of educational institutions, hospitals, etc., I should like to suggest that it should be simply defined as a 'wage earner'. Whoever earns a wage, in whichever activity he may be employed, should be considered as a workman. I should again like to suggest that 'industry' should be simply defined for purposes of the Trade Union Act and the Industrial Disputes Act as any activity in which an employer-employee relationship persists. Whatever be the activity, any activity in which employer-employee relationship persists should be taken as 'industry' for purposes of trade union and the Industrial Disputes Act.

So far as 'unfair practices' are concerned, which constitutes the last para of this Bill, I should like to say that in Maharashtra, the Maharashtra government had constituted a committee some three years back. The report of the committee is a very valuable document. It gives guidance on the problem of unfair practices and how to prevent them. Though the legislation passed subsequently is not satisfactory, so far as the report on the unfair labour practices is concerned, it is really valuable. So, based on that report, we should have some sort of legislation regarding unfair labour practices. Also I am sure that if our hon'ble Labour Minister is earnest about maintaining industrial peace – and I know he is earnest about it – he will consider the suggestion about recognition of the plant, industrial and national level.

Labour Provident Fund Laws (Amendment) Bill, 1971–Motion for Consideration[271]

Mr. Deputy Chairman, while I welcome this measure, I must point out that a number of suggestions and demands made by the workers from time to time, workers from all sections, have been ignored by the government. For example, they have demanded that every employee must be brought within the purview of the Provident Fund by which they meant that there should be no exemption for any industrial or commercial establishment on some plea or other, either of the number of employees therein or any other plea, so much so that I should like to insist that any activity, not only industrial or commercial establishment, but any activity which consists of employer-employee relationship should be brought within the purview of the Provident Fund. Secondly, our Labour Minister has done well in dealing at length with the problem of the steadily growing arrears of Provident Fund. He has also spoken of the proposed deterrent and enhanced penalties to defaulting employers. We had suggested earlier that whatever penalties are imposed for default regarding income-tax under the Income-tax Act should also be made applicable to the defaulting employers in this respect, but I also doubt whether this alone would suffice because there may be employers who would prefer to receive such severe penalties rather than to pay their dues in proper time, and, therefore, I should like to suggest that there should be certain structural changes in the scheme itself. In every factory, there should be constituted a Provident Fund Committee comprising of the representatives of employers and

271. *Rajya Sabha Debate* dated 6th April, 1971.

employees, and periodically whenever the Provident Fund dues are collected from workers and employers, the same should be deposited promptly in the name of both, one representative of the workers and one of the employers, and the workers' representative should have a right to complain to the appropriate authorities whenever, within the proper time, the employer fails to pay his own dues of the Provident Fund.

Secondly, last time, we had seen the list of defaulting employers and the amounts due from them. So, there should be a law that after a particular amount, if the due rises, in that case, the factory or the mine should be taken over from the employer and should he entrusted to workers therein for management. I think it would be a really deterrent thing rather than just introducing a few amendments in the existing penal provisions.

Then there is the contribution of the workers. So far as the provision for workers' contribution to the PF scheme is concerned, it is understandable, it is just. But the burden of gratuity and of family pension should be borne, in fairness, by the government. It may be that that burden may be shared by the concerned employers. There may be mutual negotiations between the employers and the government on that point. But, in general, the workers should not be allowed to shoulder the burden of gratuity and family pension scheme, and particularly workers receiving anything below the need-based minimum wage should be certainly exempted from this burden.

Then, sir, so far as this particular measure is concerned, there are two points of detail that I want to mention. The rules are to be framed by the executive as usual, and this is but proper. But the rules thus framed should be laid on the table of Parliament or there should be some provision made through which Parliament also would be able to scrutinise and exercise control over the rules because these apply both to governmental as well as private industries. Secondly, there is nothing specified as to what will be the check on the inspectors. So, some provision should be made regarding that.

Then, again, the workers have been demanding that there should be a special legislation regarding gratuity and also there should be legislation regarding unemployment insurance and that there should be an integrated social security scheme, an integrated social security law under an integrated social security authority. I think the time is ripe when these demands of the workers must be taken very seriously and considered. Instead of bringing in piece-meal legislations–which also we welcome, it would be much better if the Labour Ministry takes pains to evolve such an integrated system so that in one measure itself, it is possible for us to cover all the social security measures.

Coal Mines Provident Fund and Bonus Schemes (Amendment) Bill, 1965[272]

D. Thengadi: Madam, the provisions of this Bill are good and welcome so far as they go, but the workers would very much like that the Provident Fund scheme and bonus scheme for coal mine workers should be brought on par with or amalgamated with the Employees Provident Fund scheme and bonus scheme. It is welcome that the definition of 'coal mine' is made wide and realistic. There should be no limit on the number of employees employed by a coal mine, to make it included in the definition of a 'coal mine'.

The redefinition of the term 'coal mine' has been on the lines of the definition of 'mine' in the Mines (Amendment) Act, 1959. This is more comprehensive.

Now the term 'coal mine' includes a lignite mine, colliery offices, and ancillary undertakings, such as coke ovens, workshops, hospitals, etc. and this has removed or helped to remove certain anomalies in the working of the Act.

The definition of 'employee' now includes employees employed by or through contractors, *malis* [garderner], sweepers, domestic servants, and teachers, employed by coal mines, and apprentices and trainees who receive wages or stipends from the employer. I feel that workers doing a clerical job of a non-technical kind should also be included in the definition of "employee".

The term 'employer' has also been redefined. According to this redefinition, in the case of a coal mine owned by a company, such company or the managing agent who manages the colliery shall be deemed to be the employer.

Under Clause 10(b), certain persons are named as persons who will be regarded as 'employers' within the meaning of this Bill. This is good so far as it goes. But the definition of 'employer' should be made still wider so as to include the parasitic class of royalty-owners in it. This class must be done away with. It is good that the employees employed by or through contractors have been brought within the purview of this Act. They have

272. *Rajya Sabha Debate* dated 30th November, 1965.

been provided with the Provident Fund as well as a bonus scheme. But it is also necessary to find out ways and means of counteracting the usual mischief of contractors, that is, of continuing their workers as temporary for years together by not allowing them to complete the stipulated number of days during a year. In the case of contract labour, both the contractor and the principal employer should be made responsible for the payment. Neither should be allowed to escape or evade. In view of the manoeuvring nature of contractors and the helplessness of the workers under them, it seems to be more practical to reduce the stipulated number of days in case of the contract labour.

Inclusion of teachers in the definition of 'employee' is a step in the right direction. In this respect, this Bill has given a correct lead to other industrial establishments and educational institutions also. In fact, it is necessary to evolve a Provident Fund scheme and bonus scheme for the entire teaching profession in the country.

The Bill seeks to bring this Act in line with, firstly, the Mines Act; and secondly, the Employees' Provident Fund Act, 1952. It would not be proper to obstruct the passage of this Bill on the plea that there is a distinction between social security legislation and the other type of legislation which concerns itself with controlling operating conditions, such as the Mines Act or the Factories Act, because I apprehend that such a plea may be taken up by the coal-mine employers.

Clause 10F imposes penalty on employers for default. But our experience about the penalising clauses in the earlier Bills is not encouraging. At the all-India level, we have seen how the cotton textile industry is made to confront or to face a crisis because of the wrong attitudes of the employers. Even this Clause 10F would be useless if the government does not implement it effectively.

Proper implementation is important. Punishment for default should be more severe. The punishment provided for here is not adequately deterrent. The Provident Fund Commissioner and his officials have failed so far in this respect.

Employers' violation of the Coal Mines Provident Fund scheme has become a regular feature. According to the annual report of the Coal Mines Provident Fund, the amount outstanding up to 31st March, 1963 was as much as Rs. 1.75 crores. As has been stated earlier, for failure to remit contributions in time to the Fund, apart from 543 prosecutions under trial, there are 788 recovery proceedings for the realisation of a sum of Rs. 1.2 crores. These defaults delay the issue of annual statements of members' Provident Fund accounts, leading to dissatisfaction among them.

It is a matter of grave concern that the government should feel helpless in realising completely from employer money due from them. Roughly, it comes to 12 per cent of the total amount which is to be collected from the employers. Even the contribution made by the employees is not deposited by the employers; even that is consumed by the employers. With due respect to Patna High Court, which has been mentioned by the hon'ble minister, I want to state that if there are employers who swallow the amounts of employees' contribution, there should be a penalty imposed, and interest should be charged on that money if the employers do not pay it or if they delay the payment of that money to the government. There should be some provision to compel the employers to deposit the employees' money in the Fund and in the bank within proper time.

A word about the rate of interest. A fixed deposit for five years earns 7 per cent interest. But the employees receive only 4½ per cent interest. They must be given at least 7 per cent interest. The Coal Mines' Provident Fund Scheme has pooled the individual savings of workers and has provided a source of finance for the planned development of the country.

The progress of the scheme during the last 16 years has been commendable. Originally, the Coal Mines' Provident Fund Act applied only to Bengal and Bihar. Now it is extended to different states. The rate of compulsory contribution to the Fund has been enhanced from 6¼ per cent of the basic wage in the beginning to 8 per cent of the total emoluments now. The number of subscribers to the Provident Fund increased from 2.96 lakhs in 1948 to 4.25 lakhs in 1965. All these are quite welcome features. Now it should be possible for an employee to take loan from his Provident Fund amount. There should be some provision to this effect, some machinery for this purpose. Paradoxically enough, it is easier to secure loan in factories not covered by the Provident Fund scheme and extremely difficult to secure the same in factories covered by the Act. This should not be the case. Otherwise, poor workers will have to allow themselves to be entrapped by money-lenders. Under the present scheme, the paraphernalia for the granting of loan is quite elaborate. The process must be quick and simple.

I am happy that at long last, the government has decided that the employers' contribution should be at the same rate as that of the employees. That is good. But why should we not require the employers to pay more than their workers? The two cannot be equated.

Now if a worker dies and even after three or six months his widow or minor children do not get the payment, the object of the scheme stands defeated. Six months' time is given in other cases and three months' time in the case of coal-mine workers. There are, however, cases of inordinate delay, say, even for over a couple of years. Machinery must be geared up to see that bona fide claimants get their dues in proper time.

Deputy Chairman: How much more time would you take, Mr. Thengadi?

D. Thengadi: Some five minutes more.

The Deputy Chairman: Then you may continue tomorrow. The House stands adjourned till 11 a.m. tomorrow.

The House then adjourned at till 11 o'clock on Wednesday, 1st December, 1965.

Central Labour Laws (Extension to Jammu & Kashmir) Bill, 1970 – Motion for Consideration[273]

D. Thengadi: Mr. Deputy Chairman, I welcome the Bill, but I feel that this piece of legislation is piecemeal, halting, haphazard, in more than one sense. In the broader context, it can be questioned why all the central labour laws should not be made applicable to Jammu & Kashmir, why the state of Jammu & Kashmir should not be brought at par with the rest of India, why Article 370 of our Constitution should not be scrapped. These are broader questions, and even from this point of view, as I said, this piece of legislation is piecemeal, halting and haphazard. Secondly, from the point of view of industrial laws also, while the government has gone a step ahead in a welcome direction, it has not gone ahead enough, and that has been our complaint for long. For example, the working class of our country has been clamouring for integration of the various labour laws and uniformity in them in various states, but this has not been done so far.

We had pleaded before the National Labour Commission that a common labour code should be evolved, that at least there should be an integration of the different labour procedures and that a Labour Procedure Code should be formulated. Now the National Labour Commission has given the plea that in case there is any formulation, the states that are advanced would suffer, workers in those states would suffer. But we had already argued that we could have a common Labour Code on common

273. *Rajya Sabha Debate* dated 2nd December, 1970.

problems giving the minimum requirements of law and without any prejudice to the existing rights and amenities of the workers in the different states, wherever the states are advanced. But that has not been accepted by the National Labour Commission. It is surprising because the Commission had appointed a Study Group which gave a draft of such a common labour code. We had also submitted our formula of the common labour code. But that has not been taken cognisance of. Consequently, there has not been an integration of labour laws, wherever that is necessary. For example, regarding social security, we know that there are inadequacies in the social security laws. But whatever laws are already existing, those laws and machineries under them, the schemes under them have not been properly integrated. Similarly, we know that there has been a demand from all the sections of working class that the definition of workmen should be uniform in all the Acts. The government also, if I remember alright, had promised that an attempt would be made in that direction. But there has been an inordinate delay. Similarly, we know that there are uniform norms, standards and conventions regarding some vital problems affecting the labour world. For example, to bring home the fact to the government, in its own administration, the Central Government had inaugurated the Joint Consultation Machinery.[274] There was much drum-beating about it. Now, the Joint Consultation Machinery has failed to abide by any norms and standards so much so, to give a recent example, it is true that the Comptroller and Auditor-General has his own special status and position for the purpose of regulation of industrial relations and the functioning of the Joint Consultation Machinery, even his department is brought within the purview of the Joint Consultation Machinery. And still we find that the Comptroller and Auditor-General has launched unilaterally a proposal to introduce what is described as the scheme of decentralisation which is actually a scheme of victimisation. And when his employees, their association, the recognised association, demanded that the authorities should establish the necessity, the advisability, the utility of this scheme, that the CAG and the other officials should sit round the table and have discussions, that has been refused and unilaterally the authorities are proceeding to demand who are going to volunteer for transfers. Now, this arbitrary approach and attitude of the CAG goes against the very principle and spirit of the Joint Consultation Machinery

274. A scheme for consultation between the employees and the government or the Organisation.

and I may forewarn the government that in the last fortnight, agitations have been launched, though on a modified level, in Madras, Calcutta, Delhi and Nagpur, but if this adamant attitude persists, probably in all these four centres, the employees of the Audit and Accounts Department will be forced by the CAG to go on an indefinite strike for which they are not to be blamed. So, even in its own home administration, the Government of India has failed to bring about any uniformity of norms, standards and conventions.

There is the vital problem of the recognition of unions. There is a difference of opinion, some asserting that the verification of the membership should be the criterion and others saying that it should be a secret ballot of all the workers. Our own organisation, the Bharatiya Mazdoor Sangh has said that it should be a secret ballot of all the unions, that is, of workers, those who are workers of some union or the other in the industry.

There may be different attitudes and approaches, but there should be some uniform law. In the absence of uniformity in the law of recognition, we find some ridiculous positions created in the dealings of different authorities with their employees. For example, we know how the state governments are not subject to any conventions in their dealings with the employees. We also know that in the sector of nationalised banking, which is directly under the government, in two of the major banks, that is, the Bank of Baroda and the Indian Overseas Bank, the agitation is going on for a very funny thing because the managements have refused to hold bipartite talks with the duly recognised unions and have tried to impose certain agreements to which their recognised unions were not a party. Why should the Government of India not direct the managements of the Bank of Baroda and the Indian Overseas Bank to hold bipartite talks with the representatives of the recognised unions?

Sir, we know how regarding recognition, there are some differences in the provisions of the Central Industrial Disputes Act and the Bombay Industrial Relations Act, which is described by workers as a black Act. Why should the government not try to bridge the gulf and, thus, all the Industrial Disputes Act in the country at par, on one level? As a matter of fact, it can be said without entering the problem of the Centre-state relationship, which is a broader question, that my own organisation, the BMS has pleaded for making labour a central subject so that uniformity and integration should be perfect. I am saying this without entering into the main controversy about Centre-state relationship. From all the points of view, I should like to suggest that a more comprehensive, either labour procedure code or a common labour code or both, should be evolved. There should be integration of various laws and schemes allowing uniform benefits in regard to assets or even liabilities for the working class of the country.

The Employees' State Insurance (Amendment) Bill, 1966[275]

D. Thengadi: Madam, the Bill has been introduced with a view to making the administration of the scheme simpler and to eliminate various complicated formalities envisaged in the scheme. No doubt, this Bill confers certain additional benefits upon the workers and, in that sense, it is an improvement upon the 1943 Act. For example, the raising of the wage limit from Rs. 400 to Rs. 500 would bring a larger number of workers within the purview of this scheme. The term 'family' has been redefined so as to include the parents of widows who are also among the working classes. The redefinition of the term 'employee' is also welcome. Those connected with the distribution or sale of the products are also now covered by the scheme. The rate of Employment Injury Benefits as well as the rate of Disablement and Dependents' Benefits are being enhanced. The qualifying conditions for eligibility to sickness and maternity benefits are simplified and the scope of the maternity relief benefit is enlarged. These, among others, are some of the welcome features of this Bill. I, therefore, welcome broadly the provisions of this Bill.

To be sure, this is already a belated measure; such a measure ought to have been introduced earlier. Again, I think it would have been advisable to introduce a fresh Bill instead of such an amendment Bill. I am saying this because of the vast ground covered by this particular amendment Bill.

Now I want one clarification. Probably, the provisions of the Bill are not being extended to Jammu & Kashmir. If that be so, there is no reason why the workers in Jammu & Kashmir should be deprived of the benefits under this measure. The workers of seasonal factories should also not be deprived of the benefits of this scheme. They should be brought on par with the workers of perennial factories.

According to the statement of the hon'ble minister on 30th September, 1966, the total coverage of this scheme was 31 lakhs of employees. In view of the large number of industrial workers in the country, this seems to

275. *Rajya Sabha Debate* dated 23rd November, 1966.

be a very poor figure. Serious and sustained efforts ought to be made to expand the coverage.

The administration, particularly of the provisions for medical, should not be left to state government only. The Central Government should directly take over the administration of the provisions for medical care.

The funeral benefit has been introduced. It is a welcome thing but, at the same time, the benefit as stipulated in the Bill is very poor. A sum of Rs. 100 is nothing when you take into account the present cost of living and the present prices. I would, therefore, request that if the government cannot allow a decent living to the workers, at least, it should give them the comfort or happiness of having a decent burial or funeral. I, therefore, suggest that the funeral benefit should be raised from Rs. 100 to at least Rs. 200. I understand the additional cost would be to the tune of Rs. 20 lakhs or so. Whenever we talk about employers, the government is not in a mood to speak in terms of lakhs or crores; they only talk of percentages, but in the cases of the employees, they talk in terms of thousands or lakhs or crores of rupees, I think though this will cost an additional amount of Rs. 20 lakhs, it is worthwhile and we can give them the satisfaction of having a decent burial or funeral.

M. Ruthnaswamy: Does the hon'ble member want to increase the cost of dying in the country?

D. Thengadi: Unfortunately, if you will kindly enquire into the prices, you will find that within a sum of Rs. 100 there cannot be any funeral. You kindly enquire into the prices.

P.K. Kumaran: Because of the growth of population, he wants to give them an incentive for death.

D. Thengadi: The exemption limit for employees' contribution should be raised to below Rs. 3 so that those who are earning less than Rs. 3 would not be required to contribute.

To a worker who has contributed to the scheme but who has never had any occasion to receive any benefit under the scheme, a 'no-claim rebate' should be given. The employees' contribution should not be recovered as arrears of land revenue. In this respect, it would be very unfair to equate the poor employees with the rich employers.

The corporation does not take early and effective steps for recovery of dues from defaulting employers. A few cases cited sometimes from the government side are only exceptional in character. That for Employees'

Provident Fund and other funds, the unrecovered amounts are bigger is hardly a consolation.

The rate of contribution from employers should be enhanced to the prescribed maximum of 5 per cent of the total wage bill and an equivalent or corresponding relief should be given to workers from the point of view of their contribution.

A special committee should be appointed to go through the working of the hospitals and dispensaries and the provision of other medical benefits because everywhere the workers are complaining about improper implementation of this scheme. The specialists' medicines are never available. The doctors usually hesitate to give certificates, being under the pressure of employers. The number of beds at a number of places is inadequate. Generally, beds for T.B. patients are not provided at all. The time limit of 56 days is unreasonable and inadequate. Actually, there should be no time limit and the benefits should continue as long as he does not recover.

Clause 26 leaves out an important contingency, that is, protection for old age. This has to be remedied. Needless to add that these omissions and defects in the Bill are only illustrative; they are not exhaustive.

Madam, I want to point out one more aspect of the working of the corporation. The Public Accounts Committee has also made certain comments about the functioning of this corporation. In the 54th Report of the PAC of 1965-66, it has been said:

"The Audit Reports will be presented to Parliament soon after they are submitted by Audit, so that they are available to the Members of Parliament and the Public Accounts Committee for examination without delay."

The committee has said that the government should ensure this but this has not been ensured so far. The committee has criticised the delay in presenting the report to Parliament. The PAC further says:

"It is all the more surprising that the corporation has not been able to recover its dues even from a government body (Rajasthan State Electricity Board) which are pending for the last 14 years."

Here, on the one hand, government is complaining that additional benefits cannot be given to the employees because of lack of funds while, on the other hand, we see that for 14 years, they could not recover their legitimate dues from a government body. According to the Report of the PAC:

"There was undue delay at every stage in this case which resulted in locking up of the amount of Rs. 1 lakh sanctioned for the construction of a hospital. All correspondence in adjusting this amount against the dues to be paid to Delhi Administration remain unattended to."

The government must pay due attention to this lapse on the part of the corporation.

There is one more aspect I want to bring to your notice. When the Corporation employees were on hunger strike, we learnt reliably from the leaders of the employees that a solemn assurance proceeded from the government side that once the agitation was withdrawn, their demands would be considered and conceded. This assurance proceeded from one hon'ble M.P. of this House. I am sorry to say that the movement was withdrawn relying upon the assurance of the government and now nothing is being done regarding the demands of the employees. It is also being said that there was no assurance from the government side. It is really strange that an hon'ble M.P. had conveyed to the employees that an assurance is there. That was why the movement was withdrawn but now actually the employees are left in the lurch. They withdrew the movement in good faith. When it was in full swing, they could have continued it. Now the movement has been withdrawn and now they are left in the lurch. They are told, rather they are betrayed, that after all, no assurance came from the government. I request the government not to make this a prestige issue now that there is industrial peace prevailing in the ESI. The government should come forward with magnanimity and extend its hand of co-operation to the employees, who are prepared to co-operate with the government and see that their demands are settled amicably.

The *Beedi* and Cigar Workers (Conditions of Employment) Bill, 1966[276]

D. Thengadi: Regarding amendment No. 8, I want to suggest that there should be no distinction made on the point of maternity benefit between a regular employee and a home worker. Indeed, in the entire Bill, such a distinction has been sought to be made. A home worker is not a self-employed person. She is working for either a contractor or a proprietor and in that sense, she is also an employee. Therefore, there

276. *Rajya Sabha Debate* dated 10th November, 1966.

should be no discrimination against her so far as the maternity benefits are concerned.

G. Ramachandran[277] (*nominated*): Does the minister admit that there is such a clear distinction as pointed out by Mr. Thengadi?

Shah Nawaz Khan:[278] There is a distinction and the reason is that many of the female workers who work at home are not regular employees of any contractor or proprietor. They work at home. There are no fixed hours of work. So, this provision has been brought in to give some benefit to them – maternity benefits and also some annual leave but we cannot give them all the benefits which are given to all the regular workers because they stay at home and work whenever they like. There are no regular hours of work and so it is not possible to give the same benefit.

The Dock Workers (Regulation of Employment) Amendment Bill, 1967[279*]

D. Thengadi: Madam, I have not much to add but I should like to stress that the process of decasualisation should have been prescribed or laid down in the Bill itself. Secondly, even ports that are not major should be treated as a Central subject for the purpose of implementation of labour laws. I think that is essential that ports that are not major should be treated as a Central subject.

The term 'port authority' should be properly defined in the Act. Also the election of workers' representatives to the Dock Labour Board[280] should be through secret ballot. There need be no hesitation in adopting the method of secret ballot in this election.

---

277. G. Ramachandran (1905-1995) – Gandhian, freedom fighter, educationist, founded Gandhigram, founder Vice Chancellor of Gandhigram Rural University, founder Secretary, Gandhi Peace Foundation, editor of *Gandhi Marg*, studied at Visvabharati, Santiniketan, was conferred Desikottama, chairman, All India Khadi & Village Industries Commission (KVIC). Ramachandran was member, Kerala Legislature and served as Minister of Health and Education of Kerala in Pattom Thanu Pillai's ministry between 1960-62; was member, Rajya Sabha, 1964-1970.

278. Shah Nawaz Khan (1914-1983) – close collaborator of Netaji Subhas Chandra Bose, was Maj-General in the INA, Khan was among those who faced the famous Red Fort trial that generated a wave of indignation in support of the INA members across the country, was member, 1st, 2nd, 3rd and 5th Lok Sabha from Meerut in Uttar Pradesh, held various portfolios over the years, was Deputy Minister of Railways & Transport, Minister of State in the Ministry of Steel and Mines, Minister of Food & Agriculture, was chairman of the Food Corporation of India. In 1956 he headed the three-member committee constituted by Nehru to go into the episode of Netaji's disappearance.

279. **Rajya Sabha Debate* dated 5th December, 1967.

280. Which administered the National Dock Labour Scheme of Labour Department.

The term 'staff of the Dock Labour Board' should also be properly defined, whether inspectors are included in the staff or not.

Very recently, the hon'ble Labour Minister had an occasion or opportunity to conciliate in the dispute between port and dock labour and managements. I think it would have been better had he taken into consideration all the various points raised in the dispute, on which he himself had to opine, and brought a comprehensive Bill so as to cover all disputable points. That would have been still better. A comprehensive Bill could have been welcome.

Resolution Seeking Disapproval of the Essential Services Maintenance Ordinance, 1968 (No. 9 of 1968) and the Essential Services Maintenance Bill, 1968[281]

The ordinance which forms the subject-matter of the Bill as well the resolution have already been challenged in the Delhi High Court. A writ petition has been filed. It has been admitted. The High Court has not given its verdict. Therefore, at this stage, when this matter is subjudice, it will be a contempt of the Delhi High Court to discuss the matter, whether the resolution or the Bill.

It is now very clear that regarding mere procedural technicalities, some difficulties have arisen. I should like to suggest that the leader of the House should take into confidence the leaders of different parties and should have a private sitting. Now it is already 5 o'clock...

The matter should be easier for the Chair if the Chair kindly accepts my suggestion that the House adjourns now and the Leader discusses with various parties.

The hon'ble leader of the House presumes that the resolution and the Bill should be taken together as certain time is allotted. That is not the understanding. It is better we adjourn the House now. We can thrash out that proposal.

I will speak on the resolution brought by Mr. Bhandari.[282]

दत्तोपंत ठेंगड़ी: मैं इस संकल्प पर अपना विचार प्रकट करना चाहता हूँ कि यह सभा राष्ट्रपति द्वारा 13 सितंबर, 1968 को प्रख्यापित किए गए अत्यावश्यक सेवाएँ अनुरक्षक अध्यादेश 1968। 1968 की संख्या 9 का अनुमोदन नहीं करती है।

281. *Rajya Sabha Debate* dated 23rd December, 1968.

282. Member of Parliament, Rajya Sabha.

Regarding the views of revered Mahatma Gandhi, whose centenary we are to celebrate this year, Mr. Khandubhai Desai,[283] one of his closest followers in the labour field, has elaborated in the following fashion – I am quoting from *Peaceful Industrial Relations* [Navajivan Publishing House, 1957] by Mr. R.J. Soman:

> "All industrial disputes should be settled by mutual consultation, negotiations and arbitration. They should not resort to any direct action so long as they have not exhausted all avenues of a peaceful settlement. They should, however, be prepared to strike if the employer refuses arbitration or does not carry out the award of the arbitrators."

These are the views of revered Mahatma Gandhi according to Khandubhai Desai. That is why, when the INTUC was formed and its constitution was formulated, Clause 3 of the constitution laid down that it will pursue in the matter of strikes:

(i) to establish just industrial relations;

(ii) to secure redress of grievances, without stoppage of work, by means of negotiation and conciliation and failing these by arbitration or adjudication;

(iii) where adjudication is not applied and settlement of disputes within a reasonable time by arbitration is not available for the redress of grievances, to have recourse to other legitimate methods including strikes or any suitable form of *Satyagraha*;

(iv) to make the necessary arrangements for the efficient conduct and satisfactory and speedy conclusion of authorised strikes or *Satyagraha*.

Later on, the spirit of Gandhism has been violated by the ordinance. It is true, madam, that while Articles 14 to 32 of our Constitution describe the fundamental rights and the right to strike is not mentioned therein, it is also a fact that it is derived from the right to organise and from the prohibition of forced labour. It is also a derived right and except in a few cases, a statutory right but not accepted as a fundamental right. The legitimate character of strike has been accepted by the judiciary in a number of cases. To quote a few instances, in 'Ramrao L. Shirkhedkar & Anr. vs. Accountant General, Maharashtra', the Supreme Court has stated:

283. Khandubhai Desai (1898-1975) – Congress leader from Gujarat, trade unionist, president of INTUC, was member, Bombay Legislative Assembly, member, Constituent Assembly, member, Provisional Parliament, and member of the 1st Lok Sabha. Desai was Union Minister for Labour, 1954-57 and member, Rajya Sabha, 1959-1964 and 1964 to 1968, and also served as Governor of Andhra Pradesh.

"A strike is a legitimate weapon in the hands of the workers to redress their grievances."[284]

In 'India General Navigation and Railway Co. Ltd., and their workmen',[285] the Supreme Court says as follows:

"To determine the question of punishment, a clear distinction has to be made between those workmen who not only joined in such a strike, but also took part in obstructing loyal workmen from carrying on their work, or took part in violent demonstrations or acted in defiance of law and order, on the one hand, and those workmen who were more or less silent participators in such a strike, on the other hand. It is not in the interest of the industry that there should be wholesale dismissal of all the workmen who merely participated in such a strike. It is certainly not in the interest of the workmen themselves. An Industrial Tribunal, therefore, has to consider the question of punishment, keeping in view the overriding consideration of full and efficient working of the industry

---

284. Ramrao Laxmikant Shirkhedkar v. Accountant General, 1962 (SCC OnLine Bom 100) : In this case the hon'ble High Court has held, "There is yet another aspect of the matter which must also be considered. The very concept of strike postulates a joint action that is more than one person withdrawing from work in spite of there being a contract or an obligation to work. Rule 4(A), as it is cast, would seem to apply even to an individual worker. Therefore, it does not contemplate a case of joint action. Rule 4(A) is a rule of conduct for each single employee. We cannot conceive of an association going on strike. The association never works under the government as such and no question can possibly arise of the association going on strike."
Therefore, the SC had held that "there was no question of association being prohibited from going on strike. It is in that aspect that rules regarding recognition of association of employees have to be read and we do not think that there is anything wrong if an employee is prohibited from going on strike. We, therefore, do not think that r. 4(A) is liable to be struck down as violative either of Art. 14 or Art. 19(1)(c). We do not accept this contention of the petitioners. Thus, the result is that both the petitions are allowed. The two orders passed by the respondents in each case are hereby quashed and it is declared that each of the petitioners continues to be in service."

285. ***India General Navigation and Rly. Co. Ltd. v. Workmen (1960), 2 SCR 1 : AIR 1960 SC 219 :***
In this case the issue was of illegal strike whereby the hon'ble SC has distinguished between two types of workmen – one who have violated the public order and part of the illegal strike and the other who has not committed any such violation of IPC. The Court had declared the strike illegal and held that "the appeal is, therefore, allowed in part, as indicated above, that is to say, (1) the order of reinstatement in respect of Jahangir Sardar and Keayamat Hussain, is set aside, (2) similarly, the order of reinstatement in respect of the 37 workmen, who had been convicted under Section 188 of the Indian Penal Code, is also set aside, and (3) the order for payment of full back wages, etc. is modified by reducing those amounts by half, for the period aforesaid. As success between the parties has been divided, they are directed to bear their own costs in this Court.

as a whole. The punishment of dismissal or termination of services has, therefore, to be imposed on such workmen as had not only participated in the illegal strike but had fomented it, and had been guilty of violence or doing acts detrimental to the maintenance of law and order in the locality where work had to be carried on."

Madam, in 'Swadeshi Industries Ltd. vs. Their Workmen,'[286] the Supreme Court has said:

"Collective bargaining for securing improvement on matters like basic pay, Dearness Allowance, bonus, Provident Fund and gratuity, leave and holiday is the primary object of a trade union and when demands like these are put forward and thereafter a strike is resorted to in an attempt to induce the employer to agree to the demands or at least to open

286. ***'Swadeshi Industries Ltd. v. Workmen', AIR 1960 SC 1258***
In this appeal, the appellant, a public limited company engaged in the manufacture of cotton textile, art-silk products and certain other goods, challenges the correctness of an order made by the Labour Appellate Tribunal of India, Calcutta, by which in reversal of the order made by the Industrial Tribunal in a reference of an industrial dispute between the Company and its workmen, the Appellate Tribunal reinstated 230 workmen. These 230 workmen along with other workmen were represented at that time by a trade union registered under the name of Swadeshi Industries Mazdoor Union, struck work on 27-4-1951. On 24-5-1951, the Company terminated the services of all the workmen. On 8-6-1951, however the Company issued a general notice asking the workmen to come back on 9-6-1951. Not a single workman responded to this; but after a similar notice was issued on 17-6-1951, intimating that the factory would reopen on 18-6-1951, and asking the workmen to come to their work, a large number of workmen but not including these 230 workmen, joined and were employed. Later on, SC held the strike legal and, dismissing the appeal filed by the Company ordered for reinstatement of these workers also. It has held, "The position therefore is that the conclusion of the Appellate Tribunal that the strike was not illegal and that it was justified remained unassailable. It was within a few days after the strike was launched that a general order terminating the services of all the workmen was made. The Appellate Tribunal thought that this order was made vindictively and mala fide, the purpose being to break the strike and weaken the position of the Mazdoor Union. Before us the Company's counsel has tried to suggest that these 230 members were guilty of violent activities. If that was the reason for which their services were sought to be terminated, it was necessary that it should be decided as a matter of fact by proper enquiry after giving reasonable opportunity to each workman to show the contrary that he was so guilty of violence. But no enquiry was held, no charge-sheet was framed and none of these 230 workmen had an opportunity to show that they were not guilty of any violence. Indeed, the very manner in which a general order terminating the services of all workmen was made shows that the termination was intended to be the punishment, not for any violent conduct or any other misconduct, but for the mere fact of taking part in the strike. Besides no attempt had been made to prove by satisfactory evidence before the Tribunal the charge that any of their workmen were guilty of violence. In these circumstances the order of reinstatement made by the Appellate Tribunal is fully justified."

negotiations, the strike must prima facie be considered to be justified unless it can be shown that the demands were put up frivolously or for any ulterior purpose."

Strike has not been clearly defined and there is no uniformity in the definition of strike. For example, the Industrial Disputes Act defines strike as follows:

"Strike means a cessation of work by a body of persons employed in any industry acting in combination, or a concerted refusal, or a refusal under a common understanding, of any number of persons who are or have been so employed to continue to work or to accept employment."

Under the Bombay Industrial Relations Act, the cessation or the refusal to work must take place in consequence of an industrial dispute. Accordingly, protest strikes or *hartals* as they are usually styled and sympathetic strikes, will not be 'strikes' under the BIR Act.[287]

Now, so far as the other strikes are concerned, such as the stay-in strike, go-slow or pen-down strike, of course, these are not included in the definition of strike. Hunger strike is also excluded from the definition of strike. But regarding the right of workers to go on a strike, we have always stressed and we have demanded that in the schedule of fundamental rights, the right to work should be included. We also simultaneously demand that the right to strike which is a natural corollary to the right of work must also be included in the schedule of fundamental rights.

Now, regarding the right to strike, various authorities here and abroad have given their views, and I should like to state a few of them. For example, GDH Cole[288] in his *British Trade Unionism Today* [1939] has said:

> "Employers and workmen may be, in the eyes of the law, equal parties to a civil contract, but they are never equal parties in fact. The workman, under contract, is bound to serve his employer; the employer is entitled to order the workman about. The relation between them is, thus, essentially unequal. The workmen can do nothing to change the terms of employment without the employer's consent; the employer who wishes to change them needs only to give an order, which the workman is expected to obey. The employer, therefore, never needs to break his contract by locking out his workmen without notice. He issues an order, and they have either to obey it or go on strike

287. The Bombay Industrial Relations Act, 1946.

288. GDH Cole (1889-1959) – English political thinker, proponent of the co-operative movement, writer and historian.

in breach of contract, and, thus, put themselves legally in the wrong. It is easy for employers to talk about the 'sanctity' of the contracts, because they are seldom under any inducement to break them. But the workmen have sometimes to choose between breaking their contracts and breaking faith with their fellow-workers, in such a way as to allow the employer to worsen the conditions of employment. Under such conditions, workmen cannot be expected to keep their contracts; indeed, they would be wrong to do so, if it is in their power to resist."

Madam, about how the strikes can be avoided or can be rendered superfluous, some opinions have been expressed. These are the opinions of authorities. For example, Mr. Knowles [British Labour Party leader, trade unionist] states:

"Yet as trade unionism has developed, there has emerged a steady tendency to restrict the use of the strike weapon."

He quotes the following from the 2nd November, 1946 issue of *The London Times*:

"The long and painful transition from the barricades to the board room has at length been accomplished, and today the TUC [Trade Union Congress] exerts its influence not so much through strikes and demonstrations, as through reasoned arguments before an independent arbitrator or an industrial Court, or in the Cabinet Room."

But this has been done because of the strength of the unions, not because of any suppression of the trade union rights.

Madam, Sir Hartley Shawcross,[289] a prominent member of the then Labour Government, drew pointed attention in the course of a debate in the British Parliament in 1946 to the strike-control function of the trade unions. He is reported to have stated that it was impossible to prevent strikes by the processes of the criminal law but that trade unions could do it. That is why he asserted, and I quote, that:

"Most people nowadays realise that it is in the interests not only of industry but of the State to have strong and powerful trade unions of which all the workers in the industry are members, and which are able to lead and guide their members."

---

289. Hartley Shawcross (1902-2003) – British Labour Party leader, Member of Parliament, Attorney General, 1945-1951.

Mr. Knowles again states:

"It has not, of course, been by legal prohibitions that strikes have been controlled so much as by the development of a powerful union leadership and the evolution of voluntary and statutory procedures for negotiating wages and working conditions as well for avoiding disputes."

"A strike is not merely an economic struggle for securing some demands. It is also a sociological phenomenon."

Authorities have said that the various aspects of this phenomenon must be studied. Another authority says and I am again quoting:

"Can a developing economy, it is asked, afford the luxury of strikes?"

This is exactly the question posed to the government:

"It cannot be denied that if an economy is to progress rapidly, there should be no interruptions in the processes of production, which means that there should be no, or as few, strikes as possible. The easiest remedy would be to ban strikes as in totalitarian countries. But the remedy will be worse than the disease. It will pave the way for the abolition, as pointed out earlier, of all democratic rights and liberties. Moreover, denied the normal channels, workers' discontent and dissatisfaction will find expression in absenteeism, changing jobs, malingering, go slow, fall in quality, neglect of machinery and similar other more damaging acts of commission and omission. The remedy is, thus, self-defeating."

If a feeling of belonging and participation is created as happened in Great Britain during the days of the Second World War, workers will be prepared to avoid strikes and work harder. But to come with a heavy hand to suppress their trade union rights is hardly a way that would succeed.

Madam, some other independent views and opinions have been expressed on this point. I should like to state them here. For example, shortly after the airline strike of 1966, a group of Protestant Churchmen and laymen in USA with an interest in labour relations were called together by the Committee on Church and Economic Life, National Council of the Churches of Christ in the USA. They were asked to look into the growing sense of conflict of interest between the right of strike and the general welfare. To this subject, they brought a background of Christian ethical concern and an unusual detachment, for not a single member of the committee is a partisan in labour-management relations. Now, I quote what they say.

"The right to strike is simply the right of any person entering into a contract to decline to sell, until he has an agreeable contract with the buyer as to the terms under which he will sell."

It should be further noted that the right to strike has historically been one of the first casualties wherever totalitarian political regimes have come to power:

"In sum, the right of collective bargaining with its ultimate weapon of the strike has proved to be a significant means of achieving social justice for workers."

The committee has come to conclude – and I will not quote extensively – that "Strikes produce good as well as harm."

The other conclusions are that "the management must share with unions the responsibility for strikes", still other being that "losses due to strikes are given exaggerated emphasis".

Now, here I should like to quote:

"For example, industrial accidents cost some 244 million man days of lost production in 1966 – nearly 10 times the number of man-days lost from strikes during the same year. Or again, the work-days lost because of unemployment far outweigh those lost in strikes. During the 10-year period: 1952-1961, a total of three billion, nine hundred thirty million man-days were lost due to unemployment over and above a minimal fractional unemployment rate of 2½ per cent. This amounts to 12 times the number of man-days lost because of strikes during the same period."

Now, madam, the conclusion drawn by this committee which has a detached interest – an impartial committee – is:

"Any broad-scale limitation of the right to strike would mean either that industrial disputes would generally be resolved by default in favour of management or that the equitable resolution of disputes would fall upon the shoulders of government. It is essential that the system of free collective bargaining in private employment, including the right to strike, be preserved and strengthened as the major technique for resolving labour-management conflicts and achieving an approximation of justice. The freedom of workers to withhold their labour should be preserved."

Deputy Chairman: I think it is 7. You may continue tomorrow.

Essential Services Maintenance Bill, 1968 Ordinance, 1968[290]

D. Thengadi: Madam Deputy Chairman, while talking on the resolution of Mr. Bhandari, I had quoted the verdict of Protestant Churchmen of the United States. Now, inaugurating the ILO Asian Regional Seminar on Personnel Management at Jamshedpur on 23rd October, 1968, Mr. P.C. Mathew, Secretary, Ministry of Labour, Government of India, stoutly defended the right of the government to ban strikes. But even he had to say:

> "This ban cannot be construed as an unreasonable invasion of an inviolable right as long as provision is made for an alternative method of settlement of the grievances of the concerned workers, say, through compulsory arbitration. Such compulsory arbitration would bind the State also, unless a Parliament decides otherwise in any specific case."

Madam, you are very well aware that our Joint Consultative Machinery has been qualitatively very much inferior to the Whitley Council Machinery of Great Britain, and notwithstanding the existence of the Whitley Council Machinery, it is well known that in Great Britain, there is no ban on the right to strike of the government employees. Recently, in Great Britain, the Royal Commission on Trade Unions and Employers' Associations had to go through this whole question and one of its conclusions is as follows:

> "...Every individual employee has the legal right to cease to work for his employer on giving whatever notice is required by his contract of employment. The right to strike is, basically, a right to withdraw labour in combination without being subject to the legal consequences of acting in combination which would, in the past, have followed. This situation is now well recognised."

The ordinance has put our Socialist government in a very awkward position, so much so that now even the capitalists have come forward with the 'holier than thou' attitude, and here is what Mr. Tata has to say about the ordinance and about the move of the government to ban strikes by government employees:

> "It is rather strange that, after years of lip-sympathy in favour of working classes in support of fundamental freedom for the trade union, the government suddenly refuses to accept the right to

290. *Rajya Sabha Debate* dated 24th December, 1968.

strike by government employees as legitimate. There is abundant evidence both in our national labour laws as also in international conventions of the ILO that, after all efforts at conciliation, mediation, arbitration and adjudication have failed, both the parties to the dispute have a reciprocal right to strike or a lock-out. It is also true that our government has been party to such labour conventions passed in Geneva and have also, through their action, blessed similar legislations with their moral and legal support."

And again, if our objective is to reduce the incidence of strike, then all this should be directed, not towards ending the right to strike, but mending the situation under which it is indiscriminately resorted to. As I have already said, it is an irony of fate that Mr. Tata should sermonise to the so-called socialist government on this point. I am again inclined to refer to one remark by a very sober leader of thought about whom I am sure there is high regard even in the mind of Mr. Yeshwantrao Balwantrao Chavan.[291] He is Mr. V.B. Karnik [prominent trade unionist and leader of the Indian Federation of Labour (IFL)] who in no sense can be described as an irresponsible leader. He has given his opinion in this fashion:

"If workers are free to sell their labour power, they must be free to demand for it a price which they consider fair and reasonable, i.e. a fair wage and fair conditions of work, and in case such a fair price is not available, they must also have the freedom to refuse to sell or to withdraw their labour power. If strikes are altogether prohibited, it will be necessary to deny workers the right of organisation as well as freedom of speech, press and assembly. Totalitarian regimes have recognised this and along with the abolition of the right to strike, they have also abolished all other fundamental rights. The abolition is not restricted to workers; it is inevitably extended to the society as a whole. The society then becomes a slave society as distinguished from a free society, which has been the aim and aspiration of man throughout the ages."

---

291. Y.B. Chavan (1913-1984) – one of the most prominent Congress leaders from Maharashtra, was Chief Minister of Bombay state, served as first Chief Minister of Maharashtra, replaced V.K. Krishna Menon as Union Defence Minister, over many years in Delhi Chavan held various crucial portfolios such as Finance, External Affairs; post-Emergency he split away from the Indira Gandhi faction, became Deputy Prime Minister and Home Minister in the Charan Singh ministry; post 1980, returned to the Congress.

Madam, we have been opposing this ordinance on various grounds. We have serious objection to the definition of 'strike' in Section 2(1)(b) of the Ordinance. Carried to its logical limits, it spells of slavery, forced labour and *beggar*. Section 2(l)(b) of the ordinance is, therefore, ultra vires Article 23(1) of the Constitution. Any artificial extension of the meaning of 'strike' beyond its ordinary and natural meaning is a serious invasion of the fundamental rights guaranteed under the Constitution. The government cannot altogether ignore the Directive Principles of State Policy and is obliged to give effect to the provisions of Part IV of the Constitution. The artificial extension of the meaning of 'strike' is absolutely unjustified and, in fact, prohibited under Articles 39(a), 42 and 43 of the Constitution. Sub-clause (ii) of clause (b) of sub-section (1) of Section 2 of the ordinance confers on the Executive an unchannelised, unguided and arbitrary power which is indefinite in its scope and mischief. Clause (b) of sub-section (4) of Section 3 of the ordinance enables the government to enact a retroactive criminal law and this is expressly prohibited under Article 20(1) of the Constitution. Section 4 of the Ordinance is also violative of Article 20(1) of the Constitution. The ordinance is also violative of the rights guaranteed under Article 10(1), (b) and (c) and also Article 19 of the Constitution. The power conferred under the Ordinance is unguided and arbitrary and offends Article 14 of the Constitution by treating differently the workers under the government from other workers similarly circumstanced without any reasonable basis. Sections 2, 3 and 4 of the ordinance are more rigorous than those of the general law relating to industrial disputes.

Again, madam, the provision to exact extra work from the...

D. Thengadi: Yes, there is. Even under the law it is guaranteed. There are regulations regarding this right to strike. It is a derived right...

The Deputy Chairman: That is his interpretation.

D. Thengadi: Again, madam, the provision to exact extra work from the employees contravenes Convention No. 29 of the International Labour Organisation which has been ratified by India in 1964. The reasons for wide and sweeping powers given by this ordinance are unconvincing. According to the up-to-date information, madam, under the powers given by the ordinance, only yesterday, 14 employees of Telephone Traffic – all from Bangalore – have been arrested on the ground of mere participation in the 'token strike of 19th September. Similarly, the services of one telephone employee from Gwalior have also been terminated yesterday. That means the government is vindictive, and the Ordinance has armed the government with extra and sweeping powers, and all the employees feel themselves insecure under the present conditions. If this Ordinance is incorporated in any Bill, it is but natural that there would be very great resentment. I am sorry to say, madam, that the government is under an impression that the alternative is whether strike or no strike. That is not the alternative. The alternative would be strike or revolution, because if the right to strike is denied, then there would be no other alternative but to resort to revolution which is not a very democratic and palatable thing.

Madam, in conclusion, I should like to state that such a sweeping power is also not in consonance with the tradition of our country. We have been managing industrial relations in this country for hundreds of years though under different conditions and various authorities on labour jurisprudence in Bharatvarsh have stated as to how industrial relations could be properly regulated. Here I want to quote from Shukraneeti.[292] He says:

> That is, if scoundrels can be united for the sabotage of a nation, why should it not become possible for the State and its employees to stand united for annihilating the enemy of the nation?

Then, Shukra proceeds to give five reasons for industrial disputes amongst which inadequate wages is No. 1. So far as the need-based minimum wage is concerned, Shukra states:

That is, wages are termed as 'ordinary' if they are adequate to procure the necessaries of life. He again says:

> That is, the necessaries of life are to be purchased from the amount of wages. The wages of an employee should, therefore, be so determined as to enable him to procure all the necessaries of life.
>
> He also enjoins:
>
> That is, wages should never be forfeited, nor their payment withheld or postponed. Ultimately, he says that if the government continues to give low wages to its employees, the government will have created its own enemies–Low-paid employees are the enemies created by the government against itself.
>
> And, therefore, he enjoins:
>
> That is, satisfied with adequate wages, promoted honourably, and consoled or cheered up by soft words, the employees would never desert their employer. This is the spirit of the tradition or our Bharatvarsha. Therefore, I urge the government not to proceed with

292. Shukraniti - popular treatise on polity and politics by Sage Shukracharya.

such arbitrary, dictatorial, totalitarian measures, and to come to terms with its employees and united with the employees, serve the nation.

The Essential Services Maintenance Bill, 1968: Continued[293]

Clause 5: Penalty for Instigation, etc.

D. Thengadi: If outsiders are prohibited from helping any cause of the workers which is, according to them just and fair, then it would be very difficult for us to conduct normal, democratic, free trade union activities. Now, whether a strike is legal or illegal, whether it is declared to be illegal or not, if anybody spends money on it, naturally he would do it in his own right and there is no justification whatsoever for bringing him to book. So far as abetting it directly or indirectly is concerned, even under the criminal law of the land, there is enough provision for bringing to book such persons, who are abetting any illegal act, directly or indirectly. Therefore, to my mind, this particular clause has a restraining effect upon our freedom, democratic rights and also legitimate activities. Therefore, I have brought forward my amendment, suggesting that the period of one year be reduced to one week and the fine reduced to one rupee.

D. Thengadi: Madam, this clause gives very wide powers to the ordinary police officers to arrest without warrant. Now, it is well known that when such arbitrary powers are vested even in high officials, they are abused, much more so in the case of petty officials. So, we are opposed to this particular clause and we suggest that the authority or power to arrest without warrant should not be vested in petty police officers.

D. Thengadi: Madam, in the first place, the provisions of the Industrial Disputes Act are themselves quite stringent. Be it as it may, those provisions have not yet been found to be inadequate to deal with any situation of industrial unrest or industrial dispute, and, therefore, this clause seems to be superfluous. Secondly, madam, if this clause is adopted, naturally there will arise a discrimination between the workers covered by the Industrial Disputes Act and those covered by this Bill. And this discrimination is against the spirit and letter of our Constitution. Thirdly, if this practice is followed and encouraged, even the workers in the private sector will be gradually brought within the purview of any such legislation under pressure from the private employers. Fourthly, there is no alternative machinery for redressal of grievances provided for when this clause is

---

293. *Rajya Sabha Debate* dated 27th December, 1968.

being sought to be enacted. Therefore, I am bringing forth this amendment.

D. Thengadi: I move:

2. "That at page 1, line 3, for the word 'maintenance', the word 'dislocation' be substituted."

D. Thengadi: I move:

10. "That at page 1, line 9, for the words 'expiry of three years', the words 'first day of January, 1969' be substituted."

D. Thengadi: Madam, I want to replace the word 'maintenance' by the word 'dislocation' because I am convinced that the Bill as introduced is bound to have the reverse effect. It is bound to irritate, agitate and provoke the employees who are otherwise patriotic, loyal and law abiding and, therefore, since this is going to dislocate the services, creating some sort of reaction amongst the employees, I wish that the word 'maintenance' be replaced by the word 'dislocation'. Secondly, madam, now that the Bill is brought, in order to pay some respect to the hon'ble Home Minister we have said, well, let it be passed but it should cease to have effect on the 1st day of January, 1969 so that even due respect will have been shown to the authorities and at the same time, the Bill will not have the misfortune of continuing longer than it is tolerated by the employees.

D. Thengadi: Madam Deputy Chairman, this is a self-defeating measure. It is doing a great disservice to the very cause it proposes to serve. It reminds me of the legendary figure sitting at the end of a branch with an axe and trying to cut the very branch on which he is sitting. It would be wrong to believe that employees can be terrorised or coerced into submission or discipline or dutifulness. Employees are expected to perform their duties. Dutifulness must be inspired from within, like love and affection. It cannot be imposed from above. Employees have already demonstrated their patriotism, dutifulness, discipline and sense of responsibility particularly during both the emergency periods that is, in 1962 and 1965, and government has no justification whatsoever for disbelieving in their goodness.

Madam, while I am opposing this measure, I should like to urge upon the government that having brought it forth and making a bid for getting it passed, the government should at least show now a sense of justice, if not of generosity and withdraw all victimisations subsequent and consequent to the token strike of 19th September, by which I mean that all prosecutions against those persons who may have participated in the token strike should be withdrawn. Particularly, the termination orders against the temporary employees should be withdrawn. In the cases of suspension, dismissal, discharge, termination or break in service, all the orders should be withdrawn, and an atmosphere of cordiality, congeniality and mutual trust should again be created so that the new machinery proposed to be created by the government may function in a proper environment.

One of the measures adopted by the government to victimise the collective leadership of workers has been withdrawal of recognition to the participating unions or associations. One may or may not agree with the views and inclinations of those various unions and associations, but in the name of democracy, I urge that all those recognitions should be restored so that, it would help promotion of industrial peace and cordiality.

Again government has talked of bringing forth a comprehensive Bill regarding the machinery for joint consultation. I urge that this consultative machinery to be created should not be weak and inferior in quality as compared to the Whitley Council Machinery of Great Britain, so that there should be no other occasion for the employees to lose their faith in the Joint Consultative Machinery and again resort to strike. It seems to me that the government has particular wrath against the outside leadership of the various unions. I think the Minister of State for Home Affairs has not consulted his own rank and file, his own colleagues on this point because, while the Home Ministry would very much like that outsiders should be withdrawn from these associations, probably this proposal may not be palatable to the trade union leaders from his own party. Therefore, I think he has shown indecent haste in saying that outsiders should be withdrawn.

Madam, to conclude, I will say that this is a measure by the temporary government against the real permanent government because everybody knows that the government employees constitute the real and permanent government. Ministers are temporary; they come and go. As in Tennyson's *The Brook*, our government employees say that ministers may come and ministers may go but 'we go on forever'.

Bhupesh Gupta: But they do not go usually.

D. Thengadi: Therefore, it is unfortunate. That the temporary government should come forward with this measure against the permanent government. I wish that even at this last stage, government should show commonsense and withdraw this measure.

D.Thengadi: Normally, we are not in favour of walk-outs, but this measure is exceptionally deplorable, unconstitutional, undemocratic, anti-labour, anti-social, and we cannot be a party to the passing of this Bill.

Contract Labour (Regulation and Abolition) Bill, 1970[294]

Going through the various clauses of this Bill, I may agree that the intentions of the government are alright but the drafting is extremely faulty and it gives loopholes to those who are experts in utilising them. For example, as Mr. Menon[295] said, the limit on the number of employees has been prescribed and it is said that only to such establishments that employ 20 or 30 workmen, this Act will be applicable.

This need not be there because we know how various devices have been employed by the employers to circumvent the provisions of the present Act. Now there is reference to casual work. It is already a controversial subject. Let alone the private sector, even in industries that are directly under the government, like the Railways, this casual labour is a very controversial subject. Workmen are employed continuously even for a number of years and still they are termed as casual. Similarly, the term 'seasonal' is also controversial... and we all know how these powers will be abused. So, the Bill needs to be redrafted, and the powers of the licencing officers, particularly the power to exempt certain establishments and employers and contractors from the provisions of this law should be curbed. Otherwise, a licensing officer would, by himself, become an employer. Similarly, there should be no right given either to the licensing officers or even to government to exempt any category from the operation of this law, and also the government should not be allowed to exempt the special cases referred to in Clause 31, and in Clause 32 the sub-section (1) also would be misused and the said subsection (1) reads as follows:

"No suit, prosecution or other legal proceedings shall lie against any registering officer, licencing officer or any other government servant or against any member of the Central Board or the State Board, as the case may be, for anything which is in good faith done or intended to be done in pursuance of this Act or any rule or order made thereunder."

Now, sir, it is very difficult to establish 'good faith' or to establish 'bad faith', whatever it is and, therefore, such special exemption should not have been given to members of the Boards or the registering officers or the licensing officers.

---

294. *Rajya Sabha Debate* dated 18th August, 1970.

295. Balachandra Menon (1911-1985) was a CPI leader and trade unionist from Kerala. Menon was member, Kerala Legislative Assembly, 1957 and 1960 and member, Rajya Sabha, 1967-1973.

We welcome the provision under which principal employers are made liable for payment of wages and for other amenities of labour employed by contractors. We also welcome the other provisions regarding canteens, medical facilities, drinking water and all these things. We understand the intentions of the government.

But regarding violation, the penalty proposed is too light. It ought to have been more severe. The punishment must always be deterrent; otherwise they would think all right, even if I have to pay Rs. 1000/- or Rs. 500/-, I can pay it as fine if I can earn huge profits thereby. Therefore, they will be prepared to pay these penalties.

Short Duration Discussion Regarding Government's Employment Policy in Public Sector Undertakings[296]

D. Thengadi: Sir, firstly regarding the recruitment of the local people, I think the criterion should not be the amount of salary received; it should be the nature of the work. That is the unskilled and the semi-skilled people should be necessarily, invariably and without exception recruited from amongst the local people. But for the recruitment of highly skilled and technical people, an all-India perspective should be had. Regarding reservations or other facilities to the Scheduled Castes, the Scheduled Tribes, the nomads and semi-nomad tribes and the ex-criminal tribes and those backward classes, they should be given encouragement but not merely by way of reservations, but by providing for them special training programmes so as to bring them on par with others.

Then there is the question of overstaffing and understaffing also. The problem of overstaffing arises because the original estimates are very often incorrect. But it is not the fault of those who are in the public sector undertakings that they are found to be surplus. It is the mistake of those who made the original estimates. And, therefore, it should be seen that there is no retrenchment, that they are absorbed in the same undertaking, and the employment given to them should be with no loss of seniority or grade.

There is also the question of understaffing. I know of many of the departments; their workload is so high that needs to be shared by a greater number. So, a workload analysis should be conducted in the different departments of every undertaking, and wherever there is necessity of further recruitment, it should be done expeditiously.

296. *Rajya Sabha Debate* dated 15th March, 1969.

Our policy should be of progressive elimination of foreign technical knowhow. Now, that cannot be arranged unless proper precaution is taken at the time of arriving at agreements with the foreign collaborators. So, right from the beginning, this precaution should be taken so that, in course of time, we should be able to replace the foreign technical know-how with our own.

One rule should be strictly followed that there should be no direct recruitment to the higher posts wherever suitable persons are available for the same in the lower grades, which is generally one of the causes of heartburning.

Now, the general experience is that the public sector undertakings have failed so far to attract the best talents in the land. The reasons are obvious. Our values of life are materialistic, economic, and the private sector can give alluring and more attractive pay scales. Some way should be found out to stop this diversion of talents to the private sector. And for this purpose – I do not know whether it would be feasible but it is worth experimenting – even as we have got the standardisation of nomenclature or description of jobs and designation of jobs, we should explore the possibility of evolving standardisation of pay scales for the different jobs, whether those jobs are in the private sector or in the public sector or in the co-operative sector.

Regarding top managerial posts, if these posts are manned by bureaucrats who have no business acumen or knowledge or intimate understanding of industrial psychology, naturally the undertakings will have a very bad employer-employee relationship and they will fail in making profits. Therefore, it is necessary, it seems, that we must have, as suggested by Mr. Krishan Kant,[297] a sort of All-India service for the public sector undertakings for recruitment to them of people with the necessary qualifications.

Regarding deputationists also, I think the time is ripe when we should not allow things to drift. Some norms and standards should be evolved about deputationists in the different undertakings and these should be uniformly implemented.

297. Krishan Kant (1927-2002) was the tenth Vice President of India, part of the 'Young Turks' in the Congress, Kant left the party in protest against the imposition of Emergency, later joined the Janata Party and Janata Dal. Kant served as Governor of Andhra Pradesh and became the 10th Vice President of India between 1997-2002; he died in office. Kant was also the General Secretary of the Peoples' Union of Civil Liberties (PUCL).

Short Duration Discussion Regarding Delay in Implementing the Report of the Gajendragadkar Commission[298]

D. Thengadi: Madam Deputy Chairman, I am here to stress that the government should go beyond the recommendations of the Gajendragadkar Commission. We are not satisfied with these recommendations because, in the first place, the commission has not enunciated any principle or formula about the protection of real wage. I do not know whether it is so because the terms of reference were rigid. Nevertheless, no principle or formula has been enunciated.

Secondly, the Commission has failed to indicate any solution to the wage-price spiral. In this respect, it has been argued by the government that if there is rise in D.A. or wages, naturally prices would rise. But the very fact that without any additional payment of D.A. or wages we are having, after the last raise, a rise of 20 points in the index which goes to prove that there can be price rise even without wage rise. As a matter of fact, we are of the firm opinion that wage rise cannot be held responsible for price rise, and that wage rise can be responsible for price rise only to the extent to which the wage rise is in excess of productivity rise.

Now, my hon'ble friend, Akbar Ali Khan, had posed a very valid question, namely whether all sections of population should not be called upon to shoulder the burden of price rise. As a casual reference, I might say that while the question is very valid, there should be justice about the shouldering of the burden also, and to ensure this justice, it is necessary even in our country as in some of the Western countries that there should be a cause-wise break-up of price rise and the percentage of price rise which is due to deficit financing should be borne by the government, whatever is due to profiteering should be borne by the profiteers and whatever is due to scarcity, that should be borne by all the 50 crores of people, including employees. Unless there is this cause-wise break-up, it is not possible for us to locate – what is the percentage to be borne by the general consumers including the employees. That is what I want to suggest to our friend, Akbar Ali Khan.

P.K. Kumaran: How to do all these things? It is easy to pass it on to the workers.

D. Thengadi: The Commission has not done justice to the subsistence-level workers. As a matter of fact, we differ from the Gajendragadkar

298. *Rajya Sabha Debate* dated 17th August, 1967.

Commission regarding the definition of subsistence level. In view of the prevalent prices, we think that the economic limit of subsistence level should be up to Rs. 300, that of vulnerability up to Rs. 750, while the Commission has prescribed these limits to Rs. 150 and Rs. 575, respectively.

Now, these subsistence-level workers must be given full neutralisation. There should be no compromise about this fact. Again, we know that the formula of a one-year and 10-point rise creates much discontent among the workers. As a matter of fact, the period of six months and a rise of 5 points should have been accepted even by the Commission. On account of these facts, the employees are thoroughly dissatisfied with the Gajendragadkar Commission report. Therefore, I urge that the government should go beyond the report of the Gajendragadkar Commission and do justice to the employees in general and those on the subsistence level in particular.

Again, to think of deferred payment by making payment in bonds or in any other form is highly unjust because whatever is given to him is meant to meet his present requirement, and if the payment is deferred, that means I will receive the money in 1980, so that I may satisfy my hunger in 1967. This is ridiculous. Therefore, all payments should be only in cash. There should be no compromise even on this point.

Madam, without going into details, because there is hardly any time for all that, I must say that ours is not a cost inflation. To say that because there is increase in the wage bill the prices are rising rather is not relevant to the situation obtaining in the country today. In Great Britain, two-thirds of the national expenditure is the wage bill. In our country, the wage bill constitutes roundabout one-third of the national expenditure. Therefore, the analogy of Great Britain cannot be made applicable to India. At the same time, the Government of India seems to have made this a prestige issue. It should not be so. I remember some of the ministers saying that they are also as much public servants as the Class IV employees. If it is so, then they should not make it a prestige issue, and before September 11, I would request the government to come to senses to see through reason and to do justice to the employees.

I remember a sort of statistics generally given that if the Gajendragadkar Commission is accepted, the Central Government will have to bear Rs. 64 crores more, state governments Rs. 60 crores more, Corporations Rs. 22 crores more and local-self governments Rs. 28 crores. All the statistics were given. The total figure was Rs. 174 crores. But, at the same time, I must say that this is only one part of the argument. We cannot forget that while the government has come forward with the plea that various measures are to be adopted for checking the price rise and holding the price line, we, on behalf of the Opposition, assure the government that in case the government comes forward with a comprehensive plan – that is important – to hold the price line, all the Opposition parties will extend their whole-hearted support to the government's policy. But, very unfortunately, the effort of the government in checking the price rise begins and ends with the throttling of the Class IV employees and nothing is done to check profits, government expenditure and other things. Therefore, we are compelled to say that if there is a wage-freeze without being preceded by a profit-freeze or price-freeze or expenditure-freeze, then, being helpless, the workers will unfortunately have to resort to a work-freeze and the entire responsibility for this will rest with the government and not with the employees.

Resolution Seeking Disapproval of the Essential Services Maintenance Ordinance, 1968 (No. 9 of 1968) and the Essential Services Maintenance Bill, 1968: Continued[299]

D. Thengadi: Madam, I move:

14. "That at page 2, for lines 21 to 23, the following be substituted, namely:

'(viii) any other service which both Houses of Parliament may decide from time to time by a majority of not less than seven-eighths of the total membership of each House to be an essential service.'

The Deputy Chairman: Are you reading it? It is not necessary. They have been circulated.

D. Thengadi: Madam, I move:

29. "That at page 3, for lines 4 to 15, the following be substituted, namely:

'(2) No notification shall be issued unless it is approved by a majority of seven-eights of the total membership of each House of Parliament.'*

D. Thengadi: Here the point is that essential service should be declared by a vote in Parliament. That authority should not be given to the government, that is, to bureaucrats. Secondly, there is the question of overtime. As I referred to it in my speech also, India has ratified the ILO convention which enjoins that there should be no exacting of work against

---

299. *Rajya Sabha Debate* dated 26th December, 1968.

the wishes of the employees. It is against overtime work, and this working of overtime has been legislated upon. We are opposed to it because it is against the spirit of our Constitution as well as the convention of the ILO. Then whenever any notification is to be issued, it should be issued with the prior consent, prior approval of both the Houses of Parliament. Not that Parliament or both the Houses should be confronted with a fait accompli that already the government has issued the notification and only the Houses have to endorse it. For this reason, I have given this amendment.

D. Thengadi: Madam, I move:

35. "That at page 3, for lines 16 to 19, the following be substituted, namely:

35. "That at page 3, for lines 16 to 19 after referring a dispute to arbitration by mutual consent, feels that in the public interest it is necessary or expedient so to do, it may, by a general or special order, prohibit strike in any essential service specified in the order:

Provided that no order prohibiting the strike in any essential service shall be issued unless the same is approved by both the Houses of Parliament by a resolution adopted in each House by a majority of seven-eighths of the total membership of that House:

Provided further that an order issued when Parliament is not in session shall cease to operate unless it has been approved by resolutions of both Houses of Parliament at the commencement of the immediately subsequent session."

44. "That at page 3, for lines 23 to 26, the following be substituted, namely:

'(3) An order made under subsection (1) shall be enforced for one week only, but it can be extended for further periods, one week at a time, if approved by both Houses of Parliament by a resolution adopted in each House by a majority of seven-eighths of the total membership of that House'."

53. "That at page 3, line 29, the words 'or remain' be deleted."

Resolution Seeking Disapproval of the Essential Services Maintenance Ordinance Bill, 1968[300]

D. Thengadi: Madam, my amendments are against giving sweeping powers to the government regarding prohibition of strikes. Before any order prohibiting a strike is issued, I have suggested that there should be

300. *Rajya Sabha Debate* dated 26th December, 1968.

a precondition imposed. The dispute should have already been referred to arbitration by mutual consent and Parliament's approval must be sought at the earliest opportunity. If Parliament is in session, each House by a majority of seven-eighths should pass or should consent to such an order. If it is not in session, there should be approval at the earliest opportunity in the immediately subsequent session. I think unless this restraining power of Parliament is accepted and unless, in principle, arbitration by mutual consent is made a pre-condition, this particular clause is going to confer upon government unrestrained, totalitarian, dictatorial powers.

Secondly, I have suggested in Clause 3(3) that an order shall be enforced for one week instead of six months. It can be extended for a further period of one week at a time. This is a power which should be used very sparingly and, therefore, I have suggested one week instead of six months.

Thirdly, sub-clause (4) authorises the Government to give retrospective effect to the order issued. Now, this is unfair, unjust and unprecedented. When a man does a particular act, which is legal, and subsequently an order is passed which gives retrospective effect making it illegal, it is something unjustified. Therefore, such retrospective effect should not be given and that power should not be conferred upon the government. These amendments I am moving.

D. Thengadi: Sir, I am opposed to this clause and I am suggesting certain amendments. In the first place, as I have said earlier, it would be unfair, unjust and illegal to give retrospective effect to any order issued by the government. Secondly, the wording of this clause is very vague. "Any person who commences a strike which is illegal under this Act or goes or remains on, or otherwise takes part in…" which means that the whole clause can be construed in any way favourable to the government. And, thirdly, since I am opposed to the very issuing of an order prohibiting strikes, as a matter of fact, I am not convinced that for going on strike anybody should be punished; but now that there is a legislation and some punishment or other is to be imposed, I have suggested through my amendment that the period of six months of punishment be reduced to one week and a fine of Rs. 200/- to Rs. 1/-. I am quite aware that the hon'ble Minister of State is going to say that this is absurd. Certainly, this is absurd. I agree with him. But I also remind him that the absurdity of our amendment is only the effect of the absurdity of the original clause. So, the absurdity of our amendment flows from the absurdity of the original clause. If the original absurdity is removed, following it, the incidental absurdity will not have any justification for its existence.

Statutory Resolution Seeking Disapproval of the Payment of Bonus (Amendment) Ordinance, 1969 and The Payment of Bonus (Amendment) Bill, 1969[301]

D. Thengadi: Madam, the Statement of Objects and Reasons of the Bill states very clearly that the Bill has been brought with a very limited purpose, the intention of the government being that the available surplus under Section 5 should be so computed that the amount of tax rebate accruing to the employers on account of bonus paid or payable under the Act becomes a part of the available surplus of the succeeding year, instead of the same going entirely to the employers. A very limited purpose has been set forth and, therefore, extraneous considerations need not have been brought in.

So far as the object of the Bill is concerned, I wholeheartedly support it. Regarding the other points referred to by our friend Mr. Chinai, I want to state that he is not correct in saying that bonus is an ex-gratia payment. No, bonus assumes two characters. So long as there is a gap between the living wage and the actual wage, bonus has the character of deferred or supplementary wage. But once the actual wage attains the level of living wage, then only bonus has the character of profit-sharing. Therefore, as wage, deferred or supplementary, bonus must be given its priority or precedence over all other allocations. Therefore, now that he has referred to other points, I want to say that instead of bringing in this piecemeal amending legislation, we should have welcomed the government to come forward with a comprehensive amending Bill in which this definition of bonus ought to have been incorporated as deferred or supplementary wage so long as there is a gap between the living wage and the actual wage; secondly, doing away with the tampering with the number of workers employed for purposes of the application of the Act as well as doing away with the ceiling of percentage of available surplus for purposes of distribution of bonus and, in the same way, granting to the workers the right to go behind the balance-sheets of their respective concerns and scrutinise the profit and loss accounts and also the propriety or impropriety of the various expenditures incurred. In this fashion, if a comprehensive Bill had been brought, we would have further welcomed it. I would request the government to bring forward such a comprehensive Bill.

---

301. *Rajya Sabha Debate* dated 26th February, 1969.

D. Thengadi: By way of clarification, I want to ask one question. I quite appreciate the point that giving retrospective effect may be opening the Pandora's Box. But the hon'ble minister must have consulted the Law Minister on this point as to how to cover the present pending cases. This is the main point.

Jaisukhlal Hathi:[302] So far as the first point is concerned, in fact, I myself have examined and thought of this, whether we can do it from 1967 onwards, but I understand that it will lead to many complications. Many cases might have been settled or many cases where bonus was given, may not have been pending. Then, all those questions will have to be reopened if we want to be just to all the workers. Those who accepted bonus, did not raise the dispute because they thought, 'This is an Act, this is the interpretation.' Therefore, that will lead to further complications, otherwise, I myself thought of it. Then about Mr. Bhadram's[303] second amendment, the provision, as it is, is just consistent with the scheme; as it is, the allocable surplus is 60 per cent and 40 per cent. They have had it. But now, at present, we cannot change it. Then, so far as Mr. Thengadi's point is concerned, for the accounting year 1968, they will all be covered under this new legislation...

Resolution Seeking Disapproval of the Additional Emoluments (Compulsory Deposit) Ordinance, 1974 (No. 8 of 1974)[304]

Sir, with your permission, I move:

"That this House disapproves the Additional Emoluments (Compulsory Deposit) Ordinance, 1974 (No. 8 of 1974 promulgated by the President on 6th July, 1974."

Sir, in this connection, I do not know what the position is, as had been objected to earlier, whether the matter is subjudice and we are not competent to discuss it here. But it is for you to decide. That is your

302. Jaisukhlal Hathi (1909-1982) – Congress leader, was member, Constituent Assembly, 1946-47, member, Provisional Parliament, member Lok Sabha, 1957-62, and Rajya Sabha 1952-1957, 1962-1968, 1968-1974. Hathi served as Union Deputy Minister, Minister of State and Minister holding portfolios of Irrigation and Power, Supply, Home Affairs, Defence and Labour and Rehabilitation,1952-69; he was leader of the Rajya Sabha between 1967-69. Was chairman of the Commission on Drugs & Pharmaceuticals in 1974, was also closely associated with Bharatiya Vidya Bhavan and was also a trustee of the Somnath Temple Trust..

303. M.V. Bhadram, (1918-1991) – CPI leader from Andhra Pradesh, served as member of Rajya Sabha between 1966-72.

304. *Rajya Sabha Debate* dated 29th August, 1974.

jurisdiction. Our first objection is that before the ordinance was promulgated, the workers' representatives were not taken into confidence; there were no prior consultations with them; as a matter of fact, the Government of India is committed to prior consultation with workers' representatives in all matters concerning them. But this time they were completely ignored. As a matter of fact, objection has been raised that there was no case for promulgation of an ordinance when Parliament was to meet so soon after. I do not know whether even the Finance Minister had any prior knowledge about the drafting of this scheme; but anyway, it is their domestic affair with which I am not concerned. On moral grounds, it is obvious that the government that cannot freeze prices has no moral right to freeze wages; the government that cannot freeze huge, exorbitant profits of monopoly houses and foreign collaborators has no moral right to freeze wages; the government that is incompetent to guarantee a need-based minimum wage is hardly competent morally to freeze workers' wages. A government that has failed to evolve – not to speak of implementing – aduring the last 27 years has no justification in freezing wage of workers. It is not just a wage-freeze. It is actually a wage cut because wages are going to be reduced through this measure. You will have noted already that while the surplus remuneration of workers has been immobilised, whatever surplus is left beyond the ceiling on dividends has not been taken over as compulsory deposit which is left with the companies for further investment. That is a sort of discrimination or difference between these two measures. It is a well-known sound principle of economics that every wage rise is not responsible for price rise. Wage rise is responsible for price rise only to the extent to which the wage rise is in excess of productivity rise and in our country, even an independent and impartial body like the National Labour Commission has said that in India, productivity rise has always been in excess of wage rise so that prices are going ahead; they are being chased by productivity rise and both are chased by wage. Therefore, according to the sound principle of economics, government is not justified in saying that because wages are rising, there is price rise.

This measure covers two aspects of our national policy. One is inflation and the other, our wage policy. Every one of us is interested in curbing inflation and we should have liked to co-operate with the government on this point, provided they would have made a proper move. If inflation is to be curbed, the proper point to start with would have been the black money regarding which Wanchoo Committee had suggested certain measures. But the government is not prepared to introduce demonetisation for obvious reasons. They do not want to offend their patrons.

Sir, money supply is entirely regulated by the government and is also a sound principle that the growth rate in money supply should be corresponding with the growth rate in national income. Today I may not be exaggerating if I say that our growth rate is almost nearly zero per cent, whereas the growth rate in money supply has been 15 per cent. This principle also has been violated.

There should have been a drastic curtailment in the unproductive, administrative expenditure. But, presently, the administrative expenditure has risen from 2 per cent to 14 per cent. Wasteful, vulgar and ostentatious consumption has been continuing and the government has no courage to introduce a consumption tax so as to curb such ostentatious expenditure on consumption. Deficit financing is also another matter completely within the hands of the government. Though they are saying times without number that deficit financing would be progressively reduced, actually it is on the rise. All of us know about it.

The patterns of production can also be regulated to a considerable extent by official policy. There should have been a complete ban on production of luxury goods and they should have done everything to boost up production of consumer goods. But the pattern of taxation is such that luxury goods production is encouraged while that of consumer goods is discouraged. It is wrong to presume, as the government seems to, that the criterion for assessing the national prosperity is the Gross National Product. It is not so. As a matter of fact, it is necessary to encourage the consumer goods industries because that is the only way to give wider employment and also to ensure decentralisation of money power. Sir, the patterns of production have an inherent and built-in mechanism which would resist any pattern of distribution which is not consistent with the pattern of production. Therefore, to say that even by boosting up the production of luxury goods, we will increase our national income and then we will have proper distribution is ridiculous. Today, it is the consumer goods which are neglected and it is the luxury goods which are receiving the special favour from the government. Then, sir, there is a heavy dose of indirect taxation. Many of the so-called Supplementary Budgets are nothing but proposals for indirect taxation, although our Finance Minister is not admitting this fact. Sir, we should have utilised to the fullest extent the idle capacity in our public sector for the non-utilisation of which the bureaucratisation of industries is responsible. But the government is not doing anything in that direction.

Then, sir, about corruption, I need not say much. Also, tax evasion cannot be there from the side of the capitalists without the active co-operation from the other side also. Many measures in these directions must have already been taken. But, instead of starting from the right point, they have started with the workers first. Sir, this is an onslaught on the workers who are already below the poverty line. Sir, in this case, I must say, the Government of India has been very callous to the plight of the poorer sections of the population. As an example, I must point out one thing. While the biggest problem in our economy is that of unemployment, of course, along with the problem of price rise, but the Planning Commission and the Government of India are not in a position today to give us the correct assessment of the extent of unemployment and underemployment. Most of us know that while the figures relating to unemployment were given in the documents of the first three plans, in the document of the Fourth Plan it was mentioned that they were not in a position to give any figures because they said that so far, that is, till the time the draft was prepared, they did not have the correct methodology for assessing the extent of unemployment and underemployment and that the one-dimensional methodology used for the three plan documents was not suited to the Indian conditions! It is a matter of wonder that this revelation was there after three plans were there and this is an example to show how callously the poorer sections of the people are being treated by the government. Sir, even the term 'poverty line' is not properly defined. Quite apart from removing poverty, they have made poverty and poverty line a matter of discussion. A per capita income of Rs. 40 p.m. is supposed to indicate the poverty line. I do not know whether Mr. Chavan will maintain himself and his family at this rate of Rs. 40 p.m. Anyway, sir, how many people are below the poverty line and how many people are above it are matters of debate now in this country. Sir, it is true that in the absence of any national wage policy, there is going to be chaos and there is chaos and the government is preparing itself for another onslaught on the working class by introducing what is wrongly described as the rationalisation of the wage policy. We know that according to the reports published unofficially and not contradicted officially, that this policy is going to be introduced, this policy of rationalisation of differentials. Sir, we understand that there must be job evaluation and on the basis of the job evaluation, wage differentials should be fixed. This process can be resorted to only after the minimum, that is, need-based minimum wage has been guaranteed for every unskilled worker. Now, we are far away from the policy of need-based minimum wage. Therefore, this policy of the government, at this stage, through which the government wants to set the unorganised working class against the organised working class, the general population against the working class, is going to help only in creating chaos and aggravating the problem of poverty in the country.

Sir, I must say that regarding wage policy, some rationalisation is necessary – Compulsory Deposit Scheme I admit. But what that rationalisation should be? In the Directive Principles of our Constitution, the minimum living wage is thought of. People have not been given that. Even whatsoever has been given is now being snatched away by such ordinance and Compulsory Deposit Scheme. Sir, this cannot be tolerated. The working class has an apprehension that probably this particular attack, that is, of CDS, is not an isolated act. They apprehend that this is a link in the chain, and that particularly after being emboldened by their military operation against the Railway employees, now the government feels that they are in a position to crush the working class and their movement and, therefore, it is the first link in the chain. They apprehend that more such measures would follow.

Sir, I must say – and I want to remind our Finance Minister in all seriousness – that we have demanded that our national policies should be formulated not in the air-conditioned rooms of the Planning Commission but that a round table conference of all economic interests should be conveyed to formulate on the basis of a consensus national policy regarding employment, productivity, prices and incomes. But no such step has been taken by the government. Sir, I will not talk about any ambiguities if they are there, because this is not the proper time to talk about them. I will not discuss the various problems that are going to arise out of the implementation of this Compulsory Deposit Scheme because there is no time for that. There are various problems that we will have to face immediately about the daily, rated workers, about the piece-rated workers, about the workers who have entered into an agreement immediately before the promulgation of this ordinance regarding wage rise. For example, I learn that one industrialist from Maharashtra has even declared that in spite of this ordinance or Act, he would give the full amount of additional wage and additional dearness allowance to his workers. I do not know how far it is true. In our own House, we have the case of our Lakshmana Gowda,[305] who, along with his colleagues in the plantation industry in Karnataka and in Tamil Nadu, has entered into an agreement with the workers, enhancing the daily rate from 50 paise to 60 paise in the month of June, and now when first payment was to commence in July, there is difficulty for both the employers and the employees. Sir, many such difficulties are there; I am not going to take the time of the House by going into the details of implementation. For example, objection has already been raised that the duplication of accounts is unnecessary and wasteful and that could have been avoided. These are all minor points.

The main point is whether the government is justified in attacking the existing meagre wages of the workers in the name of curbing inflation. Sir, I want to say that because of this Compulsory Deposit Scheme, inflation is not going to be affected; inflation will be there. It has its own pace and tempo. Only our workers will suffer.

Sir, they have been very generous in saying that they have offered 11 per cent interest rate. But are we not aware, sir, that the rate of inflation is 27 per cent, and after that period, the period of five, even during that period, prices are to rise, and, therefore, the value of the rupee will go down. It is a postdated cheque. I do not know whether Mr. Chavan will be there to implement it. But still if this postdated cheque is to be valid, even then the value of the rupee is going to be reduced. And, therefore, they will suffer a loss, from the point of view of not only workers, but from the point of view of national economy, in view of the fact that the real cause of inflation is left untouched, and also in view of the fact that the Government of India is completely unwilling to take any action against blackmarketeers, hoarders, profiteers, smugglers, monopoly houses and foreign capital in the country. This onslaught appeals to be just a measure to appease monopolists and foreign collaborators who are probably not behaving in the way government wants them to behave, thinking that if the working classes are active if their trade union movement is strong, they will not have their own way, they cannot get away with their huge profits. Therefore, with a view to assuring monopolists and foreign collaborators, probably government wants to show that they have crushed the working-class movement and this one measure is a step in that direction. The Indian

305. U.K. Lakshmana Gowda (1919-2017) – Independent member of Rajya Sabha and served for two-term between 1968-1980.

working class is determined to fight out this measure inside the Parliament, outside Parliament, from all forums through a chain of mass struggles. And if our government is really earnest about increase in production, then, this is not the way to seek the co-operation of all workers. Unless workers are co-operative, production cannot increase. And they always say production must be increased; otherwise, we will further go down. Workers are willing to offer co-operation provided government adopts right policies. So, in the absence of co-operation from workers and with a chain of mass struggles at every level, it would be very difficult for the Government of India to continue to appease their patrons, whether Indian or foreign. It is high time that the Finance Minister saw the writing on the wall, that he saw that this policy cannot continue for long, that this will throw the country into a sort of economic chaos, and that, therefore, he should withdraw this measure and earn the co-operation of the working class.

Sir, when I am moving this Resolution, I am not agreeable to this position. I want that the two should be taken up separately. In the absence of any agreement, I am requesting the Chair to kindly take up these two matters separately.

Sir, the hon'ble minister has failed to give any argument in favour of his stand. I would like to add certain facts to whatever has been said earlier.

Regarding wages, the position has been that workers' share in the VAM [Value Added by Manufacture] has been constantly declining while employers' share is on the increase. The National Commission on Labour has said:

To sum up, we know that increase in money wages of industrial workers since Independence has not been associated with the rise in real wages, nor have real wage increases been commensurate with improvement in productivity. Simultaneously, wage costs as a proportion of total costs of manufacture have registered a decline and the same is true of workers' share in the VAM.

According to the *Reserve Bank Report:*

For all the 1,650 companies studied, the component of manufacturing expenses in the total value of production rose from 62.6 per cent in 1970-71 to 63.1 per cent in 1971-72, while there was a marginal fall in the component of remuneration to employees from 15.4 per cent to 15.3 per cent.

The burden of indirect taxation on workers is increasing, but his real wage has been going down progressively. Under the circumstances, it is very unfair and impractical to expect that this policy of the government ensures the workers to give higher productivity, which is the need of the hour. What is necessary is all-out co-operation of all the parties to the industrial relations to enhance production at this juncture. But at such a critical situation, government is coming on with a heavy hand upon our poor workers. Sir, some appeal has been made about sacrificing for the cause of the national prosperity. Sir, I must say that our workers are patriotic and on all occasions of national emergency, they have exhibited their sense of patriotism. In 1962, when there was the Chinese aggression, in 1965, when there was war with Pakistan and in 1971, when there was the Bangladesh crisis – on all these three occasions, the workers were the first and the foremost to suffer and sacrifice for the country. But they must be guaranteed that their suffering is for the cause of the nation, that their suffering is for stabilising the national economy and that their suffering is not for tightening the stranglehold of the black money and its partners, that is, the Ministers and others, on the national economy. Therefore, sir, the workers are demanding that this Additional Emoluments (Compulsory Deposit) Ordinance must be withdrawn and it should not be made into an Act, that the entire economic policy should be altered in favour of the poorer sections of the population, that a proper financial discipline should be evolved and implemented and that the Government of India itself should strictly follow this financial discipline instead of giving sermons to all others that such a discipline should be followed. These are the things which are demanded by the workers of the country.

Sir, I am at a disadvantageous position since our hon'ble Finance Minister has utterly failed to say anything in favour of his stand and, therefore, I request my hon'ble friends here to support this resolution and oppose the ordinance.

Calling Attention to a Matter of Urgent Public Importance Regarding Boycott of the One-Man Independent Body for Dearness Allowance by the Central Government Employees' Unions[306]

D. Thengadi: Sir, with your permission, I rise to call the attention of the Minister of Finance to the situation arising out of the total boycott of

306. *Rajya Sabha Debate* dated 29th September, 1964.

the 'one-man Independent Body for Dearness Allowance' by the Central Government Employees' Unions.

D. Thengadi: What is the total membersnip of the unions that have co-operated with the work of the Commission and also of those who have not co-operated with it?

B.R. Bhagat: It is difficult to give the membership list, but I only suggested that it is not a total boycott. Many unions are coming forward. Many have not come forward. That is true.

D. Thengadi: The hon'ble minister has said that there have been no serious developments during the last four or five years that would call for a review of the basic principles of the formula of the Pay Commission. Does he not consider the unprecedented spiralling of prices during recent years such a serious and noteworthy development, which would call for a revision or a review of the Pay Commission's formula?

B.R. Bhagat:[307] When the Pay Commission recommended it, the average index was 115. Now, subsequently, up to an average index of 135, it has been neutralised. So, progressively, the Pay Commission's recommendations were implemented and no situation has arisen so that the formula itself should be changed.

D. Thengadi: One more clarification. Now, that the period of the recommendations of the Pay Commission has already expired on 1st July last, what are the technical difficulties in constituting another Pay Commission?

B.R. Bhagat: Well, sir, the hon'ble member refers to the Joint Consultative Machinery. As you know, there is a recommendation that after five years, it may be revised. May I bring to the notice of the hon'ble member that the employees have not accepted that formula. When they have not accepted the formula, they cannot raise any objection to its implementation.

---

307. Bali Ram Bhagat (1922-2011) – Congress leader from Bihar, was a seven-term member of Lok Sabha from Arrah, and served in the 1st, 2nd, 3rd, 4th, 5th, 7th and 8th Lok Sabha between 1952-1989. Bhagat was Union Deputy Minister of Finance, 1956-1963; Minister of Planning 1963-67, Minister of State for Finance, Minister for Defence Production, Minister of State for External Affairs, Cabinet Minister for Foreign Trade and Supply, Cabinet Minister for Steel and Heavy Engineering, 1970-1971; Bhagat was also Speaker of the Lok Sabha, 1976-1977; he served as External Affairs Minister in Rajiv Gandhi's cabinet between 1985-1986 and also served as Governor of Himachal Pradesh and Rajasthan.

Calling Attention Notice Regarding Stay-in-Strike on 9th December, 1965 by the Employees of the Press Trust of India[308]

D. Thengadi: Sir, in view of the fact that the PTI is a national agency, as admitted by our hon'ble Labour Minister, it is within the competence of the hon'ble Labour Minister to advise that there should be proper settlement across the table, and also it is within his competence to introduce an amending legislation in the Industrial Disputes Act, and also because he is aware of the fact that what the management seeks to do is to actually reduce the existing benefits of the employees, and the plea of paucity of funds or that funds have fallen because the gratuity reserve has to be built up gradually, in view of all these facts, apart from natural justice, the fact that the PTI employees have rendered distinguished service to the national cause during the last national emergency, will the hon'ble Labour Minister bring appropriate pressure to bear, or advise the management to settle matters across the table?

D. Sanjivayya: I know, sir, that I am competent to introduce an amending Bill and also competent to bring in the central sphere labour relations pertaining to this particular industry, but before I do that, I have to consult the state governments, and more often than not, the state governments do not agree with any proposal of this type.

Coming to the other question, sir, namely the amount set apart by the management towards a fund for gratuity, I must say that they have set apart more than Rs. 2 lakhs and the employees say that the management need not have been in such a hurry to build up that fund. They could have contributed only Rs. 1 lakh or Rs. 80,000 so that the demand of the employees could be fulfilled. It is for the management to consider. In fact, we in the Labour Ministry do not wish that any employee or any worker should get less bonus than he has been getting earlier. That is why, we have made a provision in the Bonus law. But even that is not a fool-proof one.

Calling Attention Notice Regarding Reported Mass Agitation by Employees of Office of the Comptroller and Auditor-General of India[309]

D. Thengadi: May I know, sir, if it is not a fact that all the delegates who attended the annual session of this Association in 1960 were chargesheeted and penalised, thus making it impossible for them to

308. *Rajya Sabha Debate* dated 10th December, 1965.

309. *Rajya Sabha Debate* dated 9th March, 1966.

function in a regular democratic trade-union fashion? Is it also a fact that in May 1965, the Home Minister gave a decision that the question of the recognition of the Association should be reconsidered? So far as the status of the Auditor-General is concerned, is the government aware of the fact that in an affidavit made before the Nagpur Bench of the Maharashtra High Court, the Auditor-General, Bombay, submitted that what happened on the floor of the House of the Lok Sabha had no relevance? And one more thing, sir. Our Constitution provides for the impeachment of the Auditor-General for incapacity or misbehaviour. There are serious allegations of misbehaviour against the Auditor-General. The exact position of the Auditor-General had been clarified by Dr Ambedkar in the Constituent Assembly on 30-5-49 when he said:

"On comparing the articles about the Supreme Court and the articles relating to the Auditor-General, I cannot help saying that we have not given him the same independence which we have given to the judiciary."

On this ground, because of the misbehaviour, will the government impeach the Auditor-General?

B.R. Bhagat: I am sorry, sir, that the hon'ble member without substantiating any charge says that there are serious allegations and, therefore, he should be impeached. He has drawn his own conclusions.

D. Thengadi: What is the charge sheet against the Auditor-General ?

B.K.P. Sinha:[310] I have a point of order. The point is that the Constitution confers a certain status on the Auditor-General. Now the Auditor-General is not present in the House. Even in his absence, to say that there are serious charges and he must be impeached, is that appropriate and should that remark be allowed to be a part of the proceedings of this House?

Mr. Chairman: I think we should be a little more careful because there are limitations to our freedom.

Calling Attention Notice Regarding Demonstration by Development Officers of Life Insurance Corporation[311]

D. Thengadi: Sir, I have given a calling attention notice inviting the attention of the government to the Development Officers of the Life Insurance Corporation of India, who are staging a demonstration today

---

310. Braja Kishore Prasad Sinha (1909-1996) – Independent member of Rajya Sabha from Bihar, Sinha was member, Provisional Parliament and member, Rajya Sabha for three terms from 1952-1970. Between 1941-1949, Sinha was also General Secretary of the Bihar Pradesh Congress Committee.

311. *Rajya Sabha Debate* dated 10th November, 1966.

before Parliament for their demands. In view of the important role played by them in the national economy, I would request the hon'ble Minister of Finance, through you, sir, to make a statement on this issue.

Mr. Chairman: Yes, we have received the notice and we have passed it on.

Calling Attention Notice Regarding Reported Cancellation of Flights of Air India Owing to the Strike Notice Served by the Indian Flight Navigators Guild[312*]

D. Thengadi: Is it not a fact that on a number of occasions, earlier the Government of India came forward with modifications to the awards of industrial tribunals allegedly for maintaining industrial peace, etc.? If that is so, what has prevented the government from intervening after the strike notice was served and before the flights were cancelled?

N. Sanjiva Reddy:[313] I do not think it is necessary that we should modify this award. It is there, good, bad or indifferent. The moment you amend it – the Flight Engineers have given notice – they are going to strike. It is a tussle between the two, the Flight Engineers and the Navigators. The point is the Flight Engineers' emoluments have been increased by about Rs. 400 while the Navigators' emoluments have been increased by Rs. 150. But the Navigators have lost nothing. Therefore, we do not want to modify the Award.

Calling Attention to a Matter of Urgent Public Importance Regarding Reported Mass Agitation by Development Officers of Life Insurance Corporation[314]

D. Thengadi: Sir, may I with your permission call the attention of the Minister of Finance to the reported mass agitation by the Development Officers of the Life Insurance Corporation?

---

312. *Rajya Sabha Debate* dated 21st March, 1966.

313. N. Sanjeeva Reddy (1913-1996) was the sixth President of India and was president of the Indian National Congress for three terms between 1960-1963. A freedom fighter, Reddy was member, Madras Legislative Assembly, 1946 and member of the Constituent Assembly, a Minister, government of Madras, 1949-51; Deputy Chief Minister of Andhra Pradesh, 1953 and Chief Minister of Andhra Pradesh, 1956 and 1962-64. Reddy also served as member, Rajya Sabha, 1952-1953, 1964-1966, 1966-1967; Union Minister for Steel and Mines and Transport, Aviation, Shipping and Tourism, 1964-67; Reddy was Speaker, Lok Sabha, 1967-69 and March 26 to July 13, 1977; President of India, July, 1977 to July, 1982.

314. *Rajya Sabha Debate* dated 23rd March, 1966.

The Minister of State in the Ministry of Finance (*B.R. Bhagat*): Sir, the Development Officers of the Life Insurance Corporation have launched a programme of agitation on the following issues:

(i) Payment of Annual Bonus to Development Officers;

(ii) To protest against the continuance of Clause 10(b) of the Government of India Order No. 53(l)-INS(l)/57 dated 30th December, 1957; and

(iii) Reinstatement of G.S. Vaish.

The Payment of Bonus Act, 1965 specifically exempts the Life Insurance Corporation of India from the operation of that Act for payment compulsorily of annual bonus to employees. However, the Life Insurance Corporation has been paying even before the commencement of the Payment of Bonus Act non-profit-sharing bonus to Class III and Class IV employees.

The relevant clause 10(b) of the Government of India Order mentioned above is reproduced below:

"10(b): The services of any Development Officer may, with the prior approval of the Chairman of the corporation, be terminated without assigning any reason after giving the Development Officer three months' notice thereof in writing."

This order was issued in December 1957. There is a similar provision in the Life Insurance Corporation of India Staff Regulations, 1960 for other employees also. Even if this clause is revoked, the provisions of the Life Insurance Corporation Staff Regulations, 1960 would still operate. A similar provision exists in the regulations of a number of other public sector undertakings.

As for the third, that is, the termination of the services of G.S. Vaish,[315] it is entirely a matter for the Life Insurance Corporation of India to decide. It is an autonomous body set up under the Life Insurance Corporation Act, 1956, and is fully competent to deal with such matters.

D. Thengadi: In view of the fact that Mr. Vaish was ousted from service after reinstatement through a Court order, is it not advisable for the government to see that he is again taken on the service and, secondly, is the government aware of the fact that under Clause 10(b), since the services of a field worker can be terminated without rhyme or reason, as many as 14 field workers have been done away with from service even

315. G.S. Vaish, communist trade union leader, was all-India president of the National Federation of the Insurance Field Workers of India (NFIFWI) for three terms from 1957.

after they won their cases in the High Courts? In view of this legal position, and also of the fact that Clause 10(b) is ultra vires the Constitution, will the government advise the LIC, to scrap this clause? And, secondly, sir, is it not a fact that the Bonus Act has made employees "in receipt of salary or wages not exceeding Rs. 1,600 per month eligible to bonus", that the maximum salary of field workers is only up to Rs. 605 per month, that the Class III and Class IV employees of the corporation are availing of this privilege since earlier, and that the erstwhile insurers used to grant bonus to all their employees without discrimination?

Mr. Chairman: I am afraid you are putting too much into one question and it may be difficult for the minister to remember and answer all the questions put in one. I shall allow you another question if you like.

D. Thengadi: Just half a minute, sir. And since the government has already taken the decision to extend the provisions of the Bonus Act to different public sector undertakings, will the government advise the LIC to bring these field workers, these Development Officers also within the purview of the Payment of Bonus Act?

B.R. Bhagat: Sir, a number of questions have been bunched together. As for the question of the reinstatement of Vaish, the practice not only in this case but in many other cases has been that even if the Court judgement has been in favour of the appellant, we have been taking departmental action if we think that a particular employee's continuance in service or his activities have been prejudicial to the interests of the department. And this matter has been raised even before; it is a very old matter. All these considerations had been gone into earlier and the LIC, has taken the action in the interests of the corporation, and they are competent to do so.

As for bonus, as I said, they are paying non-profit-sharing bonus to Class III and Class IV employees. The Bonus Act makes exemption to them, but even then they are being paid. Now they did not consider payment of bonus to Class I and Class II employees necessary, but it is for them to decide.

D. Thengadi: Sir, actually, field workers draw only between Rs. 130 and Rs. 605 and, secondly, in principle, the government seems to have accepted in their communications that bonus should be paid to Class I employees of the corporation. In view of all these facts, will the government assure that it will consider the case of extension of bonus to the field workers and, secondly, that the decisions of the High Courts...

Mr. Chairman: You have secondly in this question also...

D. Thengadi: And, then, sir, if the decisions of the LIC... are not in keeping with the decisions of the High Courts, may I know whether appropriate changes will be suggested or advised by the government?

B.R. Bhagat: Decisions of High Courts, in which respect?

D. Thengadi: In the matter of those 14 workers, in the matter of their reinstatement in service.

B.R. Bhagat: That, sir, I will look into. I do not have the details with me, details of those 14 cases, but certainly I will see.

Calling Attention Notice Regarding Strike by Government Employees and the Consequent Law and Order Situation in Uttar Pradesh[316]

D. Thengadi: Madam Deputy Chairman, I have also given a Calling Attention Notice on the same subject. Much has been said about the subject and as far as possible, I shall see that there is no repetition of what has been said.

D. Thengadi: Madam Deputy Chairman, I had also the permission from the Chair to speak on the situation in Uttar Pradesh.

The Deputy Chairman: Yes, you have the permission from the Chair, but be very brief, Mr. Thengadi.

D. Thengadi: Madam, now the situation in Uttar Pradesh, as has been evident, is extremely serious, and the Centre cannot shirk its responsibility just by arguing that it is a state subject. The Centre has to prevail upon the state government to restore normalcy by conceding the demand of the people in general, and the government employees in particular. Now these demands include a judicial inquiry.

D. Thengadi: Madam, the demands of the people of U.P. in general, and of the government employees in particular are that they have demanded that a judicial inquiry be held into the *lathi*-charge within the precincts of the Secretariat on the 15th of this month, that the Chief Secretary, Mr. K.K. Das, be removed immediately, that government should assure that there will be no victimisation of the U.P. state government employees, that there should be the transfer of the District Magistrate and Superintendent of Police of Banda [city in Uttar Pradesh], and that compensation should be given immediately to the families of the people shot dead in the police firing. Unless the Centre brings appropriate pressure to bear upon the state government to concede these demands, it would be impossible to

316. *Rajya Sabha Debate* dated 25th July, 1966.

run the government there. The law and order situation has already broken down there, and, therefore, I urge upon the Central Government to bring that pressure and see that these popular demands are conceded.

D. Thengadi: I want a clarification.

The Deputy Chairman: What is the constitutional point?

D. Thengadi: I want to ask whether any objective criterion for the satisfaction of the President is prescribed to determine whether or not the governmental machinery under the Constitution has failed?

Jaisukhlal Hathi: It would be when the President is satisfied that the government cannot be run. There can be no criterion. It depends upon the situation arising in different parts at different times and at different places. It may be that when a ministry resigns and there is no other Ministry or a party which can take it over, the government can come to the conclusion that it can be done. It may be that there may be a disaster of a vast magnitude, where it may be found that the government cannot function. So, it all depends upon certain circumstances prevailing in different parts at different times. There cannot be one standard to determine that. But the main thing is that the President must be satisfied that the position has arisen.

Calling Attention to a Matter of Urgent Public Importance Regarding Recent Judgement of the Supreme Court of India Declaring Certain Provisions of the Payment of Bonus Act, 1965 ultra vires the Constitution[317]

D. Thengadi: Now that the government is aware that because of the judgement of the Supreme Court, the workers are worsted and particularly the cases that are pending would be adversely affected, will the government convert this difficulty into an opportunity or make the best out of the worst and come forward to remove the basic omission in the Act, that is, absence of any clear-cut definition of bonus so that while recasting the measure, we may come out with a definition incorporated in the Act itself that bonus is a deferred wage so long as there is a difference or gap between the living wage and the actual wage, so that all further lacunae would be made up?

Jagjivan Ram:[318] If the hon'ble member feels that by revising the definition of bonus, the problem that has arisen by certain provisions of

317. Rajya Sabha Debate dated 10th August, 1966

318. Jagjivan Ram (1908-1986) – one of the most well-known Dalit leaders of the Congress Party from Bihar, was a key leader in the founding of the Indian Depressed Classes League, member of the Constituent Assembly, served as minister in the Union Cabinet

the Act being held unconstitutional will be surmounted, I will welcome the suggestion.

Calling Attention to a Matter of Urgent Public Importance Regarding Five-week Old Strike in Rubber Plantations in Kerala[319*]

D. Thengadi: According to the statement of the hon'ble minister, it is more than two years that the last relief was provided, and the government would take quite some time to examine the report and come to some final decision. In the meanwhile, will the government give some ad hoc interim relief to the people so that till the examination is over, the workers can wait?

Shah Nawaz Khan: The Wage Board has made no such recommendations. I can assure the House that the government will not take a long time to examine this report.

Calling Attention to a Matter of Urgent Public Importance Regarding Reported Hunger-strike by Employees of the Exploration Wing of the Geological Survey of India and the Indian Bureau of Mines[320*]

D. Thengadi: While an immediate decision may not be possible on account of financial implications, the government should accept at least in principle some of the major demands because, for example, we have to find out whether the government is prepared to accept the principle that after a continuous service of 240 days, every worker should be absorbed against a regular vacancy and also that there should be no wage difference

for over four decades, held various portfolios, was Minister for Labour in interim Cabinet and then became India's first Labour Minister in free India's first Cabinet, was elected to the Lok Sabha from 1952-1984, was Deputy Prime Minister of India (1979). In his decades-long stint in public life Jagjivan Ram held several portfolios, such as Union Minister for (i) Labour, 1946-52, (ii) Communications, 1952-56, (iii) Transport and Railways, 1956-57, (iv) Railways, 1957-62, (v) Transport and Communications, 1962-63; resigned under Kamaraj Plan for revitalising the party; again Union Minister for (i) Labour, Employment and Rehabilitation, 1966, (ii) Food, Agriculture, Community Development and Co-operation, 1967-70 (holding additional charge of the Ministry of Labour, Employment and Rehabilitation, 1969-79), (iii) Defence, 1970-74, (iv) Agriculture and Irrigation 1974-77, (v) Defence, March 1977-July 1979; also Deputy Prime Minister, January 1979-July 1979. Jagjivan Ram left the Congress, post-Emergency, was made Defence Minister in the Morarji Desai Cabinet and joined the Charan Singh government as Deputy Prime Minister. Ram later formed his own political party, the Congress (J) and was re-elected to the 8th Lok Sabha in 1984.

319. *Rajya Sabha Debate* dated 16th August, 1966.

320. *Rajya Sabha Debate* dated 17th August, 1966.

between daily-wagers and regular employees because the regular employees are getting double the amount as compared to the daily-wagers and the present wages were fixed before eight or 10 years. Whether they should be linked up with the present cost of living index, this principle at least should be accepted by the government. Also whether the Mines Act is applied to them or not, at the same time, the government should give them the minimum wages. About medical facilities, safety provisions, etc. in principle, the government can accept even today that these things would be provided to the employees.

Also, so far as the house rent and the city compensatory allowances are concerned, is the government prepared to accept in principle that this should be done? Can the government also say that whether it would be practicable or not would be examined?

S.K. Dey: The government, in principle, also accept the socialist pattern of society, equality of opportunity to everybody, everybody to be free from starvation, free from disease, everything for everyone, etc. I am sure the hon'ble member would like to have something much more concrete than the mere acceptance of something in principle. In today's conditions or in the conditions that we can foresee within the immediate future, I do not feel that it would be possible for the government to concede it that all contingent workers will hereafter be absorbed on the regular payroll of the government. Now, the hon'ble member must appreciate that we have a very large number of workers, casual labourers, who have to be recruited every day, irrespective of any qualifications, irrespective of their age, because they have to work in obscure places. And depending on the demand for labour and the availability of the workers willing to work in such difficult places, we have to make recruitment in order to see that the work progresses. When the government takes people on the permanent pay-roll, naturally those will be against regular posts and regular posts will have regular qualifications prescribed for them. I wish that it were possible for the government and we were affluent enough as a country and as government to be able to ensure that everyone receives the minimum wage which can ensure certain basic amenities. But the mere acceptance of this theory in principle, I do not believe, will advance the cause very much further. Medical facilities, canteen facilities and other such amenities they must have. There are certain essential amenities which every person must have in every camp. We are trying to ensure that even before they make their demand. And I may mention that during my recent visit to Nagpur, I had the opportunity of meeting the president of the workers' union and I found him an extremely reasonable person and I was very deeply impressed by his attitude in regard to all the problems that he presented. And I discussed with him the difficulties of the government and I also discussed with him what we could immediately do and what we have to do for the future to solve the difficulties. I think he was quite reasonable about it and quite receptive. My only regret is that they had to resort to this hunger-strike in order to demonstrate their protest. It should not have been necessary. But I can assure the House that everything, that the government can do, will be done. But the hon'ble member will appreciate the financial difficulty through which the government is passing today. And I hope members will attach some importance to what can reasonably be expected of an organisation without sacrificing the overall programmes.

Calling Attention to a Matter of Urgent Public Importance Regarding Recent Arrest of an Employee of the All India Congress Committee, New Delhi[321]

D. Thengadi: Is it not a fact that Mr. Mohit Choudhury was arrested in April and in May, he made a full and frank confession and gave the details of the conspiracy? He also revealed Mr. Sunil Ranjan Das'[322] implication in this shameful affair in May last. If so, what is responsible for this inordinate delay in taking action against Mr. Sunil Ranjan Das if it be not pressure from the big guns of the ruling party and also from the government? Then is it a fact that smuggled gold and ornaments worth over Rs. 40,000 were recovered from Mr. Sunil Ranjan Das' AICC residence? And, thirdly, may I know whether the government has ascertained that utilising...

An hon'ble member: That is not a fact.

D. Thengadi: It is for the Home Minister to say... his position at the AICC office, Mr. Sunil Ranjan Das and his gang have not proceeded to form similar cliques in the State Congress Committee Offices or among their employees, particularly in the border States?

321. *Rajya Sabha Debate* dated 19th August, 1966

322. An office bearer of the All India Congress Committee.

Calling Attention to a Matter of Urgent Public Importance Regarding Hunger Strike and Demonstrations by the Employees of the Hindustan Lever Limited, New Delhi[323*]

D. Thengadi: Sir, may I bring it to the notice of the government that the agreement that has been referred to by the hon'ble Deputy Minister confines itself to the problems and disputes of field workers only and not to the disputes of other categories? That is number one.

Secondly, the Hindustan Lever has its centres all over India and it would be unfair to treat it as a state subject and entrust the whole thing to the state governments. So, the demand of the workers for a National Tribunal is fully justified and there is no ground for rejecting it since the centres of the Hindustan Lever are scattered throughout the length and breadth of the country.

Thirdly, while certain employees of certain categories, such as drivers and market research girls, are being declared as un-absorbable surplus, their work has actually doubled or trebled, but the whole thing is being got done through contract labour. Is the government not aware of the fact that the system of contract labour has been discouraged and not approved of officially? And if this work is being got done through contract labour, is it not the duty of the government to see that injustice is not done to these market research girls and drivers?

Another thing. The Company has assured the government and the government seems to have been satisfied that there will not be any retrenchment, but the fact is that till now, there were three establishments for three divisions and they are to be integrated. That means there would be surplus staff and though not in a direct or straightforward way, every Company has got its own way of retrenching the staff through harassment, through undue transfers, through fraudulent retrenchment, under the pretext of voluntary retirement and under pressure. So, through all these means and devices, there would be retrenchment and this rationalisation cannot be tearless. Is the government not aware of this fact and in view of all these considerations, will the government assure us that a National Tribunal will be appointed to do justice to the employees of the Hindustan Lever Limited?

323. *Rajya Sabha Debate* dated 19th August, 1966.

Calling Attention to a Matter of Urgent Public Importance Regarding the Threatened Strike by the All India Port and Dock Workers Federation at Major Ports[324]

D. Thengadi: Now that negotiations are going on, I would not like to say anything that will affect the smooth course of the negotiations adversely. The problem is industrial but it has two aspects: economic as well as psychological. While the economic implications of the various demands are being worked out, I should like to say that psychologically the hon'ble minister is convinced that the union and its President have adopted a constructive approach. It is quite obvious, even regarding the movement of foodgrains; earlier they have shown this attitude. In view of the fact that the hon'ble minister is convinced of their constructive approach, I would seek from the hon'ble minister a categorical assurance that he will see to it that the strike is not forced upon the workers because their constructive approach is already assured. It is only the part of the government which remains to be seen whether that same cooperative and helpful attitude is shown to the demands of the workers. So, I want this categorical assurance that a strike will not be forced upon the workers and that the government will see to it.

Prof. V.K.R.V. Rao:[325] I am very hesitant to give a categorical assurance excepting in psychological terms. I can certainly give a categorical assurance in psychological terms that we have no complaint about the patriotism or other characteristics of the particular federation. In fact, I know Mr. Kulkarni and whenever there has been difficulty, he has been coming to the rescue of the country. Therefore, the psychology is very good and we are very anxious to see that the strike is not forced upon the workers. I am sure that the House will agree after hearing the long list of demands that I read out and the various parties whom they concern, that it will not be possible for the government to say in a matter of 24 hours that all these things will be given. Actually, yesterday we had arrived at a great deal of understanding. We have sorted out certain points. All that I want from the House is the assurance of moral support for all of us.

---

324. *Rajya Sabha Debate* dated 9th August, 1967.

325. V.K.R.V. Rao (1908-1991) – economist, educationist, thinker, politician from Tamil Nadu; founder and Director of Delhi School of Economics, Rao founded a number of institutions for economic research, was Vice Chancellor of Delhi University, member Planning Commission and served as Union Minister Transport-Shipping (1967-69) and Union Education Minister 1969-1971, Rao was conferred the Padma Bhushan in 1974.

We want to see that this is settled because of the great difficulties in which the country finds itself otherwise.

Calling Attention to a Matter of Urgent Public Importance Regarding Modifications Made in the Unanimous Recommendations of the Wage Board for Electricity Undertakings[326]

D. Thengadi: The hon'ble minister is well aware that our judiciary has viewed with disfavour any discrimination made against a section of workers in the same industry on the ground that either it is a public sector undertaking or it is a government Department. In the Pimpri Antibiotics case,[327] the Supreme Court has said that if within the same area, there is a private sector undertaking and a public sector undertaking, there should be no discrimination in the wage policies between the two simply on the ground that this is a public sector undertaking and that is a private sector undertaking. In the bonus case of Maharashtra Electricity Board workers, the Bombay High Court in its recent judgement has not allowed the Maharashtra state government to escape its liability of granting bonus to the electricity workers. Now in view of these judgements of the High Court and the Supreme Court, is it not the view of our hon'ble minister that exclusion of the government-owned electricity undertakings from the operation of this award is in violation or is at variance with the spirit of the various judgements of our judiciary and, in view of this, will the government modify or set aside its own modifications regarding the government sector undertakings and allow the workers of those

326. *Rajya Sabha Debate* dated 9th August, 1968.

327. Hindustan Antibiotics Ltd. v. Workmen, AIR 1967 SC 948:
The Hindustan Antibiotics Limited is a government undertaking and is incorporated under the Indian Companies Act. Its registered office is at Pimpri, Poona district, state of Maharashtra, and its main business is the manufacture and distribution in bulk of antibiotics like penicillin, streptomycin, etc. A dispute arose between the workmen of the Company and the management thereof and the workmen presented a charter of fifteen demands to the Company. The government of Maharashtra referred the said dispute to the Industrial Tribunal, Bombay, for adjudication under Section 10(1) (d) of the Industrial Disputes Act, 1947 (14 of 1947). The hon'ble SC upheld the Tribunal Award on all counts of the award except one. It has held, "We do not think it is proper to give a discretion to the Company to raise the age of retirement or not to do so, for, the vesting of such uncontrolled discretion in the employer might lead to manipulation and victimisation. We would, therefore, following the trend of judicial opinion, hold that the retirement age of the employees of the Company should be raised to 60 years." Finally, the Civil Appeal No. 406 of 1964 preferred by the Company was dismissed with costs; and Civil Appeal No. 407 of 1964 preferred by the workmen was also dismissed with costs, except that the award is modified in regard to the age of retirement.

undertakings to enjoy the same benefits as being enjoyed by other workers in the electricity undertakings?

Jaisukhlal Hathi: So far as the public sector and the private sector are concerned, there is no discrimination, the wages are equal; they would be governed by the Wage Board. Here the question is of government servants. Now the hon'ble member talks of discrimination, but, government servants get pension. I think the workers under this Board or in other industries or factories do not get pension. Is it not then discrimination? If it is discrimination, it is in favour of government servants. They are governed by the same pay scales, gratuity, pension and everything else. The other workers do not get these things. So, although we say there should be no discrimination, discrimination is there. Government servants do get pension while other servants do not get it.

Calling Attention to a Matter of Urgent Public Importance Regarding Strike by Tea Garden Workers in West Bengal[328]

D. Thengadi: Is it not a fact that in some other states, such as Kerala and Mysore, agreements have been arrived at in the tea industry, that the present strike cannot be described as confined to any particular political party as the INTUC is also a party, and that the adamant attitude of the employers has made the strike inevitable? In that case, will the government declare categorically that if it is established that it was because of the adamant attitude of the employers that the nation is incurring such huge losses, some heavy penalty will be imposed on the employers, and that if the government is not adequately armed with powers to impose heavy penalties, such powers will be assumed?

Jaisukhlal Hathi: I am happy that the hon'ble member has referred to the strikes and settlements in other states, like Mysore, Kerala, etc. There also there was a strike and the Central Government did not intervene. The matter was ultimately settled by the state government itself with the union leaders and the employers. Here also the state government is doing it, and therefore, the next step will only depend upon the result of the discussions. If the employers see reason and settle with them, with the unions, that is all right.

328. *Rajya Sabha Debate* dated 19th August, 1968.

Calling Attention to a Matter of Urgent Public Importance Regarding Demonstration by state government Employees in New Delhi[329*]

D. Thengadi: Sir, I do not expect the Central Government to help the cause of the state governments' employees inasmuch as the Central Government cannot cater justice to its own employees. But, that apart, the whole question of wages is being treated in a slipshod manner. I should like the government to apply its mind to the question of evolving a National Wage Policy and the national policy questions cannot be treated in an isolated manner. So, will the government think of evolving a National Wage Policy in the next plan period? And, secondly, will the government appoint, at least for the Central Government employees, a Third Pay Commission so that in the light of the recommendations of the Third Pay Commission, which would be meant for the Central Government's employees, the pay scales, emoluments and other things of the state governments' employees also can be refixed? So, regarding the evolution of a National Wage Policy and the appointment of the Pay Commission, I should like the government to clarify its stand.

Vidya Charan Shukla:[330] Sir, as far as the National Wage Policy and other things are concerned, I have already made my position clear that whatever policy we might evolve, it will only be concerned with the Central Government's employees. It would not cover the state governments' employees. As far as the Pay Commission and other questions are concerned, I do not think there is any proposal to appoint any Pay Commission.

Calling Attention to a Matter of Urgent Public Importance Regarding Situation Arising out of the Indefinite Strike by Engineering Workers in Jamshedpur and Other Towns in Bihar[331]

D. Thengadi: Sir, I want clarification on three points. Firstly, it is customary for the government to examine all the recommendations and to

329. *Rajya Sabha Debate* dated 20th August, 1968.

330. Vidya Charan Shukla (1927-2013) – Congress leader from Madhya Pradesh/ Chhattisgarh. Shukla's father Pandit Ravi Shankar Shukla was a prominent freedom fighter, Congress leader and first Chief Minister of Madhya Pradesh; his brother Shyama Charan Shukla was Chief Minister of Madhya Pradesh for three terms, Shukla won nine elections to the Lok Sabha and held various portfolios in the Union Cabinet from Planning, to Defence Production to External Affairs, etc. A close confidante of Indira Gandhi, Shukla is best remembered for his excesses as Union Information and Broadcasting Minister during Emergency in censuring the media.

331. *Rajya Sabha Debate* dated 25th November, 1969.

approve some of them or all of them. May I know whether the government has shirked its responsibility of approving the recommendations in this particular case so that they are leaving everything in the lurch?

Secondly, in view of this experience in Bihar, may I know whether the government has come to realise that the present recognition in law is not the real recognition when the recognised union does not command enough influence to control, guide and direct the workers and, therefore, does the government realise that the rules for recognition must be changed, so that instead of relying upon verification of membership, secret ballot of either all the workers or of unionised workers is introduced for this purpose?

Thirdly, in view of the expenditure incurred and the time lost in this process of Wage Boards, will the government think of converting the Wage Boards in future by changing their character and composition into tripartite forums for collective bargaining?

Bhagwat Jha Azad:[332] Sir, it is a fact that when Wage Board recommendations used to come before the government in the past, we used to call the different parties, know their views and we have taken decisions as in the case of cotton textiles. In this case, as I had impressed upon the House, this Wage Board had no unanimous or even near-unanimous recommendations. There were four sets of recommendations, one by the Chairman and the independent members, second by the private employers, third by the public sector employers and fourth by the workers and that also with some dissent note. Therefore, when we called the Tripartite Committee[333] of the trade unions, the state governments and the employers, they themselves agreed that it should be left to region-wise settlement. Therefore, we have not shirked our responsibility; we have acted according to the decision of the Tripartite Committee where there were the workers' representatives also.

Secondly, about recognition, it is known to hon'ble members that recognition is by verification. We had referred this matter to the National Labour Commission; they have also not suggested whether it should be by verification or by secret ballot. They have left it to the Industrial Relations Commissions to decide what should be done. When I called a meeting

332. Bhagwat Jha Azad (1922-2011) – Congress leader from Bihar and Chief Minister of the state, 1988-89. Azad was member of the 1st Lok Sabha and was re-elected for a number of terms upto the 7th Lok Sabha and served as Union Minister, holding various portfolios between 1960s-1980s, ranging from Education, Labour-Employment, Civil Aviation, Food & Civil Supplies.

333. Committee of workers, employers and independent field experts on labour issues.

of the state governments at the Indian Labour Conference, excepting Delhi and West Bengal the consensus was for verification. Therefore, this process continues. I do not agree with the hon'ble member that the recognised union in Jamshedpur has not got the following because we go by verification.

About Wage Boards, I have already said it should be looked into as to whether in future, it should be a decision by the collective bargaining strength of the workers and employers or whether the government should enter in each stage and set up Wage Boards, which take time. It is an important question which we are considering.

Calling Attention Motion Regarding Strike by the Dock Workers of the Madras Port[334]

D. Thengadi: Sir, the hon'ble minister has said that the matter can be settled within half-an-hour.

My question is that since this is not the first instance of misinterpretation by the authorities and since this is likely to recur, if it is not checked in time, will the government think it proper to take to task and punish the authorities who are found to be misinterpreting willfully? Will the government take steps so that such things do not recur in future?

Calling Attention Motion Regarding Reported Strike in the Bharat Heavy Electricals Limited, Haridwar[335*]

D. Thengadi: With a view to creating a congenial atmosphere, sir, there should be no victimisation.

Sir, obviously the hon'ble minister has been misinformed by the local management on certain points. I would not go into all the details. But the Bharatiya Mazdoor Sangh Union is not unregistered as suggested by him. Also the procedure of progressive reduction in the project allowance as followed in Tiruchi was not followed at Haridwar. You may enquire about it. And it is certainly a violation of Section 4(1) of the Industrial Disputes Act. Now in view of the fact that the government is in a mood to settle the dispute, may I ask whether the government will assure that there will be no victimisation as a result of the strike action? Secondly, the talks should be conducted at Haridwar itself because in that case, the local labour leaders will be in a position to be in communion with their co-workers. Thirdly, because it is not possible for the local management and the local labour leaders to arrive at

334. *Rajya Sabha Debate* dated 8th May, 1970.

335. **Rajya Sabha Debate* dated 15th May, 1970.

any agreement because of the strained relations, will any special officer be sent for this purpose so that he can bring about such a settlement?

In order to create a congenial atmosphere for bringing about a settlement, I would urge the government not to stand on prestige. It is common decency that the government should assure that there shall be no victimisation. Then only the atmosphere will be congenial.

Calling Attention Motion Regarding Reported Lay-off of 1,50,000 Workers in Asansol and Bharia Belts[336]

Is the government aware – the government must be aware – of the fact that the conspiracy referred to by Mr. Kalyan Roy[337] that ICI, is not an isolated affair and that it is a link in the chain of the general policy of coal employers themselves following the practice for long of manoeuvring strikes, even by offering money to labour leaders just to bring about strikes or manoeuvre situations, leading to layoffs or manoeuvre situations leading to strikes whenever they feel that there is over-production, or the production – whatever the production is there – cannot be disposed of. So, it is being felt since long that a standing machinery should be set up to investigate into every case of lay-off and strike in the coal industry, and whenever it has been established or it is found that the coal employers have themselves been responsible for strike or layoff, they should be brought to book and a heavy penalty should be imposed on them. Will government consider this proposal to setting up such a standing machinery to bring to book such employers who bring about national losses?

What I have said, I have said from personal experience.

Calling Attention Motion Regarding Reported Strike in Durgapur Steel Plant and other Public Sector Industries at Durgapur[338*]

May I know whether, notwithstanding the observations by Mr. Chatterjee,[339] the union concerned is not affiliated to CITU, which was sponsored by the CPM under its own auspices?

---

336. *Rajya Sabha Debate* dated 13th August, 1970.

337. Kalyan Shankar Roy (1929-1985) – CPI leader from West Bengal, trade unionist, senior leader of the AITUC, Roy's father, Kiran Shankar Roy, was a well-known Congress leader from Bengal. Roy was Member of the Rajya Sabha from 1969-1975, 1975-1981 and 1982-1985.

338. *Rajya Sabha Debate* dated 14th August, 1970.

339. Arun Prakash Chatterjee (1921-2000) – CPI-(M) leader from West Bengal. Chatterjee was a well-known lawyer; member, Rajya Sabha, from 1966-1972.

Secondly, while there were certain elements out for disturbance, the management initiated an experiment of Joint Consultative Machinery informally, that is, consultation with various unions for maintaining industrial peace, and this has been of great help. I want to know whether a similar experiment on an informal basis would be conducted in other steel plants, including Durgapur. Thirdly, I want to know whether in view of the recent disturbances, the government would advise the appropriate authorities to revise the decision on recognition and to have a secret ballot of workers for the purpose of according recognition so that industrial peace could be effectively maintained.

Calling Attention Motion Regarding Strike by the Employees of the Ashoka Hotel, New Delhi[340]

Sir, I should like to know what were the reasons recorded by the conciliation machinery for the failure of talks, number one? Secondly, I want to know precisely the time sequence? It was on the night of the 18th that the failure report was given by the conciliation machinery, and early morning on the 19th, the strike commenced and only after the strike commenced, there was reference to adjudication. I want some precise reply – number two. Thirdly, I want to know what was the number of guests prior to the strike and subsequent to the strike, and then whether, in view of the seriousness of the situation, the government would come forward even at this late stage, whether the minister himself would take the initiative, invite the leaders of the unions and personally try to bring about some sort of solution, assuring them that there would be no victimisation so that normalcy could be established in industrial relations?

About the time sequence, I want precisely to know whether it is not a fact that the strike commenced after the failure report and before reference to adjudication?

The other question has not been answered as to the number of guests prior to the strike and the number subsequent to the strike. Secondly, I want to know whether it is not a fact that the strike commenced after the failure report was submitted but before there was reference to adjudication.

---

340. *Rajya Sabha Debate* dated 21st August, 1970.

Calling Attention Regarding Reported Serious Situation Arising out of Jute Strike in West Bengal[341*]

Sir, I will not cover the ground which has already been covered. So, I would like to ask some specific questions. No.1, what were the suggestions made by Labour Unions on 14th of February, and in what respect they differed from the proposals of Dr Gopal Das Nag[342] made on 18th February? Secondly, in what way the proposals of Dr Nag seek to compensate for the cheating of workers on account of the fraudulent cost of living index number? That cheating has been there is accepted by all. Has it taken note of the fact that the prices of essential commodities in West Bengal are different from the prices taken for granted by Simla Bureau? Has this fact been taken note of? Thirdly, sir, what is the decision of our friend Raghunatha Reddy on the proposals by Dr Gopal Das Nag; or has the whole issue been evaded? That we should like to know.

In the proposals of Dr Gopal Das Nag on 18th February, Dr Nag made certain proposals to the trade union. So, on the proposals or recommendations, what is the decision taken by Mr. Raghunatha Reddy; or whether the whole thing has been evaded?

One question arises. On 18th February, the West Bengal government made certain proposals and the employers accepted them. The strike is continuing. The report that the strike is withdrawn is false. In view of the fact that the strike is continuing, I should like to know whether further negotiations are going to be held and what steps are going to be taken for the settlement of the issue? According to the government, is it their case that the whole thing has now ended? One more point. Sir. From the statement of Mr. Chattopadhyaya, it appears that the jute industry is going down and the poor jute employers are running the industry only to oblige the workers and the people. So, this is not...

Because the industry is in bad shape and it is going from bad to worse, under such conditions, instead of forcing the jute employers to perform such great sacrifices for the people, will the government take over the jute industry and hand over all the mills to the workers themselves, so that they can manage their own affairs?

341. *Rajya Sabha Debate* dated 20th February, 1975. Jute mill workers went on a 48 day strike in West Bengal between 6th January–18th February, 1975.

342. Dr Gopal Das Nag was Labour Minister in the Siddhartha Shankar Ray Cabinet in West Bengal.

I would like to know the difference between the suggestions of labour unions and the proposals of Dr Nag. In what respects do they differ?

I would like to ask whether the proposals of Dr Nag did not concede the essence of the demands or suggestions made by the labour unions on 14th February.

Motion Regarding Statement in Connection with Demonstration near Parliament House on 7th November, 1966[343]

D. Thengadi: I object to this. If he wants to quote Mr. Golwalkar,[344] he should give his entire statement, but not tear it out of context.

Bhupesh Gupta: You are perfectly right. I can read out the whole speech delivered on August 20th, but that will not be very palatable to you. I will read out, all my speech will be taken up by Mr. Golwalkar. How can I do that...

Mr. Chairman: I think it is not necessary to read all that. If there is something else, then some other members might point that out.

D. Thengadi: I was myself present at the meeting and I can say that it is torn off the context and it is misleading.

Bhupesh Gupta: I will never do such a thing. I have marked all those portions, but it will take time. It says here:

"They who can have the cow killed, can also have the country sold."

This is the heading. I am not misleading you. Then Guruji commented: "Hasn't the government been campaigning that people should change their food habits? Why can't they who take beef be asked to change their food habits and switch on to some other diet?"

Guruji wryly recalled that a Congress minister had lately advised people even to eat rats. Why not give this counsel to the beef-eaters?

The approach is communal. Now I do not read this thing.

---

343. *Rajya Sabha Debate* dated 17th November, 1966; the cow-protection agitation referred to earlier.

344. M.S. Golwalkar, 'Sri Guruji' (1906-1973) was the second Sarsanghchalak of Rashtriya Swayamsevak Sangh between 1940-1973. A direct disciple of Swami Akhandananda, who was among the first batch of adherents who had gathered around Sri Ramakrishna, Sri Guruji's long tenure as Sarsanghchalak, laid a deep, wide, extensive and comprehensive foundation of the Sangh's work in India and across the world. His tenure saw some of the most tumultuous period in post-Independent India's history, starting with Partition, to the formation of the Bharatiya Jana Sangh, to the 1962 India-China war, to the 1965 India-Pakistan war, to the cow-protection agitation, to the formation of new states and more. One of the most authentic voices of Indian nationalism and cultural self-expression, Sri Guruji was widely revered as a leader, socio-spiritual thinker and organiser.

D. Thengadi: We want him to quote the whole speech. He is quoting it torn out of the context.

Mr. Chairman: He is quoting something which suits his argument. If there is something else in the speech which does not suit his argument, you can in your turn point it out.

Bhupesh Gupta: They do not quote the whole thing. On 11th September, there was a meeting. It is headlined here. They will not object to it. Now, sir, it is here, our friends are objecting to it; on September 15th, cow protection in Delhi. It was a Hindu feeling. I can understand the position. If we cannot defend the cow, we cannot defend the country. Therefore, defence of the cow is everything; defence of the cow is defence of religion, defence of the cow is defence of the country; defence of the cow is everything that is noble and good in this world.

Lokanath Misra: May I interrupt? Defence of the cow is also defence of the election symbol.

Bhupesh Gupta: I will come to that. Here he said, this is the speech: 'Is the Government going to heed this demand only after bloodshed?' It is in bold print. I think followers of Guruji...

D. Thengadi: I am very sorry to interrupt. Here again to take out one single sentence out of context and quote it is mischievous.

Mr. Chairman: As I said, he is quoting something that suits his argument and he is quoting it from a paper.

Motion Regarding Central Government Employees' Strike on 19th September, 1968[345]

D. Thengadi: While analysing the situation, the hon'ble Home Minister distinguished between the employees proper and outside leaders. I will reserve to myself my views on that topic. But will he maintain the same distinction while determining the punishment to be given? And in view of the fact that they are the employees of government and government has to conduct smooth functioning of administration, will he think of resorting the status quo ante, that is, the position before 19th September...

Y.B. Chavan: No.

D. Thengadi: ...in view of the fact that he himself has distinguished outside leaders from the employees.

345. *Rajya Sabha Debate* dated 20th November, 1968.

Motion Regarding the Situation Arising out of the Token Strike by Central Government Employees on 19th September, 1968[346]

D. Thengadi: I should be very happy if Mr. Chavan corroborates the facts now narrated by Mr. Krishan Kant.[347] He should have at least corroborated from Mr. Chavan.

Madam, I need not repeat all the facts that are already publicly known. One thing is obvious that the greatest responsibility for the token strike of September 19th rests with the Government of India. Had the government any intention of avoiding the strike possibility, it was within their reach, but it seems the government was determined to provoke the workers. That is why they did not abide by whatever has been laid down in the scheme of Joint Consultative Machinery. The scheme in unmistakable terms provides for arbitration in case of disagreement on certain questions, including salaries and allowances. There was no reason why the government should not have agreed to arbitrate but this particular fact and again the fact that on behalf of the government, there have been attempts to terrorise and provoke simultaneously the government employees even in subsequent periods goes to prove that more than the employees, the government has been responsible for the strike on 19th September. Now the propaganda by the government regarding the demands has outdone even Dr Goebbels. The government had agreed in principle in the 15th ILC [Indian Labour Conference] about the need-based minimum wage. We do not understand why there should be no co-ordination between the Labour Ministry and the Finance Ministry? It has been said that the government employees constitute a fixed income group – that is correct – that crores of people in the rural areas are starving – that is also true – that this is not true – the government employees are aspiring to thrive at the cost of the starving millions, as if the government employees are out to snatch the morsel of foodgrains from the mouths of the starving millions in the rural areas. That is not so. If our agricultural labourers and the petty *kisans* are on starvation level, the government employees are not to be blamed for their miserable plight. It is the wrong economic policies and planning of the government that are responsible for this. Again, while mentioning one extreme of starvation, the government has conveniently ignored or forgotten that there is the other extreme also. Thousands of crores of black money through tax evasion – of anything between Rs. 200 to Rs. 300

346. *Rajya Sabha Debate* dated 19th November, 1968.
347. Ibid.

crores every year – concentration of wealth in the private sector – at least the lion's share of wealth – in 75 industrial houses – all these facts are conveniently ignored by the government and only the starving millions are referred to. This is unfair.

We want to suggest – we have already said – that the national income policy, the national price policy and the national production policy of the country during the Fourth Five-Year Plan period should be determined at least now. Now we are on the threshold of the Fourth Five-Year Plan and this is the appropriate time when all these three national policies regarding price, production and income should be determined, and for this purpose, we had suggested that the government should convene a round table conference of all the economic interests – I am not mentioning political parties – a round table conference of all the economic interests so that, through the conference, on the basis of some sort of consensus, all the three national policies can be evolved. I am very confident, madam, that if such a round table conference is convened, the representatives of the Central Government employees, or for that matter, of all the workers in general, would be able to prove that a need-based minimum wage is possible even under the present circumstances. But that apart, what was highlighted in the government propaganda was the fact that the workers demanded a need-based minimum wage. But they conveniently forgot to highlight the fact that what they actually wanted was arbitration on the point. Therefore, some sort of a misunderstanding about the demand of the workers was created.

Recently, we were amused to read in the newspapers that our Finance Minister, Morarji Desai, had declared that the Centre was prepared to give Rs. 100 crores to the states for the implementation of the policy of prohibition. If a hundred crores could be given for prohibition, why the same amount could not be diverted for the benefit of government employees is something un-understandable.

Now the point has been raised by our friend that the National Labour Commission is going into this question. As a matter of fact, it is controversial whether this point was already specifically referred to the National Labour Commission; I will not go into the controversy but, apart from that, it is but logical to say that the National Labour Commission would have been greatly helped if this important problem would have been referred to arbitration so that the proceedings of arbitration and the arbitration award would have greatly helped the National Labour

Commission in arriving at right conclusions on this most important point.

Secondly, madam, it was said – rather an impression was created – that these employees were out for an all-out revolution – as if they wanted to go on an indefinite strike and as if the government had come down heavily upon these alleged revolutionaries and curbed the revolution. Now this is all false. It is a well-known principle that a strike is an outlet for discontent so that a revolution should become superfluous. Those who want revolution do not resort to strikes, and those who resort to the legitimate and constitutional weapon of strikes are not out for a revolution. Still, there was a calculated effort on the part of the government to create this misunderstanding, and also to create the impression that the Home Ministry had behaved in a very strong manner and proved themselves strong administrators. Madam, in this connection, I cannot but be reminded of a story, which every one of us has read, about one Don Quixote. He attacked a windmill thinking that it was a demon, and when the windmill was stopped by his attack, he paraded himself as a brave man and said that he had killed a demon. Actually, there was no demon but only a windmill, and there was no killing. In the same way, here there was no revolution and there were no revolutionaries, yet an impression was created that a revolution had been suppressed. To say so is very unfair to the government employees.

Now so far as the present plight of the employees is concerned, I am sorry to say that the various departments of the Government of India were not uniformly implementing the decision about termination of the services of temporary employees on the 18th of October. First of all, we find, madam, that there is no uniformity even in the policy of victimisation; there are no uniform criteria for victimisation of the employees in different states. For example, out of about 7,600 total arrests, nearly 6,000 were confined to five states; they are Delhi, Punjab, Haryana, Rajasthan and Madhya Pradesh, though in other states also, the degree of the success of the strike was no less than in those States. This indicates that more than any policy, the petty prejudices of local officials had a free hand in victimising the employees and there was no uniform policy. Now we find, for example, how uniformity is lacking even in victimisation in the Audit and Accounts Departments where some 416 are suspended though only 80 out of them were actually arrested and their services since terminated, but the others have been suspended even when they had not been arrested.

Now regarding the suspended employees, different policies are followed in different offices. For example, at Ranchi, the suspended employees are required to mark their attendance in office every day, whereas in the office of the AGCR [Accountant General of Central Revenue] in Delhi, the suspended employees are not even allowed to enter the office. Thus, there is no uniformity of policy even in the matter of victimisation.

In the Railways, 3,616 are suspended and 935 are dismissed. But suspension apart, many of the Railway employees were arrested on the 18th of September, that is, on the previous day, while they were alighting from buses or returning from office and proceeding homeward. In the first place, the arrests, such mass arrests were unjustified and, secondly, curiously enough, without a chargesheet being given, those who were arrested on the 18th of September have been accused of staying away from work on the 19th of September. This pattern of accusation has been followed in similar cases in the case of employees of other ministries also. In the Railways, the policy of withdrawing termination notices against temporary employees has not been implemented in a large number of cases, and wherever it is implemented, it is done on the basis of discrimination – the whims and fancies of local bureaucrats. There have been cases of deliberate, calculated moves and manoeuvres by local bureaucrats to victimise employees out of vindictiveness. To cite an example, I will not repeat, to cite a single example – a telegraphist – we do not know whether at the instance of official instigation or not – reported to the police on 23rd September that he was assaulted by nine persons on the 20th of September. He did not report it to the officer in-charge nor was it reported to the police for three days. Now after three days, he is reporting, and merely on that report, these nine persons were arrested and then suspended from service. Out of the nine, four were temporary and they were discharged from service. And one of them, Mr. S.R. Gupta, a telegraphist, he died in hospital out of shock. The point to be noted is that the complaint was made three days after the alleged assault though it was alleged to have happened within the office premises. The officer in-charge was not informed, nor was there any investigation by the officer in-charge. Thus, the arrests and suspensions were made without any investigation. Such examples of vindictiveness can be multiplied, but I have cited a single example.

One of the more important problems, madam, is about the termination of temporary employees; most of the temporary employees were not at all arrested and yet discharged without giving them any opportunity to explain their cases. At the most, they could have been suspended, show-cause notices served on them, and further action based upon the replies received from them. In the absence of show-cause notices the termination is obviously arbitrary. So, all temporary employees, whose services are, thus, terminated, should be immediately reinstated. This is the demand of justice.

Now, even in the case of such temporary employees, who happened to be arrested, the injustice done is equally obvious. Their cases are pending before law courts. Still they are terminated. Now, suppose some of them are acquitted subsequently, what will be the position of those terminated employees? Clearly, their termination should be withdrawn. At the most, suspension orders should be served.

The Ministry of Works and Housing, madam, has withdrawn many termination orders and served orders of suspension on such employees. I think the same procedure should have been followed by other ministries also. The postal services in Delhi are not yet normal. The government is claiming that they are normal but the claim is false to the knowledge of the government. New recruits are pressed into service, but, naturally, they cannot dispose of the work that efficiently.

In response to the government's decision on October 18th to cancel the termination notices served on temporary employees, the National Federation of Posts and Telegraphs Employees withdrew its work-to-rule programme – this was a gesture of goodwill – and extended its co-operation to the government in running the services efficiently. But, the Communications Ministry has not implemented the decision of reinstating the terminated temporary employees. Thus, the offer of co-operation has been cold-shouldered. Along with the temporary employees, the plight of extra-departmental staff is also miserable. At least, a thousand extra-departmental staff have been victimised. Their wages are only from Rs. 40 to Rs. 60. Madam, I would urge that the extra-departmental staff should be treated as a special case and all of them reinstated immediately.

Madam, there have been cases of unwarranted firing and *lathi*-charges. At Pathankot, without any provocation on the part of the workers or the citizens, there was firing in the course of which six persons died and 33 were injured, mostly with bullets, and the wonderful part of it was that as in Sarai Rohilla in Delhi, there in Pathankot also the police entered even into the family quarters. Even women were assaulted–all this without any provocation–and an officer junior to the one who ordered the firing was appointed as Enquiry Officer. Similar cases have occurred in Bikaner, Guwahati, etc. There were *lathi*-charges in Ferozepore, Jodhpur, Sarai Rohilla and there was also the case of a person who was run over and killed at Jagadhri [Haryana]. Now, in all these cases, we demand that there should be a judicial enquiry and that adequate compensation should be paid to the persons aggrieved and the concerned officers punished. In the particular case of Pathankot, we demanded that the report of the Executive Magistrate who conducted the enquiry, should be laid on the Table of the House.

Madam, we wish that there should be perfect co-ordination between the government and its employees and it is the responsibility of the government, because government is stronger, to take the initiative in creating an atmosphere of congeniality, an atmosphere of cordiality. Out of vindictiveness, only vindictiveness would grow. Now some time also has elapsed and we are in a more calm atmosphere. Therefore, I urge upon the government to withdraw, all gestures of vindictiveness and withdraw all victimisation. I will not enumerate and say that the terminated employees should be reinstated, that suspension orders should be withdrawn and so on. It is not necessary to say all that; the entire victimisation should be withdrawn and a proper atmosphere for the functioning of the Joint Consultation Machinery should be created. That is the only way to ensure the smooth functioning of the government administrative apparatus in the country. I hope the Home Ministry will prefer to be wiser rather than vindictive.

In Response to the Statement Regarding Recommendations of the Bonus Commission[348]

D. Thengadi: May I know whether the acceptance of all direct taxes and tax concessions as prior charge was not demanded even by employers, that is, by Mr. Dandekar? That is one thing. Secondly, where there is no agreement, will the formula prevail?

D. Sanjivayya: What is the last portion?

D. Thengadi: Where there is no agreement, will the LAT formula prevail?

D. Sanjivayya: Yes, if there is no agreement, the bonus will be calculated both on the basis of the LAT formula and the present formula; whichever is higher, the worker will get it.

348. *Rajya Sabha Debate* dated 18th September, 1964.

Then with regard to the direct taxes, in the Minute of Dissent by Mr. Dandekar, he has certainly made a mention of that.

In Response to the Statement Regarding Applicability of the Payment of Bonus Act, 1965 to Public Sector Undertakings[349]

D. Thengadi: Section 32 referred to by the hon'ble minister probably mentions the Reserve Bank of India. I want to know categorically whether the employees of the Reserve Bank of India would be entitled to bonus and, secondly, what was the reason for excluding Railways and Defence establishments also from the benefit of bonus?

Clarifications in Relation to Statement Made on Calling Attention Notice Regarding Threatened Strike by LIC Employees[350*]

D. Thengadi: I want to know whether the Study Group of the Administrative Reforms Commission has stated that in the LIC automation is not necessary, whether on the point of automation in the LIC – I am addressing Mr. Hathi, I want the attention of Mr. Hathi – no unanimous decision could be taken in the tripartite meeting and in view of both these facts, the question of automation and consequences flowing from automation were not referred to the Tribunal.

Jaisukhlal Hathi: So far as the report of the Administrative Reforms Commission is concerned, I am not aware of it. So far as the question of automation in the LIC is concerned, in fact, this matter had been gone into in detail in 1966. The Committee on Petitions of the Lok Sabha also examined this and they said that in view of the assurances given by the Corporation and the Ministries, this matter need not be pursued further. And, moreover, in the tripartite conference, we wanted that the management should assure that there would be no retrenchment and that categorical assurance had been given.

Reference to Strike by Employees of government Press in Delhi[351*]

D. Thengadi: Sir, yesterday our Rajya Sabha and Lok Sabha could not get printed their papers because on the 28th and 29th of August, there was a successful token strike by the employees of the government Press in Delhi. In view of the united will of the employees as expressed through

349. *Rajya Sabha Debate* dated 9th December, 1965.

350. **Rajya Sabha Debate* dated 5th December, 1968.

351. **Rajya Sabha Debate* dated 30th September, 1968.

their token strike, I request the government to take serious cognisance of their demands and to cater justice to them expeditiously.

Reference to the Negotiations on Jute Workers' Strike[352*]

D. Thengadi: Sir, the stage has now reached that if the Government of India strongly intervenes, the employers have to succumb; they have to yield. It is only reluctance on the part of the Government of India that they are prolonging this particular dialogue. So, we urge upon the government that they must take a strong attitude and put appropriate pressure upon the employers. The stage has reached now.

□

352.**Rajya Sabha Debate* dated 9th December, 1970.

7
External Affairs

On India's external affairs, Thengadi was concerned about India's dependence on information from other than its own sources. He questioned the efficiency of the External Affairs Ministry and felt that India's intelligence was not functioning properly. He wanted to know as to why should India not aspire to become a first-rank military power. Thengadi wanted the country to develop into a nuclear power. He was not happy with other countries dictating terms to India on this account.

Short Duration Discussion under Rule 176 Regarding Supply of the U.S.-Made Arms to Pakistan[353]

D. Thengadi: Every time we conduct discussions regarding any development concerning the External Affairs Ministry, our discussions unfortunately are based upon information furnished by sources other than our own. The point is: what exactly our diplomatic representatives abroad are doing? Are they not alert about different developments which directly concern the interests of India and are they not apprising the Government of India about those developments? Every time we have to rely upon sources other than our own. Secondly, madam, we are glibly swallowing formal assurances from various governments and not trying to ascertain the veracity of these assurances. Now we have been hearing that we have been surprised. Very often we are surprised. To be surprised so often is a sad commentary on the efficiency of the External Affairs Ministry. Now every incident takes us by surprise. That means that our intelligence is not functioning properly and that the approach of the External Affairs Ministry is not realistic. Now, in this particular context, I feel that the ministry is not very clear in its mind about certain facts. For example, is the United States in a position to restrain West Germany,

353. *Rajya Sabha Debate* dated 28th July, 1967.

if West Germany does not abide by the advice of the United States, from supplying arms to Pakistan, directly or indirectly, because West Germany is being pressed to accept arms or purchase arms for balance of payment reasons? Is there any power with the United States to restrain effectively West Germany from supplying arms to Pakistan? I should like to know the position from the hon'ble minister. Secondly, the position of Iran is also not very clear. It has been said that Iran would assist Pakistan only if India attacks Pakistan. But it is well-known that which country is the aggressor cannot be decided and so it is very easy for Iran to assist Pakistan even if Pakistan is the aggressor. So, on these two points, I would like our hon'ble minister [M.C. Chagla was then Union External Affairs Minister] to give us some clarification.

I wonder whether we should always keep ourselves in a position of only recording protests. Why should we not aspire to become a first-rank military power? Germany which was razed to the ground during the Second World War has now become a military power to some extent. We know that we have got man-power; we have got our own resources. What is lacking is the determination on the part of the government to become a military power.

What prevents us from deciding that we should develop ourselves into a nuclear power also? India is a peace-loving country and a peace loving country like India become a nuclear power, would be guaranteeing world peace. Why should the world be deprived of such a guarantee? Then there is another point. Have we conveyed to all the concerned nations that supply of arms to Pakistan would be considered by us as an unfriendly act? Why have we not conveyed this to the concerned nations? Madam, our External Affairs Ministry's policies have so far been very weak-kneed. I should like to urge that instead of depending upon the mercy of any nation, like the United States or China or Russia, we should try to develop ourselves into a military power. Now America has adopted a peculiar attitude. They are thinking as if they are entrusted by God with the work of policing, what they describe as, this subcontinent, as if they are entrusted with the work of maintaining an arms ratio between India and Pakistan. Who are they to dictate terms to us? Who are they to police this so-called subcontinent? Therefore, it is all because of our weakness, because of the inefficiency of our External Affairs Ministry, of our diplomatic representatives abroad and therefore, I urge that there should be a reorientation of our policy and there should be a determination to become a first-rate military power, so that the world need not look to Moscow and Washington only so far as military affairs are concerned but New Delhi should be at par with Washington and Moscow.

Calling Attention to Matter of Urgent Public Importance Regarding–(i) Position of Indian Nationals in Congo; and (ii) Alleged Anti-Indian Demonstration held at Nairobi on 26th November, 1964[354]

I beg to call the attention of the Minister of External Affairs to (i) the position of Indian nationals in Congo and (ii) the alleged anti-Indian demonstration held at Nairobi on 26th November, 1964.

The Deputy Minister in the Ministry of External Affairs (*Dinesh Singh*):[355] Hon'ble members are aware of the landing of Belgian paratroopers in Stanleyville on 24th November [1964].[356] This move has evoked a sharp reaction from many African capitals. In Nairobi, the Kenya African National Union Party organised a protest demonstration on 26th November outside the Embassies of Belgium and the USA. Slogans protesting against Western interference in Congo were raised and many demonstrators carried placards against Belgium, the USA, Mr. Tshombe[357] and others. One of the placards exhorted the Indian High Commissioner in Nairobi to quit Kenya.

1. The demonstration was primarily a reaction to outside interference in the Congo. No undue significance need be attached to the single placard against the Indian envoy. The demonstrators, however, in the course of their march through the streets damaged four cars bearing CD plates, including those of the Swedish Ambassador, the British Information Secretary and the personal car of our High

354. *Rajya Sabha Debate* dated 1st December, 1964.

355. Dinesh Singh (1925-1995) was once Indira Gandhi's chief troubleshooter and a principal member of her 'Kitchen Cabinet', till he felt out with her and was sidelined. Singh was elected to the Lok Sabha for multiple terms from Pratapgarh in Uttar Pradesh. Her served as Union Deputy Minister/Minister of State/ Minister of External Affairs, Commerce and Industrial Development and Internal Trade, 1962 and 95. Singh's last assignment was as External Affairs Minister in the Narasimha Rao Cabinet.

356. Operation Dragon Rouge by the Belgian military in 1964, to rescue hostages who had been held captive in Stanleyville, Congo.

357. M.K. Tshombe (1919-1969) – secessionist Congolese leader, Tshombe controlled the mineral-rich province of Katanga and seceded from newly-independent Congo with support of Belgium. A controversial figure, Tshombe also briefly served as President of Congo.

Commissioner in Kenya. The Ambassador's car bore a CD plate but had no marking to indicate its ownership.

2. The Indian High Commissioner has lodged a strong protest with the Government of Kenya on these incidents and has personally called on some ministers of the Government of Kenya in the same connection.
3. In regard to events in the Congo, Belgian paratroopers, after landing in Stanleyville, have evacuated the Europeans and some other people of various nationalities. Among these are included 43 Indian nationals and 4 children.

According to reports received, there were 43 Indian nationals and 415 people of Indian origin in Stanleyville. Of these, 455 have been flown out to Leopoldville. One person of Indian origin is presumed to be killed and two others are missing; these three are not Indian nationals.

The Indian nationals or people of Indian origin were not treated as hostages nor were ill-treated either. The danger to them may have grown with the panic which seized the Stanleyville troops and from which even the Congolese civilians were not exempt. The Indian refugees who are in destitute condition are receiving necessary assistance through our Embassy in Leopoldville.

D. Thengadi: Madam, have we received an assurance from the Congo government about the safety of all Indians in that country, and what measures are being adopted officially, that is, on governmental level, and unofficially, that is, through the voluntary organisations of the Indian community in Kenya to remove all misunderstandings between the Africans and the Indians there?

Dinesh Singh: Madam, so far as the first part of the question is concerned, the whole difficulty has arisen because the Congolese government is not in a position to guarantee the safety throughout the Congo. So the question of asking them for safety of Indian nationals does not arise. So far as the second question is concerned, we have very good relations with the government and the people of Kenya; this incident need not cause misunderstanding. We continue to make every endeavour to strengthen the friendly relations that we have.

Resolution Regarding Withdrawal of India from the Membership of the Commonwealth[358]

D. Thengadi: I am led to believe that the future historians would have to record that our link with the Commonwealth had been a very uncommon phenomenon because every country looks after its own national self-interest first and is not carried away by high-sounding phrases and in this particular matter, it seems that we are influenced more by phraseology than by reality. Our late Prime Minister, who sincerely believed that this Commonwealth was a partnership of people with different ideologies, political systems and policies and a challenge to the world and that the Commonwealth was a lesson in agreement and harmony through arguments and debate, even he had come to doubt the real utility of any such organisation and in March 1962, on the floor of the Lok Sabha, he even dropped a hint that it may be possible for India to go out of the Commonwealth, though he was careful enough to point out that the particular issue that was being discussed – that was the U.K. Immigration Bill[359] – was not sufficient enough to quit the Commonwealth. That remark of Pandit Nehru had removed the impression that might have been created in certain quarters that the Commonwealth link was a sacrosanct one and that it was not open to revision. By implication, Pandit Nehru had made it clear that India could quit the Commonwealth if and when the need for it arose. The arguments in favour of continuing in the Commonwealth are too simple, namely, that it gives India a sense of belonging, that it helps many practical projects that we have undertaken on socio-economic plane, etc. but we cannot be oblivious to the fact that the Commonwealth has already ceased to be as homogeneous as it was intended to be.

For example, on colonial matters junior members of the Commonwealth were not seeing eye to eye with the senior members. The courtesy of mutual consultation also was not shown on a number of crucial occasions. For a number of years, Britain's policy towards South Africa[360] was based upon its indifference to the attitude of the other Commonwealth countries. The Common Market brought up further incompatibilities. Great Britain clearly

---

358. *Rajya Sabha Debate* dated 3rd December, 1965. Mohan Dharia had moved a short resolution in the House "...I beg to move the following resolution: "This House is of opinion that India should withdraw from the membership of the Commonwealth."

359. Legislation which controlled immigration of all Commonwealth passport-holders (except those who held U.K. passports) in 1965.

360. U.K. policy about South Africa pulling out of the Commonwealth.

put its own national self-interest above that of the other Commonwealth countries. The division on the basis of colour was not also negligible. So far as India is concerned, we know that we have been discriminated against by Great Britain rather consistently. It has been siding practically with Pakistan as against India and the episode is so recent that it need not be recapitulated. It was Great Britain's policy of divide and rule that was responsible for the partition of our sacred motherland and also on the issue of Kashmir, Britain has been persistently siding with Pakistan as against India. Great Britain is also soft to China whose attitude towards India has been hostile. British strategy is mainly responsible for the antagonism of the various native communities in Burma, Ceylon, Fiji, Mauritius, East Africa and British Guiana towards Indians. We should not be enamored of mere dreams or visions. We must be aware of our needs or realities and like every other nation in the world, we must also consider our national self-interest supreme and therefore, on the criterion of national self-interest I think that this entire question requires reconsideration.

Enquiries Regarding Calling Attention Notices about the Reaction of the Government of India to the Explosion of a Hydrogen Bomb by China[361]

We have also given a calling attention notice regarding the reaction of the Government of India to the explosion of a hydrogen bomb by China. It is a matter of life and death for our nation, and we should like to know very much whether as a reaction to it and as a safeguard, our own government would be prepared to go in the direction of nuclear weapons? We want this clarification.

Calling Attention Motion Regarding Hydrogen Bomb Explosion by China[362*]

In view of the fact that the possession of nuclear weapons by China is found to disturb the balance of power in the Afro-Asian part of the globe, that it is a serious threat to our national existence and also to the maintenance of world peace and further that India is reputed to be a peace-loving country, does the government not feel convinced that the possession of nuclear weapons by India would serve as a deterrent to China and as the only guarantee to world peace?

361. *Rajya Sabha Debate* dated 10th May, 1966.
362. **Rajya Sabha Debate* dated 11th May, 1966.

Calling Attention to a Matter of Urgent Public Importance Regarding the Chinese government's Decision not to Allow an Indian Diplomat, K. Raghunath to Leave Peking for India[363*]

D. Thengadi: Regarding the public trial of Mr. Raghunath, we have received information this morning. Now, during the last seven hours, have we tried to contact the different countries having diplomatic relations with China to convey the whole thing to them and to ensure that they also bring appropriate pressure to bear upon China in this respect?

M.C. Chagla:[364] The first thing that I did this morning was to get the British High Commissioner here to send a wireless message to our Embassy. As regards contacting the other embassies, China is not on good terms with anybody excepting Pakistan. (interruptions) Hon'ble members will not expect me to go to the Pakistani High Commissioner and ask him to use his good offices with China.

Calling Attention to a Matter of Urgent Public Importance Regarding Reported Decision of the U.K. Government to Apply for Membership of the European Economic Community[365]

D. Thengadi: May I know whether, because of its progressive indifference to the national interests of other members of the Commonwealth, may I know whether it has been categorically put to the United Kingdom that, if this continues, then we would quit the Commonwealth?

Dinesh Singh: No, sir, we have not communicated this.

---

363. **Rajya Sabha Debate* dated 13th June, 1967. Indian diplomat K. Raghunath, who was then Second Secretary and his colleague P. Vijay, who was Third Secretary at the Indian Embassy in Beijing, were arrested by the Chinese authorities in early June 1967 on unsubstantiated charges of 'espionage.' Since Raghunath and Vijay had visited the 'Sleeping Buddha Temple' in Beijing and had clicked photographs, they were arrested, and a Court ordered them to leave. While they were leaving both Raghunath and Vijay were assaulted and manhandled at the airport by Red Guards in full public view. This issue of unprovoked assault on Indian diplomats became a major issue with India taking retaliatory measures as well. Raghunath rose to become a distinguished diplomat, becoming India's Foreign Secretary and also Ambassador to Russia.

364. Union Minister for External Affairs, 1966-67.

365. *Rajya Sabha Debate* dated 25th May, 1967.

Calling Attention to a Matter of Urgent Public Importance Regarding Reported Announcement by the U.K. government to set up Military Bases in the Indian Ocean in Cooperation with the United States[366*]

Niren Ghosh:[367] Sir, I beg to call the attention of the Minister of External Affairs to the reported announcement by the U.K. government of its decision to set up military bases in the Indian Ocean in co-operation with the Government of the USA.

D. Thengadi: May I know whether we have approached the various countries encircling the Indian Ocean, excluding of course Australia, New Zealand and Malaysia and ascertained the reaction to the British mover so that the pressure of collective protest from all the various countries can be brought to bear upon the U.K.?

M.C. Chagla: Certainly, we will take up this matter. This is a matter of recent occurrence. We will mobilise public opinion in countries which are equally interested in the Indian Ocean as we are and we will also do what we can through the platform of the U.N.

In Response to the Statement Regarding Recent Developments in Bhutan[368*]

The Minister of State in the Ministry of External Affairs (*Lakshmi N. Menon*):[369]

Sir, the government should understand the concern displayed by many members of the House about recent developments in Bhutan.

On November 27th an authoritative statement was issued by the Druk Gyalpo's[King of Bhutan, then Jigme Dorji Wangchuk] government which should set at rest any fear or apprehension or any further speculation about these developments in Bhutan, which are internal in character. As the statement issued by the Druk Gyalpo's government on November 27th

366. **Rajya Sabha Debate* dated 6th April, 1967.

367. Niren Ghosh, (1915-2001) was a CPIM leader from West Bengal and member, Rajya Sabha, for two terms from 1962-1975.

368. **Rajya Sabha Debate* dated 2nd December, 1964.

369. Lakshmi Menon (1899-1994) – educationist, lawyer, politician, a Congress leader elected to the Rajya Sabha from Bihar and served as Minister of State for External Affairs. Menon served in the Rajya Sabha from 1952 to 1966; she was parliamentary secretary to the then Prime Minister Jawaharlal Nehru, 1952-57; Union Deputy Minister/Minister of State in the Ministry of External Affairs, 1957-62. Menon was conferred Padma Bhushan in 1957. She was also president of the All India Women's Conference.

said, the situation in Bhutan is fully under control. Altogether, two Army officers, including the Deputy Commander-in-Chief of Bhutan Army and four civilian officers fled the country, they appear to have done so under an exaggerated sense of fear of action that may be taken against them on the King's return from Switzerland for dereliction of duty during his absence. The statement added that the King has taken steps to replace the officers, who deserted their duty.

To the best of Government of India's knowledge, there is no disturbance or disorder of any kind, whatever, in Bhutan. The King has resumed full responsibility for the administration.

Our relations with Bhutan, one of our closest and nearest neighbours, are most cordial and friendly. The King of Bhutan is deeply interested in the modernisation of his country and the rapid economic, social and educational advancement of his people. In this task, the Government of India remains committed and anxious to give all possible assistance to the Government of Bhutan.

D. Thengadi: What was the precise nature of the dereliction of duty?

Lakshmi N. Menon: I just pointed out.

The Deputy Chairman (*M.P. Bhargava*):[370] It is an internal matter. How can she reply to that?

In Response to the Statement Regarding the Commonwealth Prime Ministers' Conference in London[371]

D. Thengadi: It should be read because we are not provided with copies of the statement.

D. Thengadi: I have three questions to ask. Firstly, can it be said that on the point of the application of economic sanctions against Rhodesia the view of Great Britain is completely identical with that of India? That is number one.

Secondly, while matters of bilateral interest might have been left out of the final communiqué, have we brought it to the notice of the Commonwealth that recently there have been intrusions in Bhutan by the Chinese forces and in that case, what was the reaction of the Commonwealth nations?

---

370. M.P. Bhargava (1917-1992) from Uttar Pradesh, member of Rajya Sabha, 1956-1970. Prasad served as permanent secretary, AICC and was vice-chairman, Rajya Sabha, 1960-63.

371. *Rajya Sabha Debate* dated 7th November, 1966.

And thirdly, can the government assure us after this meeting that the interests of Indians in Mauritius would henceforth be properly safeguarded?

Sardar Swaran Singh:[372] Sir, about the first question my reply is that the Indian view and the U.K. view is not identical on the use of sanctions. Whereas we are all in favour of the application of all mandatory sanctions and the use of force to enforce them, the British were not completely in line with our thinking and the maximum agreement that could be achieved is incorporated in the communiqué.

About intrusions from the Chinese side, it is not a matter for the Commonwealth. We want to establish a convention very firmly. Whatever may be our problems either with another country of the Commonwealth or with a third country, whereas we can talk about them with the friendly countries which might be interested, there is no use raising this in the Commonwealth and in fact we want to establish a custom whereby these things are kept out of the Commonwealth meetings.

Then about the last question, there are no Indians in Mauritius. What probably the hon'ble member means is Mauritians who are persons of Indian origin. We are interested in Mauritians as such and I am sure the application of the normal principles of democracy would be applicable in the case of Mauritius when they get their independence.

In Response to the Statement Regarding Siege of Indian Embassy in Peking[373]

D. Thengadi: Really, we fail to see any point in continuing our diplomatic relations when the position is such that even our diplomatic personnel cannot be safe in China. That is one thing. Secondly, at least now we should not have any more illusions about the designs of China. These

372. Swaran Singh (1907-1994) – one of the most well-known Sikh leaders in the Nehru and Indira cabinet, Singh had a long stint in the Union Cabinet and held important ministerial portfolios. Singh was External Affairs Minister during the Bangladesh Liberation War of 1971. Singh was Minister of Works, Housing and Supply, 1952-57; member, 2nd, 3rd, 4th, 5th Lok Sabha, and was also Minister of Steel, Mines and Fuel. Singh also assisted Prime Minister Nehru for the Sino-Indian border question talks that the latter held with Chinese Premier Chou-En-Lai in 1960; was part of the talk that led to the signing of the Canal Waters Treaty between India and Pakistan in 1960. he led the Indian delegation for India-Pakistan talks on Kashmir in 1962-63; was Minister of Railways, Minister of Food and Agriculture, Minister of Industry and Supply, and Minister of External Affairs, Minister for Defence, Agriculture and had two stints as Minister for External Affairs.

373. *Rajya Sabha Debate* dated 20th June, 1967.

designs have adversely affected not only our country but many. Afro-Asian countries are also similarly affected. Therefore, in order to contain Chinese expansionism, will the government consider the convening of some formal or informal conference of such Afro-Asian countries so as to evolve a formula through which we could contain Chinese expansionism? It is just immediately after this aggressive move by China against our personnel, they have exploded their hydrogen bomb. So I would like to know whether in view of the changed circumstances, Government of India would not reconsider its decision and decide that we should also become a nuclear power in the immediate future? I say this because a peaceful country, a peace-loving country like India possessing nuclear weapons is the only guarantee of peace in the world.

Sardar Swaran Singh: As for the first question I would like to say that there is no proposal for convening any informal conference of Afro-Asian countries of the type that the hon'ble member has indicated in his question. About the exploding of a nuclear bomb, I have already promised to make a statement tomorrow and I hope the House will bear with me and have these questions discussed at the time when I make that statement.

Discriminatory Practices in Nepal Against Persons of Indian Origin and Indian Nationals[374]

D. Thengadi: May I know whether these restrictions on Indian citizens are just an inadvertent slip or they are due to some shift in the foreign policy of Nepal so far as India is concerned?

Dinesh Singh: I do not think there is any question of shift in the foreign policy so far as India is concerned. The Government of Nepal has given certain protection to their nationals and we feel that the Treaty should be honoured and people of Indian origin in Nepal should not be discriminated against.

□

374. *Rajya Sabha Debate* dated 2nd December, 1966.

8
Defence

Calling the attention of the Defence Minister on reported massing of troups and military exercises by Pakistan on India's borders, Thengadi enquired about steps taken to revive civil defence activities in our border areas. He drew the attention of the government towards Sino-Pak conspiracy against India and wanted India's border police to be reinforced.

Calling Attention to a Matter of Urgent Public Importance Regarding Reported Continuous Firing from Across Pakistan Territory by Pakistani Forces in Cooch-Bihar District[375]

D. Thengadi: Madam, in the first place, are these attacks the outcome of any Sino-Pak conspiracy against India, and is the government in a position to assure us that the foreign nationals who were reportedly seen alongwith the Pakistani forces were certainly not the Chinese nationals, that they were not the Chinese? Can the government assure us? Secondly, in view of the fact that the Pakistani Border Police is being reinforced by Pakistani Armed personnel, why are we not reinforcing our Border Police with our armed personnel?

Sardar Swaran Singh: This question has been put as to whether those people who were deported or who went to the other side, there were any in Chinese. No one has deported anybody. I do not know where from...

An hon'ble member: Reported.

Sardar Swaran Singh: Reported? There is no report at all that there were any Chinese nationals who were moved from one part to the other. The only report that appeared in a newspaper was that there were some foreign troops. No one had mentioned that they were the Chinese. (interruptions) May I at the same time say that we may have our difficulties, conflicts and the like? But let us not try to see danger even when it does

375. *Rajya Sabha Debate* dated 22nd March, 1965.

not exist, let us not exaggerate things. Let us try to see it with a certain measure of calmness.

The other question is put as to whether there is any deep Sino-Pak conspiracy or arrangement and whether as a result of that, all this is happening? Now, we know the relations between China and Pakistan. They are becoming quite thick, and they are functioning to the prejudice of India. But that is a bigger political issue and to connect that with each incident that takes place anywhere, perhaps will not be a very safe conclusion, at any rate, without any concrete evidence.

Calling Attention Regarding Reported Intrusion of Pakistan-Occupied-Kashmir Troops in the Poonch Area on 17th September, 1964[376]

D. Thengadi: Sir, with your permission, I rise to call the attention of the Minister of Defence to the reported intrusion by Pakistan-occupied Kashmir troops in the Poonch area of the ceasefire line in Jammu & Kashmir on the 17th September, 1964.

Minister of Defence (*Y.B. Chavan*): Mr. Chairman, on 17th September, 1964, at 9.30 a.m. our patrol consisting of one officer and 4 other ranks was ambushed by Pakistan-occupied Kashmir troops in an area about 8½ mile south-west of Poonch. The place of ambush was approximately 1,000 yards on our side of the ceasefire line. Simultaneously two of our posts in the same area were fired upon for 30 minutes with medium machine guns from four places across the ceasefire line. Three other ranks of ours have been killed and one officer is missing, presumably taken prisoner by the Pakistanis. Besides, we have lost one sten gun and two rifles with ammunition.

Our troops inflicted two casualties on Pakistan-occupied-Kashmir troops. One of them was a regular soldier and the other was a *Razakar* [paid Islamist mercenary, especially patronised by Pakistan]. Our troops also recovered a bag containing 2 grenades and 5 sten magazines full of ammunition from the dead bodies. Ceasefire violation complaints have been lodged. The decision of the Chief Military Observer is awaited.

D. Thengadi: Have there been any cases during the last fortnight of the United Nations' vehicles or United Nations' observers being fired upon by Pakistani intruders and what steps do government propose to take? Do government propose to take it up with the United Nations to prevent the recurrence of such firings?

---

376. *Rajya Sabha Debate* dated 29th September, 1964.

Y.B. Chavan: Yes sir, unfortunately, for the last few days there has been an increasing number of such incidents of continuous firing which are certainly going on in that sector of Poonch-Nowshera area. I have also heard about some sort of firing at the United Nations' vehicle and personnel. Naturally, we are all concerned about it and we do not like this position because we do not want any incident to take place on the ceasefire line because we do not want any wrong relationship on that side. Well, sir, the matters are brought to the United Nations organisation there and possibly we will have to take it up with the High Commissioner also, if necessary.

D. Thengadi: Is there any proposal to increase the strength of the United Nations' Observers' team?

Y.B. Chavan: Well, sir, we have mentioned it before on the floor of the House that we had asked for a larger number of observers. I think, to a certain extent, this request has been conceded.

Calling Attention to a Matter of Urgent Public Importance Regarding Reported Massing of Troops and Military Exercises by Pakistan on our Border[377]

D. Thengadi: Sir, I beg to call the attention of the Minister of Defence to the reported massing of troops and military exercises by Pakistan on our border with Pakistan and the situation arising therefrom.

Minister of Defence (*Y.B. Chavan*): Mr. Chairman, sir, for the last one month or so, movements of Pakistani troops on to our borders of Jammu and the Punjab, have been coming to our notice. The movements and other measures taken by the Pakistan government have caused us some concern. Even assuming that these troop movements are in the nature of exercises, closeness of troops to the border is something which is not expected normally, and certainly not in the context of the Tashkent Agreement[378] and the agreements between the Chief of the Army Staff, India and Commander-in-Chief, Pakistan Army under which the withdrawals took place on both sides.

On 23rd August, 1966, Pakistani official sources in India, which could only mean the Pakistan High Commission, incorrectly briefed two foreign correspondents about so-called Indian troop movements on to the borders near Sialkot, Punjab and Kutch. That this kind of briefing was only

377. *Rajya Sabha Debate* dated 2nd September, 1966.

378. The Tashkent Declaration signed on 10th January, 1966.

a cover for Pakistan's own troop movements is obvious. We denied the Pakistani allegation and gave facilities to foreign and Indian journalists to visit our western border. They have seen for themselves that there are no troops on our side near the border and, what is more, they have obtained confirmation, locally, of the fact of the deployment of troops, including armour, etc., just across the border on the Pakistan side.

Troop movements by Pakistan on to our western borders, and their continued retention there, is something which we cannot look upon with equanimity, however restrained we may be in our approach. We must, in the face of this continuing phenomenon take precautionary steps. However on assessment of the situation, I do not anticipate any imminent threat. I would like to assure the House that we are keeping a careful watch over the situation and have plans to meet any eventuality. We are also exploring various other methods to reduce the tension on our borders.

I hope that this assurance which I have given will give confidence to our people who are living on our western borders and who have been perturbed by the Pakistani troop movements on the other side.

I have been giving to the House an idea of the expansion of Pakistan's armed forces and other steps like improvement and construction of roads and airfields in both West and East Pakistan. While we are aware that Pakistan has been taking measures of military significance in East Pakistan as well, the reports that have been appearing in papers regarding concentration of Pakistan troops near our eastern borders are highly exaggerated.

D. Thengadi: In view of the statement may I know what steps have been taken so far to revive civil defence activities in our border areas to stop the large-scale demobilisation of our officers to ascertain whether Russia will stand by its commitment notwithstanding the violation of the Tashkent Agreement by Pakistan and to assess whether this time China and Pakistan propose to launch a joint attack?

Y.B. Chavan: So far as civil defence measures are concerned, I have convinced myself that the state governments concerned are quite vigilant about this particular matter. About the other thing we thought it necessary to bring to the notice of both the USA and Russia and the Pakistan government about the significance of the movements that the troops are making on the other side of the border and I think they have also shown some concern about it.

Calling Attention to a Matter of Urgent Public Importance Regarding Reported Concentration of Pakistani Troops on Rajasthan Border and other War-like Activities by Pakistan[379]

D. Thengadi: The hon'ble minister said that topmost priority has been given to this problem of the Rajasthan border area. That is all right but we would like to know as a consequence of giving the topmost priority to this question, what concrete steps have been taken, how much more money has been spent to tackle the water scarcity problem and other problems in this area?

B.R. Bhagat: As I said, I will require notice to give all these details.

In Response to the Statement Regarding Chinese Firing on Two Indian Outposts in the Dongchui La Area on Sikkim-Tibet Border[380*]

D. Thengadi: May I know. Sir, how many times before the Chinese resorted to such unprovoked firing?

A.M. Thomas:[381] I have also mentioned the number of times in which intrusions have been committed.

Calling Attention Notice Regarding Withdrawal of Indian Troops from the Sialkot Sector[382]

D. Thengadi: Sir, an attempt is being made to minimise the gravity by saying that the acreage is only 36. Consequently may I ask whether apart from the 30,000 sq. miles of area in Jammu & Kashmir which is under illegal occupation, this episode of 36 acres is not a link in the chain so that Pakistan has not yet withdrawn from various areas from which it ought to have withdrawn according to the Tashkent Declaration? If that is so, may I know what is the total area from which it ought to have withdrawn and has not yet withdrawn?

---

379. *Rajya Sabha Debate* dated 5th June, 1967.

380. **Rajya Sabha Debate* dated 15th November, 1965. A.M. Thomas, then Minister for Defence Production in his statement on the Chinese intrusions had said: "They have committed seven intrusions into Sikkim. This is the third intrusion over the Dongchui La'. The earlier two were on 20th September [1965] and on 26th September" [1965].

381. A.M. Thomas, (1912-2004) – Congress leader from Kerala, at 39 became Speaker of the Travancore-Cochin Legislative Assembly, was Minister for Agriculture & Farmer's Welfare in Nehru and Shastri Ministry and was elected from Ernakulam to the 1st, 2nd, 3rd Lok Sabha.

382. *Rajya Sabha Debate* dated 7th April, 1966.

Sardar Swaran Singh: Sir, I am not minimising any gravity of it. I am making a factual statement. When it is 36 acres, I cannot make it 360. You should read nothing more in it than what is stated.

The second question asked is whether Pakistan continues to be in illegal possession of areas from which Pakistan should have withdrawn according to the Tashkent Declaration. I would like to make the position categorically clear and say that there is no area in the possession of Pakistan from which Pakistan, under the Tashkent Declaration, was required to vacate. All that has been vacated by the Pakistani forces.

In Response to the Statement Regarding Reported Supply of the U.S. Sabre Jets to Pakistan through Ottawa-Bonn-Tehran Axis[383*]

D. Thengadi: May I know the date on which these Sabre jets first reached Pakistan, the date on which this came to our notice, and the date on which we lodged our first protests with Iran, West Germany and Canada? That is one thing. And, secondly, though ourselves and Pakistan are at loggerheads, both belonging to the British Commonwealth, Canada is the third member of the British Commonwealth and it is involved in this matter. Is it the opinion of the government that our link with the British Commonwealth has been of no avail so far as our internal India-Pakistan affair is concerned and, therefore, have we conveyed it to the U.K. that in case other members of the British Commonwealth persist in such anti-Indian attitude, we shall sever all connections with the Commonwealth?

□

383.**Rajya Sabha Debate* dated 2nd September, 1966.

9
Print Media

Speaking on the Press Council Bill, 1963,[6] Thengadi emphasised that the Press Council should not become a medium and instrument of official repression. He felt that in case the Press Council was to depend upon the government for its finances, it would cease to be a really autonomous body. He strongly pleaded for safeguarding the autonomy of the Press. According to him, allocation of newsprint, disbursement of advertisement, printing machinery and printing equipment should in no way affect the autonomy of the Press.

The Press Council Bill, 1963[384]

I do not know whether it was quite inevitable to refer to the qualifications of journalists in general and youngsters among them in particular. I may tell my hon'ble friend that though any Tom, Dick or Harry is capable of entering the field of journalism, neither Tom nor Dick nor Harry will be able to continue long in that field for the simple reason that it will also require specialised knowledge. The Press Council, as envisaged under this Bill, has certain unique features. It is a clear deviation in certain respects from the recommendations of the Press Commission. It does not follow the pattern of the British Press Council. In certain other respects it is not quite on par with our Bar Council or the Medical Council. In view of all these facts, it has become necessary to consider in detail the merits and demerits of this Bill so that in our enthusiasm to create a Press Council, we do not throw up a Frankenstein that we are capable of creating but quite incapable of controlling. The Press Council as envisaged under the Bill should not become a medium and instrument of official repression. Therefore, since the Bill is going to be referred to the Joint Select Committee, it would not be out of place to go into certain details also.

384. *Rajya Sabha Debate* dated 14th September, 1964.

Now, in the first place I would suggest that in the Preamble, wherever the word 'liberty' is used it should be replaced by 'freedom'. The difference in the shade of meaning is quite obvious.

In Clause 2, the following should be added:

"For the purposes of this Act the expression 'newspaper' includes 'news agencies'"

Because news agencies, like the Press Trust of India, the Hindustan Samachar, the U.N.I, should also be represented on the Press Council. According to the definition of a 'newspaper' as given in the Press and Registration of Books Act, [1867]' a newspaper does not include a news agency. Therefore, inclusion of this clause is necessary.

In Clause 12(1) for the word 'liberty' substitute 'freedom' and for the word 'newspaper' substitute the word 'journalism'.

In Clause 12(2)(b) omit the words:

"and, in particular, to prevent the use of any information obtained by journalists for purposes of blackmail."

In the first place these words are redundant in view of the first part of that clause. Secondly, it casts an unnecessary aspersion. It may be noticed that the Press Council Bill, 1956 did not contain these words.

Clause 15 of the Bill dealing with 'Payments to the Council by the Central Government' should be omitted.

Clause 16(1) should be redrafted as follows:

"The Council shall have its own funds created from out of a cess levied on newsprint consumed by newspapers and earmarked specifically for the purposes of the Council."

Subsequent sub-clause should be suitably redrafted. If the Press Council is to depend upon the government for its finances, it would cease to be a really autonomous body. It would ultimately degenerate into an instrument of official repression. It is noteworthy in this connection that the Press Commission[385] [1952] had recommended that a cess of Rs. 10 per ton should be levied on the consumption of newsprint and expenditure on Council and its ancillaries be charged to the fund thus collected. The Press Council must be self-supporting financially, otherwise it would be forfeiting its autonomy.

385. The first Press Commission set up under Justice Rajyadhaksha of Mumbai High Court with the mandate of looking 'into the state of the Press and its present and future lines of development.' Some of the prominent names who were members of Commission were, 'Acharya Narendra Deva, Dr Zakir Hussein, C.P. Ramaswami Iyer, Dr V.K.R.V. Rao among others.

In Clause 13, sub-clause (4), the whole thing should be omitted, namely:

"The decision of the Council under sub-section (1) shall be final, and shall not be questioned in any court of law."

I may mention here that the Press Council Bill, 1956 did not contain any such clause. Though it has been said that this will not curb considerably the freedom of the Press, I think we are not moving, if we accept this wording, in the direction of progressivism. The whole thing should be dropped. I may also point out that the Press Council Bill, 1956 did not contain any clause similar to sub-clause (2) of Clause 13 which runs thus:

"Where any newspaper, editor, or journalist has been censured more than once under sub-section (1), the Council may report the matter to the Central Government together with a recommendation in regard to the action which may be taken by that government against the newspaper editor, or journalist." The point is, why bring in the Central Government here? As a matter of fact, as somebody has remarked just now, the government is too much mixed in the whole thing.

Clause 14 of the Bill, under which the Press Council can force a journalist to produce documents and also divulge his source of information, would obstruct the free flow of information in the journalistic world. Correspondents, reporters, etc. must have necessary protection. In this respect, the regard for the freedom of the Press demands that the Press Council be placed on a par with the Bar Council and the Medical Council. There are certain other matters which also deserve our serious consideration. In the first place, there are general complaints regarding allocation of newsprint. The government has large authority in respect of this and that authority is being misused. The legitimate requirements of every paper must be fulfilled and the government must give appropriate assurance to that effect. Today it is a well-known fact that certain newspapers purchase newsprint in the black market and there are others who sell it in the black market which means that certain newspapers are not given their required quota and others are having more than what they require. It is so because there is no correct ascertainment of the circulation of each paper. The figures given are wrong. So, it is the duty of the government to see that there is correct ascertainment of the circulation and for this purpose necessary action should be taken. And it would be better if once the Press Council is created, the work of allocation of newsprint from within the foreign exchange made available is entrusted to the Press Council. The Council should also be entrusted with the work which is presently being conducted by the Directorate of Audio-Visual Publicity (DAVP) and till such time as this proposal is implemented, the DAVP should be required to publish and place before the House, its Annual Statement containing the following details:

(1) The names of the papers that are given advertisements.
(2) The quantum in each case.
(3) The rate in each case.

Today the government is showing discrimination in the matter of allocation of advertisements also. The government has wide powers in the matter of granting of foreign exchange for buying of machinery, both for maintenance and for normal expansion and other materials required for newspaper production and granting of foreign exchange for newspaper correspondents abroad. In this matter also, the government is showing discrimination against papers whose policies are independent. This discrimination also must be ended.

I now come to one important clause, that is Clause 4 dealing with the composition of the Council. According to this clause, the Council would consist of 13 members from among working journalists; out of them not less than six would be editors. Now, there are editors and editors. There are working editors, and non-working editors. There is nothing in this clause to prevent nomination of proprietor-editors in all the six cases, in which case the number of working journalists would be reduced to seven and that of non-working proprietors or their representatives would go up to 12. It should be, therefore, specified that only working editors should be nominated to the Council.

Mulka Govinda Reddy:[386] They are already.

D. Thengadi: Not working editors.

Now, much has been said against them and almost all our newspapers have been charge-sheeted. Nevertheless, in order to maintain the autonomy of the Press, the Press Council should also protect our journalists from interference from official quarters and it would be necessary that our Press Council should have the authority to go into complaints of interference from governmental agencies, politicians or other individuals. As I said,

386. Mulka Govinda Reddy (b1916-) – Congress leader from Mysore, who was also associated with the Praja Socialist Party (PSP) and was member of Rajya Sabha from 1952 to 1968.

much has been said against our newspapers, and while the article by Mr. Frank Moraes[387] has come under criticism, I must say that his views and also those of Mr. Mani have been supported by the Press Commission also, and I would like to read a small passage in support of my contention – this is from the Report of the Press Commission:

"*Yellow journalism, only among small sections* – In concluding this survey of the performance of the Press, it is necessary to state that the well-established newspapers have, on the whole, maintained a high standard of journalism. We are glad to state that they have avoided cheap sensationalism and unwarranted intrusion into private lives. They represent a decisive majority of the total circulation in India. Objectionable features have been noticed in a small section of the Press."

This is what the Press Commission has to say. My friend, Mr. Anwar,[388] seems to have cultivated some aggressive love for Mr. A.D. Mani and directed all criticism against the gutter Press. I want to inform you that there are adequate provisions in some other Acts to curb the undesirable activities of what he described as the gutter Press.

A.D. Mani: What about gutter politicians?

D. Thengadi: Yes, there must be certain Acts, but on the whole we should not include anything in this Bill which would cast aspersions upon our journalists and upon our journalism.

Press Council Amendment Bill[389]

The Bill has been introduced for a limited purpose. Nevertheless, the factors that are responsible for the introduction of this Bill are worth stating. I must say without any prejudice that the entire question of Press Council has been dealt with by the government so far in a very casual manner. I know that journalists owe to the government the constitution of two Wage Boards. Under the Working Journalists Act[390] there is a proposal for a third Wage Board also. But, so far as the Press Council is concerned,

387. Frank Moraes (1907-1974) – leading journalist, was one of India's most well-known journalists. Moraes was editor of the Indian Express for many years and a close associate of the doyen of Indian journalism, Ramnath Goenka.

388. N.M. Anwar (1915-1972) – Congress member of Rajya Sabha from Tamil Nadu. Anwar served in the Rajya Sabha, 1960-1966.

389. *Rajya Sabha Debate* dated 3rd December, 1973.

390. An Act to regulate certain conditions of service of working journalists and other persons employed in newspaper establishments.

the matter has been treated in a very casual, tardy manner. The very time sequence of different events would illustrate this. I need not go into the details. The Press Commission submitted its report in 1954. The Press Council Act was passed in 1965, i.e. 11 years after the Press Council was set up in 1966. The Advisory Committee of MPs was constituted in 1968. The committee submitted its Report on 31-10-1968 and the Press Council Act was amended on 31-3-1970. Under the provisions of the amended Act, the Press Council was reconstituted on 1-10-1970. The very time sequence can illustrate in what casual, shabby manner, the subject of Press Council has been treated by the government.

Then, sir, so far as the nominating committee is concerned, I agree with some of my previous hon'ble friends who spoke earlier that the Chief Justice, the Chairman, Rajya Sabha and the Speaker, Lok Sabha, should be requested by all of us to resume their work as members of the nominating committee because that is the best available personnel for the purpose. If these dignitaries refuse to work on the nominating committee, the nominating committee would lose the confidence of the people and therefore I request the government to persuade all the three of them to resume their work on the nominating committee. Now, what led to their resignation is also equally well-known. One of the organisations of working journalists, i.e. Indian Federation of Working Journalists did not receive representation on the Press Council. That is a fact.

But it is also a fact that the technical omission was on the part of the Indian Federation of Working Journalists. They did not submit their panel within proper time though the time limit was extended for them and because of this technical omission, they could not be represented on the Press Council. It is also a fact that some allegations, undignified and indecent, were made by some journalists against these dignitaries but I think no intellectual takes seriously such allegations or accusations by so-called progressives and radicals because, after all, now all intellectuals are aware in our country that the words 'progressive' and 'radical' have no specific meaning. Progressive is one whom I love; reactionary is one whom I do not like. Now since these words have lost all significance, these allegations and accusations need not be taken seriously and, therefore, I think the government would be in a position to persuade these dignitaries to resume their work on the nominating committee. Now when we are thinking about the constitution or the continuance of the present Press Council, some of the aspects we will have to consider, particularly the status of the Press Council. It is true that in many Western countries, no statutory status is conferred upon the Press Council but in such countries, like Great Britain, people are governed as much by conventions as by the Constitution and the British Press Council by convention enjoys status equal to that of statutory one. In our country, we know, how even the state governments flout the verdict and the decision of the Press Council. In a conflict between the Haryana state government and *Tribune* we know how the decision of the Press Council was treated by the state government. There are various examples of the state governments trying to crush or suppress the papers that refuse to tow the official line. So it is necessary, that statutory status should be conferred on this Press Council.

Then, Sir, it has rightly been mentioned that the question of diffusion of ownership should be seriously considered and a decision taken upon. Now this diffusion of ownership is a vague term. No doubt we are all opposed to the monopoly of press and it is also true to say that today the freedom of press is equivalent to the freedom of press baron, that is monopoly of press barons. That is true. But at the same time we are to be careful that the monopoly of private capital should not be replaced by the monopoly of state capitalism and, therefore, this diffusion of ownership should be properly worked out. I should like to suggest that the newspaper industry is confronted with so many problems today and a number of aspects deserve serious consideration and serious thought. Right from the case of a *mofussil* [rural] correspondent, one of the most neglected sector, to the big question of decentralisation of ownership, all these various problems and questions deserve serious consideration and, therefore, I should like to urge that a Second Press Commission should be immediately appointed to go through the entire problem of newspaper industry.

Motion Regarding Report of the Registrar of Newspapers for India[391]

Madam, I welcome the changes that have been introduced in the report this year. I, however, feel that there is still some scope for improvement in the next edition. To cite just one example this report informs us that the combined circulation of the foreign mission publications was 9.35 lakhs. The total number of such publications is 74. The country-wise break-up of the circulation would be necessary, as well as helpful, particularly because

391. *Rajya Sabha Debate* dated 17th November, 1965.

there is great disparity in the numbers of publications by different countries. The country-wise break-up of circulation would help us in ascertaining, though roughly, their respective spheres of influence.

Yet another change that I should like to suggest is this. In the next report we should be furnished with a separate break-up of publications of the Left Communists, the SSP, etc. Now, the pattern of ownership is very important and it has been rightly said that ownership influences the presentation of news and views. The circulation of the common ownership papers has increased and the trend towards monopoly is obvious. The big business houses that run newspapers are as strong, if not stronger, today as they ever had been. While I cannot suggest that Article 19 of the Constitution should be scrapped, I do suggest that we must encourage through all possible measures the trust form of ownership of newspapers. Newspapers and news agencies started by co-operative societies should also be given greater facilities and financial aid.

Regarding newsprint, I am constrained to say that, apart from the import difficulties, we have not yet been able to evolve a rational basis for the allocation of newsprint to different papers. It is well-known that very often bloated figures of circulation are furnished by the papers from the basis of allocation of newsprint.

Recently in the name of crisis 5,000 tonnes of newsprint had been distributed by the government to papers. It was a good gesture because our Press played a very important role during this emergency. Their performance was splendid, but the distribution of newsprint was made in an arbitrary fashion with no reference to the comparative figures of actual circulation. The quota of newsprint is based on the circulation figures of 1962. What would be the fate of papers that have increased their circulation during the intervening period? Should they be strangulated on account of the rigidity of this rule? While we cannot rely too much upon the imported newsprint, it is necessary that we must increase our indigenous production. It would be advisable that for this purpose we should impose restrictions upon the profits of our paper mill owners. In the name of emergency they are making huge profits. The quantum of paper produced in India justifies relief to consumers through the reduction in the prices of papers. This can be done only by limiting the profits of the proprietors. This will help us considerably in bridging or overcoming the difficulties of newsprint.

Banning obscene publications is yet another measure that can be helpful in this direction. Personally I feel that these obscene publications create moral confusion in the public even as Chinese communists create political confusion.

Today there is a great emphasis on self-sufficiency. I think that there should be self-sufficiency in the matter of printing machinery and printing equipment also. Appropriate measures should be adopted in this direction.

It had been assured times without number that there would be no discrimination on political grounds in the matter of disbursement of advertisement and that the standing and the position of the papers would be the sole criterion of disbursement.

But this has not been followed, and it is necessary that we strictly adhere to our advertisement policy.

Language papers and language news agencies should be given greater support. Though the Supreme Court has given a verdict adverse to the introduction of the price page schedule...

Deputy Chairman: You will have to wind up now. Only salient points you can give now.

D. Thengadi: I must say that small papers must be given adequate protection.

It is also necessary that we must have our own correspondents abroad. Today the PTI and the UNI have arrangements with certain foreign news agencies, but this makes us look at the events abroad through foreign eyes. I think some arrangement has to be made so that the bigger news agencies are facilitated to appoint correspondents in distant countries and the smaller news agencies in the neighbouring countries, particularly in South East Asia, and for this purpose appropriate aid should come forward from the government.

The working journalists have been totally neglected in this report. Also the non-working journalists deserve special attention. The Press Trust of India which is by far the biggest news agency of the land is not doing justice to its employees. Their pay scales and working conditions are far from being satisfactory and it is necessary that the government must come forward so as to transform the PTI into a public corporation and give representation to the employees of the PTI on the managing body or Board of Directors. It is also necessary to give further interim relief to the working journalists and non-working journalist employees because after the last interim relief, there has been an increase in the cost of living index number.

Motion Regarding the Report (1965) of the Enquiry Committee on Small Newspapers[392]

I beg to move:

"That the report (1965) of the Enquiry Committee on Small Newspapers, laid on the table of the Rajya Sabha on the 9th March, 1966, be taken into consideration."

We are satisfied with the labour taken and the earnestness exhibited by the members of this committee, but the response to their questionnaire has been poor. Secondly, the accuracy of the conclusions that flow naturally from the various replies received remains questionable.

The percentage of replies received was only 6.37. However, on the strength of the replies received, some generalisations become inescapable.

Majority of small newspapers have no branch office for collection of advertisements and for sale of newspapers. Majority of small newspapers are not economically viable. Majority of newspapers did not apply for an import licence for printing machinery. At least two-thirds of the papers did not own the premises housing them. Majority of newspapers did not own the equipment used by them. Majority of papers did not have their own presses and majority of the press-owning papers had to allow their presses to undertake job work, i.e. work other than printing of newspapers. Majority of papers did not subscribe to the services of any news agency. About 53.72 per cent of these papers did not maintain any staff correspondents. Most of the papers preferred to have news service in their own languages. The news service in Hindi was preferable to papers in U.P., M.P., etc. while in the replies from Madras, the opinion was equally divided. That is interesting to note. Two-thirds receive information service from the Central Government, 70 per cent of those papers receive information services from the state governments. Majority of newspapers receive information services from foreign embassies in India. Some papers that do not receive any information service either from the Central or the state governments are getting information service from the foreign Embassies, namely, USIS [United States Information Service], USSR, Britain, West Germany, etc. More than half the papers receive feature articles from the Central or the state governments. While more than half the papers were illustrated, majority of them did not maintain their own staff photographers. Most of the papers do not own block-making facilities. Majority of papers enjoy postal facilities and rail facilities. The

392. *Rajya Sabha Debate* dated 5th December, 1967.

advertisement bills relating to government departments, it is curious, were not settled in a large number of cases within 75 days of their submission. 55.91 per cent, of these papers receive advertisements from the Central Government while the percentage of those receiving advertisements from the state governments is 62.5. More than 50 per cent of the papers do not receive advertisements from *zila parishads*, municipalities and *panchayats*. Majority of them are of the view that different rates of advertisements are not justified for English and Indian Language newspapers. While paper supply to nearly 50 per cent of the small papers has been regular, paper supply to majority of them has been unsatisfactory and inadequate. Now these are some of the conclusions which can be drawn from the replies received.

Now, sir, as has been rightly stated by the committee, a newspaper is the only commodity in the world which is sold at below its production cost, the difference being made up largely by advertisement revenue. While for commercial reasons it will take time to persuade national advertiser to patronise adequately the small papers, the government in their own interest as well as in the interest of the small papers should take a bold step in this direction. The government must give more assistance to small press through its increased advertisements. No advertising agency should be allowed to negotiate a rate lower than the trade rate. Small papers should not be compelled to pay higher commission. No paper should allow more than 15 per cent commission to recognised agencies and more than 10 per cent to provisionally recognised agencies. Payments for advertisements should be prompt even from the government. Regional advertising agencies equipped to handle advertising business of small advertisers on a district level should be organised. The scope for classified advertisements in the district areas should be fully explored, for example, PWD [Public Works Department] tenders, court notices, employment notices, college and school admissions, matrimonials, etc. Small papers should also be supplied the university examination results. That would help a lot. Government advertising should be handled only by Indian advertising agencies and not by foreign agencies. There should be no ceiling placed on advertisement expenditure on newspapers and periodicals. The income-tax rules in respect of allowable advertisement expenditure should not be too harsh. Restrictive policies of the government in regard to newsprint and import of machinery should be liberalised.

The committee has considered the various aspects of the problem of newsprint and made various appropriate recommendations. According to the committee – and we endorse that view – the government should review the newsprint import policy. Small newspapers should be spared the necessity of having supplies of costly white printing paper as well as Nepa newsprint. They should be supplied imported newsprint only. The import duty on newsprint for small papers should be totally removed or considerably reduced and the newsprint required by them should be exempted from sales tax, municipal, octroi and all such other duties. The newsprint should be treated by the Railways as an essential commodity and given 'A1' priority in rail movement. A satisfactory procedure for the clearance of newsprint consignments should be evolved. One or more newspaper factories should be started in the public sector. The Nepa newsprint mill should regard it as an act of public service to supply quality newsprint to newspapers. An institute for pulp, paper and allied industries should be set up on the lines of the Textile Industry Research Association.

The committee has also discussed the various aspects of the problem of price-page schedule. With regard to this problem, I should like to say that the price-page schedule should be followed voluntarily but that may fail. In that case, the schedule to the Essential Commodities Act can be utilised for that purpose. But I am not in favour of amending Article 19 of the Constitution only for this purpose because it would open the Pandora's box.

Now there are various other suggestions made by the committee which deserve not merely serious consideration but immediate implementation. They are regarding transport, communication facilities to staff correspondents, organisation of an institution for training journalists, etc. All these are serious suggestions which deserve immediate implementation.

Now, the balanced progress of the Press as a whole is necessary for the proper functioning of democracy. Big newspapers – I will not comment upon them here – have their own utility and place. But small papers and periodicals also have their distinct role to play.

This reminds me of a poem in which a squirrel says to a mountain that the latter should not be puffed up with pride because of its size, and that even a squirrel had its own place in the scheme of things. The squirrel says:

"Everything is well and wisely put,
Talents differ;
If I cannot grow forests on my back
Neither can you crack a nut."

The big Press is often termed as capitalistic Press. Small papers and periodicals constitute the people's Press or the common man's Press. But to fulfil the expectations of the people from it, this people's Press must follow, in the matter of news coverage and news display, a policy different from that of the big Press.

In the first place, the news of state importance and that of local and regional importance should be given larger coverage and better display. Even editorials should relate more to regional and local problems rather than to national and international problems.

Similarly, social events and economic news of local and regional importance should find a better place in these papers. Radio programmes, local engagements, readers' correspondence, films, commercial and market news, and local and regional sports should also be allotted some space.

Fortunately, by and large, it has been found that our small papers are not after sensationalism or blackmail, and they do not devote more space to sex or crime. Their news presentation is also more objective and less coloured. To compensate for this commercially, humour columns, poems, book reviews, fiction and features, photo-blocks, illustrations, cartoons and strips may be better utilised, more so in Sunday editions, if there be any.

News services catering to regional and other news in regional languages should be strengthened and subsidised for the benefit of the small papers.

One more point. I believe that the questionnaire should have been sent by the committee to publishers of even other periodicals, such as market reports, publicity journals, journals of astrology, serialised fiction, publications of religious nature, and other things.

On the whole we are satisfied with the work done by the Committee and we only urge that the government should take the follow-up steps, so that these recommendations are implemented properly and promptly.

Mr. Vice-Chairman, I am thankful to the hon'ble minister for the sympathy he has expressed for the cause of small newspapers.

We have gone through the recommendations that are accepted by the government, but I must say that our experience in the past has been that there is a wide gap between profession and practice, and even when certain good recommendations are accepted, while implementing them they are susceptible to various corrupt practices. In view of all this...

In view of the experience, one thing I should like to insist upon is that whatever recommendations have been accepted should be properly and promptly implemented. This is one thing. And, secondly, so far as advertisements, newsprint quota and concessions to staff correspondents' courses of journalism and other things are concerned, I think that much help can be sought from the general public and also from the newspapers themselves, if the proper consciousness is aroused in that respect. As I have said, when the big Press is termed as the monopolistic Press, that cannot represent the public opinion to the same extent to which the small Press can represent. So it is our duty to strengthen the hands of this democratic Press and everything possible within our power should be done to that end.

Calling Attention to a Matter of Urgent Public Importance Regarding Decision of STC to Raise Newsprint Prices and the Shortage of Newsprint[393]

Instead of 1,16,000 metric tonnes, we have now raised the ceiling to 1,30,000 metric tonnes but still the difficulties continue. The big newspapers offset the enhanced prices by a surcharge on advertisements but the *mofussil* papers or the language papers with small circulation cannot adopt this measure. May I know in what way the government proposes to subsidise these small papers or the language papers so that they can overcome this difficulty?

Manubhai Shah:[394] On the question of subsidisation of small papers, there is already a Small Papers Committee which has gone into this matter and the recommendations of the same are under the consideration of the Information Ministry. Whether it takes the shape of one type of assistance or the other, I cannot just now say in advance.

393. *Rajya Sabha Debate* dated 11th August, 1966.

394. Manubhai Shah (1915-2000) – Congress leader from Gujarat, was member of the Saurashtra Legislative Assembly, 1948-56. Shah was member of Rajya Sabha, 1956-1957 and again from 1970-1976. He was also member of the 2nd and 3rd Lok Sabha from Madhya Saurashtra and Jamnagar and was Union Minister for Industries from 1956-67.

Calling Attention to a Matter of Urgent Public Importance Regarding Lock-out Declared by the Management of the *Times of India*[395*]

D. Thengadi: It is obvious that these talks are a part of the dilatory tactics on the part of the management. We have full faith in the noble intentions of the minister but the bona fides of the management are challengeable. In view of this, I want to know precisely and specifically what the legal impediment is in directing the management to lift the lockout and to give the interim relief? What is the legal impediment since there is no stay order?

Jaisukhlal Hathi: The question of payment of interim relief is certainly there and that of course can be recovered as revenue dues by the Collector; that can be done but I am only putting a practical thing, not a theoretical thing. They have today gone to the High Court and immediately again they would further go and ask for stay order. So why create this difficulty? If we find ultimately that they are simply using these dilatory tactics – it is only two days or so since this has been taken up – if it is found that they are not doing anything, then certainly all the available steps will be taken.

Calling Attention to a Matter of Urgent Public Importance Regarding Permission Given by the Government of India to the Government of Andhra Pradesh for the Introduction of the Andhra Pradesh Special Powers (Press) Bill[396]

D. Thengadi: Sir, this Bill leads us to a very fundamental problem. Without entering into personalities or party politics I want just to ask if there is any competent authority in this country which can restrain the state governments from encroaching upon our fundamental rights and freedoms, including the freedom of the Press in this country. Is the Central Government to play the role of a helpless spectator if any state government encroaches upon our fundamental rights? That is the main problem. I do not agree that the hon'ble Home Minister is so ignorant or so innocent as not to understand the mischief inherent in this Bill. He certainly knows all the clauses. For example it says, "if satisfied that it is necessary so to do"; it can lead to discrimination. There is no objective criterion laid down for the subjective satisfaction of the authorities. I am confident that he is well aware of all the facts. He also knows that this is like a *Frankenstein*

395. **Rajya Sabha Debate* dated 23rd March, 1967.

396. *Rajya Sabha Debate* dated 22nd September, 1968.

or *Bhasmasur* and is likely to be misused. So without being so innocent or pretending to be so, I want to categorically know from him whether there is any competent authority to save us, to protect us from encroachment upon our fundamental rights and, if it is the Central Government, why is the Central Government feeling so helpless in this respect ?

Y.B. Chavan: Naturally, sir, the Central Government has certain obligations under the Constitution. When certain matters are referred to them for sanction, they have got to be looked into. But at the same time the basic authority to protect the fundamental rights is the Legislature itself and the Supreme Court.

□

10
Home Affairs

While participating in the discussion on the Anti-Corruption Laws (Amendment) Bill,[397] Thengadi praised the Santhanam Committee[398] for its splendid work but observed that the Bill had left out many of its important recommendations. He said that the Bill should have been taken up after the debate on Santhanam Committee in the House. He categorically said that so long the government fails to root out corruption at the top, it should not expect that corruption amongst the low-paid government servants would be eliminated.

Speaking on the Police Forces (Restriction of Rights) Bill, 1966, he felt that curtailment of rights of police force was unfortunate. He wanted the government to withdraw the Bill. Police forces, according to Thengadi, could not be treated at par with other Central Government employees or civilian employees. He questioned the need for haste in which the Bill was introduced when the Police Commission's Report was awaited.

Dwelling on the Central Industrial Security Force Bill, 1966, Thengadi

---

397. Amendment of anti-corruption law in relation to certain pending trials.

398. Committee on Prevention of Corruption constituted by Lal Bahadur Shastri as Union Home Minister in 1962, headed by K. Santhanam, prominent Congress leader and public intellectual from Madras. On objectives of the committee Shastri told Parliament, "It is desirable that there should be exchange of views between them and public men of experience. Perhaps, hon'ble members might have read in the papers that I have suggested that a formal committee should consider the important aspects of the evils of corruption. But I do not want to make it a formal committee as such and wait for its report. Since we know most of the problems, the real point is to take remedial action. I, therefore, propose to request some members of Parliament and, if possible, other public men to sit with our own officers in order to review the problem of corruption and make suggestions." K. Santhanam, (1895-1980) was member, Central Legislative Assembly, 1937-42, member, Constituent Assembly, and member of the Provisional Parliament, 1950-52. Santhanam was Union Minister of State for Railways, 1949-52; Lt. Governor, Vindhya Pradesh, 1952-56; Chairman, Finance Commission, 1956-57 and member, Rajya Sabha, 1960-1964.

observed that the Bill not only cast reflection upon the ability and efficiency of the state governments but also cast aspersions on the patriotic character and sense of responsibility of our workers. He wanted the Bill to be withdrawn for being referred to a Select Committee.

Besides these Bills, Thengadi spoke on the imposition of President's Rule in West Bengal and Kerala too. He actively participated in many Calling Attentions on matters of urgent public importance. He also reacted on various statements made by the Union Minister of Home Affairs.

The Anti-Corruption Laws (Amendment) Bill, 1964[399]

I congratulate the Santhanam Committee for its splendid work. I am also thankful to the Home Ministry for moving a bit in the right direction but this amending Bill has left an impression that so far as corruption is concerned, the government is willing to strike but reluctant to wound.

In the first place this amending Bill is based upon the recommendations of the Santhanam Committee. It would have been more appropriate or in the fitness of things to discuss this report in the House and then to introduce a Bill in the light of the discussion in the House. Somehow this has not been done. The Santhanam Committee has taken pains to submit comprehensive recommendations. It should not have been difficult or impossible for the government to introduce a comprehensive Bill on its strength but the Bill that is introduced has left out many of the important recommendations of the Santhanam Committee. There are in all 12 sections in the report. It is true that all of them do not deal with recommendations involving legislation, yet their content and import ought to have been taken into consideration by the government before introducing this amending Bill. As it is, this amending Bill takes cognisance of the recommendations in only one section of the report, viz. Section 7. Even there, all the recommendations have not been accepted. Out of 29 paragraphs, only 5 to 24 are incorporated in this Bill. Paragraphs 1 to 4 dealing with social offences and 25 to 29 have not been touched. In all, there are 137 recommendations of the committee; out of these, 49 have not been accepted so far. Thirty-nine have been accepted with or without changes but they are not yet implemented. Fifty-one recommendations have been accepted, not in toto, but with modifications and these alone have been implemented. Thus only 51 out of 137 recommendations have reached the stage of implementation and that too not without

399. *Rajya Sabha Debate* dated 7th December, 1964.

modifications. We do not advocate adventurism but at the same time the pace with which the government is moving, is overcautious and this is not going to meet the need of the day so far as the problem of elimination of corruption is concerned. Some of the important recommendations that have been overlooked deserve our attention. For example, I do not understand why in keeping with the recommendations of the Santhanam Committee abetment of offence should not have been made a substantive and non-bailable offence. There is no reason why this should not have been done. The committee had recommended that for two years after his retirement, a public servant should not be permitted to accept any employment in a commercial enterprise or business. This also deserves to be incorporated.

Now, in Sections 4 and 5 of the committee's report, they deal with the Conduct Rules and Disciplinary Rules. In the light of the recommendations in those two sections, appropriate changes ought to have been introduced. For example, there is a recommendation:

"A thorough review of laws, rules, procedures, and practice should be undertaken for the purpose of listing the discretionary powers, levels at which such powers are exercised, the manner of the exercise of such powers, the control exercised within the hierarchy over the exercise of the powers, the points at which citizens come into contact with the ministries and departments and the purpose for which they do so."

The committee further suggested:

"A thorough study be made in respect of each ministry/department/ undertaking of the extent, the possible scope and modes of corruption, preventive and remedial measures prescribed, if any, and their effectiveness."

The amending Bill has not taken cognisance of these important recommendations in Sections 4 and 5. On the contrary, this Bill seeks to introduce some procedure which has not been recommended by the Santhanam Committee. Here I am referring to the procedure of in camera trial. I must say that this is a very dangerous procedure and it will minimise the extent of justice, which is really the purpose of all trials.

Now, there are certain powers with which the public, in general, is concerned, for example, the Central Public Works Department, the Import and Export Control Organisation, DGS and D and the Director General of Technical Development. The Santhanam Committee has made certain specific recommendations regarding these departments, but they have also been cold-storaged.

There is a demand from the general public that the Home Ministry must go thoroughly into the question of procedure of licensing. The organisation of the Director General of Supplies, which first scrutinises the applications, must itself be subjected to a thorough scrutiny. In the matter of public relations, every officer must be above suspicion and for this, appropriate safeguards must be prescribed. There should be a proper enquiry into the grant of licences.

We would also like to know from the Home Minister whether the government proposes to implement the recommendations of the Santhanam Committee relating to the judiciary.

Section 21 of the Indian Penal Code is very important. Clause 2 seeks to expand the definition of 'public servant' under that section, but this expansion is not as much as would satisfy the recommendations of the Santhanam Committee. Now, some categories, whose inclusion in the definition of 'public servant' was recommended by the committee, have been left out. The committee wanted the inclusion of the president, secretary or other office-bearers or a member of a managing committee of a registered co-operative society, office-bearers or employees of educational, social, religious and other institutions, in whatever manner established, which receive aid in any form from the Central or state governments, in the definition of 'public servant'.

Now, the Bill does not provide for inclusion of all these people. The hon'ble Home Minister has argued that their inclusion will discourage them from entering public life. I believe that this casts a reflection upon those noble social workers. They are men of character and integrity. They would welcome their inclusion in the definition of 'public servant'. They have nothing to fear from such an inclusion.

The committee has stated that it should be made clear that all Ministers, Ministers of State, Deputy Ministers, Parliamentary Secretaries and members of local authorities, etc. should also come within the definition of 'public servant'. Now, on the strength of the judgement of the Supreme Court in Rao Shiv Bahadur Singh of 1953, the hon'ble minister has suggested that it is not necessary to make a specific reference to the inclusion of ministers in the category of public servants. Now, the point is, if according to the Home Ministry, ministers are already included in the definition, what harm would be there if it is specifically included...

Now, in the Santhanam Committee's report there is a chapter regarding legislators and political parties. Now, that has not been dealt with. Regarding legislators it has been said by the committee:

"It may be that some legislators are in the employment of private undertakings for legitimate works. In such cases, it is desirable that such employment should be open and well-known and should be declared by the legislators concerned. It should be a positive rule of conduct – that such legislators should not approach ministers or officials in connection with the work of their employers and they should refrain from participating in the discussion or voting on demands or proposals in which their firms or undertakings are interested. Other legislators, who are not bona fide employees, should on no account undertake, for any valuable consideration or other personal advantage, to promote the interests of, or obtain favours for any private party either in the legislature or with government."

I am sure that the Home Minister agrees with this recommendation. I would very much like to know the reason for not incorporating this particular provision in the amending Bill.

Now, the main cause of corruption, at least one of the main causes of corruption, is the practice of receiving political donations. A few days back, Mr. Atal Bihari Vajpayee had introduced a Bill to this effect. Unfortunately, the ruling party did not choose to support it. Now, this is what the Santhanam Committee has to say on the subject:

"We consider that, in Indian conditions, companies should not be allowed to participate in politics through their donations. It is true that this matter was debated at length during the discussion on the Companies (Amendment) Bill of 1960 and it was decided to permit such donations, subject to restrictions of amount and condition of publication. We do not think that this is sufficient and feel that nothing but a total ban on all donations by incorporated bodies to political parties and purposes will clear the atmosphere."

Now, the Santhanam Committee dealt with ministers' sons and relatives being appointed to high posts on huge salaries, mostly without qualifications. Such persons are generally appointed as Public Relations Officers because this is one post which does not require any specific qualification; now, the committee says:

"There is a widespread impression that failure of integrity is not uncommon among ministers and that some ministers who have held office during the last 16 years have enriched themselves illegitimately, obtained good jobs for their sons and relations through nepotism, and have reaped other advantages inconsistent with any notion of purity in public life. The general belief about failure of integrity among ministers is as damaging as actual failure."

Now, all these recommendations of the Santhanam Committee deserve to be incorporated in the Bill and there is no reason why there is delay or they should have been avoided.

Now, there are certain general observations, which must be made, so far as the low-paid government servants are concerned. To my mind, it would be absurd to expect integrity from them, incorruptibility from them, so long as we do not provide them with at least a need-based minimum wage. I am reminded of a famous story, when the great sage, Viswamitra, preferred to steal dog's meat from somebody else, in place of being starved to death. If that can be the case of a great sage, those who are low-paid government servants, who cannot get their common basic minimum needs, are very much unlikely to live up to the standards unless the government is very earnest about providing them with the minimum basic needs. Secondly, if we are out to root out corruption, the process must start, must be initiated from the top. It has been aptly said: 'The laymen follow whatever examples are set by the higher-ups.' Very unfortunately, I will not repeat whatever has been already said, but very unfortunately, even the Chief Ministers and other higher-ups are not above blemish and the Government of India is not earnest in rooting out corruption at such top level. So long as government is showing reluctance, disinclination in rooting out corruption at the top level, the Government of India has no right whatsoever to expect that corruption amongst the low-paid government servants would be eliminated. So let the process start from the top.

With these remarks I conclude.

The Police Forces (Restriction of Rights) Bill, 1966[400]

The introduction of this Bill is most unfortunate and there is no propriety of necessity for the introduction of this Bill. That discipline is the primary need, must be admitted by all. At the same time, we all know that discipline has been the primary need ever since the Constitution came into being. That being so, this curtailment of the right of these people in

---

400. *Rajya Sabha Debate* dated 14th November, 1966.

the police is unfortunate and I must say it is rather unprecedented. So far as the Jana Sangh is concerned, it lays equal stress on discipline and liberty for the police and it has not been established by the government that there was any necessity for the introduction of this Bill because the police force had become unrestrained or had taken to any anti-social activities. As a matter of fact, this Bill brought forward by the government is a sort of condemnation by it of its own police force and this is bound to result in very tragic conditions being created. Therefore, I think that this Bill should be withdrawn.

So far as the assertion of the government that no member of the police force should participate in or address any meeting or take part in any demonstration 'organised by any body of persons for any political purposes' is concerned, we may agree with much of it, though I must say that we are not in entire agreement with the policy of the government regarding the right of government employees to participate in political activities. In Great Britain, I may point out that only 16 per cent of the government employees are subjected to as many restrictions as are imposed on government employees in India. Here our government employees are subjected to cent per cent restrictions. Only 16 per cent of government employees are under such restrictions in Great Britain and then 22 per cent of them are allowed even to participate in election campaigns, though they cannot contest elections. And then as many as 62 per cent are allowed even to contest elections there. In view of the fact that we are following the pattern of Great Britain in a number of respects, there is no reason why similar latitude or similar opportunities should not be allowed to government employees in India also.

So far as the police forces are concerned, I would concede that they cannot be treated at par with other Central Government employees or civilian employees. That is true. But at the same time, they also cannot be treated at par with the armed forces. Therefore, they need not be subjected to all the restrictions that are now imposed on the armed forces. That the members of the police force should not be allowed to form any political associations would be agreed to by all. But at the same time the explanation given in the Bill, I submit, is fraught with disastrous consequences. The explanation reads:

> "If any question arises as to whether any society, institution, association or organisation is of a purely social, recreational or religious nature under Clause (b) of this subsection, the decision of

the Central Government thereon shall be final." We know that in its anxiety to retain power, the ruling party is accustomed to equate politics with the entire span of public life and the ruling party has conveniently accepted that politics and public life are co-extensive. I submit that if the government itself is given the discretion to decide what is political activity and what is non-political activity, then probably there will be no non-political association or activity. Therefore, this is a very sweeping explanation that they have put in here. It may cover ground which it is not legitimately expected to cover.

So far as trade union activities are concerned, I have just said that while the police need not be treated at par with civilian employees, they are also not to be treated at par with the armed forces. I think it would be much better to see that the police do not feel the necessity to resort to any trade union activities. Conditions should be made helpful to them. A Police Commission has been appointed and now I feel the government is introducing this Bill in an indecent haste. Why not wait for the recommendations of the Police Commission which the government itself has constituted?

The government is introducing this Bill in indecent haste. Why not wait till the recommendations of the Police Commission[401] are finalised, it has also been stated by the government that some sort of a machinery is under contemplation for the redress of the grievances of the police forces. That machinery has not been finally decided upon. What I would suggest is that until and unless an alternative arrangement is finalised and implemented, so that the formation of a trade union becomes a superfluity, a Bill prohibiting them from forming any association or union should not be introduced. After that also, it should not be the government's right to ban the right of these people to form associations or trade unions. The real thing is conditions should be so helpful to the policemen themselves that they would find it unnecessary or superfluous to form associations or trade unions. I would recommend the creation of such a congenial condition, rather than the denial of this right, which is there already in the Constitution.

---

401. Delhi Police Commission constituted in 1966 and headed by Justice G.D. Khosla. Delhi police was largely restructured based on the recommendations of the Khosla Commission. One of the recommendations it made was the introduction of the Commissioner of Delhi in the system.

The Central Industrial Security Force Bill, 1966[402]

Without entering into the controversy over which the Chair has given its ruling, I must say that this Bill casts a reflection upon the ability and efficiency of the state governments. I would like to know specifically from the minister how many and which of the state governments have conveyed their inability to the Centre in maintaining law and order in the public sector undertakings within their respective territories? Were they even consulted before this Bill was introduced? If they were consulted how many of the states have supported this measure? How many others have opposed this? All this information we are entitled to have from the minister before he proceeds further.

Secondly, this is also casting an aspersion on the patriotic character and sense of responsibility of our workers. Our workers have exhibited and demonstrated a high sense of patriotism during both the periods of national emergency. They have donated their blood and sweat, they have worked for extra hours without overtime allowance and thus they have established beyond all doubt that they are 101 per cent patriotic. To doubt their bona fides would be doing an injustice to them and this is precisely what this measure seeks to do. This measure is putting the cart before the horse. This is superfluous. If certain other measures which are easy for adoption, are adopted, probably this measure would not be necessary. For example, if we refer to the Statement of Objects and Reasons, we understand that if there is planned recruitment, adequate supervision, training and discipline, the problem will not arise. Instead of remedying all these deficiencies, this Security Force is being imposed upon the patriotic workers.

Another thing, this Security Force is not going to function either independently or as a third party, but it will be the Managing Directors who use the force to crush genuine trade union activities of the workers. As a matter of fact, it is a well-known fact that our public sector undertakings are not functioning properly. Their in-charge is not possessing sufficient business acumen or knowledge of industrial psychology. In the case of those industries that are nationalised, we expected a better deal to workers and consumers. But I must say that we are disappointed in this respect. As a matter of fact, the Managing Directors are only the bureaucrats coming from the former ICS steel frame and they are still persisting in their bureaucratic attitude. They do not know how to handle their works.

402. *Rajya Sabha Debate* dated 1st June, 1967.

And through this measure, innocent workers are being made to pay for the sins of bureaucratisation. I have personal knowledge of the conditions obtaining in a number of public sector undertakings. Workers are in a very miserable condition, no adequate housing facilities are provided to them. Their pay scales are meagre and attempt was made by the public sector undertakings to give their workers lesser pay and lesser amenities as compared to the workers in the private sector undertakings in the same area. And the Supreme Court has given its judgement only on the plea that this is a public sector; such a discrimination cannot be practised. We also know that public sector undertakings are trying to convert the entire mass of workers into political slaves. A number of restrictions are being imposed upon them regarding their political activity, which are going against the spirit and letter of our Constitution. In a recent case before a month-and-a-half, where one LIC employee from Bombay was victimised for having participated in the election campaign of a particular party, the Bombay High Court has given its judgement that the very Staff Regulation 25(1) of the LIC violates Article 19 of our Constitution. Thus, our public sector undertakings have become slave camps, which goes against the spirit of our Constitution.

Again, we are already having the watch-and-ward staff in every undertaking, and so constitution of this Security Force will only duplicate matters. The functions of the watch and ward staff and this Security Force would, to a considerable extent, be overlapping.

In case there is amalgamation, I really fear – this is my genuine fear – that there will be some sort of retrenchment under some guise or other, and this is another danger signal so far as the employment position is concerned.

If our Managing Directors in the public sector undertakings are given training or apprenticeship or lessons in industrial psychology, the whole problem would not arise. It has been said that certain anti-social elements are misleading the workers. If so, it is always open for the government to locate those anti-social elements, to bring them to book. But, instead of following this regular procedure, you are creating a Security Force which will be at the beck and call of the Managing Directors who are out to suppress the genuine trade union activities of workers, and thus another type of dictatorship will be seen in all the public sector undertakings. As a matter of fact, I must point out that even this so-called Security Force is itself not secure so far as their service conditions and other things are concerned. I may draw your attention to Clause 8 and Clause 20 of the Bill. Clause 8 relates to dismissal, removal, etc. of the members of the Force, in which superior officers are given arbitrary powers; they can do anything they want. And Clause 20 specifies that certain Acts are not to apply to members of this force. It means that they will be deprived of the regular legal protection which they ought to enjoy under other industrial legislation. In this way even the Security Force is left insecure. Instead, I should like to suggest that instead of disbelieving in the patriotism of our workers, the government should try to adopt a different approach, an enlightened approach. It is possible for us to have a proper psychological handling of workers and we can and to inculcate a spirit of dutifulness and discipline in the workers provided the bureaucrats, who are in-charge of the public sector undertakings, change their own attitude. But, with the present set-up, the workers are likely to be misled, and for that the Managing Directors and the bureaucrats are responsible, not the poor innocent workers.

When I heard from the government that certain anti-social elements are misleading the workers, I am reminded of something that was said by our ancient Acharya Sukra. If for anti-national designs all the anti-social elements can forge their unity, why should it not be possible for the State and the State employees to forge unity for nation building? This is possible, but the attitude of the bureaucrats, who are in charge of the public sector undertakings, must be changed. And for this purpose it would be necessary to have a basic approach and to introduce certain basic changes in the pattern and structure of the ownership and management of our public sector undertakings. Now there is over-centralisation and bureaucratisation. Instead, I should like to suggest that public sector undertakings should really become public, should really become nationalised. In that case all those who are interested in that particular industry should have their representation on the board of management. Even the workers should have their representation on the board of management of every public sector undertaking so that, along with the consumers, even the workers should be able to carry the feeling that they are also participants in the management and they are also having a hand in the framing of the policies of their own public sector undertakings. In this way, if we take the workers into confidence, it will be possible for us to make them more disciplined and more dutiful. Instead of following this right approach, the government, I am very sorry to say, is placing a handle in the hands of the Managing Directors for the suppression of legitimate trade union activities and, in this way, the workers will be antagonised against their managements. It will not be possible for the managements to maintain smooth industrial relations because of the very presence of the Security Force.

For all these reasons, I oppose this measure and I request the hon'ble minister that either it should be withdrawn or else it should be circulated for opinion or else it should be referred to a select committee. But it should not be passed as it is.

The Andhra Pradesh and Mysore (Transfer of Territory) Bill, 1968[403]

D. Thengadi: As has been said, this is a simple and non-controversial Bill. One suggestion I wanted to put forth was, instead of having such piecemeal legislation, it would have been better if all the problems concerning Mysore state – because it has disputes with Kerala, Maharashtra, Andhra Pradesh – had been taken cognisance of and a comprehensive Bill had been brought forward, it would probably have been better even administratively.

Now, it is true that both the legislatures, that is, Andhra and Mysore, have agreed on this particular thing but at the same it is clear that linguism has created a number of difficulties and has been a hurdle in the way of National Integration and so long as this linguism is not properly superseded by the spirit of nationalism, it is impossible to safeguard the interests of linguistic minorities. Though we are not dissatisfied with the work of the Commissioner for Linguistic Minorities, I think from this point of view this question should be treated more as psychological rather than as administrative and this would require us to adopt constitutional provisions which will be inclined more towards unitary form of government rather than towards federalism. Unless such a psychological change is adopted it would not be possible for the government with all the best intentions it has to solve the problems between the different states. So a psychological shift in the stand towards unitarism must be insisted upon. That is the suggestion I want to make at this stage.

---

403. *Rajya Sabha Debate* dated 5th August, 1968.

The Central Industrial Security Force Bill, 1966: Motion for Consideration[404*]

The House reassembled after lunch at half-past two of the clock with, The Deputy Chairman in the Chair.

दत्तोपंत ठेंगड़ी : उप सहमति महोदया, यह बिल जो हम लोगों के सामने लाया है, उससे यह बात स्पष्ट हो जाती है कि यह भारतीय मजदूरों के प्रति एक तरह से नो-कॉन्फिडेंस मीशन है। हमारे मजदूर हमेशा देशभक्त रहे हैं। पाकिस्तान और चीन की लड़ाई के समय उन्होंने सब तरह से अपनी देशभक्ति का परिचय दिया है। यद्यपि यह बात सच है कि कुछ समाजविरोधी और राष्ट्रविरोधी तत्त्व उन्हें बहकाने की कोशिश करते रहते हैं, फिर भी हमारे देश के मजदूर पूरी तरह से राष्ट्रभक्त हैं। इस दृष्टि को सामने रखते हुए जो बिल इस समय सदन में लाया गया है, वह मजदूरों के खिलाफ है और उनके प्रति एक बड़ा अन्याय है, यह मैं समझता हूँ।

दूसरी बात मैं यह कहना चाहता हूँ कि यह जो बिल है, वह राज्य सरकारों को क्षमता के विषय में अविश्वास प्रकट करने वाला बिल है। एक बात यह है कि राज्य सरकारों के असहकारिता के विषय में अब तक किसी ने भी शिकायत नहीं की है। दूसरी बात यह है कि जिन राज्यों में शांति और सुव्यवस्था का काम ठीक ढंग से चल रहा है, वहाँ पर यद्यपि आवश्यकता है कि संविधान की धारा-355 के अंतर्गत कोई भी राज्य सरकार शांति व सुव्यवस्था के लिए केंद्रीय सरकार से सहायता की याचना कर सकती है और उनको केंद्रीय सरकार सहायता दे सकती है। किंतु राज्य सरकारें, जहाँ कांग्रेस की सरकारें भी हैं, उन्होंने भी इसका विरोध इसलिए किया है कि कई जगहों पर इस बिल के कारण केंद्र और राज्य सरकारों के संबंधों में बिगाड़ आ सकता है। यहाँ पर रेलवे प्रोटेक्शन पुलिस फोर्स के बारे में जो बात कही गई है, मैं यह बतलाना चाहता हूँ।

महाबीर प्रसाद भार्गव : पुलिस फोर्स नहीं है, प्रोटेक्शन फोर्स है।

दत्तोपंत ठेंगड़ी : यू आर राइट। यह भी एक बात है कि यह प्रोटेक्शन फोर्स है। दूसरी बात भी है। जिस समय इस फोर्स के डायरेक्टर श्री गामा गवाही देने के लिए आए तो उस समय यह बात स्पष्ट रूप से आई थी कि जिन कारणों से रेलवे प्रोटेक्शन फोर्स का निर्माण किया गया था, वही कारण बराबर चरितार्थ नहीं हो रहे हैं, उस तरह के कार्य नहीं हो रहे हैं। अभी रेलवे प्रोटेक्शन फोर्स का निर्माण हो चुका है, फिर भी फ्रेज बढ़ते ही जा रहे हैं। अगर स्टेट पुलिस की सहायता से शांति व व्यवस्था का काम अच्छे ढंग से चलाया जा सकता है तो यह काम भी अच्छे ढंग से किया जा सकता था, यह बात सामने आई है। वैसे तो रेलवे प्रोटेक्शन फोर्स और इंडस्ट्रियल सिक्योरिटी फोर्स में कुछ अंतर है। रेलवे प्रोटेक्शन फोर्स को एक राज्य से दूसरे राज्य में जाना पड़ता है, जबकि इस फोर्स को एक स्थायी जगह पर ही रहना पड़ता है। इस दृष्टि से भी इस फोर्स की ओर रेलवे प्रोटेक्शन फोर्स की तुतना नहीं की जा सकती है। जिस तरह से बातें कही गई हैं, उसके आधार पर यह कहा जा सकता है कि रेलवे प्रोटेक्शन फोर्स का वाइंड-अप करने के लिए अच्छा केस है और जो दूसरा इंडस्ट्रियल सिक्योरिटी फोर्स बनाया जा रहा है, उसकी कोई आवश्यकता नहीं है। इस दृष्टि से मैं समझता हूँ कि केंद्र तथा राज्यों के बीच अच्छे संबंध कायम रहे, उनको देखते हुए भी इस बिल को वापस ले लेना अच्छा होगा।

---

404. **Rajya Sabha Debate* dated 23rd February, 1968 (in Hindi).

दूसरी बात मैं यह कहना चाहता हूँ कि हम जो यह इंडस्ट्रियल सिक्योरिटी फोर्स बना रहे हैं और उनके नाम पर हम पुलिस रख रहे हैं तथा उसको सुपर पॉवर्स दे रहे हैं, वह एक दृष्टि से हर राज्य में एक पैरलल पुलिस फोर्स के रूप में हो जाएगी। दोनों के अधिकार क्षेत्र, ज्यूरिडिक्शन क्या रहेगा, यह अभी तक स्पष्ट नहीं हुआ और इस तरह से दोनों फोर्सों में राइवैलरी और जैलेसी किसी भी इश्यू के बारे में हो सकती है। इतना ही नहीं, दोनों में किसी भी इश्यू के बारे में विवाद हो सकता है और इस तरह की परिस्थितियाँ हो सकती हैं।

इस तरह से इस संबंध में और भी उलझनें बढ़ती जा रही हैं, यह बात स्पष्ट है।

यहाँ दूसरी बात है सेक्शन 10 की, 10सी और सेक्शन 14 है। अगर इनको इकट्ठा पढ़ा जाए तो यह बात ध्यान में आती है कि जो सेंट्रल अंडरटेविगंज है, पब्लिक अंडरटेविगंज है, उन्हीं के लिए फोर्स नहीं है, बल्कि जो अंडरटेविगंज इनको माल सप्लाई करते या कोई और किसी–न–किसी तरह से संबंधित है, जहाँ भी इस फोर्स की नियुक्ति की जा सकती है। इस तरह से 10बी, 10सी और 14 के अंतर्गत जितने भी अंडरटेविगंज हैं, उनके लिए यह इंडस्ट्रियल सिक्योरिटी फोर्स लागू की जा सकती है। इस तरह से यह सरकार औद्योगिक क्षेत्र में तानाशाही और डिक्टेटरशिप लाना चाहती है। इस तरह से सरकार ने इस बिल के द्वारा एक अच्छा जरिया खोज लिया है, जो कि लोकतंत्रीय जनता और मजदूरों को पसंद नहीं हो सकती है, यह बात स्पष्ट है।

यह बिल क्यों लाया गया है, इन बातों को सरकार की ओर से प्रभावशाली ढंग से नहीं बताया गया है। एक भी पब्लिक सेक्टर अंडरटेविगंज मैनेजमेंट ने या सेंट्रल ने यह बात नहीं बताई। इस तरह के फोर्स का निर्माण होना चाहिए। यह बात ठीक है कि वाच ऐंड वार्ड की जितनी क्षमता होनी चाहिए थी, उतनी नहीं है। अगर उसके रिक्रूटमेंट की कोई··· बनाई जाए, ताकि उनके सर्विस कंडीशन को ठीक रखी जाए, ट्रेनिंग आदि की अच्छी व्यवस्था की जाए तो आज जो हमारी वाच ऐंड वार्ड है, वह अच्छे ढंग से कार्य कर सकता है और इस तरह से फिर हमें किसी दूसरे फोर्स की आवश्यकता नहीं होगी। इस दृष्टि से जो मैनेजेरियल कैडर है, उसने सेलेक्ट कमेटी के सामने इस बात की माँग नहीं की कि हम इस तरह का फोर्स चाहते हैं। इतना ही नहीं, जो इंडस्ट्रियल सिक्योरिटी एडवाइजर टु दी गवर्नर ऑफ इंडिया है, जो अधिकार रखते हैं कि हमने जो कल्पना की है, वह भी यह नहीं बतला सके कि उन्होंने कौन से सेचुएशन का अध्ययन किया था, जिसके आधार पर इस तरह के फोर्स का निर्माण किया जाना आवश्यक है, वरना काम नहीं चल सकता है। इस तरह की बात जो गवर्नमेंट ऑफ इंडिया के इंडस्ट्रियल सिक्योरिटी एडवाइजर हैं, वे भी नहीं बतला सके। ऐसी परिस्थिति में सरकार और सरकार के इरादों के विषय मजदूरों के मन में अनावश्यक ढंग से एक गलतफहमी पैदा होगी और इसके अलावा इस बिल से कोई फायदा होनेवाला नहीं है। इस समय मैनेजमेंट और मजदूरों के बीच जो खाई है, जो अंतर है, वह इस बिल के द्वारा अनावश्यक ढंग से बढ़ने वाला है, यह हम कहना चाहते हैं।

फिर इस बिल में जो पावर्स दी गई हैं ऐसेस्ट करने की, वे डिक्टोरियल पावर्स हैं। मैं सरकार से पूछना चाहता हूँ कि जब 1962 में इमरजेंसी थी तो उस समय क्या हुआ था? सन् 1962 से लेकर आज तक इस तरह की सुपर पुलिस फोर्स नहीं रखी गई थी। हमने उन समय देश को अपने औद्योगिक संस्थानों को आसानी के साथ चलाया और किसी तरह की गड़बड़ी का सामना नहीं करना पड़ा। इमरजेंसी के समय में भी हमें इस तरह के फोर्स की आवश्यकता नहीं पड़ी। अब

जबकि इमरजेंसी हट गई है तो क्या कोई सुपर इमरजेंसी आ गई है, जिसके कारण सरकार नई फोर्स का निर्माण करने जा रही है ? यह प्रश्न हम लोगों के सामने आता है।

फिर इसकी एक बात और भी आँखों से ओझल की गई है और वह यह है कि औद्योगिक संस्थानों को, जो संबंध को ठीक ढंग से बनाए रखने से जुड़ा हुआ है, को अलग नहीं किया जा सकता है। औद्योगिक संस्थानों की सुरक्षा तथा उनके जो संबंध है, वे एक-दूसरे से जुड़े हुए हैं। यदि किसी संस्थान में औद्योगिक संबंध अच्छे रहते हैं तो फिर उस संस्थान में औद्योगिक सुरक्षा का प्रश्न जटिल नहीं होता है।

इससे ऐसा माना गया है कि औद्योगिक सुरक्षा अलग सवाल है और औद्योगिक संबंध बिल्कुल अगल सवाल है, इसमें एक का दूसरे से कोई संबंध नहीं है। मैं समझता हूँ कि यह सरकार की गलती है और इस दृष्टि से औद्योगिक संबंधों को अच्छा बनाने में इस बिल के कारण बहुत बाधा आने वाली है। विशेष रूप से जहाँ यह बात मैंने पहले कही कि सरकार जिस तरह से अपने मजदूरों पर अविश्वास प्रकट कर रही है, वहाँ दूसरी बात यह है कि इस बिल के अंतर्गत मैनेजिंग डायरेक्टर को यह अधिकार दिया गया है कि कई समय लगेगा वही बुलायेगा अपने फोर्स को और इस तरह से मैनेजिंग डायरेक्टर जो कि आरोपी के रूप में हो सकता है, इसलिए कि औद्योगिक संबंधों का एक पक्ष यानी मजदूर है, जो किसी भी डिस्प्यूट, किसी भी विवाद में एक पक्ष के नाते, एक पार्टी के नाते आता है, उसी को अब न्यायाधीश बनाया जा रहा है, या किस ढंग से पुलिस की सहायता करनी चाहिए, यह सोचने वाला अधिकारी आप उसको बना रहे हैं। आरोपों को आरोपी के पिजड़ें में खड़ा करने के बजाय न्यायाधीश की कुरसी पर बैठाने वाला काम इस बिल में किया हुआ है। ऐसा भी नहीं हुआ कि इस फोर्स के मोबेलाइन··· हो, चाहे डिप्लाय कर सकता था, लेकिन मैनेजिंग डायरेक्टर को ये सारे अधिकार दिए गए हैं। चूँकि मैंनेजिंग डायरेक्टर औद्योगिक संबंधों का एक पक्ष है इसलिए वह अपने हाथ मजबूत करने के लिए इतनी बड़ी ताकत का उपयोग कर सकता है। अतः अब तक जो हमारे अनुभव हैं मैनेजिंग डायरेक्टर, नौकरशाही, ब्यूरोक्रेट्स के विषय में, उनको न औद्योगिक मनोविज्ञान का कुछ ज्ञान है और न उनको बिजनेस अक्यूमन है। अपने ब्युरोक्रेटिक ढाँचे में जैसे चलते आएँ हैं, वे उसी ढंग से चलना चाहते हैं और उसके दुष्परिणाम जो अभी तक होते आए हैं, वे और भी ज्यादा होंगे, उससे दस गुना ज्यादा होंगे तथा उसमें यह इंडस्ट्रियल सिक्योरिटी फोर्स सहायक होगा, समर्थक होगा। यह बात स्पष्ट है कि इस ढंग से यह बिल मजदूरों के खिलाफ जाने वाला है। यह बात स्पष्ट है कि मजदूरों के जो ट्रेड यूनियन के अधिकार हैं, उन अधिकारों का हनन करने के लिए इसका उपयोग ज्यादा होने वाला है। आज सरकार के द्वारा कुछ गुडी-गुडी टाक क्यों न हो, लेकिन इसका ज्यादा उपयोग ट्रेड यूनियन राइट पर आक्रमण के लिए होने वाला है। इतना ही नहीं, इसके कारण जो नॉर्मल ट्रेड यूनियन एक्टिविटी है औद्योगिक सस्थानों प्राइवेट सेक्टर और सेंट्रल गवर्नमेंट में, अब नहीं चल सकेगी। इस तरह ट्रेड यूनियन दोनों के खिलाफ जाने वाला, तानाशाही की तरफ देश को बढ़ाने वाला और मैनेजिंग डायरेक्टर्स की तीसरी तानाशाही खड़ी करने वाला बिल है। मुझे स्मरण होता है कि एक अच्छी किताब में मिस्टर जेम्स बर्नहम ने एक विश्लेषण दिया है कि हम इस इज्म का नाम लेते हैं, उस इज्म का नाम लेते हैं, किंतु उन्होंने कहा कि एक तीसरा इज्म आने वाला है। उन्होंने किताब का नाम दिया 'मैनेजेरियल स्टेट'। उसमें न एंप्लाई का कोई बस चलेगा, न एंप्यलायर का। मैनेजर्स का सबकुछ चलेगा, उनका आधिपत्य

चलेगा। मैं समझता हूँ कि मिस्टर जेम्स बर्नहम ने जिस मैनेजेरियल स्टेट की कल्पना की है, यह उसकी ओर बढ़ने वाला कदम है। इसमें किसी भी ढंग से हमने ऑडिट वगैरह पेश किया तो भी बिल का जो उद्देश्य है, वह इतना विषैला है, इतना दुष्ट है, लोकतंत्र विरोधी है, मजदूर विरोधी है कि इसमें डमेट लगाने से ओर पास करने से भी कोई मौलिक परिवर्तन और सुधार नहीं हो सकता। इस दृष्टि से मैं पूरी ताकत के साथ इस बिल का विरोध करता हूँ और सरकार से प्रार्थना करता हूँ कि उन्हें इस बिल को वापस लेना चाहिए।

The Central Industrial Security Force Bill, 1966[405]

On this amendment I would suggest that the Industrial Security Force should not be allowed to have the worst of both the worlds in the sense that they are denied the benefits that could have accrued to them as a regular police force but burdened with those liabilities undergone by a regular police force. Thus they are having the worst of both the worlds. The latter should be avoided. Secondly, one can, for the sake of argument, accept the position that probably full-fledged trade union rights may not be granted to this special force. As a matter of fact, we stand for full-fledged trade union rights, but under special circumstances, even if it is conceded, for the sake of argument, that all the rights may not be granted, still it is necessary that some grievance procedure must be evolved, a machinery for redress of grievances must be set up, and some forum for joint consultation must be held. Otherwise, the resultant discontent will explode, if there will be no outlet for it. Therefore, I should like to suggest that, before rejecting this amendment, the government should come forward with an assurance that there would be some sort of grievance procedure or some forum for joint consultation or some machinery for redress of grievances.

The Minister of state in the Ministry of Home Affairs (*Vidya Charan Shukla*): Madam, this amendment seeks to insert subclause under Clause 22. This matter, as the hon'ble members may remember, was discussed exhaustively in the Select Committee, and then we decided not to amend it. Now it will take away the basic scheme of the Act if this amendment is accepted. Therefore, I am not in a position to accept this.

The Central Industrial Security Force Bill, 1966[406*]

D. Thengadi: I am opposed to this clause and I support the amendment of Mr. Basu. I also propose that it should be for the machinery of the

405. *Rajya Sabha Debate* dated 13th May, 1968.
406. *Rajya Sabha Debate* dated 29th April, 1968.

Labour Department at the Centre to require the officers and members of the Force to be deployed in a particular situation. We are opposed totally to this Bill. We have expressed our opposition but now that the clause by clause consideration is going on, I say that this is a very ridiculous clause in the sense that the Managing Director, who is the root cause of all the industrial troubles and who is the would-be accused is given the opportunity to be the judge of the situation. So practically, one who is to be accused, if he is given the power of a judge, naturally the other party would suffer a great injustice. The trade union rights of the workers would be crushed by the Managing Directors who are not known for their enlightenment throughout the country. Therefore, I oppose this particular part of the clause. I support the amendment and I request that it should be so amended that the power to deploy should be entrusted to the Labour Department machinery and not to the Managing Directors.

The West Bengal State Legislature (Delegation of Power) Bill, 1968[407]

दत्तोपंत ठेंगड़ी : उपसभापति महोदया, मैं उन बातों को दोहराना नहीं चाहता हूँ, जो कल इस संबंध में कही गई थीं कि जब इस तरह का कॉन्स्टिट्यूशनल क्राइसेस बड़ा हो जाता है तो उस परिस्थिति में प्रेसीडेंट रूल लागू करना पड़ता है। लेकिन मैं यह निवदेन करना चाहता हूँ कि किन परिस्थितियों में प्रेसीडेंट रूल लागू किया जाए, इस विषय में एक सर्वविदित नियम बनाना आवश्यक है और इस दृष्टि से कॉन्स्ट्टियूशन में सुधार लाने की आवश्यकता है।

हमारे सामने जो बिल लाया गया है, उसके द्वारा पश्चिमी बंगाल में राष्ट्रपति का रूल लागू हो गया है या हो जाएगा, किंतु इस समय हमें यह आश्वासन मिलना चाहिए कि 6 महीने की अवधि से ज्यादा समय तक इसको लागू करने का प्रयास शासन दल की ओर से नहीं होगा, क्योंकि केरल में यह देखा गया था कि हर 6 महीने के बाद वहाँ पर राष्ट्रपति के शासन को एक्सटेंड किया गया और इस तरह की बात वहाँ के संबंध में हमारे सामने आई। इसलिए मैं निवेदन करना चाहता हूँ कि 6 महीने की अवधि के पश्चात् पश्चिम बंगाल में राष्ट्रपति का शासन लागू नहीं किया जाना चाहिए। यह बात हम शासन से चाहते हैं।

दूसरी बात मैं यह कहना चाहता हूँ कि आज इलेक्शन कमिश्नर का एक बयान अखबार में निकला है। वैसे तो बंगाल में भी इस तरह की बात की अफवाह फैली हुई है कि वहाँ इलेक्शन देर से होंगे। इस दृष्टि से एक बहाने का उपयोग किया जा सकता है जो कि मतदाताओं की सूची है, खासकर औद्योगिक केंद्र के मतदाताओं की जो सूची है, वह गलत हो गई है। इस नाते इस सूची को रिवाइज्ड करने के बहाने से वहाँ पर इलेक्शन बाद में करवाने की बात कही जा रही है, इस तरह की शंका लोगों के मन में है। इसलिए मैं सरकार की ओर से आश्वासन चाहता हूँ कि इस तरह से मतदाताओं की सूची का बहाना नहीं किया जाएगा और वहाँ जल्द-से-जल्द इलेक्शन करवाए जाएँगे।

---

407. *Rajya Sabha Debate* dated 13th March, 1968 (in Hindi).

साथ ही, इस बिल में जो कंसल्टेटिव कमेटी की बात कही गई है, उनके संबंध में मैं यह चाहूँगा कि उसमें जो मेंबर्स की संख्या 10 और 20 दी गई है, यह बहुत बड़ी मालूम होती है। दूसरी बात इसमें यह कही गई है कि इस कमेटी में जो मेंबर रखे जाएँगे, उनको स्पीकर और चेयरमैन अपने डिसकशन के मुताबिक रखेंगे। तो मेरा निवेदन यह है कि इस तरह के मेंबर्स को नियुक्त करने में पहले किसी गाइडिंग प्रिंसिपल्स का खयाल रखा जाएगा। अगर यह बात तय हो जाती तो बहुत अच्छा होता, क्योंकि यह तो प्रेसीडेंट रूल की अवधि है। उस कालावधि का दुरुपयोग कांग्रेस के फेवर में किया जा सकता है। इस समय केंद्र में कांग्रेस की सरकार चल रही है और वह अपना प्रभाव बढ़ाने के लिए तथा विरोधी दल को बदनाम करने के लिए इस कालाविध को अपने फायदे के लिए इस्तेमाल कर सकती है। इसलिए हम चाहते हैं कि इस तरह की चीज न हो और उसका किसी तरह से दुरुपयोग न किया जाए। इस दृष्टि से मैं समझता हूँ कि यह जो कंसल्टेटिव कमेटी बनाने की बात कही गई है, उसमें पश्चिम बंगाल की असेंबली में विभिन्न पार्टियों की जो स्थिति है, उसके अनुपात से प्रमोशंनल रिप्रजेंटेशन के आधार पर कमेटी में मेंबर्स की नियुक्ति की जानी चाहिए। यह एक सुझाव मैं यहाँ पर देना चाहता हूँ।

साथ–ही–साथ मैं यह भी कहना चाहता हूँ कि इस समय वहाँ पर जो राजनीतिक अस्थिरता है और पी.डी.ए. के अंतर्गत जिन लोगों को रखा गया है, राष्ट्रपति के शासन लागू होने पर उन लोगों को ग्रेसफुली छोड़ देना चाहिए या फिर हर एक व्यक्ति के केस को कोर्ट के सामने लाया जाना चाहिए। राष्ट्रपति शासन के अंतर्गत किसी व्यक्ति को बिना ट्रायल नहीं रखा जाना चाहिए। मैं जानता हूँ कि सरकार यह बात कह सकती है कि कुछ दल के संबंध में उनके पास कुछ एविडेंस हैं, जिनके आधार पर इस तरह लोगों को पी.डी.ए. के अंतर्गत रखा जाता है। मैं सरकार से यह प्रार्थना करूँगा कि पी.डी.ए. के अंतर्गत रखने के बजाय यह अच्छा होगा कि अगर किसी दल के खिलाफ इस तरह के एविडेंस हैं तो उसे व्हाइट पेपर के रूप में पार्लियामेंट के सामने रखा जाना चाहिए। अगर सरकार इस तरह की बात करेगी तो जनता के मन में जो आशंका है, वह भी दूर हो जाएगी। ये सारे सुझाव मैं सरकार के सामने रखना चाहता हूँ और अगर सरकार इन सुझावों को स्वीकार करेगी तो इससे राष्ट्रपति की प्रतिष्ठा बढ़ेगी और अगर वह अस्वीकार करती है तो राष्ट्रपति की प्रतिष्ठा घटेगी। इस बात का सरकार खयाल रखे यही मेरी प्रार्थना है।

Resolution Regarding Proclamation by the President under Article 356 of the Constitution in Relation to West Bengal[408]

दत्तोपंत ठेंगड़ी : महोदया, इस अवसर पर अपने विचार व्यक्त करते हुए बड़ा दुःख हो रहा है। मैं समझता हूँ कि दूसरे महायुद्ध के पश्चात् हिंदुस्तान में यदि कोई एक राज्य ऐसा होगा, जिसमें राजनीतिक अस्थिरता का सबसे अधिक अनुभव किया होगा, तो वह राज्य बंगाल है।

Deputy Chairman (M.P. Bhargava) in the Chair

आज यह जो समस्या वहाँ खड़ी हुई है, उसके दो संदर्भ इमीडिएट कॉन्टवेस्ट है और वाइडर ऐंड लॉन्ग रेंज कॉन्टवेस्ट है और जहाँ तक इमीडिएट कॉन्टवेस्ट का संबंध है तो मैं समझता हूँ कि अभी तक जो भाषण हुए है उनमें उस पर काफी प्रकाश डाला गया है। विभिन्न दल हैं, युनाइटेड फ्रंट और कांग्रेस है, इनमें आपस में खींचातानी चल सकती है। टैक्टिस और स्ट्रेटजी भी अलग–अलग

408. *Rajya Sabha Debate* dated 12th March, 1968 (in Hindi).

तरह की है। इसकी गइराई में न जाते हुए मैं समझता हूँ कि इसमें जो सैद्धांतिक सवाल सन्निहित है, जो वाइडर ऐंड लॉन्ग रेंज कॉन्टवेस्ट इसमें आता है, जो देश की दृष्टि से अधिक महत्त्वपूर्ण है, उधर आपका ध्यान आकृष्ट करना आवश्यक है।

हम लोगों ने ऐसा तय कर लिया कि संविधान और लोकतंत्र के आधार पर हिंदुस्तान का कारोबार चलेगा, किंतु जिस समय हमारा संविधान बनाया गया था, उस समय यह स्वाभाविक है कि कई संभावनाओं और कॉन्टिजैगीज का विचार उस समय हम लोगों के मन में नहीं आया था। आज राजनीतिक परिस्थिति में जैसा फर्क होता जा रहा है, परिस्थितियाँ बदलती जा रही हैं। नई समस्याएँ खड़ी होती जा रही हैं, ऐसा प्रतीत होता है कि संविधान के अब तक के प्रावधान अधूरे हैं, विशेष रूप से गवर्नर की भूमिका क्या रहे, अधिकार क्या रहे, जिम्मेवारी क्या रहे और स्पीकर की भूमिका, अधिकार एवं जिम्मेवारी क्या रहें? दोनों विषय ऐसे हैं, जिनके बारे में हमें फिर से विचार करने की आवश्यकता है, ऐसा मैं समझता हूँ। वैसे देखा जाए तो हमारे यहाँ गवर्नर की जो भूमिका है, वह एक तरह से ब्रिटिश सावरेन की तुलना में आ सकता है, दोनों समकक्ष आ सकते हैं और साथ-ही-साथ जहाँ गवर्नर को यह जिम्मेवारी दी गई कि मंत्रिमडंल बनाने के लिए वह किसी-न-किसी को आमंत्रित करें। वहाँ किस आधार पर यह आमंत्रण देना चाहिए, जिसको चीफ मिमिस्टर के नाते बुलाना चाहिए, यह सब तय करने के बारे में कोई नियम या कोई कन्वेंशन अभी तक डाले नहीं गए। यह बात ठीक है कि इस विषय में गवर्नर को कुछ डिस्कशन का भी उपयोग किस तरह से होना चाहिए, इसके बारे में कुछ नियम बनाने की आवश्यकता थी, ऐसा मैं समझता हूँ। हमारे संविधान के आर्टिकल 164 में चीफ मिनिस्टर के अपॉइंटमेंट के बारे में जो कुछ भी कहा गया है, उसमें कोई भी नॉर्म्स स्टेंडर्ड या गाइडिंग प्रिंसिपल्स इस तरीके के अभी तक बनाए नहीं गए।

मैं ऐसा जानता हूँ कि कॉन्सिटट्यूएंट असेंबली की जो ड्राफ्टिंग कमेटी थी। उसके सामने यह विषय विचारार्थ आया था और उस समय यह सोचा गया था कि इंस्ट्रूमेंट्स ऑफ भी कॉन्सिटट्यूशन के शेड्यूल में डाल दिया जाए, वैसे इंस्ट्रूमेंट्स में गवर्नर के लिए कुछ गाइडिंग प्रिंसिपल ऐसे ग्रिथत किया जाए, जिसके अनुसार सरकारी नेता का चुनाव करना चाहिए, उसको बताना चाहिए, किंतु वह बात उस समय शायद इतनी अर्जेंट मालूम नहीं हुई, जितनी वह आज अर्जेंट हो गई और इस दृष्टि से इस तरह का इंस्ट्रूमेंट ऑफ इंस्ट्रेक्शन, जिसका विचार पहले किया गया था, बाद में उसको अधूरा छोड़ दिया गया, वह बनाने की अब आवश्यकता है, ऐसा मैं समझता हूँ। इस तरह का कोई इंस्ट्रूमेंट ऑफ इंसट्रेक्शन न होने के कारण संविधान के अंतर्गत रहते हुए भी गनर्वर का व्यवहार किस तरह से और स्वेच्छाचारी हो सकता है, मनमाना हो सकता है, उसका यदि थोड़ा-सा उदाहरण देखें तो पता चल सकता है। जो शासक दल है, वह माइनॉरिटी में आ जाता है। मैं उदाहरण बताऊँ कि यह परिस्थिति तीन जगह आती है। राजस्थान में पिछले आम चुनाव के पहले छह महीने में नवंबर के महीने में यह परिस्थिति आई थी, वहाँ असेंबली को न प्रयोग किया गया, न डिजॉल्व किया गया, चुनाव तक वैसे ही कारोबार चलता रहा। यही परिस्थिति बंगाल में आ गई। वहाँ असेंबली को डिजॉल्व किया गया और आज अंडर सिमिलर सर्कमस्टेंस पंजाब के गवर्नर ने असेंबली का प्रयोग कर दिया है, किंतु असेंबली को अभी तक डिजॉल्व नहीं किया, यानी मध्यावधि चुनाव का मौका अभी तक नहीं दिया गया। इस तरह से लगभग एक ही जैसी परिस्थिति में राजस्थान, पंजाब और वेस्ट बंगाल के गवर्नर अलग-अलग ढंग से व्यवहार कर चुके हैं। इसको देखते हुए इस तरह का इंस्ट्रूमेंट ऑफ इंस्ट्रेक्शन बनाने की आवश्यकता मैं समझता हूँ। जो बात गवर्नर के बारे में है, वही

बात स्पीकर के बारे में है। स्पीकरों ने जो भूमिका निर्वाह की है उसके विषय में एक और से निंदा की बात एक ओर से प्रशंसा की बात कही गई, किंतु मैं यह समझता हूँ कि स्पीकर की भूमिका क्या है, यह निश्चित होना चाहिए और किसी तरह से स्पीकर अपने अधिकारों को संविधान को व्यवहार में लाने के रास्ते में बाधा न ला सके, यह भी ध्यान रखना होगा। वेस्ट बंगाल के स्पीकर ने अच्छा किया या बुरा, पंजाब के स्पीकर ने अच्छा किया या बुरा, इसके बारे में अलग-अलग दल के लोग अपनी अलग-अलग राय दे सकते हैं। किंतु जो परिस्थिति है, उसके कारण बाधाएँ कैसे निर्माण होती हैं, यह हम देख सकते हैं। पंजाब के स्पीकर ने साइने डाइ एडजॉर्न नहीं किया, स्पेसिफिक पीरियड के लिए एडजॉर्न किया। यह स्पष्ट था कि चूँकि बजट 31 मार्च के पहले पास होना चाहिए, तो एक तरह से कॉन्स्टिट्यूशनल क्राइसिस खड़े करना, यह उद्देश्य उसके पीछे था।

दूसरी बात स्पष्ट है, हालाँकि वेस्ट बंगाल के बारे में स्पीकर ने किसका बहुमत है, किसका बहुमत नहीं है, इसके विषय में शक्ति परीक्षण होने देना चाहिए था। स्पीकर को ट्रायल ऑफ स्ट्रेंथ होने देना चाहिए था। उससे आगे आने वाली क्राइसिस टल जाती। लेकिन वह नहीं होने दिया और उससे भी अलग बात कि किसी भी तरह से जो सरकार बनाई गई है, जो गवर्नर ने बनाई है, वह सरकार कॉन्स्टिट्यूशनल है, लीगल है या नहीं, यह बताने का

अधिकार वास्तव में हमारे स्पीकर को कॉन्स्टिट्यूशनल के अंतर्गत नहीं है। तो इस तरह से स्पीकर अपने अधिकारों के बाहर न जाएँ, अतिक्रमण न करें, अपने अधिकारों को इस तरह से उपयोग में न लाएँ कि जिसके कारण संविधान को व्यवहार में लाने में असुविधा निर्माण हो, बाधा उत्पन्न हो, यह भी देखना आवश्यक है। और इस दृष्टि से मैं समझता हूँ कि गवर्नर और स्पीकर, दोनों की भूमिका, अधिकार एवं जिम्मेवारियों का स्पष्ट विवरण इसमें होता है। इस तरह का एक लॉन्ग रेंज खयाल करके इंस्ट्रूमेंट ऑफ इंस्ट्रेक्शन निर्माण करने की आवश्यकता है, यह बात मैंने कही।

साथ-ही-साथ मैं यह भी बताना चाहता हूँ कि केवल कॉन्स्टिट्यूशन में परिवर्तन करने मात्र में कुछ कार्य होगा, ऐसा नहीं समझा जा सकता। विभिन्न दल होते हुए भी राजनीतिक स्तर पर बहुत खींचातानी होते हुए भी यदि हम इसका अनुभव नहीं करेंगे कि राष्ट्र की ओर भी अपनी एक जिम्मेवारी है तो कॉन्स्टिट्यूशन हम कितना भी अच्छा बनाएँ तो भी उससे काम बनने वाला नहीं है। मैं कांग्रेस या विरोधी दल, दोनों में से यह नहीं कहूँगा कि कौन सही या कौन गलत है, किंतु हमें जो कॉन्स्टिट्यूशन के अंतर्गत स्वातंत्र्य दिया गया है, यदि उसका दुरुपयोग होता है तो उसे भी राष्ट्रवादी शक्तियों को रोकने की आवश्यकता है। अभी जो बात चली थी कि तरह-तरह का प्रचार हो रहा है—कहीं वॉशिंग्टन का नाम आता है, कहीं मॉस्को का, कहीं पीकिंग; का उससे तीन दिन पहले की एक घटना मुझे याद आती है। जैसे मैंने यह कहा कि भाषण स्वातंत्र्य का, प्रचार स्वातंत्र्य का, जो कॉन्स्टिट्यूशन के अंतर्गत है, दुरुपयोग न हो उसके बारे में हमें ध्यान देना होगा। हमारे मित्र डाह्याभाई पटेल ने कहा कि किसी एक पार्टी को बैन करना चाहिए। मैं बैन के पक्ष में नहीं, किंतु उस प्रचार का कोई भी गलत परिणाम अनपढ़ जनता के मन पर न हो, यह देखना भी राष्ट्रवादी शक्तियों का काम है। पिछले शुक्रवार को मैं देहरादून में था। वहाँ कुछ मजदूर भाइयों से मेरी बातचीत हुई। अब कितना अपप्रचार हो सकता है कॉन्स्टिट्यूशन के अंतर्गत स्वातंत्र्य का दुरुपयोग हो सकता है, इसका छोटा सा उदाहरण हमारे मजदूर भाई ने बताया—"आप जानते नहीं हैं, माओ त्से तूंग साहब की नीति क्या है?" मैंने कहा, "भाई, मैं नहीं जानता, तो बोला कि भारतीय संरूकति के अनुसार वह चलते हैं।"वह क्या करते हैं?" तो मजदूर ने हमें बताया कि जैसे राजा रामचंद्रजी लंका पर आक्रमण

करने के लिए गए, लंका को जीत लिया और लंका के ही एक आदमी को सिंहासन पर बिठाकर वापस चले आए, उसी तरह से माओ त्से तुंग भी यहाँ सेना लेकर आएँगे, हिंदुस्तान को जीत लेंगे और आपको, हमको सिंहासन पर बिठाकर वापस चले जाएँगे। राजा रामचंद्र जी के अनुयायी माओ त्से तुंग है, यह बात एक मजदूर ने हमें बताई। यह बात मजदूरों तक कैसे पहुँचती है ? मतलब यह है कि अपप्रचार होता है, भाषण स्वातंत्र्य का भी दुरुपयोग होता है। तो इस दृष्टि से हममें, आपस में राजनीतिक मतभेद हो सकता है, संवैधानिक ढाँचे के अंतर्गत हम आपस में लड़-भिड़ सकते हैं तो भी यह राजनीतिक दल के हित के भीतर है, यह सबको मन में रखने की आवश्यकता है। कॉन्स्टिट्यूशन के अंतर्गत आज जो पार्टियाँ हैं, गवर्नर और स्पीकर की भूमिका के बारे में, उनको हम दूर करते हैं तो इस तरह की आपत्ति बार-बार झेलने की बात नहीं आएगी, ऐसा मेरा विश्वास है।

जहाँ तक इमीडिएट कॉन्टेस्ट की बात है तो मैं यह कहना चाहता हूँ कि सरकार को यह गलती नहीं करनी चाहिए कि हर छह महीने के बाद फिर से वही बात, पोस्टपॉन्ड करते जाना, एक्सटेंड करते जाना। यह गलती नहीं करनी चाहिए। यह सबके हित में है, देश के हित में है कि बंगाल से तुंरत मिड टर्म पोल होना चाहिए, मध्यावधि चुनाव होना चहिए। सब लोगों को अपना-अपना प्रचार करने की स्वतंत्रता रहेगी और इस मध्यावधि चुनाव से नई लोकतांत्रिक सरकार आनी चाहिए, यह आवश्यक है। और इस दृष्टि से मध्यावधि चुनाव की माँग करते हुए यह जो बातें कॉन्स्टिट्यूशन के ग्रमेंडमेंट के बारे में कही, उसको फिर से दोहराकर मैं अपने भाषण को पूरा करता हूँ।

Government Resolution Regarding Continuance of the Proclamation under Article 356 of the Constitution in Kerala for a further Period of Six Months*[409]

D. Thengadi: Madam, before I proceed to the subject proper, I have to refer to some of the observations of Mr. [K.K.] Shah who tried to make his speech very substantial though there was no substance in it. One fact that I want to mention is this: He said that 36 MLAs of the Indian National Congress and 24 of the Kerala Congress could make 60. He knows it – and I am only reminding him – that in Kerala 36 plus 24 could never make 60, and this is a demonstrated fact that in politics 2 plus 2 very rarely makes 4 because of internal differences. I need not enter into a speech on that. Computation or percentage of votes is another point raised by Mr. Shah. I think for him it would be a boomerang because, is it not a fact that with less than 35 per cent of the votes to its credit, the Congress is in the Centre? So, I wish he had never referred to this trend.

K.K. Shah: Forty-four.

D. Thengadi: The hon'ble Minister has said that there was no assembly and that now it is too late to order fresh elections and all that. These

409. **Rajya Sabha Debate* dated 7th November, 1966. The Congress ministry led by R. Shankar lost the vote of confidence in September 1964; President's Rule was imposed a second time in Kerala on 10th September, 1964. Elections were held in March 1965 and no party won a majority; thus, President's Rule was reimposed in Kerala.

arguments are being repeated. As a matter of fact, it would not have been difficult to order fresh elections before the government made a bid for the extension of President's Rule last time. In Punjab just on the eve of the next General Elections, they had the audacity to carve out two state assemblies, ministries and the other paraphernalia; there is no reason why the government found itself incompetent to allow the Assembly to function there or in the alternative, to order fresh elections and thus to have the popular ministry functioning in the state of Kerala before six months. So, this plea seems to be not plausible. From the example of Punjab, one is tempted to believe that the Government of India is adopting double standards, one for the states in which the Congress is powerful and the other for the states in which the Opposition is likely to come to power. Now, it cannot be said that the people of Kerala are satisfied with the President's Rule. As a matter of fact, we have very often repeated the slogan that even a good government is not a substitute for self-government. But even then, under the President's Rule, that good government was denied to the people of Kerala. Our friend, Mr. Shah, said that there was a discussion about declaring Malayalam as the state language. Had there been a popular ministry in Kerala, I think that by now Malayalam would have been declared as the state language. But this has not been done so far under the President's Rule. For so many months, the people have been urging that the provisions of the Land Reforms Act, particularly those pertaining to land ceilings, should be implemented. They have not been implemented so far and this has aggravated discontent in the rural areas. No measures have been adopted to ameliorate the conditions of the fishermen who are quite huge in number. And therefore, on that side also we are facing great discontent. The people of Kerala feel that had there been a popular ministry to assert the claims of the state while the draft of the Fourth Plan was being prepared, probably it would have secured for itself a just and fair share. But the same has been denied in the absence of a popular ministry.

All these facts go to indicate that the people there are extremely dissatisfied and they are justified in remaining dissatisfied under the President's Rule. It is no use denying any state its popular ministry, and the plea forwarded for committing this injustice is also very feeble, not tenable. I really challenge the bona fides of this resolution. This is a very serious thing in view of the statement made by Mr. Vidya Charan Shukla at Raipur only last week. He is stated to have said it was reported in the Press that "if in any state, any party other than the Congress, comes to power, well, that state would become another Kerala." It has been reported in the Press. There has been no contradiction from Mr. Shukla. That indicates the tendency of the Congress government. I think this is against the spirit of our Constitution. Mr. Shukla should be asked to clarify the position. Since he has not contradicted the statement that has appeared in the Press, we have reasons to believe that he did say all these things which were objectionable and against the spirit of the Constitution, and that also indicates that Kerala, or the treatment given to Kerala, was not just an accidental affair but that it was a pre-meditated, calculated injustice committed against the state in which the Congress had no likelihood of coming to power.

The Congress government is opposed to the Communist Party. We are also opposed to it. But at the same time the votaries of democracy would not like the Communist Party to be defeated by undemocratic methods. Even if it is to be defeated in the battle of the ballot box, it should be through democratic measures. And therefore, as a votary of democracy, though I am opposed to communism, I am very much against the spirit of this resolution and I feel that we would be strengthening the forces that are against democracy by adopting such measures. I really feel that today our country is standing on the crossroads. On the one hand, there is a possibility that the institutions that are democratic may continue to function properly if appropriate precautions are taken by the government and also by the Opposition parties. Also there is an apprehension that the situation may further deteriorate and the country may be thrown into chaos which would be worse than the Congress rule. And then thirdly there is the possibility that if we do not properly safeguard the future of democratic institutions in our petty individual or party interests, we may invite dictatorship which would be to nobody's benefit. Thus, we are on the crossroads. What is our choice? Furtherance of democratic institutions or plunging India into chaos or the advent of dictatorship? And I fear that the present resolution is going to help the two other alternatives except the furtherance of democratic institutions. I believe that the Congress Party is treating this country as an estate of some individual or a party. This is a wrong attitude and therefore, I urge that this resolution should be withdrawn.

Resolution Regarding Proclamation Relating to the State of Kerala[410]

Much has been spoken about the efficacy and utility of the Consultative Committee. This tempts me to suggest that if this be the better method, probably we should use it in the case of the Central Parliament and Central ministries so that both should be dispensed with and replaced by the Central Consultative Committee. (interruption.) I oppose this resolution because the move contemplated under it is a negation of democracy and gross abuse of the powers granted by the Constitution. The period specified is six months but are we going to hold elections just within a couple of months before the General Elections? So, it is but natural that the period will be extended up to the General Elections and this would lead anyone to suspect that probably this extension of the period was already decided upon. Rainy season has also been under discussion. I may remind our hon'ble friend that in Kerala also, where rains are torrential even some of the battles in historical times were fought during the rainy season, in spite of rains. I am referring to the history of Pazhshi Raja.[411] It has been accepted by the hon'ble minister that even a good government would not be a proper substitute for a democratic, popular and responsible government. But unfortunately, I must say that this President's rule has not done justice to the people of Kerala and they are dissatisfied on every score. I will try to mention just some of the problems of the people of Kerala in regard to which the Centre has not been able to satisfy them.

The first problem is in regard to language. Every state has been jealous in safeguarding the interests of its language. Only a couple of days back, Maharashtra declared Marathi as its state language, but even now Malayalam has not been recognised or declared as the official language of Kerala. Madam, in 1958 [1957] a committee was appointed under the chairmanship of Komattil Achyuta Menon[412] to recommend measures to be adopted for making Malayalam the official language. The committee made various recommendations with a view to making Malayalam the

410. *Rajya Sabha Debate* dated 3rd May, 1966.

411. Kerala Varma (1753-1805) – popularly known as Pazhashi Raja was one of the most valiant Kings of Malabar. Varma had defeated in Malabar, Arthur Wellesley, also known as the 1st Duke of Wellington, who had defeated Napoleon in the battle of Waterloo.

412. Komattil Achutha Menon (1887-1963) was a lawyer, judge, historian and founder of the Kerala History Association. Menon authored books on the history of ancient Kerala. In 1957, the EMS Namboodiripad ministry appointed a committee headed by Menon to study the feasibility of declaring Malayalam as the administrative language of the state.

official language by 1965. The committee proposed a 7-year scheme but the scheme has been cold-storaged. I think just five months back or so an officer had been appointed at state level for this purpose but dilatory tactics as usual are being resorted to. Even procurement notices given to illiterate agriculturists are in English. Even in the smallest courts the proceedings are still being conducted in English. The Centre has failed miserably in according Malayalam the status it deserves.

The Centre has further failed to improve the state of affairs in the private-managed school in Kerala. They receive money for admission of students, as well as for appointment of teachers. Private schools have become a regular business and the Centre is quite aware of it. A suggestion has been made that there should be established an independent or autonomous state-level corporation for the management of schools but in this direction the Centre has not made any move.

In the areas of the former states of Travancore and Cochin, there are no private forests, but in the former British Malabar there are vast areas under private control. Now some of these forests are being owned by *devaswoms*. There has been unauthorised encroachment on the private forest areas in north Kerala, particularly Tellicherry-Cannanore area, through the active connivance and conspiracy of the *devaswom*[413] managers. The Centre has not been able to put an end to this malpractice.

It is the duty of the government to give proper attention to the poor fishermen. Today they are like labourers under the owners of the fishing boats. Lion's share of the profits goes to these owners and those who go to the sea get very little. They are only the wage-slaves. The government ought to have brought forth a Bill enabling the fishermen to become owners of their boats. Further appropriate credit facilities should have been granted to them to tide over the off-season period. I must say that the fishermen of Kerala are not happy at the formation of the Fisheries' Corporation since they feel that the corporation would be a poor substitute for their own co-operatives. They further suspect that at least one of the motives behind the formation of the corporation is the continuance of employment to one of the retired officials, which is not a good practice. The ice-plants for freezing fish which are today only at two places but should have been installed on the entire coastal area. For fast transport of fish from the coastal areas to the interior, appropriate arrangements have not yet been made.

413. Devaswom Boards – Government-appointed Boards in Kerala to administer selected temples under it.

The people of Kerala have demanded introduction of some Railway lines, for example, broad gauge from Cochin to the further south, extension of Railway line from Trivandrum to Kanyakumari, Trichur to Guruvayur, Kollengode to Trichur and Mangalore-Calicut-Bangalore direct line. It has been stated by the hon'ble minister that the various ministries concerned take some co-ordinated action. Probably as usual, this has escaped their attention.

The government has not increased the amount earmarked for minor irrigation and wells which the people of Kerala demanded. They have also not given adequate loan facilities for installing pumps and for consumption of electricity by the agriculturists.

The absence of a thermal station is Kerala's big problem. A thermal station should have been already installed, preferably in central Kerala. After the year 1962, there have been recurring power-cuts in Kerala, and this year the power-cut had started as early as in January. The power-cut this year is affecting not only industrial concerns but also domestic consumption. In the first place, there is a less number of industries in Kerala. On the top of that, whatever industries are there, they are also suffering from frequent power-cuts. But the Centre has totally ignored this problem. The small-scale industries in Kerala suffer not only from power-cuts but also from the non-availability of raw materials, particularly iron. What has the Centre done all these months, I would like to know, to help the small-scale industrialists?

The Centre has not yet fully implemented the Kerala Land Reforms Act, i.e. Act I of 1964. Particularly the provisions relating to ceilings have not been implemented. As a matter of fact, even these provisions are not fully satisfactory because there are certain loopholes. For example, the lands in Kuttanad area are exempted from the operation of these provisions. More than 80 per cent of the tenants are tenants under 'small holders', i.e. holders having less than eight acres of double crop lands. These tenants are denied the right to purchase the landowner's right or title.

Provisions regarding fixation of 'fair rent' are not equitable. For example, in some cases, the fair rent exceeds the contract rate, especially in the case of tenants under small holders.

Again, today the government procures paddy from a cultivator at a lower rate, while he has to pay to the landlord a higher price for the similar quantity. This disparity has been persisting under the Central rule. This procurement of paddy from the cultivators is at a low price and it does not leave sufficient margin for cultivation expenses and for domestic consumption.

The problem of the NGOs has already been referred to. Their demands for weightage, Dearness Allowance and house-rent allowances are perfectly justified and they would be supported in any of their struggles by all the Central labour organisations of the land.

The Centre has also failed to provide adequate funds so that the pay-scales of college teachers could be brought on a par with the recommendations of the University Grants Commission.

In view of all these facts and I have mentioned only a few as illustrations and not given an exhaustive list, I must say that the Centre has failed to do justice to Kerala. Even the hon'ble minister accepted that even good government was no substitute for a democratic, responsible, popular government. This Central Rule cannot be even described as good government. Therefore, on both these scores, firstly, because this is a negation of democracy and secondly, since the Central Rule has failed to do justice to Kerala, on both these scores, I oppose this resolution.

Resolution Regarding Appointment of a High-Powered Commission to Examine the Constitutional and Legal Position of the Police in India[414]

D. Thengadi: You are attributing motives to Mr. Shukla.

M.P. Bhargava: I am not attributing motives to Mr. Shukla. He said the intentions of Mr. Bhargava's resolutions are good, and that gives out the working of his mind. But because he has to abide by the decision taken, he had to oppose the resolution. Now my position is absolutely clear.

A.P. Chatterjee: You are withdrawing the resolution? Is it your position now?

M.P. Bhargava: This is what I am saying now. My position is absolutely clear. I have impressed upon this House the need for an all-India Commission, and my stand has been fully vindicated by the speeches made in this august House. Now the test will be Mr. Mani's amendment. If Mr. Mani's amendment is accepted, I shall certainly press my resolution. But if the House in its wisdom throws out Mr. Mani's amendment, I have no other go but not to press my resolution, which, if done, will meet the same fate as Mr. Mani's amendment.

---

414. *Rajya Sabha Debate* dated 6th December, 1968.

Short Duration Discussion under Rule 176 Regarding Abolition of Privy Purses, etc. of Rulers of Former Indian States[415]

D. Thengadi: Deputy Chairman, a couple of days back the hon'ble minister had stated on the floor of this House that the entire issue was under examination. I do not know what progress has been made so far in the process of examination, but to our mind certain aspects of the problem are very clear.

Firstly, I am convinced that this problem or issue of abolition of privy purses has no international aspect or implications. Kashmir and Kutch are entirely our domestic problems and therefore, they cannot be described as having any international implication. So far as the legal and constitutional position about the abolition of privy purses is concerned it appeared in the Press today that the Law Department has given a certain opinion which says that there would be no legal or constitutional difficulty in the abolition of privy purses. I do not know how far the report is correct. The decision of the Supreme Court in the case of family allowance of the ex-rulers of Orissa has also been cited. Personally I am not a constitutional pundit, but I know that pundits of Constitution will certainly interpret the various relevant provisions in different ways. But I doubt very much whether that sanctity is attached to Constitution by the ruling party also, in view of the fact that the number of amendments to the Constitution is greater than the number of years that have rolled on since the adoption of the Constitution.

The moral aspect has also been referred to. There is some substance in it, but I must also say that this status of super-citizenship that has been accorded under the law, under the Constitution, is at least unmoral if not immoral. The human aspect of the problem has also to be considered, but there is only one human aspect of the problem; that is, if the privy purses are abolished, how to rehabilitate the princes who will have no other means of livelihood? That can be considered compassionately. But this problem has some other important aspects that must be taken into consideration.

Firstly, I am astonished why the ruling Party has chosen this particular moment for passing this resolution. I have great admiration for my friend, Mr. Dharia, and between myself and Mr. Dharia the area of agreement is much wider than the area of this agreement. But we are not discussing individuals. We are considering the functioning of the collective mind

415. *Rajya Sabha Debate* dated 31st July, 1967.

of a particular party. Therefore, I really fail to understand what was particularly auspicious about this *muhurtham* because the Congress has been wedded to a socialist pattern of society or socialism right from its Avadi session.[416] How is it that the *muhurtham* was chosen only after the General Elections of 1967? I am really inclined to agree with the remark passed by Mr. D.P. Mishra[417] – though we disagree everywhere else – that there may be some element of anger in the AICC decision to abolish privy purses because certain princes had gone against the Congress. It appears as if so long as the princes invariably sided with the Congress, the socialist Congress did not find it necessary to pass any resolution and now that the pro-Congress attitude of the princes is undergoing a certain change, in order to pressurise them, this resolution is being brought. Therefore, the political motive of the ruling Congress Party has also to be taken into consideration. There is one more aspect to the problem. So far as the ex-rulers are concerned, we do think and we do believe that these privy purses should be abolished. There is no doubt about that. But there is another aspect to it. Shall we allow the party, the ruling party, to create a bad precedent on the strength of which they can go back upon their earlier assurances given to other sections of the population? For, there are commitments not only to the princes but to other sections – the middle classes and even to the working classes regarding living wage. Now there has been breach of trust. They have not kept their word and we have condemned them for that. Wherever there has been breach of trust, we have condemned it. Now, if we endorse or sanction this breach of trust, will they not be emboldened to go back upon their commitments in other cases? Therefore, it is necessary, according to me, to find out a way whereby such a precedent will not be created but the purpose of abolition of the privy purses also will be achieved.

Therefore, a new approach is required and here I am reminded of the procedure followed by Sardar Vallabhbhai Patel. We know that before the provision was incorporated into the Constitution, Sardar Vallabhbhai Patel had negotiations with the princes – he was an iron man and indeed,

416. Indian National Congress session was held at Avadi on 10th January, 1955 and passed the resolution on the need to establish a socialistic pattern of society. At Avadi, Nehru had declared that, "Planning should take place with a view to the establishment of a socialistic pattern of society."

417. Dwarka Prasad Mishra (1901-1988) – Congress leader from Madhya Pradesh, was twice Chief Minister of Madhya Pradesh and was also a freedom fighter, journalist and poet.

he proved his mettle and brought round all the princes to his way of thinking which was difficult and only after the matters were settled, it was incorporated in the Constitution. I think that if we follow this procedure then without bringing in any legal sanction or legislative sanction, it should be possible for us to do it. The hon'ble Home Minister is a statesman and I think this is a challenge to his statesmanship to bring round the princes even at this stage. Sardar Patel was called upon to deal with real living tigers. Now they have become paper tigers. Is our Home Minister not capable of dealing with these paper tigers? So we should like that the procedure followed by Sardar Vallabhbhai Patel should be followed by our hon'ble Home Minister also now. And while the examination of the issue is going on, I should like to know from him whether he is also simultaneously conducting negotiations on this problem with the princes, because the entire environment is such that public opinion has been mobilised to such an extent that even the princes will have to come down and in this way, if matters are settled, then we will not be sanctioning or endorsing another breach of assurance by the government so that their assurances to every section of the population also remains inviolable.

Half-an-Hour Discussion Regarding Points Arising out of Answers to Starred Questions Nos. 96 and 105 Relating to Demands of the Delhi Policemen[418]

D. Thengadi: The Prime Minister has laid great stress upon discipline. That is one aspect of it. I would like to know whether he has enquired into another aspect, namely, whether tactlessness and high-handedness of some particular officials were also responsible for provoking the police? Whether that aspect has been enquired into, that I should like to know specifically?

Secondly, now that the agitation has been called off and the minister has rightly said that right from the smallest constable up to the hon'ble minister, all belong to one family – he is preserving the family of India – may I know what measures have been adopted after the calling off of the agitation up to this day by the Home Minister for the redressal of their grievances? At least has any move been initiated in that direction? That is number two.

Thirdly, when this Police Forces Bill was under discussion it was clearly stated that if the police are to be deprived of the trade union

418. *Rajya Sabha Debate* dated 5th June, 1967.

rights, some appropriate machinery must be devised for redressal of their grievances and also for mutual consultations. In the absence of such a machinery, aggravation of the discontent was but natural. Will the government consider setting up of such a machinery in the near future?

Y.B. Chavan: I thought I had explained these points. I will answer his last point first, that the association of the policemen was recognised, its constitution approved and its office-bearers properly elected and it had started functioning quite all right. So there was no question of any lack of any organisation which can look after their problem. It was there. It was a representative body.

The second point that he mentioned was whether any steps have been taken or not. As I said, this Khosla Commission and its report is one of the most important steps, because allowances and pay scales were the most important controversial aspects of the matter. The Commission has gone into them and made certain recommendations. That has to be gone into. About the other steps to be taken, I mentioned the housing problem and other problems. They have also been gradually dealt with. About whether tactlessness and high-handedness were not responsible for the present trouble, I would say 'no'. I do not say that there was not or there cannot be any but on this occasion which ultimately led to their *morcha*, etc., high-handedness was not responsible.

Alling Attention to a Matter of Urgent Public Importance Regarding Reported Firing by Police on Displaced Persons from East Pakistan at Coimbatore[419]

D. Thengadi: May I know, madam, whether anybody from the police force was suspended for firing? Who ordered the firing and was he competent enough to order the firing?

Deputy Chairman: That investigation is going on.

Mahavir Tyagi:[420] As I have just submitted, the matter is under investigation. If the policeman is found at fault, not only suspension but definitely something further might come. If it is proved action will be taken. Immediately action has been taken on the very day. A magistrate

419. *Rajya Sabha Debate* dated 15th December, 1964.

420. Mahavir Tyagi (1899-1980) – freedom fighter, well-known Parliamentarian and Congress leader, was member, Uttar Pradesh Legislative Assembly for 9 Years, Constituent Assembly, member, Provisional Parliament and member of Lok Sabha, 1952-57, 1957-62 and 1962-67. Tyagi was also Union Minister holding portfolios of Finance, Defence and Rehabilitation between 1953-66 and member, Rajya Sabha, 3-4-1970 to 2-4-1976. After the split in the Congress, Tyagi continued with the Congress (O).

has gone there. He is making a thorough enquiry and as soon as the result of the enquiry is in the hands of the authorities, they will take proper action either against the police or the person concerned.

Calling Attention to a Matter of Urgent Public Importance Regarding Demand of the Mizo Union for the Formation of a Mizoram State within the Indian Union*[421]

D. Thengadi: Has the Pataskar Commission[422] conveyed its reaction to the government, and is what is described as adequate autonomy by the Home Ministry consistent with the reactions of the Pataskar Commission?

Gulzarilal Nanda: I could not follow the question.

Mr. Chairman: Has the Pataskar Commission communicated its reactions to the government in this regard?

Gulzarilal Nanda: No, sir, the Pataskar Commission is still at work and these people also can present, and I am sure, are presenting their case before the Pataskar Commission.

Calling Attention to a Matter of Urgent Public Importance Regarding Recent Correspondence between the Prime Minister and Sant Fateh Singh and the Situation Arising out of Sant Fateh Singh's Reported Announcement to go on Fast Unto Death from 17th December, 1966 and to Immolate Himself*[423]

D. Thengadi: So far as the statement of minister goes, I think it is merely a reiteration of the stand taken earlier – by earlier I mean after

---

421. *Rajya Sabha Debate* dated 29th November, 1965.

422. The Pataskar Commission (Commission on the Hill Areas of Assam 1965-66), set up by the Govt. of India during Lal Bahadur Shastri's tenure as Prime Minister. The Commission was, headed by Hari Vinayak Pataskar to look into the political affairs of the Mizo Union and its terms of reference was to "recommend a detailed scheme for reorganizing the administrative set-up of the hill areas having regard to the main objectives of conferring a full measure of autonomy on the hill areas, subject to the preservation of the unity of the State of Assam, the continuance of a common legislature for the whole State and the maintenance of the cabinet form of government functioning on the basis of collective and joint responsibility to the State Assembly." The Commission was also required to recommend "the administrative, financial and legal measures necessary for giving effect to the proposed reorganization." H.V. Pataskar (1892-1970), Congress leader from Maharashtra, was member of the Constituent Assembly, member of the 1st Lok Sabha, was Minister of Civil Aviation (1956-57) in the Nehru cabinet, Governor of Madhya Pradesh, Vice Chancellor of Poona University and was awarded Padma Vibhushan in 1963.

423. *Rajya Sabha Debate* dated 8th December, 1966.

Sant Fateh Singh[424] has made his declaration. I agree with the minister that the life of Sant Fateh Singh is very valuable for the country. I also must point out that in not following the majority recommendation regarding the status of Chandigarh, government has already gone out of its way. Under the circumstances I want to know – because there is an imminent danger of some tragedy so far as self-immolation is concerned – what concrete steps the government proposes to take to avoid the tragedy of self-immolation.

Y.B. Chavan: The step is the statement that I have made before Parliament.

Calling Attention to a Matter of Urgent Public Importance Regarding Reported Statement by the Chief Minister of Jammu & Kashmir, Blaming the Union government for Uncertainty in the Affairs of the State[425]

D. Thengadi: In his talks with the Prime Minister, did J.P. Narayan convey what topics he wanted to discuss with Sheikh Abdullah? The Government of India has declared times without number that accession of Jammu & Kashmir to India is final and irrevocable. In view of this, our firm stand, what other topics remain to be discussed? Did J.P. Narayan convey any idea?

Calling Attention to a Matter of Urgent Public Importance Regarding Condition Prevailing in the Naxalbari Area in West Bengal*[426]

D. Thengadi: The hon'ble Home Minister has said that he would not like to add anything. I can appreciate it that there should be some restraint, but I should like to know whether he has investigated another aspect of the matter? Since a few months we are receiving reports of concentration

424. Fateh Singh, (1911-1972) was an Indiana leading Sikh religious and political leader and proponents of Sikh rights. Fateh Singh , and was a key figure in the Punjabi Suba movement along with Master Tara Singh. In 1962, Fateh Singh took control of the Shiromani Akali Dal and the SPGC. He was revered as Sant Fateh Singh among his followers. The 1966 debate pertained to the period when Fateh Singh had announced that he would again resort to a fast-unto death and self-immolation in protest about Chandigarh and some other portions being left out the new Punjab state that had come into being in November 1966. Fateh Singh was eventually talked out it by the Chief Minister of the newly formed Punjab state, Giani Gurmukh Singh Musafir and others.

425. *Rajya Sabha Debate* dated 26th August, 1966.

426. **Rajya Sabha Debate* dated 14th June, 1967.

of Pak troops on our borders. Since a few weeks operations by the anti-national elements in Naxalbari are being conducted and only three days back an aggressive move by China against our Indian embassy was launched. I want to know whether he has already conducted investigations in these affairs and whether there is any common link between the three. Are they the links of the same chain? May I know whether he would advise the MPs to look into these aspects also?

Y.B. Chavan: These are all matters which normally the Defence Ministry, the Home Ministry and the different branches of the government always take into consideration while making an assessment.

Calling Attention to a Matter of Urgent Public Importance Regarding Offical Copy of the CBI Report on Certain Allegations against Biju Patnaik[427]

D. Thengadi: In the first place the statement by the hon'ble minister is self-contradictory. On the one hand he says that all the parts of the CBI report can be available to the Orissa government because they are traced from their own files. On the other hand, he says that the C.B.I, report is a secret document. The two are self-contradictory. If everything is available to the Orissa government, then how is it treated as secret? If it is secret, how it is available to the Orissa government? Secondly, I want to know categorically whether the hon'ble minister considers it superfluous to hand over the report to the state government because according to him the C.B.I, report in the possession of the opposition is authentic? That I should like to know.

Thirdly, this is a very serious matter. It affects the relationship between the state government and the Central Government. It shall not always be a one-way traffic. One state government has requested you for a certain report. Tomorrow probably your ministry would demand a document from the state government. If your ministry or the government persists in such an adamant attitude, do you mean to say that we will be required to evolve a new code of conduct in a conference of Central Ministers and also state chief ministers to deal with all such matters, as relationship between

427. *Rajya Sabha Debate* dated 8th June, 1967. The Union Home Minister Gulzarilal Nanda and the Congress High Command ordered a CBI enquiry against Biju Patnaik pertaining to corruption that had taken place during his tenure as Chief Minister of Odisha. Biju Patnaik (1916-1997), one of the most well-known political figures of Odisha, post- independence, assumed charge as Chief Minister of Odisha from, for the first time in June 1961 and resigned in October 1963, ostensibly under the Kamaraj Plan.

the Central Government and the state governments? Is the government prepared for such a conference and evolve a new code of conduct between the Central and state governments?

Vidya Charan Shukla: There is no contradiction in what I have said earlier. As far as this question of providing the reports to the state government is concerned, I have already made it repeatedly clear that the notings or the report which are used for internal purposes in interministerial discussion, which are considered by the Cabinet, are not usually made available to any outside agency outside the Government of India and there is no question of evolving a code of conduct. This has been the standard practice so far.

In Response to the Statement Regarding Rishi Swarup Brahmachari[428]

While condemning severely the callous, brutal and inhuman attitude the government adopted in meting out such treatment to the dead body, I should like to ask whether the government is aware that it is for the disciples and not for the relatives of the *sannyasi* to perform the last rites? Secondly, in view of the fact that the situation is taking a serious turn, on account of the adamant attitude of the government, will the government consider the proposal for convening a round table

428. *Rajya Sabha Debate* dated 2nd December, 1966. Union Home Minister Y.B. Chavan's statement had thus described the episode, "Shri Rishi Swarup Brahmachari aged about 74 had undertaken a fast on the night between 22nd and 22rd November, 1966 in the Office of the All India Dharam Sangh, Delhi. Shri Rishi Swarup Brahmachari was reported to be a resident of Meerut District of Uttar Pradesh. He was found dead on 30th November at about 4 A.M. The District Authorities had suggested a postmortem examination, but on account of the opposition of the members of the Dharam Sangh, it was not performed. As desired by the members of the Dharm Sangh, the body of Shri Rishi Swarup Brahmachari was taketj by truck to Garh Mukteshwar for cremation. The truck left the Dharam Sangh office at 3.15 P.M. The cremation took place at about 10.30 A.M. on 1st December at Garh Mukteshwar. The last rites were performed by the grandson of the deceased in the presence of other relations."Chavan's statement was followed by Thengadi's intervention on the callous and careless attitude shown by the government towards Brahmachari. Rishi Swarup Brahmachari had undertaken the fast against cow-slaughter which had shaken the country in November that year with police firing on protestors in front of Parliament and killing sadhus. In course of the discussion Chavan, at one point, vehemently asserted his "Hindu" credentials when he said, "a *Sannyasi* does not recognise any relation. I know that...I am a Hindu and I am glad that I am a Hindu. I am not sorry for it. My "Sanskars" are the same." True to their vicious opposition to the cow-slaughter movement, Bhupesh Gupta called the movement "obscurantist and revivalist" and called on the government to come out "clearly and sharply against the anti-cow slaughter movement."

conference of all the concerned parties to thrash out the problem, because, as we know, the government did not take a stiff attitude towards Pakistan or China when there was aggression, but in this case against the cow-slaughter movement, the government has adopted a stiff attitude? May I know whether some such steps would be taken by the government in this matter?

Y.B. Chavan: The hon'ble member's questions are not related to this particular question. I regret that the hon'ble member, while asking questions, has used superlatives in his questions. No brutal treatment was shown. Naturally it was our duty to be very respectful to the body of the late *rishi*. We wanted to give all the help that was necessary. A truck was provided. Though a *sannyasi* does not recognise relations, the other relations do recognise him, the relations on the side of the *sannyasi*. He has no relations, but the other people do not forget that he was a *sannyasi*. If the disciples wanted to go, nobody prevented them from going.

In Response to the Statement Regarding Detention of Shankaracharya of Puri[429*]

D. Thengadi: Is the hon'ble Home Minister aware that his appeal to Jagatguru Shankaracharya has come rather too late in the day in the sense that his indefinite hunger strike was already declared? It was open to the hon'ble Home Minister to have made a similar appeal earlier. Secondly, he has said that it was a very difficult and delicate decision. Of course, there are balancing factors, but if, according to him, continuance of the indefinite hunger strike by Jagatguru Shankaracharya would provoke his followers, is he aware of the other side of the picture that the arrest of Jagatguru

429. *Rajya Sabha Debate* dated 22nd November, 1966. Union Home Minister Y.B. Chavan's statement weas as follows: "the House is aware that agitation for a complete ban on cow slaughter is continuing in different parts of the country in spite of the policy statement made on behalf of Government on 4th November. On 20th November Jagatguru Swami Niranjana Deva Tirtha of Puri Commenced an indefinite fast in the compound of the Dharam Sangh, Kash-meri Gate, Delhi. Delhi Administration, who are responsible for the maintenance of law and order in the Union Territory of Delhi, gave full consideration to the likely repercussions of the fast undertaken by Swami Niranjana Deva Tirtha especially in the light of the unfortunate events of November 7, 1966. In their view the action of Swami Niranjana Deva Tirth was prejudicial to the maintenance of public order in Delhi. He has accordingly been detained under section 3(a) (ii) of the Preventive Detention Act in pursuance of an order issued by the Deputy Commissioner, Delhi." Following Chavan's statement Atal Bihari Vajpayee intervened asking him whether it was believable that the decision to detain Shankaracharya was only that of the Delhi administration and why was he detained despite assuring the authorities that his agitation would be entirely peaceful.

Shankaracharya would be more provocative and it is to the credit of his followers and also followers of the *'Go Raksha Andolan Samiti'*[430] that they have restrained themselves? They did not allow themselves to be provoked, though the government deliberately or inadvertently took such a step which was provocative. Is he aware of it?

Y.B. Chavan: That is why I described the decision as rather a difficult decision and delicate decision. That is why I am making an appeal to his followers, the most important and influential followers who are sitting in this hon'ble House to give some sort of co-operation, and that in order to keep peaceful conditions in the country, they should persuade him by supporting my plea and appeal to Shankaracharya to give up his fast.

In Response to the Statement Regarding Grave Concern Reported to have been Expressed by Assam Chief Minister about Activities of Saboteurs in Assam*[431]

The Minister of State in the Ministry of Home Affairs and also Minister of Defence Supplies in the Ministry of Defence (*Jaisukhlal Hathi*): Sir, government have obtained the text of the statement made by the Chief Minister, Assam, [B.P. Chaliha served as Chief Minister of Assam from 1957-1970] to which attention has been called. There is nothing in the statement that is not already known to this House. The Chief Minister's statement referred only to Pakistan's help to subversive and anti-national elements in this country, like the MNF [Mizo National Front] rebels and the Naga hostiles. The Chief Minister especially mentioned the training camps run in Pakistan where training in guerrilla warfare is imparted to the MNF rebels and Naga undergrounds. In this connection, the House will recall that information available to government regarding the assistance provided by Pakistan to the Naga hostiles and MNF rebels has already been placed before this House in reply to a number of questions and the whole subject has been thoroughly discussed.

The Chief Minister of Assam also mentioned the brisk war preparations going on in Pakistan. In fact, while doing so, he quoted the Union Defence Minister's recent statement in Parliament on the subject. He ended his statement by saying that Government of India as well as the state government were aware of these activities and were taking all

430. Forum formed to spearhead the movement demanding ban on cow-slaughter in 1966. Then Shankaracharya of Puri, Swami Niranjana Deva Tirtha, had undertaken a fast, pressing for the ban on cow-slaughter.

431. *Rajya Sabha Debate* dated 5th September, 1966.

necessary steps to meet the situation. That states the correct position and I have nothing to add by way of comment.

D. Thengadi: The explanation given by the hon'ble minister that the Chief Minister had in his mind only activities of the Mizos and the Nagas is not convincing, for he has referred to forces which have been let loose all over the country to create subversive activities. It is obvious that the Mizos and the Nagas alone are not referred to because they are not scattered all over the country. So I want to know what particular forces the Chief Minister has referred to when he says that all over the country subversive activities are there and, secondly, what effective steps have been taken so far by the government to isolate Indian saboteurs and agents provocateur from the inimical powers abroad by sealing the border? What is the difficulty in our sealing the border?

Jaisukhlal Hathi: Now, so far as the statement of the Chief Minister of Assam is concerned, I requested the Assam government to send me the relevant extract of the statement and for the purpose of clarifying anything, if any doubt is there, I shall only read out what he has mentioned:

> "Mr. Speaker, sir, particular news item referred to by the hon'ble member has given some information with regard to some preparations that are going on in Pakistan for subversive activities inside our country. Hon'ble members, in the meantime, must have seen the statements issued by the Defence Minister... He has categorically stated in his statement that there is very brisk preparation in Pakistan against India. Along with it, there is evidence to show that Pakistan, through their various secret agencies, have been trying to organise subversive activities in our country. There are reports that they have been running training camps inside Pakistan officered by Chinese in guerrilla warfare and hon'ble members are aware how Pakistan has been helping the underground Nagas and Mizo National Front volunteers with arms and ammunition and otherwise. The Government of India as well as the state government are quite aware of these activities and we are taking all necessary steps to prevent creating further mischief by these forces."

So far as subversive activities are concerned, it may refer to other agents, who may be working as the agents of these countries. That may be the interpretation. Now, so far as sealing the border is concerned, on one side we have completely sealed it. On the other side, we have increased our security forces and the Border Police has been strengthened. We have taken all precautions to see that the border is safe from infiltration.

Motions Regarding Reports of the Union Public Service Commission for 1962-1963, 1963-64 and 1964-65*[432]

D. Thengadi: In the first place, I would like to request the minister to assure us that in the future there will be no occasion for us to discuss reports for two or three years simultaneously. I would suggest that the number of posts and services, which have been excluded from the Commission's purview from time to time since the issue of the UPSC (Exemption from Consultation) Regulations, 1958, and which remained so excluded as on 1st April, 1965, should be progressively reduced, emergency or no emergency. In regard to matters mentioned in sub-clause (e) of Clause (3) of Article 320 of the Constitution,[433] the government should not be allowed to ignore the authority of the Commission.

Regarding selection tests, I want to suggest that personality tests should be considered at least as important as the written examination. Equal marks should be allowed for both because the recruitment is not merely for clerical jobs but for executive services also. The personality test should include aptitude test and for these tests, the techniques of the aptitude tests should be adopted from the Western countries. Modern advanced knowledge of psychology should be brought to bear in this respect. At least some members of the Personality Test Board should be very well acquainted with modern psychology.

The decision of the government to reduce the maximum marks for personality test is, according to me, a retrograde step. In this context,

---

432. **Rajya Sabha Debate* dated 4th April, 1966.

433. (a) Clause (3): The Union Public Service Commission or the State Public Service Commission, as the case may be, shall be consulted.

(b) Sub Clause (e): "on any claim for the award of a pension in respect of injuries sustained by a person while serving under the Government of India or the government of a state or ... under the Government of an Indian state, in a civil capacity, and any question as to the amount of any such award, and it shall be the duty of a Public Service Commission to advise on any matter so referred to them and on any other matter which the President, or, as the case may be, the Governor of the state, may refer to them: provided that the President as respects the all-India services and also as respects other services and posts in connection with the affairs of the Union, and the Governor, as respects other services and posts in connection with the affairs of a State, may make regulations specifying the matters in which either generally, or in any particular class of case or in any particular circumstances, it shall not be necessary for a Public Service Commission to be consulted."

it is necessary to insist that the test should be conducted not merely in English, but also in Hindi and other regional languages. Firstly, it would be unwise to deprive the country of the talents simply because the persons concerned are not proficient in expressing themselves in English and secondly, it is high time that English should be replaced by Hindi and other regional languages.

This may lead us to the problem of evaluation in Hindi and English or other languages and to maintain the standard in both languages. It would be necessary to decide the percentage allotted to matter and manner. Though form and content cannot be dissociated, still it would be possible for us to evaluate form and content separately. The candidate should also be acquainted with our national objectives. We are in the process of development of national reconstruction and it is necessary that these candidates who are to become the pillars of the nation, are very well acquainted with the objectives of the nation and also with the psychological climate suited to those objectives. It is claimed that the UPSC is not a money-making machine. It is as it should be but there are instances which give rise to doubts about the veracity of this statement. For example, on 23rd October, 1965, the UPSC advertised for the posts of Income tax Officers in the Ministry of Finance. The closing date for the applications was 6th December, 1965. After a lapse of nearly six months, the UPSC has informed some of the candidates that they are not eligible to appear for the ITO competitive examination when many of them have spent a lot of money and time in preparing for the said examination. Originally the minimum qualification prescribed was: (i) degree of a university; and (ii) five years' experience in a responsible position in a government department. The UPSC did not specify as to what was meant by 'responsible position'. Now the Commission has come out with the decision that only assistants of five years' standing or persons drawing a basic salary of Rs. 250 will be allowed to appear for the examination. Now a fee of Rs. 28 was to be sent along with the application form. A sum of Rs. 15 was to be returned to the candidates found unsuitable for the examination. The remaining amount, the balance of Rs. 13, is unreturnable. It is pertinent to ask whether the UPSC would be justified in retaining with itself the balance of Rs. 13 in each case, since a number of persons who were disqualified by the subsequent notification, applied and submitted their fees under a wrong impression. Who is responsible for this mistake? Is it the ministry or the Commission but whoever is responsible, the candidates are to suffer. The original notification was ambiguous and vague and because of this vagueness or ambiguity of the advertisement, these people have spent their money and time. This is unjust, unfair and it goes to prove that the UPSC also aspires in a way to become a mere money-making machine.

The UPSC should be like Caesar's wife, above suspicion. I am sorry to say that I have come across certain instances which are not above board. For example, I will cite some concrete cases. In four consecutive tests, a Scheduled Caste candidate was refused selection though he was better qualified than those who were actually selected and the posts were reserved for Scheduled Castes and Scheduled Tribes only. The occasions were:

(i) Recruitment to the post of Research Officer (Climatology), 1960.

(ii) Recruitment to the post of Research Officer (Artificial Insemination), 1962.

(iii) Recruitment to the post of Research Officer (Farm Animal Genetics), 1963.

I do not say that an undeserving candidate should be selected only because he belongs to the Scheduled Caste but I do insist that no candidate should be discriminated against, simply because he belongs to the Scheduled Caste. True, in keeping with Article 335[434] of the Constitution, the claims of the members of the Scheduled Castes and the Scheduled Tribes should be taken into consideration consistently with the maintenance of efficiency of administration but the case I am citing is a case of discrimination affecting adversely the much-prized efficiency of administration. Steps should be taken to further reduce the time lag between declaration of the final results by the Commission and the appointment of selected candidates. The number of cases where the offer of appointment was delayed by the government is quite impressive – 160 in 1963-64, and 171 in 1964-65.

434. "The claims of the members of the Scheduled Castes and the Scheduled Tribes shall be taken into consideration, consistently with the maintenance of efficiency of administration, in the making of appointments to services and posts in connection with the affairs of the Union or of a state:
Provided that nothing in this article shall prevent in making of any provision in favour of the members of the Scheduled Castes and the Scheduled Tribes for relaxation in qualifying marks in any examination or lowering the standards of evaluation, for reservation in matters of promotion to any class or classes of services or posts in connection with the affairs of the Union or of a state."

The would-be candidates from the Scheduled Castes and the Scheduled Tribes should be given special, appropriate, intensive training before they appear for the examination. The number of training centres for them should be increased. In view of the inadequacy of number of suitable candidates for the fields related to medical, metallurgical, engineering, scientific and technical, and educational, that is, teaching posts, it seems imperative to popularise these fields and to take care of the proper standard of instruction in them. For these fields, apart from advertisements in newspapers, it would be advisable to circulate information to students regarding these posts through educational institutions.

The number of posts for which requisitions were cancelled after advertisement, but before interview, was 3 in 1963-64, and 21 in 1964-65. The number of posts for which requisitions were cancelled after advertisement and interview was 5 in 1963-64 and 13 in 1964-65. Who is responsible for this? The Ministries or the Commission? The reasons for cancellation are stated and can always be stated. But this is an unfortunate trend that deserves to be checked immediately. The candidates suffering losses, physical, psychological and also financial, must be compensated for properly. The 12 Class II officers of the Ministry of Rehabilitation, who are still out of job, should be provided with alternative employment as early as possible.

There should be a more sustained and liberal effort to absorb retired military officers in suitable civil posts.

The new scheme, drawn up during 1964, under which overseas candidates could be assessed along with candidates in India, not only for specific posts for which requisitions may be pending with the Commission at a point of time, but for all posts which may be entrusted to them for recruitment within a period of a year or so, is commendable – an improvement over the earlier system. It needs, however, to be watched carefully. The problem of Indian talent abroad, being made available to meet the requirements of the country, had always been a knotty one. In the light of this experience, there should be introduced further suitable changes in this scheme.

Sir, the exclusion of talents on the basis of mere prejudice would be criminal and suicidal. I should like to know whether highly qualified candidates, placing their services at the disposal of the country, were not denied such opportunity simply because they were associated with the Rashtriya Swayamsevak Sangh. The Rashtriya Swayamsevak Sangh is a cultural organisation moulding the character of patriotic citizens, and the talents associated with this organisation should be utilised for the work of national reconstruction. I should like to know from the government what exactly their policy on this point is.

Sir, it is regrettable that the Government of India does not accept the advice of the Commission on a number of points. The reaction of the government to the advice of the Commission on the disciplinary action against an officer of the Indian Police Service is a glaring example of the government's high-handedness. This is a case of bungling on the part of the Government of India, which has clearly disregarded the authority of the Commission. People are bound to lose faith in the government's sense of justice and fairness if such examples are multiplied.

There must be specified some independent authority to which are referred the cases regarding which there is disagreement or difference of opinion between the Commission and the government. To my mind, the Attorney General would be the appropriate authority for this purpose.

There should be no irregularity in implementing the Recruitment Rules approved by the Commission. If the ministries hold a different view on any matter, it is open for them to convey the same to the Commission and request that the latter should change or modify its decision. But, without formal approval of the Commission, no changes in the Recruitment Rules should be introduced. The lapse, this year on the part of the Ministry of Community Development, is regrettable.

The decision that cases relating to the grant of quasi-permanency to officers governed by the Central Civil Services (Temporary Service) Rules and to those governed by the civilians in Defence Services (Temporary Service) Rules, need not be referred to the Commission, is unwise and likely to give rise to cases of discrimination and favouritism. In these cases, reference to the Commission must be made compulsory.

As in previous years, cases where consultation with the Commission was inordinately delayed, and cases where appointments made were irregular ab initio, continued to occur during the year 1964-65 also. According to the Commission, the number of delayed references relating to temporary appointments was 35 in 1963-64, and 59 in 1964-65. Probably, in reality the number is greater. This undesirable tendency is on the increase. This must be put to an end. The departments should not be allowed to thus bypass the Commission.

Even after so many years of functioning of the Commission, we are not free from the cases of irregularities in appointments. This is a sad commentary on the conscientiousness of the government departments. Effective measures must be introduced so as to ensure that the *Sixteenth Report* of the Union Public Service Commission does not contain any case of such irregularity.

Reference to Incidents Reported from Thanjavur District[435]

D. Thengadi: May I, through you, draw the attention of the government to the gruesome incidents reported from Thanjavur district. Forty-three persons have been burnt alive according to reports in a faction fight. Obviously four factors have been responsible: (1) casteism; (2) inefficiency of the Police Department; (3) latitude given to local landlords for bringing agricultural workers from outside to replace the local workers, and (4) non-extension of the Minimum Wages Act to agricultural workers throughout the country. May I know from the government whether the Home Ministry has received any report or asked for any report from the state government and whether in this connection the Home Ministry has given any advice to the state government?

□

435. *Rajya Sabha Debate* dated 27th December, 1968. Thanjavur in Tamil Nadu. On 25th December, 1968, 44 members of the Dalit community were killed by a gang let loose on them by their landlords for demanding higher wages. C.N. Annadurai as Chief Minister headed the DMK ministry in the state.

11
Education

Speaking on the UGC [University Grants Commission], Thengadi admired the Commission for doing a lot to improve the pay scales and service conditions of the teachers. He felt the need to make agriculture courses more attractive and suggested that state engineering colleges should also be placed under UGC. Thengadi also stressed on the need for autonomy for universities. He suggested that grants should be distributed only after proper scrutiny and education should be separated from politics. Thengadi wanted the medium of teaching to be Indian languages and felt the need for a well-organised translation service as well.

Welcoming some of the unique features of the Jawaharlal Nehru University Bill, Thengadi said that the post of Chancellor was superfluous. He suggested that not more than one Rector should be provided. According to him, not only the teachers but the educationists also should be entitled to become Vice Chancellors. He was in favour of removal of teachers on the ground of misconduct. He cited Buddhist tradition to put forward his views that universities should be named only after particular individuals, howsoever great the individual may be.

While speaking on the Benaras Hindu University (Amendment) Bill,[436] *Thengadi strongly opposed the dropping of the word 'Hindu' and suggested that the original intentions of the revered founder of this university must be respected.*

Motion Regarding Report of the University Grants Commission[437]

Since the hon'ble Minister of Education has to leave the House earlier, I will take my last point first. I support the amendment by A.D. Mani and urge upon the hon'ble minister that an impartial enquiry should be held

436. Amendment to the Banaras Hindu University Act.

437. *Rajya Sabha Debate* dated 23rd November, 1964.

into the student disturbances in Orissa. I also support the amendments of Vimal Kumar Chordia.

Regarding the medium of instruction, we have entered a vicious circle. The Indian languages are not competent to become the mediums of instruction because they suffer from certain disabilities and we know that those disabilities shall never be removed unless and until they are actually recognised as mediums of instruction. Therefore, this is a vicious circle. No hen without an egg and no egg without a hen. This circle has to be broken; otherwise, there will be no end to the domination of English. We have no particular hatred for the English language. They say it is an international language; there are other international languages also. We aspire that our own Indian languages should become international languages as early as possible but, at the same time, while we may give the status of international languages not only to English but to German, French and other languages also, as medium of instruction, English should be discarded and our national languages should be recognised. To my mind, all the languages spoken by Indians are national languages and Hindi is the state as well as the national language. Therefore, all the national languages should be recognised as mediums of instruction. I should like our hon'ble Minister of Education to enlighten us on one point – whether the advanced non-Anglo-Saxon countries have accepted English as medium of instruction and if not, whether they have suffered for want of English as medium of instruction?

Now, I congratulate the University Grants Commission because it has done a lot to improve the pay scales and service conditions of our teachers. Our teachers have been asked to suffer and sacrifice but this advice can be given to all sections of the population and why should teachers alone be asked to carry a cross on their shoulders? I would point out one fact that though much has been done, yet much remains to be done and their pay scales are not as attractive as those obtaining or prevailing in business, administration or industry. Even the pay scales prescribed by the University Grants Commission are not implemented in some of the universities, such as Madras, Baroda, Utkal, Jammu & Kashmir, Osmania and Andhra. Dearness Allowance and medical facilities are denied to the teachers in three Central Universities of Delhi, Aligarh and the Benaras Hindu University. The associated colleges of the Allahabad University have denied their teaching staff the pay scales prescribed by the University Grants Commission. I know that there are technical niceties involved but

I should like to request the University Grants Commission not to stand on technical niceties but to allow these teachers to profit from the pay scales granted by the Commission.

Again, in Delhi University when a college teacher is taken into the University, he is denied his service benefits such as Provident Fund and leave facilities. That should not be the case. Further, in the colleges of Delhi University, it has been complained that the staff ratio is not properly maintained and the University Grants Commission should go into this matter. The leave rules should be liberalised in favour of young teachers. Then, evening classes for B.Com. and M.Com. should be conducted in Delhi. The University Grants Commission should maintain a panel of all-India qualified teachers so that different universities can draw from that panel according to their requirements. For qualifying teachers, properly in-service training should also be organised. Apart from pay scales, there is the question of quarters for the teaching staff. This is an urgent question and it should be given the priority it deserves. All this would mean allocation of more funds. At the same time, unless these funds are allocated, the teaching profession will not be as attractive as it should be.

Then, according to the report it seems that some of the important subjects, which deserve priority, are not drawing sufficient number of students; agriculture, for example. I will not dilate upon the importance of agriculture which is the biggest industry of India but the percentage of students taking up agriculture is very poor, probably the lowest with the only exception of France, so far as other civilised countries are concerned. The agriculture courses should be made more attractive and also cheaper. Then, the percentage of students taking up technical education is also very poor. We need more engineering colleges and technological institutions. In this connection, I would say one thing that the state engineering colleges should also be placed under the University Grants Commission. Engineers should be given more effective representation in the All India Council of Technical Education and the distinction between higher and lower courses, that is, the degree and the diploma courses, should be properly appreciated and both should not be placed under the same body.

Regarding grants, first of all I should like to suggest that the grants should be distributed only after proper scrutiny and without undue haste. At least for some specific objectives there should be total grants. All grants should not be matching grants. Again, the grants should be selective for more essential objectives; for hostels, for instance, and not for the

University Film Council though the latter has its own utility. The grants from the University Grants Commission for increasing the salaries of teachers and for providing other amenities to them should be continued and this is not fantastic for at least a quarter of a century. I may remind the House that in the USA, similar recurring expenses are provided for about that period. Our universities should be granted autonomy. Even in England, the University Grants Committee was devised as via media through which economic aid could be obtained without inviting direct departmental control. Our Vice-Chancellors should not be official nominees. They should be duly elected but they should be elected from amongst the educationists.

There is much discussion about starting of fresh universities. It is true that power politics has entered here also. Actually, education should be divorced from politics but here certain fresh universities are started because of power politics. Certain universities that have been approved are not started because of power politics. I am referring to Kanpur and Meerut. I may also suggest that for humanities, wireless universities as suggested by Mr. Harold Wilson[438] in England, can be organised even in India.

As I said that the medium of instruction should be Indian languages, it becomes imperative that the translation work should be expedited – translation of scientific and technical terminology from foreign to our Indian languages. There should be one central agency for the preservation and utilisation of manuscripts. A translation service should be efficiently organised for translating select passages of literature from one Indian language into all other Indian languages. That would bring about National Integration. For example, why should not the entire Thirukkural by Thiruvalluvar be translated into all other Indian languages? Similarly, the southern languages should be made compulsory in the northern universities. Our libraries and laboratories require to be better equipped. In Oxford, for example, there are no less than three million books, while our Calcutta University Library has less than six lakhs. Laboratories also require expansion and better equipment.

The UGC has realised the importance of hostel accommodation. I should also like to suggest that as in England it is high time that we introduced the system of authorised houses and approved houses for students' lodging. (time bell rings). With these words, I conclude.

438. Prime Minister of the United Kingdom, 1964-1970 and 1974-1976.

The Jawaharlal Nehru University Bill, 1964[439]

Today we read in the newspapers that the University Grants Commission has asked the proposed Raipur University not to name itself after the late Pt. Ravishankar Shukla. Now, the university they have suggested in this Bill should not be named after personalities. We know they are particular about the decision of the government regarding the Raipur University. Therefore, what I suggest is that we should not adopt double standards.

Secondly, the size of this university is also important. True, Delhi requires another university, but, at the same time, the question of raising a memorial to Pt. Jawaharlal Nehru should not be confused with the problem of ever-increasing student population of a big city. Delhi is already a problem city with so many problems – problem of accommodation, problem of water, problem of electricity and all that. Therefore, a more appropriate thing would be to situate this university in a place like Allahabad. I think Allahabad is better suited for this particular purpose.

Yet there was another subject which always fascinated Pt. Jawaharlal Nehru – the problem of National Integration. I feel that it is necessary to conduct scientific research in the problem of Indian culture. The word 'culture' denotes a trend of impression on the mind of the society which is peculiar to itself. It has a cumulative effect towards passion, emotion, speech and action throughout its history. The problem of National Integration has become extremely difficult in the absence of scientific research in Indian culture. I think if such a study is undertaken, it will bifurcate culture from religion, so that the compact national culture of India, which is the outcome of its history of thousands of years, will be properly brought forth.

The Jawaharlal Nehru University Bill, 1964: Continued[440]

I welcome some of the unique features of this proposed university, for example, its truly national character, introduction of some interdisciplinary courses, its non-affiliating character, association of some eminent organisations without their losing in the least their much-priced autonomy or their dignity, constitution of the academic advisory committee and machinery for reviewing the progress of the university.

439. *Rajya Sabha Debate* dated 1st September, 1965.
440. *Rajya Sabha Debate* dated 2nd December, 1965.

[*Deputy Chairman in the Chair*]

While these, according to me, are some of the welcome features, there are others which are not quite as welcome. Proposing to take the first question last that is about the name of the university–I will just. . . some of the points, because in clause by clause consideration we will take them up in detail.

To my mind, the post of Chancellor is really superfluous. After apportionment of the top responsibilities between the Visitor and the Vice-Chancellor, I wonder what exactly is left behind for the Chancellor to do. There is a trend, and it is a healthy trend to do away with merely ornamental or decorative posts, and therefore I think that this university can dispense with the post of Chancellor.

We also should not provide for more than one Rector. I feel that an increase in the number of Rectors will reduce the efficiency of administration. I can understand the utility of de-centralisation of administration, but in the case of a university or any educational institution, unified supervision and unified management would be more helpful.

I do not subscribe to the view that only teachers should be entitled to become Vice-Chancellors, but at least it should be an educationist who should be a Vice-Chancellor and also the powers of Vice-Chancellor should not be as unlimited or autocratic as they have been laid down in the present Bill.

In the Second Schedule, the power of the Registrar to take disciplinary action should be subject to subsequent approval of the Vice-Chancellor, and if that is not done, at least the employee should be given the right to appeal to the Vice-Chancellor, not only in cases of the penalty of the withholding of increment, but also in cases of all penalties, penalty of every variety. Similarly, an employee should have a right to appeal to the Executive Council against the order of the Vice-Chancellor, whether the penalty imposed is that of dismissal or of a less severe type. It has been laid down that a person shall be disqualified for being chosen as, or for being a member of any of the authorities of the University if among other things "he has been convicted by a court of law of an offence involving moral turpitude and sentenced in respect thereof to imprisonment for not less than six months." Now this qualifying clause seems to weaken the main purpose of this provision. If he is convicted of an offence involving moral turpitude, that should suffice. About the duration of the sentence, there should be no qualifying clause because moral turpitude is moral turpitude, and if we want to set an example of any ideal before the students, it is necessary that we should be very strict in this respect.

Regarding removal of teachers on the ground of 'misconduct', I am all for it and I would urge upon the authorities to be very strict on this point. But may I suggest that the term 'misconduct' is so vague and it is likely to be misused. The term must be properly defined, at least as properly as it is possible, lest any member of the teaching fraternity should be discriminated against. The same holds good in the case of the non-teaching staff also.

I welcome the provision for voluntarily membership of students' organisation and also the provision of the constitution of a council of students' affairs consisting of teachers and students. This would go a long way in establishing cordial relationship between the teacher and the student. In this context, I should like to insist on the proper maintenance of the teacher and the student ratio, 1:20.

Now I come to the First Schedule. It is stated that this university is expected to fulfil the ideals that Jawaharlal Nehru stood and worked for during his lifetime. Now all of us have a very high regard for the late revered Pandit Jawaharlal Nehru. He was one of the greatest leaders of humanity and scientific outlook was his special characteristic. Now through this wording, I think we are trying to create almost a church out of the theories or ideals that he stood for. This task, howsoever noble, comes hardly within the legitimate jurisdiction of a university. This is the work of a church, not of a university. The university should be expected to encourageand to conduct research in the philosophy of Pandit Nehru, but not to 'fulfil the ideals' he stood and worked for. Madam, through this fulfillment of the ideals through the medium of a university, I fear we will be carving an 'ism' out of his philosophy, and this is something damaging to the personality of the late revered Pandit Jawaharlal Nehru. This is very unfortunate because, as all of us know, Pandit Jawaharlal Nehru's thinking was dynamic, not static, and every 'ism' is necessarily, invariably and inevitably a closed system of thinking. The moment it ceases to be closed, it ceases to be an 'ism' and therefore, to carve out Nehruism would be doing some damage to the great dynamic personality of Pandit Jawaharlal Nehru. In this connection, it is worth noting that Lord Buddha has said something very relevant and we all know how Pandit Nehru respected Lord Buddha. Now he says I am quoting a translation by Dr Ambedkar –

"Do not believe what your teacher tells you, merely out of respect for the teacher. But whatsoever, after due examination and analysis, you find to be conducive to the good, the benefit, the welfare of all beings that doctrine believe, and cling to and take as your guide." "Be lamps unto thyselves," that was his last advice to his disciple. Buddha, whom Pandit Nehru respected so much, was opposed to scripturalism, and also to the personality cult. He observed, and again I am quoting Dr Ambedkar's translation–"If principle needs the authority of man, it is no principle. If every time it becomes necessary to invoke the name of the founder to enforce the authority of *Dharma*, then it is no *Dharma*."

On this ground Buddha refused to appoint his successor. He said "*Dharma* must be its own successor." As Dr Ambedkar points out, Buddha whom, I again repeat, Jawaharlal Nehru respected so much kept his teachings separate from his personality. Principle, Buddha remarked, must live by itself, and not by authority of any man, not even of himself. That is why I feel that none of us can respect Pandit Jawaharlal Nehru more than what Kassyappa, the President of the first Buddhist Congregation held after the death of Buddha, praised and respected Lord Buddha, and in that first congregation, Kassyappa conducted only two enquiries to the August assembly, about the *Dharma* of the body and about the *vinaya* of the body, and nothing about his personal biography or life. I think that this spirit is necessary for maintaining the dignity of the personality we are going to respect.

Regarding the name of the university, much has been said. I need not repeat the decision taken by the Ministry regarding the naming of the university, also the endorsement of the decision by the university Grants Commission, but I may only say that Pandit Jawaharlal Nehru himself would not have appreciated or liked the idea of naming any university after his own name for the simple reason that we all know how sincerely, how earnestly he respected the late revered Mahatma Gandhi. But still, during his lifetime, he never tried to set up – he could have done it, had he wanted to, any university after the name of Mahatma Gandhi. We also know that in our India, also in the Buddhist tradition, which Nehruji loved so much, universities had been set up. But they were not named after any particular individual, howsoever great the individual may be. We have had the Nalanda University. It was not named after Buddha or Ashoka. As Carlyle said, 'No truly great religious teacher ever intended to found a new sect.' Did Pandit Nehru teach anything which was not part of our national culture?

[*Vice-Chairman* (*M.P. Bhargava*) in the Chair].

D. Thengadi: I agree with the hon'ble Education Minister when he says that whatever was taught to us by Pandit Nehru has become a part of our national culture. I want to supplement it by adding that whatever he taught was also a part of our national heritage, and in this sense I think that, if we tried to name the university after Pandit Jawaharlal Nehru, we would be trying to degenerate the dynamic personality of Pandit Nehru into the status of a sectarian leader because, as we have seen in a number of cases, in times historical and modern, out of the misguided over-enthusiasm of followers, persons who stood for rationalism, for scientific outlook, have been reduced to the status of leaders of ordinary sects. I think that this injustice should not be done to the late revered Pandit Jawaharlal Nehru.

The Jawaharlal Nehru University Bill, 1964:[441] Continued

D. Thengadi: I have some clarification to seek. Does the word 'secular' mean non-spiritual and is it in this sense that we have accepted the term 'secular'?

D. Thengadi: Madam, I move.

5. "That at page 1, line 10, for the word 'hall', the word '*niwas*' be substituted."

8. "That at page 2, line 6, for the words 'Jawaharlal Nehru University' the words '*Rashtriya Vishwavidyalaya*' be substituted."

(These amendments also stood in the name of V.M. Chordia).

The questions were proposed.

Deputy Chairman: Mr. Thengadi, you have your amendments.

D. Thengadi: Madam, in this context I want to suggest a change for the word 'hall' occurring here. I am not very particular about using the word '*Niwas*' that I have suggested. All that I want is some word from an Indian language should be used instead of 'hall' which is an English word. This university is going to be a national thing and it is high time that we dispensed with English terminology.

As for my other amendment, I am happy that the hon'ble Minister of Education [M.C. Chagla] has appreciated some of the points raised by us the other day. Though I am not a steno, I may try to quote him. He said that this university stands for "certain basic national principles Pandit Nehru believed in." Also, that "these are the principles to which the whole nation subscribes." He also said that this university was "not to study

441. *Rajya Sabha Debate* dated 6th December, 1965.

the principles as Nehru believed in them." As a matter of fact, we are next to none in our high regard for Pandit Nehru, and my hon'ble friend M.M. Dharia has done us a great service by quoting extensively from what Atal Bihari Vajpayee said in this House while paying his tribute to the memory of the late Jawaharlal Nehru. That is precisely the reason why we should try to see that no injustice is done to the memory of Pandit Nehru, which we may do, though with the best of intentions. To put the thing in a nutshell, what I want to say is, whether it is intended by the hon'ble Education Minister today or not, in course of time, this is going to convert this university into a sort of school of thought, if the First Schedule is adopted. Therefore, we want to repeat that this formulation of an ism is going to do some injustice and damage to the memory of Pandit Nehru, and that for two reasons. I shall try to put it as briefly as I can. First of all, isms are static, while situations are dynamic. Again, all isms are close systems of thought while the frontiers of human knowledge are ever expanding. And so, I think to convert any institution into a school of thought and associate that institution with the name of any great dignitary would be doing injustice to that great dignitary. As a matter of fact, the facts placed before us by the hon'ble Education Minister are all correct, but I am unhappy to see that on the basis of those correct facts he has according to me – I may be wrong and I shall be happy if I am wrong in this – the conclusions drawn do not naturally and logically flow from the facts he has mentioned. Therefore, I request that in view of the fact that, as mentioned by the hon'ble the Education Minister, these are principles to which the whole nation subscribes, the name *Rashtriya Vishwavidyalaya* would be more appropriate and it should be adopted.

D. Thengadi: I may request the hon'ble minister to...

Deputy Chairman: He has opposed the amendment.

M.C. Chagla: May I point out that both the Delhi University Act and the Aligarh University Act have the word 'hall' used in them and it is more than a hostel. It is not merely meant for students residing, but also for students' activities and so on. It is an English word, of course, but we all use English words and the whole Bill is in English. So, I said I oppose the amendment.

D. Thengadi: I beg leave of the House to withdraw my amendment No. 5. *Amendment No. 5 was, by leave, withdrawn.

D. Thengadi: Madam, I move:

12. "That at page 2, line 11, the words The first Chancellor and' be deleted."

(The amendment also stood in the name of V.M. Chordia).

The questions were proposed.

D. Thengadi: As the hon'ble Education Minister has put it, this is going to be a unique university and I think in this university, particularly superfluous posts should not be there. I have not been able to understand the propriety of having a Chancellor's post and after the apportionment of some responsibility between the Visitor and the Vice-Chancellor, there remains nothing left to be done by the Chancellor. I will, therefore, request the hon'ble Education Minister to make this university unique in this respect also. All the other universities are having these ornamental posts and our unique university should drop this convention.

D. Thengadi: Madam, I beg leave to withdraw my amendment No. 12.

* Amendment No. 12 was, by leave, withdrawn.

D. Thengadi: Madam, I move:

16. "That at page 2, lines 20 to 22, the words 'and by the example and influence of its corporate life and in particular the objects set out in the First Schedule' be deleted."

(The amendment also stood in the name of V.M. Chordia).

D. Thengadi: Madam, the arguments in favour of this amendment have already been put forward and I need not repeat them. Whatever I have said against naming this university after any great dignitary remains in this case also. Either the First Schedule should be dropped or should be redrafted.

Clause 5–Powers of the University

D. Thengadi: Madam, I move:

19. "That at page 2, lines 24-25, the words 'including correspondence courses' be deleted."

(The amendment also stood in the name of V.M. Chordia).

D. Thengadi: Madam, I move:

22. "That at page 2, after line 29, the following be inserted, namely:

'(1A) to provide for instruction and research in *Bharatiya* culture, comparative study of religions and of Western socio-economic philosophies;'

(The amendment also stood in the name of V.M. Chordia).

D. Thengadi: Madam, I move:

24. "That at page 2, lines 30-31, for the words 'within the Union territory of Delhi or outside that territory' the words 'in India' be substituted."

(The amendment also stood in the name of V.M. Chordia).

D. Thengadi: Madam, I move:

30. "That at page 3, at the end of line 24, after the word 'recognition' the words 'subject to subsequent approval of the Visitor' be inserted."

(The amendment also stood in the name of V.M. Chordia).

D. Thengadi: Madam, I move:

32. "That at page 3, lines 26 to 28, the words 'having in view the promotion of purposes and objects similar to those of the university' be deleted."

(The amendment also stood in the name of V.M. Chordia).

D. Thengadi: Madam, I move:

34. "That at page 4, line 11, and the words 'representing such property' be deleted."

(The amendment also stood in the name of V.M. Chordia).

The questions were proposed.

D. Thengadi: Madam, regarding my amendment No. 19, I am prepared to withdraw it provided the hon'ble Education Minister assures me that the quality of education will not suffer adversely because of these correspondence courses.

M.C. Chagla: The university will not introduce correspondence courses the quality of which is likely to suffer. It will take every precaution to see that quality is maintained.

Deputy Chairman: Are you prepared to accept the amendment?

M.C. Chagla: No, no.

D. Thengadi: Madam, I withdraw my amendment No. 19.

Deputy Chairman: You may do it later when I put the amendment. Is the Minister accepting any amendment?

D. Thengadi: In amendment No. 22, I want that at page 2, after line 29, the following be inserted, namely:

'(1A) to provide for instruction and research in *Bharatiya* culture, comparative study of religions and of Western socio-economic philosophies'.

As our hon'ble minister said, being a democrat, he is not nervous about or afraid of study in different philosophies, socio-economic and political. I think it is necessary that such studies should be conducted. Similarly, it is necessary that there should be comparative study of religions because I again beg to differ with our hon'ble Education Minister on this point. The word 'secular', as our friend, Prof. Ruthnaswamy has explained, has also a meaning 'sceptical of religious truth or opposed to religious education'. I think that secularism of our revered Mahatmaji was not opposed to religious instruction. It supported instructions in all the religions, and in that sense, comparative study of all religions should also be one of the items for instruction. Also, in *Bharatiya* culture, the character of *Bharatiya* culture needs to be explored and properly explained and people should be educated in the great character of *Bharatiya* culture.

In amendment No. 24, I have said: "for the words 'within the Union Territory of Delhi or outside that territory' the words 'in India' be substituted". I think there is nothing much in it and the hon'ble Education Minister will not be reluctant to accept it. In amendment No. 30 I want that at page 3, at the end of line 24, after the word 'recognition' the words 'subject to subsequent approval of the Visitor' be inserted. That is also only a formal amendment.

In amendment No. 32, I want that at page 3, lines 26 to 28 the words 'having in view the promotion of purposes and objects similar to those of the university' be deleted, because I have also opposed the insertion of objects and purposes in the Schedule. That is all, madam.

The Deputy Chairman: Mr. Thengadi, you are withdrawing?

D. Thengadi: Yes, madam. I beg leave to withdraw my amendment No. 19.

* Amendment No. 19 was, by leave, withdrawn.

D. Thengadi: Madam, I beg leave to withdraw my amendment.

* Amendment No. 24 was, by leave, withdrawn.

D. Thengadi: Madam, I beg leave to withdraw my amendment.

* Amendment No. 30 was, by leave, withdrawn.

D. Thengadi: Madam, I move:

41. "That at page 4, lines 30 to 32, the words, 'unless the Central Government, after consultation with the University of Delhi, authorises the Jawaharlal Nehru University to do so' be deleted."

(The amendment also stood in the name of V.M. Chordia).

D. Thengadi: I move:

44. "That at page 4, lines 33 to 36 be deleted."

(The amendment also stood in the name of V.M. Chordia).

The questions were proposed.

D. Thengadi: If this idea of Jawaharlal Nehru University materialises and it is going to be – naturally the University of Delhi will be like a dwarf by the side of this giant and some protective walls should be raised. This has been recognised by the first part of sub-clause (2) of Clause 6 which says:

'Notwithstanding anything contained in clause (13) of section 5, the Jawaharlal Nehru University shall not grant recognition, either in whole or in part, to any institution which has already been recognised by the University of Delhi...'

So, this first part of the clause recognises the necessity of some protecting wall but subsequently there is a qualifying clause for which I have objection. It says:

'...Unless the Central Government, after consultation with the University of Delhi, authorises the Jawaharlal Nehru University to do so.'

My objection is that though we have all faith in the justness and fairness of our present Education Minister, we have to err on the safe side and here consultation with the University of Delhi has been provided for, but approval has not been explicitly provided for and, therefore, it would always be possible for the government to bring pressure to bear upon the Delhi University authorities to accept this particular recognition of their institution by the Jawaharlal Nehru University even against their will. So, either the word 'consultation' should be substituted by 'approval' or else, the entire thing 'unless the Central Government, etc., should be dropped and consequently sub-clause (3) also should be dropped.

D. Thengadi: If this be the condition governing recognition then, instead of the word 'consultation', the word 'approval' should be used.

D. Thengadi: I beg leave to withdraw my amendment No. 44.

* Amendment No. 44 was, by leave, withdrawn.

Sharda Bhargava:[442] Madam, I move:

49. "That at page 6, lines 1 to 4 be deleted."

(The amendment also stood in the names of D. Thengadi and V.M. Chordia).

Prof. M.B. Lal:[443] Madam, I move:

---

442. Sharda Bhargava (1912-1999) – Congress leader from Rajasthan. Bhargava was member, Jaipur Legislative Council, 1945-49 and member, Rajya Sabha, 1952-1956, 1956-1962 and 1963-1966; she also served as Vice-Chairman, Rajya Sabha, 1956-57.

443. Prof. M.B. Lal (1901-1981) – Praja Socialist Party leader from Uttar Pradesh, Lal was member, Uttar Pradesh Legislative Council, 1952-54 and member, Rajya Sabha, 1960-1966.

52. "That at page 6, line 11, for the words 'one or more Rectors' the words 'a Rector' be substituted."

(The amendment also stood in the names of, D. Thengadi and V.M. Chordia among others).

D. Thengadi: Madam, the post of Rector has been created, first, to assist the Vice-Chancellor in carrying out his duties effectively. But I fear that if there are more than one Rector, then none of them would acquire the stature necessary for assisting effectively and substantially for such duties. The multiplicity will weaken the authority of a Rector, and further, it will affect adversely the unity of administrative responsibility and authority. Therefore, I think that there should be only one Rector, not more than one.

D. Thengadi: Sir, barring the members of the staff from being members of the Academic Advisory Committee by implication would mean as if the members of the staff are lower in stature when compared to those persons who will be appointed on this committee. I think there is no valid reason for preventing a member of the staff from becoming a member of this Advisory Committee also.

M.C. Chagla: As I visualise the functioning of this university, as I had occasion to tell the House, as soon as this Bill is passed by this House and the other House, and it has received the assent of the President, the first thing is to appoint the Vice-Chancellor and give him this Academic Advisory Committee. This will consist of the best educationists we can get in India. They cannot be members of the staff. This advisory body will plan the university.

D. Thengadi: Sir, I beg to move:

69. "that at page 9, line 24, for the words 'and shall be considered' the words 'for consideration and approval' be substituted."

I want that the annual report of the university should not only be considered by the Court, but that it should also be approved by the Court. The Court is a larger body and a more democratic body and, therefore, the approval of the annual report by the Court would be conducive to the democratic atmosphere.

The question was proposed.

M.C. Chagla: I am sorry, I cannot accept. It would lead to serious difficulties.

D. Thengadi: I beg leave of the House to withdraw the amendment, sir.
Amendment No, 69 was, by leave, withdrawn.

D. Thengadi: Sir, I move:

78. "That at page 11, line 4, the words 'and fulfil the ideals' be deleted."

D. Thengadi: Sir, I move:

83. "That at page 11, line 10, for the word 'composite' the word 'national' be substituted."

D. Thengadi: Sir, whatever has been said by the hon'ble Education Minister goes to prove that he wants this university to conduct an objective study and research into the ideals of Pandit Jawaharlal Nehru. As I said, the fulfilment of those ideals cannot be the legitimate work or task of the university. It is the work of the society, not of the university and, therefore, this fulfilment of the ideals should be dropped and the university should be entrusted only with the work of conducting an objective study and research into the ideals of Pandit Jawaharlal Nehru.

Secondly, the phrase 'composite culture' is a very unhappy one. Let it be replaced by the phrase 'national culture' because our culture is compact, not composite. A number of factors have contributed to its evolution and, therefore, I think the word 'composite' should be replaced by the word 'national'.

D. Thengadi: Sir, I move:

105. "That at page 16, lines 11-12, after the words 'withholding of increment' the words 'subject to the subsequent approval of the Vice-Chancellor' be inserted."

106. "That at page 16, line 16, for the word 'Vice-Chancellor' the words 'Executive Council' be substituted."

107. "That at page 16, lines 17-18, for the words 'the penalty of the withholding of increment' the words 'any penalty' be substituted."

108. "That at page 16, line 25, for the words 'the penalty of dismissal' the words 'any penalty' be substituted."

The questions were proposed.

D. Thengadi: Sir, what I suggest is that the power of the Registrar to take disciplinary action against the employees belonging to the ministerial staff and to suspend them pending enquiry, to administer warnings to them, or to impose on them the penalty of censure or the withholding of increment should be subsequent to the approval of the Vice-Chancellor. This is just to see that personal whims and caprices do not play their own part.

Again, there should be right of appeal not only to the Vice-Chancellor but, may be, through the Vice-Chancellor to the Executive Council. And, again, it should not be confined to the right of appeal in cases of withholding of increments, but whatever be the penalty, in every case he should have a right of appeal to the Executive Council.

Again, the proviso says:

'Provided that an appeal shall lie to the Executive Council against the order of the Vice-Chancellor imposing the penalty of dismissal.'

Here I have suggested that only in case of the penalty of dismissal, but in every case of any penalty, he should have a right to appeal to the Executive Council. Now as a matter of general policy, sir, the employees of the university will not be granted protection under any of the labour laws, the Indian Trade Union Act or the Industrial Disputes Act. I will not quarrel with the verdict of the judicial authorities that a university is not an industry inasmuch as it is not a profit-making concern. It cannot be denied that, after all, the employer-employee relationship does persist between the authorities and the employees of the university, and since we are not going to extend protection of the labour laws to the university employees, it is but proper that adequate provision should be made for protecting them against the caprices or whims of any individual authority. I do not doubt that the Vice-Chancellor, to be appointed, would be probably the best possible one. But at the same time, we cannot prefer, even in educational institutions, benevolent despotism to democracy, particularly so far as the rights of employees are concerned. So provision should be made for adequate protection to employees.

Statue 11–The Court

D. Thengadi: I am not moving No. 113.

D. Thengadi: I do not move Nos. 119 and 121.

Statue 14–Powers of the Executive Council

D. Thengadi: Madam, I beg to move:

137. "That at page 23, lines 3 to 6 be deleted."

D. Thengadi: Madam, I have moved my amendment seeking the deletion of the following proviso:

'Provided that, in matters of discipline and punishment, where the final power has been vested in the Vice-Chancellor or any other officer of the university, no appeal shall lie to the Executive Council.'

I feel that while it is necessary for the Vice-Chancellor or some other officer of the university to have the authority to punish and to maintain discipline, nevertheless, the right of appeal should not be denied, otherwise a sort of autocracy would be created. Unrestrained power or unlimited power should not be vested in any authority, even in the Vice-Chancellor. If that is done, then that would give rise to what I said earlier, a benevolent despotism and I say this despotism must not be created.

Statue 23 - Disqualifications

D. Thengadi: Madam, I move:

161. "That at page 28, lines 12-13, the words 'and sentenced in respect thereof to imprisonment for not less than six months' be deleted."

Madam, Statute 23 states that a person shall be disqualified for being chosen as, and for being, a member of any of the authorities of the university if, among other things enumerated there, he has been convicted by a court of law of an offence involving moral turpitude and sentenced in respect thereof to imprisonment for not less than six months. Now I do not know what is in the mind of the hon'ble Minister of Education because if he feels that no person is likely to be sentenced for less than six months for moral turpitude, then this wording is superfluous and, therefore, should not be there but if he feels that some persons are likely to be sentenced for less than six months, in that case this is an objectionable wording because moral turpitude is moral turpitude, the duration of the sentence notwithstanding, and it is necessary in order to maintain proper atmosphere in educational institutions that the students should have before them ideal examples of character of teachers. Therefore, I feel that this qualifying clause should be deleted.

The question was proposed.

D. Thengadi: Madam, I beg for leave to withdraw my amendment.

*Amendment No. 161 was, by leave, withdrawn.

D. Thengadi: Madam, I move:

169. "That at page 29, (i) in line 33, for the word 'Chancellor' the words 'Executive Council' be substituted; and (ii) in line 34, for the word 'he' the word 'it' be substituted."

The questions were proposed.

D. Thengadi: Madam, in Statute 26, Clause (8) I want that a person aggrieved by an order of withdrawal under Clause (7) may, within three months from the communication to him of such order, appeal to the Executive Council, instead of to the Chancellor, who may pass such orders thereon, as he thinks fit.

Now, it is a matter of principle. Our hon'ble Education Minister is reluctant to put much faith in the sense of responsibility on our Executive Councillors, because examples in different universities might have discouraged him. But we are saying that we are going to carve out some unique university and, therefore, not withstanding any discouraging examples of Vice-Chancellors of other existing universities, he has been able to pin down some faith in the quality of the Vice-Chancellor to come in the case of this University. I do not know why he does not share our hope that just like the new Vice-Chancellor of better quality, we will also have better type of Executive Councillors. Therefore, I wish that instead of the Vice-Chancellor, the Executive Councillors should be vested with this authority. Let us believe that our Executive Councillors will have much sense of responsibility and the entrusting of authority to one individual should be discouraged as far as possible.

M.C. Chagla: I accept the amendment of Mr. Thengadi.

The Benaras Hindu University (Amendment) Bill, 1964: Continued[444]

Vice-Chairman, sir, I congratulate the hon'ble Education Minister for taking the initiative for putting an end to the ordinance and for initiating this particular Bill. In the meetings of the Select Committee, the hon'ble minister has conducted himself in such a way that we all came to know that he is a perfect democrat, for which also he deserves our congratulations.

Before I proceed to the subject proper, I have to express my fear that probably I have misunderstood one of the points raised by our senior-most colleague, Ruthnaswamy, when he said that through this Bill we are inaugurating a new era. I hope I have misunderstood him, because if really he means to say that it is the inauguration of a new era, then it is casting a reflection upon the history of nearly five decades which has been highly creditable.

[Deputy Chairman in the Chair]

The contribution of the Benaras Hindu University to the nation has been splendid. It has served on the national plane as a nucleus of freedom fighters and on the educational plane, it has initiated studies in mining, metallurgy, mechanical engineering, electrical engineering and other subjects. I hope what my hon'ble friend meant was only this, that a new development is there which is quite significant in the history of the Benaras Hindu University. There has been some talk about the word "Hindu". It is pertinent to note that the word 'Hindu' had been inserted at the instance of one who was not a Hindu by birth, that is, Dr Annie Besant

444. *Rajya Sabha Debate* dated 4th November, 1965.

and the word 'Hindu' did not denote any religion. It was in the sense of nationality that the word was used. Even in the first Minute of Dissent, while pleading for the omission of the word 'Hindu', they have said:

"It is clear that the founder of the university, the great late Madan Mohan Malaviya, used the word 'Hindu' in English version only to emphasise that it is a national institution..."

"Madam, it is in the sense of a nationality and not of a religion that the word 'Hindu' has been used. We cannot but take into consideration the feelings of those donors and other promoters of the Benaras Hindu University in the initial stages at whose instance the word 'Hindu' was inserted. I am particularly amazed to find that those who are condemning the use of the word 'Hindu' in this particular context are quite enthusiastic in accepting or welcoming the word 'Indian' though. As a matter of fact, the term 'Indian' is derived from the word 'Hindu' and, therefore, it is very amazing to find that while the original word is rejected, its derivatory form is being welcomed."

This Bill contains more welcome features than the unwelcome ones. In the first place, a number of superfluous posts or ornamental posts have been done away with, those of Pro-Chancellor, Chief Rector, etc. Even the post of Pro-Vice-Chancellor has been abolished on the plea that it is almost co-equal with that of the Vice-Chancellor because of which many difficulties might be experienced or have been experienced in the smooth functioning of the university. Nevertheless, a new post called Rector has been created. It is an executive post to assist the Vice-Chancellor.

Another welcome feature is the replacement of Treasurer by the Finance Officer. In the very nature of things, it is necessary that anyone shouldering this particular responsibility should be a full-time officer. Formerly, the Executive Council was empowered to nominate members of the committee charged with the duty of recommending a panel of names to the Visitor for appointment to the post of Vice-Chancellor. This function has been assigned to the Court, which is a higher and more representative body. This is certainly more democratic and therefore we welcome it. Nevertheless, I should like to suggest that it would have been more appropriate had the election of the Vice-Chancellor been left to the Court itself, subject to the subsequent approval of the Visitor. The Standing Committee of the Academic Council is a new set-up. There was much discussion and it was approved finally. This Bill provides for the submission of the audited accounts to the Court, instead of to the Visitor.

This also is a democratic gesture. The deletion of the original Clause 14 is really a drastic change. As a consequence of this deletion, all colleges and educational institutions within a radius of 15 miles from the university would be admitted to the privileges of the university. I can quite appreciate the anxiety of our hon'ble Education Minister that this deletion should not be allowed to vitiate the original character of the university. That is understandable but at the same time there are certain developments which probably were not clearly foreseen by the founders of the university or it was not necessary to foresee these developments during that period and we cannot quarrel with the facts. It would be really anomalous or ridiculous that any college 3 or 4 miles away from the university area should be allowed to be affiliated to Gorakhpur University. So, instead of quarrelling with the facts, I think a compromise or discretion was the best thing and this deletion of Clause 14 is perfectly justified, though the anxiety of our Education Minister is quite understandable.

While in the case of every other officer it has been laid down that he will continue to hold his office until his successor enters upon the office, in the case of the Vice-Chancellor and the Registrar, it has been provided that they shall vacate their offices on the commencement of this Act. Now, that has been a very controversial point and all that I want to suggest is that it would not be wise to bracket the Vice-Chancellor and the Registrar together. The post of Registrar is mainly executive in character and, therefore, it should not be put on the same footing as that of the Vice-Chancellor. There are certain contractual obligations and though we may, for argument's sake, concede that a particular person might have done things detrimental to the welfare of the university and his continuance might be detrimental to an extent, we have also to consider the fate of other universities. I think no competent or talented person would come forward to accept this post of Registrar in any university in the country because this bad precedent has been created. A sense of security is necessary even for talented persons and, therefore, while trying to do justice according to our own convictions to the Benaras Hindu University, we should not do something which would be detrimental to the welfare of other universities in future.

Clause 5(c) of the Statute provides for appeal to the Executive Council against an order of the Vice-Chancellor imposing the penalty of dismissal on an employee of the university. This right of appeal is also a welcome feature. The power to appoint the Librarian has been delegated not to the

Executive Council but to the Vice-Chancellor as before. The membership of the Court has been increased and now it has a non-official majority. People were clamouring for it and the Joint Committee has done justice to the demands of the people. The registered graduates have been given more representation and the regional representation in their case has been done away with. The donors' representation is made more democratic. Another point that was insisted upon by the hon'ble Education Minister was that the membership of the Students' Union should be voluntary. Of course, it is quite in keeping with the freedom of association, with the principles of democracy and, therefore, all votaries of democracy would welcome this change also.

There are certain points which are not quite as welcome as those enumerated earlier. There is a possibility of the power to withdraw degrees, diplomas, certificates and other academic distinctions being abused and, therefore, the circumstances under which this power would be exercised should also have been specified. In Clause 12(b)(ii), mere imprisonment for an offence involving moral turpitude should have sufficed because if it is once accepted that imprisonment for any period less than six months will not be a bar, then we would be defeating considerably the very purpose of this clause. Another thing that we would have to consider is what effect it would have on the minds of the students if persons undergoing imprisonment for any period less than six months for moral turpitude are allowed to continue as office-bearers. There will naturally be demoralisation. In view of that fact, this qualification of less than six months should be dropped. In sub-clause (3) of Clause 16B proposed in Clause 17 of the Bill, it is said that the decision of the Tribunal of Arbitration shall be final and shall not be challenged in any Court of law. This is unjust and not in keeping with the provisions of the Arbitration Act. The doors of the law courts should not be shut against the poor aggrieved teachers. A regular provision for appeal should be made. In the case of suspension of teachers, there is already a provision in the proposed Clause 7C (5) to cope with emergency conditions. Statute 30(a) empowers the Vice-Chancellor to suspend a teacher though the Executive Council may have the order subsequently revoked if it so thinks it necessary. Now this is wrong. The power to suspend a teacher must vest in the appointing authority, that is, the Executive Council. The teacher must be given a reasonable opportunity to explain his case before any action is taken against him. If in any case the Executive Council subsequently revokes the suspension order. it would certainly have an adverse effect on the prestige and dignity of the Vice-Chancellor.

This Bill also ignores the needs of employees other than the teachers. They also need some protection against the whims and caprices of the authorities.

Now, Statute No. 59 deals with the problem of students' discipline. It vests in the Vice-Chancellor unlimited autocratic powers. Even according to eminent educationists, the Vice-Chancellor should not have autocratic power for in this field as in every other field of activity the principle holds good that power corrupts and absolute power corrupts absolutely. Statute No. 59 confers such absolute powers on the Vice-Chancellor. It must be borne in mind that it is not the controlling authority but the sterling merit and character of the Vice-Chancellor that really moulds the mind of the students. Even, in our ancient *gurukuls*, instruction through word of mouth was considered to be secondary and that through the life lived primary.

There was also discussion about the right of the Rector. A regular provision should be made to ensure the presence of the Rector in the meeting of the Executive Council. Though he is not an ex-officio member of the Executive Council and therefore not entitled to vote, he should be given the right to participate in its deliberations so as to extend the benefit of his knowledge to the Executive Council.

These are some of the suggestions that I should like to make in this context. There was one more discussion about which I am not going to say one way or the other but I would just suggest about the tenure of the Vice-Chancellor whether it should be five years without eligibility for further election or it should be three years with eligibility for further election, that I personally feel – though I may not press the point – that a tenure of three years with eligibility for re-election at least once would be more appropriate.

The Benaras Hindu University (Amendment) Bill, 1964: Continued

D. Thengadi: Madam, I feel that there is no case for changing the original name of the Benaras Hindu University. The term 'Hindu' is not denominational; it is national, and the hon'ble Education Minister had rightly said that the sentiments and emotions that are evoked by a particular word are important. Now during the last five decades nobody could prove that the insertion of the word 'Hindu' had created any communalism in the Benaras Hindu University. Actually, even those who have raised an objection against the word 'Hindu' have conceded that originally the word 'Hindu' was inserted in the title of the Act in the national sense and not in the denominational sense. Secondly, even if it is taken for granted that all denominational names should be dropped, then it would be more appropriate to bring forward a separate Bill banning all denominational titles of educational institutions, so that in one Bill we can achieve the purpose, which is sought to be achieved. Thirdly, it would be more appropriate to allow the educational institutions themselves to decide what names they should adopt or should not adopt, instead of our legislating on the point. In view of the fact that the word 'Hindu' denotes national and not denominational sense, I oppose the dropping of the word 'Hindu'.

The Benaras Hindu University (Amendment) Bill, 1964[445]: Continued

D. Thengadi: Sir, the term 'moral and spiritual values' is quite a comprehensive term, all of us stand for democratic ideals and principles and even if you call it secularism or secular nationalism, it is the same. My difficulty is this that if we try to enumerate all the various ideals that we stand for, then this will have to be a very exhaustive list. Instead of that, I think it would be better to maintain the original term 'moral and spiritual values'.

A.D. Mani: Even the minister has said in advance his willingness to accept the amendment.

M.C. Chagla: No, I have not expressed my willingness to accept.

Mr. Chairman: He has not had his say.

M.C. Chagla: I have not had my say yet.

D. Thengadi: Madam, the original intentions of the revered founder of this university must be respected by all. That is true. He wanted it to be of a residential character but there are reasons to believe, and there is no disrespect when I say this, that probably during those early days, certain developments may not have been envisaged or anticipated and the springing up of new colleges or educational institutions within that radius is one such development. Already we have four such colleges, two of them had already been admitted to the privileges of the university and even according to this amendment, the remaining two would be admitted.

445. *Rajya Sabha Debate* dated 11th November, 1965.

There is no reason to presume that there would be mushroom growth of colleges within the same radius. After all a few more may come up and for them to be barred from the affiliation to this university would be highly unjust. Any college situated within the radius of this university and being affiliated or required to be affiliated to Gorakhpur certainly is unfair. So far as the charge against U.P. is concerned, I may say with all modesty that U.P. is one of the few states that do not suffer from provincialism.

The Benaras Hindu University (Amendment) Bill, 1964:[446*] Continued

This amendment moved by the hon'ble Education Minister has wider implications. Through this he is giving a constructive lead even to other educational institutions in the country because we know that there is a sort of deterioration in the relationship between the teacher and the taught and if the teachers are asked to participate and co-operate with the students' welfare activities and organisations, naturally there will be a marked improvement in the relationship between the teacher and the taught. So, without standing on any technical ground, I think we should support the move.

I fail to reconcile the bid for compulsory membership with the spirit of democracy which has been advocated here earlier. This is a student's organisation and its functions are limited. I believe the functions of the Council for Students' Welfare and those of the voluntary organisations are not going to overlap and if anybody is bent upon mixing up politics with education, he can do so whether the organisations are voluntary or compulsory. I think it would be more in keeping with the democratic traditions to support the provision.

The task we are accomplishing is of great importance, but it is not that I agree with every provision of the Bill as it is being passed now. Personally, we have expressed our differences or opposition to some of the provisions, for example, those that seek to change the original name or to deny new colleges the admission to the privileges of the university or to vest unlimited authority in the Vice-Chancellor. But still, though we continue to hold the same views and are sorry to say that there is no proper appreciation of them here, I say that the task that is being accomplished is really very important. Particularly, so far as the name is concerned, I may inform the hon'ble Education Minister that I had on the last Saturday

446. **Rajya Sabha Debate* dated 16th November, 1965.

and Sunday been to some parts of U.P. and really the people are agitated over the point, and I should request the hon'ble Education Minister to reconsider his decision of changing the name because the people have genuine affection and affinity for this particular name, particularly because, as I have said, the name, according to them, denotes a national and not denominational sense. In a way and to a certain extent, this has set a model for the other universities though every university does have and it is but proper that it should continue to have its own distinctive characteristics. I must mention here that the progress of this measure has been mainly due to the sincere and sustained efforts of our hon'ble Education Minister and I feel that but for him, the process would not have been so much expedited. We could find in him the rare blending of the democratic spirit and the unyielding idealism.

Now that the Bill is in its final stage, I cannot but pose myself a few questions. To what extent will we succeed in achieving our broad objectives in the field of education? First of all, we are all aware of the evils that flow from the mixing up of politics with education. Will the provisions of this Bill help us in eradicating or overcoming these evils? The country is confronted with the serious problem of the teacher-and-the-taught relationship. The problem is of supreme importance in that; in the absence of a proper relationship between the teacher and the taught, it would be simply impossible to bring up the younger generation in a healthy atmosphere. Will this Bill help us in bringing about such an atmosphere?

Administration in the educational field is not comparable with administration in the political or the governmental sphere. The contexts differ and so differ the objects. In the sphere of education, what is sought to be achieved is the all-round development of human personality. This necessitates an appropriate balance between democracy and discipline so far as the administration of the educational institutions is concerned. In this respect we have to welcome democracy without allowing it to degenerate into licentiousness, and discipline without allowing it to degenerate into regimentation. We, in India, have a very characteristic example of such 'elastic discipline' – a disciple seeking guidance on the point of his duty in a spirit of perfect discipline – (Hindi Words) and the *guru*, after having, explained all the pros and cons of the problem in 18 chapters, telling the disciple that the latter should do whatever he is inclined to do after taking into consideration all the facts placed before him.

(Hindi Words)

This spirit of elastic discipline should be the guiding light of all such measures.

Have we incorporated in this Bill this spirit?

I feel that we should test the success of this measure on this basis and be open-minded enough to introduce amendments further in the light of fresh experience.

The Aligarh Muslim University (Amendment) Bill, 1965[447]

Before I turn to the events of April 25, let me state that even before that date, the affairs of this university were not in proper order and it was sensed that there was something rotten in the State of Denmark. Serious allegations against the affairs of this university in the report of the Accountant General of Uttar Pradesh on the university finances were as follows:

> "The alleged irregularities are of a serious character, and related almost to every aspect of financial management in the university. More serious audit objections related to embezzlement and misappropriation of funds, defalcation and tampering with the records, unauthorised revision of estimates in respect of sanctions by government, complete mismanagement of large construction projects, non-observance of financial procedure, and inefficient and tardy collection of dues from students."

Even in general, the government was right in noting that the administration of the university was inefficient, and untrustworthy. There were inordinate delays in important administrative matters. Official secrets were not preserved. The standards and the basic characteristics of the university as an academic institution were going down, and it was losing its all-India character. It may be noted that the Aligarh Muslim University is a university and not a theological convent. Entry 63 of Union List I of the Seventh Schedule describes this university as an "institution of national importance", along with the other three Central universities. Now, sir, some apprehension has been expressed in this House regarding the fate of minority institutions. In India there is no reason for minorities for getting panicky. The Anglo-Indians who are a microscopic minority as compared to the others are conducting 300 educational institutions of their own and there has been no encroachment or interference by

447. *Rajya Sabha Debate* dated 15th September, 1965.

either the so-called majority community or by the State in their internal affairs. The hon'ble Education Minister is a great believer in the autonomy of universities and he has assured us categorically that this amending Bill is going to be a temporary measure. This is an emergency measure justified by unusual and extraordinary circumstances. It is not a normal affair for a Vice-Chancellor to get beaten to death. The events of April 25th are self-eloquent. Even a coffin was already prepared for the Vice-Chancellor and his survival was accidental or miraculous. The unholy alliance as mentioned in a statement by my senior colleague, Abid Ali, between the communists and the communalists, was responsible for this conspiracy. Aligarh has already become the hotbed of communalism. During a certain period, even the Shia-Sunni controversy was raised. This is not the first time that the police had to be called and the constitution of the university suspended. During the twenties, during Mr. Ziauddin's regime, similar things did happen. Then Sir Ross Masood was appointed the Vice-Chancellor, the university constitution was suspended and a triumvirate consisting of the Vice-Chancellor, the Pro-Vice-Chancellor and the Treasurer administered the affairs of the university. The record of the office-bearers of the University is worth noting. Dr Yusuf Hussain Khan, the Pro-Vice-Chancellor, has been a Razakar [reactionary Islamists pro-Pakitan elements who sided with the Nizam of Hyderabad and resisted the state's integration with India] leader. After the police action, he fled to Pakistan, and from there went to UNO to plead for an independent Hyderabad. Sardar Patel vowed that he should not come back to India. After the passing of the Sardar, he persuaded New Delhi to let him in. Dr T. Saifuddin, Chancellor of the university, is also having an unclean record. He was closely associated with the movement that culminated in the Partition of the country.

The Vice-Chancellor[448] was expressing the bare truth when he wrote to the hon'ble Education Minister:

> "I left a distinguished career of service in my country to take up my duties at Aligarh, hoping to serve my community in a national context and for high academic aims. I have never touched dirt in my life, and I do not wish to go where, evidently, I am not wanted. In any case, I

448. Nawab Ali Yavar Jung (1906-1976) – distinguished diplomat and educationist, was Vice-Chancellor of Aligarh Muslim University between 1965-68 when the minority status agitation in the university reached a crescendo. Jung had opposed religious reservation in the university.

can do nothing there – nobody can under the constitution as it exists."

This is the background against which the hon'ble Chagla has thought it advisable to introduce this measure. Chagla is a man with a mission, is endowed with courage of conviction. He has stood firm like a rock in the midst of a slander campaign conducted by the communalist press which wanted him to go to the *jehanum* [hell]. His steadiness and courage of conviction cannot but remind me of the great Abraham Lincoln.

In the context of this Bill, sir, certain articles of our Constitution are referred to. There is reference to Clause (2) of Article 28. Now, nobody would object to any educational institution being run on sectarian lines provided it does not depend for its maintenance upon parliamentary grants. In fact 95 per cent of the expenditure of the Aligarh University is being met through Parliamentary grants. Consequently, Clause (1) of the same article comes into operation which runs thus:

> "No religious instruction shall be provided in any educational institution wholly maintained out of State funds."

The critics of this Bill are leaning heavily on Article 30 of our Constitution but no article of the Constitution can be considered in isolation. The following passages occurring in the judgement of the Supreme Court dated the 16th March, 1954, are noteworthy.

The Supreme Court said:

"We may refer in this connection to a few American and Australian cases, all of which arose out of the activities of persons connected with the religious association known as 'Jehova's Witnesses'. This association of persons, loosely organised throughout Australia, United States of America and other countries, regard the literal interpretation of the Bible as fundamental to proper religious beliefs. This belief in the supreme authority of the Bible colours many of their political ideas. They refuse to take oath of allegiance to the king or other constituted human authority and even to show respect to the national flag, and they decry all wars between nations and all kinds of war activities."

In 1941, a company of 'Jehova's Witnesses', incorporated in Australia commenced proclaiming and teaching matters which were prejudicial to war activities and the defence of the Commonwealth, and steps were taken against them under the National Security Regulations of the State. The legality of the action of the government was questioned by means of a writ petition before the High Court, and the High Court held that the action of the government was justified and that Section 116 which guaranteed freedom of religion under the Australian Constitution was not in any way infringed by the National Security Regulation," vide 67 C.L.R. 116, at page 127.

These were undoubtedly political activities though rising out of religious belief entertained by a particular community.

"In such cases," as Latham C.J. [prominent Australian lawyer politician, who served as Chief Justice of Australia between 1935-1952] pointed out, "the provision for protection of religion was not an absolute protection to be interpreted and applied independently of other provisions of the Constitution. These privileges must be reconciled with the right of the State to employ the sovereign power to ensure peace, security and orderly living without which constitutional guarantee of civil liberty would be a mockery."

When the interpretation of Article 25 of the Constitution came before the Bombay High Court, the Chief Justice observed:

> "It may be said that both Articles 25 and 26 deal with religious freedom, but, as I shall presently point out, religious freedom, as contemplated by our Constitution, is not unrestricted freedom. The religious freedom which has been safeguarded by the Constitution is religious freedom which must be envisaged in the context of a secular State. It is not every aspect of religion that has been safeguarded, nor has the Constitution provided that every religious activity cannot be interfered with."

Now, sir, clarification of certain concepts in the context of this Bill seems to be necessary. We have very often been using the word 'secular' and I could follow the spirit behind the word 'secular' and 'secularism'; but I must say by way of suggestion that the choice of the word is not correct. Holyoake[449] was right in initiating the movement of what he described as 'secularism' in Britain in 1846, but his choice of the word was not happy; 'secular' means 'non-spiritual'. This is not the sense in which we are using the word. What we mean is a 'non-theocratic' or a 'non-denominational' or a 'jurisdictionalist' State. In this sense the State has always been non-theocratic in India and that is the significance or characteristic of *Bharatiya* culture.

The term 'communal' has often been used in this House and that also needs to be properly defined. Communalism is the attitude of mind

449. George Holyoake (1817-1906) – British journalist and editor who coined the term 'secularism'.

and can flourish even in a country consisting of only one religious group. Turkey, for example is certainly a Muslim country. Nevertheless, when Mustafa Kamal Pasha introduced for the first time the Turkish rendering of *Koran* in all mosques, the vested interests revolted and there were riots throughout Turkey. This was the revolt of communalism against Turkish nationalism. Similarly, communalism asserted itself when the rising tide of nationalism in Egypt and Iran revived the glorious patriotic memories of the Pharaoh kings and Pahlavi kings respectively. Afghan nationalism spearheaded by King Amanullah[450] had to suffer reverses at the hands of the communalists. It may be noted that all these are hundred per cent Muslim countries.

In all these Muslim countries, nationalism had to face stiff opposition from communalism though both these tendencies were represented by Muslims only. In India also the tussle is not on the basis of religion; it is a fight between communalism and nationalism; it is not a fight between Hindu and Muslim.

The expression 'Muslim culture' has been used. I am unable to comprehend the meaning of this particular expression 'Muslim culture'. I have very high regard for Islam and also for Mohammed the Prophet. I believe, sir, that all religions lead to the same goal, be it described as Allah or Jehovah or Father in Heaven or Brahman or Ahur Mazd. I further believe, sir, that the ultimate truth preached by all prophets is essentially the same though the expressions of different prophets are different so as to suit the different spiritual and intellectual levels of their respective audiences. This means that had Shankaracharya been born in Arabia before 14 centuries, the *Koran* would have been revealed to him and had Mohammed the Prophet been born in India in the 8th century he would have written a thesis equivalent to *Shankara Bhashyam*.[451] Thus there can be no conflict between any two religions. The conflict arises because of the political ambitions of the non-religious persons who exploit religion to promote their materialistic political ends. *Bharat* is the land of religions. We welcome all religions of the world. The treatment accorded to the Parsis and the Jews, whose numerical strength is insignificant, indicates the true spirit of the *Bharatiya* culture. We have welcomed Islam also. All religions that are being followed by the patriotic Indians are *Bharatiya* religions.

450. King of Afghanistan from 1919 to 1929.

451. Adi Sankaracharya's commentaries on Vedas, Brahmasutram and Bhagavad Gita.

This is so far as religion goes but culture is something different.

An hon'ble member: May I know how it is all relevant?

D. Thengadi: As I stated once earlier, the word 'culture' denotes a trend of impressions on the mind of a society which is peculiar to its own and which again is the cumulative effect of its passion, emotion, thought, speech and action throughout its history. Culture is much more comprehensive than, and cannot be identified with, religion. Religion is only a relationship between a man and his Maker. Culture should not be confused with religion.

Joseph Mathen:[452] Is it a sermon that you are preaching?

Mr. Chairman: He is clarifying concepts, but I am afraid we have very little time left.

D. Thengadi: In the West, two world wars were fought between the nations professing the same religion because though their religion was one and the same, their national cultures were different. Even different Islamic countries have different national cultures. This has been made amply clear by Gokalp, the Prophet of Turkish nationalism. There are as many cultures as there are nations. It would be inappropriate, therefore, to talk of Muslim culture. All *Bharatiyas* have but one culture which is equally respectful to all the religions. Let us, therefore, talk in terms of *Bharatiya* culture which is equally helpful to studies and researches in Muslim theology and Muslim religion.

We are the most ancient nation but let me state that even the youngest nation of the West, that is the United States, is extremely particular about the process of acculturation of different racial groups. But for the accomplishment of the process of acculturation of the various groups the United States would never have attained its present status of nationhood. We believe that all *Bharatiyas* put together constitute one nation having one culture whose distinct characteristic is the principle of unity in the midst of diversity, unity without regimentation and diversity without disruptionism.

Motion Regarding Kerala University (Amendment) Act, 1966[453]

The question of salaries of teachers and the staff of colleges has been agitating their minds for very long. Their demand that they should be brought on par with the recommendations of the UGC is quite natural and justified and would be supported by all. I know that the Central Government

452. Joseph Mathen (1916-1995) – Congress leader from Kerala. Mathen was member of the erstwhile Travancore-Cochin Legislative Assembly, 1949-52 and member of Rajya Sabha, 1960-1966.

453. *Rajya Sabha Debate* dated 12th May, 1966.

is anxious to see that justice is done to them in this respect. At the same time, now that Kerala is being administered centrally, it is the direct responsibility of the Central Government and now there can be no shirking of responsibility as in the case of other states, as between the Centre and state governments.

Regarding the management of some of the colleges, I have to request the Central Government to see that the managements do not behave in an arbitrary fashion and do injustice to their staff. Recently a very important case has been brought to my notice, which I want to place before you. It is one of the many examples in which the management has been harassing the employees, even the officials, without any rhyme or reason. This is the case of the Principal of Guruvayurappan College, Calicut. He has been threatened with disciplinary action by the Board of Management, without the previous permission of the University Syndicate, which is conducting the enquiries into the charges against the Principal. The Board has not given any provision of law, statute or ordinance that sanctions such disciplinary action. The University Inspection Commission had specially requested the President to see that neither he nor the Board would proceed to take any action regarding any matter, which would come up for consideration before the University Commission. True, after the motion was served on 18th April, 1966, Samuel Mathai, Vice-Chancellor, University of Kerala, did write to the Chairman of the Board of Management of the Guruvayurappan College in course of which he said:

> "You are aware that the Syndicate has appointed a commission to look into the affairs of the Guruvayurappan College, Calicut. The management of the College itself had requested the University to enquire into the affairs of the college. We wrote to you some time back (Registrar's letter No. GC.1668/65, dated 17-12-1965) that till after the University had, had an opportunity to examine the problems connected with the college, no precipitate action should be taken by the management against the Principal of the college on any differences of opinion that may exist between them. You are also aware that the University Commission visited the college on the 5th and 6th of this month. The Commission's report is expected in a few days and the Syndicate will be considering the report most probably at its next meeting in May 1966. Meanwhile, I understand that the Board of Management has framed certain charges against the Principal very recently and asked the Principal for his explanation within 10 days. It would appear that

the management has not given the consideration to the advice of the university and wishes to pursue action against the Principal in a hurry. I once again advise you and through you the Board of Management of the college under the powers vested in me as Vice-Chancellor not to proceed with any action against the Principal..." Now, this is one of the many cases and I would request the hon'ble Minister to go through this case and see that injustice is not done.

M.C. Chagla: As regards my friend, Mr. Thengadi, he has drawn my attention to the case of a particular college. I have not got the facts here, but I promise him that I will look into it and see what can be done about it.

There is nothing else I have to answer, sir, and I ask you to put the motion to vote.

Calling Attention to a Matter of Urgent Public Importance Regarding Reported Hunger-strike and other forms of Agitation by Teachers Throughout the Country[454*]

D. Thengadi: In view of the fact that the minister, in spite of his best efforts, has not succeeded so far in bringing about uniformity in the pay scales in all the states and also in getting the increased cost of living neutralised and also of the fact that he has suggested that the teachers should not resort to agitation, what other channels would he like to suggest for the teachers to get their grievances redressed? What are the other channels for the teachers?

M.C. Chagla: Democracy prescribes certain channels.

Bhupesh Gupta: What are they?

M.C. Chagla: The channels are, meet the minister, explain to him, meet

454. *Rajya Sabha Debate* dated 26th February, 1965. Besides Thengadi a number of leading members took part in the discussion such as Bhupesh Gupta, A.D. Mani, Ruthnaswamy, I.K. Gujral, Mohan Dharia, Chandra Shekhar among others. Chagla, then Union Education Minister made a detailed statement on the strike, the demands and the situation arising out of it. Some of the prominent teachers organisations which were active in the strike were the All-India Primary Teachers Federation, Kerala Aided Primary Teachers' Union and the All-India Secondary Teachers' Federation. The demands were mainly to do with emoluments and other facilities, uniform pay-scale, security of services etc. In his statement, Chagla made the following reference to the increasing cost of living, "The difficulty resulting from the low emoluments of teachers particularly in some States has been greatly aggravated by the increase in the cost of living, particularly since the proclamation of the Emergency. It is felt that whereas there was a necessity to raise the emoluments of teachers even earlier, a substantial increase is needed now only to neutralise the effect of the higher cost of living. It is felt that this is a broader issue and should be dealt with in the same manner as the increase in the dearness allowance of other employees."

the ministers of their own state, get public support but no direct action, not to say that and what will be the effect on or 'I will go on strike'. How could a teacher say that and what will be the effect on students?

Calling Attention Motion Regarding Recent Incidents in Benaras and Allahabad Universities[455]

D. Thengadi: Now that the name of the RSS has been dragged in by Mr. Raj Narain in this discussion, may I ask whether it is not a fact that the RSS is having its branch for nearly a quarter of a century...

---

455. *Rajya Sabha Debate* dated 18th November, 1968. This issue merits a background in some detail because shows, how even then, the RSS would always be unfairly and maliciously blamed for episodes and incidents in which it had no role. Raj Narain's casting aspersions on the RSS in the BHU episode, was strongly countered and exposed by Thengadi. Noted educationist Dr Triguna Sen (1905-1998) was then Union Education Minister (1967-70) he had also been Vice Chancellor of Banaras Hindu University (BHU) (19665-66). Dr Sen made a detailed statement on the episode also mentioned that then Vice Chancellor of BHU through its Executive Council had decided to set up a "Committee to enquire into the state of constant unrest and frequent agitations in the University and to make such recommendations as may be considered necessary or expedient for removing the situation and for improving the general tone of discipline and law and order in the University." Describing the events as they unfolded at BHU, Dr Sen told the House, that "the recent disturbances in some of the Universities in U.P. commenced on August 30, 1968 with the Banaras Hindu University. Soon after the announcement of the election results of the Students' Union, some stray cases of assault on the students were reported. On September 25, a group of students stopped the car of the Vice-Chancellor and the Rector and beat two peons who tried to protect the Vice-Chancellor from physical assault. On account of this indulgence in violence and gross acts of indiscipline, 3 students were expelled by the Vice-Chancellor. On October 28, the agitators tried to force their entry with loudspeakers in the University Campus. When this was resisted by the proctorial staff of the University, the students threw brickbats on them and used lathis. On November 6, a procession was taken out in the University Campus, led by the expelled students pressing for the withdrawal of the expulsion orders. The demonstrators stormed the University Central Office. They also threatened the Vice-Chancellor that he would be dragged and killed if he did not withdraw the expulsion orders. The Vice-Chancellor requested for help of the police and the District Magistrate and Senior Superintendent of Police reached his residence. The students broke the gates of the Vice-Chancellor's residence, stoned his house and indulged in brick bating, causing considerable damage. As a result of this, a number of police officers and some students were injured. In the University and nearby areas Section 144 was promulgated for 15 days from the same date. On November 7, the students set fire to certain deposits of hay of the Agriculture College and the timber of a contractor. Their efforts to set fire to adjoining buildings was foiled by timely arrival of the fire brigade and the police. The situation has started returning to normal since November 9 and there has been no significant incident since then. From the same date, police in uniform has remained confined to the Vice-Chancellor's lodge, power station, water works and university press. The teaching work in the University is continuing with normal attendance."

And that there were no reports about disturbances in which the RSS people were involved, till Mr. Raj Narain entered the politics of the university court?

That is No. 1.

Banka Behary Das: You have started doing it because he has done it.

D. Thengadi: Secondly, may I know from the hon'ble minister whether the proposed enquiry committee will also be asked to go into one aspect, i.e. the responsibility of Mr. Raj Narain personally in the entire episode of the disturbances.

D. Thengadi: May I know whether it is not a fact that Mr. Raj Narain's followers had alleged that the RSS people had committed a cold blooded murder of one peon and demanded with bravado, which is usual with Mr. Raj Narain, that his dead body should be produced and that the RSS people were concealing the body of the murdered man? Also, is it not a fact that subsequently the murdered man appeared before the Vice-Chancellor and said that he was asked by interested parties to go to his village and abscond, so that a murder charge could be framed against the RSS people? These three questions I want to ask.

□

Dr Sen's statement was followed by a detailed and at times heated debate, both Sunder Singh Bhandari, Thengadi and Pitamber Das from the Jana Sangh participated in it. Some of the members made a demand for shutting down the university, for appointing a central enquiry committee etc. But for our purpose, it is interesting to note, that after Thengadi had made his three points exposing Raj Narain's false statements, Dr Sen, cited from the BHU enquiry's committee's report on the RSS's activities in the campus. It demolished the contentions of the likes of Bhupesh Gupta and Narain that the RSS was complicit in the violence. Following Thengadi's intervention, Dr Sen told the House that "Since, again and again, the question of RSS activities is coming up, I am compelled to read out from the Report: "It is correct that 4 Sakhas of R.S.S. are functioning inside the University and some teachers are associated with them. I am told that only a small number of students, about 40-50 out of nearly 9000, are active members of the R.S.S. It may be noted that R.S.S. has been functioning in the University from the thirties. The University branch was opened with the blessings of late Pt. Madan Mohan Malaviyaji and the Executive Council vide resolution No. 20 of April 20, 1941, agreed to havs a small pavilion in the university grounds for the Rashtriya Swayam Sewak Sangh. However, when the Law College building was completed the pavilion of R.S.S. was found to affect its frontage. Request was, therefore, made to the Secretary, Rashtriya Swayam Sewak Sangh, Varanasi, and Dr P. K. Banerjee, Sanchalak, R.S.S., Varanasi, to vacate the building. A reminder was also issued on February 20, 1967. On February 24, 1967, he replied that the pavilion and the adjacent fields have been used by the R.S.S. University Branch without any objection or complaints from any quarter. He has also intimated that since he was only the Head of the R.S.S. Branch at Banaras, he had to refer the matter to the Head Office to seek its direction. He also intimated that if the use of the pavilion was causing any inconvenience to the

12
Judiciary

Thengadi was of the firm opinion that to attract the best talent in the legal profession, High Court judges should be offered more attractive terms and conditions of service. He felt that the judiciary should be completely free from the influence of the Executive and suggested the need to make a clear departure from the British bureaucratic ways.

The High Court Judges (Conditions of Service) Amendment Bill, 1964[456]

Deputy Chairman, as has been rightly said, this Bill in itself is a consequential and therefore non-controversial one. But I feel that the situation demands introduction of a non-consequential, that is, a more comprehensive and maybe a more controversial Bill. Now there are certain important points which have been discussed here. First of all, it is with regard to the selection or appointment of judges. Notwithstanding whatever was said earlier by some of my friends, it is a fact that directly

---

Law College, he would be ready to alter or modify the uses that it would not cause any inconvenience to anyone till the matter was finally settled. It is understood that when Dr T, Sen was Vice-Chancellor here he had a talk with Dr P. K. Banerjee about the R.S.S. pavilion. Dr Banerjee agreed to vacate it if he was given some alternative accommodation. Dr Sen appears to have agreed with the proposal, but there is no record in our office. With the General Elections of 1967, the complexion of the Government in U.P. changed. Dr Sen left for Delhi. In the changed circumstances the matter was not pursued." Dr Sen concluded thus, "we are not concealing anything. There was a pavilion and the students used it for physical exercises and other activities. A request was made that they vacate the building and they were prepared to do so. About the allegation that the RSS students were responsible for the murder, this and that, I do not personally believe it and the reports that I have received also do not justify in any way that the boys are responsible for it." Following this, the debate which ended soon, had degenerated into name-calling and attempts to divert the issue, since there were no points to make though CPI's Bhupesh Gupta tried to continue heaping calumny on the RSS.

456. *Rajya Sabha Debate* dated 29th September, 1964.

or indirectly the Executive exerts its influence in this matter. I should like to emphasise that the state Chief Ministers should not be allowed even indirectly to influence the selection or appointment of High Court judges. The matter should be left entirely to the Chief Justice of the state and also the Chief Justice of India. The High Court judges should be offered more attractive terms and conditions of service because it is necessary to attract the best talent in the legal profession for these posts. Unless the talents are the best, it is quite possible, quite likely, that the independence of the judiciary may not be maintained. They may be susceptible to certain pulls and pressures from the Executive, and therefore this would necessitate the introduction of a more comprehensive Bill so as to improve the service conditions of the High Court judges.

In the case of transfers from one state to another, I should suggest that some compensatory allowance should be offered to the judges transferred. That would facilitate the mobility of talents.

Another point is that those in authority should not attack the High Court judges on the floor of Parliament, because judges are neither present nor represented here. Therefore, it would not be decent to attack them here. Unfortunately, the age of High Court judges has recently been a matter of some controversy. I would suggest that the age should be ascertained at the time of appointment. Subsequently, it should be treated as a non-contestable issue, and even if it is questioned at a later stage, it should be decided upon by the Chief Justice of India and he should be the final authority in this matter. The executive should not arrogate to itself either the rights or the responsibilities of ascertaining the age.

In short, the judiciary should be completely free from the influence of the Executive, and the Executive should learn to pay due regard to the judiciary. In this context I should like to quote Justice P.N. Mukherjee who has said:

> "While Judges are doubtless bound by their oath to uphold the Constitution and so to permit no infraction of Articles 106 and 194, they may justly and reasonably claim for the safe, due discharge of their duties that others in authority ought similarly to be alert that constitutional protection and immunity of judges under Article 121 is not violated."

There is one more important problem, madam, which is also discussed. The present Chief Justice of India, Mr. Gajendragadkar has said that it is only in the fitness of things that the judiciary should have to deal with the Ministry of Law rather than the Ministry of Home Affairs. This view must be taken into consideration with the seriousness it deserves, and we must make a departure from the British bureaucratic ways. In no democratic country the judiciary is placed under the Home Ministry. With these remarks, madam, I conclude my speech.

The Goa, Daman and Diu Judicial Commissioner's Court (Declaration as High Court) Bill, 1964[457]

This Bill is not, as our hon'ble Minister of State would have us believe, as simple or as innocent. In the first place this Bill ignores the obvious geographical facts, Diu and Daman are hundreds of miles away from Goa, and the residents of these tiny places would have to suffer untold hardships if justice is to be administered to them from Goa. Again, there is difficulty of language also which I need not mention. As a matter of fact, it could have been more natural, rational and logical to place Diu and Daman under the Ahmedabad High Court. Secondly, the present measure cannot be considered or treated as an isolated gesture. It is part and parcel of the broader policies of the Government of India. If these policies be correct, this measure deserves our support. But if they are not correct, this deserves to be opposed and I am convinced that these broader policies of which the present Bill is just a part are thoroughly detrimental to National Integration.

There is a general impression that the leaders of the government are out to maintain Goa as a separate entity. They are trying to make out a case that Goa has a separate culture. Recently there was a report that one Mr. Chopra was found taking films of religious institutions or of a particular community, which has given rise to suspicion in Goa that the Government of India is behind the move of maintaining Goa as a separate cultural entity. I want to know whether government sincerely believes that Goa has its own culture? If not, there is no justification whatsoever for making arrangements which would perpetuate separation of Goa from the rest of the country. Before I speak anything on this point, I feel it is necessary that I should clarify my stand regarding Christianity.

I am a great admirer and even a follower of Jesus Christ. I fully believe when the Son of Man asserts: I and my Father are one, I am the way, the truth and the life. But I cannot forget the fact that it was Jesus who said: 'Give unto God what is God's and unto Caesar what is Caesar's.' By this he

457. *Rajya Sabha Debate* dated 4th May, 1964.

meant that religion is a relationship between man and his Maker and that it should not be allowed to interfere with the national and political loyalties. Therefore, Jesus never hankered after political power; not merely that, but he firmly rejected the plea of Satan who offered him a sway over all the kingdoms of earth. For his followers to conduct political maneuverings with anti-national bias is bringing his fair name into disrepute. Had Jesus been alive, he would have condemned it. First, he would have condemned the anti-national maneuverings of the so-called Christian missionaries. He was not after political power. It was his lot to say: 'The foxes have holes, the birds of air nests, but the Son of Man hath not where to rest his head.' Here is an attempt to carve out a State to the detriment of the nation. He could never have supported it. Here I am thinking of the so-called Christians or missionaries who are conducting anti-national activities. I am not to be misunderstood as a disbeliever in Jesus. I am a good Hindu. Being a good Hindu I am automatically a good Christian because nobody can be a good Hindu without being a good Christian in the real sense of the term, not in the political sense. Therefore, I want to proceed to consider there is any justification for maintaining Goa as a separate cultural entity.

It is said that Goa has its own characteristics. I want to point out madam, that every state, every city even, has certain local characteristics. These local characteristics are not to be confused with culture. If local characteristics be the criterion for conceding separate states, I fear we will have to concede separate states for every city. I hail from Kanpur. I am sure that Kanpur has its own local characteristics which are distinct from other cities. Should I demand a separate city state for Kanpur on the pattern of Greek city states? No. Local characteristics are different and are to be distinguished from culture. The word 'culture' to my mind denotes a trend of impression on the mind of the society, which is peculiar to itself and which again is the cumulative effect of its passion, emotion, thought, speech and action throughout its history. According to this criterion I feel, madam, that entire India, from Sheikh Abdullah's Kashmir to Kanyakumari is one cultural entity. (interruption) It is one cultural entity. All the states, all the religious groups, castes and communities notwithstanding their distinct characteristics belong to one culture, and that is the *Bharatiya* culture. Therefore, this talk of separate culture of Goa is mischievous politics and has nothing to do whatsoever with the fair name of Jesus Christ. I am very unhappy to find that his name is being exploited by political agitators for carving out a separate state. Therefore, this is my request that the Bill which is just a step in the direction of a separate existence of Goa should be immediately withdrawn. The general trends in the country and the general policies that are being pursued by our government are very disturbing. There was Partition, then Kashmir, then Nagaland. Now regarding Goa, the government has been forewarned, but it refuses to be forearmed. All these things are extremely disturbing. I am a great admirer of our beloved Prime Minister. I wish that the future historians should not be tempted to describe him as a Partition specialist. After the Second World War, Mr. Winston Churchill firmly said that he had not become the Prime Minister of Great Britain to liquidate the British Empire. I want an assurance from our beloved Prime Minister that he is not continuing as Prime Minister of India to liquidate the Indian nation. With these words, I conclude.

The Goa, Daman and Diu Judicial Commissioner's Court (Declaration as High Court) Bill, 1964:[458] Continued

I am thankful to you for giving me this opportunity of clarifying only one point. It seems that my speech here yesterday has been inadvertently misreported and an impression has been created that I wanted Goa to be placed under the jurisdiction of the Ahmedabad High Court. This misreporting I know is inadvertent, not deliberate, and I, therefore, would read out the text of my speech so far as this part is concerned:

> "In the first place this Bill ignores the obvious geographical facts. Diu and Daman are hundreds of miles away from Goa, and the residents of these tiny places would have to suffer untold hardships if justice is to be administered to them from Goa. Again, there is difficulty of language also which I need not mention. As a matter of fact it would have been more natural, rational and logical to place Diu and Daman under the Ahmedabad High Court."

The only point I want to clarify is that I want Diu and Daman to be placed under the Ahmedabad High Court, not Goa. So far as Goa is concerned, it should be placed under the Maharashtra High Court. Simultaneously I want to state that this misreporting is not deliberate. It is inadvertent and as a working journalist, I myself know that such slips are common.

458. *Rajya Sabha Debate* dated 5th May, 1964.

In Response to the Statement regarding Judgement of the International Court of Justice on South-west Africa[459]

D. Thengadi: On account of this judgement we have lost confidence in the International Court. May I know, madam, if we have conveyed this reaction to the International Court?

Sardar Swaran Singh: I think my statement itself will be seen by them. This is the most effective way of conveying our views with the support of this august House.

□

459. *Rajya Sabha Debate* dated 2nd August, 1966. This discussion followed the statement made by Swaran Singh regarding the "Judgment of the International Court of Justice." Ethiopia and Liberia had filed a case in 1960 ICJ arguing that South Africa had not complied with its mandatory obligation vis-à-vis South West Africa which it continued to dominate. The UN General Assembly had passed numerous resolutions on the issue, the one passed in 1965 – Resolution 2074 (XX) emphasized the right of the people of South West Africa to independence and had called upon South Africa to relinquish its hold and remove its bases. The disappointment expressed by Thengadi and other members was on the issue of the ICJ's ruling in 1966 that Liberia and Ethiopia had no locus standi to bring the issue to the Court. Excerpts from Swaran Singh's statements read thus, "...the Government of India has seen with deep disappointment the judgment of the International Court of Justice on South West Africa. The Government of South Africa has persistently refused to place the territory of South West Africa under UN Trusteeship as required under the Charter. On the other hand, the South African Government has been taking measures to incorporate South West Africa as one of its provinces applying to it all the evils of apartheid to which it has subjected its own non-white population....The judgment is not likely to inspire confidence in the International Court or in the establishment of the rule of law in international affairs. The fact that it took nearly six years for the Court to decide that Ethiopia and Liberia have not established, any legal right or interest in the subject matter of their complaint is regrettable. In 1962 the Court rejected the preliminary objection of South Africa that the Court had no jurisdiction and that Ethiopia and Liberia had no standing to bring the case. Yet four years later the Court has decided that Ethiopia and Liberia have no locus standi in the matter...India's attitude has been throughout to strongly support the African countries in their legitimate demand for the grant of independence to South West Africa. As early as 1946, the Government of India were the first to raise this issue at the United Nations, and expressed their opposition to what amounted to the annexation of South West Africa..." (Rajya Sabha, 2nd August, 1966)

13
Matters of Public Importance

The Maternity Benefit (Amendment) Bill, 1965[460]

D. Thengadi: Before I deal with the subject proper, I must clarify that so far as the amendment of Shrimati Shakuntala Paranjpye[461] is concerned, I will pass no comment, either for or against it, because being a bachelor I consider myself not qualified and...

I consider that it is beyond my jurisdiction. Madam Deputy Chairman, this measure is one that I welcome, so far as it goes. As a matter of fact, it should have been brought in much earlier. Nevertheless, as the saying goes, it is never too late to mend. But the present amending Bill is again, as usual, an inadequate step in the right direction. As the government is well aware, even today there is no uniformity in the rates of benefit and the relief given is not related to the reality of the existing prices. As such, piecemeal measures do not provide appropriate relief to those for whom they are meant.

The subject of maternity benefits in India was taken up for discussion, for the first time by the Commission on the Employment of Women of the Washington Conference, i.e. the first session of the International Labour Conference, 1919, which adopted the Childbirth Convention. This means that the subject is quite old. In 1924, N.M. Joshi[462] made an unsuccessful

460. *Rajya Sabha Debate* dated 26th July, 1966.

461. Shakuntala Paranjpye (1906-2000) – well-known Marathi writer and social worker. Paranjpye was nominated to the Rajya Sabha for one term 1964-1970. She was also member, Maharashtra Legislative Council, 1958-64. She also wrote plays, novels, stories. Paranjpye worked in the ILO, Geneva in the 1930s and was conferred the Padma Bhushan in 1991 and did pioneering work in the field of family planning.

462. N.M. Joshi (1879-1955) – trade union leader, acolyte of Gopal Krishna Gokhale. Joshi was among the founders of the All India Trade Union Congress and was its general secretary between 1925-29 and 1940-48.

attempt to place an all-India Maternity Benefit Law on the Statute Book of the Central Government.

In 1929, the Bombay government passed the first maternity benefit law, to be followed in 1930 by the Madhya Pradesh government.

An hon'ble member: You mean the Central Provinces of those days?

D. Thengadi: Yes, the Central Provinces and Berar. And then other provinces followed suit in course of time.

The Royal Commission on Labour[463] examined this question, but the guiding principles laid down by the Royal Commission were found to fall far short of the standards laid down by the Childbirth Convention.

It is a matter of great regret that even today, that is to say, 19 years after our attaining Independence, we are not free from the inadequacies, the defects and the drawbacks of the maternity benefit legislation, and have not been able to ensure fully the two essential features of a maternity benefit scheme, namely, compensation and medical care. Whatever legislation is there, suffers from the absence of proper enforcement. Insecurity of service is still a menace that women workers are required to face constantly. The paucity of women doctors including women workers, is still a handicap. Ignorance of women workers is also another obstacle.

The point to be considered seriously by us is this. Immediately after Independence, we had set before us as an ideal in respect of maternity benefit, some measures including the International Labour Conference regulations concerning the problems of maternity protection. These were:

(i) The Childbirth Convention of 1919 (Convention No. 3).

(ii) The Childbirth (Agriculture) Recommendation, 1921. (Recommendation No. 12).

(iii) Articles 10 and 24(3) of the Income Security Recommendation, 1944 (Recommendation No. 67).

(iv) Article 31 of the Recommendation concerning Minimum Standards of Social Policy in Dependent Territories, 1944 (Recommendation No. 70).

(v) The Havana Code of 1939.

(vi) The Social Security Resolution of the Asian Labour Conference, 1947.

463. The Royal Commission on Labour, 1929.

(vii) The Medical Care Recommendation, 1944.[464]

The point is this. After 19 long years, how far have we progressed in this direction? I am confident that even the hon'ble minister cannot claim that our performance so far has been satisfactory. But what is most important is the evolution of an integrated social security scheme, covering all aspects of social security, from workmen's compensation to unemployment insurance.

In 1939, New Zealand took the lead in creating a comprehensive social security social assistance and schemes that provided scheme by

---

464. The Childbirth Convention of 1919 (Convention No. 3), also called the Maternity Protection Convention 1919, was an International Labour Organisation Convention convened at Washington by the Government of the United States of America on the 29th day of October 1919. It decided upon the adoption of certain proposals regarding "women's employment, before and after childbirth, including the question of maternity benefit". Then it was decided that these proposals shall take the form of an international Convention.

The Childbirth (Agriculture) Recommendation, 1921 (Recommendation No. 12), also known as the Maternity Protection (Agriculture) Recommendation, 1921 (No. 12) a general conference of the International Labour Organisation convened at Geneva by the Governing Body of the International Labour Office. It decided upon the adoption of certain proposals regarding the protection before and after childbirth of women wage-earners in agriculture.

Articles 10 and 24(3) of the Income Security Recommendation, 1944 (Recommendation No. 67), also called Income Security Recommendation, 1944. A general conference of the International Labour Organisation was convened at Philadelphia by the Governing Body of the International Labour Office on 20th April, 1944. It decided upon the adoption of certain proposals regarding income security, workmen's compensation for accidents and occupational diseases, sickness insurance, provision for maternity, old-age, invalidity, and widows' and orphans' pensions, and provision for employment.

Article 31 of the recommendation concerning Minimum Standards of Social Policy in Dependent Territories, 1944 (Recommendation No. 70) was discussed at a general conference of the International Labour Organisation convened at Philadelphia by the Governing Body of the International Labour Office on 20th April, 1944. It decided upon the adoption of certain proposals regarding minimum standards of social policy in dependent territories.

The Medical Care Recommendation, 1944, also called Medical Care Recommendation, 1944 (No. 69) was made at the general conference of the International Labour Organisation convened at Philadelphia by the Governing Body of the International Labour Office on 20th April, 1944 and it decided upon the adoption of certain proposals with regard to the question of medical care services and to take further steps for the improvement and unification of medical care services, the extension of such services to all workers and their families, including rural populations and the self-employed, and the elimination of inequitable anomalies, without prejudice to the right of any beneficiary of the medical care service who so desires to arrange privately at his own expenses for medical care.

bringing together a series of old age, invalidity and survivors' pensions, unemployment benefits and family allowance adding sickness benefit and all forms of health services. Other advanced countries also followed the example of New Zealand, one by one.

In 1942, as is well-known, Sir William Beveridge,[465] in his historic report on Social Insurance and Allied Services [also known as the *Beveridge Report* which argued for the founding of the welfare State in Britain], pleaded for improvement of State insurance to quote his words:

> "by means of improving the present schemes of social insurance in three directions:
> (i) by extension of scope to cover persons now excluded,
> (ii) by extension of purposes to cover risks now excluded,
> (iii) by raising the rates of benefit."

The 26th session of the International Labour Conference made two recommendations, i.e. Recommendation No. 67 and Recommendation No. 69 and I quote:

> "to bring together in a single scheme all provisions for assuring maintenance in case of inability to work or to obtain work, and to extend these provisions to all workers whether employed or self-employed, and whether urban or rural."

It has now become obvious to all thinking minds that there can be no real freedom from fear or worry, in the absence of an integrated social security scheme.

Our Constitution states:

> "The State shall, within the limits of its economic capacity and development, make effective provision for securing the right to work, to education and public assistance in case of unemployment, old-age, sickness, disablement and other cases of undeserved want."

Obviously, the Constitution envisages an integrated social security scheme. In the past we had evolved a characteristically *Bharatiya* socio-economic order which ensured fullest social security to all, but that order is now disintegrating. And a new order is not yet evolved. Thus, ours is a case of unborn tomorrow and dead yesterday. Against this background, I urge upon the government to make an early and determined effort to realise our long-cherished dream of full comprehensive social security.

---

465. William Beveridge (1879-1963) – British economist and liberal politician.

The Maternity Benefit (Amendment) Bill, 1967[466]

D. Thengadi: I welcome the Bill. There is not much to add, but I should like to stress that it is high time that an integrated social security scheme was evolved and there was an integration of social security legislations. This very amending Bill indicates or illustrates how lack of integration creates problems. So, I should like to know from the hon'ble minister what prevents him from evolving such a scheme. I should also like to suggest that once such an integrated social security scheme is evolved, the same can be placed under tripartite management and it can be followed up by similar appropriate legislation. So, this is the point that I would like to stress.

Jaisukhlal Hathi: I am grateful to both the hon'ble members for making these suggestions. So far as the maternity benefits are concerned, as far as I know the benefits under the Maternity Benefit Act are not in any way less. The only idea was that a woman worker should not get benefits under both the Acts, but the benefits are not less. On the contrary, when the Employees' State Insurance Act applies, she will get other benefits which are not available to her under this Act. Then so far as Mr. Thengadi's point is concerned, I think we should bring in a comprehensive social security Bill, but what kind of other social security is to be given we shall have to consider. Today we are giving them medical benefits; then we are having the Provident Fund; we are also thinking of some unemployment scheme and various other measures. All these measures are under consideration and perhaps the hon'ble member knows that the Labour Commission has appointed a Study Group which will look into all these social welfare measures to be taken, and that matter is under consideration. So far as management by a tripartite body is concerned, perhaps the hon'ble member knows that the Provident Fund is under the management or administration of a Board of Trustees which consists of both workers and employers. In this corporation also, the workers and the employers are there. So we have tried and we are trying, and it is my sincere endeavour, to take the workers into confidence as much as possible because all that we are doing is for them. And if they do not feel satisfied with what is being given to them, then the very object of taking these measures is frustrated. Therefore, these two schemes which we have, the Provident Fund and social insurance, are already under tripartite management.

466. *Rajya Sabha Debate* dated 5th December, 1967.

Whenever other schemes come, it shall be my duty to see that the workers are associated in a big way, that is, it would be under a tripartite body.

Resolution Regarding Appointment of Committee to Suggest Remedial Measures to Check Influx of Rural Population to Urban Areas[467]

D. Thengadi: This is a very important problem and we are discussing it rather 25 years late. Our Planning Commission has not taken cognisance of this problem and therefore we find that our rural areas are almost totally ignored. Is it not a fact that thousands of villages are not having access even to drinking water in the summer season? The very first economic problem before the country was what should be the character of our industrialisation? It is well known that the developing countries cannot profitably imitate the developed countries in point of technology, location and size of the industry. Sir, a British economist, Dr Schumacher,[468] toured the South-east Asian countries and came to the conclusion that the Western technology type of production will not be useful in Asian conditions and, therefore, he evolved an intermediate technology which is now being named as appropriate technology, the peculiar characteristic of which is that without decreasing considerably the efficiency of the industry, the employment potential should be increased and that should be the characteristic of our technology. Therefore, he has insisted upon the location of industries in the medium cities and also in the rural areas and he has suggested decentralisation of industries and also he has suggested that in the existing techniques of our traditional industries, there should be some innovation, technological innovation, without decapitalising our managerial skill and the skill of our traditionally self-employed persons and also the small capital available in the rural areas.

We are having the problem of investment now. It is so because we are concentrating only on heavy industries. If we channelise all the small sums available in the rural areas into industrial investment through small-scale savings and again investing them in small-scale industries, the very industrial map of India would have been altered. Therefore, I suggest that an expert committee should be appointed to study the technological and locational aspects of our industries. I say this because in the rural areas there is not sufficient electrification and we have not tried to imitate the

467. *Rajya Sabha Debate* dated 10th May, 1974.

468. E.F. Schumacher (1911-1977) – British-German economist and author of the 1973 best-selling book *Small is Beautiful: a Study of Economics as if People Mattered.*

Japanese way. In Japan, sir, electricity is there in all the huts in the villages and the hamlets and the processes of production are decentralised and in every hut some part of a commodity, some part of an article, is being produced according to specifications and standards and all such parts produced separately are assembled at one place and in this way, sir, the agricultural population, which is underemployed and unemployed for at least five or six months in a year, gets additional employment without losing its contact with its land. If we adopt some such techniques, it is possible for us also to decentralise the processes of production and in this fashion, industrialisation suited to our conditions can take place in our rural areas.

Our entire planning has been heavily loaded in favour of the richer classes using luxury goods and it is known to the Planning Commission that the processes of production also condition the processes of distribution. Our government is talking of socialism and under socialism there should be equitable distribution of wealth. Now, sir, to say that with very high-production techniques we will increase our luxury goods and thus our GNP will be increased and our total national wealth will be increased and once it is increased, we will try to distribute it equitably is, I think, a self-defeating theory. As a matter of fact, if there is a ban on luxury goods and if we give impetus to the production of consumer goods, naturally, sir, employment will increase because the consumer goods can be produced by low-production techniques in the rural areas and then, naturally, the income distribution problem will be solved. Now, with the production of luxury goods, there is concentration of wealth in the cities and from the rural areas people are inclined to flock to the cities for getting employment. Urbanisation, over-urbanisation, has its own problems. Because of over-urbanisation, sir, those who come from the rural areas are cut off from their moorings and they do not have the family life and its affects their total personality and also the problems of sanitation and transport and other such problems we have not been able to solve in the cities. Moreover, we also find that because of over-urbanisation our cultural standards are also going down. Instead of concentrating our industries in the urban areas, if we decentralise our industries in the rural areas, it will be possible for us to have equitable distribution of wealth and, at the same, to have a healthier atmosphere. You know, sir, that nowadays even the Western countries have taken cognisance of the fact that industrialisation with no regard for the ecological aspects is a dangerous thing and is detrimental to the health of mankind as well as to the other living creatures. This is detrimental to the health of mankind as well as of all living creatures. In the West, special committees are being appointed in different countries to solve ecological problems. Our industrialisation has also created ecological problems. Only in Kanpur, it was stated by experts, as many as 3,000 chemical substances, which are not helpful to living things, are present in the atmosphere. Now, if the ecological problems are to be solved, the only way is to decentralise our industries. But, sir, in blind imitation of the West, we have brought in heavy industries. And now we find that we have reached a stage where we cannot fully utilize the capacity of installed machinery. Idle capacity has also become another problem before our country. If the technology is changed – I am sure, our technologists, if properly engaged, are competent enough to take care of this problem – if technology is changed to suit the Indian conditions, it should be possible for us to have widely scattered small- and medium-size industries throughout the rural areas so that our problems of economics and equality will be solved, and, sir, simultaneously the problems arising out of over-urbanisation which are mainly cultural in character, will be solved. Therefore, I urge that an expert committee should be appointed. I support this resolution. This Expert Committee should go into the entire problem and see that our industries are decentralised and incomes properly distributed – not through any mechanism of governmental machinery but through the very process of production, so that there is equitable distribution of wealth.

Minister of State in the Ministry of Planning (*Mohan Dharia*): I am happy that the hon'ble member has not yet lost his faith and confidence in the constitution of new committees.

The Salaries and Allowances of Members of Parliament (Amendment) Bill, 1964[469]

While I agree with some of the arguments put forward by the mover, Mr. Bhargava, I sincerely feel that this measure seeks to put the cart before the horse. True, there has been an unintermittent spiralling of prices but then this has hit one and all, not only Members of Parliament and, therefore, the real and effective remedy would have been to reduce the prices, instead of increasing the salary of a few persons. Instead of trying to reduce the prices through this measure, we are seeking to increase our own emoluments. I understand that even Members of Parliament

469. *Rajya Sabha Debate* dated 8th May, 1964.

require some more money because prices are going high but then that is the universal malady, I may say and, therefore, universal remedy is to be found out which is reduction in prices. Secondly, we will have to consider what our masters, the masses whom we represent, would feel when they learn that we have passed such a Bill because they are our masters and when they find that their representatives would be enjoying a better position. I will give one concrete example. Our textile workers in Bombay used to get 30 rupees in 1939. Broadly, it can be said that now the price level has risen five times. It is also admitted by the authorities that during 1951-58 there was an additional increase in industrial production of 20 per cent. Therefore, the industrial workers feel themselves justified in demanding that their wage should be six times higher compared to the 1939 level. According to this calculation, we would be justified in fixing the national minimum wage at Rs. 180. While all these things have not been practicable so far, we are trying to increase our own salaries, and, therefore, my humble request is that we must consider what our masters, the masses, would feel outside. But at the same time I do accept that the arguments put forth by Mr. Bhargava have validity and therefore I feel that the entire situation is such that this particular measure has both the sides which are equally valid. As Sir Roger de Coverley's[470] famous remark goes, much can be said on both sides. Both the sides have been put forth vehemently and at the same time I feel that there is some uniqueness in this measure.

An hon'ble member: On which side are you?

D. Thengadi: I am going to say that. While on all other occasions when we decide things we give our verdict about somebody else's cases here, we are passing a verdict about our own salary. Therefore, this is a delicate matter and as I said, arguments on both sides have validity. Therefore, I would request that our hon'ble Chairman should follow some unusual procedure so far as this particular measure is concerned. Instead of trying to rush through and getting this Bill passed by the majority vote, I would request that the hon'ble Chairman should invite leaders of all the groups for consultations and try to arrive at a unanimous decision which would be acceptable because all are responsible citizens of the country and such a unanimous decision would be the only proper course so far as this unique measure is concerned.

---

470. A fictional character conjured by English writer and essayist, poet Joseph Addison, who was also a leading contributor to *The Spectator*.

Resolution Regarding Continuance of Proclamation under Article 356 of the Constitution in Relation to the State of Kerala[471]

The plea put forward by the government in favour of such an extension of the President's Rule for a period of another six months in Kerala is not quite convincing. Matters would have been different had it been argued by the government that because of the national emergency, because we are in an armed conflict with Pakistan instigated by China, it has become impossible or difficult to hold elections in any part of the country. As a matter of fact, if I remember aright, a responsible, leading member of the ruling party had the audacity to suggest that elections should be brought out earlier. For what reason, we do not know. And in the face of such a statement from a leading member of the ruling party, just to suggest that because of national emergency the elections should not be held, is not convincing. I should have liked the government to establish beyond all doubt that in order to augment, to reinforce, our defence efforts, it was necessary to extend the President's Rule there for another six months. But that argument has not been put forth. The extension has been based upon the report of the Governor of Kerala which states: "The general opinion in the state is that if elections are held now, the results will be much the same as they were in the mid-term elections."

Here, the government has tried to predict the election results I do not know with the help of which astrologer because when he mentions 'general opinion', whose opinion it is? Is it the opinion of a few vested interests who surround him? As a matter of fact, this extension involves the question of principle. Even otherwise, to say that even after six months of President's rule, the situation in Kerala has not improved, does no credit to the government. But that apart, even if the President's Rule would have been beneficial to the state, it would not have been in the interests of the state and in the interests of democracy to continue to extend such a rule because as Burke said: 'For form of government, let fools contest; that is best which administers best.' We know, as the votaries of democracy, that inefficient democracy is preferable to benevolent despotism. Again, this is not the case of Kerala alone. This trick of imposing the President's Rule can be repeated in the case of any other state which is likely to have a non-

471. *Rajya Sabha Debate* dated 8th November, 1965.

Congress majority. So, in the interests of democracy it becomes necessary to oppose this extension. Of course, there is a provision in the Constitution and it can be resorted to for imposing the President's Rule. Article 356 of the Constitution says:

> "If the President, on receipt of a report from the Governor of a state or otherwise, is satisfied that a situation has arisen in which the government of the state cannot be carried on in accordance with the provisions of this Constitution, the President may, by proclamation:
>
> (a) assume to himself all or any of the functions of the government of the state and..." etc.

Now this has been given, but the satisfaction must be objective, not merely subjective. And it is difficult to say that in the case of Kerala, the satisfaction has been objective. There were five other earlier instances of President's Rule being imposed. In the first place in June 1951, Dr Gopichand Bhargava's[472] Ministry resigned and on 28th June, 1951 the first Proclamation under this article was signed by the President. Secondly, when the Prakasam Ministry[473] [Andhra Pradesh] was defeated on 15th November, 1956, the President signed a proclamation under this article. Again, on 23rd March, 1955 when the Travancore-Cochin ministry[474] resigned and no other ministry could be immediately formed, powers under this article were invoked. Again, the power was invoked when on 31st July, 1959 the Namboodirapad ministry[475] was dismissed

---

472. Gopichand Bhargava (1889-1966) was the first Chief Minister of Punjab. His second stint from 1949 came to an end due to internal tussle within the Congress legislative party and President's Rule was impose in Punjab in June 1951.

473. T. Prakasam, (1872-1957) Andhra Kesari, formed the first ministry after the creation of Andhra Pradesh on 6th October, 1953, with himself as Chief Minister and N. Sanjeeva Reddy as Deputy Chief Minister. The ministry resigned on 6th November, 1954, when it lost a no-confidence motion and President's Rule was imposed on 5th November, 1954.

474. The PSP-led coalition of Pattom Thanu Pillai resigned on 10th February, 1955 when it lost a no-confidence motion after the Congress withdrew support.

475. The first communist party in the state took office on April 1957 with E.M.S. Namboodiripad (1909-1998) as Chief Minister. Despite the government being stable and having a majority in the Assembly on 31st July, 1959 after 28 months, the government was dismissed, President's Rule imposed and the Assembly was dissolved.

and lastly on 25th January, 1961 when the Mahatab coalition ministry[476] resigned and no other ministry could be formed, President's Rule was imposed on Orissa. But in every one of these cases, a ministry was already there. It was functioning but there was a political breakdown. The existing ministry simply could not continue to function and the President's Rule became inevitable. These are genuine cases of subjective satisfaction. But in the present case, no ministry was allowed to be formed. The legislature was not allowed to meet. No party leader was called upon to try to constitute a coalition ministry. The normal machinery of the government was not allowed to function. It would be ridiculous to assert that the government of the state of Kerala cannot be carried on in accordance with the articles or provisions of the Constitution when such a trial has not been given. Merely party position cannot be a deciding factor.

To say that since there is no absolute majority of any party in the General Elections, President's Rule becomes inevitable would not be correct because there are cases of coalition ministries being formed

476. On 22nd May, 1959, Harekrushna Mahatab (1899-1987) formed a coalition government with Ganatantra Parishad in order to provide a stable administration to the state. This coalition continued in office till 23rd February, 1961. The Chief Minister resigned during the Budget session on February 21st. Odisha was brought under President's Rule on 25th February, 1961." After the fall of the Sankar [R. Sankar (1909-1972), third Chief Minister of Kerala,1962-64] Ministry on 8th September, 1964, President's Rule was imposed in Kerala on 10th September, 1964, because none of the parties in the Assembly" were ready to form a government. Mid-term elections were held on 4th March, 1965 and though the CPI(M) with 40 seats was the largest party, itwas not given a chance to form the ministry. Namboodiripad is said to have told the then Governor of Kerala that the CPI-M was ready to support the PSP from outside so that a non-Congress government could be formed, "but the Governor, after making his own assessment, came to the conclusion that a stable government was not possible. Hence, he recommended the imposition of President's Rule and the dissolution of the Assembly and on his report, the Assembly was dissolved before it could meet even once." Experts and political observers had then questioned on "how far the imposition of President's Rule on March 30th, and the dissolution of the Assembly within 26 days of the election (without giving a chance to the largest party in the Assembly which was ready to explore the possibilities of forming the government and to face the Assembly immediately), was constitutionally proper." For a comprehensive survey and analysis of the politics of President's Rule in India, *see* e.g. J.R. Siwach, *Politics of President's Rule in India*, Simla: Indian Institute of Advanced Study, 1979. This was the argument that Thengadi, a member of Jana Sangh was making. He was questioning the constitutional validity of the move of continually imposing President's Rule and thus throttling democracy. When it came to constitutional propriety and norms; it did not matter to Thengadi that the CPIM was an arch-political adversary of the Jana Sangh. He took up its case because Constitutional propriety and the democratic spirit had to be safeguarded, the CPIM's ideological ambivalence towards parliamentary democracy did not deter him in defending their parliamentary rights.

and functioning properly and there is no reason why in any other state of India such a coalition ministry should not be given a trial. Against this background I am led to agree with the observation of an eminent, impartial and independent person like Mr. M.C. Setalvad[477] who remarked in his article in the *Indian Advocate* of 2nd November:

"What is more reprehensible is the use of arbitrary and extensive powers obtained by the Executive in the name of emergency, not for the real purpose of the emergency, but for the ordinary purposes of government."

Again I want to insist upon the point that if it is established beyond all doubt that for national emergency and for augmenting defence efforts, postponement of elections is inevitable, we would support the measure. But in the absence of such an argument and a categorical statement from the side of the government, it is difficult to support such an extension.

The Goa, Daman and Diu (Extension of the Code of Civil Procedure and the Arbitration Act) Bill, 1965[478]

D. Thengadi: In the context of the current political and national issues, the Bill is non-controversial and the time taken for introducing the Bill is also understandable, because certain preliminaries were to be arranged and prerequisites to be fulfilled. It is true that the original system as obtaining in Goa was different from our system here. We follow the British pattern while the continental pattern was followed in Goa. But that is no reason why our system should not be introduced now. Now that would be a step ahead in the direction not only of legal integration, but also of National Integration. To that extent it is also welcome. But I should like to say, as has been already suggested, that this is a piecemeal legislation, and in view of the present political and national situation, it would have been better had this Bill not been introduced at all. True, we are facing great problems, particularly on our frontiers, and therefore we would observe a sort of moratorium so far as our domestic problems are concerned. This is all right but at the same time, now that this particular Bill is being introduced, I must say that this is yet another indication of the government's policy of vacillation and procrastination regarding the future of Goa.

---

477. M.C. Setalvad (1884-1974) noted jurist, one of the longest-serving Attorney Generals of India, (1950-63) and Chairman of the 1st Law Commission.

478. *Rajya Sabha Debate* dated 9th September, 1965.

I may say that the Goa problem has been handled in a very tragic way. Perhaps that is the mildest word that I can use and it has been allowed to drift in such a fashion as to allow vested interests. As a matter of fact, make Goa the cockpit for conflicting vested interests. As a matter of fact, it was in the interest of the nation that Goa, Daman and Diu should have been merged with the adjacent state or states. I am using the words state or states, because Goa, Daman and Diu are not contiguous areas. But the question of their merger should have been finally settled. Therefore, I say that instead of introducing such piecemeal measures, the Government of India should come forward at the proper time, immediately after this national emergency is over, with a measure to merge Goa, Daman and Diu with the adjacent state or states, and then it should become unnecessary or superfluous to introduce such a Bill as is being introduced now.

□

Index

A

B

C

D

H

I

J

K

L

M

N

O

P

Q

R

S

T

U

V

□□□